CRIME AND JUSTICE IN EARLY MODERN ENGLAND: 1500-1750

Gregory Durston, MA, DipL, LLM, PhD,
of the Middle Temple and Lincoln's Inn,
Barrister

Barry Rose Law Publishers Limited
Chichester, West Sussex

ISBN 1 902681 41 X

Barry Rose Law Publishers Limited
Little London
Chichester

*This book is dedicated to William Adams (Miura Anjin),
English mariner and samurai (1564-1620)*

Acknowledgements

I would like to acknowledge the invaluable assistance provided by the staff of the British Library, the Institute of Advanced Legal Studies, and the libraries of Kingston University, Niigata University, the LSE, Cambridge University, Lambeth Palace, the Middle Temple and Lincoln's Inn. Additionally, I would like to thank the Public Record Office in Kew, the City of London Record Office, the London Metropolitan Archives, the Sussex Record Office in Chichester, the Kingston Local History Room, Kingston on Thames, the Surrey History Centre, Woking, and the many archivists, from numerous institutions, who have been extremely generous with their time in assisting me. I am, as once before, indebted to the Faculty of Law, Niigata University, Japan, where the bulk of this book was written. As with all such works, there is also a huge debt to the many scholars, past and present, who have laboured in the same field, and whose works can be found in the bibliography and footnotes. Thanks are due to Philippa Russell for assistance with the preparation of the manuscript. On a personal basis, I would also like to thank Philippa, Reiny and L.B. for their constant support and encouragement.

Gregory Durston
Niigata

Preface

In recent decades, the study of crime and criminal justice in early modern England has become academically 'fashionable'. In response to this, some scholars have suggested that the importance of the criminal law to the operation of the wider society has been exaggerated and is not deserving of such close scrutiny. Others have stressed the large amount of work that remains to be done. Nevertheless, whatever view is taken, it is certainly legitimate to ask why another book on the subject is justified. Part of the answer to this question lies in the general tendency for existing studies to focus primarily on crime (largely the province of social historians) or procedure (the province of legal historians) although the two were inextricably interlinked; crimes were defined by their legal consequences. The aim of this study is to treat the subject holistically, from initial deviance, via detection and prosecution, to final penal disposal. Additionally, in a field that has become increasingly dominated by micro-histories, at the expense of geographically and chronologically broader studies, this book aims to explore wider themes pertaining to early modern crime and justice. It is hoped that it will provide a thorough account of the era's crime and criminal justice system.

Contents

PART ONE: CRIME

Chapter 1

General Introduction

Many recent studies of early modern crime and justice have been heavily circumscribed, geographically, institutionally and chronologically, focusing on the detailed scrutiny of a restricted area, a single decade, or the work of one court. Unfortunately, this has often been at the expense of pursuing the 'wider' picture and has not resulted in very stimulating generalisations about either crime or the criminal law of the period.[1] However, one of the primary reasons for such caution amongst historians is also readily apparent, namely, the era's lack of precise 'system' and the parochialism of early modern society. Thus, if a man spoke of his 'country' he usually meant not his nation but the county community in which he was born or resided. Sussex, a county only 50 miles from London (already one of the largest cities in Europe), was notorious for its isolation and bad lines of communication. This localism makes drawing generalisations inherently difficult, if not positively dangerous. Almost everywhere, exceptions to 'ideal typical' national patterns for any phenomenon, both legal and criminal, can readily be found, whether it is Halifax's

---

1.   J. McMullan, "Crime, Law and Order in Early Modern England," *British Journal of Criminology,* 1987, vol.27, no.3, p.252.

unique system of execution, the exclusion from the assizes's system of the counties palatine, or simply local variations in administering the 'standard' system, such as the qualifications required for jurors. This was especially true in the sixteenth century, before the expansion of printing and a growth in legal primers in English helped to disseminate a degree of knowledge and a modicum of 'standard practice' throughout the country. The first printed work devoted solely to English criminal law, the judge Sir William Staunford's *Les Plees del Coron*, was only published in 1557. Generalisations can be drawn - must be drawn in a work of this nature - but it is important to remember that that is all they are.

This book is about English crime and justice, albeit that, because of its intimately linked relationship, some mention is made of Wales. Although, in theory, English law applied to much of Ireland, its influence outside a few confined areas was modest until the era was well advanced. As Sir Edmund Spenser noted in the 1590s, there were: "... many wide countries in Ireland, in which the lawes of England were never established." Even where it did operate, alternative, traditional, systems of administering justice were often used by the Gaelic inhabitants.[2] However, comparisons will regularly be made with the situation in other parts of Western Europe, such as Germany, Holland, Spain, Scotland and France, so that similarities can be

---

2.   E. Spenser, "A Veue of the Present State of Ireland," (1596) in A.B. Grosart (Ed.), *The Complete Works in Verse and Prose of Edmund Spenser*, London, privately published, 1884, vol.9, p.19.

identified and contrasts drawn. For the same reason, extensive use is made of the observations of foreign visitors to England on criminal justice matters, though language problems, a lack of specialist interest and limited length of exposure mean that such sources must often be treated with caution. Most foreign visitors to England confined themselves to London (entirely *sui generis* in the early modern period), Oxford, Cambridge, Windsor and the royal palaces.[3] Nevertheless, it is to be hoped that these foreign comparisons and opinions will allow the reader to gain an insight into those aspects of English crime and justice that were 'typical' over much of Western Europe, being a natural response to early modern structural determinants, and those that were special to the country.

Some aspects of early modern crime were so widespread that several continental works on the subject were translated into English. Thus, Paul Godwin translated the *Histoire Des Larrons*, or *The History of Theeves* from French, publishing it in London in 1638. In the same year *The Sonne of the Rogue*, or *The Politicke Theefe With the Antiquitie of Theeves* translated from the original Spanish by 'W.M.' was published (it had already been translated into Dutch and French). Nevertheless, some characteristics of English crime were already unusual, largely confined to one of Europe's most singular nations. However, even more peculiar than its pattern of crime, was the nation's criminal justice system. As a Flemish legal historian has observed, the extraordinary

---

3.   M. Misson, *Memoirs and Observations in his Travels over England* (J. Ozell Trans.), London, 1719, p.337.

thing about English law is its distinctness from that found on the Continent (and even in Scotland) although in other respects England's cultural, linguistic, religious and (albeit to a very much smaller extent) political history broadly match that of its European neighbours.[4] In retaining its ancient common law England had stood out against the reception of Roman civil law elsewhere in late medieval Europe.

Perhaps because early modern society is both alien to us, and yet, in some respects, strangely familiar, there is a constant danger that its historians will be guilty of 'presentism', a temptation to introduce anachronistic concepts that accord to a modern agenda but which are of limited relevance in a historical context. Thus, to discover a 'crisis' in gender relations in the years between 1540 and 1640 is attractive to many who witnessed the enormous changes in the position of women and the growth of feminism and 'women's studies' in the twentieth century. However, the evidence for such a crisis, as opposed to historically longstanding tensions between the sexes, is relatively modest. Similarly, before the 1990s, the dominance of conflict models of society, premised on class struggle between groups of unequal power locked in permanent opposition, was sometimes projected back across the centuries in unsubtle forms. This is not to suggest that such approaches have not produced valuable insights. It would be equally mistaken to propound a consensus model

---

4.   R.C. Van Caenegam, "Judges, Legislators and Professors:" *Chapters in European Legal History*, Cambridge, CUP, 1987, at pp.5-6.

of early modern society, in which its various social stratum worked in harmony within an organic hierarchical framework.[5] According to a Somerset JP, in the harsh 1590s at least, many of the poor attributed their misfortunes to the upper social orders and complained that "ritche men have gotten all into their hands and will starve the poor."[6] Nevertheless, early modern England was not dominated by acute class conflict.

Sources of Knowledge

The post-modernist assumption that independent, objective reality does not exist, that truth is always 'constructed' and that history is little more than literature, has to be eschewed in a work of this nature. Nevertheless, abstracting 'reality' from the main sources available for the study of early modern crime and criminal justice, whether statutes, literary accounts or criminal statistics, is difficult, as all are inherently flawed. As a result, many popular modern portrayals of the era's crime and criminal justice system are based on a seamless web of truths, half-truths, legends and simple falsehoods. Thus, the black letter law of statutes often reflected pressures on legislators, sometimes from

---

5. J. Samaha, "Gleanings from Local Criminal Court Records: sedition amongst the 'inarticulate' in Elizabethan England," *Journal of Social History*, 1975, vol.8, p.62.

6. E. Hext, "Letter written to Lord Burghley on September 25, 1596," reproduced in *Tudor Economic Documents*, R.H. Tawney and E. Power (eds.), London, Longmans, 1951, vol.2, at pp.340-341.

relatively small groups, and their sense of the social and political needs of the moment. In reality, such laws might be widely ignored, or applied in ways that differed markedly from their wording and from the intentions of those who drafted them. Consequently, it is essential to examine the criminal justice system in action to determine its role in society.[7] However, this is easier said than done, as both the remaining sources of information also pose problems. Early modern statistics are extremely unreliable, because the passage of the centuries has seen many records completely or partially lost, and because they suffer from major problems of changing offence definition, levels of public sensitivity, enforcement, ease of prosecution, interpretation and collation. Statistics are also unreliable because the relative importance of different types of crime changes, as new opportunities present themselves and others wane. As a result, it is very difficult to decide whether variations indicate alterations in the reality of crime, its *modus operandi*, or contemporary attitudes towards it. The factors affecting the relationship between 'real' and prosecuted levels of crime are so numerous and difficult to measure over a vast historical period, the resulting patterns so difficult to interpret, that quantification to establish long-term trends has proved to be of limited value. Although more confidence has been placed in indictment-based time series used to examine short-term fluctuations in criminality (over, for example, a decade) even these cannot be viewed with

---

7. D. Paton, "Punishment, Crime and the Bodies of Slaves in Eighteenth-Century Jamaica," *Journal of Social History*, 2001, vol.34, no.4, pp.923-925.

total confidence. Thus, it has been observed that the well known correlation between war and a reduction in criminal prosecutions in the eighteenth century *might* be explained not by the greater employment opportunities afforded by hostilities to the poor, as is commonly suggested, but by the widespread practice of allowing suspected offenders the option of enlisting rather than facing trial. Frequently, this occurred after suspects had been apprehended but before an indictment was brought, the accused man consequently not showing up in any statistics. Thus, at Leeds, in 1762, a burglar was produced before a magistrate: "... who gave him his choice, whether he would enlist into His Majesty's service, or be committed to York Castle, the former of which he accepted."[8] Further complicating matters, the distinction between civil and criminal actions was also more fluid during this era than it is today. By way of illustration, Sir Robert Townshend brought a civil action against the three yeomen who broke into, and stripped, his empty town-house in Norwich, under cover of the disturbance occasioned by Ket's revolt in 1549. Why he brought a civil writ of trespass, rather than informing the JPs and having it treated as a crime, is not clear. He may have been more interested in recovering damages than in seeing the men punished; he claimed forty pounds in compensation and ultimately was awarded twenty pounds plus costs by the jury at the Lammas assizes in Norwich Guildhall in 1554 (the case having been sent back *nisi prius* from the Court of

---

8. J. Styles, "Crime in Eighteenth-Century England," *History Today*, 1988, vol.38, issue 3, p.36.

Common Pleas at Westminster). His decision may also have reflected the fact that the offence charged was house breaking (committed in daytime) rather than burglary (committed at night) and that juries were less likely to convict in such cases. Perhaps Townshend merely felt that his delay in bringing the case compromised any criminal action.[9] However, modern academics are not unique in attributing more significance to historical criminal statistics than they warrant. According to Sir William Petty (1623-1687), a noted Oxford statistician and surveyor of Ireland, it would be possible, having ascertained the number of people in England, by calculating, *inter alia*: "... the number of Corporall sufferings and persons imprisoned for crimes, to know the measure of Vice and Sin in the nation."[10] Even so, a positivist approach to crime in early modern England is slightly easier than in other early modern societies because, in theory, all Englishmen were subject to the same substantive criminal law, with a few small exceptions, such as the 1671 Game Act and various (largely ineffectual) pieces of sumptuary legislation. Additionally, a small number of noblemen apart, they were also subject to the same adjectival (procedural and evidential) law. Most educated Englishmen throughout the period would have acknowledged that 'fur collar' crime was crime, even on the occasions when it was not prosecuted

---

9.   C. Moreton, "Mid-Tudor trespass: a break in at Norwich 1549," *English Historical Review*, 1993, vol.107, pp.387-398.

10. Sir W. Petty, *The Petty Papers: Some Unpublished Writings of Sir William Petty*, edited from the Bowood Papers by the Marquis of Lansdowne, New York, Augustus M. Kelley Publishers, 1967, vol.1, p.197.

through influence or extra-legal pressure.

Literary sources, the other form of available information, are also flawed, not least because of their socially determined nature. Given the low levels of literacy until late in the period, they usually have a distinctly upper class or clerical provenance, social groups which might be expected to have a distinct 'take' on the phenomenon of crime, though less on the mechanics of law enforcement and prosecution. Additionally, their authors are almost invariably male and significantly older than the average age for the general population. However, towards the end of the period, a few alternative literary sources emerge. In particular criminal 'autobiographies' (actually usually ghosted works) became popular in the eighteenth century, especially in London. They purported to be written by criminals or those, like the prison chaplain Henry Goodcole, who had become intimate with them, though their accuracy and even authenticity is sometimes questionable.[11]

Dates

All dates to delineate historical periods, especially those premised on centuries and half-centuries, are artificial. This is especially the case for the early modern criminal justice system as Tudor legal innovations were frequently *ad hoc* adaptations of medieval practices, rather than a self-

---

11. P. Rawlings, *Drunks, whores and idle apprentices: criminal biographies of the eighteenth century*, London, Routledge, 1992, at pp.1-4 and pp.11-23.

conscious administrative revolution.[12] Arguably, a group of imaginative Elizabethan and Jacobean lawyers and writers, such as Coke and Kitchin, were still adapting England's medieval legal institutions to suit early modern needs a century and more after 1500. As a result, there were numerous continuities between late medieval and Tudor society and their criminal justice systems, as well as major differences. Where relevant, some sources from the 1400s will be cited, if only to establish such continuities or changes. Additionally, aspects of the early modern criminal justice system survived into the nineteenth century, so that a few post-1750 sources will also be referred to. Nevertheless, 1500 and 1750 provide useful dividing lines. As the era opened, the criminal trial was slowly completing a transformation that got underway in the late medieval era. As it ended, another transformation was about to take place. Trial procedure in the early 1700s still bore a close resemblance to that portrayed in the 1560s by Sir Thomas Smith, though it was slightly more formal, and the role of judge, prosecution and defendant more clearly delineated.[13] However, the second quarter of the eighteenth century, and the 1750s, witnessed developments that presaged a change in the criminal justice culture of the nation. The advent of counsel in the felony trial, modest provision for state compensation for prosecutors in 1753, the arrival of De Veil

---

12. C. Herrup, review of "Crime, Law and Society in Late Medieval and Tudor England" by J.G. Bellamy (1984), *American Journal of Legal History*, 1987, vol.31, p.165.

13. T.A. Green, *Verdict According to Conscience: Perspective on the English Criminal Trial Jury*, Chicago, University of Chicago Press, 1985, p.270.

as an innovative magistrate at Bow Street in 1739, the Fielding brothers' experiments in detection, the slow strengthening of exclusionary rules of evidence and the expansion of penal transportation, all suggest that change was afoot. Insofar as an 'early modern' criminal justice system exists, one that is significantly different to both its medieval ancestor or its modern descendant, it can be identified in the decades from the middle of the sixteenth century to the early years of the eighteenth century, and these will provide the focus for this book. Nevertheless, this should not blind us to developments within this large period of time. London, in particular, witnessed significant changes in both policing and prosecution in the century after 1660. Crime and the English criminal justice system of the era can be treated holistically, but only with great caution.

Social Change

The period witnessed a mixture of radical change and profound conservatism. This provided the backdrop to developments in the nature of both crime and the nation's justice system. Sixteenth and early seventeenth century England was wedded to a static view of society and the universe, in which all of creation, angelic, human, animal, vegetable and mineral had its allotted place in a great chain of being that stretched from God to the soil. As the *Homily on Obedience* of 1547 noted, on earth, God had "assigned and appointed Kings, Princes, with other governours under them, in all good and necessary order."[14] Within the human part of this chain, each social group, gender, age cohort, and functionary had its designated position, so that according to a contemporary observer, in England people were commonly divided into "gentlemen, citizens or burgesses, yeomen, and artificers or labourers".[15] However, in reality, even by 1500, there was already far more social mobility than the model allowed for, something that became increasingly apparent as the period advanced. There were great social and economic changes in the years between 1500 and 1750. Massive population growth, inflation and the increasingly wide dissemination of literacy all had an impact on the incidence and type of crime that English society experienced and on the agencies tasked with dealing with it.

In 1500, foreigners had been struck that so rich and fertile a land as England remained "very thinly inhabited".[16] The country's population had expanded only slowly after the demographic reverses of the fourteenth century. After c.1520, however, growth accelerated swiftly, so that the number of Englishmen increased from about 2,400,000 to approximately 3,500,000 by 1580, and to about 5,000,000 in 1640. This engendered numerous social and economic

---

14. Anon, *Certaine Sermons or Homilies appointed to be read in Churches ...*, London, John Bill, 1623, p.69.
15. Canon W. Harrison, *A Description of England* in Raphael Holinshed's *The First Volume of the Chronicles of England, Scotland and Ireland*, London, John Harrison, 1577, pp.103-104.
16. Anon, *A Relation, or Rather a True Account of the Island of England ... About the Year 1500* (C. Sneyd Trans.), London, Camden Society, 1847, p.3.

pressures and changes. A peasantry that had benefited from the labour shortage engendered by the Black Death found the terms of life changing against them. The rise in population was accompanied by inflation, making life difficult for those with fixed incomes. Prices, which had been relatively stable in the fifteenth century, had trebled by the 1570s, with foodstuffs being particularly affected. By the end of the period, the increase was six-fold. There was also the ongoing, and very complex, phenomenon of enclosure, depriving the poor of access to common lands, while lease-holds were increasingly being purchased and taken out of husbandry by graziers and sheep farmers.[17]

Throughout Europe, whether Protestant or not, there were important religious developments in the period, and especially in the sixteenth century. Both Catholicism and reformed Christianity became more assertive and interventionist. It is possible that this, too, had an influence on offending. However, it is important not to exaggerate the impact of religion on crime rates, at least for serious offences. England was a Christian country and, faced by impending death, many were sincerely influenced by faith. Even the worst felons could be contrite and repentant at the gallows, shedding genuine tears and urging moral reform on others. However, the presence of widespread religious belief, on its own, does not appear to have prevented their initial offending. To an extent, this phenomenon is matched in the modern era. Religion, of all denominations, tends to

---

17. G.R. Elton, *Reform and Reformation: England 1509-1558*, London, Edward Arnold, 1977, pp.2-3.

be strong in 'high-crime' Africa and the Southern States of America, and weak in 'low crime' Japan. This is not to suggest any correlation between belief and crime, as the burgeoning offence rates in secular modern Britain indicate. Nor does it mean that the small number of personally highly devout believers found in nearly all societies are not markedly less prone to committing crime. It merely indicates that even in 'religious' societies, the power of belief to influence general human conduct is limited. This was appreciated by some of the most devout men of the early modern era, who were sometimes candid about the limited capacity of the here-after to regulate behaviour, and accepted that: "... in rewarding vertue, and in punishing vice, the Parson endeavoureth to be in Gods stead, knowing that Countrey people are drawne, or led by sense, more then by faith, by present re-wards, or punishments, more then by future."[18]

Radical social change must also be seen in context. Despite the impact of the Renaissance, the Reformation, enclosure, industrialisation and the eighteenth century Enlightenment, with accompanying advances in science and medicine, many aspects of 'traditional' English rural life remained unchanged until well into the nineteenth century. It was only in the 1800s that increased agricultural mechanisation and the development of a global market for meat and grain, combined with emigration and urbanisation, finally led to the separation of rural

---

18. G. Herbert, *A Priest to the Temple*, London, 1652, p.21.

communities from the ancient 'rhythms' of agricultural life.[19] Nevertheless, with this reservation, the England of 1750 was manifestly different to that of 1500.

19. O. Davies, "Witchcraft: The spell that didn't break," *History Today*, 1999, vol.49, issue 8, p.7.

Chapter 2

Theoretical Perspectives on Crime 1500-1750

Introduction

Some studies of early modern crime and punishment expose lurid and often untypical detail at the expense of wider themes and arguments. Others provide 'explain all' paradigms for crime that lack empirical support. A balance must be struck. It is vital to recognise that crime is both a cultural and a situational phenomenon. These are so intimately intertwined that it is often difficult to separate the two. There has to be a motivation or 'stimulus' to commit crime, and these are limitless: greed, need, reputation, honour, excitement, revenge, etc. However, crime does not exist in a cultural vacuum. Whether stimuli are ultimately conducive to violence or theft depends heavily on the wider social environment. This chapter examines one cultural explanation, mainly pertinent to crimes for violence, and one social stimulus (need) primarily germane to instrumental crime.

The Cultural Background

Despite the presence of numerous records and published materials, it can be difficult to 'understand' early modern English society. This has produced radically different portrayals, in the work of, *inter alia*, Professors Stone,

Sharpe, Herrup and Cockburn. To some, it was a relatively cohesive and harmonious society, not enormously concerned, for most of the time, about crime and disorder, and possessed of a strong sense of community and neighbourliness. To others, it presents a bleaker visage, a highly violent, fissiparous world, wracked with internecine conflict, mutual suspicion, malicious gossip, disorder, and characterised by fractured communities, given to spying on their neighbours, litigation and assaults. Often, the 'harmonious' interpretation of English society draws heavily on the enormous amount of contemporary literature extolling the value and importance of being 'in charity' with one's neighbours. By contrast, the 'fractured' portrayal relies on the available statistics of violence, especially homicide, and inter-personal litigation and dispute.

However, both portrayals are flawed to some extent. Contemporary 'neighbour' literature was descriptive, not normative. It portrayed an ideal society rather than social reality. Indeed, frequently, paying lip service to specific virtues is most prevalent in societies where they are notably absent. (Few modern Scandinavian politicians would make an issue about the importance of non-corrupt government, many contemporary politicians from the Indian sub-continent might do so.) In their wills, numerous early modern English landlords piously urged their sons not to rack-rent their inherited property, despite their own personal history when alive of doing just that. There were probably very few individuals or villages that managed to live up to the highest standards of neighbourliness. Nevertheless, this does not render such portrayals entirely meaningless. Paying lip service to ideals has practical social consequences, limiting blatant departures from the model. Interpretations that draw heavily on the raw statistics of violence *might* be exaggerating the tensions of early modern society.[1] Thus, it has been argued that the 'feel' of surviving court records and accounts does not suggest that early modern England was a fundamentally violent or affectionless society.[2] Notwithstanding apparently high levels of interpersonal conflict, most people were horrified by potentially lethal violence. Indeed, in some respects it is their antipathy to murder, in a world in which levels of mortality from other, natural, events were so high that seems surprising.[3]

A Violent Society

Nevertheless, a society with a high incidence of lethal violence can preserve a deep rooted horror of murder (as evidenced in some parts of modern America), and, with some reservations, England in the years around 1500 does appear to have been an exceptionally violent and lawless society. Proponents of a more benign interpretation are probably rightly criticised for having an excessively roseate

1. J.S. Cockburn, "Patterns of Violence in English Society: Homicide in Kent 1560-1985," *Past and Present*, 1991, no.130, p.106.
2. J.A. Sharpe, "Debate: The History of Violence in England, Some Observations," *Past and Present*, 1985, no.108, p.215.
3. W.B. Robison, "Murder at Crowhurst: A Case Study in Early Tudor Law Enforcement," *Criminal Justice History*, 1988, vol.9, pp.44-45.

view of late medieval and early modern villages and their levels of harmony.[4] The fifteenth century world of the Pastons was one of endemic disorder, danger and insecurity. Typically, in correspondence from early 1452, there were complaints that influential men in Norfolk were assembling a "great multitude of misruled people". These would sally forth at will, in groups up to 30 or more strong, and commit numerous "abominable deeds". Amongst their crimes, they stole livestock and other goods, dispossessed local people from their lands, and assaulted, wounded, abducted, fired arrows at and sometimes murdered others. Even the priest of Snoring and six of his men were captured in connection with a murder and many "horrible robberies". This prompted Margaret Paston to write to her husband on July 18, 1461 asking him to arrange for a special 'oyer and terminer' (i.e., an assizes) for the county to try the cleric.[5] England had many of the characteristics of a 'high crime' society. Thus, crime avoidance appears to have been a prominent organizing principle in everyday life. The institutions of social control (whether courts, JPs or sheriffs) were often partisan or highly erratic in their performance. Many noblemen's retainers doubled as hired 'bullies' in their masters' personal quarrels with their tenants and fellow aristocrats. Such traditions were to die hard, as evidenced by the four servants of Lord Stourton who were executed with him in 1556. They had joined a large band of

---

4.   L. Stone, "Debate: The History of Violence in England, A Rejoinder," *Past and Present*, 1985, no.108, pp.220-222.
5.   J. Warrington (Ed.), *The Paston Letters*, London, Everyman edition, J.M. Dent, 1956, vol.1, pp.65-69 and p.183.

their master's followers, including 15 or 16 of his servants, sundry tenants, and even some JPs, in 'arresting' two men with whom Stourton had quarrelled bitterly and exchanged bullets on an earlier occasion. The murders, however, were conducted much more secretly, the four servants being sent by Stourton to kill the two bound prisoners in private and then burying them in a pit.[6] The Tudor regime was to spend over a century persuading the servants and tenants of such powerful magnates that loyalty to their masters should not extend to pursuing their employer's interests by force of arms.[7] Along with such high level disorder there was also widespread low-level robbery and violence.

From the early 1500s, however, rates of violent crime and disorder seem to have begun what was to be a long, and very slow, decline, one that would last for several centuries. The Elizabethan magistrate Sir Nathaniel Bacon sat as a JP for same area of Norfolk as several prominent members of the Paston family a century and more earlier. Nevertheless, a perusal of their writings quickly makes clear that they helped to police very different societies. There was nothing special about England in this respect, the long-term decline of serious criminal violence from the late Middle Ages appears to have been shared by most parts of Europe, including Scandinavia and Germany.[8] Historically, physical

---

6. J.L. Rayner and G.T. Crook (eds.), *The Complete Newgate Calendar*, 1926, vol.1, at pp.27-28.

7. Stone, *The Crisis of the Aristocracy 1558-1641*, Oxford, OUP, 1967, p.98.

8. E. Lacour, "Faces of violence revisited. A typology of violence in Early Modern rural Germany," *Journal of Social History*, 2001, vol.34, no.3, pp.649-668.

conflict seems to have been a common, and almost tolerated, form of dispute settlement in many pre-modern societies, a situation that decreased throughout Europe in the centuries after 1500. Perhaps surprisingly, the era's expanding cities do not seem to have had exceptionally high levels of violence when compared to rural areas.[9] In England, by 1750, crime, particularly violent crime, was much less of a social problem than it had been, even if tolerance for it had dropped even faster than its incidence. As was noted in March 1731, even allowing for the tiny size of the county: "It [wa]s remarkable, that at the assizes held at Oakham for the County of Rutland, there was no Prisoner, nor one Cause try'd."[10] By then, the Old Bailey itself very occasionally recorded 'Maiden' sessions, in which no death sentence was passed (white gloves being worn by the presiding judge to mark the occasion). Any satisfactory historical explanation for violence needs to account for its decline in the early modern centuries. Why this occurred has been termed the 'violence we have lost' debate.[11]

Modern studies on the history of violence generally, and homicide in particular, have employed a variety of explanations for the phenomenon: economic, demographic, political and cultural. Sometimes, these have distinguished instrumental from 'expressive' violence. It has been argued that for the latter, an excess of young men, a 'culture of

---

9.   J.A. Johnson and E.H. Monkkonen, (eds.) *The Civilization of Crime: violence in town and country since the Middle Ages,"* Urbana: University of Illinois Press, p.13.
10.   *The Gentleman's Magazine,* 1731, vol.1, p.124.
11.   Cockburn, "Patterns of Violence in English Society," p.71.

honour' that encourages aggressive responses to perceived insults and threats, and the absence of alternative methods to achieve status, or pursue quarrels have all been factors that have influenced levels of lethal violence. More recently, the role of recreational violence in providing popular entertainment and the raw material of excitement in pre-industrial societies has been emphasised.[12] All of these approaches provide insights. However, perhaps the most plausible general explanation for the early modern decline in violence was that advanced as far back as 1939 by the German scholar Norbert Elias (1897-1990), in his major work *Über den Prozeß der Zivilisation* (first published in Switzerland). Unfortunately, the translation of much of Elias's work into English did not occur until the 1980s, despite his tenure of an academic position at Leicester University, leading to the neglect of his ideas in the Anglophone world. Elias stressed the role of long-term social changes in the decline of private violence. Amongst them, he particularly focused on the growth of social interdependence. As more and more people were required to adjust their conduct to that of other people it was necessary for their actions to be regulated increasingly strictly.[13] Ultimately, this would come to characterise the bourgeois market society, where self-control and consideration for others were vitally important, and manifest in the development of widely accepted notions of

---

12. C. Conley, "The agreeable recreation of Fighting," in *Journal of Social History*, 1999, vol.33, no.1, p.57.

13. N. Elias, *The Civilizing Process, vol.2, State Formation and Civilisation*, Oxford, Blackwell's, 1982, p.232.

personal restraint. However, and crucially, Elias also linked this 'gentling' process to the emergence of powerful early modern states in Western Europe, political entities that possessed a hitherto unprecedented monopoly on the use of force and a novel willingness to intervene in everyday life. Thus, in England, the post-medieval era saw the state gradually claim exclusive competence over the administration of justice, religious organisation, fiscal, military and even social matters such as the administration of charity via the poor law and the licensing of taverns. According to the Elias paradigm, this new state power curbed individual aggressiveness, so that in the long-term most people, with the state acting as: "... superego, have learned to behave in a more rational and less routinely and impulsively violent fashion."[14] In turn, this allowed the creation of social spaces that were normally free from private violence.[15] As a result, dispute settlement gradually became the province of law courts rather than upper class internecine conflicts, or the tavern and street brawls found amongst all social groups. Elias's work is especially significant as it challenges the arguments of those theorists, such as Michel Foucault, for whom the key developments in patterns of crime and justice only occur after 1770, and who contrast a supposedly static early modern era with an age of dynamic change in the late eighteenth and the early nineteenth centuries. Such theorists mistakenly present the

---

14. R. Lane, Review of "The Civilisation of Crime: Violence in Town and Country Since the Middle Ages," *Journal of Social History*, 1998, vol.31, no.3, pp.750-753.
15. Elias, *The Civilizing Process*, vol.2, p.235.

administration of criminal justice in the (supposedly) pre-reform era as being irrational, inefficient and unchanging.[16]

According to Elias, the leading actors in the initial stages of the civilising process were courtiers and city merchants. Under government pressure, noblemen gradually abandoned 'martial' pursuits and their attendant fortifications, and moved to royal courts. These fostered an increased emphasis on social graces and non-violent conflicts. In England, some observers, such as Daniel Defoe, claimed to have been aware of a general improvement in upper class manners from the time of Edward VI, though Defoe ascribed this to the Protestant Reformation and its production of a 'sober Nobility'. In the Elias paradigm, much of this new court engendered culture of restraint and control allied to more 'refined' manners, gradually spread downwards from the nobility to the bourgeoisie and yeomanry, and was ultimately reflected in a mass of diverse social indicia, such as nose blowing, table manners, levels of modesty about bodily functions and, most importantly, aggressiveness.[17] Thus, although the 'Reformation of Manners' is particularly associated with the societies by that name which operated between the 1690s and 1730s, in its *broadest* sense, the phrase (used by Cromwell in the 1650s) captures a historical phenomenon that stretched back into

---

16. T.C. Curtis and Sharpe, "Crime in Tudor and Stuart England," *History Today*, 1988, vol.38, issue 2, p.23.
17. Elias, *The Civilizing Process*, vol.1, pp.84-204.

the fifteenth century, if not earlier.[18] As part of this process, both the ecclesiastical and secular authorities condemned many popular and traditional rituals, entertainments and games and took measures to suppress some of them. Those aspects of popular culture that survived increasingly came to be viewed as 'vulgar' by educated people.[19]

Societies with low homicide/violence rates necessarily develop effective legal alternatives to physical confrontation as well as inculcating personality traits into their members that inhibit aggressiveness.[20] The traditional 'cult of honour' had defended the vital commodity of personal reputation amongst one's social peers. It was not found solely in the upper classes, having a mirror in the lower orders. A 'tall man' would little more tolerate an insult than would a nobleman, even if the weapons he might use to avenge it were different. Arguably, this feudal concern for honour gradually yielded to a bourgeois concern about status and money, and so encouraged a move from inter-personal violence to litigation.[21] Legal action could sometimes be a very thinly veiled substitute for physical confrontation. As late as 1781, in the case of *Howe v. Dive*, an action for defamation over an allegation of sodomy, the plaintiff's counsel explicitly warned the jury that an award of "small

---

18. M.J. Ingram, "Reformation of Manners in Early Modern England" in *The Experience of Authority in Early Modern England*, P. Griffiths, A. Fox and S. Hindle (eds.), London, Macmillan, 1996, pp.49-51.
19. Ingram, "Ridings, Rough Music and the 'Reform of Popular Culture' in Early Modern England," *Past and Present*, 1984, no.105, p.78.
20. E. Leyton, *Men of Blood: Murder in Modern England*, Harmondsworth, Penguin Books, 1997, pp.17-18.
21. Stone, "Debate: The History of Violence in England," pp.214-216.

damages" would signify that his client had made a mistake in relying on the law, and must, in future "carve out his own satisfaction, by plunging his sword into the heart of the offendor".[22] During the transitional stage from violence, litigation might be expected to show a major increase, and this seems to have been the case in England. There was a fivefold growth in the work of the central common law courts in Westminster between 1560 and 1606. The Bar and attorney's profession also grew rapidly. However, by the 1690s, civil litigation in England was falling rapidly.[23] There was a major reduction in business in all the principal common law courts in the years after 1680, something that reached a nadir around 1750, when the courts of King's Bench and Common Pleas were hearing only about a sixth as many suits as they had 80 years earlier.[24] This suggests that the transitional stage was long over.

In England, the 'gentling' process appears to have proceeded somewhat faster and developed slightly further than some other parts of Europe, so that as early as the 1620s the country may have had a lower rate of serious violent crime than many of its major European counterparts.[25] Nevertheless, progress was slow, and improvements were not always apparent to contemporary observers. The innate

---

22. J.C. Oldham, "Truth-Telling in the Eighteenth-Century English Courtroom," *Law and History Review*, 1994, vol.12, no.1, p.113.
23. Stone, "Debate: The History of Violence in England," pp.220-222.
24. D. Lemmings, "Blackstone and Law Reform by Education: Preparation for the Bar and Lawyerly Culture in Eighteenth-Century England," *Law and History Review*, 1988, vol.16, pp.221-222.
25. Leyton, *Men of Blood*, pp.17-18.

human tendency to believe that one is living through the worst of times was found throughout the era. Complaints in the late 1650s that "Knavery of late is so epidemically practised" linked an alleged deterioration in the nation's morals to other changes, including sartorial developments such as the move from trunk-breeches to wide-breeches![26] Similarly, in November 1699, John Evelyn noted that the previous months had seen: "Horrible roberys, high-way men, and murders committed such as never was known in this nation since Christian reformed."[27] Even in the capital, there was, by 1731, a degree of nostalgia for a secure remembered past, however illusory: "A few years since, London was as remarkable for the safety of its inhabitants, as it is now notorious for the danger Persons are exposed to who walk the Streets after ten at Night."[28]

Additionally, the 'civilising process' did not develop in a continuous, uniform or unhindered manner. A Scandinavian historian, applying Elias's paradigm to early modern Sweden, found it to be a valuable explanation of change, but not without interruptions and setbacks, for example the many homicides occasioned by that country's numerous soldiers during Sweden's period as a great martial power in the seventeenth century. As a result, she

26. Anon, *The Caterpillars of this Nation Anatomised*, London, 1659, p.1.
27. J. Evelyn, *The diary of John Evelyn*, Oxford, Clarendon Press, 1955, vol.5, p.366.
28. *The Gentleman's Magazine*, 1731, vol.1, pp.59-60.

termed it a "civilizing process with obstacles".[29] Such an analysis could equally be applied to England. Thus, after 1660, a rakish upper class counter-culture, given to duelling and drunkenness developed, especially in London. Its members certainly did not avoid 'emotionally charged instructions and cues' that validated violence as a manly and correct response to life's everyday frustrations and humiliations.[30] Defoe was convinced that there had been a general deterioration in manners in the 40 years following the Restoration of 1660, something he attributed to the decline of Puritanism and the bad example set by a dissolute court, many members of the gentry and even clergymen.[31] Arguably, the libertine culture of the Restoration period was a conscious rejection of, or reaction to, the new notions of civility. Thus, there was no general internalisation of a monolithic code that produced increased levels of inhibition. Not all aristocrats embraced 'civility'; some had reservations about the 'artful' behaviour that they feared it engendered. Nevertheless, it can also be argued that, because Restoration libertines were trying to set themselves apart from others by their very misbehaviour, this itself is indicative of the prevalence of the new culture of manners, already so powerful that it could prompt the creation of a

---

29. E. Osterberg, "Criminality and the Early Modern State in Scandinavia" in *The Civilization of Crime: violence in town and country since the Middle Ages*, J.A. Johnson and E.H. Monkkonen (eds.), Urbana: University of Illinois Press, 1996, p.41.
30. Leyton, *Men of Blood*, pp.17-18.
31. D. Defoe, "The Poor Man's Plea" in *The Shortest Way with the Dissenters*, Oxford, Basil Blackwell, 1927, pp.2-5.

'counter-culture' to distinguish certain men.[32]

Crime and Need

Even in the early modern period, thoughtful men suspected that economic conditions affected contemporary levels of crime. In the early 1500s, Thomas More had argued that, rather than savagely punishing felons, it would be much better to make provision for everyone to earn a living: "... so that no man should be driven to this extreme necessity, first to steal, and then to die."[33] Such views were to be shared by other senior members of the judiciary in the ensuing centuries. Thus, Sir Mathew Hale was convinced that the prevention of poverty, idleness, and the promotion of education among the poor would do more good than: "... all the Gibbets, and Cauterization, and Whipping Posts, and Jayls in this Kingdom, and would render these kinds of Disciplines less necessary and less frequent."[34] In the harsh closing decades of the sixteenth century, in particular, numerous observers accepted More's suggestion that there was a link between crime rates and an economy suffering from the combined effects of harvest failure, war, plague

---

32. C.D. Hemphill, Review of "From Courtesy to Civility: Changing Codes of Conduct in Early Modern England" by Anna Bryson, *Journal of Social History*, 2000, vol.33, issue 3, p.747.
33. Sir T. More, *Utopia*, Ware, Wordsworth Classics, 1997, p.31.
34. Sir M. Hale, Professor to *A Discourse Touching Provision for the Poor*, London, William Shrowsbery, 1683, p.103.

and an apparent industrial stagnation.[35] The equation appeared simple; as Robert Hitchcock noted in 1580, a starving man: "... in his great want, will take with force and courage from them that hath, to serve his necessity."[36]

Such an analysis has also been supported by several modern academics, who argue that the patterns of prosecution produced by the records of Elizabethan and Jacobean courts reflect real changes in the level of property crime, and that these changes were rooted in economic conditions.[37] Such scholars have usually (tentatively) suggested that crime, as measured by assizes indictments, was increasing during the Elizabethan period.[38] Thus, according to Professor J.S. Cockburn, a superficial examination suggests that the *per capita* level of indictments for crime increased in the 40 years prior to the end of the sixteenth century. It then stabilised and began to fall slowly until the early 1620s, when another gradual increase set in. Accordingly, Essex produced eight indictments per 10,000 people in the 1560s, rising to 14 in the 1570s and about 20 by 1600 (estimating levels of population size and growth in this period is always difficult). However, slightly limiting the

---

35. P. Lawson, "Property Crime and Hard Times in England, 1559-1624," *Law and History Review*, 1986, vol.4, p.96.
36. R. Hitchcock, "A Politic Plat for the honour of the Prince," in *Social England Illustrated: A Collection of XVIIth Century Tracts*, A. Lang and E. Arber (eds.), Westminster, Archibald Constable, 1903, pp.86-87.
37. Lawson, "Property Crime and Hard Times in England, 1559-1624," p.127.
38. L. Knafla, "Sin of all Sorts Swarmeth: Criminal Litigation in an English County in the early Seventeenth Century" in *Law, Litigants and the Legal Profession*, E.W. Ives and A.H. Manchester (eds.), London, Royal History Society, 1983, p.52.

conclusions that can be drawn from these figures, the increase for Sussex was more modest, and the indictment level for Hertfordshire almost unchanged during the same period. Even so, there would appear to be enough evidence to suggest a significant, if not spectacular, real increase in the rates of indicted crime in the latter decades of the sixteenth century, followed by a gradual decline.[39] Such an analysis at least raises the possibility that there was a genuine increase in crime during this period.

More generally, Professor Cockburn has identified a correlation between the incidence of crime and high prices in the sixteenth century, and a weaker link between them in the early seventeenth century, leading him to conclude that a significant amount of theft was motivated by economic necessity.[40] (Such an analysis has also been applied to the similarly straitened early decades of the fourteenth century.) Thus, in Elizabethan Essex, the reasonable harvest years of 1592-94 saw an average of 78.6 prosecutions for theft, the years of dearth in 1595 to 1597 produced an average of 178.3 There was also an increase in the proportion of thefts that involved foodstuffs. A similar pattern is discernible in early seventeenth century Somerset, Wiltshire and Lancashire.[41] There were specific crimes that were clearly attributable to need. The Somerset JP Edward Hext noted a case, in the

---

39. Cockburn, "The Nature and Incidence of Crime in England 1559-1625: A Preliminary Survey" in *Crime in England 1550-1800*, J.S. Cockburn (Ed.), London, Methuen, 1977, at pp.53-54 and p.70.
40. Cockburn, "The Nature and Incidence of Crime in England 1559-1625," p.70.
41. K. Wrightson and J. Walter, "Dearth and the Social Order in Early Modern England," *Past and Present*, 1976, no.71, pp.23-24.

1590s, in which a band of 80 poor men had waylaid a cart loaded with cheese, and divided it amongst themselves. Others were apparently heard to declare "boldlye they must not starve, they will not starve".[42] However, it is by no means a simple picture, even in this period. Heydon in Essex experienced extreme poverty with up to two-thirds of the village receiving parish relief in difficult times, yet it produced only one identified felon in the period between 1558 and 1603. By contrast, the small weaving town of Halstead saw a sharp increase of crime during the difficult 1590s.[43] Additionally, an increase in prosecution levels does not necessarily mean a real increase in theft. As wealthier people saw the arrival of dearth they may have become more alarmed for their own security and been willing to initiate a higher proportion of prosecutions out of criminal incidents, in a system that contained massive discretion not to take formal action. Rather than producing a crime wave, harsh times might have produced a law enforcement wave. An increasingly interventionist early modern state may also have been keen to crackdown firmly during periods of hardship. Thus, the proclamation of the Caroline Book of Orders on January 31, 1631 was typical of the longstanding and traditional response to economic problems and rural crisis, in this case a series of harvest failures and slumps in the manufacturing trades. It reminded local governors of

---

42. E. Hext, "Letter written by Edward Hext, a Somerset JP, to Lord Burghley on September 25, 1596," reproduced in *Tudor Economic Documents*, R.H. Tawney and E. Power (Eds.), London, Longmans, 1951, vol.2 at pp.340-341.
43. Wrightson and Walter, "Dearth and the Social Order in Early Modern England," pp.23-24.

their existing statutory duties. On a positive note, poverty was to be relieved, unemployed and idle people provided with work and children apprenticed. However, it also stipulated that vagrants be vigorously punished, houses of correction built, and ale-houses shut, etc.[44] Similarly, behind Hext's concern about sturdy rogues were thinly veiled social fears, anxieties that had been exacerbated by the harsh conditions present at the end of the sixteenth century. Hext felt that the apparent impunity of many beggars set a bad example to the ordinary poor in a 'tyme of dearth'. Some vagrants apparently demonstrated open 'contempte both of noble men and gentlemen'.[45]

However, despite regular harvest failures, and constant population growth, demographic studies have indicated that in early modern England, at least, and unlike some other European countries, dearth rarely gave rise to crises of subsistence.[46] Food became scarcer and much more expensive, food of an inferior quality was consumed and life generally became 'harder'. Nevertheless, apart from isolated villages in a few remote areas, such as the fells of Cumberland and Westmoreland in the 1590s, people did not actually starve. This must be factored into any analysis. On the whole, the evidence does suggest a significant, albeit complex, link between hard times in the late sixteenth

---

44. H. Langeluddecke, "Patchy and Spasmodic?: The Response of Justices of the Peace to Charles I's Book of Orders," *English Historical Review*, 1988, vol.113, no.454, p.1231.

45. Hext, "Letter written by Edward Hext to Lord Burghley on September 25, 1596," pp.340-341.

46. Wrightson and Walter, "Dearth and the Social Order in Early Modern England," p.23.

century and an increase in the number of prosecutions for theft during that era, with harvest crises depressing living standards and rising offences. However, it requires a sophisticated paradigm. Thus, dearth frequently prompted migration, especially from the north to the south, and particularly to London. As migrants got into difficulties, away from their native parishes, the temptation to steal increased. This might explain both an apparent 'lag' between dearth and prosecution levels and also the clusters of criminal cases around migratory routes, such as Ermine Street. Such an analysis avoids focusing entirely on the workings of the criminal justice system and elite mentalities, while being more sophisticated than a simple 'unsatisfied hunger produces crime' model.[47]

Generally, however, the late 1500s apart, most observers consider that the link between economic hardship and the incidence of crime is uncertain. There was little apparent direct correlation between economic crises after the early 1600s and crime rates. Serious property crimes appear to have declined steadily from then onwards, and especially after the Restoration, a process that continued until the late eighteenth century.[48] Of course, the century after 1650 witnessed a generally improving situation with a considerable expansion in the economy. Better root crops, grains and grasses increased agricultural yields, while internal and foreign trade expanded, promoting wealth and

---

47. Lawson, "Property, Crime and Hard Times in England 1559-1624," pp.109-123.
48. J. McMullan, "Crime, Law and Order in Early Modern England," *British Journal of Criminology*, 1987, vol.27, no.3, p.253.

the demand for labour.[49] By 1704, Defoe was convinced that it was labour, not work, that was lacking in England, so that: "No man in England, of sound limbs and senses, can be poor meerly for want of work."[50] It might be expected that this would have a long-term affect on crime rates.

In any event, whatever the role of 'need', it must be remembered that it was never more than a factor in the commission of offences. Such records as exist, indicate that a considerable number of serious crimes were not motivated by the survival imperative, nor were they 'social' crimes, prompted by class resentment. Rather, like the murder of a wealthy collier by his social 'superior' in Crowhurst, in 1532, they were committed as 'short-cuts' to increased wealth.[51] An examination of the occupations of 98 male convicts, transported to the Americas in the early 1720s aboard two ships, provides a proportionately representative cross-section of English society. Unsurprisingly, almost half (48 out of the 98) were unskilled labourers, with over a fifth (21 men) being low-skilled labourers (for example weavers and fishermen). However, just over a quarter (27 men) were made up of skilled craftsmen and tradesmen (such as barbers, carpenters, tailors, shoemakers and perukers); another two per cent were wealthy tradesmen and

49. A.L. Beier, *Masterless Men: the vagrancy problem in England 1560-1640*, London, Methuen & Co., 1985, p.172.
50. Defoe, *Giving Alms to Charity*, London, 1704, p.9.
51. Robison, "Murder at Crowhurst," p.42.

professionals (an attorney and a prosperous miller).[52]

---

52. A.R. Ekirch, "Bound for America: A Profile of British Convicts Transported to the Colonies, 1718-1775," in E.H. Monkkonen (Ed.), *Crime and Justice in American History, The Colonies and Early Republic,* London, Meckler, 1991, Part 1, vol.1, at pp.101-102.

Chapter 3

The Pattern of Crime in Early Modern England

> ... there is no country in the world where there are so
> many thieves and robbers as in England; insomuch, that
> few venture to go alone in the country, excepting in the
> middle of the day, and fewer still in the towns at night,
> and least of all in London.
>
> *Venetian Diplomat, c. 1500[1]*

Introduction

In some respects, England's crime profile made it a singular
early modern society. For much of the period, and especially
after 1600, it was characterised by contemporary European
standards (though not by modern English ones) by a
relatively low level of serious interpersonal violence even in
the 'lawless' North, and by an absence of social banditry.
The reasons for this are not entirely clear. Of course, it was
a small country, a fraction of the size of France or Spain, and
lacking large areas of mountain, moor or forest, its highest
fell being little over 3,000 feet. It was surrounded by water,
apart from its Scottish and Welsh borders (the latter
Principality being legally incorporated into England in
1536). Thus, it was inherently easier to police than some
continental countries. Nevertheless, other, social and

---

1.   Anon, *A Relation, or Rather a True Account of the Island of England ... About the Year 1500*, C. Sneyd (Trans.), London, Camden Society, 1847, p.34.

cultural, factors appear to have been at work as well.[2] However, although, in some respects, an unusual society, in many others similar social determinants to those found on the continent meant that patterns of crime, the incidence of offences, and their immediate social background, were very much like those elsewhere in Europe. In foreign eyes, piracy was the only crime that the English were particularly associated with, being "good sailors, and better pirates, cunning, treacherous and thievish".[3] This was, perhaps, unsurprising in a maritime nation.

The Profile of Early Modern Crime

What was a 'typical' English crime? The criminal profile provided by a statistical analysis of the cases heard before the country's courts (themselves a minority of offences) depends heavily on the tribunal investigated. Thus, a break-down of the assizes indictments for Kent in the early seventeenth century would suggest that 73 per cent of prosecuted crimes were for offences against property, 21 per cent for crimes against the person and six per cent for offences against the peace. Of the property offences, 61 per cent were cases of grand larceny (theft of items worth over 12d. in value). Additionally, they indicate a rate of seven indictments per 10,000 people in the county (then c.130,000

---

2. A. Macfarlane and S. Harrison, *The justice and the mare's ale. Law and disorder in seventeenth century England,* Oxford, Blackwell, 1981, at pp.186-187.
3. P. Hentzner, *Travels in England during the reign of Queen Elizabeth,* London, Cassell & Co., 1889, p.82.

inhabitants). Neighbouring counties appear to have produced a strikingly similar proportion of property crimes at their own assizes, about 75 per cent in Essex, 77 per cent in Sussex and 79 per cent in Hertfordshire, although the per capita rate of indictments was sometimes much higher (up to three times greater than in Kent). However, taken alone, this division gives a misleading picture of English crime, as, in Kent, the assizes courts dealt with only seven per cent of all criminal cases (broadly defined). The quarter sessions dealt with 20 per cent of cases, and the many local courts, such as the Faversham and Dover borough sessions, another 73 per cent. This profile *still* excludes any manorial leet courts that had continued to deal with criminal matters (though, in Kent, they appear to have been exceptionally rare by then). It also ignores any quasi-criminal offences determined in local ecclesiastical courts. Even excluding such forums, the profile of crime revealed by considering assizes, quarter sessions and borough courts together is very different to that provided by the assizes alone. Taken together, property offences make up only 10 per cent of crimes, with offences against the person being 22 per cent of cases, those against the peace 20 per cent, moral crimes 22 per cent, and public nuisances 25 per cent.[4] Not only do the proportions of various types of crime vary greatly with the court(s) surveyed, but so also do the numbers. Thus, in Essex, the recorded crime rate in c.1630 increases from

---

4.   L. Knafla, "'Sin of all Sorts Swarmeth.' Criminal Litigation in an English County in the early Seventeenth Century" in E.W. Ives and A.H. Manchester (eds.), *Law, Litigants and the Legal Profession*, London, Royal History Society, 1983, p.58. Other categories account for the remaining one per cent.

approximately 100 per 100,000 of population when based on the assizes alone, to approximately 700 per 100,000 when based on the assizes and quarter sessions combined. The rate would probably increase at least as much again if all the other lesser courts and church courts with criminal jurisdictions were included.[5]

Of course, the cases handled by these different courts were not all of the same gravity; the assizes usually claimed the most serious offences, county and borough sessions matters of lesser seriousness. It is also possible to exaggerate the significance of some minor offences dealt with in lesser forums. A qualitative distinction can frequently be drawn between different types of 'crime', and this was something that English early-modern jurists were very willing to do. Largely untroubled by modern notions of moral relativism, common lawyers from the end of the fifteenth century until at least the time of Jeremy Bentham - men such as Coke, Hale, Hawkins and Blackstone - accepted, almost without question, that there was a crucial distinction between crimes that were *mala in se*, which offended against God and religion, such as murder, robbery, theft and rape, and offences that were *mala prohibita*, created to promote good administration by a municipal legislator. Obviously, breaches of the Mosaic Law that were also secular crimes were in the former category, those of bye-laws in the latter. Blackstone even went as far as to claim that laws that were *mala prohibita* were not binding on conscience, individuals

---

5. T. Curtis and J.A. Sharpe, "Crime in Tudor and Stuart England," *History Today*, 1988, vol.38, issue 2, p.23.

could choose to pay the penalty prescribed for not obeying them instead.[6] Unfortunately, this does not mean that the work of (for example) the church courts can be neatly distinguished from that of the quarter sessions and assizes. Some of the cases dealt with by ecclesiastical forums would have been considered mainstream crimes by any definition, and included matters which *could* have been brought in secular forums. Additionally, many moral (but not secular criminal) offences were considered *mala in se*. Thus, great caution is necessary before making sweeping generalisations based on the evidence of a single court. Perhaps more valuable than studies of individual courts are examinations of all the cases recorded in a county in a single year, such as Professor Knafla's masterful study of Kent in 1602.

Versatility of Criminal Careers

It is necessary to classify offences and offenders for purposes of analysis. This has historical precedent. Many early modern English observers, such as Thomas Harman, had a near mania for producing refined distinctions and elaborate hierarchies within the criminal underworld. However, the value of such classifications is limited. In the modern era, despite a popular belief in criminal 'specialisms' encapsulated in terms such as 'burglar', 'robber' etc., criminal careers appear to be fairly versatile

---

6. P.J. Fitzgerald, "Crime, Sin and Negligence," in *Law Quarterly Review*, 1963, vol.79, pp.351-354.

and offender specialisation is comparatively rare.[7] Early modern criminal careers were equally fluid. Many offenders varied their enterprises as opportunities presented themselves, switching freely between picking pockets, burglary, shoplifting and robbery. Thus, Jack Hall, executed in 1707 for house breaking and shooting a constable, was also reputed to be an expert footpad, shoplifter and general pilferer of anything that he could find, even if it were 'but mops and pails'.[8] Similarly, Dick Turpin was, in turns, a receiver of poached meat, burglar, house robber and highwayman, before eventually being hanged for horse theft. Additionally, then as now, some men would drift in and out of criminal activity, interspersing their criminal careers with lengthy periods of legitimate work. Thus, in 1661, the notorious highwayman William Nevison, having robbed a rich country Brazier of 450 pounds, returned to Yorkshire, after an absence of eight years, and: "... lived very honestly with his father till he died, and then returned to his old courses again, committing such robberies as rendered his name the terror of the road."[9]

Gender

Crime is, and always has been, a predominantly male

---

7.   M. Gottfredson and T. Hirschi, *A General Theory of Crime,* Stanford, Stanford University Press, 1990, p.91.

8.   J.L. Rayner and G.T. Crook (eds.), *The Complete Newgate Calendar,* London, privately printed for the Navarre Society, 1926, vol.II, p.196.

9.   C. Johnson, *A General History of the Lives and Adventures of the Most Famous Highwaymen, Murderers, Street-Robbers,* London: J. Janeway, 1734, p.104.

activity. However, although always in a minority, the proportion of females involved in crime has varied significantly over the centuries. Nevertheless, with some reservations, those formally accused of crimes in early modern England were overwhelmingly men, irrespective of the court, county or decade selected for scrutiny. Typically, between 1591 and 1618, women made up less than 15 per cent of all those prosecuted on indictment in Hertfordshire, at that county's quarter sessions and assizes courts.[10] The generalisation is almost true irrespective of the individual offence considered, with the exception of a few mainly 'female' crimes, such as witchcraft and infanticide.[11] In Hertfordshire, women committed 10 of 11 cases of infanticide and most offences of witchcraft in the same 27-year period.[12] There were a few other crimes, among them various ale-house offences and the receiving of stolen goods, where the number of females involved was also often significant. The Hertfordshire study appears to be consistent with equivalent studies conducted for Sussex (Herrup) and Essex (Sharpe), though it seems that heavily urban and sub-urban areas, such as the Metropolis, were *sui generis* in witnessing higher rates of female prosecution. Thus, in London, women made up c.30 per cent of defendants in serious cases at the Old Bailey in 1687, rising to a peak of

---

10. Anon, *The Caterpillars of this Nation Anatomised*, London, 1659, p.4.
11. Curtis and Sharpe, "Crime in Tudor and Stuart England," pp.23-33.
12. P. Lawson, "Patriarchy, Crime and the Courts: The Criminality of Women in Late Tudor and Early Stuart England" in *Criminal Justice in the Old World and the New*, G.T. Smith (Ed.), Toronto, Centre of Criminology, University of Toronto, 1998, pp.21-27.

c.40 per cent in 1715, before declining inexorably to a level of only 10 per cent by the end of the nineteenth century.[13] Nevertheless, predominantly rural Cheshire also appears to have witnessed a slightly higher number of female indictments than the national average.[14] It should be noted that there was nothing unusual about England's gender distribution in prosecuted crime. In Frankfurt, in the years from 1562 to 1646, 318 men were executed compared to only 25 women, though in Nuremburg they appear to have made up almost 30 per cent of seventeenth century executions.[15]

More controversially, it has been argued that not only were women less prone to offending and prosecution but they were also unlikely to commit offences without male assistance, and were more likely to play a passive and dependent role in the execution of crime than men.[16] Such generalisations are probably justified, albeit that numerous qualifications must be made to the general pattern. Even the highway woman who held up an astonished butcher at pistol point in "very Gallant Manner", near Romford, Essex, in 1735, was backed up by an armed male colleague.[17] Of the Hertfordshire selection of women, 58 per cent worked with

---

13. M. Feeley and D.L. Little, "The Vanishing Female: The Decline of Women in the Criminal Process, 1687-1912" in *Law and Society Review*, 1991, vol.25, no.4, p.719.

14. G. Walker, "Women, theft and the world of stolen goods," J. Kermode and Walker (eds.), *Women, Crime and the Courts in Early Modern England*, London, UCL Press, 1994, pp.81-87.

15. R. Van Dulmen, *Theatre of Horror: Crime and Punishment in Early Modern Germany*, Cambridge, Polity Press, E. Neu (Trans.), 1990, p.80.

16. Curtis and Sharpe, "Crime in Tudor and Stuart England," pp.23-33.

17. *The Gentleman's Magazine*, 1735, vol.5, p.680.

accomplices, a much higher figure than for their male counterparts; these were usually, though not always, men.[18] (However, Garthine Walker has recently challenged the generality of some assumptions about women's criminal involvement, suggesting that their involvement was greater than sometimes proposed, that they were not mainly the assistants of male criminals and that they did not necessarily steal goods of lesser value than men.)[19] Many of the differences between the proportions of men and women indicted for different types of crime are unsurprising. Female instrumental crime was more likely to involve stealth (theft) rather than violence (robbery) compared to that of male criminals. In particular, many pick-pockets were female, especially in London, where it was noted in the 1650s: "Of this sort there be as many women as men, especially whores."[20]

There are two possible explanations for the generally low incidence of early modern female prosecution (arguments that have also been advanced for the medieval and recent modern eras). One is that women really were less likely to commit crime; the other is that they were more leniently treated by the criminal justice system when they did so, being less likely to be reported or prosecuted. The most likely explanation is a combination of the two, with a heavy emphasis on incidence rather than differential treatment within the justice system. Nevertheless, women

---

18. Lawson, "Patriarchy, Crime and the Courts," pp.21-27.
19. Walker, "Women, theft and the world of stolen goods," pp.81-99.
20. Anon, *The Caterpillars of this Nation Anatomised*, p.4.

did, sometimes, benefit from leniency in a manner that was denied to men. Early modern England, like everywhere else in Europe, was a male dominated society. As an anonymous author noted in 1632: "Women have no voyse in Parliament. They make no Lawes, they consent to none, they abrogate none." (Like many in that era, he attributed this to the consequences of Eve's role in precipitating man's fall in the Garden of Eden.) However, in the criminal law at least, this 'legal passivity' did not always work to their disadvantage. Obviously, a woman acting on her own, "without the privitie of her husband", could become "either principall or accessory" in committing felony. Nevertheless, if she worked with her husband, unless in an overtly active role, the law was often reluctant to find that she was implicated. Indeed, some even argued that: "If a man and his wife commit felonie joyntly, it seemeth the wife is no felon, but it shall be wholly judged the husband's fact." Moreover, if a man became aware that his wife was involved in theft or receiving stolen goods he could only absolve himself from complicity by drastic steps; her "husband so soone as he perceive it [must] waive and forsake their company." By contrast, assuming she did not get excessively involved in her spouse's crimes, his wife, even though: "... not ignorant of it may keepe his Company still notwithstanding, and not be deemed accesory."[21] Perhaps because of this, women were also more likely to be acquitted if tried. Thus, at the Hertfordshire assizes, in the 50 years from 1573, only 30 per

---

21. Anon, *The Laws Resolutions of Womens Rights*, London, John More, 1632, pp.6 and 206.

cent of the women arraigned for felony were convicted, compared to 52 per cent of men. (This appears to have been a change from the medieval period when conviction rates for the two sexes were closer.)[22]

Nevertheless, with this reservation, the primary explanation for the low numbers of women being processed through the criminal justice system appears to be incidence; then as now, women committed fewer offences. Why this should be so has perplexed sociologists for decades. Some observers, particularly feminists, have argued that female crime was (and is) socially contextualised in a patriarchal society, reducing its occurrence. Certainly, women's criminal activity, especially instrumental crime, was limited by situational factors which were a reflection of the economic and social realities of their lives. Significantly, female servants, who, unlike many others of their gender, *did* have ready access to stealable goods, appear to have been almost as likely to commit theft as their male colleagues. Thus, in 1725, Defoe could complain that: "Our sessions' papers of late are crowded with instances of servant-maids robbing their places."[23] Others have attributed low levels of crime, especially violent crime, to women's inherent biological or psychological natures.[24] Women do appear to have committed markedly fewer

---

22. J.G. Bellamy, *The Criminal Trial in Later Medieval England: Felony Before the Courts from Edward I to the Sixteenth Century*, Toronto, University of Toronto Press, 1998, p.124.

23. A. Moreton (D. Defoe), *Every-Body's Business is No-Body's Business*, London, 1725, p.6.

24. Lawson, *Patriarchy, Crime and the Courts*, pp.56-57.

homicides (infanticide apart) though they were also much less likely to be armed or intoxicated. Again, a combination of the two appears most likely, crimes of violence being more influenced by innate factors (strength and aggression) and the incidence of female instrumental crime being more likely to be socially determined.

Social Profile of Crime

In the modern era, conventional crime (as opposed to white collar crime) has tended to be disproportionately concentrated in a criminogenic 'underclass'. Arguably, such a class also existed in the early modern period. However, crime was not its special preserve, having a more socially variegated basis than it does today. This was especially true for offences of violence and robbery (the incentive for petty theft amongst the wealthy being largely absent). In the 1590s, William Harrison deplored England's large numbers of robberies. However, he identified their perpetrators as being of two social types, one seeking a better quality of life, rather than its necessities, the other merely trying to survive: "... the first by young shifting gentlemen, which oftentimes doo beare more port than they are able to maintaine. Secondlie by servingmen, whose wages cannot suffice so much as to find them breeches."[25] Despite the softening in manners amongst the upper social orders (previously

---

25. W. Harrison, *A Description of England, 2nd Book*, 2nd edn., 1587, London, New Shakespeare Society, 1877, p.230.

discussed), something that gradually discouraged the commission of violent offences, change was a very slow process.

Upper Class Crime

Throughout the period, there was a continuing tradition of upper class violence. Many aristocrats and gentlemen demonstrated a capacity for extreme aggression, both to each other and to their social inferiors, often in the most inappropriate places. Thus, Henry Pierrepont, the 1st Marquis of Dorchester, a doctor, lawyer and regular brawler, assaulted a man during divine service in Westminster Abbey in 1638. Alcohol could turn even apparently innocuous upper class social gatherings into brawls. In 1663, soldiers were called to the Earl of Oxford's London house after a dinner party degenerated into "high words and some blows and pulling of perriwigs". In 1685, the obstreperous and bellicose 19-year-old Lord Sunderland was beaten up, while drunk, by a group of London constables.[26] In what was almost an anthropological study of the breed, an observer during the Interregnum laid the origins of Metropolitan 'Hectors' on the presence of civil war veterans, including many officers, who had been discharged after the conflict and then gravitated to London. There, lacking employment, they formed into groups, whored, gambled, frequented taverns, picked fights and

---

26. K.M. Brown, "Gentlemen and Thugs in 17th Century Britain," *History Today,* 1990, vol.40, issue 10, pp.27-30.

duels, extorted money, pimped and robbed as the opportunity presented itself. They were likely to die violently, of sexually transmitted diseases or on the gallows.[27] Peace did not bring an improvement, complaints continuing about: "The madness of many debauched Hectors being of late [1677] become so great." As a result, it was claimed that it was a "dangerous adventure for an honest person to walk along the streets especially in the evenings."[28] Similarly, after one Mr St Johns, himself the son of a Knight, killed another Knight in a tavern in December 1684, it was observed that "so many horrid murders and Duels about this time being committed (as was never heard of in England) gave much course of complaint and murmure universally."[29] In London, in the early 1700s, the phenomenon manifested itself again in vicious street attacks by upper class 'Mohock' hooligans and their imitators. As a result, Whitlocke Bulstrode, addressing the grand jury for the Middlesex quarter sessions, held at Westminster Hall in October 1722, could complain of "men of quality" who sat up into the small hours drinking before sallying forth into the Metropolitan streets "inflamed with Burgundy and inspired with madness." In this condition, they frequently resolved to commit some "outrageous wickedness", often

---

27. Anon, *Notable and pleasant History of the Famous renowned Knights of the Blade*, London, Richard Harper, 1652, pp.1-3.

28. Anon, *A true relation of all the Bloody Murders that have been committed in and about the Citie and Suburbs of London since the 4th of this instant June 1677*, London, D.M., 1677, p.3.

29. J. Evelyn, *The Diary of John Evelyn*, Oxford, Clarendon Press, E.S. de Beer (Ed.), vol.4, p.401.

manifested by attacking anyone that they encountered. Bulstrode noted that two such 'gentlemen' had recently been hanged in London for killing a Watchman.[30]

As these cases suggest, there were often lamentable failings in the behaviour of the upper social echelons. Indeed, the circumstances surrounding the hanging of Colonel Vrats and his accomplices for murder, in 1682, may be indicative of a fairly widespread upper class belief that some rules, even religious and legal ones, did not apply to the 'quality'. According to John Evelyn, Vrats went to his execution "like an undaunted hero ... and hoped and believed God would deal with him like a gentleman."[31] Arguably, however, upper class misconduct was more dangerous that that of the lower orders, if only because of the bad public example it set, a: "Rich Man's wickedness affects all the Neighbourhood, gives offence to the Sober, encourages and hardens the Lewd."[32] As Bulstrode observed, aggravating upper class violence was the widespread practise of "every giddy-braine'd huffado's wearing a Weapon."[33] Even magistrates were not immune from this habit and from what to modern eyes sometimes appears a bizarre degree of sensitivity. Thus, in March 1731, Justice Webster and Justice De Veil clashed in a coffee-house in Leicester-fields: "... words arising, the former [Webster]

---

30. W. Bulstrode, *The Third Charge of Whitlocke Bulstrode, Esq.*, London, 1723, pp.6-7.
31. Evelyn, *The Diary of John Evelyn*, vol.4, pp.273-274.
32. D. Defoe, *The Poor Man's Plea, in the Shortest Way with the Dissenters*, Oxford, Basil Blackwell, 1927, pp.1-11.
33. Anon, *A true relation of all the Bloody Murders*, p.5.

struck the other; on which Mr De Veil retreating to draw his Sword, Mr Webster stab'd him in the Belly about 5 inches deep." The quarrel arose because Webster, an Irish magistrate, had 'superseded' a warrant issued by De Veil against a fellow Irishman.[34] The outcomes could be even more tragic. In 1677, it was reported that as the keeper of a victualling house in Bishopsgate Street was quietly walking with his female partner, a man: "... better arm'd with a Sword, than seasoned with Discretion, took some impertinent occasion to quarrel with him about taking the wall justling him, or the like trifle; and drawing his weapon most valiantly upon this naked man, presently laid him dead at his feet." The killer was arrested and taken to Newgate for examination.[35] The *cassus belli*, a dispute over walking on the wall side of the pavement away from the gutter, was a common one; Paul Hentzner, a visiting German lawyer, noted that Elizabethan Londoners "give the wall as the place of honour". In 1725, John Gay's 'Peachum' was still alluding to upper class violence generally when observing that: "Murder is as fashionable a Crime as a Man can be guilty of. How many fine Gentlemen have we in Newgate every Year, purely upon that Article!"[36] Upper class children were not immune to such bellicosity. In March 1731, two youths at Eton College quarrelled while playing together, at which one drew a penknife and stabbed the other through the heart. The killer, a boy named Dalton, was

---

34. *The Gentleman's Magazine*, 1731, vol.1, p.125.
35. Anon, *A true relation of all the Bloody Murders*, p.5.
36. J. Gay, *The Beggar's Opera*, 1728, Act 1, Scene 4.

the son of a senior Irish judge; his victim, Edward Cochran, the offspring of an Antiguan merchant. Dalton, though apparently charged with murder, was subsequently convicted of manslaughter at the Buckingham assizes in August of that year, probably being clergied and released. Although the boys were described as being of about 12 years of age, Dalton's tomb in the Eton cemetery indicates that he was actually 14. Some press reports suggest that the quarrel arose as the two boys were playing marbles.[37]

As Harrison's remark suggests, gentlemen were also well represented amongst the ranks of robbers, especially highwaymen. In the Elizabethan Jesuit Robert Parson's words, such men were often of "no base condition". If John Aubrey is to be believed, Sir John Popham (1531-1607), who ultimately became a Lord Chief Justice, had a roistering youth during which he neglected his legal studies but spent his time in "profligate company, and was wont to take [rob] a purse with them". Fortunately, his wife ultimately forced him to mend his ways.[38] Similarly, in 1618, Sir George Sandys was hanged for highway robbery. He had already been acquitted and pardoned for the same crime on two earlier occasions, and his son appears to have followed his father's trade, though executed for rape in 1626.[39] However, such high-ranking men were rare. Most 'genteel' robbers were less distinguished and fell into certain well defined categories. Some were younger sons, without inheritances,

---

37. *The Gentleman's Magazine*, 1731, vol.1, p.130 and p.351.
38. J. Aubrey, *Brief Lives*, Woodbridge, The Boydell Press, R. Baxter (Ed.), 1982, p.252.
39. G. Spraggs, *Outlaws and Highwaymen*, London, Pimlico, 2001, pp.101-102.

who, having indulged in idleness and gaming, had no attractive and remunerative alternatives open to them. Others, though originally wealthy, were forced into crime having become impoverished because they had "no government of themselves, but [spent their time] banqueting with whores, and making late suppers". Their victims were frequently of a lower social class, being "honest poor men" who were often totally undone by their losses.[40] A group of 'gentlemen' who were executed for highway robbery and murder in 1608 were typical of such individuals. After taking up a roistering existence in London they found they could no longer afford their extravagant lifestyle without resorting to crime.[41] Such men often became especially desperate after falling into debt, so that some blamed money-lenders to the gentry for making Newmarket Heath and Royston Downs (favourite locations for robbery) so full of highwaymen at Christmas that: "... poor country people cannot pass quietly to their cottages, but some gentleman will borrow all the money they have."[42]

Upper Class Immunity

Upper class lawlessness was aided because, treason apart, aristocrats and substantial gentlemen had a considerable,

---

40. S. Rid, "Martin Markall, Beadle of Bridewell," in A.V. Judges (Ed.) *The Elizabethan Underworld*, London, George Routledge, 1930, pp.415-416.
41. B.L., *The Lives, Apprehension, Arraignment and Execution of Robert Throgmorton, William Porter, John Bishop*, London, Henry Gosson, 1608, f.A3.
42. W. Fennor, "The Counter's Commonwealth 1617," in A.V. Judges (Ed.), *The Elizabethan Underworld*, London, George Routledge, 1930, p.446.

though not unlimited, immunity in practice from the workings of the criminal law. This had a long historical basis. In the fifteenth century, landed and titled felons only rarely faced the judicial consequences of their crimes, especially when they involved violence. Medieval noblemen could exert enormous influence over their era's criminal justice system, intimidating, kidnapping, assaulting and even murdering witnesses, jurors, judges and court officials. Frequently, however, even these steps were unnecessary, simple bribery or family influence being enough. Thus, a fourteenth century JP could openly inform a young nobleman that: "For the love of your father I have hindered charges being brought against you and have prevented execution of indictment actually made." Not surprisingly, only 14 out of 10,500 felony indictments in that century involved noblemen, and most of these ended in acquittal or were never heard.[43] Even when charges were brought, they could easily be undermined by an appeal to the King. An examination of fifteenth century indictments determined in the court of King's Bench suggests that, normally, almost anyone of rank could rely on receiving a pardon, if facing any crime short of high treason. However, as the poet Thomas Hoccleve observed in 1411, granting well-connected murderers pardons merely encouraged further killings. As a result, the chief deterrent to murder amongst the landed classes was usually the threat of private vengeance. The

---

43. B.A. Hanawalt, "Fur Collar Crime: the Pattern of Crime amongst the Fourteenth-Century English Nobles," *Journal of Social History*, 1975, vol.8, p.3 and p.7.

failings of royal justice in this area also had disastrous consequences in undermining the wider 'rule of law', legitimising violent crime throughout society and undermining the operation of the criminal justice system for all social groups.[44]

This highly privileged position did not survive the end of the medieval period unscathed. Nevertheless, change was slow and incomplete in the 250 years after 1500, so that the class bias that lay behind much early modern justice remained readily apparent to contemporary observers. Thus, Shakespeare's King Lear famously observed that: "Through tatter'd clothes small vices do appear; Robes and furr'd gowns hide all. Plate sin with gold, And the strong lance of justice hurtless breaks: Arm it in rags, a pigmy's straw does pierce it."[45] Over a century later, Daniel Defoe was still noting that members of the upper social orders might commit offences of immorality or worse and escape totally unpunished, while those from the lower classes would be put in the stocks or sent to the House of Correction for the same matters. As a result, legislation to prevent vice often produced "Cobweb Laws, in which small Flies are catch'd, and great ones break through." A few whores might be whipped, some poor inebriates stocked, and those who sold alcohol on the Sabbath fined, but: "The man with a Gold Ring, and Gay Cloths, may Swear before the Justice, or at the Justice; may reel home through the open Streets, and

---

44. S.J. Payling, "Murder, motive and punishment in fifteenth century England: two gentry case-studies," *English Historical Review*, 1998, vol.113, no.450, pp.1-20.
45. W. Shakespeare, *King Lear*, Act 4, Scene 6.

no man take any notice of it."[46] Such socially variegated law enforcement applied as much to the church courts as to the secular ones. George Herbert thought it necessary to urge churchwardens to treat rich parishioners on the same basis as poorer ones when it came to presenting offenders, and "by no means to spare any, though never so great."[47] Members of the political nation were also usually wary about passing any legislation that might impinge on their own lives and pleasures. When 'Puritan' legislation was passed, it was often in the knowledge that it would only be used against the 'meaner sort'. Indeed, some thoughtful MPs expressly condemned such legislation specifically because of this. Thus, in 1601, a century before Defoe was writing, Edward Glascock criticised a bill against drunkenness as a "meer cob-web to catch poor flies in". Similarly, John Bond opposed another bill, the same year, punishing absence from church on the Sabbath, arguing that: "The poor commonality (whose strength and quietness is the strength and quietness of us all) he only shall be punished, he vexed. For will any think that a Justice of Peace will contest with so good a man as himself?"[48]

Even worse, selective enforcement of the law in the early modern era was not confined to minor offences of morality. Whatever the crime, upper class miscreants were more

---

46. D. Defoe, *The Poor Man's Plea*, pp.6-7.
47. G. Herbert, *A priest to the Temple*, London, T. Maxey and T. Garthwait, North door of St Paul's, 1652, p.30.
48. J. Kent, "Attitudes of Members of the House of Commons to the Regulation of 'Personal Conduct in Late Elizabethan and Early Stuart England," *British Institute of Historical Research*, 1973, vol.46, pp.41-71 and pp.60-61.

likely to be ignored, pardoned or, if penalised, dealt with informally or by alternative sanctions to formal prosecution. Thus, in August 1731, Philip Nichols, a Doctor of Laws and Fellow of Trinity Hall, Cambridge, was unanimously expelled from the college, and a copy of his 'sentence', written in Latin, was fixed to the college gate, signifying that he had been guilty of: "... dissolute living and of stealing many valuable Books out of St John's College Library, and elsewhere, to the great Scandal and Dishonour of that University."[49] He could have been transported had the matter come before a court. Similarly, in August 1690, the participation of James Seton, brother and heir to Viscount Kingston, in the robbery of mailbags on the London to Edinburgh highway was tactfully 'overlooked', not even a trial resulting.[50] Occasionally, until late in the period, quite blatant class bias can be discerned *after* formal proceedings were invoked. At Winchester, in February 1731, Sir Simon Clarke and Lieutenant Robert Arnott were convicted of a highway robbery in a court crowded with local gentlemen. However, Sir Simon made an emotive and moving speech to the court. After hearing it:

"The High Sheriff and grand jury, considering the antiquity, worth and dignity of Sir Simon's ancestors, the services they had done their king and country, together with the youth and melancholy circumstances

49. *The Gentleman's Magazine*, 1731, vol.1, p.351.
50. K.M. Brown, "Gentlemen and Thugs in 17th Century Britain," *History Today*, 1990, vol.40, pp.30-32.

of that unhappy gentleman, agreed to address his Majesty in their behalf; upon which a reprieve *sine die*, which implies for ever, was granted them."

The same report recorded many executions for crimes committed by ordinary felons elsewhere in the country.[51] Financial and personal influence with jurors might also produce a satisfactory outcome for well-to-do defendants. John Gay's 'Peachum' alluded to this in 1728, when observing that many gentlemen accused of murder: "If they have wherewithal to persuade the Jury to bring it in Manslaughter, what are they the worse for it?"[52] Manslaughter was a clergyable offence.

Rank continued to provide protection, as Sir John Fitz, a Devon gentleman of dissolute habits, found in the Elizabethan period. Having quarrelled over dinner with a friend, he followed his erstwhile dining partner as he rode home. Accompanied by four retainers (an echo here of Lord Stourton's case), Fitz killed him and abandoned the dead man's "livelesse carkasse" by the road. He then escaped to France, where he stayed while the uproar occasioned by the murder died down. In his absence, his wife sought a pardon, using all the means that the "procurement of her woorthy freendes could effect, or her owne industry labour". Fitz was allowed to return with a "reprieval, if not a pardon, but with thys proviso, of his good behaviour ever

---

51. *The Gentleman's Magazine*, 1731, vol.1, p.124.
52. J. Gay, *The Beggar's Opera*, 1728, Act 1, Scene 4.

after."[53] Similarly, and also in the Elizabethan period, Sir John Dayrell, who murdered the newborn baby of his mistress, used his fortune and influence at court to secure a *nolle prosequi* (abandonment of proceedings).[54] Even in the seventeenth century, and despite the widespread presence of 'unreformed' manners, only a handful of substantial gentlemen and aristocrats were executed for conventional felonies, most notable amongst them being the Earl of Castlehaven, who was beheaded in 1631 for sodomising his servants and participating in the group rape of his wife. Almost no aristocrats were executed for felony in the century preceding the hanging of Lord Ferrers for murdering his valet in 1760.

However, although outrageous by modern standards, it is also apparent that early modern upper class criminals did not have the same protection from the reach of common law punishment as their ancestors had enjoyed in the later middle ages, and also that such exemption as they enjoyed declined slowly throughout the era. The Crown was very gradually abandoning its indulgent attitude towards aristocratic and gentry crime. Exactly when this change occurred is difficult to establish. Nevertheless, the process seems to have been underway by the early 1500s. The execution for murder of Lord Stourton in 1557 indicates a considerably lower tolerance for aristocratic felony.[55] Bias was increasingly less blatant than it had been in the 1400s.

---

53. Sir J. Fitz, *The bloudy booke, or, the tragicall and desperate end of Sir John Fites (alias) Fitz*, London, Francys Burton, 1605, ff.B1-3 and C3.
54. Aubrey, *Brief Lives*, p.252.
55. Payling, *Murder, motive and punishment in fifteenth century England*, pp.1-20.

Even Sir John Fitz had "but a conditionall and no speciall pardon".[56] Indeed, by European standards, early modern England was noteworthy for the relative equality of its inhabitants before the criminal law. As a patriotic Jacobean Englishman could observe, the country's yeomen could: "... complaine to the Justice, if a farre better man doe him wrong: and in this who can come neere us?"[57] Significantly, only five years after Nichols's lucky escape, a barrister, Henry Justice, was accused of a very similar crime, stealing books from the library of his own *alma mater*, Trinity College, Cambridge. In this case, however, Justice received appropriate justice (for the era) and was transported.

One of the largest problems thrown up by the honour culture, and upper class privilege, yet also indicative of wider social attitudes towards violence and the criminal law was the practice of duelling.

Duelling

Duelling had its roots in the medieval period, and occasional, informal, duels were recorded in Kent in the early 1500s, with all elements of society being potential participants.[58] However, it only became modestly fashionable amongst upper class Englishmen in the 1570s, replacing earlier large scale communal feuds in which

---

56. Fitz, *The Bloudy Booke*, ff. B1-3 and C3.
57. T.C., *The Glory of England*, London, 1618, p.308.
58. J.S. Cockburn, "Patterns of Violence in English Society: Homicide in Kent 1560-1985," *Past and Present*, 1991, no.130, p.83.

servants supported their masters. Indeed, in 1614, the English fencing master George Hale specifically alluded to this as one of the potential benefits of single combat duelling, promoting as it did "Publique good abroad, for avoyding bloud".[59] The cult of honour, especially prevalent amongst gentlemen, also encouraged it. Vincento Saviolo, an Italian swordsman plying his trade in Elizabethan London, was well aware of the prickly upper class male code that prevailed throughout Europe: "I have seene and noted in diverse partes of mine owne countrie and in other places of the world, great quarrells springing from small causes, and many men slayne uppon light occasions." Nevertheless, he accepted that some discords and quarrels between gentlemen of honour and reputation, if they could not be settled by law or reason, had to be determined by "armes and combat". This made it only prudent to master the rapier.[60] However, the style of duelling changed considerably between 1550 and 1750. In the sixteenth century, a plethora of weapons were used: rapiers, broad swords, bucklers, daggers, etc. Subsequently, the rapier, favoured by Italian Masters, slowly became dominant, and, as the sixteenth century advanced, lighter, ultimately ending up as purely a thrusting, rather than cutting, weapon.[61] It ruled the field until challenged by pistols in the eighteenth

---

59. G. Hale, *The Private Schoole of Defence,* London, John Helme, 1614, 'Dedicatorie' (unpaginated).
60. V. Saviolo, *Vincentio Saviolo his Practise,* London, J. Wolfe, 1595, p.B1.
61. Captain A. Hutton, *Old Sword-Play, The Systems of Fence in vogue during the XVth, XVIIth and XVIIIth centuries with lessons arranged from the works of various ancient masters ...,* London, Grevel & Co., pp.1-36.

century. The social value of duelling was never accepted unreservedly in England, being vigorously condemned in a proclamation issued by James I in 1613.[62] Even so, this did not prevent George Hale dedicating his book, *The Private Schoole of Defence*, to that monarch's son, Prince Charles, the following year. However, Hale was well aware that fencing masters were the subject of much criticism: "Many are the imputations laid upon this Art ... the chiefe whereof is, the increasing our bloudy and irreligious Duels." In response, he sought to justify his profession by arguing that the science of swordsmanship did not increase murders, and that in an already violent society such training was valuable for self-defence, being a: "Remedie to an unavoyded disease, in opposing sodiane assaults."[63] Like others, he also pointed out that fencing provided healthy exercise and prepared potential soldiers for an emergency. For this reason, George Silver deprecated the training provided in London by fashionable Italian instructors whose rapiers ('bird-spits') were useless for anything other than duelling or murder: "... most shameful, they teach men to butcher one another here at home in peace, wherewith they cannot hurt their enemies abroad in war."[64] However, fencing schools could themselves be the breeding ground for dangerous grievances. In 1607, a Scottish gentleman, Robert Creighton, had an eye put out while playing at foils (a

---

62. Brown, *Gentlemen and Thugs in 17th Century Britain*, pp.27-30.
63. Hale, *The Private Schoole of Defence*, London, 'Dedicatorie' (unpaginated).
64. G. Silver, *Paradoxes of Defence*, London, Edward Blount, 1599, p.A5.

training weapon) with John Turner, a London fencing master. He resolved to be revenged and, five years later, hired Scottish assassins to shoot Turner dead in a tavern. Although his killers fled back to their native land, they were subsequently extradited, tried and executed.[65] Additionally, men who became adept at swordplay could become bullies. Even Saviolo deprecated lusty men who, feeling themselves to be: "... expert in this science, presuming thereupon, thinke that they may lawfully offer outrage and injury unto anie man, and with crasse and grosse termes and behaviour provoke everie man to fight."[66]

Nevertheless, as a Swiss visitor noted, although Englishmen made fine soldiers they were culturally adverse to duelling, so that, compared to much of continental Europe: "... very few are partisans of duelling, so there you do not often hear of this mode of settling quarrels."[67] To some Englishmen it was a 'Frenchified' custom, to others, irreligious. Additionally, by the eighteenth century, swords were giving way to pistols as the preferred duelling weapon. This may have encouraged caution, as duels were less likely to end in minor flesh wounds that satisfied 'honour', as occurred in the celebrated St James's park engagement between Lord Hervey and William Pulteney, in 1731. After "several passes on both sides, [they] were parted

---

65. Rayner and Crook (eds.), *The Complete Newgate Calendar*, vol.1, p.36.
66. Saviolo, *Vincentio Saviolo his Practise*, p.B2.
67. M. Van Muyden (Trans. and Ed.), *A foreign view of England in the reigns of George I and George II. The letters of Monsieur Cesar de Saussure, to his family*, London, John Murray, 1902, pp.179-180.

and disarm'd" by their friends and seconds.[68]

Another important explanation for the country's relatively modest incidence of duelling was the very strong antipathy of English criminal law towards the practice. Unfortunately, this was fettered by the era's frequently confused (and often indulgent) legal definition of murder. Nevertheless, in 1620, magistrates were enjoined not to: "... tollerate those single combates, that rise upon Quarrels and vaine pleas of reputation."[69] During the Interregnum, an ordinance issued on the 29th June 1654 outlawed the practice as un-Christian and "contrary to good order and government". It provided that any death that occurred as the result of a duel should be treated as murder.[70] However, this was merely a reinforcement of the existing common law position. JPs were often willing to charge successful duellists with murder.

In such situations, grand juries might still only indict for manslaughter, and, even if they did not, trial juries would rarely return a verdict that was more serious than manslaughter; being clergyable, this usually allowed immediate release. An outright acquittal was common. Thus, on the 18th May 1711, Mr Richard Thornhill was tried for the murder of Sir Cholmley Deering. The dead man had struck him and given satisfaction with pistols at Tothill Fields, the two men firing simultaneously (within four yards

---

68. *The Gentleman's Magazine*, vol.1, 1731, p.28.
69. T. Cooper, *The Cry and Revenge of Blood: Expressing the Nature and haynousnesse of wilfull Murther*, London, Nicholas Okes, 1620, p.24.
70. N.L. Mathews, *William Sheppard, Cromwell's Law Reformer*, Cambridge, CUP, 1984, p.171.

of each other) and the Knight being mortally wounded. Significantly, and indicative of the duel's lack of legal status, as Thornhill was leaving a person stopped him, told him he had killed a man, arrested him and took him before a JP, who committed Thornhill to prison. Fortunately for him, witnesses at the Old Bailey established that the dead man was "unwarrantably contentious", and the deceased had, like a gentleman, absolved his killer before expiring. As a result, after a lengthy retirement the jury eventually acquitted Thornhill of murder, but found him guilty of manslaughter, so that he was clergied and released.[71]

Where a conviction for murder was gained in such cases, it was usually because jurors were troubled at the 'fairness' of the duel, as can be seen in the case of two naval officers, Captains Innis and Clarke, who fought in Hyde Park on an August morning in 1749. Innis was mortally wounded, and the subsequent coroner's jury returned a verdict of wilful murder against Clarke, as a result of which he was arrested and tried at the Old Bailey, found guilty, and sentenced to death. Fortunately for Clarke, he was respited *sine die*, and the King granted him a free pardon in recognition of his earlier naval service. The two juries appear to have been heavily influenced by an apparent disparity in the terms of the combat, Captain Clarke's pistols (unusually for the time) were rifled with seven inch barrels, while those of Captain Innis were common pocket-pistols with smoothbore three

---

71. Anon, *A True Account of what past at the Old Bailey ... relating to the tryal of R. Thornhill, Esq., indicted for the murther of Sir Cholmley Deering*, 2nd edn, London, 1711, pp.4-14.

and a half inch barrels. Additionally, there were suggestions that Clarke had turned and fired early. He, too, was fortunate that the dying man absolved him, making the granting of a pardon easier.[72]

It was inherently difficult to define a duel's parameters. Where did a murderous quarrel between gentlemen end and a duel begin? Indeed, where did 'gentlemen' begin? In any event, given that an argument amongst members of any social group that descended into lethal violence would frequently be treated leniently, often producing a manslaughter verdict at most, it is not surprising that duelling was also treated benignly even by juries that were made up of tradesmen. A very late, but overt, judicial acceptance of such attitudes, can be seen at the Armagh Assizes in 1808, when a Major Campbell was tried and convicted of murder, and subsequently executed, for killing a fellow officer. The trial judge informed the jury that there was no legal defence of duelling, but reminded them that there was a: "... thing called the point of honour - a principle totally false in itself, and unrecognised both by law and morality, but which ... has usually been taken into consideration by juries." However, he also stressed to them that in such a case there must have been great provocation, true consent by both parties to the duel, and the contest must have been scrupulously fair. Unfortunately for the accused officer, he also reminded the jury that the dying man's final words to the prisoner were: "You have hurried me: I wanted you to wait and have friends. Campbell, you

---

72. *The Gentleman's Magazine*, 1750, vol.20, p.233.

are a bad man."[73] In the previous century, the judiciary were sometimes more robust. Nevertheless, even then, overstepping the boundaries could be disastrous. In 1729, the experienced duellist Major John Oneby was shocked to find himself convicted of murder and sentenced to death for what he felt was an affair of honour. His mistake was to fight indoors, at a gaming house, without witnesses or pre-arrangement, to be discovered holding his wounded opponent, and, earlier, to have publicly vowed to "have the blood" of the dead man (something that the eminent judge Lord Raymond felt had great weight against him).[74]

Upper Class Faction Fights

The Tudor era witnessed a marked reduction in the internecine conflicts amongst the propertied and wealthy that were common in the late medieval period. Litigation and, to a very much smaller extent, the duel, replaced them. Nevertheless, in an age where retainers and large and extended families were common, they continued a modest existence, even outside the border country. Thus, in 1589, Sir Thomas Langton led 80 men in an attack on Thomas Houghton and his own band of 30 men at Lea Hall in Lancashire, killing Houghton. Although such incidents declined rapidly during the 1500s, a few cases still occurred in the following century. In 1617, Sir Thomas Metcalfe

---

73. Rayner and Crook (eds.) *The Complete Newgate Calendar*, vol.v, pp.26-27.
74. Rayner and Crook (eds.) *The Complete Newgate Calendar*, vol.iii, p.56.

besieged Frances Robinson in Raydale House Wensleydale, one of the besiegers being killed when her relatives raised the siege.[75] Disputes over property were especially common. Typically, in a letter to Nathaniel Bacon JP, in 1582, Edward Clere complained that his "Cousin Heidon" had forcibly seized one of his properties, in Saxlingham (it was the subject of a family quarrel that went, ultimately, to the Court of Chancery). Heidon's entry to the property had been made "with great countenance, & numbers of persons". These had been heavily armed and terrified those of Clere's own servants who were there, several of whom were knocked down by: "... three unknowen persons with long picked staves besydes others with swords & bucklers." The attackers had subsequently 'garrisoned' the house to prevent repossession.[76] Such cases were common enough for Michael Dalton to address them specifically, even in the 1600s. He felt that where such forcible entry, holding, or deteiner of lands took place, a JP, without making a judgment as to the rights of either party, ought go to the property concerned with appropriate support: "... sufficient power of the County, or Town, by his discretion, and the Sheriff also if need be to aid him for the better execution of this business." He should then arrest and remove any men he found there who physically resisted him, seizing their weapons, harness, and armour before conveying them to jail. If the doors of a

---

75. K. Wrightson, *English Society, 1580-1680,* 2nd edition, London, Routledge, 1998, p.160.
76. Sir N. Bacon, *The Official Papers of Sir Nathaniel Bacon of Stiffkey, Norfolk as Justice of the Peace 1580-1620,* H.W. Saunders (Ed.), London, Royal History Society, Campden Third Series, 1915, vol.26, p.8.

seized house were barred against the JP and he was refused entry, he could break in to seize the occupiers. However, if those who had taken the property did not "make shew of any force" they could not be arrested or removed. Even if the JP evicted occupiers, he should not upon "his own view, restore the party ousted" before the matter had been determined at trial.[77]

Lower Class Crime

At the opposite end of the social scale to the country's well-born offenders, there appeared to be a large criminogenic underclass. These were the nation's itinerant rogues, vagabonds, and 'sturdy beggars', to employ a generic phrase first used in an Elizabethan proclamation. A few of them were hereditary travellers, foremost amongst these being gypsies. Some observers believed that gypsies had first appeared in Germany at the start of the sixteenth century before rapidly spreading throughout Europe. Becoming troublesome, most states took action against them. Thus, they were formally 'expelled' from France in 1560 and Spain in 1591. England imposed controls on them by statute in 1530 (22 Hen. VIII) blaming them for "many heinous felonies" and widespread trickery. In theory, gypsies who remained in the country for more that a month could be executed, though in practice this provision was usually

---

77. M. Dalton, *The Country Justice, Containing the Practise of the Justices of the Peace out of their Sessions ...* London, Company of Stationers, 1661, pp.64-65.

ignored.[78] More commonly, their goods might be seized. However, although associated with crime, especially horse theft, the number of gypsies in England was quite small, a few bands in each county, and they were certainly a minor element amongst the country's itinerants, most of whom were of native stock. The literate classes of early modern England thought that mobile but destitute people were proliferating rapidly, seeing a "continuell encrease of vacabundes in to infinite nombres".[79] By the Elizabethan and Jacobean periods, there were fears that vagrants swarmed in: "... every corner of the Realme, and not only lie loytering under hedges, but also stand sturdily in Cities, and begge boldly at every doore, leaving labour which they like not."[80]

However, not all of the country's impoverished inhabitants were rogues. According to William Harrison, writing in the 1560s, there were three sorts of very poor people in England. Some had been created by 'impotence', amongst them being orphans and the permanently incapacitated. Others were "casualties", such as wounded soldiers and people afflicted by sickness. Finally, however, there were the "thriftles poore" who provided the country's rogues.[81] This frequent division was used as the basis for action in 1552, after Nicholas Ridley, the Bishop of London,

---

78. W. Blackstone, *Commentaries on the Laws of England*, vol.4, Oxford, Clarendon Press, 1769, p.166.
79. Sir T. Elyot, *The Boke named the Governour*, London, J.M. Dent & Co., 1962, p.120.
80. Rid, "Martin Markall, Beadle of Bridewell," f.B3.
81. T.C., *The Glory of England*, p.217.

made a "Godley exhortation to the riche to be merciful unto the poore". This resulted in a consciously three-fold attempt by the City authorities to deal with urban destitution. It included the foundation of Christ's Hospital for London's abandoned orphans, the use of St Bartholomew's and St Thomas's hospital to deal with the sick, diseased and wounded, and the establishment of the Bridewell to accommodate thriftless vagabonds.[82]

There was little that was novel to England in this respect. The division of beggars into 'deserving' and 'undeserving' or 'able-bodied' occurred throughout Europe. The deserving, usually orphans and the disabled, were normally provided with alms by their city authorities or given official 'begging letters' allowing mendicancy. By contrast, the able-bodied were forbidden to beg and punished if they did so. Thus, an apparent flood of vagrants prompted Seville's government to license approved beggars in 1597. A panel of council members, royal justices and medical doctors examined mendicants. Afterwards, the incurably sick were sent to a hospital, the able-bodied were ordered to work, and the disabled and very old were authorised to seek alms. People without licences were forbidden to beg and would be whipped and exiled if they were caught doing so. Over 40 years later, in 1639, Seville's orphanage for girls petitioned the city council reiterating the importance of differentiating the genuinely impoverished from those who could work but instead went about "in little

82. E. Blunden (Ed.), *The Christ's Hospital Book*, London, Hamish Hamilton, 1953, pp.3-21.

bands, running through the city, and taking alms from the truly poor who cannot work."[83] Similar, largely unavailing, attempts to exclude beggars and the poor from entering and lodging in their city were made by the Leipzig city council. In 1701, councillors wrote to their Electoral government declaring: "... we constantly strive to capture the females who are rumored to follow a suspicious and obscene life and turn them from this city."[84]

Rogues were 'masterless men' who lived outside the highly structured society of early modern England, were geographically mobile and supposedly unwilling, rather than unable, to work. As if it was hard to envisage such an existence, observers frequently gave them a complicated, albeit inverted, social hierarchy, cohesiveness and organisation, creating almost an underworld mirror image of their own society. Sometimes, the attributed level of organisation reached absurd degrees, with secret county-wide meetings hundreds strong. This was clearly a literary construct, adding to their menace and consequent interest, rather than an accurate reflection of reality. Similarly, some of the criminal trades described were probably invented by pamphleteers, and almost never witnessed outside print. Nevertheless, such portrayals were not purely invention. Thomas Harman, a minor Kentish gentleman living close to London, who had been a JP during

---

83. M.E. Perry, *Crime and Society in Early Modern Seville*, Hanover (N.H.), University of New England Press, 1980, pp.163 and 184.
84. T. Kevorkian, "The rise of the poor, weak and wicked: Poor Care, Punishment, Religion and Patriarchy in Leipzig, 1700-1730," *Journal of Social History*, 2000, vol.34, no.1, p.163.

Queen Mary's reign, published one of the most important in 1567 (his account was influenced by earlier works). Forced by sickness to 'tary and remayne at home' for long periods, he had got into the practice of conversing with the beggars who regularly appeared at his house asking for alms. His proximity to London and a main arterial route meant that there were quite a few of these, and he appears to have been the victim of crime on several occasions, once losing a prized horse. He hoped to warn the wider country against the menace posed by the apparent wave of thieving and fraudulent beggars, though, where he felt cases were deserving, he continued to provide charity.[85]

Were rogues really able-bodied but idle rascals, deliberately shirking labour in favour of crime and begging? Did an: "... infinite nombre of englisshe men and women at this present time wander in all places throughout this realme, as bestis brute and savage, abandonyng all occupation, service, and honestie?"[86] In reality, much of the European wide concern with vagrancy was probably engendered by the social and economic changes sweeping across the continent, changes that meant that subsistence and employment were not guaranteed to everyone. As a result, although a vagabond's existence was harsh and his life on the road relatively short - Harman suggested an average of between 10 and 16 years before they were convicted and hanged for a felony or died of "filthy and

---

85. T. Harman, *A Caveat or Warning, for Common Cursitors vulgarly called Vagabones*, London, Wylliam Gryffith, 1567, p.Aiii.
86. Elyot, *The Boke named the Governour*, p.119.

horyble diseases" - as fast as they died out, their ranks would "dayly renew" with fresh recruits.[87]

However, not *all* itinerants were forced by necessity into their nomadic lifestyle. It has become fashionable to argue that contemporary portrayals of the threatening nature of vagabonds, even when made by those, such as Harman, with personal experience of them, are unreliable because they do not 'tally' with the picture contained in the court records. It is suggested that such portrayals were largely shaped by prejudice. In reality there were sound reasons for vagabonds 'in the woods' being so much more fearsome than those produced in court. It was one thing to detain a single female itinerant, or an elderly, exhausted or ill man. It was quite another to intervene when there was a group of young men, perhaps armed with blades and cudgels. The law enforcement agencies were not equipped to deal with such bands, and, except when their members were blatantly committing crimes, it must have been easier to wait for them to 'move on'. The mass of evidence seems to suggest that there was a genuine crime problem associated with rogues who, unlike some other criminals, would "spare neither rich nor poore".[88] The respective proportions of those wandering the roads of early modern England who were genuinely looking for work, and those attracted to a nomadic life of ease, theft and robbery has been the subject of heated debate. According to Professor Beier, few people who became vagrants had any real choice in the matter, with

---

87. Harman, *A Caveat or Warning, for Common Cursitors*, p.Aiii.
88. Canon W. Harrison, *A Description of England*, p.231.

most being recruited from economically vulnerable sections of English society, such as cloth-workers, servants, the young, etc. By contrast, Doctor Pound places the number forced by economic necessity into vagrancy and genuinely seeking honest labour at a somewhat lower level, and identifies a higher proportion of "professional villains".[89]

It was the Tudor vagabonds' mobility that made them qualitatively different to the medieval poor, or even those very poor but non-mobile early modern Englishmen who remained within the social control of their villages. Vagrants could move considerable distances across the country. Thus, in January 1585, William Lambarde recorded that while at his Kentish seat: "I sent to the gaol as rogues Gabriel Lilly of Yorkshire and John Nicolson of Lincolnshire, brought by John Hawles, constable."[90] Some were Welsh or Scottish, and many others were Irishmen. It was also genuinely easier for itinerants to steal. For those living in intimate and small communities, instrumental crime poses inherent difficulties, unless directed against outsiders who are passing through

---

89. J.F. Pound and A.L. Beier, "Debate: Vagrants and the Social Order in Elizabethan England," *Past and Present*, 1976, no.71, pp.126-134.

90. W. Lambarde, "Ephemeris," *William Lambarde and Local Government, 1580-1588*, C. Read (Ed.) 1962, New York, Cornell University Press, p.29. William Lambarde (1536-1601) was a pioneering, if retiring, legal scholar and historian. He inherited the family manor of Westcombe in Greenwich from his father, while still young, something that allowed him to pursue his academic interests. In April 1556 he was admitted to Lincoln's Inn, taking a lengthy 11 years to complete his training, and being called to the Bar in 1567. During this period, Lambarde associated with other Elizabethan humanist scholars, and was prominent amongst a group of common lawyers who used antiquity to justify their country's unique legal system, and its difference from civil law.

the locality (often few and far between), or those living well away from the offender's parish (difficult in an era of relatively poor communications). If local theft goes beyond the taking of cash or small amounts of foodstuffs for personal consumption it is likely to be rapidly discovered, just as stealing a neighbour's motorcar and then using it would be today. Even stolen food and money can only be used secretly, otherwise other villagers will wonder how the thief can keep such a good table, or afford little luxuries, on an apparently low income. The thief's own children must be kept in the dark, if they are not to talk to their friends, who will, in turn, very likely, tell their own parents of what they have learnt. Not surprisingly, intra-village crime is often small scale, the theft of a few chickens, eggs or coins left carelessly lying about, etc. These constraints do not apply to outsiders.

Whatever their origins, the existence of apparently draconian laws seemed to make no difference to their numbers: "The punishment that is ordeined for this kind of people is verie sharpe, and yet it can not restraine them from their gadding, wherefore the end must needs be martiall law."[91] As this comment suggests, this acted as a spur to some observers to demand ever more rigorous penal laws (such as rule of the Marshall). Others, however, suspected that repression alone, whether public whippings or brandings, would not solve the problem. Such men rejected a harsh penal approach in favour of ameliorating what they saw as the problem's root causes. Thus, in 1571, when a new

---

91. T.C., *The Glory of England*, p.219.

'Bill against Vagabonds' was read for the first time in the Commons, one MP (a Mr Sands) argued that it was: "... over sharp and bloody, standing much on the care which is to be had for the poor; saying, that it might be possible with some travail had by the Justices, to releive every man at his own house and to stay them from wandring."[92] Large numbers of equally punitive Bills regulating personal conduct failed to reach the statute book because of similar resistance.

Several specific social problems that contributed to England's vagrancy problem have been identified. Some appear more significant than others; most have some plausibility. They include the abolition of the monasteries under Henry VIII, the unprecedented numbers of discharged servicemen on the roads and the economic effects of enclosure. Perhaps most important, however, was the rapid population growth of the era. It produced a devaluation of labour and an increasing polarisation amongst the common people. In this process, some were 'winners' but numerous others lost out. As a result, many unfortunate people were no longer anchored to one place by the possession of a small amount of land, nor could they eke out an existence by working their own plots. Indeed, the loss of peasant subsistence farmers appears to have gone further in England than in other parts of Europe, producing an unprecedentedly mobile society. The enclosure of intensively farmed arable land, by greedy nobles, gentlemen and (before the Reformation) monasteries, often using

---

92. Sir S. D'Ewes, *A Compleat Journal of the Votes, Speeches and Debates, both of the House of Lords and House of Commons*, London, 1613, p.71.

forced purchases, illicit tricks and even physical pressure, aggravated these problems. According to Thomas More, its subsequent replacement with sheep pasture (which required few hands to work) meant that numerous displaced families were forced onto the roads and, in the absence of available work, given the choice of stealing (and execution) or begging, which led to them being "cast in prison as vagabonds". Thus, men were 'devoured' by sheep.[93] As a result of such changes, in late medieval and early modern society, those in need were no longer confined to the aged, the infirm and pilgrims, but also included large numbers of apparently destitute agricultural workers and tradesmen.[94]

To an extent, the authorities recognised that such developments were engendering crime, and, periodically, there would be feeble attempts to intervene in the process. JPs (if not themselves the perpetrators of enclosure) might be petitioned and become involved in regulating economic changes. These could involve a grey area, on the fringes of criminal and civil law. Thus, Nathaniel Bacon entertained a complaint from the inhabitants of Eccles in Norfolk about John and Robert James, local farmers involved in enclosing and ploughing up: "... heath groundes wheare not only we but our predecessors from tyme to tyme without mynd of man had our comon feed according to our aunceant use & custome." This petition was 'signed' by 12 men (half making a mark), at some time between 1604 and 1620. The

---

93. Sir T. More, *Utopia*, Ware, Wordsworth Classics, 1997, p.34.
94. A.L. Beier, *Masterless Men: the vagrancy problem in England 1560-1640*, London, Methuen & Co., 1985, at pp.4-5.

signatories sought the reformation of these wrongs on behalf of the "poor tenauntes".[95] To such individuals, the James's behaviour must have seemed criminal. Enclosing land was usually bitterly unpopular with the lowest social classes, however profitable it might be for the rich. Its legality was also often doubtful. Even supporters were forced to acknowledge that there was no statute that gave "full power to enclose all the Common Fields, in the Kingdom". As a result, there was frequently active resistance to the process from the "beggarly multitude". Such people would pull down fences and spoil the corn. One brutal answer to this problem, supposedly based on the experience of a JP, was that instead of creating narrow ditches and high banks round the newly enclosed land, which could easily be pulled down or filled in, broad ditches, up to ten feet wide and six deep, should be dug, and the spoil removed from the field to prevent them being refilled.[96]

The ongoing social and economic changes also engendered a change in attitudes towards the poor. Ultimately, this was most clearly manifest in Renaissance humanism and Calvinism, with their emphasis on worldly success. In particular, the willingness to idealize poverty that was sometimes found in the High Middle Ages, to see the face of Christ in the beggar, most obviously manifest in Franciscanism, waned. Even in 1349, the preamble to the Statute of Labourers had complained of "some rather willing to beg in idleness, than by labour to get their living".

---

95. Bacon, *The Official Papers of Sir Nathaniel Bacon*, pp.50-51.
96. Anon, *England's Great Happiness*, London, J.M. for E. Croft, 1677, pp.15-16.

By the beginning of the early modern period such attitudes were widespread. An absence of honest employment was seen as not merely impoverishing to the commonwealth and offensive to God but also highly corrosive to the personal morality of the unemployed. Thus, George Herbert considered that idleness was the worst national sin: "For when men have nothing to do, then they fall to drink, to steal, to whore, to scoffe, to revile, to all sorts of gamings."[97] Growing numbers shared Daniel Defoe's fear that England's apparent plethora of vagrants was being created by misplaced compassion, both personal and institutional, allowing mendicants to pursue their lives because it was easier and better remunerated than labour.[98] However, such views did not entirely replace older attitudes towards the poor, which continued to the end of the period, pursuing an uneasy co-existence with a stricter approach. In 1550, although Robert Crowley was convinced that some beggars actively encouraged their sores to spread so as not to appear able bodied he still gave alms where there was even a mild doubt about authenticity, urging that others "cesse not to gyve to all, without any regard".[99] This, too, was a European wide phenomenon. Despite the best efforts of the authorities in early modern Leipzig, and their willingness to finance incarceral institutions, many burghers in the city continued to give alms to 'undeserving' beggars in the street, and some even interfered when beadles

---

97. G. Herbert, *A Priest to the Temple*, p.33.
98. D. Defoe, *Giving Alms no Charity*, London, 1704, pp.10-15.
99. R.H. Tawney and E. Power (Ed.) *Tudor Economic Documents*, London, Longmans, 1951, vol.3, p.406.

arrested such people, prompting the city council to issue fresh laws forbidding obstruction.[100] Perhaps, deep down, many contemporary observers instinctively appreciated that vagrancy was often not purely a matter of choice.

Regulation of Rogues

Vagrancy was primarily a crime of status, not conduct. Thus, the early Act of 1531 had defined a vagabond as: "... any man or woman being whole and mighty in body and able to labour, having no land, master, nor using any lawful merchandise, craft or mystery whereby he might get his living."[101] As a result, campaigns against vagrants were difficult to conduct and fraught with the risk of mistakenly arresting respectable (albeit poor) travellers. This had been apparent even in the late fifteenth century, when assorted pilgrims, soldiers travelling to join their military bands, and those journeying to take part in major construction projects, such as the Archbishop's palace at Lambeth, had been detained on suspicion of being vagabonds. If they were not too distant from home, arrest might prompt their neighbours to report them as being of "honest rule and conversation, and of good name and fame", securing their release.[102] If they were far from home it was often difficult to establish their credentials. The criminalisation of such people was not confined to England. In Frankfurt, the

---

100. Kevorkian, *The Rise of the Poor, Weak and Wicked*, p.163.
101. Beier, *Masterless Men,* p.9.
102. M.K. McIntosh, *Controlling Misbehaviour in England, 1370-1600,* Cambridge, CUP, 1998, p.122.

Verdachtsstrafe allowed the punishment of those deemed to be 'suspicious', the growth in the incidence of its use coinciding with a precipitous increase in property crime sentences.[103]

In theory, those found to be rogues would be whipped and then passed back via parish constables to their village of origin, carrying appropriate documentation. A typical "Testimonial for a Vagrant Rogue", including any unusual identifying marks, prepared by JPs, might run in the following terms:

"X Is a sturdy Vagrant Beggar, of low Personage, red-haired, and having the Nail of the right Thumb cloven, was [date] openly whipped, at D.. in the County of M. for a wandring Rogue, according to the Law, and is assigned to pass forthwith from Parish to Parish, by the Officers thereof, the next strait way to S. in the County of D. whereas he confesseth he was born; Or dwelt by the space of one whole year; and if the case be such. And he is limited to be at S. afore-said, within 10 days now next coming, at his peril."[104]

However, as with all mass-produced early modern documents, forgery was endemic. Harman noted that rogues would often carry passports specifying details about the home parish to which they were supposedly returning,

---

103. M.R. Boes, "Jews in the Criminal-Justice System of Early Modern Germany," *Journal of Interdisciplinary History*, 1999, vol.30.3, pp.407-435 at p.422.
104. H. Twyford, T. Dring and F. Place, *Justice Restored: Or a Guide for his Majesty's Justices of Peace*, 2nd edn., London, Th. Roycroft, 1660, p.32.

which, in reality, had been created by a specialist fraudster and were amendable at will. In 1585, Edward Hext sent a copy of such a counterfeit pass to Lord Burghley, citing it as an example of the very high standard that could be achieved by forgeries. Given that communications were slow and difficult, provided than an issuing parish that was fairly distant (to the vagabond) was specified on the document, it was very unlikely that anyone would check its authenticity. Rogues correctly assumed that "none will send two or three c [hundred] myles to discover them for a whippinge matter".[105]

Further aggravating the situation, parishes might go to considerable lengths to avoid the cost and security risks associated with rogues. In 1603, Richard Riplinghams was bound over to appear at the following Norfolk sessions for fraudulently appealing a Minister's refusal to grant a passport to a "vagerant boy" who had appeared in Warham. The boy was aged between 10 and 12 and "sick of an ague", this being the reason for the cleric's refusal of the formal document that would facilitate his removal. Riplinghams appealed the Minister's decision to Sir Nathaniel Bacon, his local JP, so that the boy could be expelled and then passed from village to village, until he reached his place of birth. There, he could be punished and his own village obliged to support him or set him to work. To effect this Riplinghams persuaded Bacon that the boy was at least 12, the statutory

---

105. E. Hext, "Letter written by Edward Hext, a Somerset JP, to Lord Burghley on September 25, 1596," *Tudor Economic Documents*, R.H. Tawney and E. Power (eds.) London, Longmans, 1951, vol.2, p.343.

minimum age for compulsory removal, and that his sickness was not so serious that he could not travel without danger. Bacon accepted his arguments as to age and that the illness was largely feigned, and granted the passport. However, the January cold swiftly exacerbated the ailing lad's condition, and he died on the way to Bynham, his body being dumped at the gate of the village constable there. Bacon was evidently chastened by having facilitated this tragedy, and summonsed Riplinghams for: "... abusing a Justice of peace, in seeking to be directed by him, did concele the weaknes of the partie and danger of his sicknes ... to dischardge the towne of him."[106] However, even when successfully returned, rogues' 'home' parishes were often reluctant to receive them. As late as 1742, the Middlesex JPs were summonsed for having played 'shuttle cock' with an octogenarian. Two Worcestershire JPs from Yarley had sent this old woman back to St Margaret's Westminster, the place of her last legal settlement. At this, the Middlesex justices, rather than take responsibility for her, made an order returning her to Warwickshire, trusting, it was claimed, that a combination of unseasonably hot weather and age meant she would die on the way. Unfortunately for them, she proved very resilient and survived the journey in a cart, promptly being sent back to Westminster, where the justices, "not at all discouraged", sent her back to Warwickshire once again, almost killing her in the process, and finally prompting a legal complaint. The magistrates emphatically denied being party to a "Confederacy to saddle another

---

106. Bacon, *The Official papers of Sir Nathaniel Bacon*, p.62.

Parish with this old Woman". (Their counsel also argued that JPs who served their country for nothing ought to be treated with leniency.) Fortunately for them, the woman finally died before a verdict could be reached.[107]

Discharged Servicemen

Ex-servicemen were a major component in the ranks of itinerant rogues everywhere in Europe. They were especially feared because they were often still armed on discharge, skilled in the use of weapons, far from their family homes, and likely to roam about in small groups without any means of support. Thus, in Germany, it was thought that some resorted to street-robbery, and many others were believed to steal cattle.[108] Worse still, some had originally been recruited in lieu of punishment for crimes of which they had already been convicted or charged. Even the Spanish army of the sixteenth and seventeenth centuries, though famous for its battlefield discipline, was largely made up of anti-social elements, often taken from the country's prisons. The inhabitants of Seville complained repeatedly of murders, thefts and other crimes and misbehaviour committed by local soldiers.[109] Throughout Europe, military service seemed to have a corrupting effect on 'true men', so that even those that "went out honest,

---

107. *The Gentleman's Magazine*, 1742, vol.12, p.260-261.
108. E. Lacour, "Faces of Violence revisited. A typology of violence in early Modern rural Germany," *Journal of Social History*, 2001, vol.34, no.3, pp.649-668.
109. Perry, *Crime and Society in Early Modern Seville*, pp.95-96.

returne home againe like Roysters".[110] It was notorious that former soldiers found adjusting to civilian life difficult, and that it was normal for the "more idle sort, having once served ... to shake hand with labour for ever".[111] As was noted in 1610, such men became so used to their new lifestyle, that they could not apply themselves to "any honest trade of life, but, loving to live in idleness, betake themselves to robbing and stealing". As a result, it was also widely believed that crime rates went up after wars, with society witnessing "more robbing, theeving, begging and murdering then before".[112] This also meant more executions. Another observer noted, in 1580, that at the: "... breaking up of wars, there are a great number of worthy and valiant soldiers [who] ... if they tarry in England, hanging is the end of the most part of them."[113] In any event, after a short time on the roads, such men were often almost unemployable in legitimate work. According to More, their threadbare attire and "pale sickly faces" deterred gentlemen from taking them on, and small farmers knew that their previous lives as soldiers meant that they would be unwilling to do "true and faithful service to a poor man with a spade and mattock for small wages and hard fare".

In England, the reign of Henry VII had been largely

---

110. Rid, *Martin Markall, Beadle of Bridewell*, p.B3.

111. Harrison, *A Description of England*, p.231.

112. Rid, *Martin Markall, Beadle of Bridewell*, p.B3.

113. R. Hitchcock, *A Politic Plat for the honour of the Prince*, in *Social England Illustrated. A Collection of VIIth Century (sic) Tracts*, 1580, A. Lang (intro.) E. Arber (Ed.), *English Garner Series*, reprint edition, Westminster, Archibald Constable, 1903, pp.86-87.

peaceful, at least after 1487. However, after his death in 1509, the country was involved in persistent conflict, against France, Spain and Scotland. Additionally, there were several major internal risings, the suppression of which required considerable armies. Thus, in 1516, Thomas More identified veterans of the then recent French wars and Cornish Rebellion, too weak and lame to carry out their former trades and too old to learn new ones, as a fertile source of itinerant criminals.[114] Under Elizabeth I alone, almost 116,000 men were conscripted for military ventures. There was also increased navigation generally, as well as maritime conflict, producing more sailors, who shared some, if not all, of the problems faced by soldiers when paid off.

Kent, in particular, suffered from being the natural conduit for discharged soldiers coming back from the continent. Typically, in 1596, three soldiers who had landed at Dover with only seven shillings between them, after returning from service near Boulogne, stole books from Charing church, planning to sell them on in Faversham. Significantly, they had already been detained, and released, for being 'suspicious' by the Watch at Ashford. A decade later, in 1606, George Mannage, a former silk weaver from London who had served in Holland as a soldier, been captured and freed, shipped from Calais to Margate. After 'wandring up and downe' this area for several days, he stole some shirts that were drying on a hedge.[115] London appears

---

114. More, *Utopia*, p.32.
115. E. Melling (Ed.) *Crime and Punishment, Kentish Sources VI*, Maidstone, Kent County Council, 1969, p.142.

to have acted as a honey pot for former soldiers and sailors. As the Lord Mayor of London, Sir Richard Gresham, observed in a letter to Edward VI urging enhanced charitable provision for the urban poor, during Henry VIII's reign after the: "... ending of the king's warres, yt appeareth that there were greate nombers of poor lame ydell and maysterless men dispersed in dyvers parts of this Realme, but chiefely aboute this Cittie of London."[116] This situation was not helped by the later introduction of a policy of paying sailors' wages in arrears by means of promissory notes that could only be redeemed at the London Pay Office. The reforming MP James Oglethorpe deprecated such a practise in his *The Sailors Advocate* of 1728. Aggravating these problems, there was little formal provision made for discharged servicemen, despite Elizabeth I complaining to the JPs about their negligence in this area. In the 1641 version of his major work on the law pertaining to constables, William Sheppard protested that returning soldiers were liable to be deemed felonious rogues under the provisions of the Act of 39 Eliz. I if they were driven by circumstances to beg. He suggested providing financial support for them to make the journey home. The exigencies of the Civil War encouraged some reform in this direction; in 1647 improved provision was made for returning soldiers and sailors (as well as their widowed and orphaned dependants).[117]

---

116. E. Blunden (Ed.) *The Christ's Hospital Book*, London, Hamish Hamilton, 1953, pp.3-4 and pp.6-21.
117. Mathews, *William Sheppard, Cromwell's Law Reformer*, p.76.

Chapter 4

Instrumental Crime

> Theaft is counted so horrible amongest some nations, that men commonly will rather sterve then steale, and here in England he that can robbe a man by the hygh waye is called a tall felowe.
>
> *Thomas Wilson, A Discourse Upon Usury, 1572*

Instrumental crime was the most common form of serious early modern deviance, albeit not as statistically dominant as in the present era. Thus, it has been observed that Elizabethan criminals did not normally murder, rape or pillage, they merely stole things. Additionally, their thefts were not usually committed against the rich and powerful, but more commonly victimised other poor people.[1] According to Cesar de Saussure, those who stole from the person could be separated into "three divisions - highwaymen, footpads and pickpockets".[2] The first two were robbers; the last merely thieves. Burglars and housebreakers can be added to complete the list of instrumental criminals (being nocturnal and diurnal

---

1.   J. Samaha, "Gleanings from Local Criminal Court Records: sedition amongst the 'inarticulate' in Elizabethan England," *Journal of Social History*, 1975, vol.8, p.62.
2.   M. Van Muyden (Trans. and Ed.) *A Foreign View of England in the Reigns of George I and George II; The Letters of Monsieur Cesar de Saussure, to his Family*, London, John Murray, 1902, p.128.

respectively). However, crimes of dishonesty produced a somewhat different profile to that of the modern era. Theft by servants, the employment of whom was universal in prosperous houses, but almost absent today, was a very significant problem, though one that is now of little importance. Theft from the person, 'pick-pocketing', was probably the most important form of instrumental crime, much more so than burglary, a reversal of today's situation. In any crowded Metropolitan environment pickpockets or cutpurses were prevalent: "Their Exchange is Tyburne or any great Show, but especially Bartholomew Fair."[3] The last was especially notorious, Paul Hentzner noted that while watching a side-show there, one of his medical companions: "... had his pocket picked of his purse, with nine crowns du soleil, which, without doubt, was so cleverly taken from him by an Englishman who always kept very close to him, that the doctor did not in the least perceive it."[4] Such thieves were not deterred by proximity to the gallows, being: "... so impudent, they steal under the gibbet. There never is any execution without handkerchiefs and other articles being stolen."[5] Even the crowded court rooms of the era presented regular criminal opportunities, though with the added risk that justice was likely to be both prompt and draconian if a thief was apprehended. In the 1680s, the inexperienced David Hughes picked a pocket in open court at the Kingston Assizes. Sadly, he was caught, immediately tried, and

---

3. Anon, *The Caterpillars of this Nation Anatomised*, London, 1659, p.4.
4. P. Hentzner, *Travels in England during the reign of Queen Elizabeth*, London, Cassell & Co., 1889, p.37.
5. Van Muyden, *A Foreign View of England*, p.130.

condemned to be: "... hanged upon a gibbet within sight of the Bench, as a terror to others."[6]

Craft Crime

Nowadays, the existence of an early modern 'criminal underworld', dominated by professionalism, long distance networks, and criminal fraternities is usually attributed to the febrile imagination of contemporary observers and the gullibility of mid-twentieth century historians. There is almost a consensus that early modern criminal organisations were largely *ad hoc* and amateurish, and that the era's criminals were essentially opportunistic, a few acknowledged exceptions apart. Amongst the latter were large-scale coiners, horse thieves and, perhaps, some Metropolitan underworld groupings. Generally, however, it is argued that the early modern criminal vanishes into the 'ordinary' poor.[7] Given this, it must be asked why contemporary observers, such as Thomas Harman, laboured under such monumental misapprehensions. Undoubtedly, what has been termed the 'ingenuity fallacy', the myth of the brilliant and daring criminal, the general human tendency to exaggerate the offender's cleverness and skill, has been present throughout history.[8] On its own, however,

---

6. Rayner and Crook (eds.) *The Complete Newgate Calendar*, vol.ii, p.55.
7. J. McMullan, "Crime, Law and Order in Early Modern England," *British Journal of Criminology*, 1987, vol.27, no.3, pp.254-255.
8. M. Felson, *Crime and Everyday Life. Insights and Implications for Society*, London, Pine Forge Press, 1994, p.5.

this does not fully explain the era's belief in the prevalence of professional crime. One answer is that the period produced a considerable amount of 'craft crime', which required the mastery of relatively sophisticated techniques, even by 'amateurs'. These were necessary in an era that had fewer offence friendly environments, such as, for example, modern self-service shops. Thus, the versatile Jack Hall (executed in 1707) was a master of, *inter alia*, the "drag", in which a hook was fastened to the end of a stick and used to pull goods out of shop windows at night, and an expert at the "lob", in which the thief went with a companion into a shop to change a gold coin, and having received about half of his change in silver abandoned the exchange and returned the money, but with such dexterity that he left a shilling or half crown sticking to the palm of his hand, which he carried off without suspicion. Hall was also accomplished at the "whalebone lay", using a thin piece of whalebone to retrieve money from shop tills while the shopkeeper was distracted.[9] Towards the end of the period, an Irishwoman named Mary Young was equally skilled. She was known as 'Jenny Diver' because of her abilities as a pickpocket. Young led a gang of thieves prior to her execution at Tyburn in March 1740. On one occasion, she used a pair of false arms to steal gold watches during divine service at a prominent City church. Like Selman, over a century earlier, she had attended the service "very genteely dressed", and sat among the wealthier elements of the congregation, with a criminal associate in livery pretending

9.   Rayner and Crook, *The Complete Newgate Calendar*, vol.ii, pp.196-197.

to be her footman. As this case suggests, a frequent technique for those who were articulate, personable and could afford the appropriate costume, was to rely on the social deference of the era to infiltrate upper class environments, where rich pickings could be expected. Thus, Diver often secured entrance to people's houses by pretending to be a pregnant lady in distress, stealing their valuables while they were distracted.[10] Similarly, if less spectacularly, in 1676, two well-attired men "pretending to be Persons of Quality" rode away on a pair of expensive horses, belonging to another traveller, which they took from outside the *King's Arms* at Darbing in Surrey.[11] More daringly, in the early 1700s, Benjamin Child would effect his criminal designs by dressing in the "habit of a man of distinction", meeting wealthy merchants and claiming to have been at school with them 20 years earlier.[12]

Changing fashions during the period meant that criminal techniques also necessarily had to evolve. Thus, in the 1650s, it was noted that pickpockets: "... of late have inlarged of their Trade since gold buttons on cloaths have been in fashion, which they will cut from behind."[13] Similarly, almost a century after the death of Simon Fletcher, an expert Metropolitan pickpocket who was executed in 1692, it was noted that: "The chief sort of thieving [from the

---

10. Rev. Gordon, *The Life and Circumstantial Account of the extraordinary and Surprising Exploits, Travils, Robberies and Escapes of the Famous Jenny Diver*, London, 1745, p.8.
11. *The London Gazette*, no.1089, 24-27 April, 1676.
12. Anon, *The Whole Life History of Benjamin Child*, London, 1722, at p.12.
13. Anon, *The Caterpillars of this Nation Anatomised*, p.4.

person] at that time was cutting off people's purses or pockets, which was in use long before the modern and more dexterous practice of picking out the money and leaving the case behind."[14] The widespread advent of tailored pockets had changed the trade.

Theft by Servants and Employees

The one major example of theft committed by the poor against the better off was that committed by domestic servants and commercial employees.[15] Sometimes they could be large-scale thieves, as they had access to, and knowledge of, their master's premises. However, in such cases, detection and pursuit were almost certain, and, unless the servant was willing to travel a considerable distance, capture was likely. London was a partial exception to this pattern, as it was sometimes possible to disappear into what was already a large and anonymous city. Nevertheless, even there, escape was difficult. Thus, in June 1733, Rose Moreton was sentenced to death at the Old Bailey for stealing 24 guineas and some silver from her master.[16] However, servants usually posed a more insidious and subtle threat. As Defoe noted, at least if a maid was a "downright thief she strips you, at once, and you know your loss". More problematic were those who would beggar their employers

---

14. Rayner and Crook, *The Complete Newgate Calendar*, vol.ii, p.85 and *The Gentleman's Magazine*, 1742, vol.11, p.162.
15. Samaha, *Gleanings from Local Criminal Court Records*, p.62.
16. *The Gentleman's Magazine*, 1733, vol.iii, p.325.

"inchmeal" by pilfering. He felt that this practice, along with that of taking commission on household purchases from tradesmen, was often ignored, although receiving stolen goods and confederating with felons were "not a jot worse". Pilferage by ordinary workers from their employers was also widespread. However, automatically defining it as stealing presents interesting problems as to where the realm of legitimate work-connected perquisites ended, and theft began. In many trades and occupations there were longstanding customary rights to, for example, spillage and leftover materials. Even in the early 1700s, pilfering servants usually did not view themselves as thieves: "Tea, sugar, wine, &c., or any such trifling commodities, are reckoned no thefts, if they do not directly take your pewter from your shelf, or your linen from your drawers, they are very honest."[17] Additionally, the doctrine of possessorial immunity protected many workers from criminal allegations for much of the period (though statute gradually eroded it). Nevertheless, not everyone took a benign view of 'customary' behaviour, however widespread. Thus, a popular continental work on crime, published in England in the 1630s, noted that there was endemic 'theft' amongst artisans and professionals. Tailors and shoemakers specified more material and leather than they needed so that they could keep the balance for their own use. Most radically, it complained that lawyers exaggerated their client's prospects of success, encouraging them into costly and unsuccessful

---

17.   Moreton (Defoe), *Every-Body's Business*, pp.7-9.

litigation.[18]

Horse and Animal Theft

Horse and animal theft was a particularly serious problem, throughout the era. It was often the province of well organised networks. Casual thieves were likely to be detected because they attempted to sell horses too close to home and too soon after they had stolen them.[19] Thus, Dick Turpin was ultimately convicted and executed at York in 1739, for stealing a mare and a foal in Heckington in Lincolnshire, after the loser, a man named Creasy, went to considerable lengths to obtain information about the missing animals. He hired men and horses and "rode 40 miles round and about us to hear of them, and got them cry'd in all the Market Towns about us". Eventually, one John Baxter came forward and told him that, while at Pocklington Fair in Yorkshire, he had heard of a man (Turpin) that had recently been arrested and committed to the House of Correction at Beverly for shooting a game cock (the offence for which Turpin was initially detained). Baxter claimed that this individual was in possession of two horses that closely matched the description provided by Creasy. Fortunately, the animals marks were highly distinctive, something that

---

18. W.M. (Trans.), *The Sonne of the Rogue, or the Politicke Theefe*, London, 1638, pp.104-114.
19. J.M. Beattie, *Crime and the Courts in England 1660-1800*, Oxford, OUP, 1986, p.169.

was stressed in court when identification was in issue.[20] Similarly, if livestock were stolen near a market or fair, there was a strong likelihood that the losers would go to the market as quickly as possible and inspect the animals on offer there. Thus, in the 1580s, when John Oborne tried to sell an ox at Warwick fair that he had taken from a nearby village, his victims swiftly appeared, "owned the oxe", and were bound over to give evidence against Oborne.[21] As a result of such common precautions, William Harrison could note that even in the 1590s valuable stolen beasts would frequently be sold at distant (from the crime scene) fairs.[22] Some professional horse thieves were very large-scale operators, and might graze up to 60 stolen horses at a time. William Smith was typical of such men, prior to his conviction and execution for the crime at the Chelmsford Assizes in August 1731. He had graduated to crime after training as a clothier, working as a gentleman's servant and serving in the military. Smith was primarily involved in receiving animals taken by others, though he also personally "bit a person of 6 good horses [while] pretending to buy them". He returned some stolen animals to their owners for a reward. Others were transported to distant parts; in some cases, it seems, even out of the country. He also sold horses

---

20. T. Kyll, *The Trial of the notorious Highwayman Richard Turpin, at York Assizes on the 22nd day of March, 1739, before the Honourable Sir William Chapple, Kt. Judge of Assize*, York, 1739, pp.1-3.

21. T. Kempt (Ed.) *The Book of John Fisher, Town Clerk and Deputy Recorder of Warwick 1580-1581*, Warwick, Henry Cooke & Son, 1909, p.50.

22. W. Harrison, *A Description of England*, 2nd Book, 2nd edition (1587), London, New Shakespeare Society, 1877, p.230.

more locally after carefully "altering their marks" to prevent identification. Smith appears to have been fairly ruthless about this. He was convicted at the same time of stealing a woman's cows, and, when caught, was "cutting off the Cows Ears to deface 'em". While awaiting execution he made money by providing information about stolen goods to their losers.[23]

John Owen, a habitual seventeenth century Shropshire thief also specialised in animals. On one occasion he used an ingenious if cruel method to acquire a plump heifer. While drinking with drovers at an inn, he killed the animal by inducing internal bleeding, so that it died during the night, allowing him to buy its carcass for a song the next morning. He regularly stole cattle and horses using more conventional methods. These would be hidden on a piece of rough ground, owned by one George Pickstock, in a neighbouring village. Ultimately, however, this was to be the cause of his downfall as one of the horses was recognised and Pickstock immediately implicated Owen, who was promptly arrested. Owen, like any modern burglar attributing his possession of stolen goods to a purchase in a public house: "... confessed that the horse was his, and made that idle excuse which every silly theife will doe, that he bought him of a stranger on the road." He was convicted and executed at the Shrewsbury Assizes.[24]

---

23. *The Gentleman's Magazine*, 1731, vol.1, p.351.
24. R. Gough, *The History of Myddle, 1701*, D.Hey (Ed.) Harmondsworth, Penguin, 1981, pp.149-150.

Burglary and Housebreaking

Burglary entailed entering a house at night with the: "... intente to robbe, though they take nothynge awaye, it is burglary, which in it selfe is felony." As with robbery, the amount actually stolen was irrelevant. Housebreaking entailed entry during the day, and was viewed slightly less seriously. Perhaps unsurprisingly, modern research indicates that the single most important factor facilitating successful burglaries (day and night) is an unoccupied house. Some estimates place its presence in as many as 80 per cent of present day cases.[25] In the modern era, with double income couples, working far from their homes, children away at school for long periods, frequent absences due to vacations, and many single occupancy homes, such buildings are easily found. However, in the early modern period they were notably absent. In richer houses there would be the constant presence of servants. In poorer homes, although the men-folk might be out in the fields for most of the day, especially when ploughing, sowing and harvesting, women not only took care of the children at home, but also swept out their houses, brewed, cooked and tended the family's domestic animals, garden and any fruit trees close by.[26] Unsurprisingly, in these circumstances, Divine service provided attractive opportunities for burglars, as it readily allowed them to identify where other

25. M. Gottfredson and T. Hirschi, *A General Theory of Crime*, Stanford, Stanford University Press, 1990, p.25.
26. B.A. Hanawalt, "Narratives of a Nurturing Culture: Parents and Neighbours in Medieval England," *Essays in Medieval Studies*, 1995, vol.12, pp.1-20.

parishioners were, and were likely to be, for an hour or so. Thus, in August 1626, John Reeks, of Cerne Abbas in Dorset, noticed John Harris quietly leave evensong one Sunday, and subsequently found £130 stolen from a trunk in his bedchamber, and tools belonging to Harris abandoned nearby.[27] Outsiders could also exploit this opportunity. Hence, at 11 a.m. one Sunday in October 1726, two horsemen went to the house of the Reverend Goodwin, asking for the Minister of Tankersley. Not surprisingly, at such an hour on the Sabbath, there was only a (very brave) maid and his two small children in the house. The maid told them that her master was at church and refused to admit them. At this, they swore at her and attempted to break in. However, she put the children in a closet, seized a: "... spit and run it at them; flung hot broth in one of their faces; they discharg'd a pistol at her, and missed her: then they went to a door, broke it open; she barricaded the in-door with chairs and stools, and made a great noise." Alarmed that those in the nearby church might hear her, the robbers fled, taking only a dirty shirt with them. After the church service was over, Goodwin's man pursued them until his horse tired.[28] Given the lack of unattended premises, and the relatively modest amount of valuable domestic items available in most homes, it is not surprising that burglary did not have its modern importance in the scale of crimes.

If housebreakers targeted a wealthy home they were

27. J.H. Bettey (Ed.) *The Casebook of Sir Francis Ashley JP, Recorder of Dorchester: 1614-1635*, Dorchester Record Society, 1981, p.97.
28. J. Hobson, "John Hobson's Diary" in *The Making of Barnsley*, B. Elliott, Barnsley, Wharncliffe Publishing Ltd., 1988, pp.86-87.

likely to conduct a close reconnaissance of its bolts, locks and weak windows, before attempting entry. If it appeared too hard to break into from outside, but was thought to contain valuable items, burglars might attempt to enlist the assistance of a servant already inside the house, or put a small boy into the building through an aperture to let them in. Once inside, any occupants would be tied and gagged.[29] Sometimes, blatant force rather than stealth was used to effect entry. Early in his criminal career, Dick Turpin joined Samuel Gregory's large gang (up to 20 strong) of armed robbers and took part in brutal attacks on substantial isolated properties. In one farmhouse robbery, an elderly man was beaten and had a kettle of boiling water thrown over him while his servant was raped. In others, the occupants were tortured into revealing their valuables.

Robbery

Robbery was theft accompanied by force. In an agrarian society it was most frequently committed in remote areas which were crossed by arterial routes: "Robbery is where a man lyeth by the Kynge's hygh waye to market townes, in woddes, dykes, or in any other secret places, where people come forth by, and robbeth them." In large urban areas, like London, it might also be conducted in the streets. Unlike larceny, it was the use or threat of violence that made robbery such a serious offence, not the value of the goods

---

29.   Anon, *The Caterpillars of this Nation Anatomised*, p.3.

stolen; consequently, even if a robber took 'but the value of a penny, or lesse, it is felony'.[30] This could occasion problems, as the dividing line between robbery and aggressive begging was a fine one. Thomas Gent, a celebrated eighteenth century printer, recorded the execution of two men at York in September 1716. The pair had been companions of another man, who, it was claimed, had received three half-pennies from a traveller, from whom he 'beg[ged] a little money to get a drink'. However, the traveller's companion, a Mr. Jackson, treated their request as being with menaces and: "... seemed a hero in defence of what he had, and told him, if he expected any [from him], he must fight for it first." The trio had immediately indicated that they had no interest in fighting and left. When the two men were subsequently seen in York by Mr. Jackson, he had them arrested by the constables and prosecuted to conviction as accessories to robbery, for which crime they were hanged (many thought unfairly).[31] Robbery could be committed either by highwaymen or footpads, the difference being that: "The first sort are called gentlemen robbers, or thieves, and these ride on horses well appointed, and go in show like honest men. The other rob on foot, and have no other help but a pair of light heels and a thick wood."[32]

---

30. W. Middleton, *The Boke for a Justyce of Peace*, London, 1545, p.9.
31. T. Gent, *Thomas Gent's autobiography*, 1832 edition, Rev. J. Hunter (Ed.) p.56.
32. S. Rid, "Martin Markall, Beadle of Bridewell," in A.V. Judges (Ed.) *The Elizabethan Underworld*, London, George Routledge, 1930, pp.415-416.

Highwaymen

Highwaymen viewed themselves, and were viewed by others, as the aristocracy of English crime. Indeed, their ranks included a considerable number of minor gentlemen, and some highwaymen affected an exaggerated courtesy to their victims and a well-to-do lifestyle. Many others manifested a reluctance to shed blood if it was possible to avoid it. However, as Samuel Butler noted in the 1660s, the reality of their work was usually much less glamorous: "He takes place of all other thieves as the most heroical, and one that comes nearest to the old Knights errant, though he is really one of the basest, that never ventures but upon surprizal, and where he is sure of the advantage."[33] Despite the romantic image, highwaymen were capable of extreme barbarity. William Cady shot a woman in front of her husband and then cut her stomach open to retrieve a prized wedding ring that she had swallowed to prevent him seizing it. He subsequently murdered several other men, including a cleric, whom he felt were not sufficiently 'co-operative', and went to his execution in 1687 without any show of remorse.[34] Nevertheless, in England, killings committed during the course of a highway robbery were rare.

Highwaymen were a problem throughout the early modern period. Thus, in a letter dated 4th December 1575,

---

33. S. Butler, "Character of a highwayman," in *Characters and Passages from Note-Books*, A.R. Waller (Ed.) Cambridge, CUP, 1908, p.227.
34. Rayner and Crook, *The Complete Newgate Calendar*, vol.I, pp.312-316.

the Privy Council complained to the Lord Keeper and Lord Treasurer that the Queen had been informed of numerous highway robberies which had lately been committed in divers parts of her realm. Even worse, it had been reported that it was an increasingly: "... common thing for the thieves to carry pistols whereby they either murder out of hand before they rob, or else put her subjects in such fear that they dare not resist, [consequently] their lordships are requested to take such steps as may be necessary to redress this mischief."[35] However, despite such Tudor villains, the heyday of the highwayman occurred in the years after 1600, so that by 1701 one observer feared that people would: "... shortly not dare to Travel in England, unless, as in the Deserts of Arabia, it be in large Companies, and Arm'd."[36] Even so, contemporary observers probably exaggerated the incidence of such robberies. One examination of Yorkshire records between 1650 and 1700, suggests that they accounted for less than two per cent of all crimes prosecuted at the assizes in that county, and many cases involved relatively small amounts of money or items of low value.

The flowering of the highwayman was the result of a conjunction of opportunity structures. Such robbers needed relatively busy roads, yet in a country in which there were still many isolated heaths and commons to provide ready cover. This meant that certain locations became particularly favoured. Thus, in the early 1720s, Defoe noted that Gad's

---

35. Anon, *Calendar of the Manuscripts of the Marquis of Salisbury at Hatfield House*, Part II, London, HMSO, 1888, p.123.
36. Anon, *Hanging, not Punishment Enough, for Murtherers, High-Way Men, and Housebreakers*, London, A. Baldwin, 1701, p.A2 and pp.1-5.

Hill, on the road from Gravesend, was a noted place for robbing seamen after they had received their pay at Chatham.[37] Similarly, Shooter's Hill, also in Kent, and on the heavily used London road, had a particularly bad and longstanding reputation. Famously, in 1583, a London merchant, George Saunders, and one of his servants, were murdered there while travelling from Woolwich to St Mary Cray. (The servant managed to survive for a few days, despite being wounded 11 times, and gave crucial information leading to his killers' apprehension.)[38] Lonely heaths, such as that at Hounslow to the west of London, were also favoured. Along with cover, robbers required a cash economy, so that travellers were carrying gold and silver rather than bankers' drafts. They also needed firearms that were sufficiently reliable to safely overawe their victims at a distance. Until the advent of the flintlock, the inherent limitations of contemporary ignition systems hindered the practicality of using pistols. These were the highwayman's weapon of choice, and appear to have slowly developed out of the 'dags' introduced to England in c.1544.[39] Even reliable pistols were limited to a single shot, and reloading was a slow process. However, although possession of a pair of pistols was a *sine qua non* of the highwayman's profession, much greater amounts of weaponry could be carried in

37. D. Defoe, *A Tour Thro' the Whole Island of Great Britain*, London, Everyman, 1962 (first published 1724), vol.1, pp.103-104.

38. Anon, *A briefe discourse of the late murther of Master George Saunders*, London, H. Bynnemen, 1573, f.B1.

39. H.C.B. Rogers, *Weapons of the British Soldier*, London, Sphere Books, 1972, pp.53-59.

saddle holsters and about the person. Thus, in the 1680s, Jack Bird armed himself with half-a-dozen pistols and a sword.[40] Such an armoury explains how considerable gun battles could occur between highwaymen and pursuers, with numerous casualties inflicted. In 1640, when Isaac Atkinson was cornered at Turnham Green by 10 men, after his horse had run off, leaving him unable to escape in his heavy riding boots, he: "... pulled out several pocket-pistols and discharged them; so that he killed four of the men on the spot, and afterwards mortally wounded another with a hanger [sword], which he wore by his side."[41]

Legal controls on the possession of firearms and other projectile weapons were virtually absent in early modern England. Where they existed, they were modest, rarely enforced and largely ineffectual. Thus, in the 1530s, anyone who had less than 300 marks annual worth of land was *theoretically* forbidden to shoot or possess cross-bows (not longbows) or handguns "upon payne of forfayture therof" and a fine of 10 pounds. There were exemptions for those living within six miles of the sea (who might need them for self-defence) and those who manufactured and traded in such weapons.[42] In practice, the provision was widely ignored. In a situational attempt at crime prevention, the law also provided that if anyone carried loaded firearms a JP could require them to find "sureties for the Peace, and

---

40. C. Johnson, *A General History of the Lives and Adventures of the Most Famous Highwaymen, Murderers, Street-Robbers*, London, J. Janeway, 1734, p.127.

41. Johnson, *A General History of the Lives and Adventures of the Most Famous Highwaymen*, p.116.

42. Middleton, *The Boke for a Justyce of Peace*, p.25.

may take away such weapons".[43] This, too, appears to have been little applied, not least because it would impinge on those carrying weapons for self-defence. Indeed, many men were actually required to hold weapons at home if they were members of the militia. Similarly, although a 1553 decree of Edward VI ordered that "all persons who shoot guns" register themselves with a local JP, this seems to have been widely ignored as well, so that by 1618 Dalton could "quaere if this now be in use". There were to be sporadic, and fairly ineffectual, attempts by James II to use the theoretically strict provisions of the Game Act of 1671 to control the possession of firearms. Generally, however, those who could afford the (considerable) cost could easily obtain firearms.[44] Even if they could not, many potential highwaymen merely followed the example of the Irish burglar, William MacQueer, who furnished himself with the necessary accoutrements for robbery at others' expense, stealing a horse and saddle from a stable in the Strand and a pair of pistols from a gunsmith in Westminster. He subsequently also stole a sword to complete his equipment.[45]

Resistance by those attacked on the highways was surprisingly frequent, at least to modern eyes. Of course, some men, even if in a position to defend themselves, would react abjectly, handing over cash and valuables: "... no

---

43. M. Dalton, *The Country Justice, Containing the practise of the Justices of the Peace out of their Sessions* ... London, Company of Stationers, 1661, p.38.

44. D.B. Kopel, "It isn't about duck hunting: The British origins of the Right to Arms," *Michigan Law Review*, 1995, vol.93, pp.1333-1362.

45. Johnson, *A General History of the Lives and Adventures of the Most Famous Highwaymen*, p.333.

sooner the word deliver is let loose, but they are surprised so with fear, that like babes they cry." Others, however, would fight back valiantly to avoid being robbed, often successfully as highwaymen were usually after soft targets.[46] Some cases of victim resistance were predictable. In 1739, two armed highwaymen accosted the Marquis of Graham and his servant near Farnham in Surrey. One of the robbers seized the Marquis's bridle and ordered him to 'deliver'. Nothing daunted, however, the nobleman drew a pistol and shot him through the head. The other man fired, missed and fled, pursued by his two intended victims. He was forced to abandon his horse and escape into a wood on foot.[47] Similarly, in the 1680s, when William MacQueer robbed an army captain on Hampstead Heath, a fight ensued. The two men fired several pistol shots at each other, all of which missed, then fell to sword-play, making a "great many pushes". MacQueer, being less accomplished at this exercise, was in difficulties, but suddenly remembered an unfired pistol that he still had in his breeches' pocket. He drew it and shot the officer dead while the latter "apprehended nothing but the sword".[48] More surprisingly, physically disadvantaged men and women could show stout resistance, even over small sums of money. Jack Bird was beaten and captured by a Dover naval pilot, who had lost both his hands years earlier, when he attempted to rob the old but "boisterous" mariner. He was lucky to escape

46.   Anon, *The Caterpillars of this Nation Anatomised*, p.4.
47.   *The Gentleman's Magazine*, 1739, vol.9, p.382.
48.   Johnson, *A General History of the Lives and Adventures of the Most Famous Highwaymen*, p.332.

execution at the following Maidstone Assizes, and resolved never to take chances again. When, near Acton, he accosted a Welsh drover who fought back with his quarterstaff, Bird shot the drover dead. Rifling through the man's pockets, he found only 1s 6d.[49] Similarly, in 1714, John Bradshaw was sheltering in a wood near Shooter's Hill, in Kent, waiting for victims when one Cecilia Fowley, a servant girl, passed by carrying a box containing her clothes, a hammer, and 15 shillings in wages. Bradshaw approached her alone, being, he thought "sufficient enough to deal with her", and took her box. However, whilst he was examining it, Fowley seized the hammer and struck him on the temple with it, felling him: "She then seconded it with the claw of the hammer, by striking it into his windpipe, of which wound the rogue instantly died." A passing gentleman carried Fowley before a magistrate, where he stood bail for her appearance at the March Assizes in Rochester. This was purely a formality, as she was swiftly acquitted of any crime in killing Bradshaw.[50]

As these cases suggest, the highwayman's life was fraught with dangers. However, they frequently also shortened their careers by drawing attention to themselves with a flamboyant lifestyle combined with an obvious lack of support. Many resided, ate and drank at roadside inns, the owners of which were often, effectively, tacit accomplices in their work, charging extortionate amounts

---

49. Johnson, *A General History of the Lives and Adventures of the Most Famous Highwaymen*, p.127.
50. Rayner and Crook, *The Complete Newgate Calendar*, vol.II, p.253.

for board and lodging and being their "close confederates and allies, though the common interest of both will not permit it to be known".[51] Such extravagance meant that for many it was a "brief life but a merry one". However, those who were cautious could survive for considerable periods. Shortly before being executed for murder at Lincoln, in 1733, the Hallam brothers admitted that they had committed "upwards of 50 Robberies".[52] The celebrated highwayman William Davis (the 'Golden Farmer') had avoided the slightest suspicion during a criminal career that spanned 42 years prior to his execution in 1689. Other than the slightly unusual habit of paying all his bills in gold, there was, apparently, nothing to distinguish him from other Wiltshire tenant farmers.[53] His agricultural occupation provided him with seclusion, shelter and also justified his frequent movements and possession of cash.

Although popular in fiction, robbing mail coaches was an especially hazardous undertaking; in 1722, Ralph Wilson claimed it was 'certain destruction' as they were heavily guarded. Perhaps as a result, between 1725 and 1730 the Bristol mail was not robbed on a single occasion, although attacked twice in the following year. Additionally, the valuable bank notes that the mail often carried were frequently 'marked' with a request that payment should not be made on them if news was received that the coach carrying them had been robbed. As a result robbers were

---

51.   Butler, *Character of a highwayman*, p.227.
52.   *The Gentleman's Magazine*, 1733, vol.3, p.154.
53.   Johnson, *A General History of the Lives and Adventures of the Most Famous Highwaymen*, pp.106-108.

sometimes convicted after being "discover'd by Indorsements on Bank Notes taken away".[54] Even if successful, strenuous efforts would be made to catch and convict those guilty of such crimes. Thus, in 1738, the mail coach for the North was robbed at Kingsland, near London, by a "middle-siz'd Man, with a Paper Mask, who took several of the Baggs and rifled others". The Postmaster promised an extra reward of 200 pounds, over and above the statutory ones available for his conviction, even if the information was provided by an accomplice (who was also promised a royal pardon).[55]

To reduce the dangers involved in their ventures, various techniques became 'standard' to highwaymen. Most obviously, they would usually quickly put a considerable distance between themselves and a major crime, something that their mounted status facilitated. A few would even lie low outside the jurisdiction, in Scotland or on the Continent. Additionally, it was common to shoot the robbed party's horse or to cut the traces of a carriage, to slow the raising of the hue and cry and prevent close pursuit. Thus, when William MacQueer robbed Lady Auverquerque's carriage he shot two of the coach horses and the horses of two footmen that were in attendance, before riding off.[56] Similarly, three inexperienced highwaymen who robbed two London merchants on Bagshot heath in 1608 "tooke also, their horses, and stripping off their bridles, turned

---

54. *The Gentleman's Magazine*, 1731, vol.1, p.122.
55. *The Gentleman's Magazine*, 1738, vol.8, p.435.
56. Johnson, *A General History of the Lives and Adventures of the Most Famous Highwaymen*, p.333.

them loose". In this case, while their attackers were distracted with another potential victim, the merchants recovered their animals and "raised up the country", leading to the speedy arrest of the neophyte robbers.[57] It was also normal to make servants stand well apart from their masters.

Most importantly, highwaymen had to be realistic about the size of their potential targets as over-ambition could be disastrous. There were situational advantages when conducting a robbery in working with accomplices, one man could search for valuables while another kept the target covered and there was more 'firepower' if resistance was encountered. However, there were also major disadvantages, groups of mounted men were much more visible and, most importantly, if any one of them was captured he might turn evidence for the Crown and implicate his erstwhile colleagues; there was little honour amongst thieves. For these reasons, many, like William Nevison (executed in 1684) worked alone, rather than with a partner "who by favour or misfortune might be drawn in to accuse him".[58] A solitary highwayman would often only expect a reasonable 'contribution' from each traveller that he stopped, the risks of conducting a thorough body search frequently being too great for a single man. Because of this, many wealthy travellers carried 10 or 12 guineas separately from their other money to handover in case they were

---

57. B.L., *The Lives, Apprehension, Arraignment and Execution of Robert Throgmorton. William Porter. John Bishop ...* London, Henry Gosson, 1608, f.A3.
58. Johnson, *A General History of the Lives and Adventures of the Most Famous Highwaymen*, pp.103-5.

stopped.[59] Things were usually different if a gang were involved: "When there are several highwaymen together, they will search you thoroughly and leave nothing."[60] Even so, in 1720, John Hawkins's notorious gang settled for 10 pounds and a watch from a Mr. Hide of Hackney, when they robbed his carriage, missing £300 in bank notes.

The mechanics of such a robbery, and the official reaction to it, can be seen in the case of five highwaymen who, in the early 1670s, would "cruise up and down" the Branford to Windsor road. After some petty robberies, they acquired intelligence about a stage-coach carrying several wealthy men. They ambushed it near Colbrook, where they took a considerable sum of money at pistol point, without resistance. Before leaving, they took the precaution of "doing the Harnesmaker the kindness of cutting the Horses Traces that they might not presently follow them". Even so, the victims immediately went to a local JP, who set the hue and cry into operation. As a result, the highwaymen were closely pursued, their unusual number making their trail relatively easy to follow. As they fled, they commandeered other travellers' horses when their own became exhausted, leaving their tired mounts as "strays to feed upon the common". The leading man of the pursuing posse, a well mounted and brave army Lifeguard, caught up with them. They flung him from his horse and rode on. Nevertheless, the soldier pursued them once more, riding one of their

---

59. J.B. Le Blanc, *Letters on the English and French Nations,* London, J. Brindley, 1747, vol.II, pp.291-3, 295-6.
60. Van Muyden, *A Foreign View of England,* p.128.

abandoned animals. The highwaymen captured him again, at pistol point, but, with considerable gallantry, "scorn'd to kill him, because they found he was a person stout and valiant". Leaving him, they continued their flight. Unfortunately, they were cornered at Hampstead by over a 100 local people, news having been sent ahead of the fugitives, across country. Only one highwayman managed to break through the cordon, and he was later arrested. The other four, knowing they could expect no mercy from the courts, stood their ground on foot and fought desperately, killing two local men and wounding several others, before they were captured.[61]

John Clavell, awaiting death for highway robbery in 1628, gave practical advice to travellers as to how they could avoid his colleagues. Most of it was anodyne and banal, in a vein that was periodically repeated over the following century. Thus, he advised them to be careful when staying in country inns about letting chambermaids discover if they were carrying money, because they might have contacts with underworld elements; to avoid travelling on the Sabbath when there were likely to be few other road users about; and that robbers frequently wore cloaks so that their attire could not be identified and neckerchiefs to use as improvised masks. Interestingly, however, and contrary to some impressions, Clavell felt that highwaymen were reluctant to operate at night as few travellers with anything of value were on the roads at such times, it was impossible

---

61. Anon, *A True and Perfect Revelation of a Robbery and Murder Committed by five Notorious Highwaymen*, London, 1674, pp.2-6.

to discern if a potential victim was armed and because even highwaymen had to keep lawful hours if they were not to attract suspicion.[62]

Footpads

Not all robbers had the means, riding ability or inclination to become mounted highwaymen, many choosing to be footpads instead. For obvious reasons, such men dominated robbery in urban areas. Thomas Sherwood, originally from Staffordshire, and Elizabeth Evans, from Shropshire, who both gravitated to London's underworld, were archetypal footpads. In Evans's case, the precipitating incident was the fairly standard one of losing her position in domestic service due to personal scandal. Indeed, the Reverend Henry Goodcole, the Newgate Ordinary, who talked to her at length after her arrest, placed some of the blame for her descent into murder on her London relations, who had disowned her. With no credit, money and "all means of livelihood failing", it was predictable that she would drift into prostitution and crime. Falling in together, the couple became notorious murderers "both hunting for one prey". They were responsible for at least three killings. Elizabeth would pose as a prostitute, closely shadowed by Sherwood. She would frequent theatres, inns and ale-houses, and lure drunk but prosperous individuals, who had been "too busy with the Pot", to secluded locations where they could be

---

62. J. Clavell, *A Recantation of an Ill led Life*, London, 1628, pp.30-40.

viciously cudgelled and robbed by her partner. Amongst their victims were a merchant and an army Lieutenant. The couple were eventually caught when they foolishly tried to sell the latter's clothes, the day after his murder.[63]

However, some footpads would also prey on mounted travellers on the main roads. To do this, they required cover close to the passing riders. To reduce the threat of such robberies, the Statute of Winchester had provided that: "... there shail no busshe growe two hundred fete of every syde of the waye."[64] Although the provision remained in force throughout the period, it was widely ignored. As a result, in June 1652, John Evelyn, riding alone on the London highway near Bromley, could make the mistake of avoiding the summer heat by keeping close to the shaded sides of the road. This allowed two footpads to surprise him from the cover of a hedgerow, something that would have been impossible had he kept to the centre of the highway (the robbers were only armed with pistols). Suddenly, there: "... started out two Cutt-throats, and striking with their long staves at the horse, taking hold of the reins, threw me downe, and immediately tooke my sworde". They then dragged him deep into an adjacent wood, threatened to cut his throat, stole his sword, money and two rings, before tying him up and removing his boots. They left his horse, partly, Evelyn felt, because its unusual appearance made it easily identifiable and "well known on that roade". They

---

63. H. Goodcole, *Heavens Speedie Hue and Cry sent after Lust and Murther*, London, N. And I. Okes, 1635, pp.A2 and B1-B2.
64. Middleton, *The Boke for a Justyce of Peace*, p.13.

were not highwaymen, had no personal use for the animal and presumably did not wish to risk selling it.[65] Their *modus operandi* suggests that they knew their trade. Footpads often necessarily had to use violence if they were to safely surprise and disable their targets. Thus, in the 1690s, a (mounted) highwayman advising a neophyte club-armed footpad, who had attempted to rob him on the highway, as to how to go about his pedestrian business, warned him that: "When you have a mind to robb a man, never take hold of his bridle and bid him stand, but, the first thing you do, knock him down, and, if he talk to you, hit him another stroke."[66]

Fencing of Stolen Goods

Stolen valuables, unlike cash, would have to be fenced unless personally consumed or otherwise used by the thief. This was often relatively easy in a world in which second-hand goods were widely sold or pawned. They might be traded in goldsmiths, silversmiths, chandlers or other businesses of doubtful probity. However, ale-houses were the most common centres for criminal and fencing networks. Typically, Thomas Phippes, examined in Hertfordshire about a theft in 1626, claimed that he had entrusted the sale of the stolen goods to a widow who ran an ale-house in

65. J. Evelyn, *The Diary of John Evelyn*, Oxford, Clarendon Press, 1955, vol.5, pp.69-71.
66. A. de la Pryme, *The Diary of Abraham de la Pryme*, Durham, Surtees Society, 1870, pp.76-77.

Ware. According to Phippes, she was a regular fence and even had a secret compartment on her premises to accommodate such items.[67] As a result of such cases, many observers, like Thomas Harman in the 1560s, were inclined to blame the very existence of rogues on: "... a number of wicked persons that keepe typlinge Houses in all shires, where they have succour and reliefe; and what so ever they bring, they are sure to receave money for the same."[68] His views were shared by the authorities who thought that the extensive opportunities available for fencing stolen goods in the Metropolis acted as the city's "Nurserie of Burglaries, Robberies, felonies, and frauds".[69] Indeed, William Fleetwood was able to specifically name a number of ale-houses and taverns, such as the *Crown* at Bishopsgate and the *Black Lion* in Shoreditch which were: "Harboringe Houses for Maisterles men, and for such as lyve by theifte."[70] Because of such establishments, Michael Dalton approvingly cited King James's warning to the Star Chamber against the excessive number of ale-houses which were: "... haunts and receits, for robbers, theeves, rogues, vagabonds, and other idle, loose, and sturdy fellowes, who loyter and inquire in these places where they may have a booty." Dalton urged JPs to consider both the quality and

---

67. P. Lawson, "Property Crime and Hard Times in England, 1559-1624," *Law and History Review*, 1986, vol.4, p.96.
68. T. Harman, *A Caveat or Warning, for Common Cursitors vulgarly called Vagabones*, London, Wylliam Gryffith, 1567, p.Aiv.
69. Anon, *A Proclamation for the better discovery and prevention of Burglaries, Robberies* ... London, 1630, pp.1-3.
70. R.H. Twaney and E. Power (eds.) *Tudor Economic Documents*, London, Longmans, 1951, vol.3, pp.338-9.

reputation of the proposed landlord and the tavern's location before licensing them. It was best that permitted ale-houses were situated in town centres and not in cul-de-sacs "much lesse in woods or places remote from Towns".[71] To prevent such abuses the terms in which ale-house licences were granted were often very strict. In 1608, a typical Norfolk licence provided: "That if anie vagabondes or suspicious persons come to your house, you [the ale-house keeper] shall acquainte the officers with it, and so allso if anie goodes be offered in your house by anie to be sould."[72] Of course, in practice, many of the restrictions imposed were flagrantly breached. Doubtless, however, if the authorities decided to make an example of the ale-house, they provided ample scope to find a violation of licence.

As in all periods, the 'fence' would expect to take a major share of the proceeds of crime: "... their host or hostess giveth them money for the same, but half their value that it is worth."[73] Half was actually quite generous; probably more typical, at least for lesser criminals, were the experiences of Evelyn's robbers: "These rogues had pauned my rings &c. for a trifle to a Goldsmith's servant."[74] Aggravating the situation, for much of the period, receiving was often only a misdemeanour. However, not all pawn brokers and dealers in second-hand goods were dishonest,

---

71. Dalton, *The Country Justice*, 1655, p.34.
72. Sir N. Bacon, *The Official Papers of Sir Nathaniel Bacon of Stiffkey, Norfolk as Justice of the Peace 1580-1620*, H.W. Saunders (Ed.) London, Royal History Society, Campden Third Series, 1915, vol.26, p.55.
73. Harman, *A Caveat or Warning for Common Cursitors*, p.73.
74. Evelyn, *The Diary of John Evelyn*, pp.69-71.

and for the thief fencing stolen items with a dealer whose dishonesty was not well established could be dangerous.

Fraud

Before the 1700s, the rule of possessorial immunity limited the scope of fraud. This legal doctrine was inherited from the medieval era, and meant that those who legally acquired possession over chattels were often not subject to criminal (as opposed to civil) liability for any subsequent mis-appropriation. Thus, in an extreme case, a goldsmith who appropriated precious metal that he had been given to work for his own use was acquitted of larceny in 1487. England was not unique in this, similar limitations on the criminal sphere were found across Western Europe. However, after 1473, when *The Carrier's Case* was decided in the Star Chamber, a number of important exceptions to the general rule developed. In 1529, parliament intervened to deny servants immunity for articles received directly from their masters (21 Hen. 8, c.7). There was further legislation in 1609 and, in 1692, tenants of furnished rooms also lost their protection with regard to the contents of their lodgings (3 & 4 W. & M.). However, subject to important qualifications, the general position between bailors and bailees prevailed into the eighteenth century.[75]

Nevertheless, fraudulent practices that could be

---

75. G. Fletcher, "The Metamorphosis of Larceny," *Harvard Law Review*, 1976, vol.89, no.3, pp.469-530 and pp.475-481.

prosecuted still abounded. White ruff crime could be profitable. In 1618, Francis Robinson, aided by a scrivener, forged a Royal commission allowing him to receive payments from counties neighbouring London. In the space of a month, before being detected, he secured more than £28. Unfortunately, his deceit had required that he forge the Royal seal, something that meant that he received a traitor's death.[76] At a more prosaic level, gaming offered many opportunities for fraudulent conduct. Dalton warned of people being "deceived by false Dice, or false Cards".[77] His concern was understandable, such devices were regularly employed by skilful tricksters. This compounded gambling's social injuriousness, which, it was feared, also engendered other forms of crime. Thomas More cautioned that dice, cards, football, tennis and quoits were all games that sent their practitioners "straight a-stealing when their money is gone".[78] Over 200 years later, Henry Fielding was still making the same point. All JPs had the power to enter public places where it was suspected such games were being played, and to bind over any players found to refrain from such activity in future.[79]

Coining

Crimes against the currency were widespread, in part

---

76. H. Goodcole, *A True Declaration of the Happy Conversion, Contrition and Christian Preparation of F. Robinson*, London, 1618, at f.C3.
77. Dalton, *The Country Justice*, 1655, p.72.
78. Sir T. More, *Utopia*, Ware, Wordsworth Classics, 1997, p.35.
79. Dalton, *The Country Justice*, 1655, p.71.

because of disparities between the face value and bullion worth of silver and gold coinage. Such offences came in many forms. They could range, at the lowest level, from clipping the edges of gold or silver coins to remove a small sliver of the precious metal or shaking them in a bag, to produce gold dust, via the more sophisticated gilding of low value coins, to full scale coining (minting) of fake money. Coining was a form of crime that nearly always involved professionalism, requiring a considerable amount of tools, skills and start-up capital, secure premises and a means of distributing the forged money. It was normally treated very seriously by the authorities. Indeed, both coining and clipping were legally treason, the only form of the crime that ordinary criminals were likely to encounter. A letter sent to the Privy Council, by an informer named Richard Baines, about Christopher Marlowe, provides an indication as to how gravely it was viewed. Amongst claims that Marlowe was an atheist and sodomist he alleged that the playwright had declared: "That he had as good a right to coin as the Queen of England, and that he was acquainted with one Poole, a prisoner in Newgate, who hath great skill in mixture of metals, and having learned some things of him, he meant through help of a cunning stamp-maker to coin French crowns, pistolets, and English shillings." (Technically, only the last one would have been treason, as Shakespeare's Henry V puns on the eve of Agincourt "it is no English treason to cut French crowns, and to-morrow the King himself will be a clipper".) Even so, many were surprised at the crime's status. In 1528, a French priest serving in the north of England was arrested for clipping.

He was sent to Westminster for examination but escaped while his keeper was at breakfast. He fled to Rye in Sussex, where, fearing the approach of his pursuers, he sought sanctuary in a nearby church. However, on the coroner's arrival, to supervise the abjuration process, the priest was mortified to discover that his offence was considered treason, making him ineligible for the protection of sanctuary.[80] Over 240 years later, even William Blackstone found it difficult to justify treating such a conventional crime in so singular a fashion.

Indicative of its more sophisticated manifestations, on 25th July 1696, at the assizes held at Gloucester, Mr Justice Rokeby tried and condemned one Elizabeth Biss of Oxenhall for coining and clipping. Appropriately, Biss was the widow of a goldsmith, and, presumably, inherited the tools for her nefarious business from him (if not the criminal organisation itself). Apparently: "She kept ye great mint of all these parts for adulterating ye coin of ye Kingdom. Many tooles & instruments for that purpose were found in her home." Metal clippings and silver ingots made from clipped money to the value of £338 were also found. At the same time, he condemned Mrs Biss's natural father, Walter Rudge, to death, also for clipping.[81] Given the draconian penalties for the crime (the death sentence was rarely commuted), it is, perhaps, not surprising that it engendered great ruthlessness amongst its perpetrators. Thus, in 1677, a coiner murdered

---

80. K. Kesselring, "Abjuration and its Demise: the changing face of Royal Justice in the Tudor Period," *Canadian Journal of History*, 1999, vol.3, p.351.
81. Justice Rokeby, *The Diary of Mr Justice Rokeby,* London, Wyman and Sons, 1887, p.47.

his daughter-in-law because she had witnessed his criminal operations, and he was afraid that she might give evidence against him.[82] However, the most vigorous attempts by the authorities to deal with the crime were largely unavailing. On 15th July 1694, John Evelyn noted that many people had recently been executed for clipping money, something that was done to such an: "... intollerable degree, that there was hardly any money stirring that was intrinsically worth above halfe the value." Periodically, currency would have to be reissued because adulteration had become endemic. This also occasioned difficulties, especially if the adulterated coinage was withdrawn prematurely; in June 1696 Evelyn complained that Parliament had been imprudent "to damne the old (tho clip't and corrupted) 'til they had provided supplies".[83]

---

82.   Anon, *Horrid News from St Martins*, London, 1677, p.7.
83.   J. Evelyn, *The Diary of John Evelyn*, vol.5, pp.186 and 246.

Chapter 5

Non-Instrumental Violence and Homicide

The background to most prosecuted cases of assault (and many homicides) is readily familiar to modern criminal law practitioners. They occurred as a result of 'spontaneous' arguments, frequently influenced by the presence of alcohol, sometimes following a longer period of hostility or feuding between assailant and victim. Some quarrels might allow for a degree of formalisation, with withdrawal to an outside yard or open space where the issue could be settled 'man to man'. These were probably the less dangerous type of conflict, especially if a crowd gathered, as they would normally ensure some measure of 'fair play'. Many others simply erupted as brawls. Not surprisingly, fairs, competitive sports and communal celebrations, especially where there was the ready availability of drink, could be dangerous: "... populous assemblies, under pretence of recreation, are usually occasions of quarrels, and so of murthers."[1] Some of these homicidal altercations appear to have been heavily nuance oriented, being precipitated by the most minor 'provocations' and manifestations of disrespect. The igniting incident could be almost anything, a dispute over cards, debts, straying animals, an aspersion on another's masculinity etc. This is reminiscent of the background to many killings amongst the modern American and (to a lesser extent) English underclass, groups that are strongly

---

1.   T. Cooper, *The Cry and Revenge of Blood*, London, N. Okes, 1620, p.24.

resistant to elite propaganda against recourse to violence, and which are frequently socialised into a culture that is pregnant with exoneration for its manifestations. In the early modern period, such a culture was found in a much wider range of the social spectrum than is the case today.[2]

The brief but turbulent life of the eminent playwright Christopher Marlowe provides a quintessential illustration of this phenomenon and its dangers. In 1589, while he was fighting one William Bradley in Hog Lane, London, Bradley was stabbed to death by the poet Thomas Watson, who had come to Marlowe's assistance. Both Marlowe and Watson were imprisoned in Newgate for several weeks before being discharged at trial. Three years later, Marlowe was summoned to appear at the Middlesex sessions for assaulting two Shoreditch constables. Finally, in May 1593, Marlowe went with friends and acquaintances, including one Ingram Frizer, to Deptford, a village near London. They spent the afternoon talking, eating and drinking in a tavern. According to the coroner's enquiry, a dispute occurred between them, over payment of the "reckoninge", and, in a passion, Marlowe drew Frizer's dagger and slashed him with it. In the ensuing struggle, Marlowe was himself mortally wounded, dying at the age of just 29. As this case suggests, the presence of alcohol and weapons were particularly important situational determinants in incidents of serious violence, and are worthy of individual consideration.

---

2. E. Leyton, *Men of Blood: Murder in Modern England*, Harmondsworth, Penguin Books, 1997, pp.17 and 206-217.

Alcohol

Alcohol was a major contributory factor in assaults and homicides, although contemporary jurists were adamant that intoxication was not an excuse for violence. A drunken killer was guilty of murder as his condition was a: "... voluntary ignorance in him, in as much as such ignorance commeth to him by his own act and folly ... [Indeed] what hurt or ill soever he doth, his drunkenness doth aggravate it."[3] The abuse of alcohol was a perennial early modern concern. At the start of the sixteenth century, it was identified as socially corrupting by Thomas More. By the late 1500s, bishops, government ministers, magistrates and Puritan preachers were becoming increasingly vociferous in their condemnation of ale-houses, places that, in the words of Christopher Hudson in 1631, were "nests of Satan where the owls of impiety lurk and where all evil is hatched".[4] This was partly prompted by their apparent proliferation, which seemed to encourage dissolute elements to "lye idlely in the ale howses daye and nyght eatinge and drynkynge excessively".[5] They were also frequently the scenes of violent drink induced quarrels, such as the murder of John Hall by two soldiers in 1731, after he refused them

---

3. M. Dalton, *The Country Justice, Containing the Practise of the Justices of the Peace out of their Sessions* ... London, Company of Stationers, 1661, p.307.
4. J.A. Browner, "Wrong side of the River: London's disreputable South Bank in the Sixteenth and Seventeenth Century," *Essays in History, University of Virginia*, vol.36, p.49.
5. R.H. Tawney and E. Power (eds.) *Tudor Economic Documents*, London, Longmans, 1951, vol.2, p.341.

admittance to a public house in Northampton.[6] It is sometimes suggested that the more disreputable ale-houses should be distinguished from 'respectable' inns and taverns, where wine might be served, and which attracted a higher class of customer rather than the 'dregs' of society. However, the distinction between taverns and ale-houses seems to have been fluid. Some contemporary observers felt that nefarious activities were rife at all levels of hostelry, and Thomas More was convinced that taverns and ale-houses were no better than the most openly infamous houses.[7] Many were concerned about the heavy drinking that such establishments appeared to engender. Typically, Robert Bolton, a Northamptonshire preacher, declared in 1625 that drunkenness threatened a "lamentable inundation to the whole kingdom". An MP suggested that the prevalence of alcohol meant England was unique in Christendom, "such looseness and lewdness was no where as here".[8]

Responding to such fears, in 1571, another MP argued the case for building a Bridewell in every town, and requiring "every tipler in the County to yield twelve pence yearly to the maintenance therof". Between 1604 and 1625, Parliament passed four Acts punishing drunkenness, a vice that was allegedly especially common amongst the "worst and inferior people". There were also attempts to limit the strength of beer by forcing brewers to restrict themselves to two sorts, the strongest selling at 8 shillings, and the weaker

6.   *The Gentleman's Magazine*, 1731, vol.1, p.124.
7.   Sir T. More, *Utopia*, Ware, Wordsworth Classics, 1997, p.35.
8.   Sir S. D'Ewes, *A Compleat Journal of the Votes, Speeches and Debates*, London, 1613, p.71.

at 4 shillings a barrel. However, enforcement of such regulations was inherently very difficult. In March 1614 it was reported that brewers were still producing more than the prescribed two varieties, some of it both dearer and stronger than the permitted maximum. Some brewers claimed, rather unconvincingly, that strong beer was brewed solely for consumption abroad and at sea (rather as modern British car sellers laud the theoretical top speeds of their vehicles as being valuable on the German Autobahns).[9]

Nevertheless, despite drastic proposals to deal with the problem, cooler heads usually prevailed. Thus, in the House of Commons, 1601 saw the defeat of a Bill to suppress ale-houses by restricting the granting of licences so that "no man shall sell, but he must be allowed in the Quarter Sessions by four justices". Sir Robert Wroth questioned the "pain and charge this will be to a poor man". Some would have to travel 20 or 30 miles to get a licence. Additionally, it would be a "monstrous trouble" to already overburdened JPs.[10] Support for strong measures was matched by a constant groundswell of political opposition, if only because many MPs feared that they would encourage magistrates to interfere with the lifestyles of men of 'quality'.[11] Even so, a variety of widely ignored Jacobean and Caroline statutes provided that no one might: "... tipple in any such Tavern, or in any Inne, Ale-house, or Victualing-house, in the same

---

9.   Browner, *Wrong Side of the River*, pp.50-51.
10. D'Ewes, *A Compleat Journal of the Votes*, p.676.
11. J.R. Kent, "Attitudes of Members of the House of Commons to the Regulation of 'Personal Conduct' in Late Elizabethan and Early Stuart England," *British Institute of Historical Research*, 1973, vol.46, pp.41-71.

Town where he dwelleth, nor within two miles thereof, except he be a traveller."[12]

Lethal Weapons

The only distinguishing factor between many lethal and non-lethal assaults was the availability of a weapon, whether improvised or designed. To a considerable extent, early modern England was an armed society. Potentially lethal weapons were everywhere, even if they were primarily intended for work or leisure rather than killing. Use of the ubiquitous knife was much more common in homicides than deliberately designed weapons such as daggers or swords. Possession of the latter type of implement was actually quite rare, gentlemen apart. An examination of inventories from the parish of Kirkby Lonsdale in Westmoreland suggest that even in this remote county, in the period between 1500 and 1720, over 90 per cent of the inhabitants had no purpose manufactured weapons (though smaller ones may have been overlooked).[13] This partly explains why various attempts to counter the deliberate carrying of bladed weapons were largely ineffectual in reducing violent crime. Thus, an old provision forbade men of inferior quality from carrying daggers or

---

12. Dalton, *The Country Justice*, 1661, p.29.
13. C. Harrison, "Manor Courts and the Governance of Tudor England," in *Communities and Courts in Britain 1150-1900*, C. Brooks (Ed.), London, Hambledon, 1997, p.191.

swords "upon payne to forfyte the same".[14] It was of no value in preventing killers using improvised weapons such as scythes, pruning hooks, etc.

Until c.1750, half the violent deaths in Kent involved the use of side-arms of some description, whether blades, cudgels or staffs. By contrast, by the nineteenth century, kicking, punching and beating had become the normal method of killing. However, even within the early modern era, the proportions of different types of lethal weapon varied considerably over time. In the 50 years from 1570 to 1620, bladed weapons accounted for 37 per cent of all violent deaths in Kent. After 1620, however, their number declined rapidly, so that in the years between 1620 and 1670, blunt instruments accounted for 30 per cent of all homicides and blades for only 13 per cent of killings. The use of firearms was extremely rare until after 1560. It is not difficult to explain why. To be used outside volley firing on the battlefield, guns needed to be reasonably affordable, accurate, portable and reliable. All of these factors were absent until the seventeenth century. As a result, Kent, despite straddling several routes from the Channel ports favoured by highwaymen, had only 14 fatal shootings in the century after 1560. Of these, only six involved the use of handguns, the remainder being long arms (muskets and guns for 'hail shot'). On close examination, even one or two of these shootings appear to have been accidents. Only one fatal shooting involved robbery. After 1660, the use of firearms became much more common, with shootings

---

14. W. Middleton, *The Boke for a Justyce of Peace*, London, 1545, p.14.

accounting for 26 per cent of homicides in the years 1720-1729 (compared to only three per cent in the century after 1560).[15]

Domestic Violence

Domestic violence was an accepted facet of everyday early modern life, and much of it was quite legal. The private use of corporal punishment was widespread and even extended to adults in some situations: "A School-master of a Grammar-School may chastise his Schollers, the like Law is of a Goaler of his unruly Prisoners, and thus is no Breach of the Peace." (However, the right to punish prisoners did not extend to the jailers' servants unless expressly authorised.)[16] Dons could beat university students, albeit that undergraduates were usually younger than their modern equivalents, masters could beat their servants and men their wives. If Thomas More is to be believed, in the early sixteenth century, some battered women sought refuge in the country's few permanent religious sanctuaries, having stripped their homes of saleable items: "Mens wyues runne thither with theyr housebandes plate, and saye, thei dare not abyde with theyr housbandes for beatinge."[17] Throughout

---

15. J.S. Cockburn, "Patterns of Violence in English Society: Homicide in Kent 1560-1985," *Past and Present*, 1991, no.130, pp.82-84.
16. W. Fleetwood, *The Office of a Justice of Peace*, London, R. Wood, 1657, p.44.
17. Sir T. More, "The History of King Richard the Thirde," in *The English Works of Sir Thomas More*, A.W. Reed *et al* (eds.), London: Eyre and Spottiswoode, 1931, vol.1, at p.47.

the period, the courts accepted the legal right of a husband to 'correct' his wife without criminal charge. Not surprisingly, occasionally this went too far and resulted in death.

However, such violence should not be exaggerated. Many observers, including eminent Puritan divines, disapproved strongly of any physical violence within marriage; some, such as William Heale in his *Apologie for Women* of 1609, even challenged its legality. All observers insisted that spousal chastisement be kept within modest limits, that it be 'reasonable' and commensurate with the behaviour to be corrected. The late eighteenth century 'rule of thumb', about the thickness of a rod that could be used on a wife, was a legal decision based on normative not approved behaviour patterns, and is remembered because even at the time it occasioned indignation.[18] Although it was accepted that a man might "chaste his wife with discretion", if it became "outrageous" his wife could petition for him to be bound over (the corollary applied for the hen-pecked).[19] In the earlier part of the period, excessive wife-beating could lead to presentation in the Church courts. In later years, if it produced serious injury, prosecution might result. The judiciary were adamant that such chastisement should not be inflicted with a: "... sword or a bar of iron, nor any other

---

18. S.D. Amussen, "'Being Stirred to Much Unquietness.' Violence and Domestic Violence in Early Modern England," *Journal of Women's History*, 1994, vol.6, pp.70-75.
19. Fleetwood, *The Office of a Justice of Peace*, p.31.

weapon or instrument to kill them."[20] Nevertheless, unless the consequences were especially grave, it was rare for prosecutions to be brought. In the years between 1620 and 1680, of the 579 assaults indicted at the Essex quarter sessions, none involved wife-beating, despite there being evidence of numerous informal complaints about the practice. This suggests that personal intervention by JPs, clerics or the binding over of perpetrators was the preferred treatment for those who assaulted their spouses.[21] Intervention by relatives and friends was probably more effective in limiting wife-beating. In many seventeenth century communities it was difficult to produce the social isolation from family and neighbours that accompanies much modern domestic abuse. An analysis of 176 recognizances issued for assault, beatings, and even threatening words, issued against husbands at the behest of their wives, found in Westminster Quarter Sessions records between 1685 and 1720, suggests that, in the liberating atmosphere of the Metropolis, wives became slightly more willing to have recourse to the courts, if only the binding over procedure, to deal with spousal violence, sometimes for quite minor matters. Nevertheless, this is still only an average of five cases a year in a city (Westminster) with

---

20. C. Robbins (Ed.) *The Diary of John Milward Esq, September 1666 to May 1668,* Cambridge, CUP, pp.167-168.
21. J.A. Sharpe, "Domestic Homicide in Early Modern England," *Historical Journal,* 1981, vol.24, p.31.

60,000 people.[22] Wife-beating could have other dangers. One Mr Fox, a notorious and profligate drunkard, attacked his wife after she went to a tavern to ask for money to feed their infants. The distressed woman went home, killed both her babies and then cut her husband's throat as he fell into a drunken slumber after his return.[23]

The same criteria of proportionality applied to the correction of young employees. In a case from Devonshire, a weaver's servant, put in charge of the apprentices in his master's absence, abused his position by cudgelling a negligent apprentice about the head with a broom stick, until the blood gushed out of every orifice, as a result of which he died. Lord Chief Justice Kelyng had no doubts as to what the consequences of this should be, also providing an illustration of judicial pressure on jurors: "The Jury would find this manslaughter; he caused them to go out again and bring it in murder, which accordingly they did." Although petitioned to reprieve the servant, Kelyng refused on principle.[24] Similarly, in 1681, Letitia Wigington, a coat-maker, disappointed at the quality of piece-work done by her 13-year-old female apprentice, "she had not done it so well as she required", reacted with rage. Feeling that her initial beating was not enough she arranged for a man to hold the girl down and then "whipped her so unmercifully, that the blood ran down". Shortly afterwards, the girl died.

---

22. J. Hurl-Eamon, "Domestic Violence Prosecuted: Women Binding Over Their Husbands for Assault at Westminster Quarter Sessions, 1685-1720," *Journal of Family History*, 2001, vol.26, no.4, pp.435-454, at p.417.

23. Anon, *The Distressed Mother: or Sorrowful Wife in Tears*, London, 1690, p.1.

24. Robbins (Ed.) *The Diary of John Milward Esq.*, pp.167-168.

Wigington was convicted and executed.[25]

'Hooliganism'

Even at the start of the 1600s, some foreign observers claimed to have discerned an aggressive 'hooligan' trait in English lower class life. This was, they claimed, especially prevalent in the Metropolis. Thus, an English recusant, dining in Rome with merchants from Spain, France, Germany and Italy who had visited London, recorded a mortifying conversation in which they had exchanged views about his fellow-countrymen. They claimed that the "baser sort" of Englishmen were "more rude and barbarous" than those of any other European country. Foreigners were likely to be jostled and abused, forced to walk in the gutter and even assaulted by the common people, and especially by the apprentices. However, on consideration, the diners decided that such conduct was not limited to foreigners and that such men were: "... so impartial, that when they meet with no strangers to misuse in the streets they will fall to jostling and shouldring of one another, and rather than faile they will find meanes by hemming one another to beget quarrels." Some Englishmen apparently held violent conflicts to be one of life's necessities, and would walk the streets with the sole intention of provoking fights, when they would start "tearing of one another's flesh; so these

---

25. Anon, *The Confession and Execution of Letitia Wigington of Ratcliff*, London, Langley Curtiss, 1684, pp.1-2.

men-beasts drawing their swords, mischief, maime, and kill one another". Their conduct was blamed, *inter alia*, on Puritan preachers railing against Catholics (significantly, all the observers were Catholics), on the absence of a sacrament of confession in the Church of England, an insular lack of contact with more civilised nations and the absence of sufficient 'shaming' punishments for bellicose individuals (such as being publicly displayed in the skins of wild beasts).[26] Similarly, in the 1660s, the pretend-German Mary Carleton complained about the: "... very great rudeness and incivility to which the mass and generality of the English vulgar are most pronely inclined, that is, to hoot and hallow, and pursue strangers with their multitudes through the streets."[27] Frenchmen and Spaniards, in particular, received harsh treatment at the hands of the mob.

According to a Swiss visitor, although upper class duelling was rare, settling quarrels with bare-knuckle fights was very popular amongst the poor and attracted crowds of onlookers when conducted in the streets. Many would lay bets on the participants. Additionally, if the Swiss observer is to be believed, Englishmen, both rich and poor, were especially prone to excessive drinking and cursing.[28] He was not alone in this belief. Daniel Defoe was convinced that the

---

26. Anon, *London's Looking-Glass: or the Copy of a Letter, written by an English Travayler, to the Apprentices of London*, Oxford, Bodleian Scholar Press, 1621, vol.7, pp.14-23.

27. Anon, *The Case of Madam Mary Carleton*, London, Sam Speed, 1663, at p.128.

28. M. Van Muyden (Trans. and Ed.) *A Foreign View of England in the Reigns of George I and George II; the Letters of Monsieur Cesar de Saussure to his Family*, London, John Murray, 1902, pp.179-180 and 192-193.

general slothfulness of the nation's poor meant that it was normal for an Englishman to work: "... till he has got his pocket full of money, and then go and be idle, or perhaps drunk, till, tis all gone."[29] Less frequently discussed by such observers was the (often vastly) greater size and anonymity of London compared to other European cities and the apparently lower level of general social deference, especially in the Metropolis, that already seems to have been an aspect of English society; Defoe was dismayed by the "saucy and insolent behaviour" of domestic servants.[30]Much also depended on the viewer's perspective. In the 1690s, the Frenchman Henri Misson noted that some foreign observers believed that the "excessive clemency" of English law (manifest via benefit of clergy etc.) encouraged crime. Nevertheless, others, like himself, considered that notwithstanding its leniency, there was: "... more vice and more Roguery at Paris than at London; more infamous Actions, more cruelty, and more Enormity."[31]

London's large complement of youthful apprentices was associated with much of the capital's disorder. It is, perhaps, not surprising that apprentices, living with their masters for up to seven years, separated from their own kin, sometimes abused, and frequently neglected by their employers, developed their own customs, traditions and literature to become what was almost a Metropolitan subculture. They

---

29. D. Defoe, *Giving Alms no Charity*, London, 1704, p.27.
30. A. Moreton (D. Defoe), *Every-Body's Business is No-Body's Business*, London, 1725, 2nd edn., p.13.
31. M. Misson, *M. Misson's Memoirs and Observations in his Travels over England*, M. Ozell (Trans.), London, 1719, p.67.

were particularly distinguished by their own fashions and celebrations, the latter being marked by boisterous forms of public behaviour.[32] The main apprentices "carnivale", on Shrove Tuesday, would produce mayhem, with the authorities almost surrendering control of the City, and the young men involved going "starcke mad", pulling down the houses of those who occasioned their disapproval, especially if they were brothel keepers, and generally behaving "as though the City were without lawes and magistrates".[33] According to Busino, both Shrove Tuesday and Mayday saw between 3,000 and 4,000 apprentices rampaging in the streets, sometimes even killing people, while only being ineffectively controlled by the Trained Bands.[34] Little had changed over 60 years later. In 1668, Richard Beasley led a mob of 500 'apprentices' (in reality some were the worst social elements attracted to trouble), armed with a sword and carrying a green apron on a pole. The mob pulled down bawdy houses and those owned by papists, and broke open Finsbury jail, aiming to release incarcerated colleagues. In the process they beat up a constable and stole his staff and fought with soldiers sent to deal with the disturbance.[35] By then, at least, the advent of a standing army made it easier to control such outbreaks.

---

32. S.R. Smith, "The London Apprentices as Seventeenth-Century Adolescents," *Past and Present*, 1973, vol.61, pp.149-161.

33. Anon, *London's Looking-Glass*, vol.7, pp.25-26.

34. T. Platter and H. Busino, *Journals of two travellers in Elizabethan and early Stuart England*, P. Razzell (Ed.), London, Caliban, 1995, p.154.

35. Anon, *The Tryals of such Persons (Peter Messenger, Richard Beasley)* ..., London, Robert Pawlet, 1668, pp.1-10.

More generally, there was frequent concern amongst the authorities over 'sporting' events, especially football matches. This was understandable; football was not the regulated Association game that developed in the nineteenth century. It was usually a 'free for all' with huge and unequal teams, up to a hundred strong, and few rules restraining foul play. Frequently, it was the occasion for violence and injury, sometimes even homicide (though these rarely resulted in convictions for murder, the parties apparently being deemed to be *volens* to the risks). Unsurprisingly, in 1531, Sir Thomas Elyot had warned that football was unsuitable for gentlemen as it resulted in "hurt and consequently rancour and malice do remain with them that be wounded". In 1576, the authorities in Middlesex took action against members of a group of 100 men from Ruislip who had assembled: "... unlawfully and played a certain unlawful game, called football, by reason of which unlawful game there rose amongst them a great affray, likely to result in homicides and serious accidents."[36]

Nevertheless, in reality, such obstreperous behaviour was not solely the preserve of Englishmen, even in London. Thus, in November 1653, five Portuguese men, including their Ambassador's brother, were hanged after committing murder during a riot occasioned by a quarrel between them and a man named Anstruther. The night after this clash, they returned to the scene with some fellow countrymen, wearing "breastplates and headpieces", searching for him.

---

36. J.A. Sharpe, *The Bewitching of Anne Gunter*, London, Profile Books, 1999, pp.15-17.

Instead, they came across a Colonel Mayo, whom they mistakenly took to be Anstruther, and so, at a prearranged signal, over 50 Portuguese men, with drawn swords attacked the Colonel who, while defending himself: "... received seven dangerous wounds, and lies in a mortal condition. They fell also upon one Mr. Greenway, of Lincoln's Inn, as he was walking with his sister in one hand and his mistress in the other ... and pistoled him in the head, whereof he died immediately." The Portuguese planned to complete their revenge by blowing up the Exchange, though they were unsuccessful in this.[37]

Infanticide

Infanticide had not been viewed in quite the same way as other homicides in medieval England. Although deprecated, its prosecution and punishment were usually left to the church courts, and the penalties they imposed were consequently limited (church courts could not shed blood). Thus, when Joan Rose was convicted at Canterbury of killing her young son in 1470, the judge ordered that she process several times around a variety of important Kentish towns and ports (Canterbury, Ashford etc.), wearing penitential garb and carrying a half pound wax candle in one hand, and a knife, the instrument used to kill her child, in the other. Other instances of infanticide in the fifteenth century were dealt with by whippings imposed by the local

---

37. *Mercurius Politicus*, November, 1653.

Commissary court. Significantly, the deaths of small children occasioned by neglect and illegal abortions were dealt with in a similar fashion.[38] Even in the early 1500s, infanticide was not viewed as being as heinous as other killings. However, the Elizabethan period saw an explosion of interest in the crime, accompanied by a major expansion in its prosecution. Having been little mentioned in early Tudor legal treatises it became a regular topic of discussion amongst legal authors. The extent to which this was part of the era's general quest for order, or a response to new social and religious mores is difficult to determine.[39] Whatever the reasons, an increasingly draconian approach was taken towards the crime and it fell into the province of the secular courts.

Indicative of a stricter approach, in 1580, a jury convicted, and a judge sentenced a defendant to death, on an infanticide indictment, even though the assizes clerk noted that "it was not directly proved" that the baby was born alive.[40] This became unnecessary, in cases involving unmarried women, after 1624, when most women accused of murdering their newborn children were tried under a new statute which provided that any woman who concealed the death of an illegitimate newborn child was presumed to

---

38. R.H. Helmholz, *Canon Law and the Law of England*, London, The Hambledon Press, 1987, pp.157-168.
39. Hoffer and Hall, *Murdering Mothers*, London, New York University Press, 1981, pp.6-9.
40. J.S. Cockburn, "Trial by the Book? Fact and Theory in the Criminal Process 1558-1625," *Legal Records and the Historian*, J.H. Baker (Ed.) London, Royal Historical Society, pp.65-68.

143

have murdered it, unless she could prove that the child had been stillborn. This was inherently difficult, unless the woman could produce at least one plausible witness to say that the infant had been born dead ('An Act to prevent the Destroying and Murthering of Bastard Children', 1624, 21 Jac. c 27.) In the decades immediately after 1624, up to 40 per cent of the women accused of this crime in England were convicted and hanged. In 1693, Parliament passed another law guiding juries in such cases, "An act to prevent the destroying and murdering of bastard children". It focused on "lewd women" and "bastard children", making it a capital offence for a woman who had concealed her illegitimate child's birth to secretly bury its body, whether the child was born alive or dead.[41]

However, as the acquittal rates suggest, these statutes were sometimes ignored, even in the 1600s. By the eighteenth century, they were increasingly being disregarded as the presumption that concealment signified murder was challenged. Apparently lenient judges and juries began to accept a range of defences, such as "benefit of linen", in which the defendant demonstrated that she had made linen in preparation for the birth of the infant, and "want of help", in which the defendant argued that the infant died despite her efforts to secure assistance. The conviction rate for infanticide decreased steadily after the early eighteenth century as juries increasingly favoured defendants. By the 1790s it was extremely rare for a woman

---

41. M. Jackson, "Infanticide: Historical Perspectives," *New Law Journal*, 1996, vol.146, no.6736, p.416.

to be convicted under the 1624 statute, which was formally repealed in 1803.[42] Infanticide then became subject to the same rules of evidence as murder, the 1803 law requiring the prosecution to prove that the infant was born alive. The revised Act also provided for a lesser offence, punishable by up to two years in prison, in those cases where the woman had concealed her pregnancy but the prosecution could not prove the infant was born alive.[43]

Although detested as an "unnatural" crime, the immediate backgrounds to cases of infanticide were often depressingly similar. An unmarried woman, having concealed her pregnancy (something that the voluminous clothes of the era assisted), gave birth in secret, killed the baby and disposed of its body. Female servants and the very poor figure frequently in the records, being particularly afraid of the consequences of exposure, so that: "'Tis well if she does not endeavour to screen herself from censure, by the commission of a more dreadful sin in the murder of a spurious infant."[44] Thus, in Sussex, in December 1646, a maid named Elizabeth White secretly gave birth and immediately threw the illegitimate and naked baby into her master's freezing cellar, where it quickly died of exposure. She was convicted and hanged.[45] Discovery usually came from a failure to conceal the telltale signs of birth or the infant's body. Hence, 19-year-old Sarah Wedderburn and

---

42. Jackson, "Infanticide: Historical Perspectives," p.416.
43. J.J. Dvorak, "Neonaticide: Less than Murder?", *The Northern Illinois University Law Review*, 1998, vol.19, pp.175-6.
44. *The Gentleman's Magazine*, 1749, vol.19, p.126.
45. R.F. Hunnisett, *Sussex Coroners' Inquests 1603-1688*, London, PRO, 1998, p.98.

her mother were arrested, prosecuted, convicted and executed in Yorkshire, after burning the body of a newly killed baby on their domestic fire, the infant's bones then being buried in their garden. A neighbour, made curious by the exceptional blaze, had peered through a window at them. In 1691, Mary Goodenough, an impoverished Oxfordshire widow of 40, with two young children and in desperate financial straits, was: "... seduc'd by a neighbouring Baker (reported infamous for like practices with others) thro' his Promises of some Allowance towards her necessary Maintenance." When she became pregnant she concealed it, right up to the birth, when she pretended that she had been taken ill. However, after two or three days, her neighbours, "suspecting the matter", visited her and "upon search" discovered from the condition of her breasts that she had given birth. When they charged her with this, she immediately admitted it and pointed out the baby's body, which was lying nearby wrapped in a blanket. She was subsequently arrested, indicted and convicted, receiving sentence of death.[46] Similarly, in 1670, a Staffordshire maid gave birth in an outhouse and then returned to the bed she shared with another servant woman. She, too, was discovered because she was "mistrusted by her neighbours" and physically examined by them; she, too, was hanged. It is hard to assess how many similar cases of infanticide went undiscovered. Nevertheless, an analysis of those cases in

---

46. Anon, *Fair warnings to murderers of infants being an account of the tryal, codemnation [sic] and execution of Mary Goodenough*, London, J. Robinson, 1692, pp.1-6.

which there was exposure would suggest that only a very small minority of unmarried pregnant women had recourse to such a drastic solution. In the years from 1559 to 1603, populous Essex indicted only 29 people for infanticide compared to 129 for other types of homicide, a similar proportion being found in Sussex (27 and 127) and Hertfordshire (7 and 24).[47] Similarly, between 1601 and 1665, there were only 60 cases recorded in total for Essex. Arguably, this apparent rarity is remarkable given the stigma attached to being the mother of an illegitimate child, with public penance enforced by the church courts, the possibility of corporal punishment from the secular ones and usually dismissal from any position held.[48]

More generally, bastardy was influenced by the late age of marriage, poor contraception and dishonoured promises of betrothal should such an eventuality occur. Illegitimacy increased throughout most of the Elizabethan period, before declining in the first 60 years of the seventeenth century. However, rates varied enormously within the country. In Puritan dominated Essex, parish rates might be as low as 0.5 per cent. In some Lancashire and Cheshire parishes it was as high as 10 per cent.[49] Of course, some desperate women may have managed to pre-empt such a situation, especially in

---

47. J.S. Cockburn, "The Nature and Incidence of Crime in England 1559-1625: A Preliminary Survey," in *Crime in England 1550-1800*, J.S. Cockburn (Ed.) London, Methuen, 1977, at p.53.
48. K. Wrightson, "Infanticide in English History," *Criminal Justice History*, vol.3, 1982, pp.6-8.
49. R.L. Greaves, *Society and Religion in Elizabethan England*, Minneapolis, University of Minnesota Press, 1981, p.679.

areas where disapproval was strongest. Illegal abortions and induced miscarriages to avoid embarrassing or inconvenient pregnancies were common, although it was a very risky and uncertain path. Thus, in 1605, Nathaniel Bacon recorded the examination of a spinster from Wiverton by local women as to the identity of the father of a child she was carrying. Reve appears to have taken some 'physicke' provided by a local man, at a cost of 12d, with a view to aborting the pregnancy. However, she swiftly regurgitated it. It transpired that the father of her child was the local Rector, the Reverend James Poynter.[50] The case of Richard Skeete shows that in the 1630s Essex supported at least one very active (and unsavoury) abortionist, albeit that he met with very limited professional success. He also dabbled in other criminal activites.[51] Abortion was not viewed as seriously as infanticide, especially in the early stages of pregnancy, prior to the foetus 'quickening'. Even afterwards, Coke considered that if a woman who was with child "by a potion or otherwise kills it in her womb ... this is a great misprison and no murder". However, he believed that if a child was born alive and subsequently died as a result of the earlier, unsuccessful, ingestion of an abortion-inducing drug, the ensuing death would constitute murder. In the following century, Blackstone shared his belief that the abortion of a quickened child was only a "very heinous misdemeanour".[52]

---

50. Sir F. Bacon, *The Official Papers of Sir Nathaniel Bacon*, p.18.
51. D. Cressey, *Travesties and Transgressions in Tudor and Stuart England*, Oxford, OUP, 2000, pp.76-83.
52. E. Steegmann, "Of History and Due Process," *Indiana Law Journal*, 1987, vol.63, pp.369 and 380.

In passing, it should be noted that the Reverend Poynter was not the only cleric to find himself in such an awkward situation. In January 1679, in a rare example of infanticide by a man, the Reverend Robert Foulkes, the Anglican Minister of Stanton-Lacy in Shropshire, was executed at Tyburn for the murder of his newly born baby. Foulkes had been made guardian of a wealthy young woman who had been orphaned. Although already married with children, he started an affair with the girl and she became pregnant. The Minister tried everything he could think of to procure an abortion but to no avail. To avoid public disgrace, both parties went to London and took rooms in the Strand, where the baby was delivered and secretly murdered. However, it was difficult to keep such things private and the girl was examined "upon the suspicion of some women, when she confessed the whole, and charged Mr Foulkes with the murder". Foulkes, who was still in London, was arrested, committed to Newgate, and convicted at the Old Bailey on the evidence of the baby's mother.[53] Infanticide by married women was rarer, and legally harder to prove, than that by single women. Nevertheless, it did occur. Thus, a dispute between a Presbyterian man and his allegedly Anabaptist wife about infant baptism led Mary Champion to cut the head off her seven-week-old baby and present it to her husband for Christening. How much this may have been influenced by post-natal depression rather than religious

---

53. C. Johnson, *A General History of the Lives and Adventures of the Most Famous Highwaymen*, p.316.

fanaticism is hard to assess.[54] Similar patterns of abortion and infanticide could be found in early modern Germany. There, relatively late marriages produced 'fornication' which was often ignored. If the woman became pregnant the union was usually regularised by marriage; in some villages, over 20 per cent of the children were conceived by unmarried couples who subsequently wed. Sometimes, however, marriage was not forthcoming, occasioning problems and encouraging drastic solutions.[55]

The Legal Status of Homicide

In early medieval times, proof of the commission of an act was sometimes enough to secure a criminal conviction, irrespective of any deliberation on the part of the offender; even accidental harm might be punished. By the twelfth century, however, notions of an 'evil' mindset as a prerequisite for guilt were slowly emerging. These had become more refined by the fifteenth century, so that lethal acts which were malicious and wilful were viewed as more culpable than those conducted with less (or no) deliberation.[56] Nevertheless, the late medieval substantive law relating to homicide remained confused. There was no

---

54. Anon, *Bloody Newes from Dover*, London, 1647, pp.1-4.
55. U. Rublack, *The Crimes of Women in Early Modern Germany*, Oxford, OUP, 1999, at pp.163-167.
56. C. Slobogin, "An End to Insanity: Recasting the Role of Mental Disability in Criminal Cases," Virginia, *Law Review*, 2000, vol.86, p.1216.

fully formulated lesser (but still culpable) offence of killing another. At the end of the 1400s, Serjeant Keble still believed that excessive chastisement that resulted in death would produce either a murder or a misadventure verdict. Definitions of homicide underwent further radical change in the sixteenth and seventeenth centuries.[57] Fairly quickly it was accepted that not all culpable killings should be defined as murder; instead, there were: "... two sorts, wherof the one is called murder, and that is, when one man upon malice preparred, and forethought, doth feloniously kill another. And the other is called manslaughter, as Chance-Medley, and that is, when two men fight together upon a suddaine heat of blood, without an malice precedent, and one of them kill the other."[58] Thus, the French word homicide became the *genus*, while, by the beginning of the 1600s, the Anglo-Saxon words manslaughter and murder represented its two most important species. They carried different legal consequences.

Murder was a pre-meditated killing of *malice prepensed*. The murderer had intended to kill his victim *sedato animo*, or had killed in circumstances where such malice was implied, for example by poisoning or, following the Statute of Stabbing of 1604, stabbing his victim while the latter had no weapon drawn. The classic common law definition of murder was formulated by Lord Chief Justice Coke in the

---

57.   J.M. Kaye, "The Early History of Murder and Manslaughter (part 2)", in *The Law Quarterly Review*, 1967, vol.83, at p.570.

58.   F. Pulton, *De Pace Regis et Regni*, London, Lincoln's Inn, 1623, p.324.

early seventeenth century: "Murder is when a man of sound memory and of the age of discretion, unlawfully killeth within any county of the realm any reasonable creature in *rerum natura* under the King's peace, with malice aforthought, either expressed by the party or implied by law, so as the party wounded, or hurt etc. die of the wound or hurt etc., within a year and a day of the same."[59] Thus, his definition provided limited exemptions for small children, lunatics and those who killed enemy aliens. However, the biggest issue was the crime's mental element (or *mens rea*) 'malice aforethought', a calculated act. Examples of 'implied' malice included, *inter alia*, killings committed by robbers while engaged in their crimes. The mental state was vital, and made murder an unclergyable felony. Unlike inchoate offences (attempt, incitement and conspiracy), the law relating to accomplices was well developed at common law, so that: "... when a man is murdered, all be principals and shall die, even he that doth but hold the candel to give light to the murderers."[60]

By contrast, the concept of 'manslaughter', a phrase first used in the *Boke of Justyces of Peas* of 1506, was developed to distinguish a class of homicides that were not as morally culpable as murder. Manslaughter usually entailed killing pursuant to 'chance medley'. The phrase was a corruption

---

59. It still forms the basis for the modern law of murder, albeit that some of the elements of the offence have been altered. (For example, what was called the "year and a day rule" was abolished by the Law Reform [Year and a Day Rule] Act 1996).

60. Sir T. Smith, *De Republica Anglorum* (written 1565) London, Henri Midleton for Gregorie Seton, 1583, p.117.

of the French term *chaud melee*. It was used because most killings committed without malice aforethought arose from unplanned and spontaneous quarrels, and were committed in hot blood. (Linguistic confusion between heated [chaud] and sudden [chance] fights was to create problems.)[61] Such killings, in which the fatal blow was intended, but not *sedato animo*, were clergyable, unlike murder, because society accepted that drunken brawlers (for example) should not be treated in the same way as premeditated killers.[62] After 1500, other forms of homicide were also gradually distinguished from being crimes at all, as greater emphasis was placed on the killer's mental state. Thus, killing *se defendendo* involved deliberation, but no choice, as the perpetrator had been attacked and could not realistically escape; it was not deemed to be a felony. Killing *necessitate* was the deliberate killing of a thief caught red-handed in the defendant's dwelling house. This, too, was not a felony. Similarly, accidental killings in the course of a lawful activity like hunting (such as Archbishop Abbot's shooting of a beater), provided that they were not grossly negligent, were *per infortunium* and were also not felonies.[63]

The leniency with which homicides arising out of quarrels were viewed, especially when it could be argued

---

61. J.H. Baker, "The Three Languages of the Common Law," *McGill Law Journal*, 1998, vol.43, p.9.
62. G. Coss, "'God is a righteous judge, strong and patient: and God is provoked every day,' A Brief History of the Doctrine of Provocation in England," *Sydney Law Review*, 1991, p.572.
63. T.G. Watkin, "Hamlet and the Law of Homicide," *The Law Quarterly Review*, 1984, vol.100, p.294.

that there was a lack of premeditation and an element of self-defence, gave considerable scope for clever individuals to engineer situations in which they could safely use lethal violence. Thus, at one point, in 1551, the infamous Mosbie, concerned at the ethics and dangers of murdering Thomas Arden in cold blood, sought to "pick some Quarrel or other" with him at the Valentine fair in Faversham. His aim was to kill him in a fight, and thus face, at most, a (clergyable) charge of manslaughter. However, Arden was apparently well used to being an unpopular man and "altho highly provoked, he would not fight".[64] Sometimes, the courts were alert to such manufactured quarrels. Thus, in a seventeenth century case, a "cunning desperate fellow" equipped himself with a concealed dagger and entered an ale-house where his intended victim was drinking. Initially, he was very friendly towards him, but then changed to "all the provoking language he could, to make the other strike him, which the other no sooner held up his stick to have done, but he stabb'd him into the Body with his Dagger, wherof he dyed". Although no "malice" could be proved in the incident, the trial judge took a pragmatic approach: "... so much of his intention by his preparation and circumstances appearing to design the stabbing of the other, that it was adjudged to be within the meaning, though not within the letter, of the statute." The judge was afraid that if he took any other course, any literate and clergyable men might follow suit in expectation of a manslaughter verdict. The

---

64. Anon, *The History of the Most Remarkable Tryals in Great Britain and Ireland in Capital Cases*, London, A. Bell, 1715, pp.248-255.

defendant was convicted and executed for murder.[65] As this case indicates, to counter the apparent escalation of killings arising out of heated quarrels, and a tendency amongst jurors to reduce murder to manslaughter whenever there had been any verbal (though not physical) provocation, the 'Statute of Stabbings' had been enacted in 1604, shortly after James I's accession to the throne (1 Jac. 1, c.8). It sought to limit the circumstances in which a killer who used a blade in a quarrel, without first being struck or physically threatened, could come within 'chance medley'. Essentially, it created a non-clergyable (and so capital) statutory manslaughter for some killings in which "malice aforethought" could not be proved.[66]

However, despite the 1604 Act, the distinction between self-defence, manslaughter and murder could be very fine (as they are today), especially in killings arising out of altercations. Obviously, if one of the parties had made no attempt to defend himself when a quarrel came to violence, a murder verdict was likely. However, in most situations, this was an improbable scenario, such disturbances usually involving an exchange of words and blows. Nevertheless, returning manslaughter verdicts in any case where "Blow had been returned for Blow" might be equally unjust. As counsel for the Crown pointed out when arguing a special verdict before the judges at Serjeants' Inn, this would mean that a killer could never be convicted of murder unless his

---

65. Sir F. Bacon, *Cases of Treason*, London, John More, 1641, p.175.
66. B.J. Brown, "The Demise of Chance Medley and the Recognition of Provocation as a Defence to Murder in English Law," *American Journal of Legal History*, 1963, vol.7, p.314.

victim was "so base a coward as to suffer another to cut his throat before his face, without resisting his assaulter". In practice, questions as to whom had initiated the quarrel, struck the first blow, the weapons of the respective parties and the proportionality of response during any ensuing escalation were important factors in allotting verdicts.[67]

Patterns of Homicide

Although murder is, historically, an offence to which a 'blind eye' is rarely shown, with a high incidence of reporting, comparing homicide rates across the centuries is fraught with problems. Legal definitions change and the broad contemporary, especially sixteenth century, definition of felonious killings meant that early modern homicides include some deaths that would probably be the province of civil actions for negligence rather than criminal prosecutions today. Most importantly, a steady improvement in medical techniques means that many crimes which today manifest themselves as assorted offences of non-lethal violence, such as assault occasioning grievous bodily harm or, more rarely, attempted murder, resulted in murder or manslaughter charges in the 1500s. Thus, it is highly unlikely that Richard Geerey, shot on the outside of his right thigh, at Hastings, in 1611, by a pellet loaded hand-gun, would have languished

---

67. Anon, *A Full and True Account of the Tryal, Examination and Proceedings against Mr John Maugridge, a Kettle-Drummer*, 1705, p.1.

and expired 10 days later in the modern era.[68] These factors have led some to argue that although there was a general reduction in lethal violence after the 1500s, it was 'much less spectacular' than the 'headline' figures suggest.[69] Against this, improvements in forensic pathology mean that cases of 'secret homicide' are more likely to be discovered today than previously.

Nevertheless, and bearing these limitations in mind, it seems that by 1600 the pattern of violence in England was becoming slightly more benign than that found in some other European countries. Harrison was adamant that in Elizabethan England, gratuitous murders, unconnected to instrumental crime and characterised by extreme cruelty, were rare. By contrast, he felt that such killings were not infrequent in other European countries.[70] Of course, such murders did occur, periodically, even in England. Some of the brutality evident in instances of violence were indicative of a predominantly peasant society in which life was lived close to the margins of survival and levels of squeamishness were lower than today. This produced occasional acts of unmitigated horror, such as the two Penshurst labourers who, for no apparent reason, stabbed a pregnant woman to death in 1589 and then cut out her unborn child.[71] Even so, most people were horrified by lethal violence. Indeed, in some respects it is their antipathy to murder in a world in

---

68. Hunnisett, *Sussex Coroners' Inquests 1603-1688*, p.61.
69. Cockburn, "Patterns of Violence in English Society," p.106.
70. W. Harrison, *A Description of England, 2nd Book,* 2nd edn, 1587, London, New Shakespeare Society, 1877, p.229.
71. Cockburn, *The Nature and Incidence of Crime,* p.54.

which levels of mortality from other, natural, events were so high, that seems surprising.

However, even if the situation was improving, the remarkably low murder rate of the early 1950s still lay many centuries away. The 'civilising process' had a long way to go in socialising Englishmen towards a cultural repugnance for lethal violence. As a result, the number of killings throughout the period was very much higher than it is today, though declining gradually for most of it.[72] Given the country's medieval inheritance, this is not surprising. It has been suggested that the per capita incidence of homicide for medieval England may have been as much as 10 times its rate in the early 1980s.[73] The fourteenth and fifteenth centuries appear to have witnessed particularly high levels of interpersonal violence, public disorder and other forms of serious crime. This extended to all social groups, with aristocrats regularly accused of committing murder, and the leaders of most large fourteenth century criminal gangs being drawn from the gentry.[74] Medieval Oxford seems to have been an exceptionally violent city, though the disproportionate congregation of young males and ongoing town/gown tensions aggravated the situation.[75]

Nevertheless, even by the late sixteenth century the

---

72. Leyton, *Men of Blood,* p.17 and pp.206-217.
73. L. Stone, "Interpersonal Violence in English Society, 1300-1980," *Past and Present,* 1983, no.101, p.22.
74. J.G. Bellamy, *Crime and public order in England in the later middle ages,* London, Routledge, 1973, pp.199-200.
75. C.I. Hammer, "Patterns of Homicide in a Medieval University Town: Fourteenth-Century Oxford," *Past and Present,* 1978, no.78, p.11.

national homicide rate had fallen to only five times its modern level, before declining quite rapidly again after 1660.[76] Thus, there appears to have been a drastic decline (at least a halving) in homicide rates between the mid-seventeenth and the late eighteenth centuries, with the downward trend starting, albeit slowly, in the early sixteenth century.[77] Such an analysis is borne out by a close examination of Kentish homicides, which suggest a dramatic decline in the incidence of lethal violence in the 400 years after 1560. Thus, Kent appears to have witnessed an average homicide rate of 4.6 per 100,000 people in the sixteenth century compared to 0.7 per 100,000 in 1970-80 (itself a marked increase from the level of the 1950s). However, it must be stressed that the decline was neither consistent nor smooth. The county witnessed its highest homicide rate of the 400 year period in the decade from 1581 to 1590 (when it reached 6 per 100,000), and by far its most dramatic fall in the 40 years between 1680 and 1720 (a reduction from 5.1 to 2.4).[78] Lawrence Stone's research confirms the notion of a rapid fall over a comparatively short period in the years after 1660, a phenomenon which appears to have been manifest throughout England.[79] However, the speed at which this process occurred varied. In some counties, it appears to have begun as early as 1660, in others it started

---

76. Stone, "Interpersonal Violence in English Society, 1300-1980," p.22.
77. J.A. Sharpe, *Crime in Seventeenth Century England*, Cambridge, CUP, 1983, p.214.
78. Cockburn, "Patterns of Violence in English Society," pp.76-78.
79. Stone, "Debate: The History of Violence in England, A Rejoinder," *Past and Present*, 1985, vol.108, pp.216-214.

slightly later; in some, it seems to have been complete by 1700, in others to have extended until c.1720.[80]

Early modern homicide, as today, was most frequently the result of domestic, social or personal stress engendering interpersonal conflict. Evidence drawn from both Essex and Northern circuit assize court records suggests that the most common background for English killings was a fight between two men or groups of men that went 'too far' and differed from many other assaults only in that a fatality occurred.[81] This might be entirely a question of luck, a knife hitting a vital spot, a head injury producing internal bleeding or the ready availability of a weapon. When the presence of weapons and alcohol were combined, tragedy was particularly likely to ensue. John Hobson, a Barnsley trader who kept a detailed diary between 1725 and 1734, recorded a typical example. In 1729, while visiting Leeds, he noted that a young army officer there had: "... run his man through with a rapier for being sawcy to him, being drunk. The cornet had absconded, it being supposed the man would die."[82] This lethal recipe for unpremeditated killings was found throughout Europe. In the early modern German city of Frankfurt am Main, 22 out of 70 manslaughter convictions (i.e. unplanned homicides) in the *Strafenbuch*, were of soldiers (men inherently likely to be carrying weapons), and 21 occurred in taverns or when the defendant was recorded as having been drunk. Given that many other

---

80. Cockburn, "Patterns of Violence in English Society," *Past and Present*, pp.76-78.
81. Sharpe, "Domestic Homicide in Early Modern England," p.34.
82. Hobson, *John Hobson's diary*, July 26, 1729, at pp.83-115.

people, not just soldiers, publicly carried weapons, and it is likely that not all cases of intoxication were accurately or fully recorded, these situational inducements were probably much more widespread. This may also explain the small number of Jews from the city convicted of violent crimes. Jews were banned from publicly carrying weapons and had more limited access to alcohol, especially in taverns, so that the environmental inducements for homicide were less likely to be present.[83] Killings in sixteenth century Picardy manifest a similar pattern, with many being the result of a sudden confrontation or quarrel in a tavern, again often encouraged by drink. The generally high level of homicides also appears to have been linked to Picardy's militarised society, something that produced a population that regularly carried weapons, and was prepared to use them. Soldiers in the province's large garrison seem to have been especially prone to such homicidal outbursts.[84]

Murder for Gain

However, despite this general pattern of killing, there was also a significantly higher proportion of murders attendant on instrumental crime, often committed by strangers, than is the case today. (Some of these have already been alluded to in the examination of robbers.) Even in the 1720s, the

---

83. M.R. Boes, "Jews in the Criminal-Justice System of Early Modern Germany," *Journal of Interdisciplinary History*, 1999, vol.30.3, p.427.
84. D. Potter, "Rigueur de justice: Crime, Murder and the Law in Picardy, Fifteenth-Sixteenth Centuries", *French History*, 1997, vol.11, no.3, pp.281-282.

frequency of potentially lethal armed crime mentioned by John Hobson in his diary is striking. In January 1725, he noted that a local man had shown him a flattened bullet that had lodged in a wall after being shot at his servant "by some persons which were supposed to have a design to robb the house. It had gone through his hat behind". Only a few months later, he was recording an attempted armed robbery on a nearby Minister's house in which a pistol was fired.[85] Some of the instrumental murders committed with a view to gain were especially grim (as they are today). Thus, an isolated and elderly widow named Fairbanks who sold bottled beer from a cellar under the *Pavier's Arms* in Piccadilly had acquired a reputation for being wealthy, something that may have been enhanced when one of her sons was seen leaving her premises with £100, which she had held for him while he was away at sea. At 10 p.m. on the 20th April 1684 several men and a woman apparently broke into her premises. They gagged her with a sea-handkerchief that was stuffed into her mouth with "so much violence, that they beat two of her teeth down her throat". She was strangled with another handkerchief. Even worse, the people who killed her were probably "no strangers to her" and aware that she would be alone at that time of night. The thieves appear to have missed most of her modest savings.[86]

Travellers' risks were not confined to highwaymen. The

---

85. J. Hobson, *John Hobson's Diary*, January 5, and October 9, 1725-1726, pp.83-115.

86. Anon, *Strange News from Piccadilly*, London, E. Mallet, 1684, pp.1-2.

legend of the demon innkeeper had a foundation in reality, men of that trade being well placed to identify rich but vulnerable targets. Thus, in the 1660s, a Civil War veteran who, after service north of the border, had settled down in Gloucestershire to run a small inn with his Scottish wife appears to have succumbed to temptation. He accommodated travellers, especially 'Scotch' merchants, attracted by his wife's nationality. However, trade was slow, because of the bad position of the inn. Despite this, and having arrived in the village as a very poor man, he appeared to flourish. His house was expensively furnished and he was always able to lend money to his neighbours when necessary. Although they found this strange, being at variance to his apparent earnings, they ignored it, the: "Man being of a fair, plausible carriage, and making large pretences of honesty and just dealing." In due course, he moved away to run a larger inn near Gloucester. His old property was bought by a local blacksmith, who decided to build a shed in the garden where he could seat his anvil. This needed deep foundations to anchor it. As the smith dug down he "found the bones and part of the flesh of a man buried there". Having spoken to neighbours, and his suspicions raised, he dug further, and swiftly found the bodies of seven other men in various states of decomposition. One rotting corpse still had a knife embedded in his chest, with the former landlord's name engraved on it. (The hand of God, rather than defendant incompetence, was seen in the discovery of this terrible crime.)[87]

Domestic Murder

An analysis of homicides in Essex in the years from 1560 to 1709 suggests that 14 per cent involved family members, or 24 per cent if servants and apprentices are viewed as part of the extended family (as they usually were). This compares to over half of homicides in England in the years 1957-1963 (though the percentage has since declined).[88] Thus, although the proportion of murders arising out of a domestic context was markedly smaller than in the present era (about half), it was still substantial. The details are depressingly familiar to modern readers of the crime columns of popular newspapers. A live-in curate seduced his elderly vicar's spouse. However, he wanted his master's home (by marrying his widow) as well as the affections of his wife. So, together, the adulterous couple smothered the old cleric as he slept.[89] Fraternal resentment could be equally lethal. In the 1650s, one of the grandsons of the distinguished JP, Michael Sondes, killed his brother. He was motivated by resentment at their father's perceived preference for his older sibling, something apparently manifested by his father

---

87.   Anon, *The Bloody Innkeeper, or Sad and Barbarous News from Gloucestershire*, London, 1675, pp.3-6.
88.   Sharpe, "Domestic Homicide in Early Modern England," p.34.
89.   Anon, *A true relation of the most inhumane and bloody murther of Master James Minister and Preacher of the word of God at Rockland in Norfolk*, London, R. Bowan, 1609, p.A2.

ordering him to give up a fine doublet in his brother's favour, after the latter soiled his own. Aggrieved, the younger son secretly took a meat cleaver from the kitchen, which he hid for three months. Then, one night, while his brother slept, he entered his bedroom and "cleft in sunder his head", finishing him off by running him through with a sword. He immediately confessed the crime to his father, subsequently being convicted at the Maidstone Assizes and executed.[90] Domestic rows between spouses could be equally lethal, and not just for the initial participants. In 1677, a lighterman had a quarrel with his wife and fell to blows, so that she ran off to escape his "bruitish fury". He pursued her with a half-pike, prompting a nearby tub-man to intervene, with "fair and gentle words [he] requested the man to forbear further beating or abusing his wife". The already incensed lighterman stabbed him in the heart, killing him immediately. As a chronicler sagely observed, often those who "intermeddle in a squabble do be more durtied and abused than such as originally begun it". As he cooled down, the astounded lighterman indicated that his defence would be based on provocation.[91] However, more commonly, marital discord would be lethal to spouses. A minor Shropshire gentleman or yeoman (the former phrase was sometimes used loosely in pamphlets), but clearly a comfortably off man, with five children, and employed as a clerk to Sir Clement Clark, fell into bad ways: "His Course

---

90. Anon, *The devil's reign upon earth being a relation of several sad and bloudy murthers committed*, London, J. Andrews, 1655, pp.4-5.
91. Anon, *A Caution to Married Couples*, London, D.M., 1677, pp.5-6.

of Life for late Years hath been very disorderly, and debauched by ill company." Part of his degeneracy involved sleeping with 'lewd women' with its attendant risks. He contracted venereal disease and then "Infected his Wife with that foul and noissom Distemper". When she found out, he threatened to kill her if she told anyone. As a result, she delayed receiving treatment for her infection until deciding to go home to her parents (by which time the disease was well advanced). Her husband followed, confronted and then stabbed her to death with a scimitar. He was pursued by passers-by, captured and committed to jail.[92] Lethal levels of child abuse were another feature of the era. Thus, a purveyor of Dullidge water, noted for its curative properties, who took the liquid to London for those who could not spare the time to drink it at source, asked his 12-year-old son to fetch his horse. The youth was late returning. His enraged father, who was "naturally of a cruel dogged Temper, and always immoderately severe to his Child", went looking for his tardy son with a "huge Cudgel" in his hand. On finding him, he beat him "so cruelly and excessively that within an hour or two after it [he] dyed". Marks on the body suggested that it was also stamped on. Having finished the boy's punishment, his father went to London, and the lad staggered home, where he collapsed shortly afterwards. Initially, when questioned on his return, the father pretended that a horse had kicked the boy; he eventually admitted administering a modest

---

92. Anon, *A true relation of the most horrib'e murther, committed by Thomas White,* London, 1682, pp.2-4.

beating. Nevertheless, it would appear that the attack was merely the culmination of a long record of abuse as there were "furrows in the childs hips, occasion'd by former immoderate Whippings".[93] More unusually, in 1618, a Cornish stepmother persuaded a father to murder his visiting adult son while he slept, to secure the £400 in gold that he was carrying.[94] Other domestic crimes were harder to explain. In August 1655, at Penard, a wife and mother of four children waved goodbye to her husband as he went away for a day. When he returned, his children, the eldest of them only nine years old, were all dead and their bodies stuffed into a large chest; his wife had disappeared.[95]

The notorious trial, in 1551, of Alice Arden of Faversham for the murder of her husband, later to be the subject of a famous (possibly Shakespearean) play, and sufficiently celebrated to be recorded by John Stow, provides an insight into aspects of serious early modern crime, especially murder.[96] In particular, it reveals the tangled skein of domestic and neighbourly grievances that could lie behind such cases. Thomas Arden's wife, a young and attractive woman, formed a relationship with a local tailor named Mosbie, an affair to which her husband appears to have turned a blind eye, "for fear of disobliging her Relations, from whom he had some great Expectations". Nevertheless, in due course, surreptitiously indulging in "lewd practises"

---

93. Anon, *Strange and Lamentable News from Dullidge-Wells*, London, D.M., 1678, pp.5-7.
94. Anon, *Newes from Perin in Cornwall*, London, 1618, pp.1-6.
95. Anon, *The Devil's Reign upon Earth*, London, p.9.
96. J. Stow, *The Annales of England*, London, R. Nebery, 1592, p.1022.

was not enough to satisfy Alice and her lover, and they started plotting Thomas's murder. Alice approached a neighbour called Green, who had earlier lost a bitter land dispute with her husband, and, as a result, hated him. She offered him £10 to procure a murderer. Apparently fortuitously, on the road from Rochester, Green ran into a well-armed former soldier named Black Will. He was a "terrible and cruel Ruffian" who had, allegedly, already committed several murders and robberies while serving near Boulogne with the English army. Green offered him the £10 to kill Thomas Arden, and Black Will swiftly agreed. There followed a series of bungled attempts to ambush Arden when he was alone. Eventually, Black Will hid in a closet in Arden's house, and emerged at an agreed signal, while Mosbie and his victim were gaming, those domestic servants who were not involved in the plot having been sent out of the house. Black Will attempted to strangle and smother Arden with a towel and gashed him in the face while Mosbie hit him with a hammer. Will was then paid off by Alice with the promised money, and also helped himself to the dead man's rings and petty cash. Alice subsequently stabbed her husband's body repeatedly to make quite sure he was dead, arranged for the disposal of the corpse and pretended to be distraught at his disappearance.[97]

Miscellaneous Motives

Then as now, the number of potential precipitants for

---

97. Anon, *The History of the Most Remarkable Tryals*, pp.248-262.

murder was almost limitless. Thus, disappointments in business or legal ventures, however deserved, could prompt desperate behaviour. In the latter case, it was, perhaps, ironical, given that a reduction in violent conflict has been attributed to a willingness to use litigation as an alternative forum for solving differences. In 1616, John Bartenham, an elderly man who had frittered away a considerable fortune in almost 40 years of vexatious litigation, became aggrieved at how a Chancery Master, Sir John Tindall, had disposed of one of his cases, the law "not running in so even and calme a streame as hee did expect". Driven frantic, he loaded a pistol with three balls and then 'stalked' Tindall, eventually ambushing the lawyer when he alighted from a carriage at his chambers in Lincoln's Inn. Bartenham demanded redress in "uncivill language". When Tindall responded by brusquely asking him to "trouble him with his clamour no more", he shot and killed him. Bartenham was immediately seized by the dead man's servants, who conducted him to a magistrate for examination. On the way to the JP, the servants made lurid threats to the arrested man, which further unsettled his already precarious mental condition. Bartenham made an attempt on his own life shortly afterwards. He was restrained and placed on the early sixteenth century equivalent of a 'suicide watch', in the King's Bench prison in Southwark, where he was detained. There he was searched carefully for blades and a keeper visited his cell regularly. However, it was to no avail; having obtained a thin piece of cord, Bartenham cheated the gallows and hanged himself. His body was swiftly discovered and cut down, and unavailing attempts were made to revive the still warm corpse. Denied a Christian burial, he was interred in the traditional manner for suicides, being: "... buried in the Common-highway passing by Saint George's fields, where now the body lies with a stake of wood driven quite throw it." (A procedure that was followed as late as 1811 for the alleged murderer and prison suicide William Hare.) Despite stressing that the victim was not a corrupt lawyer, the pamphleteer noted that there had been popular sympathy for the murderer in London (probably a reflection of the acute dislike many held for lawyers) and felt that it provided a timely warning for those judges who might be corrupt as to the possible consequences of their actions. He also lamented the practical inconvenience occasioned by the dead Master's caseload having to be assigned to another lawyer who was unfamiliar with them![98] In passing, it should be observed that loading multiple balls into a firearm intended for close range work was common practice. In 1659, Major Strangeway's victim was struck in the head by two bullets fired from a single carbine discharge, a third narrowly missing him. He, too, died almost immediately.[99]

Serial Murders

It has been suggested that serial murders were no rarer in

---

98. L.L. *A true relation of a most desperate murder committed upon the body of Sir John Tindall*, London, E. All. de. 1617, ff.A3-D3.
99. Anon, *The unhappy marksman*, London, T.N., 1659, pp.12-13.

seventeenth-century England than they are today (still very small in number compared to the killings prompted by domestic tensions and tavern quarrels). Certainly, there are several well-documented cases, though most seem to have been prompted by some instrumental incentive rather than simple blood lust. In 1619, five inmates of Bablake Hospital, Coventry, died suddenly and three others became seriously ill. All had been poisoned with ratsbane. As all the victims lived in the same residential almshouse, suspicion soon fell on another inmate, John Johnson, who had remained healthy. Shortly after being questioned, Johnson also died suddenly. His body was exhumed twice and examined, to reveal that he too had died of poison, presumably a suicide. It was thought that Johnson's motive for murdering his colleagues was a desire to become senior almsman in the Hospital. Similarly, in 1671, Thomas Lancaster of Hawkshead, Cumberland, murdered his wife, six of her in-laws and a young servant with arsenic. Cunningly, he also poisoned some of his neighbours, in an attempt to divert suspicion from himself. His motivation appears to have been greed. Lancaster's father-in-law (one of the victims) had made over his estate to him in exchange for periodic cash payments to members of the family, which were ended by their deaths. (His wife's aunt was added to the list after Lancaster received a bribe of 24 pounds from the heir to her estate.) A local magistrate claimed it was the "most horrid act that hath ever been heard of in this country". Lancaster was convicted (appropriately) at the Lancaster Assizes of April 1672, and hanged in chains with an order that his body be left to rot on the gibbet.[100]

Poisoning

As the Lancaster case suggests, poisoning elicited special horror in early modern England. Coke opined that it was the "most detestable" form of homicide. It was covert, devious and carefully pre-planned. However, if Henri Misson is to be believed, it was rare: "The English Disposition not being revengeful, there have been but few instances of poysoning in the Nation." Nevertheless, it was a regularly employed method of killing, especially amongst intimates, whether family, servants or friends. This was particularly the case where the perpetrator was a woman and so had access to the preparation of food and drink. Thus, wives might use poison to kill their husbands. Typically, Alice Arden, when attempting to dispose of her spouse, initially had recourse to a Faversham townsman who was reputed to be "vers'd in the villainous Art of Poisoning". He supplied her with a noxious potion. However, she failed to mix it into her husband's breakfast milk properly, so that he ingested only a little before he "vomited extremly", escaping death.[101] Similarly, in London, in 1641, a lazy, spendthrift young wife, who was chided for her excessive expenditure by her hardworking labourer husband, turned to poison to get rid

---

100. B. Capp, "Serial killers in 17th-century England," *History Today*, 1996, vol.46, issue 3, at pp.21-31.
101. Anon, *The history of the most remarkable tryals*, pp.248-262.

of him, having been advised to do so by her landlady. Anne Hamton secured five drams of poison and mixed it into her husband's food. He immediately suffered convulsions and expired.[102] Grace Griffin from Southwark killed her silk weaver husband in the same manner, for reasons that are not apparent. Suffering from a cold, he had asked for honey to alleviate the symptoms, and she had poisoned him by adulterating it. She was convicted and burned at Kingston on Thames, on the 6th August 1655.[103] On a surprisingly larger scale, in seventeenth century Shropshire, Elizabeth Hodden, a widow, remarried a quiet and respectable man named Onslow, but "soone grew into dislike of him and wanted to get rid of him". She found two other women in her small village who were also extremely 'weary' of their husbands. They allegedly made an agreement to poison all three men on the same night. However, only Onslow died, the other two narrowly surviving.[104]

---

102. Anon, *Murther, murther*, London, 1641, pp.3-4.
103. Anon, *The devil's reign upon earth*, p.7.
104. R. Gough, *The history of Myddle, 1701*, D. Hey (Ed.) Harmondsworth, Penguin, 1981, p.148.

Chapter 6

Moral, Sexual and Social Crimes

Moral Crimes

It is frequently suggested that, in the early modern period, there was little distinction between crime and sin. Certainly, medieval canonists had sought to keep the divergence between legal and moral injunctions to a minimum, and even Stuart clerics might list immorality with the most heinous offences: "There are some vices, whose natures are alwayes cleer, and evident, as Adultery, Murder, Hatred, Lying, &c."[1] Early modern England was, in a real sense, a Christian society. Although its interpretation provided a flexible, and not always very demanding, moral code, it imposed important limits on behaviour. Christianity was 'part' of the common law. Thus, at John Lilburne's trial for treason, in 1649, the court noted that the "law of God is the law of England". Similarly, in the prosecution of John Taylor in 1676, Sir Mathew Hale famously declared that blasphemous words were "not only an offense to God and religion, but a crime against the laws, State and Government, and therefore punishable in this Court". He explained that this was so because Christianity was "parcel

---

1. G. Herbert, *A Priest to the Temple*, London, T. Maxey for T. Garthwait, 1652, pp.26-27.

of the laws of England".[2] Many Puritan JPs and lawyers wanted such an analysis to be taken to its logical conclusion, believing that the enforcement of morals was a proper function for the civil authorities. Such men looked with envy at Calvinist Geneva, where moral sins were treated as crimes to be punished by the magistrate, the Bible being virtually a code of law. Indeed, William Lambarde believed that even in (Elizabethan) England formal action *could* be taken against sexual miscreants by the secular courts, so that if people were: "... in adulterie, or fornication together, then the officer may take companie with him, and that if he finde them so, he may carie them to prison."[3]

In reality, this was rarely the position in Anglican England. Even Lambarde appreciated that secular involvement in moral offences was, legally, questionable, especially when the parties were unmarried, and so merely guilty of fornication. In practice, the secular authorities appear to have been very reluctant to become involved in such matters, except where it was the subject of extreme local disapproval. Normally, they ignored mainstream sexual misbehaviour. The existence of a structure of church courts in England, dealing with adultery, fornication and incest allowed them to limit their engagement. Usually, only the ecclesiastical courts prosecuted fornication and adultery *per se*, and even they tended to focus on blatant examples. Theoretically, William Shakespeare and Anne Hathaway

---

2. S. Banner, "When Christianity was part of the Common Law," *Law and History Review*, 1998, vol.16, p.30.
3. W. Lambarde, *The Duties of Constables, Borsholders, Tithing men ...*, London, 1583, p.18.

could have been forced to do public penance, dressed in white sheets, after they married hurriedly, by special licence, three months into Hathaway's pregnancy with their first child. In practice, such matters were usually overlooked once regularised by marriage. Most Englishmen accepted that all breaches of Mosaic law were not the same.

At times, however, even in England, the thin division between sin and crime was eroded. With the suspension of the church courts under the Republic, and a temporary Puritan dominance, change occurred. In 1650, the Rump Parliament passed "An Act for suppressing the detestable sins of Incest, adultery and Fornication". It was potentially draconian, as adulterers faced execution, fornicators three months imprisonment for a first offence and death if convicted again. It could be prosecuted at either assizes or quarter sessions. In reality changing England's legal culture proved difficult, and the statute appears to have been enforced in a conservative and highly selective manner. In Devon, at least, it is hard to find any cases in which the death penalty was actually imposed. Adultery was largely left to be determined by the assizes, but appears barely to have been prosecuted at all. Most cases of fornication involved women who had become pregnant. (These rose from 13 per cent of all cases to 30 per cent in 1655.) There was still no general campaign against the unmarried but sexually active.[4] The provision was repealed after a few

---

4.   S. Roberts, "Fornication and bastardy in Mid-Seventeenth Century Devon: how was the Act of 1650 enforced?" *Outside the Law: Studies in Crime and Order 1650-1850,* J. Rule (Ed.) University of Exeter, Exeter Papers in Economic History, 1982, pp.1-14.

years, and the problems it occasioned suggest that the caution shown by most MPs towards extending secular involvement was justified.

Sexual Crimes

To an even greater extent than today, rape appears to have been an under-reported crime in early modern England. The immediate background to some cases, servants attacked by their masters, etc., partly explains why such matters only rarely came to court. Thus, between 1589 and 1618 the surviving records for trial on indictment in Hertfordshire (there are a few gaps) suggest that only seven men were prosecuted for rape, and none were convicted.[5] If Mathew Hale was typical, there was frequently overt judicial scepticism about allegations of rape, a claim that was supposedly easy to make and hard to defend, even if the accused man was "never so innocent". In fairness, Hale's attitude seems to have been influenced by a trial over which he had presided at the Sussex Assizes, in which a 14-year-old girl accused a 53-year-old man of raping her. The accused man demonstrated publicly that it was "impossible he should have to do with any woman in that kind". He had a huge rupture so that after he had unrobed, observers in court could not even "discern his privities".[6]

---

5. P. Lawson, "Property Crime and Hard Times in England, 1559-1624," *Law and History Review*, 1986, vol.4, p.37.
6. G. Geis, "Lord Hale, Witches and Rape," *British Journal of Law and Society*, 1978, vol.5, p.240.

177

It has been suggested that, in the early 1500s, rape was seen as being primarily a crime against (another man's) property, i.e., as a form of theft. It was not the virtue of a woman that was at stake, but the possession of her male 'owner', whether father, husband or master. Thus, a definition of the crime in 1556 declared that: "Rape is where a man ravisheth or taketh a mans wife, wydowe or maide against her will."[7] Even in the following century, some of the language used by seventeenth century English jurists, including Sir Mathew Hale, encourages such an analysis: "The husband cannot be guilty of a rape committed by himself upon his lawful wife, for by their mutual matrimonial consent and contract the wife hath given up herself in this kind unto her husband, which she cannot retract."[8] (A situation that prevailed in England until 1992.) As a result, it has been argued that daughters, wives and servants were favoured in making rape accusations compared to those who lacked such bonds.

However, a sea change seems to have occurred in attitudes towards rape during the era. By the mid-seventeenth century, legal definitions had altered, and medieval attitudes largely been abandoned. It had become primarily a sexual crime. No longer was it a man's property that was at stake, but rather the victim's resistance and innocence that was in issue. Nevertheless, in England, age and chastity appear to have played an important role in rape and allied cases. The sexual assault of children and virgins

---

7.   W. Middleton, *The Boke for a Justyce of Peace*, London, 1545, f.Bii.
8.   Geis, "Lord Hale, Witches and Rape," p.240.

was considered more unacceptable than the rape of adult women.[9] Then as now, the sexual abuse of small children was often the work of intimates, and their stratagems for avoiding detection are readily familiar today. Thus, in 1678, an eight-year-old girl revealed that a defendant had molested her every Sunday for the previous six months, initially gagging her while doing so, and giving her money afterwards to remain silent, so that she did not mention it: "... till some of her friends observing her to go as if she were very sore, examined her, and by telling her she would be in danger of hanging in Hell, got her to confess, that the Prisoner was her father's Prentice."[10] Such cases had occasioned legal problems until the Elizabethan period. The ancient statute law of rape required the victim to have been of full age (i.e. at least 10, possibly 12 or over) if the offence was to be charged as a felony, rather than merely a misdemeanor. A new statutory offence of 1576 (18 Eliz. C.7) provided that it was a felony without benefit of clergy to "unlawfully and carnally know any woman child under the age of 10 years". This Act followed the problems occasioned by the trial of a Scotsman, for raping a seven-year-old girl, a few years earlier.[11]

Although rape was normally a matter for the secular

9. M. Van de Heijden, "Women as victims of sexual and domestic violence in Seventeenth-Century Holland: Criminal cases of Rape, Incest and maltreatment in Rotterdam and Delft," *Journal of Social History*, 2000, vol.33, no.33, p.623.

10. Anon, *An exact account of the trials of the several persons arraigned at the sessions-house in the Old-Bailey for London and Middlesex*, London, G. Hills, 1678, p.14.

11. M. Levine, "A More than Ordinary Case of 'Rape'," 13 and 14 Elizabeth 1, *American Journal of Legal History*, 1963, vol.7, p.163.

forums, the importance placed on penetrative intercourse meant that many lesser sexual offences were dealt with by the church courts. Unsurprisingly, these included relatively minor allegations of indecent behaviour towards females. However, they also extended to matters that, in the modern era, would be considered grave crimes, including serious sexual assaults. Thus, at Banbury in Oxfordshire, in 1619, it was recorded that one Robert Dauber had behaved: "... incontinently towards the wife of Mr Ffauler Attorney & towards his maide called Katherin Wady also as is reported publiquely in the town of Banbury. The maner was by putting his hand under their clothes & lifting them up to feele their privities."[12] Similarly, mutual masturbation by members of the same sex might be determined by the church courts, despite clear homosexual overtones, although sodomy was seen as a heinous secular crime.

Sodomy, committed against both man and beast, was a capital offence. It is difficult to establish how common the former was. The Society for the Reformation of Manners claimed to have 'discovered' a homosexual sub-culture in London in the early 1700s. According to some, the capital's 'Mollies' ("sodomotical wretches") would "mimick all Manner of Effeminacy" and gather in certain Metropolitan taverns to practise transvestism, buggery and other forms of debauchery. Although this was, for a long period, supposedly secret, it was eventually exposed by the: "... cunning management of some of the Under-Agents to the Reforming-Society; so that several were brought to open

---

12.   P. Hair (Ed.) *Before the Bawdy Court* ..., London, Elek Books Ltd., 1972, p.175.

shame and punishment; others flying from Justice to escape the Ignominy."[13] Certainly, by the eighteenth century there were several Metropolitan locations that were notorious for such liaisons, and, as early as 1395, the City authorities had questioned a cross-dressing homosexual prostitute.

Sodomy with a man had always been viewed as a grave offence, even in the medieval era. However, bestiality came to be viewed in a much more serious light during the early modern period than had hitherto been the case, eventually being seen as an act which would uproot "God, Nature and the Law".[14] It has been argued that the apparent harshening in attitudes towards penetrative bestiality in the sixteenth and seventeenth centuries was based on fears of cross-breeding between man and beast, something which may have been fanned by strange reports from the newly discovered Americas and the widespread publicity accorded to such liaisons by books such as *Certaine Secrete Wonders of Nature* (1569). Considerable credence was given to such stories, even in England. Thus, Agnes Bowker allegedly gave birth to a cat in January 1569, appearing in the Archdeacon's court the same month. She explained to the court that the previous year a "cat had to do with her six or seven times". Some contemporary physicians believed in the possibility of bestial conception and hybridisation. As late as the 1720s, Mary Toft and her managers appear to have persuaded several reputable doctors that she had given

---

13.   Anon, *The Secret History of Clubs*, London, 1709, pp.284-288.
14.   M. Dalton, *The Country Justice, Containing the Practise of the Justices of the Peace out of their Sessions ...*, London, Company of Stationers, 1661, pp.64-65.

birth to a litter of rabbits.[15]

Perhaps because the primary concern was a fear of inter-breeding, the need for penetration in bestiality was similar to that for rape and human sodomy. Execution could turn on it, the offence having been withdrawn from benefit of clergy by Henry VIII. Without penetration, a serious crime was not committed. This was widely appreciated by potential witnesses. In 1647, William Bayly of Bingley claimed that he had watched one John Walton commit buggery with a mare for some time, so that he "might the more and fairly depose the truth therein". Presumably, Bayly waited to observe actual penetration. Accusers were regularly asked by attendant JPs if they had witnessed coitus.[16] The need for penetration also appears to have been appreciated by offenders. In 1631, a servant named William Gould put a ewe in a ditch in Dorset and was seen by the animal's owner in "such a motion and action" as to suggest that he had committed "the foule act of buggery". When questioned by a JP, Gould admitted this had been his intention, but stressed that he had been prevented by his premature discovery from committing a "filthy act with her butt".[17]

However, despite the existence of harsh penalties, cases of bestiality appear to have been a periodic feature of early

---

15. D. Cressey, *Travesties and Transgressions in Tudor and Stuart England,* Oxford, OUP, 2000, pp.10-26.
16. E. Fudge, "Monstrous Acts, Bestiality in Early Modern England," *History Today,* 2000, vol.50, issue 8, p.20.
17. J.H. Bettey (Ed.) *The Casebook of Sir Francis Ashley JP, Recorder of Dorchester: 1614-1635,* Dorchester, Dorset Record Society, 1981, p.103.

modern rural life. Thus, in 1642, Nathaniel Clegge of Netherton in Yorkshire was called to a cowshed by one Richard Broadbent to witness the activities of Edward Wilton, the cow-keeper, who "stood very suspiciously to commit buggery" with one of the animals in his charge. However, Clegge's view was obstructed so that, crucially, he: "... could not discern whether he did actually commit buggery with the said kine." In another Yorkshire case, from 1664, Matthew Ward of Eskwick deposed that he saw a grey mare standing in a ditch and one William Milner "standing astride the ditch behind the mare with her tail in his hand". Again, however, Ward did not get a view of the accused man's "privy member". A decade later, in Grindleton, John Cromlinton was also seen with a mare which he had placed: "... into a deep ditch and had put a slip upon her head, and himself standing upon the bank of the said ditch with his yard drawn, and making several attempts to enter her body with his said yard, but [the witness] doth not certainly know whether or not he entered her body."[18]

As noted, 'victimless' sexual offences were more commonly the preserve of the church courts, unless bastardy ensued. When formal action was forthcoming over such matters, women were normally treated more strictly than men throughout early modern Europe, females being disproportionately prosecuted for offences such as adultery, fornication, and producing illegitimate children.[19] Men could be (and were) charged with these offences, but the

---

18. Fudge, "Monstrous Acts," p.20.
19. Van der Heijden, "Women as victims," p.623.

authorities appear to have taken a generally more lenient attitude towards them. In the case of bastards, of course, establishing paternity was very much harder than maternity. However, there was also a marked prevalence of 'double standards'. Incest was also left to the church courts, the Interregnum apart, when a short-lived and little prosecuted statute made it a secular crime (a situation that would not be restored until 1908).

'Social' Crime

As already noted, most Englishmen viewed the commission of traditional religiously proscribed offences, such as theft, as 'criminal', morally as well as legally. However, there was also a class of offence that frequently lacked such connotations despite being criminalised by the authorities. These often involved a clash of interests and perceived rights, so that the law was lacking in popular legitimacy. It is possible that early modern population growth, producing increased pressure on fixed resources, made such cases more frequent.[20] Thus, legally, permitted coppicing of dead timber in hedgerows could easily become theft of living timber and criminal damage to the hedge, when fuel was scarce. The range of such offences is considerable, and only two will be considered here in detail.

---

20. Sharpe, "Law-Enforcement," p.106.

Gleaning Offences

Throughout the period, gleaning was recognised as both a fundamental legal right and, in the case of farmers, a Biblically sanctioned duty. Thus, Michael Dalton declared that for the: "... gleaning and leaving of the harvest &c. God commandeth that it be left for the poor, the fatherless, the widow, and the stranger." The legal entitlement was not to be challenged until the 'Great Gleaning Case' of *Steel v. Houghton et Uxor* in 1788, when the Court of Common Pleas concluded that that there was no common law "right" to glean at harvest time. Although an age-old custom in many areas, it was held to be merely a charitable indulgence not a legal entitlement. Earlier authorities cited in support of such a right, whether Mosaic law or the *obiter* comments of Mathew Hale were distinguished. (Although, in the short term, there were few practical consequences, this was a change of great portent for the future.)[21]

Nevertheless, although the legal right to glean in early modern England was unquestioned, it was rarely an unregulated process. Thus, in some villages, a morning and evening gleaners' bell would be rung, to let the villagers know when they were permitted to start, and required to finish, retrieving fallen corn from the fields. By its very nature, the right was susceptible to abuse by gleaners, and avariciousness by those whose corn was being gleaned.

---

21. P. King, "Legal Change, Customary Right and Social Conflict in Late Eighteenth-Century England: The Origins of the Great Gleaning Case of 1788," *Law and History Review*, 1992, vol.10, no.1, pp.1-32.

Dalton himself felt that JPs should consider taking action so that only the poor would have the benefit of gleaning and not richer people "which is no better than to rob the poor of what properly belongs to them". Not surprisingly, gleaning also provided the backdrop for numerous criminal actions throughout the early modern period. Thus, Essex gleaners complained periodically of being attacked and beaten by farmers as they went about their business, while farmers complained that gleaners were going beyond the permitted ambit of the practice to steal already harvested grain.[22]

Poaching

Laws against poaching were the most blatant form of class legislation in the English criminal justice system, and, not surprisingly, this (along with smuggling) has made them a favoured topic for radical, and even Marxist, modern analysis. Unsurprisingly, perhaps, they were also amongst the first criminal matters to be withdrawn from jury trials, becoming the exclusive province of the petty sessions. However, the law pertaining to poaching was extremely complicated. As Blackstone noted in the eighteenth century, the relevant statutes were "many and various, and not a little obscure and intricate". Most were badly worded, or relied on a "very loose and vague description" of the

---

22. J.A. Sharpe, "Law-Enforcement in the Seventeenth-Century English Village," *Crime and the Law*, V.A.C. Gatrell (eds.), London, Europa (1980), p.106.

categories of people exempted from the general prohibition against taking game.[23] On their face, however, they were extremely draconian. A series of earlier statutes culminated in the Game Law of 1671, which blatantly distinguished between the social classes. As a result, some observers expressed concern at the manner in which these laws had "in Effect disarm'd all the common People in England, [worth] under 100 l. a year in Landed estates". It was feared this would reduce their value as military recruits in time of war.[24] Even for poaching, there appears to have been a difference between the strictness of the letter of the law and its practise. Thus, small landholders who were, in theory, forbidden to take game on their own properties very rarely appeared in the courts. No doubt this was, in part, because they could often do so quite privately, taking their bags indoors immediately afterwards. Nevertheless, there was probably also a tacit recognition that it was harsh to punish a man for taking a bird or hare on his own land. Most prosecutions were of those who had also been trespassing while taking game, though there might be a dispute about the legal status of recently enclosed land. Despite its romantic image, poaching was not solely the preserve of men seeking to fill their family's pot. It also attracted professional gangs, aiming to feed the urban, especially Metropolitan, markets. Dick Turpin's criminal career began when he worked as a butcher specialising in game stolen by

---

23. W. Blackstone, *Commentaries on the Laws of England*, vol.4, Oxford, Clarendon Press, 1769, p.175.
24. *The Gentleman's Magazine*, 1736, vol.6, p.82.

commercial poachers.

Offences against Neighbourliness

To an extent, the parishes of Elizabethan and early Stuart England were moral communities, founded upon an expectation that their inhabitants would live 'in charity' with each other and adhere to certain generally accepted standards of conduct. This was premised on a fear that even moderate disharmony was potentially dangerous, creating social fault lines that could easily be exacerbated, as: "... where division and controversie doth arise, sad effects will suddenly follow; for no sooner can there a breach appear, but presently Sathan is ready to stop it up."[25] So important were communal good relations that there were specific offences for damaging them. Thus, in a society where gossip was a common currency, there was strong popular antipathy towards 'busybodies', who sought and secured information about others and spread rumours. To such people: "There can no act pass without his comment; which is ever far-fetched, rash, suspicious, delatory. His ears are long, and his eyes quick; but most of all to imperfections, which as he easily sees, so he increases with intermeddling."[26] Similarly, those who set men at odds were guilty of barratry. According to Dalton a barrator was either

---

25. Anon, *Bloody Newes from Dover*, p.4.
26. J. Hall, *Characters of Vertues and Vices*, London, Melch, Bradwood, 1608, Book 2, p.83.

a: "... common mover and stirrer up (or maintainer) of suits in Law in any Courts; or else of quarrels or parts in the Countrey."[27] Scolding was another offence against neighbourliness. In the medieval period scolds, although predominantly female, could sometimes be men. By the early modern period it was a woman only crime. Thus, Blackstone was convinced that common scolds were always "communis rixatrix, (for our law-latin confines it to the feminine gender)". The punishment was the same throughout most of the country: "Common Scolds that have disturbed the Peace and Quiet of their Husbands or Neighbours shall be put on the Cocking stool."[28] By the 1700s, the term cucking stool was "frequently corrupted into ducking stool". This was because its recipient would be "plunged in the water for her punishment".[29]

27. Dalton, *The Country Justice*, 1661, p.39.
28. Anon, *The Office of the Clerk of the Assize*, London, Henry Twyford, 1682, p.136.
29. Blackstone, *Commentaries on the Laws of England*, vol.4, p.169.

Chapter 7

London and the Borderlands

The bedrocks of the early modern English state were its rural lowlands and pastoral uplands. These covered the majority of the country and the great majority of its inhabitants. Where generalisations about crime are necessary, as they are in a work of this nature, it is right that they should concentrate on such areas. However, there were two exceptions to this general pattern, London and the Border country, which were sufficiently different to warrant special consideration.

London

Both crime and the criminal justice system in London were *sui generis*. (Strictly speaking, the 'Metropolis' was actually based around the neighbouring but separate cities of London and Westminster along with urban parts of Middlesex.) At the start of the period, some visiting foreigners were convinced that England was plagued with crime, one Venetian, writing in c.1500, claimed that despite dozens of people being arrested "yet for all this, they never cease to rob and murder in the streets".[1] On examination, however, such views seem to have been based largely on

---

1. Anon, *A relation, or rather a true account of the island of England ... about the year 1500*, C. Sneyd (Trans.), London, Camden Society, 1847, p.36.

Metropolitan experience. Certainly, compared to the orderliness and "Swiss honesty" of his native Cantons, London was a lawless place to Cesar de Saussure. He was sure that there were more people sentenced at each Old Bailey sessions for robbery and theft than were caught in all of Switzerland in a year.[2] Many English observers shared his views. Thus, in 1600, after his famous dancing journey from London to Norwich, William Kemp noted that four cut-purses, who had followed him from London, were caught at Brentwood. They had been attracted by the criminal opportunities presented by the crowds drawn to watch Kemp. After being arrested, two were committed to gaol, the others being flogged at the whipping cross and sent back to London, where, Kemp noted, there were "too many of their occupation".[3]

Even in the 1500s, the city's wealth and opportunities attracted immigrants from everywhere in the British Isles, Flanders and even more distant places.[4] It continued to attract numerous incomers from a continent wracked by religious conflict in the following two centuries. Influxes of Irish vagrants were a particularly regular feature with many complaining that too many Metropolitan beggars came from that island.[5] As a result, the population of London,

---

2. M. Van Muyden (Trans. and Ed.) *A Foreign View of England in the Reigns of George I and George II; the Letters of Monsieur Cesar de Saussure, to his Family,* London, John Murray, 1902, p.131.
3. W. Kemp, *Kemp's nine daies wonder. Performed in a daunce from London to Norwich,* London, E.A., 1600, p.6.
4. Anon, *A relation, or rather a true account,* p.43.
5. A Citizen in London, *The Vices of the Cities of London and Westminster trac'd from their original ...* Dublin, G. Faulkner, 1751, p.20.

Westminster and their immediate suburbs grew much more rapidly than that of England as a whole, immigration more than compensating for their high mortality rates. With a population of around 200,000 in 1600, out of a national total of no more than five million, it was more than 10 times as large as the biggest provincial cities. By 1662, the demographer John Graunt concluded that, within the hundred or so parishes of the City of London alone, numbers had increased to 384,000 people. In 1695, one informed estimate placed the population of the bills of mortality area at 530,000 and 630,856 by 1716.[6] However, population growth in the City, the 'square mile', both within and without its historic walls, though significant, was relatively modest compared to the expansion west of Temple Bar, where many richer citizens settled, and to the enormous growth in the poorer parishes to the east of the City or south of the Thames in Southwark.[7]

This population explosion sometimes appears to have been criminogenic. For many, London life lacked permanence, its social involvements being transient, so that in 1725 Defoe could complain that numerous female maids roved: "... from bawdy-house to service, and from service to bawdy-house again, ever unsettled and never easy."[8]Not surprisingly, in such an environment, anomie and its

---

6. *The Gentleman's Magazine*, 1735, vol.5, p.355.
7. J.A. Browner, "Wrong side of the River: London's disreputable South Bank in the Sixteenth and Seventeenth Century," *Essays in History, University of Virginia*, vol.36, pp.34-35.
8. A. Moreton (D. Defoe), *Every-Body's Business is No-Body's Business*, London, 1725, 2nd edn., p.7.

attendant crime (especially instrumental offences) flourished. The suburbs, in particular, with their concentration of people and the ensuing social evils of overcrowding, bad sanitation, vagrancy and disorder became notorious.[9] By 1749, robberies in and about the Metropolis generally had become so frequent that several parishes made voluntary subscriptions to maintain "extraordinary guards for the roads" and to provide money to fund rewards for capturing felons.[10] Aggravating the situation, London was the centre of aristocratic entertainment and consumption, attracting wealthy men. As a result, Esther Biddle, imprisoned at Newgate in 1662, for conscience's sake, was horrified at the city's general ungodlinness: "Drunkenness, Whoredom, and Gluttony, and all manner of Ungodliness, Tyranny and Oppression, is found in thee ... Taverns and Ale-houses are frequented day and night, and are seldom disturbed by the Magistrates."[11] Aggressive beggars were an especially serious Metropolitan problem. In 1700, one observer worried that the streets swarmed with mendicants whose "impudence is such that they often beat at our Doors".[12] Juvenile crime was also seen as a major Metropolitan issue, with complaints in the 1730s of: "Boys of seven or eight years old, taken in robbing a

---

9.   Browner, "Wrong Side of the River," pp.34-35.
10.   *The Gentleman's Magazine,* 1749, vol.19, p.522.
11.   E. Biddle, *The Trumpet of the Lord Sounded forth unto these Three Nations,* London, 1662, p.A3.
12.   J. Marriott, "Sweep them off the streets," *History Today,* 2000, vol.50, issue 8, pp.26-28.

shop; and some of 13 or 14 robbing in the streets."[13]

Although most Metropolitan criminals, like those found elsewhere in England, were opportunistic, London also appears to have been one of the few places where widespread professional and organised crime was more than a literary construct. There were a number of sophisticated and structured criminal groups.[14] Even in the Elizabethan period, William Fleetwood was convinced that London possessed a school "sett upp to learne younge boyes to cutt purses".[15] In 1552, a newcomer to the city had been warned that professional criminals there had long careers, unlike the mass of petty offenders. Although they might end up at Tyburn, it was: "... nothing so sone as a man wold suppose, they be but pety figgers, and unlessoned laddes that haue such redy passage to the gallowes. The old theves go thorow with their usies wel .xx. or .xxx. yeres together & be seldome taken."[16] At the end of the period (1751), the magistrate Henry Fielding believed that it was an unquestionable fact that London contained a criminal gang, almost a hundred strong, who were "incorporated in one body, have officers and a treasury, and [who] have reduced theft and robbery into a regular system". They were supposedly adept at disguise and armed with every method

13. *The Gentleman's Magazine*, 1731, vol.1, pp.59-60.
14. J. McMullan, *The Canting Crew: London's Criminal Underworld 1550-1700*, New Brunswick (NJ), Rutgers University Press, 1984, pp.21-23.
15. R.H. Tawney and E. Power (eds.), *Tudor Economic Documents*, London, Longmans, 1951, vol.2, p.338.
16. Anon, *A manifest detection of the moste vyle and detestable use of Diceplay*, London, A. Vele, 1552, ff.D5r-D6r.

of evading the law, should they be caught, whether by escaping physically from custody, bribing and threatening prosecutors into dropping charges or procuring great numbers of false witnesses ready to support bogus alibis.[17] The adult cut-purse, John Selman, was probably typical of such men. Although he followed no trade he was still able to dress "like unto a Gentleman". His clothes included a black velvet-lined cloak. Such finery allowed him to infiltrate upper class environments where lucrative targets might be found. Amongst these was the Royal Chapel, where he cut his last purse, on Christmas Day 1611. Without his elegant apparel he freely admitted that he would not have been admitted to the chapel. Unfortunately, Selman was seized as he left the service, after another worshipper, whose suspicions had been aroused on an earlier occasion, kept him under observation and alerted his final victim to the theft of a purse containing 40 shillings. (Selman's dexterity was such that its owner was quite oblivious of his loss.)[18] The celebrated transvestite, Mary Frith, known as Moll Cutpurse from her early criminal employment, provides an extreme (and unusual) example of a Metropolitan master-criminal. She was born at the Barbican in London, in 1589, her (honest) father being a shoemaker. It is hard to be sure about much of her career, as it appears to have been considerably embellished by legend. However, she evinced masculine traits early on, only playing with

---

17. H. Fielding, *An Enquiry into the causes of the late increase of robbers, etc.,* London, 1751, at pp.2-3.
18. B.L. *The Arraignment of John Selman,* London, W.H., 1612, pp.5 and 10.

boys.[19] Not willing to enter a suitably female employment, such as domestic service, she became a (fraudulent) 'fortune teller', but, this not proving sufficiently remunerative, swiftly progressed to picking pockets. She was imprisoned and clergied several times before graduating to highway robbery. A narrow escape scared her from further personal involvement in either theft or robbery and she became a 'fence'. Frith appears to have discovered that rather than simply selling stolen items on to the public, at far below their true value, she could make more money by returning them to their losers at a price and with 'no questions asked'. As a result, she created a brokerage for stolen items, opening a shop in Fleet Street, acting as an intermediary between criminals and victims, and thriving on the commission. This also had the advantage of allowing her to secure large sums for stolen items that had no resale value, whether personal items of sentimental value or commercial documents, 'shop books', taken from drapers, mercers and other rich traders. Frith died of dropsy aged 74.[20] The criminal system that she pioneered was to be employed by Jonathon Wild on an even greater scale in the early part of the following century.

Various, largely ineffectual, attempts were made to improve the policing of the capital. Thus, in the 1680s, following a tradition of government magistrates in the Metropolis that stretched back to the Elizabethan period,

---

19. Anon, *The Life and Death of Mrs Mary Frith, Commonly Called Moll Cutpurse,* London, W.G. Ilberton, 1662, pp.3-6.
20. Anon, *The life and death of Mrs Mary Frith,* pp.160-173.

and which would be developed in the following century by De Veil and the Fielding brothers, Sir John Reresby was specifically put into the Commission of the Peace for Middlesex: "... on purpose to serve upon great occasions, in deference to which the King did not think it below him, to give his orders with his own mouth."[21] Nevertheless, although London's size made its problems unique, such concerns were common to urban areas throughout Europe at this time. Thus, in 1708, shopkeepers and merchants in Leipzig petitioned their city council to provide intensified punishment for thieves, who, they claimed, often roamed the city in gangs. They demanded that such people should not merely be flogged but also: "... imprisoned for a few years or for life, and be put to odious work like street cleaning, construction, or digging ... in chains and on a diet of bread and water."[22]

Borderlands

Tudor England was relatively free from major internecine disturbances occasioned by essentially personal disputes. Certainly, it was nothing like Scotland, where the weak central power of the Crown produced endemic insecurity, evidenced by the widespread building and use of

---

21. Sir T. De Veil, *Memoirs of the Life and Times of Sir Thomas De Veil*, London, 1748, p.25.
22. T. Kevorkian, "The rise of the poor, weak, and wicked: Poor Care, Punishment, Religion and Patriarchy in Leipzig, 1700-1730," *Journal of Social History*, 2000, vol.34, no.1, p.163.

residential fortification throughout much of the country. However, both sides of the Anglo-Scottish border country were relatively lawless until late into the early modern period as were, to a lesser extent, the Welsh Marches. The border country was a particular thorn in the sides of both Kingdoms, prompting Henry VIII to write to his Scottish cousin suggesting joint action to 'chastise' the area.[23] Marcher Society was very different to the largely manorialised lowlands and pastoral uplands that made up most of the Tudor state. It was thinly populated, hilly, mainly given over to grazing, with considerable tracts of waste, and powerful local noblemen supported by warlike tenants. Sometimes, even quarter sessions could not be held locally because of the lack of substantial gentry to put into the Commissions of the Peace.[24] Their distant location hindered effective control from London so that the relatively centralised government suitable for lowland England was often inappropriate in these outlying parts. As a result, the existence of the wardens' courts, and 'border law', based on a mixture of common and military law, supplemented the work of the once yearly (in the Northern three counties) assizes. However, it never replaced that body, the assizes managing to keep going even in periods of acute cross-border tension.[25]

In counties like Northumberland, numerous fortified

---

23. G. Watson, *The Border Reivers,* London, Robert Hale & Co., 1974, pp.100-192.
24. S. Ellis, "Frontiers and power in the early Tudor state," *History Today,* 1995, vol.45, issue 4, pp.35-42.
25. C.J. Neville, "Keeping the peace on the northern marches in the later middle ages," *English Historical Review,* 1994, vol.109, pp.1-25.

buildings continued in regular use. Border lords and gentlemen preferred castles and pele towers to the country houses favoured by lowland gentry. As late as the early 1500s, Thomas Lord Dacre spent much of his income on building small castles at Drumburgh, Rockcliffe and Askerton in Cumberland to protect his estates there, and on strengthening those at Naworth and Kirkoswald.[26] Lesser gentlemen and farmers might occupy protected farms or 'bastle houses' (from the French 'bastille' or fortified place). These were smaller and lower than towers, being strengthened houses rather than miniature castles, with walls that were four to six feet thick, rather than the 10 foot depth commonly found in pele towers. However, both towers and bastle houses would normally have a bell and beacon on their roof to summon assistance in an emergency.[27] They also usually had slit windows, reinforced doors, a vaulted ground floor for animals and human accommodation in an upper level, providing a modicum of protection against both Scottish incursions and border reivers.

The reivers were both Scottish and English by nationality, usually being blood-related clans and families. Thus, north of the border were Scottish groups such as the Armstrongs. Within England, to the east of Gilsland, in the Northumberland uplands, lived the quasi-independent families of Tynedale and Redesdale, who made their livings

26. Ellis, "Frontiers and power in the early Tudor state," pp.35-42.
27. Watson, *The Border Reivers*, p.100-101.

largely by raiding wealthier lowland communities.[28] Bands of 50 reivers were normal in the sixteenth century, though they could exceed a thousand men on occasion. For many people in the frontier territory, robbery, raiding, arson, kidnapping, murder and extortion were everyday facts of life, pursued as much in peacetime as in war, and considered to be a quite 'normal' activity.[29] Unsurprisingly, the normal sixteenth century provision (theoretically) banning the possession and use of handguns and cross-bows by any but wealthy men did not apply to those resident in the: "... englysshe marches nere Scotland, which may keepe theym for defence of theyr howse and goodes."[30] In the late 1580s, despite (or because of) long years of peace between England and Scotland, and with dynastic union in the air, security from reivers in the borders had actually deteriorated, with increased incidents of rustling, etc. Typical of such raids, in 1596, Walter Scott of Harden led a band of 400 reivers, taking 300 cattle, burning 20 houses and stealing £400 in gold in the process. In an attempt to deal with reiving the area developed its own system of cross-border hot pursuit, this being conducted either 'hot trod' (immediately) or 'cold trod' (within six days of the crime) men being required to join pursuing bands on pain of serious punishment. After 1563, one man in each party was supposed to carry a smouldering turf on a lance to

---

28. Ellis, "Frontiers and power in the early Tudor state," pp.35-42.
29. G. MacDonald Fraser, *The Steel Bonnets*, London, Barrie & Jenkins, 1971, pp.90-96.
30. W. Middleton, *The Boke for a Justyce of Peace*, London, 1545, p.25.

signify a pursuit.[31]
However, Union of the Crowns in 1603 was the beginning of the end for the reivers. Indeed, many were encouraged to settle in Ulster or the colonies. Border fortifications were also gradually reduced.[32] In 1607, the passing of an "Act for the utter abolicion of all memory of Hostilitie ... beweene England and Scotland" (4 Jam., ch. 1, 1) established special trial procedures for Englishmen who committed crimes in Scotland before fleeing home south of the border. These could be used in the three northernmost counties, and were aimed at effecting a compromise between English and Scottish criminal procedure (interestingly, they allowed the calling of sworn defence witnesses, long before this was permitted elsewhere in England).[33] With the increased stability occasioned by the Union, reiving waned. This did not happen spontaneously. In the years between James I's accession in 1603 and 1611, a series of sometimes violent crack-downs, by government bodies such as the Border horse garrison, brought large-scale reiving to a fairly swift end. Although there were a few forays in the second decade of the seventeenth century they swiftly petered out, so that the horse garrison could be disbanded in 1621. In 1630, a royal proclamation required that major landholders on both sides of the frontier "search for all manner of felons, fugitives, outlawes". No one for 10 miles on either side of the border was to provide shelter for

---

31. MacDonald Fraser, *The Steel Bonnets*, pp.102 and 115, and pp.188-198.
32. Watson, *The Border Reivers*, pp.193-195.
33. G. Fisher, "The Jury's Rise as Lie Detector," *Yale Law Journal*, 1997, vol.107, p.609.

such men or other suspected persons, on pain of being imprisoned, with no chance of bail, until those they had accommodated gave themselves up for trial.[34] After this period, the security concerns of the border area begin to sound more like those of many parts of lowland England. There were periodic complaints about the number of ale-houses in the area and the manner in which they attracted idle men to spend 'tyme their in dyceing, cairting and uthir exerceissis, and do consult upon the meannis to prosecute their wicked pretensis'.[35]

The borders continued to be relatively lawless by southern standards. The large-scale reivers were replaced by much smaller bands of 'moss-trooper' in the mid and late seventeenth century. By then, there was no suggestion that they were anything other than brigands, engaged in stealing relatively small amounts of livestock at any one time.[36] Even so, there were enough of them to prompt complaints in the 1650s that both sides of the Anglo-Scottish frontier were ravaged by crime, including murder, robbery and arson, committed by the "bordering people of both nations". As in the previous century, this was greatly facilitated by the area's bogs, mountains and the "large waste grounds between England and Scotland, [felons] having thereby such opportunity, not onely at home to hide themselves and their prey or booties of stolen goods". They could also escape

34. Anon, *A Proclamation for the Suppressing of felons and outlawes*, London, Robert, 1630, pp.1-3.
35. MacDonald Fraser, *The Steel Bonnets*, pp.376-7.
36. Watson, *The Border Reivers*, pp.100-195.

across the border, making it hard to bring them to justice.[37] Even in 1653, George Fox was well aware of the area's reputation when he entered Gilsland "where some in that country were very thievish".[38] Nevertheless, by the end of the seventeenth century, the immediate border area aside, northern counties like Cumberland appear to have been remarkably peaceful, their patterns of crime no longer showing marked differences to those found further south. Thus, in the period 1650-1699, only half a dozen people resident in Westmoreland were suspected of homicide, and there was little arson, large scale rustling or rape. There was also an apparent absence of feuds and vendettas. Crimes such as theft and counterfeiting were far more common.[39]

Although not on a par with the Scottish border, the Welsh Marches could also be unruly, at least at the beginning of the period. According to Thomas More, writing in 1513, this was especially true of the countryside around Ludlow, which, being: "... far of from the law and recourse to iustice, was begon to be farre out of good wyll & waxen wild, robbers and riuers walking at libertie vncorrected."[40] Partly to deal with such problems, Thomas Cromwell steered legislation through Parliament in 1536

37. Anon, *An act for the Better Suppressing of Theft upon the Borders of England and Scotland*, London, H. Hill, 1657, pp.1-2.
38. G. Fox, *The Journal of George Fox*, London, Religious Society of Friends, 1975, p.167.
39. A. Macfarlane and S. Harrison, *Justice and the Mare's Ale*, Oxford, Blackwell, 1981, p.186.
40. Sir T. More, "The History of King Richard the Thirde," *The English Works of Sir Thomas More*, A.W. Reed *et al* (Eds.) London, Eyre and Spottiswoode, 1931, vol.1, pp.35-71.

integrating Wales into the English state and normalising its government with other parts of the realm. This was done in the face of considerable opposition from those who preferred to deal with the Principality's apparently high levels of crime and disorder by developing the existing tradition of special law enforcement found in the Welsh Marches. Prudently, the 1536 Act, although giving Welsh JPs the same powers and duties as their English counterparts, did not include the £20 property requirement for magistrates that was found in England, allowing ambitious minor gentry to take up the office, and so enhancing its effectiveness.[41]

---

41. J. Gwynfor Jones, *Law, Order and Government in Caernarfonshire, 1558-1640*, Cardiff, University of Wales Press, 1996, p.30 and pp.34-35.

Chapter 8

Contemporary Attitudes to Crime and Justice

He that is robbed, not wanting what is stol'n,
Let him not know't, and he's not robbed at all.
William Shakespeare, Othello, in Othello, Act 3, Scene 3

Introduction

It has been suggested that the early modern period is the
first in English history in which crime comes to be seen as a
special 'problem', rather than an unavoidable aspect of
human nature. This has sometimes been attributed to the
economic dislocation of the period and the influence of
Calvinism.[1] However, many medievalists would challenge
any suggestion that crime was viewed with equanimity
prior to 1500. Crime was also seen as a major problem in
England in the decades immediately before the Reformation
(and thus the arrival of Calvinist ideas). Thus, at the very
outset of Henry VII's administration, in 1485, the lords,
knights and gentlemen of parliament were forced to swear
not to employ, "receive, aid, nor comfort" anyone accused
of felony. This was done with a view to preventing the
country's "enormous and unheard of crimes".[2] Similar levels

---

1. T.C. Curtis and F.M. Hale, "English Thinking About Crime, 1530-1620,"
    Crime and Criminal Justice in Europe and Canada, L.A. Knafla (Ed.), Canada,
    Wilfred Laurier University Press, 1981, p.124.
2. C. Williams (Ed.), *English Historical Documents 1485-1588*, vol.5, London,
    Eyre and Spottiswoode, 1967, pp.532-534.

of concern about the phenomenon were found in Catholic countries after the Reformation. It should, perhaps, be observed that in modern historiography the discovery of a 'novel' preoccupation with crime is not confined to the sixteenth century, the same arguments being made for, *inter alia*, the late eighteenth and early nineteenth centuries.

Nevertheless, the increasingly governed and centralised states of the early modern age, faced by rapid social change, did have an unprecedented concern about crime at an institutional level. The era was pre-occupied by the need for order, and a general fear that, without it, a terrible fate awaited the commonwealth. In the words of a homily of 1547, without order "no man shall sleepe in his owne house or bedde unkilled".[3] This was to become a constant theme in the ensuing century. Thus, almost 50 years later, Sir Edmund Spenser was convinced that if people were: "... not contayned in doutie with feare of lawe which restrayneth offences, and inflicteth sharpe punishment to misdoers, no man should enjoy anie thing, everie mans hand would be against another."[4] In the middle of the following century, Thomas Hobbes famously reiterated such fears, when considering a society in which all were forced to provide for their own security. In such a state there was no place for industry or agriculture, because enjoyment of their fruits were so uncertain, and there was a continual danger of

---

3.　Anon, "Homily on Obedience of 1547," in *Certaine Sermons or Homilies appointed to be read in Churches ...*, London, John Bill, 1623, p.69.

4.　E. Spenser, "A Veue of the Present State of Ireland," (1596), A.B. Grosart (Ed.), *The Complete Works in Verse and Prose of Edmund Spenser*, London, privately published 1884, vol.9, p.16.

violent death, so that life was "poor, nasty, brutish, and short".

However, views about crime were never uniform, even in the sixteenth century. Incongruously, juxtaposed with this fear of crime, and a particular horror at crimes of blood, was a very high tolerance for the risk posed by criminals, at least by modern standards. Crime was often seen as one of life's inevitable hazards. In 1738, the Frenchman Jean Bernard Le Blanc noted that some Englishmen were even proud of the bravery and supposed courtesy of their nation's highwaymen, esteeming them as much as if they had been the country's soldiers.[5] Such perverted national pride was certainly not a new phenomenon in the eighteenth century. Almost 300 years earlier, Sir John Fortescue, ridiculing the supposed lack of courage of French robbers when compared to their English counterparts, had noted admiringly that: "It hath ben offten tymes sene in Englande, that iii. or iiij. theves ffor pouerte haue sett apon vj or vij trewe men, and robbed hem all." By contrast, he felt that in France thieves were reluctant to rob honest men even when they outnumbered them two to one.[6]

Perceptions differed greatly with social and economic background. Even where there was agreement that certain conduct should be unlawful, the motivations behind proscription might differ. Thus, although bastardy offended

5.   J.B. Le Blanc, *Letters on the English and French Nations*, 2 vols., London, J. Brindley, 1738, vol.II, Letter no.79, written to M. De Buffons, Newmarket & Co., pp.291-3, 295-6..

6.   Sir J. Fortescue, *The Governance of England*, C. Plummer (Ed.), Oxford, Clarendon Press, 1885, pp.141-2.

the morals of many observers, it also damaged the finances of everyone who paid parish rates, whether offended or not. Similarly, although to some educated believers and Puritans witchcraft was seen as being primarily a demonic threat to the nation's spiritual health, or at least a personal physical danger, for many of the rural poor it was essentially an economic crime. It allowed a witch to pursue personal grievances by blighting crops, killing livestock, preventing butter and cheese from setting, etc.[7]

In so far as a 'dominant' contemporary explanation for deviance existed, it was that crime was primarily the product of innate human sin. Thus, from the reign of James I, the Bellman of St Sepulchre's Church warned Newgate inmates awaiting execution the following day that "your own wickedness has caused all this evil to fall upon you". Nevertheless, this was never an unqualified view. Contrary to some modern perceptions, most thoughtful people in the era had a shrewd idea that other factors were also responsible, and that crime was not purely a manifestation of human wickedness, but was also founded in the nation's socio-economic problems, and the rapid changes that were exacerbating them. As a result, many suspected that crime was not amenable to a *purely* penal solution. Writing in the late 1460s, even the robust Sir John Fortescue accepted that daily experience showed: "... how men that have lost thair godis and be ffallen into poverte, be comme anon robbers

---

7.   O. Davies, "Witchcraft: The Spell that didn't break," *History Today*, 1999, vol.49, issue 8, p.7.

and theves."[8] In 1516, Thomas More specifically listed the social changes that were engendering criminality, and demanded that steps be taken to re-establish agriculture, to regulate the manufacture of wool and to find work for the "companies of idle people whom want forces to be thieves". Without a remedy for these evils, it was pointless to boast about punishing crime severely. If the state allowed people to be ill-educated and corrupted from birth, it was the state that was actively creating thieves.[9] More was not alone. Less than 70 years later, Robert Hitchcock considered that anyone acquainted with the poverty to be found in the market towns of England and Wales could not be surprised by the nation's security problems. Such municipalities were usually inhabited by a "great store of poor householders" unable to bring up their children properly. Frequently, their parents failing them, such youths would drift into: "... dicing, cosening, picking or cutting of purses: or else, if he be of courage, plain robbing by the wayside, which they count an honest shift for the time, and so come they daily to the gallows." He advocated sending these poor young men to sea in the nation's fishing fleet so that they could earn an honest living and gain self respect instead of being: "... hated, whipped, almost starved, poor and naked, imprisoned, and in danger daily to be marked with a burning iron for a rogue, and to be hanged for a

8.   Fortescue, *The Governance of England*, p.140.
9.   Sir T. More, *Utopia*, Ware, Wordsworth Classics, 1997, pp.30-34.

vagabond."[10] Similarly, in the early 1600s, Robert Burton (1577-1640) an Oxford scholar and Anglican clergyman whose *Anatomy of Melancholy* provides an insight into the psychological ideas of the time, complained that: "A poor sheep-stealer is hanged for stealing of victuals, compelled peradventure by necessity of that intolerable cold, hunger, and thirst, to save himself from starving: but a great man in office may securely rob whole provinces."[11] Another century further on, in 1731, the Reverend Francis Hare was still declaring that: "The immediate general cause of most Villainies is certainly the extreme Misery and Poverty great numbers are reduced to."[12] Arguably, the muted magisterial reaction to many grain riots, which were often characterised by negotiation and conciliation, were an implicit recognition of the pressures of acute poverty.[13]

There *were* sporadic attempts by the authorities to deal with some of these root causes of crime. Not only were there occasional efforts at controlling enclosure, but, throughout the period, the courts and JPs made periodic attempts to enforce a 'moral economy' by controlling grain prices and

---

10. R. Hitchcock, "A Politic Plat for the Honour of the Prince," *Social England Illustrated, A Collection of XVIIth Century (sic) Tracts*, A. Lang and E. Arber (Eds.), London, Constable, English Garner Series, 1903 edition, 1580, pp.86-87.

11. R. Zaller, "The Debate on Capital Punishment during the English Revolution," *American Journal of Legal History*, 1987, vol.31, p.127.

12. Ekirch, A.R., *Bound for America: A Profile of British Convicts Transported to the Colonies, 1718-1775*, E.H. Monkkonen (Ed.), *Crime and Justice in American History, The Colonies and Early Republic*, London, Meckler, 1991, Part 1, vol.1, p.101.

13. Anon, *Grain riots and popular attitudes to the law: Malden and the crisis of 1629*, p.65 and p.83.

limiting forestalling and speculation in foodstuffs. Some new institutions were established. Amongst them were Christ's Hospital, the first 'bluecoat school' and a model for others that carried a similar title (after the scholars' distinctive uniform). It was established by Edward VI in 1552, in Newgate Street in the City, so that London's "poor fatherless children [might] be there brought up and nourished at the charges of the cittizens".[14] Inevitably, however, such efforts were limited, if only because the political nation was responsible for many of the era's radical social and economic changes and problems.

Nevertheless, in a pre-Marxian age, observers were also notably free of beliefs that made human beings automatons, entirely at the mercy of social forces outside their control. Most thought that mankind was vested with free will. Seventeenth century chap books stressed the many criminals who became highwaymen or footpads despite having had advantageous starts to life, such as the three gentlemen who committed a robbery and a murder on Bagshot heath, in 1608, even though they had "well reputed ancestors" and "dignity in birth".[15] Although many believed that environment had a role in creating crime, a considerable amount of legitimacy appears to have been ascribed to the criminal law by ordinary people. Much research suggests a large degree of consent amongst the governed to the rule of law; even riots often had 'defensive' and limited aims.

---

14. J. Stow, *A survey of London by John Stow, reprinted from the text of 1603*, vol.1, C.L. Tingsford (Intr.), Oxford, Clarendon, 1603, p.65.
15. B.L., *The Liues, Apprehension, Arraignment and Execution of Robert Throgmorton, William Porter, John Bishop ...*, London, H. Gosson, 1608, p.A3.

Although 'social' criminals might sometimes defy authority, they rarely threatened it.[16] Generally, there appears to have been a clear distinction in the popular mind between crime and justified social action. Crime was normally secretive, individual and for personal benefit; social action was overt and communal. This distinction was reflected in the care sometimes taken by those attempting to enforce the 'moral economy' to avoid crossing the line into perceived felony. Thus, in 1532, rioters in Norwich who set their own price on grain being sold at the market there, were careful not to take the proceeds of such sales, initially giving them to a local official and then, subsequently, returning the money to the owner of the confiscated wheat. One of them observed that if she had put it in her purse "it should have been stolen". Over half a century later, in 1596, Kentish rioters consulted an attorney's clerk in Canterbury about the legality of their plan to prevent the commercial movement of grain. They were told that they could do so, provided that they took no weapons to effect their design or removed any of the cereal, advice which they carefully followed.[17]

Nevertheless, the legitimacy ascribed to the country's legal system was neither unqualified nor universal. An analysis of Elizabethan sedition cases suggests that the common people did have a conception of a 'just' society that was somewhat different to their own, albeit that it was, usually, merely a fairer, more equitable mirror of the world

---

16. J. McMullan, "Crime, Law and Order in Early Modern England," *British Journal of Criminology*, 1987, vol.27, no.3, p.261.
17. Anon, *Grain riots and popular attitudes to the law: Malden and the crisis of 1629*, p.65 and p.83.

they inhabited, one in which existing institutions worked more effectively and the ruling orders lived up to the patriarchal ideals that they paid lip service to. Thus, commoners might attack the Queen, but not the very notion of monarchy, and complain about the distribution of wealth, but not the existence of hierarchy or degree.[18] There were alternative social visions available. The Sermon on the Mount, contained in their bibles and preached in church, provided a radical prescription for society and hard times could swiftly radicalise perceptions. The speed with which Gerald Winstanley's 'True Diggers' took root in the 1640s on St George's common is suggestive. Additionally, legitimacy was always attenuated for a few 'crimes' that lacked any popular support, such as poaching, illicit gin selling and, in coastal areas, smuggling. Despite their relatively unusual nature these have, understandably, been popular subjects for radical historians, though it is a mistake to imagine that popular attitudes to such offences were necessarily representative of wider attitudes towards crime and the criminal law (any more than the occasional jury acquittal of a politically motivated offence is today). The era also witnessed more specific and practical theories that both accounted for the spread of crime and its discovery. Some of these are worthy of separate consideration.

---

18. J. Samaha, "Gleanings from Local Criminal Court Records: sedition amongst the 'inarticulate' in Elizabethan England," *Journal of Social History*, 1975, vol.8, pp.76-77.

Criminal Progression and Corruption

The early modern period was wedded to the notion of progressively deteriorating criminal careers, with sin needing only a small opening to flood in. It was a short journey from idleness to becoming a heinous felon. As Lambarde noted, this was one of the main reasons for the era's acute fear of: "... idle vagabounds, which be the very seede of robbers and theeves."[19] Half a century earlier, in 1531, Sir Thomas Elyot was convinced that that those who: "... dailye do transgresse the lawes made againe games and apparaile, [were on] the streight pathes to robry and semblable mischiefe."[20] He thought that this applied to all social groups, and, in 1663, Colonel Turner attributed his own downward spiral into serious crime, despite a respectable upbringing, to having acquired a taste for cursing and blaspheming.[21] Thomas Savage, a feckless young apprentice who killed a fellow-servant with a hammer while stealing from his master, also blamed his descent into murder on early peccadilloes, committed while still a boy: "Breaking the Sabbath (by his own confession, he having never once heard a whole sermon during that time) was the first inlet to all his other vices, especially

---

19. W. Lambarde, *A Perambulation of Kent*, London, Baldwin, Cradock, Joy & Co., 1828 edn., p.19.
20. Sir T. Elyot, *The Boke named the Governour*, London, J.M. Dent & Co., 1962, at p.120.
21. Anon, *The Speech and Deportment of Colonel James Turner*, London, 1663, p.3.

whoredom, drunkenness and theft."[22] As a result, many shared Elyot's view that early intervention over small matters was vital. Others stressed that it was imperative that the incentives to minor misbehaviour and disorder be removed; for example, that: "All gaming at orange and gingerbread barrows should be abolished, as also all penny and halfpenny lotteries ... where idle fellows resort, to play with children and apprentices, and tempt them to steal their parents' or master's money."[23] Many contemporary observers also subscribed to notions of social contamination. Like bad apples, malign individuals could easily lead others astray. Thus, at his execution in London, in 1612, John Selman lamented that he had been the "only corruption of many ripe witted youth, and leader of them to confusion".[24] Over 90 years later, William Fuller was particularly alarmed at the manner in which those accused of minor matters were mixed indiscriminately with hardened thieves in the London Bridewell, fearing that: "... young Lads hearing how easily they live, are often drawn to sociate with them."[25]

Belief in Providence

Early modern Providentialism, a belief in the direct

---

22. J.L. Rayner and G.T. Crook (Eds.), *The Complete Newgate Calendar*, London, privately printed for the Navarre Society, 1926, vol.I, pp.202-203.
23. A. Moreton, (D. Defoe), *Every-Body's Business is No-Body's Business*, London, 1725, 2nd edition, p.33.
24. B.L., *The arraignment of John Selman ...*, London, W.H., 1612, p.16.
25. W. Fuller, *Mr William Fuller's Trip to Bridewell: With a True Account of his Barbarous Usage in the Pillory*, 1703, London, pp.10-14.

intervention of God in the working of the world to chastise and punish or (more rarely) to reward, is sometimes associated with the growth of Puritan piety. However, in reality, it cut across class and religious belief structures, its roots going far back into the middle-ages. It was 'mainstream' and ubiquitous amongst most social groups, both literate and illiterate, for much of the period. Although rooted in a medieval world picture, it survived the Reformation almost unscathed. Indeed, it has been asserted that Protestantism, far from 'demystifying' the universe, left it "saturated with supernatural forces and moral significance". Reports of divine portents and wonders were regular features in popular ballads, cheap printed pamphlets and prophetic sermons given by eminent divines. God's hand was frequently seen in bizarre or unexpected events and disasters. Providentialism survived strongly until the Civil War, enjoying a vigorous Indian summer during that internecine conflict and the ensuing Interregnum. Its slow decline only began after 1660, as "rational religion" very gradually pushed it towards the social margins.[26] Nevertheless, it was still vigorous in the late seventeenth century and remained significant until well into the eighteenth century. Thus, even in 1666, many thought that the Great Fire of London, although apparently caused by chance was, in reality, the: "... heavy hand of God upon us for our sins, shewing us the terrour of his

---

26. J.L. Nelson, Review of "Providence in Early Modern England" by A. Walsham, *History Today*, 2000, vol.50, issue 5, p.54.

judgement in thus raising the Fire."[27] As late as 1752, the very practical and effective Metropolitan magistrate Henry Fielding could claim in *Examples of the Interpretation of Providence in the Detection and Punishment of Murder* that the divine hand was behind what another observer called the: "... most unaccountable indeed miraculous means, by which the most secret and cunning murders have often been detected."[28]

Providence was particularly likely to expose unsolved or undiscovered murders. In 1597, James VI and I was typical in believing that: "... in a secret murther, if the deade carcase be at any time thereafter handled by the murtherer, it wil gush out of bloud, as if the blud wer crying to the heaven for revenge of the murtherer, God having appoynted that secret super-naturall signe, for tryall of that secrete unnaturall crime."[29] Similarly, in 1608, some thought that the husband killer Margaret Ferne-Seede was wildly foolish to imagine that: "... hidden abhominations can be concealed from the eie of the Almightie, or that hee seeing our bloodie and crying sinnes, will not either reveale them before his Ministers of publique Justice."[30] This remained a constant throughout the seventeenth century. In 1673, it was confidently noted of an undetected killer that the: "... Just and Blood-revenging providence of Heaven (that never

---

27. *The London Gazette*, September 3-10th, 1666, p.1.
28. Anon, *A True Relation of a Horrid Murder Committed upon the Person of Thomas Kidderminster of Topley*, London, H. Hills, 1688, p.4.
29. James VI of Scotland, *Daemonolgie*, Edinburgh, 1597, pp.80-81.
30. Anon, *The Arraignement and burning of Margaret Ferne-Seede*, London, H. Gusson, 1608, p.A3.

suffers Murthers to go unpunished) will in due time bring him to light."[31] Four years later, when the body of a gentleman was found dumped in the Strand, having been run through and then (apparently) removed from the house where the killing took place, a pamphleteer expressed a similar conviction that, although it was not then known who committed the crime, Providence would bring the malefactor to light: "... it being a ruled Case in the just records if Fate, That such horrid Crimes rarely escape punishment in this world."[32] However, although God would usually ensure that murder was discovered, He might wait a very long time before doing so. His motives for such delay varied; for example, it might be to allow the offender a chance to repent of his iniquitous life and actions.[33] Thus, in a case heard at the Hertford Assizes in 1606, a girl who had had her tongue entirely cut out by her young brother's killers, having survived on her own by begging for some years, found her way back to the murderers' home and was suddenly granted the power to speak and incriminate them.[34] The sincerity with which such views were held is hard to establish. Occasionally, especially towards the end of the period, they were probably little more than pious hopes, in an era that was well aware of its lack of detective ability.

How did Providence effect such discoveries? A selection

---

31. Anon, *The Bloody Lover*, London, P. Browesby, 1673, p.7.
32. Anon, *A True Relation of all the Bloody Murders that have been committed in and about the Citie and Suburbs of London*, London, D.M., 1677, p.6.
33. T. Cooper, *The Cry and Revenge of Blood*, London, N. Okes, 1620, p.25.
34. Anon, *The Horrible Murther of a Young Boy*, London, 1606, p.8.

of cases is illustrative. Dreams were a common method. Thus, at Cripplegate, in 1695, three men strangled a tavern keeper named Stockden, after drinking late into the night at his establishment, so that they could steal his plate and money. They then escaped. However, shortly after his death, Stockden appeared to a Mrs Greenwood, a former neighbour, in a dream, and showed her a house in Thames Street where one of the murderers was. When she visited the house she was told he had left. However, later, in her sleep, Stockden "appear'd again, describe'd him, and told her a Wire-drawer must take him". She found such a man who, with an associate, captured Maynard for a reward of 10 pounds. Once arrested, he was questioned, swiftly admitted the crime and implicated three others. Stockden's shade was not finished, subsequently identifying the hiding places around London of his other killers (one was being held at the Marshalsea prison for coining). All but one of them, a man who had been against the killing and who had saved the bar maid from death, who was allowed to turn evidence for the Crown and had not been mentioned in Stockden's nocturnal appearances, were executed. After this, Stockden appeared once more and said: "Elizabeth, I thank thee, the god of Heaven reward thee, for what thou hast done. After which she repos'd at quiet."[35] Sometimes, rather than an appearance in a dream, there would be a ghostly intervention. In Lincolnshire, in the 1670s, a wastrel was moved to murder his scholarly sibling after the latter received half of their father's inheritance. He arranged for

---

35. *The Gentleman's Magazine*, 1731, vol.1, pp.394-395.

three men to ambush his brother while the latter was on his way to Cambridge to study theology, paying the killers £10 each for the service, and then shed "crocodils tears" at the student's funeral. However, the dead youth's ghost subsequently appeared to reveal the details and motives of his killers.[36] Of course, such 'divine' interventions might well have provided useful vehicles for expressing already harboured suspicions without revealing sources or bringing suspicion on the informant's own head. This may explain the case of a woman in Tottenham, just north of London, who dreamt that she heard a knock on her door, and a female voice crying out: "Mistress, Mistress, here's some one putting a child down the privy." A search subsequently revealed a new-born baby concealed in the nearby privy.

As King James' work suggests, one of the most dramatic illustrations of providential intervention was 'cruenation', in which changes in the corpse of a murder victim, especially the fresh issue of blood, occurred when the body was touched by, or in close proximity to, the killer. This belief was widespread, especially before 1660. Thus, a JP investigating the discovery of several bodies in a pond in the early 1600s, lamented that the passage of time meant they had been skeletonised, because: "Had these Parties bene newly slaine, their blood is usually a meenes to peach their murther."[37] At a less exalted level, in 1635, the notorious murderer Thomas Sherwood surreptitiously viewed the corpse of one of his victims, where it had been

---

36. Anon, *Strange and wonderful news from Lincolnshire,* London, 1679, pp.1-4.
37. Cooper, *The Cry and Revenge of Blood,* p.42.

displayed in a London Inn. On doing so: "Sherwood's Nose immediately gushed out with such issues of blood, that he feared thereby to be discovered."[38] Belief in the test lingered long after the Restoration. Thus, in 1684, Elizabeth Ridgway's murder by poisoning of her husband, Thomas, an Ibstock tailor, only came to light when, two weeks after Thomas's burial, one of his two former apprentices suspected that Elizabeth was also trying to poison them, and voiced his fears to his father, who then informed Sir Wolston Dixie, a local JP. Dixie ordered the body of Thomas Ridgway to be exhumed and viewed. The dead man's father made Elizabeth touch it, at which the corpse allegedly began to bleed. The coroner was sent for and Elizabeth was committed to Leicester jail.[39] Of course, sometimes, the fear engendered amongst guilty believers subjected to the test was itself a valuable indicator of their culpability. In the mid-sixteenth century, Sir George Vernon, a Derbyshire JP, investigating the death of a wandering pedlar whose body had been discovered, evidently murdered, ordered that everyone present should approach and touch it, declaring at the same time their innocence of the killing. The prime suspect, who had retained his composure until this point, shrank from the ordeal, refused to touch the body, and ran from the hall where it was displayed, hotly pursued.[40] Nevertheless, if properly conducted, the test was

38. H. Goodcole, *Heavens Speedie Hue and cry sent after Lust and Murther*, London, N. and I. Oakes, 1635, f.C3.
39. B. Capp, "Serial killers in 17th century England," *History Today*, 1996, vol.46, issue 3, pp.21-31.
40. W. Andrews, *Bygone Punishments*, London, W. Andrews & Co., 1899, p.5.

scientifically unlikely to produce a positive result via any other mechanism. Thus, in 1658, after being committed to Newgate on suspicion of murder by an examining JP, Major Strangeways, escorted by a guard, was taken to where his supposed victim's body lay. There, in front of the coroner's jury he was: "... commanded to take his dead brother-in-law by the hand, and to touch his wounds, a way of discovery which the defendents of Sympathy highly applaud." However, it was fruitless, there being 'nothing discoverable by this experiment'.[41]

Remorse

Closely linked to Providentialism was an enormous faith in the power of a guilty conscience to torment wrongdoers, few people being seen as completely beyond redemption. Thus, the Reverend John Sym believed that a man who had committed a capital crime, such as murder, so secretly that no one knew or would accuse him of the offence, would often be so troubled in conscience about it that he would have "no rest nor comfort; but in revenge upon himself, is strongly tempted to destroy himself". Similarly, and perhaps less plausibly, Michael Dalton thought that even perjurers could ultimately expect to be tormented by their consciences: "... for a Conscience is a witnesse accusing them, a Judge judging and condemning them."[42] Sometimes,

---

41. Anon, *The unhappy marksman*, London, T.N., 1659, pp.13-14.
42. M. Dalton, *The Country Justice*, London, Company of Stationers, 1655, p.370.

remorse might prompt felons to expose themselves long after successfully committing a crime. Thus, Thomas Wynne, a habitual Elizabethan criminal, ended his offending career by breaking into the house of a London linen draper. Not content with robbing its occupants, he also cut their throats as they were sleeping in bed to prevent discovery. This done, he took two thousand five hundred pounds from the house, and escaped to Virginia with his wife and children, where he flourished. In the meantime, a local beggar was arrested and prosecuted to conviction and execution on the most tenuous circumstantial evidence. Subsequently, Wynne, having been abroad for 20 years, returned to visit England, where "Providence pursued him". While visiting Cheapside, to buy plate his "conscience flew in his face" and he admitted the murders, being arrested, tried, convicted and executed: "Thus the just judgment of God at last overtook him for shedding innocent blood, when he thought himself secure from the stroke of justice." Indeed, Divine judgment was also visited on his wife and children for being privy to the crime and living on its fruits. His wife was driven mad by the news of his execution, and two of his sons were hanged in Virginia for a robbery and murder they had committed there. As a convicted felon, Wynne's plantations were also seized by the Crown, so that his 'posterity' were "reduced to beggary ever after".[43] Similarly, in 1642, a young widow with a baby found that its continual crying at night made her life very

---

43. C. Johnson, *A General History of the Lives and Adventures of the Most Famous Highwaymen, Murderers, Street-Robbers*, London: J. Janeway, 1734, p.135.

uncomfortable. As an attractive and still young woman, she also appreciated that her chances of remarriage would be hindered by the infant's presence. Eventually, she smothered the baby under a tub so that no marks were left on its body, and suspicion avoided. However, 33 years later, remarried and a mother again, having fallen sick, she "could not rest" until she had publicly revealed her crime. As a result, she was committed to Newgate, where she declared that "she cannot nor shall not dye [from illness] till she be hanged".[44] In 1747, a sailor, drinking in a public house at Gosport, also felt compelled to incriminate himself in a murder and robbery he had committed with other sailors two-and-a-half years earlier in the same area. Since then, he had been devoid of any "peace of mind, and could not be easy till he had made this discovery".[45] Providence might take active steps to encourage guilt. Richard Gough recalled a man in seventeenth century Myddle who murdered an infant nephew who, he feared, threatened his own inheritance. Having drowned the small boy in a bucket he fled, pursued by two villagers. He was found near London after the men saw a pair of ravens making a 'hideouse and unusuall noyse' by a haystack in which the fugitive was sleeping. This man, "tormented with the horror of a guilty conscience", immediately confessed to the crime and said that the ravens had followed him from Myddle (over 100 miles away). He was hanged and gibbeted.[46] However,

---

44. Anon, *Murther will out*, London, 1675, pp.1-4.
45. *The Gentleman's Magazine*, 1747, vol.17, p.101.
46. R. Gough, *The History of Myddle, 1701*, D. Hey (Ed.), Harmondsworth, Penguin, 1981, p.122.

although such cases were well publicised, and influenced by the role of the Church, there was undoubtedly a considerable degree of optimism about the generality of remorse.

Criminal Jurisprudence

In modern jurisprudence, criminal liability is normally formed by 'multiplying' harm by blame. The more of each factor present, the greater the liability. Early modern criminal jurisprudence placed a much greater emphasis on harm and a smaller one on blame than is the case now. This meant that some matters were criminalised that would today be considered more properly the ambit of civil actions. Even more importantly, the development of inchoate offences (attempt etc.) was rudimentary. The one glaring exception to this general situation was High Treason, where it was enough to intend or imagine the death of the King, even "though they bring it not to effect". However, here the substantive offence was itself merely to 'compasse' the death of the monarch.[47] By contrast, in felony, attempt, conspiracy and incitement were relatively little developed for much of the period. Indeed, their very existence was sometimes disputed. Ecclesiastical courts were in advance of the common law in this respect. Inchoate offences first appear to have been addressed properly in a secular forum by the Court of Star Chamber, falling into

---

47.   Dalton, *The Country Justice*, 1655, p.283.

desuetude with that court's abolition in 1640. They then slowly made the 'jump' to the common law courts in the early Restoration period. Thus, attempt was reconsidered in *Bacon's Case* in 1664. Bacon had been indicted at the Court of King's Bench for offering another party 100 pounds to kill Sir Harbottle Grimstone, the Master of the Rolls. Despite his protestations that his behaviour was not indictable, because "our law does not punish mere intent", he was fined 1,000 marks, imprisoned for three months and made to find sureties for good behaviour for life. Nevertheless, as late as the case of *Rex v. Cowper*, in 1696, the concept of attempt, as expressed by the court, was still confused.[48]

Attitudes to the Common Law

England's criminal justice system was unique. To a much greater extent than in the more abstract Roman legal systems of the Continent, exposure to the court room was desirable for those who wished to familiarise themselves with English law "for our Law is Practice".[49] Englishmen were wedded to their own legal system, especially after it became linked to the political debates of the early seventeenth century, the parliamentary opposition to the Stuarts, and a popular belief in an "ancient constitution" supposedly threatened by subversion. Even Mary Carleton would not take issue with the

---

48. F.B. Sayre, "Criminal Attempts," *Harvard Law Review*, 1928, vol.41, no.7, pp.821-859.
49. G. Herbert, *A Priest to the Temple*, London, T. Maxey for T. Garthwait, 1652, p.35.

unusual aspects of the country's criminal justice system: "I will not quarrel the English Laws, which I question not are calculated and well accommodated to the genius and temper of the people."[50] Despite Spelman's seventeenth century attempt to encourage a more critical analysis of England's legal development, students of English law and history frequently ascribed immemorial origins to the common law and considered its development in a completely unhistorical manner. In particular, it was often granted an antiquity that it did not entirely deserve. Thus, according to Michael Dalton, it was the system by which England was governed "many hundred years before the Conquest".[51] William Dugdale was prepared to go even further back, believing that the common law was: "... no less antient than the beginning of differences betwixt man and man, after the first peopling of this land, it being no other than pure and tryed Reason."[52] It was not entirely a coincidence that William Lambarde was an influential Anglo-Saxon scholar. Sometimes, the nostalgia for an idyllic pre-Conquest past extended further than many of its supporters might have anticipated. Gerald Winstanley, the radical Digger leader and Interregnum political philosopher, developed the myth of the "Norman yoke" to explain the introduction of the judges, justices, bailiffs and "restraining laws" which had supposedly subjugated the

---

50. Anon, *The Case of Madam Mary Carleton*, London, Sam Speed, 1663, p.128.
51. Dalton, *The Country Justice*, 1661, p.1.
52. W. Dugdale, *Origines Juridicales*, London, F. And T. Warren, 1666, p.3.

English ever since.[53] In reality, before c.1600, English law had been less insulated from Continental developments than some imagined.

---

53.   M. Rogers, "Gerald Winstanley on Crime and Punishment," *Sixteenth Century Journal*, 1996, vol.XXVII 3, pp.739-740.

PART TWO: JUSTICE

Chapter 9

A Self-Policing Society?

For in infamy, all are executioners and the Law gives a
malefactour to all to be defamed ... and Charity to the
publick hath the precedence of private charity. So that it
is so far from being a fault to discover such offenders,
that it is a duty rather, which may do much good, and
save much harme.

George Herbert, A Priest to the Temple, 1652, p.42

Introduction

Throughout the early modern period the law enforcement
ambitions of the English State outstripped its ability to effect
them at a local level. This was primarily due to a shortage of
resources. Unlike the large nation states of continental
Europe, England lacked the professional judges, bureaucrats
and law officers who might have gone some way towards
turning intention into reality, and even France and Spain
experienced a major dichotomy between ambition and
performance. England, and London in particular, did not
share many early modern continental policing
developments. As a result, by the latter part of the period,
there were significant law enforcement differences between
England and some other major European states, which had

gradually supplemented their historic communal arrangements. Thus, England did not witness the development of paramilitary organisations comparable to the *Marechaussee*, which was formed in 1544 (though some would place its origins in the medieval era), originally as a military police to control royal soldiers, but gradually extended its jurisdiction to civilians in rural France, and the *Santa Hermandad*, which operated in Castile. This latter, uniformed, body was the revival by Ferdinand and Isabella of a medieval brotherhood, placed under the central direction of a Crown-appointed bishop. It was charged with maintaining order and fighting crime, and was funded by a substantial annual levy imposed on the nobility. In Seville, the *Santa Hermandad* had its own court and prison as well as officers.[1] In Italy, the primarily detective *Sbirri* operated in some parts. Similarly, England did not share the urban policing reforms witnessed in a few continental cities. It had no equivalent to the *Lieutenant General de Police de Paris*, an office established by Louis XIV in 1667. This individual acquired responsibility for the supervision of street-lighting and cleaning, traffic, fire-fighting, public spectacles, markets, and, most importantly, the maintenance of law and order and the pursuit of offenders.[2]

However, the impact of these new European forces should not be exaggerated. France and Spain were ahead of most other continental countries in such developments, and

---

1. M.E. Perry, *Crime and Society in Early Modern Seville*, Hanover (NH), University of New England Press, 1980, pp.56-59.
2. C. Emsley, "The Origins of the modern Police," *History Today*, 1999, vol.49, issue 4, pp.8-14.

even in these two nations, the new 'professional' forces were limited. For example, in remote parts of the French Massif Central the power of the official forces of order have been described as 'puny' when compared to the social discipline imposed by a popular willingness to punish lapses from an accepted behavioural code with private retribution. Given that in the Haute Auvergne between 1587 and 1664 the 'vice-bailli' usually only had command of 15 'archers' to police a rugged area of 6,000 km² and between 150,000 and 200,000 people, this is not surprising. Generally, in France, the Crown's law enforcement forces became relatively ineffective at significant distances from the major towns.[3] Even in the eighteenth century, France's *Marechaussee* still had only 3,882 men, based in 600 stations, in what was Western Europe's largest and most populous country.[4] Its work was further limited by endemic problems with low pay, morale and discipline. In its metropolis, on the eve of the French Revolution, the *Lieutenant de Paris* still only commanded a body of 3,000 men to police a city of 500,000, and only half of his men were engaged on public patrolling.[5] Similarly, the *Santa Hermandad*, though quite substantial in size, was not rated very highly for ability by many Spaniards, and was absent from Aragon, Catalonia and the

3. M. Greenshieds, *An economy of Violence in Early Modern France: Criminal Justice in the Haute Auvergne, 1597-1664*, Pennsylvania, *Pennsylvania State University Press*, pp.49 and 232.
4. B. Lenman and G. Parker, "The State, the Community and the Criminal Law in Early Modern Europe," *Crime and the Law: The Social History of Crime in Western Europe since 1500*, V.A.C. Gatrell *et al* (Eds.), London, Europa, 1980, p.19.
5. Emsley, "The origins of the modern police," pp.8-14.

Basque provinces.[6]

Nevertheless, by 1725 the differences between England and France, supposedly Europe's best policed nation, were significant enough for visitors from that country, such as Cesar de Saussure, to be struck by how: "London does not possess any [military style] watchmen, either on foot or on horseback as in Paris, to prevent murder and robbery; the only watchmen you see is a man in every street carrying a stick and lantern."[7] Similarly, in the 1730s, the lack of professional highway policing in England, so much at variance to French practice, shocked Jean Bernard Le Blanc, who felt that the bad management of English roads was notorious amongst continentals, putting them on a par with those of Persia and Turkey. He also noted that this did not seem to occasion much concern amongst Englishmen, who preferred to joke about the want of security on their highways rather than admit it was a "scandalous thing, in a government otherwise so well regulated, that a man cannot travel in safety".[8] England remained largely dependent on its traditional localised forms of urban and rural security until the end of the period.

Compounding these problems, England was slow in acquiring a permanent standing army, as opposed to one

---

6. J.R. Ruff, *Violence in Early Modern Europe 1500-1800*, Cambridge, CUP, 2001, pp.88-89.
7. M. Van Muyden (Trans. and Ed.), *A foreign view of England in the reigns of George I and George II; the letters of Monsieur Cesar de Saussure to his family*, London, John Murray, 1902, p.68.
8. J.B. Le Blanc, *Letters on the English and French Nations*, London, J. Brindley, 1747, letter 79 to M. De Buffons, vol.II, pp.291-3, 295-6.

raised for specific contingencies, something that would wait until the Civil War and Restoration. In this respect, it lagged behind the great European powers. Before the 1640s, once the resources of the civil power were exhausted, the only military forces that could be summoned were usually the part-time militia and trained bands. These were often poorly trained, equipped and recruited. By contrast, their new military forces gave the continental crowns significantly enhanced powers in the face of serious disorder. This was widely appreciated, even at the time. Thus, in 1675, when the apprentices of Sheffield rioted against new measures for grain pricing, a notice summoning them to action declared: "For wee will not have it told for shame, if we will be daunted with 3 or 4 rusty halbards & ye constable and his cain."[9] Even when local part-time military forces were summoned they might initially be ineffective against determined opposition. Significantly, once a standing army was introduced, a major proportion of its time, at least a fifth by the eighteenth century, was spent on some form of policing duty.

Adding to their difficulties, throughout the early modern period, law enforcement agencies struggled with the problems posed by greatly increased mobility in an era that still possessed very limited bureaucratic capacity and, in particular, that was largely devoid of effective means to record and identify criminals. Thus, Sir Thomas Smith noted in the 1560s that it was: "... very usual for thieves to change

---

9. J.A. Sharpe, *Crime in Early Modern England, 1550-1750*, 2nd edn, London, Longman, 1999, p.193.

them [their names], because falling oftentimes into the Hands of Justice, and so often convicted of some crimes, yet thereby it appears sometimes, that when they are arraign'd at the Bar again, that is the first Time that they have been taken, and the first Crime whereof they have ever been accused."[10] In the light of this, proposals for making crime more difficult to commit in the first place were made with increasing frequency from the late sixteenth century. Some of these had a distinctly authoritarian flavour. Thus, Sir William Petty proposed that there be compulsory documentation of purchases and sales with appropriate receipts issued, that houses never be built so that they would stand alone, but rather be in clusters of at least 10, that the roads be guarded, with cattle being sold only in designated fairs and markets, and only certain ports and ships being allowed to carry people out of the kingdom. Additionally, he suggested the introduction of identity cards: "That every man have and carry about him an uncunterfitable Tickett, expressing his name, the numero of his Howse, his age, trade, stature, Haire, eye, and other peculiar marks of his Body."[11] Nevertheless, such suggestions were rarely followed. As a result, a plethora of orders from the Privy Council and royal proclamations might be issued, but they would frequently disappear into the sands of provincial inactivism. There would be little

---

10. Sir T. Smith, *De Republica Anglorum*, (1st written 1565) London, Henri Midleton for Gregorie Seton, 1583, p.163.

11. Sir W. Petty, *The Petty Papers: Some Unpublished Writings of Sir William Petty*, Marquis of Landsdowne (Ed.), *Bowood Papers*, New York, Augustus M. Kelley Publishers, 1967, vol.2, p.212.

overt defiance, simply a widespread willingness to ignore them or inability to enforce them.

The Statute of Winchester

In 1285, the Statute of Winchester laid down the basic structure of English policing for centuries to come. It reaffirmed and refined existing notions of communal and collective responsibility for law enforcement, imposing liability on the hundreds for robberies committed within them unless the offenders were caught, providing for night watchmen in cities and boroughs, and obligating all adult males under 60 to participate in the pursuit of a fugitive. It remained (substantially) in force until the nineteenth century. The 'traditional' historical analysis is that the system of constables and watchmen established in 1285 had begun to show signs of strain as early as the sixteenth century, and, by the eighteenth century, was "more or less a shambles". According to this view, the system's basic problem was that older, medieval, notions of universal, unpaid service worked poorly in an increasingly mercantile society.[12] Although exaggerated, such a portrayal contains a considerable element of truth. However, it should be noted that these traditional policing institutions were not unique to England, being of a type widely found in Europe. Thus, Monsieur Misson noted that: "What they call watch in

---

12. D.A. Slansky, "The Private Police", *UCLA Law Review*, 1999, vol.46, pp.1196-7.

England, is a Guet, that goes several Rounds in its District all night long, to prevent or remedy Disorders. This is practis'd, in all Countries, and well-governed Cities."[13] Where England differed from some other countries was in having little to supplement them at a higher level.

Constables

A pair of high constables acted as the supervisory police authority for each hundred (the administrative district between county and parish). They frequently also had responsibility for maintaining the urban watch and organising the removal of vagrants. Additionally, high constables investigated complaints made to JPs about inferior officers, passed on directives issued at quarter sessions by magistrates and assisted with the service of writs. Most high constables served for more than one year in the post. It was a position that might attract prosperous yeomen "next to the degree of Gentlemen". They were normally appointed by JPs sitting at quarter sessions.[14] However, all ordinary policing was conducted by petty constables, the lowest ranking officers in the system. According to Sir Thomas Smith, in the 1560s, "everie litle village hath commonly two Constables", though in smaller parishes the second man may have an understudy,

---

13. M. Misson, *M. Misson's Memoirs and Observations in his Travels over England*, J. Ozell (Trans.), London, 1719, p.358.
14. Sir F. Bacon, *Cases of Treason*, London, John More, 1641, p.25.

empowered to act when the primary officer was indisposed or absent. Constables were general purpose local officials, whose duties included, *inter alia*, apprehending criminals and preserving the peace.

The ancient, Anglo-Saxon, system of near total communality of law enforcement had been based on mutual responsibility and security. It was effected by groups of tithingmen entering into mutual obligations for each other's good conduct and for presenting felons in a system termed 'frankpledge'. Enforcement, or prosecution, was instituted by the presentment of the 12 senior thanes in every hundred whose duty was to accuse those guilty of committing crimes.[15] This ancient system lingered in nostalgia. Even in 1570, Lambarde regretted its passing while noting that "some shadow" of it still survived in the process of frankpledge in "those courts which we call Leetes".[16]

However, deficiencies in this system meant that it had gradually been supplemented, and eventually largely replaced, by part-time village officers with a special responsibility for law enforcement. These were termed, according to location, borsholders, tithingmen and headboroughs. In turn, these officers developed into the constables of the fourteenth century, though sometimes without changing their historic names, so that Smith could note that: "These Constables are called in some places

15. G.J. Edwards, *The Grand Jury*, Philadelphia: George T. Bisel Company, 1906, pp.3-4.
16. W. Lambarde, *A Perambulation of Kent*, 1828 edn., London, Baldwin, Cradick Joy & Co. (first published 1570), p.23.

headborowes, in some places tithingmen."[17] They were still part-time, local, temporary and untrained, but with the added facet of being officers of the Crown, charged with keeping the King's peace. Despite the continuing divergence of titles, the: "... duty is the same, though they have distinct names, according to the custom of the place."[18] Constables were most commonly elected to their unpaid office for a year or, more rarely, two years, by the jurors of the: "... Court Leate, unto which the Constable is a proper attendant and minister, for the Constables are chosen by the Jury, there they are sworn."[19] According to Sir Thomas Smith, in the 1560s, rural constables might be re-elected several times so that they sometimes kept the office for up to four years.

There was little uniformity in national practice. Sometimes, especially later in the period, the leet jury would merely confirm the nomination of the local parish vestry. Elsewhere, where leet courts were absent, constables might be chosen directly by the vestry or *ad hoc* village meetings. Nevertheless, appointment was still primarily local, and as late as 1612 the King's Bench decided that JPs had "no power nor authority" to elect or remove constables. This position prevailed, in theory, until 1662, when a Parliamentary Act authorised magistrates to fill vacancies if a leet had not been held or if a man had died in office or left the village suddenly. Informally, however, it would appear that by the 1630s, if not earlier, JPs had become increasingly

17. Sir T. Smith, *De Republica Anglorum* (1st written 1565), London, Henri Midleton for Gregorie Seton, 1583, p.109.
18. H. Twyford, *The Office of the Clerk of Assize*, London, 1676, p.111.
19. Bacon, *Cases of Treason*, p.23.

interventionist in the appointment process, making inroads into the rights of local bodies to select constables.[20] Thus, at the sessions held at Hertford on 10th July 1643, it was noted that: "No court Leete having been held at Standon for the space of one year, it is ordered that Sir John Watts shall [summon] before him the following inhabitants of Standon to be sworn constables ..." The same Hertfordshire quarter sessions, sitting later that year, ordered that the choice of one Mr Botler as a parish constable, made earlier at a court leet held at Wormely, be set aside. Their rejection of this man was blatant in its overruling of local accountability, his appointment being: "... contrary to the mynds of Thomas Touke Esquire, Lord of the Manor and of Edward Atkins, serjeant-at-law his steward, being two of the Justices of this County, it is now ordered that the said Thomas Touke shall make choice of some other in habitant of Wormley to be constable instead of the said Mr Butcher."[21] The Law of Settlement of 1662, allowed special constables to be sworn in for a specific occasion, to defend against "riot or felony".

A long literary tradition has portrayed the early modern parish constable as grossly ineffectual. However, it is now recognised that ludicrous fictional characters, such as Shakespeare's 'Elbow', were not necessarily typical of all such officers.[22] Research since the 1970s has produced a

20. J.R. Kent, "The English Village Constable, 1580-1642: The Nature and Dilemmas of the Office," *Journal of British Studies*, 1981, vol.20(2), pp.26-49 and pp.34-35.
21. W. Hardy, *Calendar to the Sessions Books and Sessions Minute Books, 1619 to 1657*, vol.5, Hertford, 1905, p.323.
22. Kent, "The English Village Constable, 1580-1642," p.26.

substantial revision of the traditional image of unbridled incompetence. Nevertheless, men such as Dogberry and Verges, and incidents such as their absurd exchange with the Watchmen, did have some foundation in reality, which is why they were selected for satire.[23] What is difficult is to assess how accurate such portraits were for most village constables for most of the time.

All contemporary observers agreed that great care was needed in the selection of parish officers, whether churchwardens or constables. In particular, it was vital to select the "most pious, well-affected, discreet, publicke-spirited, able and active men, and to make their election alwayes of those men". In theory, constables were men of modest but not absent means, with a personal reputation for integrity: "As for persons qualified for this office, they ought to be honest, understanding, and able Men; to be Men of Substance, and not the meaner Sort."[24] Similarly, it was desirable that urban petty constables should not be inferior people but rather drawn from the "better sort of residents".[25] Michael Dalton was convinced that social, educational and economic limitations meant that men of lowly station were inappropriate, if only because they were: "... either ignorant what to do; or dare not do as they should; and are not able to spare the time to execute this office."

Nevertheless, research has exposed a frequent divergence between the 'ideal' constable and the practical

---

23. W. Shakespeare, *Much Ado About Nothing*, Act 3, Scene 3.
24. W. Sheppard, *The Whole Office of the County Justice of Peace*, 3rd edn, London, W. Lee, 1656, pp.1 and 9.
25. Bacon, *Cases of Treason*, p.25.

reality. Although the Privy Council in London, and JPs at a local level, repeatedly issued edicts demanding that 'honest and substantial' men be recruited, these were often ignored.[26] Thus, in the 1560s, it was noted that frequently: "... men of small favor and abilitie be chosen unto that office, who have no great experience, nor knowledge, nor authoritie."[27] Almost 80 years later, according to William Sheppard, one of the principal reasons for a lack of order in English society was the general "unfitnesse of the men chosen to the offices". In particular, he felt that they were often ignorant, cowardly, afraid to upset their neighbours, and too busy, lazy, negligent or simply incompetent to enforce the law. Such men "wanted will or skill" rather than being "able and fit" individuals.[28] Their lack of enthusiasm is unsurprising. Few shared Bacon's confidence that constables did not greatly mind their unsalaried status because of the temporary nature of the office: "They have no allowance, but are bound by dutie to perform their Offices gratis, which may the rather be endured, because it is but annuall."[29] Many were reluctant to take on the unpaid and sometimes onerous duty, even for a year. Some hired substitutes (especially in the richer London parishes after 1660), others simply refused to serve and risked being

---

26. K. Wrightson, "Two Concepts of Order: Justices, Constables and Jurymen in Seventeenth-Century England," J. Brewer and J. Styles (Eds.), *An ungovernable people*, London, Hutchinson, 1980, p.26.
27. Sir T. Smith, *De Republica Anglorum* (1st written 1565), London, Henri Midleton for Gregorie Seton, 1583, p.109.
28. Sheppard, *The Whole Office*, pp.8-9 of the Preface.
29. Bacon, *Cases of Treason*, p.25.

prosecuted and fined at the quarter sessions for doing so. Thus, in the early 1600s (the precise date is not recorded), John Colffer of Briston in Norfolk showed contempt for his manorial leet court when it appointed him constable for the year. Despite being chosen by the 12 lecters, in the presence of over 30 tenants (to whom he set an "evill example"), Colffer not only left the court "disdainefully without licence, but utterlye refused to beare that office". The Lord and Steward of the manor sought the JP Nathaniel Bacon's assistance, asking him to: "... compell by your superior power the said Colffer to take uppon him the said office and to be sworn thereunto."[30] As a result of such resistance amongst the better social elements to taking the office, constables were "many times" drawn from what Sir Thomas Smith termed the 'fourth sort' of men, those who traditionally had little say in the commonwealth, made up of day labourers, poor husbandmen and landless craftsmen, although such men were not originally intended for the office.[31] This may also explain why, in the same decade, Thomas Harman had hoped that his book would spur constables to greater efforts when dealing with rogues, so that: "... settinge asyde all feare, slouth, and pytie, [they] may be more circumspect."[32] Similarly, according to William Sheppard, a wide circulation amongst the lower orders for his hand-book of 1641 on the duties of parish officers was necessary given how commonly: "... necessity so requiring

30. Sir N. Bacon, *The official papers of Sir Nathaniel Bacon*, p.50.
31. Sir T. Smith, *De Republica Anglorum*, pp.76-77.
32. T. Harman, *A Caveat or Warning for Common Cursitors vulgarly called Vagabones*, London, W. Gryffith, 1567, p.Aiii.

the most of you are called and enjoined to take upon you the offices of constables, churchwardens, and the like offices, that there is scarce a man amongst you (at least of the meaner rank) but sooner or later he is forced to serve in some or all of them."[33] There are numerous recorded cases of poorer villagers being encouraged or coerced into taking the position, or in which it was given to individuals of low reputation or intelligence. Such mistaken appointments could reach bizarre lengths. In 1608, Nathaniel Bacon was petitioned by the inhabitants of Wells to replace their constable, Robert Jarye, who, despite an existing reputation for misbehaviour, had been appointed by them: "... thinking thereby to have somewhat restrained him from his former unrulynes in gaming and using the ale-houses." They appeared genuinely surprised by the failure of this policy: "But nowe perceyving that nothing at all it avayleth but that rather it doth incourage him to bolster out both his owne loose behavioure and also the ill deneanour of others." They proposed a 'reputable' man to Bacon as his replacement.[34]

Nevertheless, though clearly a frequent occurrence, cases of inferior men being appointed were not typical for most of the country for most of the period. Thus, in Pattingham, Staffordshire, 63 of the 81 men who held the office between 1583 and 1642 were at least middling-sized farmers, and some had large holdings. Nine of the remainder were craftsmen or tradesmen. Many of these men

---

33. N.L. Mathews, *William Sheppard, Cromwell's Law Reformer*, Cambridge, CUP, 1984, p.73.
34. Bacon, *The official papers of Sir Nathaniel Bacon*, London, Royal History Society, Campden Third Series, vol.26, pp.41-42.

also filled the slightly more prestigious office of churchwarden (49 of them at least), sat regularly on the leet jury and were from the group of men who put their names and marks to important decisions of their vestry.[35] In larger towns and cities, especially London, the situation was probably not so healthy. Long before the end of the period many men elected to the office in the Metropolis were providing paid substitutes in lieu of personal service, or paying the appropriate fine, from which other paid officers could be recruited. Thus, London increasingly witnessed the advent of 'professional', i.e. salaried, men who made a living wholly or partly from being constables, even if the phrase is not entirely appropriate to their abilities.

Conflicting Pressures on Constables

Early modern constables were in an inherently awkward position. Originally, the constable had merely been a senior, locally appointed, village leader, of a type widely found in Western Europe, a 'first among equals' when it came to law enforcement.[36] The expansion of royal government and regulation, which subordinated it to higher, external, authorities, such as the JPs and sheriff, occasioned a conflict of loyalties. Although they retained the historic functions attendant upon being community representatives, such as

---

35. Kent, "The English Village Constable, 1580-1642," p.29.
36. W. Lambarde, *The Duties of Constables, Borsholders, Tithing men ...*, London, 1583, p.4.

calling upon villagers to participate in the hue and cry and assist in making arrests, they also acquired numerous government duties, which were still being added to in the early seventeenth century. These included novel, and unpopular, tasks like the collection of taxes, the enforcement of economic and social legislation, the maintenance of armour and shooting butts for use by the parish militia and the selection by ballot of militiamen. The gradual addition of a royal flavour to the office was reflected in the changes to the form and venue of the constables' (ever more lengthy) oath. It became increasingly common for them to be sworn in, not at the leet court, but before the local JPs, the Crown's representatives.[37]

Legally, the early modern constable owed his primary duty to the state. As a result, by the 1560s, they seemed to be "as it were the executors of the commaundement of the Justices of Peace".[38] This was regularly reiterated by magistrates such as Lambarde, who stressed that it was not for constables to question whether the orders of those set over them were "grounded upon sufficent auctoritie, or no". A constable would be excused if he enforced an illegal warrant of arrest at the behest of a JP, although the magistrate himself would have to answer for it.[39] However, their new, enhanced, responsibilities could pose acute difficulties, as the office's transformation was only partial. Unlike the centrally appointed JPs, constables were still

---

37. Kent, "The English Village Constable, 1580-1642," pp.26-32.
38. Sir T. Smith, *De Republica Anglorum*, London, 1583, p.109.
39. Lambarde, *The Duties of Constables*, pp.19-20.

selected by their own communities, at least until the late seventeenth century. They lived in those communities and were ordinary men sympathetic to the values of their neighbours. They possessed few powers that other parishioners did not enjoy (albeit under a greater obligation to exercise them), despite being agents of the state.[40] The conflict between local and central responsibilities, at a parish level, meant that national directives were often examined against their accordance with parochial custom and sentiment. This sometimes engendered acute stress, as constables sought to reconcile the demands of government with those of their fellow villagers. At times, these tensions could border on crisis. Thus, in the 1630s, demands that constables enforce the hated Ship Money, amongst other taxes, produced an increased popular reluctance to hold the office and a greater use of hired substitutes to avoid conducting it in person. Many constables were hesitant to enforce Ship Money, some even being incarcerated for their lassitude. The situation was only ameliorated because prudent sheriffs often appear to have appreciated that if they were too strict in disciplining such men they would lose a vital element of local government and bring many other functions (such as mustering the militia) to a virtual standstill.[41] Similarly, it has been argued that the main reason that the Caroline Book of Orders of 1631 was not fully implemented was due not to the justices' lack of

---

40. M. Goldie, "The Hilton gang: terrorising dissent in 1680s," *History Today*, 1997, vol.47, issue 10, p.26.
41. Kent, "The English Village Constable, 1580-1642," pp.44-46.

enthusiasm, but because they, in turn, had to rely on the parish officers of their divisions for its enforcement. Constables, normally small farmers and artisans, usually lacked both the time and inclination to transform their villages into the 'model' parishes proposed, choosing instead to do as little as reasonably possible. This dependence by central government on the goodwill of parochial officers undermined most Caroline attempts at reform.[42] Fifty years later, the reluctance of many Metropolitan constables to act on the warrants issued against dissenters' meetings, at the behest of the Hilton Brothers' gang of informers, was also partly based on concern for parish harmony. Typically, constable Halkins, a basketmaker in Newgate street, was unwilling to disturb his otherwise peaceable neighbours simply because of their religious beliefs.[43] Constables who violated community norms might not merely face social disapproval or ostracism. Thus, on several occasions, mobs succeeded in rescuing individuals arrested for illegally selling gin under the 1736 Gin Act. The officers involved might be beaten in the process. Two men convicted in Southwark were "upon their crying out Informers, rescued out of the Hands of the Constable, who with his Assistants narrowly escap'd the rough Discipline of the Rabble".[44]

---

42. H. Langeluddecke, "Patchy and Spasmodic?: The Response of Justices of the Peace to Charles I's Book of Orders," *English Historical Review*, 1998, vol.113, no.454, p.1231.
43. Goldie, "The Hilton gang," pp.26-29.
44. J. Warner, "Damn you, you informing bitch. Vox Populi and the unmaking of the Gin Act of 1736," *Journal of Social History*, 1999, vol.33, no.2, p.299.

A variety of ingenious expedients were employed by men eager to reconcile the performance of their office's duties with social obligations to their communities. Thus, a constable in West Derby, charged with serving warrants on several of his neighbours, dutifully attempted to do so having first advertised the fact, in the hope they would avoid him. Others might allow those placed in the stocks to escape, for example, by deliberately leaving them unattended while searching for a lock to 'secure' the apparatus.[45] Similarly, constables might be reluctant to enforce their strict legal rights, such as entry to premises pursuant to a warrant. Thus, in February 1645, Dorothy New was bound over to appear at the Maidstone quarter sessions for: "... denieinge the Borsholder to cum in and search upon a warrant for stollen goods."[46] Conversely, constables might participate in technically illegal, but popular, forms of social control. In one case, in early seventeenth century Burton-on-Trent, a constable even led some 40 of his neighbours in inflicting traditional summary justice on a local couple who were believed to be living immorally and cohabiting outside marriage. They broke into the house where the pair were staying, dragged them into the streets and paraded them to cries of "a whore and a knave", accompanied by the ringing of cow bells and the beating of pans and a drum. Significantly, the couple's complaint was dismissed by the local magistrates, forcing

---

45. Wrightson, "Two concepts of order," p.31.
46. H. Howle, "Henry Howle's Notebook," F. Hull (Ed.), *Kent Records - New Series*, vol.1, parts 1-3, Kent, Kent Archaeology Society, 1990, p.60.

them to repeat it to the Star Chamber.[47] To encourage them to stand up to local social pressure and the attractions of indolence, constables could be fined a huge array of sums if they failed to carry out their duties properly, even if these were extremely unpopular. Thus, any who failed to use their "best endeavours" to arrest vagabonds found wandering in their parishes, but instead allowed them to escape were to "forfaite vi.s. viii.d. for every such Rogue".[48] In 1571, an MP, fearful of the laxity of enforcement in such cases, even suggested that imprisonment should be added "to the pain of the constable for their remiss dealings".[49] More seriously, allowing serious criminals to escape might (theoretically) make a constable a party to their crimes: "... if the arrest were for Felonie, then by a willing escape, the officer himself becommeth a Felon also." In the case of laxity over lesser offences, such as misdemeanours, he could be fined to the value of all his goods.[50] There were many other, more specific, fiscal penalties for laxity. Thus, they could be fined 40 shillings under an Elizabethan statute if they failed to require that unemployed artificers and labourers help prevent the "losse of Corne, or Graine, or Hay in the time of Harvest". Constables could insist that such men take work by the day, at rates appropriate to their 'skill and quality'. Any who refused such labour could be imprisoned in the village

---

47. Kent, "The English Village Constable, 1580-1642," p.38.
48. Lambarde, *The Duties of Constables*, p.13.
49. Sir S. D'Ewes, *A Compleat Journal of the Votes, Speeches and Debates*, Londo, 1613, p.71.
50. Lambarde, *The Duties of Constables*, pp.22-23.

stocks for two days and a night.[51] However, enforcing such a provision might not be popular with those poorer villagers who preferred not to work in August. There could be more subtle pressures on constables. Thus, in London, in the 1680s, those who were dissenters might face dismissal, or have their lives made so unpleasant as to provoke resignations. In that decade the Hilton brothers, a pair of former criminals, stage-managed a regime of intimidation against Whig constables by securing warrants forcing them to do their legal duty. When they demurred, they publicly named them in the *Courant* and threatened to prosecute them for dereliction of duty. Sometimes they even printed their addresses, a veiled invitation to Tory thugs to pay them a visit.[52]

In theory, constables had no judicial role, merely being concerned with: "... repressing of all manner of disturbance and hurt of the people, and that as well by way of prevention as punishment, but yet so, as they have no judiciall power, to heare and determine any cause, but onely ministeriall power."[53] Nevertheless, quasi-judicial duties were sometimes placed on them. Thus, by the Elizabethan period, the constables of Havering in Essex had been given the task of deciding which of the many new arrivals in their community (strategically located close to London) should be whipped as vagabonds and sent out of the town. During three years around 1630 the Hornchurch constables

---

51. N. Collym, *A Briefe Summary of the Lawes and Statutes of England*, London, R. Constable, 1650, p.31.
52. Goldie, "The Hilton gang," pp.26-29.
53. Bacon, *Cases of Treason*, p.22.

whipped and returned to their parishes 28 men, nine women and four children. The Romford parish register for 1630 somewhat ambiguously records the burial of a "vagrant that died in the constable's hand as he was going".[54]

Corruption, Excess and Lack of Zeal

On a more positive note, local social pressures probably also meant that the number of constables seriously abusing their position and powers, to advance their own interests or those of their friends and families, was limited. Nevertheless, the office afforded considerable scope for small-scale corruption. Although unpaid, officers were frequently 'tipped' small sums for carrying out their duties. However, this could easily lead to improper pressure being placed on parties to 'pay' for a constable's services, something that was an offence, although probably quite a regular occurrence. Thus, in 1639, at the Trinity sessions in Worcester, the constable of Claynes was indicted for: "... extortion in taking 4d. to execute a warrant, the bill was fownd for his refusall to execute before 4d. paid him, although it was pleaded it was the common practise of the cowntry. But yf one will voluntarily give him 4d. it is a gratuity and no extorcion."[55] Control of licensing regulations also furnished significant

---

54. M.K. McIntosh, *A community transformed: The Manor and Liberty of Havering, 1500-1620,* Cambridge, CUP, 1991, p.319.
55. H. Townshend, *Notes of the Office of a Justice of Peace, 1661-3,* R.D. Hunt (Ed.), Worcester, Worcestershire Historical Society, 1967, p.91.

opportunities for abuse. In the early 1600s, it appears that local constables allowed nine ale-houses to operate in Cromer, Norfolk, on several of which they personally held the freeholds. This was far more than was necessary for the town or than were actually licensed. It was done so that the constables could increase the rent from the one pound per annum that would attach to such properties for normal occupation, to the three to four pounds that they attracted as ale-houses.[56] Bribes were also sometimes proffered, even in serious cases. Thus, in 1677, a murderer offered £10 to the constable who arrested him, albeit without success.[57]

Constables were untrained, acquiring such expertise as they possessed from observation of their predecessors or the use of an instructional manual. The resulting ignorance of the duties attendant on the office produced two problems. Occasionally, they would act "too confidently", exceeding their legal authority, for example by arresting without warrants (something that could lead to them being punished).[58] Watchmen and constables could become tyrannical, especially in the comparative anonymity of London. Thus, in December 1731, several constables were tried before Lord Chief Justice Raymond for assaulting one Charles Grey the previous year. Late at night, Grey had gone to the room of a woman that he had met in the street. Shortly afterwards, the constables arrived, seized him by the collar, then stripped, "beat and wounded" him. They

---

56.   Bacon, *The Official Papers of Sir Nathaniel Bacon*, pp.52-53.
57.   Anon, *Horrid News from St Martins, London*, 1677, p.7.
58.   Mathews, *William Sheppard*, p.73.

refused to carry him before the 'Constable of the Night' (responsible for supervising them) but eventually marched him to Wood Street Compter, where he was held overnight and his wounds dressed by a surgeon.[59] More frequently, however, constables' ignorance of their office led them to underestimate their powers, and proceed "too fearfully" in discharging their duties, sometimes ignoring some of them altogether.[60] This was undoubtedly also linked to an appreciation of the inherent risks of their office.

Dangers of the Office

Constables were faced by two main dangers when executing their duties. In all parts of the country, and especially in London, officers who exceeded their powers might find themselves being subject to litigation. As a result, in 1742, various expedients to prevent Metropolitan constables being excessively circumspect included providing that all actions brought against them for acts committed in the "faithful Discharge of their Duty" be defended by the Treasury Solicitor at the Crown's expense.[61] However, even more conducive to excessive caution was a fear of the non-legal consequences of strict law enforcement. Their work brought considerable risks of physical violence. In Essex, between 1620 and 1680, the quarter sessions heard 83 cases in which

59. *The Gentleman's Magazine*, 1731, vol.1, p.539.
60. Mathews, *William Sheppard*, p.73.
61. *The Gentleman's Magazine*, 1742, vol.12, p.657.

constables and watchmen had been assaulted, most in the execution of their duties. This was 14 per cent of the total number of assault cases listed. Thus, when Thomas Danckes, a Colchester watchman, reprimanded a man for swearing in public, and pointed out that it carried a penalty of one shilling a time, the foul mouthed individual "badd a turde in his teethe" and attacked him.[62] The risks and intimidation attendant on the office in London could be even greater. In 1744, a gang of robbers operating in Westminster became so audacious and: "... insolent, that they go to the Houses of Peace Officers, make them beg Pardon for endeavouring to do their Duty, and promise not to molest them." Several constables had to seek shelter in the security of the Bridewell prison, and one was severely wounded in the street.[63] Making an arrest was especially hazardous. Typically, in a case from Worcestershire, in 1661, an apparently intoxicated man was held for making scandalous speeches about the diocesan bishop. The local constable was summoned to pacify him: "... but seeing no persuasions could prevayle, the constable was taking him to the stockes, and their he fell upon the constable and strooke him in the face, and tore his band."[64]

Effectiveness

Nevertheless, despite their awkward social position and the

---

62. J.A. Sharpe, *Crime in seventeenth-century England*, Cambridge, CUP, 1983, p.122.
63. *The Gentleman's Magazine*, 1744, vol.14, p.505.
64. Townshend, *Notes of the Office of a Justice of Peace*, p.127.

dangers of their office, many constables *were* highly effective in preserving order and detaining felons, as even George Fox, the Quaker leader, could attest. After Fox preached, uninvited, in a church at Bootle, Cumberland, in 1653, the enraged congregation attacked him and: "... struck and beat me in the steeplehouse yard; one gave me a very great blow over my wrist ... so that the people thought he had broken my hand to pieces."However, the local constable was a "sober man" and rescued him. He was also very desirous of putting some of Fox's assailants in the stocks. Later, after he had finished preaching, the same constable escorted Fox out of the village, and subsequently addressed the mob and "charged them to keep the peace, and so made them quiet again".[65]

Churchwardens

Churchwardens were another (albeit ecclesiastical) cog in the extensive part-time, unpaid, system of social control that characterised early modern England. They held a moderately prestigious office, ranking far below the magistracy, but usually a little above that of constable. As such, it was normally filled by the yeomanry and (more rarely) the very lowest of the minor gentry, rather than mere husbandmen.[66] Nevertheless, George Herbert feared that

---

65. G. Fox, *The Journal of George Fox*, London, Religious Society of Friends, 1975, at pp.148-149.
66. K. Wrightson, *English Society 1580-1680*, London, Routledge, 1995, p.36.

even this office was occasionally "debased, by being cast on the lower ranke of people". The two positions, constable and churchwarden, were not hermetically sealed. The same men frequently held both offices at different periods in their lives. Additionally, the churchwarden's office did not, in Herbert's words, draw its "dignity from the Ecclesiastical Laws only"; it had a recognised legal status at common law, being the creation of statute. Perhaps in part because of this, the churchwardens often played a significant role in the administration of secular criminal justice, serving, effectively, as auxiliary constables in presenting certain cases to the JPs. (As well as being responsible for enforcing ecclesiastical regulations and levying penalties for "negligence in resorting to church, or for disorderly carriage in time of divine service".)[67] There were other connections between the secular and ecclesiastical institutions. Thus, in 1680, a number of men from Wansted and Layton in suburban Essex were brought before the JP William Holcroft for "tiplinge at the bowlin green" during divine service one Sunday. After they "confessed the fact", each was ordered to pay 3s 4d. into the local churchwarden's hands.[68] George Herbert stressed that clergymen had a duty to ensure that fit and proper men were appointed to the office and to stress what a great responsibility they had, given that the "whole order and discipline of the Parish is put into their hands". Those selected needed to study their special obligations, a

---

67. Herbert, *A Priest to the Temple*, p.30.
68. W. Holcroft, *His Booke Local Office-holding in Late Essex*, J.A. Sharpe (Ed.), Chelmsford, Essex Record Office, 1986, p.69.

good parson advising them to regularly read or hear the visitation articles and Church canons.

However, like the constables, the churchwardens' loyalties were divided between their office and their communities. The Root and Branch Petition of 1640 bitterly complained about the imposition of oaths about parish conduct upon churchwardens and sidesmen: "... which they cannot take without perjury, unless they fall at jars continually with their ministers and neighbours, and wholly neglect their own calling."[69] Unsurprisingly, for some, discretion was the better part of valour. Thus, at Beeford, Yorkshire, in 1743, the visitor's only complaint was that the local churchwardens failed to present delinquents as they were supposed to do. This was not due to a rational balancing of the potential harm to community relations that such presentments might occasion, but rather because of cowardice, their "forbearance proceeds from fear than principle". The reasons for this pusillanimity were readily understandable. One warden complained that the: "... last man that was presented immediately sought an opportunity of revenge upon the Churchwarden and were I to do it myself, nothing would be safe about me."[70] As well as fearing the repercussions of reporting their ordinary neighbours, churchwardens might, like constables, be intimidated by men of superior social status. Thus, George

---

69. H. Gee and W.J. Hardy (Eds.), "The Root and Branch Petition (1640)," *Documents Illustrative of English Church History*, New York, Macmillan, 1896, p.544.
70. P. Hair (Ed.), *Before the Bawdy Court ...*, London, Elek Books Ltd, 1972, p.158.

Herbert was moved to urge that members of the gentry or nobility be presented if they regularly arrived late at church. It set a bad example to the poor when the churchwardens took no action because "affrighted with their greatness".[71]

The Watch

The watch patrolled the streets of urban communities and environments at night. The obligation to perform Watch and Ward was limited to a town's residents, who could be compelled to serve on a rotational basis. Ideally, it was a duty for the better class of citizen "men of discretion, able bodies, and sufficently armed". Such men were supposed to take turns in fulfilling the duty, being selected "according to the custome and use of the place". Any qualified man who refused to take his turn could be referred to the assizes, quarter sessions, or a JP. Indeed, some held that a constable could commit such an individual to the stocks. Duty was normally from sunset to sunrise. Supervision of the Watch was in the hands of a constable who "*ex officio* is to order it".[72] The need for the employment of a Watch depended on the size of the community and the criminal threat it faced. Thus, in 1603, the Southampton leet court suggested that there: "... should be nightlie winter and sumer two honest watchmen appointed to watche uppon the keyes of the Towne for that we knowe and daylie see experience of

---

71. Herbert, *A Priest to the Temple*, p.6.
72. Sheppard, *The Whole Office*, pp.41-42.

manie pickeries [petty thefts] & other misdemeanours committed in shipps, barcks & boats in the harbor & uppon the keyes which by reason of this watche no doubt will be remedied."[73] It appears to have been well established that although Watchmen might be armed with staves, pikes and halberds they could not carry firearms.[74] When a Watchman first went on duty, he would often use his stick to check that shop and house doors had not been left open, alerting their owners to lapses in security.[75] When patrolling they would investigate generally suspicious circumstances. Thus, in 1678, two men were indicted for stealing lead from the roof of Stepney Church after a local constable, who: "... was with his Watch going the round, saw a Ladder standing on the side of the Church, and enquiring of the Clerk and the Sexton whether it were there by their Order, found it was not; and therefore taking away the Ladder, got up another way to the top of the Leads." Beside a wall, they also found three parcels of lead rolled up, which had been thrown down from the roof. On the roof they found two men whom they arrested (the suspects claimed to be investigating a suspicious noise).[76] Some Watchmen, especially in London, also called out the hour after hearing the church bells chime, and shouted out the state of the weather.

---

73. F.J.C. Hearnshaw, *Court Leet Records, vol.1, Part III, 1603-1624*, Southampton, Southampton Record Society Publications, 1907, p.375.
74. *The Gentleman's Magazine*, 1737, vol.7, p.806.
75. Muyden, *A Foreign View of England*, p.68.
76. Anon, *An exact account of the trials of the several persons*, London, Gilham Hills, 1678, p.18.

However, despite the desirability of employing men of some ability in the office, concerns about the quality of the Watch were a regular feature of the period, exceeding even those over constables. This situation was aggravated by the frequent use of substitutes, paid in lieu of personal service by those who were chosen for the duty. These deficiencies were alluded to in a satirical pamphlet from 1610: "... here one [a Watchman] lies drunk when he should stand sentinel, there another lying alone asleep upon a bench complayning how his back aches, with carrying the Tankard and burthens in the daytime."[77] Similarly, in 1604, there were complaints from the Southampton leet court that their local Watch was "disorderly sett". The court was also concerned about the poor quality of its officers: "Comon Watchmen being very olde poore weake and unhale persons." Even then, such grievances were longstanding, the leet noting that they had "oftentimes presented the same and finde no redresse". They were not to be spared this depressing task. The following year they complained again that: "The Watch is still very weak and impotent and no amendment has been made."[78] Corruption amongst Watchmen was a particular problem. Mary Frith, facing an arrest early on in her criminal career, noted that the "Watch were very unwilling (for I had alwaies some of them retained to my service) to carry [detain] me". Unfortunately, their duty constable overruled them.[79] At the end of the period, in 1751,

---

77. S. Rid, *Martin Mark-All, Beadle of Bridewell*, London, John Budge, 1610, p.B1.
78. Hearnshaw, Court Leet Records, p.414.
79. Anon, *The Life and Death of Mrs Mary Frith*, London, W.G. Ilberton, 1662, p.48.

numerous observers were still complaining that the Watch were "mostly old, lazy, and inactive, are too late before they are set upon Duty, leave it too early, and not a few of them are suspected to be in league with, or intimidated by the Rogues that infest our Streets". It was argued that they needed greater regulation, more able-bodied members, increased numbers and a more effective command structure by improved constables.[80] However, despite such criticisms, not everyone had negative views of the Watch. According to the Venetian, Horatio Busino, visiting England in 1617, the London Watch was so well organised that: "... one can really go about by night unarmed and purse in hand."[81]

Pursuit and Arrest

In most cases where an arrest was effected felons were apprehended in the immediate aftermath of their crimes, often by their victims, sometimes by the 'hue and cry' or the village constable acting on his own. Thus, Thomas Austin's uncle, after witnessing the aftermath of the mass murderer's killing spree in Devon in 1694, reacted automatically: "What he saw, however, was enough to point out the offender, whom he immediately laid hold of, and carried him before

80. A Citizen in London (1751), *The Vices of the Cities of London and Westminster trac'd from their original*, Dublin, G. Faulkner, pp.30-31.
81. P. Razzell (Ed.), *The journals of two travellers in Elizabethan and early Stuart England*, London, Caliban, 1995, p.148.

a magistrate, who sent him to Exeter Jail."[82] As Sir Thomas Smith noted, communality of enforcement meant that "everie English man is a sergiant to take the theefe".[83] An exception to this general pattern of swift post-crime arrest were the significant number of thieves apprehended when trying to dispose of stolen goods; this was usually a dangerous point in their ventures, unless they used a reliable fence. Thus, in 1678, John Baltee was caught when trying to dispose of a stolen tankard to one Elizabeth Web. Web testified that when she asked to whom it belonged, he claimed it was owned by a gentleman who had sent him to pawn or sell it, at which:

"She looking upon the Tankard, saw the Name of the Owner, and the Sign where he lived, engraven upon it, to whom she sent immediately to know whether he had given the Prisoner Order to Sell it or Pawn it: and kept the Prisoner till he came, which when he did, he owned the Tankard, but denied the Prisoner had it with his Consent, and so they carried him before the Justice."[84]

In theory, constables had a duty, *ex officio*, to arrest known felons and then to carry them before a JP for examination.[85]

---

82. Johnson, *A General History of the Lives and Adventures of the Most Famous Highwaymen*, p.348.
83. Sir T. Smith, *De Republica Anglorum*, 1583, p.107.
84. Anon, *An exact account of the trials of the several persons ...*, London, Gilham Hills, 1678, pp.5-6.
85. J. Giles, *The Compleat Parish Officer*, 7th edition of 1734, Salisbury, Wiltshire Family History Association, 1996, p.18.

They could break down doors to arrest a man who had made an affray then hidden in a house to escape. If a suspect fled and was followed and taken in "fresh suite", the constable could even arrest him in another county.[86] As today, ordinary people were also empowered to carry out 'citizens' arrests', though the law (10 Ed.4. c.6) provided that private individuals who arrested suspected felons should then promptly "deliver the offender to a constable".[87] Generally, bystanders appear to have been much more willing than in the modern era to become actively involved in detaining suspects. Arguably, the dominance of professional policing agencies in modern societies has encouraged passivity on the part of the public, and a reluctance to 'get involved' where the responsibility can be left to others.

Hue and Cry

The main early modern mechanism for the pursuit of fleeing felons, over distance and an extended period of time was the hue and cry, which "signifieth a pursuit of one or more that have committed felony".[88] William Harrison provided an account of its workings in the 1590s. It was normally raised by the victim or witness of a serious crime, such as theft, robbery or murder, who alerted a constable in the first

---

86. W. Lambarde, *The Duties of Constables*, p.16.
87. Giles, *The Compleat Parish Officer*, 7th edn, p.11.
88. Dalton, *The Country Justice*, London, Company of Stationers, 1661, p.83.

village that he came to, or was in when the crime occurred. The constable was then obliged to: "... raise the parish about him, and to search woods, groves, and all suspected houses and places, where the trespasser may be, or is supposed to lurk." If he failed to find the fugitive, he was to alert the constables of neighbouring parishes: "... and so one constable, after search made, to advertise another from parish to parish, till they come to the same where the offendor is harboured and found."[89] Little had changed in the following century, Michael Dalton describing it in almost identical terms and noting that it might be raised not just by the victim but also by someone from the "company of one murdered or robbed". All observers stressed that it was vital that the hue and cry be raised promptly and, if necessary, be passed between counties. To enhance its speed, it was desirable that horsemen as well as those on foot be employed.[90] If felons were caught in neighbouring counties to those in which they had committed their crimes, it was necessary for them to be produced before local JPs and, initially, detained in the jail of the county where they had been apprehended, before being returned to the crime scene.[91] All men between the ages of 15 and 60, from the town or villages near where the hue and cry was raised, were supposed to participate. This was clearly a major operation, and every 'false alarm' merely encouraged negligence in future cases. Not surprisingly, Dalton felt that

---

89. Canon W. Harrison, *Description of England,* Book 2, 2nd edition, 1587, London, New Shakespeare Society, 1877, p.247.
90. Dalton, *The Country Justice,* 1661, p.83.
91. Anon, *The Compleat Constable,* 2nd edn., London, 1700, p.28.

a JP should bind over anyone who raised a hue and cry without proper cause. There was nothing unique about such inter-parish liaison and co-operation. After the 1490s, some coroners ensured that abjurors reached their embarkation ports by ordering that they be passed from one parish constable to the next en route.[92] Subsequently, vagrants were passed back to their home village via parish constables.

Sometimes, the hue and cry worked very efficiently, especially if it was organised by a magistrate rather than a constable. It was particularly effective over short distances. Thus, Thomas Savage, escaping from London, where he had killed a maid at Ratcliff Cross and stolen over 60 pounds, took lodgings in Greenwich on his way to Gravesend. Next morning, however, the landlady, noticing that he had a large quantity of money in an unsealed bag "began to examine him about it, doubting he came not by it honestly". To avoid suspicion, he was forced to claim that he was carrying it for his master and agreed to leave it in her hands while he provided proof of its provenance. Continuing on his way, he had reached Woolwich shipyard when the hue and cry reached Greenwich, telling of the murder and theft that he had committed. Hearing this, his erstwhile landlady concluded that it must be the same youth who had lodged with her, and she: "... immediately dispatched several men in search of him, who found him asleep in an ale-house, with his head upon a table and a pot of beer by him." When

---

92. K. Kesselring, "Abjuration and its Demise: The changing face of Royal justice in the Tudor Period," *Canadian Journal of History*, 1999, vol.34, no.3, p.352.

confronted, Savage confessed the crime, was carried back to Ratcliff, taken before a JP and committed to Newgate prison.[93] Occasionally, given time, the hue and cry could operate efficiently over much greater distances, albeit such pursuits were usually 'cold'. There were cases of criminals being apprehended over a 100 miles away after several months had passed. Thus, in 1653, a suspected murderer who had fled from the Isle of Ely was detained five months later in Nottinghamshire, the warrant raised by an Ely JP having passed through numerous constables to the suspect's birth place (where he had returned to live).[94] In areas of high population, such as the countryside around London, the system could also produce dramatic numbers of pursuers. Thus, according to some estimates, in 1674 there were "about two hundred men" involved in the capture of a group of highwaymen on Hampstead Heath.[95]

However, frequently, the operation of the hue and cry was unsatisfactory. In theory, a failure to participate, or allowing a fugitive who had already been arrested by the hue and cry to escape, would render the parish officers concerned liable to punishment. Despite this, the theory and the practice often parted company. In Harrison's own experience, felons held in the stocks after capture had been allowed to escape or to be rescued by their fellows "for want of watch and guard". Worse still, thieves had been allowed

---

93. Johnson, *A General History of the Lives and Adventures of the Most Famous Highwaymen*, p.136.
94. M. Gaskill, *Crime and Mentalities in Early Modern England*, Cambridge, CUP, 2000, p.249.
95. Anon, *The Confession of the Four High-Way-Men*, London, 1674, pp3.-4.

to go because the "covetous and greedy parishioners would neither take the pains nor be at the charge to carry them to prison". Sometimes, even constables, asked to their faces to make hue and cry, had refused to participate and merely replied: "God restore your loss! I have other business at this time."[96] Harrison's fears were shared by his contemporary Edward Hext, a magistrate who felt that some arrested felons were: "... delivered to simple constables that sometimes wilfully, other times negligently, suffer them to escape."[97]

A surviving aspect of the medieval communal responsibility and liability for local crime and law enforcement, one designed to encourage diligence, was that if the hue and cry failed to catch a robber, having been summoned by his victim, the hundred in which the crime occurred was liable to make reparation to the victim.[98] In some circumstances, under an Elizabethan statute, liability might be extended to neighbouring hundreds as well. It was for this reason that Samuel Butler, in the 1660s, could note that when a highwayman "dispatches his business between sun and sun he invades a whole county". The system survived throughout the period. Thus, in 1599, Christopher Taylor successfully sued the inhabitants (i.e. the Corporation) of Kingston hundred, under the Statute of Winchester (13 Ed.1), at the Surrey assizes, because they had

96. Harrison, *Description of England*, p.247.
97. E. Hext, "Letter written by Edward Hext, a Somerset JP, to Lord Burghley on September 25, 1596," *Tudor Economic Documents*, vol.2, R.H. Tawney and E. Power (Eds.), London, Longmans, 1951, p.340.
98. Edwards, *The Grand Jury*, pp.3-4.

failed to catch the men who had earlier robbed him in Kingston or to make good his loss within 40 days of his raising the hue and cry. Taylor, the native of a neighbouring Surrey borough, appears to have been awarded £12 by the presiding judge.[99] Similarly, 68 years later, when Thomas Watts, a tax collector, was robbed of a large amount of money while bringing it from Frimley to Guildford he petitioned for proceedings to be stayed against him until the money could be recovered from the relevant hundreds. This was supported by a certificate issued by four magistrates to the effect that Watts had reported the matter promptly to George Woodruff, JP, and been examined on oath about the circumstances of the crime.[100] Even in the 1720s, according to Cesar de Saussure, when one of his friends was robbed of 200 guineas on the highway, during daytime, and reported the crime to the appropriate authorities before the sun went down that same day, he: "... had no difficulty in recovering the amount from the sheriff of the county of Hertfordshire."[101]

However, in reality, the process of recovery was normally much harder than the Swiss traveller believed or the theory suggested. Litigation could drag on for years and the authorities often evinced suspicion about claims. This was widely appreciated. William Davis, a highwayman who had had the process unwittingly explained to him by a Bristol JP, Sir Thomas Day, whom he subsequently robbed,

---

99. Kingston Local History Room, Doc. KB 16/4/1-4.
100. Surrey History Centre, Copy of petition re. tax collectors robbery 1667, Reference No. Zs 104.
101. Muyden, *A Foreign View of England*, p.129.

returned Day's lecture as a way of taunting the magistrate. Day had assured Davis that if the latter was the victim of highway robbery during the day the "county, upon your suing it, would have been obliged to have made your loss good again". When Davis later robbed him of 60 pounds he mocked that what the magistrate had parted with was not lost "because he was robbed betwixt sun and sun, therefore the county, as he told him, must pay it again".[102]

Nevertheless, both Sir Thomas and Butler were correct in noting that there were several important technical prerequisites for a successful claim. According to an Elizabethan clerk of the Court of Common Pleas, at Westminster, a considerable body of case law developed on when, exactly, a hundred would be liable for failing to organise an effective hue and cry after a crime had been committed. Much of this was established by the senior judges of that court, after jurors returned 'special verdicts' finding certain facts proved and asking for directions on the appropriate law. Thus, it did not matter that any money lost had only been in the robbed individual's hands in his capacity as agent for its true owner. Nor did it matter that the parish that was given as the scene of the robbery was incorrect, provided that the specified hundred was accurate. Because it was a collective responsibility that pursuit be made by the "Hundreders", residents of the hundred itself could not seek compensation if robbed in their own areas,

---

102. A. Smith, *A compleat history of the lives and robberies of the most notorious highwaymen, ... for above an hundred years past,* London, Briscoe, 1719, vol.1, pp.4-5.

unlike strangers passing through. There was also a considerable dispute as to whether it was reasonable to expect the hue and cry to be arranged after sunset, the crime having been committed shortly beforehand. Some argued that as towns traditionally had to close their gates at that hour, it was not practicable to arrange a pursuit. Lord Chief Justice Anderson, however, was more moved by the fact that evening was a prime time for armed robbery, and a conviction that if the hundreds were doing their jobs properly such highwaymen would not be lurking on the roads in the first place: "... it seemeth clearly that the Inhabitants ought to guard the Country in such sort, as men may safely travel without robbing." Nevertheless, cases where robbery indisputably occurred during the night were not covered by this extension. Thus, a man who had been robbed at 3 a.m. at Dunmow in Essex was not able to recover compensation: "... because the Robbery was done in the nights, and not in the day, therefore the Hundred shall not be charged."[103] In 1628, John Clavell warned that people who had been robbed while travelling on the Sabbath were also unlikely to receive compensation, as judges would rarely require the county to make restitution in such cases. Additionally, Clavell noted that highwaymen's victims frequently not only exaggerated the numbers of their assailants and the resistance which they had shown, but also the extent of their losses, with a view to making an excessive

---

103. W.S., *Reports of that Learned and Judicious Clerk, J. Goldsborough Esq.*, London, 1653, pp.24, 55, 60 and 70.

claim against the county.[104]

Detection by Accomplices

With the exception of investigations instigated following information provided by 'turned' felons, it was comparatively rare for criminals to be taken by post-crime detection organised by the authorities. Getting captured felons to inform and then give evidence on behalf of the Crown became an increasingly important stratagem during the era, and probably explains the brutal behaviour of a group of five burglars whose colleague was wounded by a servant during a break in at East Wittering, in 1582. Although they helped their injured associate to escape to Fishbourne, the gravity of his wound meant that he would hinder their escape and, presumably, risk exposing them when he was found. The rest of his gang beat him to death with their cudgels.[105] However, such accomplice information and evidence was fraught with dangers, as suspects of no probity sought to secure their own lives at the expense of others. Typically, Jack Hall and Richard Low, a pair of habitual housebreakers escaped execution "by their turning of Evidence, and Hanging several of their Companions". Nine or ten men were executed as a result of their testimony. They were ultimately hanged themselves after

---

104. J. Clavell, *A Recantation of an Ill Led Life*, London, 1628, pp.33-39.
105. J.S. Cockburn, *The Nature and Incidence of Crime in England 1559-1625: A Preliminary Survey*, Princeton, Princeton University Press, 1977, p.54.

returning to crime and wounding a constable.[106] Nevertheless, throughout the period, JPs did sometimes engage in other, more conventional, types of detective work.

JPs as Detectives

There has been considerable dispute about the extent to which the early modern JP fulfilled the role of both detective and *juge raporteur* in the era's criminal justice system. At their best, it is clear that some JPs would take their inquisitorial function far beyond simply conducting the examination of felons already produced before them, even to the level of becoming virtual detectives in serious cases, especially homicides. Thus, the elderly Sir John Gaynesford, investigating the murder and robbery of Robert Grame near Crowhurst in 1532, not only took statements from potential witnesses and defendants, but visited the crime scene in the company of observers, questioned those nearby, examined the body in detail, and carefully recorded its condition, injuries and position, as well as the location of the victim's empty purse. He subsequently held one important potential witness to the crime in isolation for a day, at his own house, until the man was more forthcoming with information, and later detained and questioned one of the suspected killers in front of five neutral observers. (This was despite Gaynesford

106. Anon, *Jack Hall and Richard Low ...*, London, 1707, p.1.

being well into his 70s.)[107] Similarly, when Thomas Arden's body was discovered lying in the snow some distance from his house in Faversham, the Mayor, an *ex officio* justice for the town, and several other local notables, were immediately suspicious and conducted a careful investigation. They were well aware of Alice Arden's "ill-conduct" during her marriage and noticed foot-prints leading from the Arden house towards the body. As a result they "very strictly examined her about her husband's murder". Searching the premises they also found some of the dead man's blood and hair near his house and the bloodied knife used to stab him. In the light of this, and under firm questioning, the killers and their accomplices soon cracked: "... they urg'd these things so home, as Evidences against them that they all confess'd the Murder." Mosbie was arrested nearby and, after blood was found on his clothes, also confessed.[108] In February 1583, a suspected double spouse poisoning was equally thoroughly investigated by William Lambarde and Sir Christopher Alleyn, despite their inquiry being held long after the event. They: "... examined sundry persons at Sevenoaks concerning the suspicion of willful poisoning of William Brightmede by Thomas Heyward and Pernel, his now wife, then wife of the

---

107. W.B. Robison, "Murder at Crowhurst: A Case Study in Early Tudor Law Enforcement," *Criminal Justice History*, 1988, vol.9, pp.34-88 and p.43.
108. Anon, *The History of the most Remarkable Tryals in Great Britain and Ireland*, London, A. Bell, 1715, pp.248-262.

said William."[109] Five days later, the two men, joined by a third JP, John Lennard, examined several other people over the death of William Brightmede and the: "... like suspicion of poisoning of Joan, late wife of the said Heyward." They then committed Heyward and Pernel to jail. Less than a week later, at the Rochester assizes, held on March 4, Lambarde certified the examinations of the two suspects (together with the witness recognisances to give evidence).[110] Similarly, after John Perry had (falsely) implicated his brother and mother in a (non-existent) murder, in 1661, the examining JP, Sir Thomas Overton, gave orders that the pair be arrested, that the drain where the victim's body was said to have been abandoned be searched, that the fish-pools in Campden (Gloucestershire) be drawn and that the ruins of Campden House, which was "not unfit for such a concealment", also be searched.

Publicly displaying significant items belonging to either victim or criminal seems to have been common practice in investigations. Thus, in 1606, a tailor was able to identify a murdered boy whose dead body had been found in a ditch, after his coat was hung up at various local towns; the tailor had been much struck by its fine quality and had hoped to replicate it.[111] Some investigative techniques were much more ingenious. A multiple murder from Suffolk that came to trial in 1620 involved a magisterial investigation that

---

109. W. Lambarde, "Ephemeris," *William Lambarde and Local Government*, Conyers Read (Ed.), New York, Cornell University Press, Ithaca, 1962 (written 1580-1588), p.27.

110. Lambarde, "Ephemeris," p.28.

111. Anon, *The Horrible Murther of a Young Boy*, London, 1606, p.2.

would not have embarrassed a modern police department. The bodies of the victims had been abandoned in a pond, several years earlier, so that they were skeletal when discovered. The JP ordered the: "... carcases to be taken out the mud, and using the helpe of a chyrurgeon herein, caused each carcase to be layd out severally by it selfe, in its proportion, so fare as the bones would afford it." There was then a careful search of each skeleton for distinguishing marks. One body, when reassembled, proved to be tall for the era, being "high of stature, six foote long". Additionally, two teeth were missing from its skull, due to a much earlier accident. Local people were summoned to examine the skeletons, and, with the tall corpse's features pointed out, a woman quickly identified it as being that of her missing son, something that then led to the identification of the other bodies.[112] Equally thorough was the Elizabethan magisterial investigation held after Sir John Dayrell impregnated his wife's maid, and then arranged for a midwife to be conducted, blindfold, to a chamber where the servant gave birth, at which Dayrell killed the baby and burnt it on the fire. Despite being well paid for her services, the midwife's conscience began to prick her and she eventually reported the matter to a JP. By an ingenious piece of detective work, based on calculations as to time (and thus distance) ridden and the nature of the building "the very chamber was found".[113] Occasionally, intimate samples might even be

---

112. T. Cooper, *The Cry and Revenge of Blood*, London, N. Okes, 1620, p.42.
113. J. Aubrey, *Brief Lives*, R. Baxter (Ed.), Woodbridge, The Boydell Press, 1982, p.252.

compared, as they are today. This occurred in a case involving the murder of an apprentice, in 1657, who was found with clumps of another man's hair in his dead hands. When a suspected killer was detained at the behest of an investigating coroner: "... some of his Hair being plucked off to be compared with the Hair which was found in the young mans hand that was murdered." He was also strip searched in the presence of the coroner and two constables, blood stains being discovered about the suspect's person.[114]

In a *cause célèbre*, quite exceptional steps might be taken. These were seen in February 1682, after Anthony Thynne was shot and mortally wounded by three foreigners acting at the behest of the Swedish Count Coningsmark, a romantic rival of Thynne's for the hand of one Lady Ogle. Not only did the case involve a prominent victim, but, Thynne being "deeply engaged in the Duke of Monmouth's interest", there were fears about the "ill constructions" which the anti-Court party might place on the killing. The Metropolitan magistrate Sir John Reresby was interrupted while going to bed, and asked to initiate a hue and cry. Reresby also immediately attended the dying man and issued warrants to search for suspects or those who could provide intelligence about them. Eventually, a sedan chairman gave information that he had conveyed one of the suspects from his lodging in Westminster to the Black Bull tavern. This, with other intelligence meant that the constables were able

---

114. Anon, *A Full and the Truest Narrative of the most Horrid, Barbarous and Unparalled Murder, Committed on the Person of John Knight, Apprentice*, London, T. Mabb, 1657, pp.3-5.

to arrest a Swede, who: "... confessed that he served a gentleman, a German captain, who had told him that he had a quarrel with Mr Thynne, and had often appointed him to watch his coach as he passed by." He also provided an approximate address for where this man and his two friends might be found. Reresby personally arrested the captain shortly after dawn following a night of searches. He also subsequently conducted the examinations of those detained.[115] Towards the end of the period, it was noted that one of Reresby's successors, the magistrate Thomas De Veil, was successful in fighting Metropolitan crime because he was willing to take pains in conducting investigations.

In serious crimes, once an arrest had been made, the assistance of the authorities, whether JPs, coroners or peace officers, sometimes allowed suspects to be indicted, and weak cases to be bolstered before trial. Thus, one Mrs Harris, a robbery victim at her home in Hornsey, Middlesex, in the 1670s "took particular notice of the burglar's physogmony" during the break-in. When a man was subsequently held, she and her maid were asked to make an identification at the New Prison. Although a formal, modern, type of ID parade was not conducted, she viewed him amongst a group of other prisoners and, assisted by a number of distinctive features and blemishes on his face "no sooner did she see him, but singled him out from amongst a number of other Prisoners".[116] Nevertheless, despite the

---

115. Sir J. Reresby, *The Memoirs of Sir John Reresby*, London, 1734, pp.78-79.
116. Anon, *The Narrative of the Confession and Execution of the three Prisoners at Tyburn*, London, 1679, pp.2-3.

impressive activism of the assorted JPs in these cases, such conduct should not be taken as typical.

Private Detection

Although sophisticated detection by the authorities was rare, ordinary people, especially if 'well to do', could turn detective on their own initiative. Thus, when one of Edward Bushell's sheep was stolen in Worcestershire in the 1650s, his servant, Richard Mountford, tracked its hoof prints to a nearby wood, finding evidence that an animal had been recently slaughtered there. This prompted him to go into the local village of Roxley, and make inquiries as to whether any villagers had come into possession of a large amount of mutton over the previous few days. The trail swiftly led back to a village butcher.[117] The simplest approach was to broadcast details of the crime, accompanied by a reward. After being robbed and tied up for two hours by footpads, in 1652, John Evelyn, having freed himself, set out for a prominent local JP, Colonel Thomas Blount, who immediately organized a hue and cry. However, Evelyn did not rely entirely on the authorities to produce success. Most of his property was recovered after he had 500 handbills swiftly printed and distributed to businesses that were likely to 'fence' the stolen items. One of the two robbers was

---

117. Anon, *Crime in the Vale of Evesham 1651-1670*, Evesham, WEA Evesham History Workshop/Hereford and Worcester County Libraries, 1987, p.1.

also captured shortly afterwards.[118] Horses, often more notable than their riders, figured heavily in such published descriptions of thieves and robbers or the animals they had stolen. (There were even cases recorded of criminals' horses being placed on an equine identification parade.) For this reason, when, early in his criminal career, William Nevison stole a horse to make the journey to London, he cut the throat of the animal: "... within a mile or two of the town, for fear it should prove a means of his discovery if he should have carried it to an inn."[119] Occasionally, crime victims, especially commercial ones, might use complicated entrapment stratagems to identify and convict suspected thieves. Thus, in 1678, a London goldsmith named Stephen Higgins accused Mary Read of stealing a ring worth seven shillings. The defendant had been a regular customer in his shop for almost a year but, despite frequently haggling, rarely purchased anything. During this period, a number of rings went missing and Higgins began to suspect Read, so that he resolved to "lay wait for her". When, on her next visit, she asked to see a ring of a certain value, Higgins left out a tray of them and: "... to give her an Opportunity, turn'd his Back, and she took hold on it, and put one into her Bosom. When he turn'd about he presently miss'd the Ring, and affirming the Box was full, tax'd her with it." She denied any involvement and offered to be searched. However, and perhaps not coincidentally, a gentlewoman

118. J. Evelyn, *The Diary of John Evelyn*, E.S. De Beer (Ed.), Oxford, Clarendon Press, 1955, vol.III, pp.69-71.
119. Johnson, *A General History of the Lives and Adventures of the Most Famous Highwaymen*, p.103.

who was also in the shop had seen her conceal the ring and helped to search Read in the premises' kitchen, where "opening her Bosom the Ring drop'd upon the Bricks in the Floor".[120]

Some personal detective initiatives went much further than these relatively modest efforts. In the winter of 1730 to 1731 the librarian of St John's College Cambridge noticed that certain books were missing from his library. The ensuing detective work into their disappearance was to be a model of thoroughness. In January 1731, a college fellow, James Tunstall, was appointed to investigate. He contacted all the book shops in Cambridge, enlisting the assistance of a book seller named William Thurlbourn who had recently lost stock. Tunstall also examined past copies of the *Daily Post* for book sales, until he found one, from the previous November, at which a selection that matched the missing books was advertised. This sale had occurred at a coffee-house near St Paul's in London, and Tunstall and Thurlbourn duly went there to make inquiries of the man who had organised it. This individual identified the purchasers of some of the books in question, who were questioned in turn by Tunstall, until one of them thought that he remembered the name of the man who had sold them, a Dr Nicols of Trinity Hall. Thurlbourn then arranged to meet Nicols in a Bishopsgate tavern, and questioned him robustly. After initial evasiveness, Nicols confessed to the

---

120. Anon, *An exact account of the trials of the several persons arraigned at the sessions-house in the Old Bailey for London and Middlesex*, London, Gilham Hills, 1678, pp.7-8.

crime.[121] Occasionally, intimates and bystanders might also initiate quite complicated forensic examinations on their own initiative. In 1641, when a young London woman poisoned her husband's food, so extreme were his death throes that those that saw the body "all easily perceived that he was poysoned". A surgeon, summoned to the deceased's residence, carried out an *ad hoc* autopsy and "rippd up his body"; he allegedly 'found' poison near the dead man's heart. A further search quickly found the packet in which the poison had come lying nearby, and a constable was summoned to the scene. On being examined, the wife and her landlady swiftly confessed to the crime.[122]

Locating the whereabouts of stolen property, by use of the 'secret arts', was a mainstay of the work of 'wise women' and 'cunning men' (exponents of 'white' magic), many of which were active well into the eighteenth century. However, some men offered more practical help for their fees, becoming virtual professional private detectives in the process. A few managed to combine both occult and forensic investigations. Thus, in March 1653, William Studwell of East Sutton in Kent had two horses stolen from his field. Having "enquired after them with all the diligence he could and not hearinge of them", he had recourse, on the advice of neighbours, to one White who lived at Sutton Vallance, and had a reputation for recovering stolen goods. White claimed

---

121. O. Chadwick, "The Case of Philip Nichols, 1731," *Transactions of the Cambridge Bibliographical Society*, vol.1, part 5, 1953, pp.422-31. I am grateful to Dr Elizabeth Leedham-Green, Cambridge University Archives, for this reference.
122. Anon, *Murther, murther*, London, 1641, pp.3-4.

to have "helped a great many in his dayes", and like any modern CID officer, produced a small book of pictures showing potential suspects. Studwell recognised one of them as having been seen in his vicinity. At this, White confidently declared that the suspect had his horses, and for 10 shillings arranged for them to be left in a nearby wood, some weeks later. By then, they were very "leane and galled with traces as if they had been hard rerought". Exactly what had happened in the meantime is hard to establish. Perhaps the horses had been taken merely for ploughing and the thief was willing for them to be returned. Alternatively, White may have threatened to invoke the law, or offered to share his reward with the thief. Whether Studwell was breaking a 'gentleman's agreement' by subsequently going to the authorities is also unclear.[123] Ultimately, as this case suggests, the existence of rewards, both state and private, spawned the emergence of professional 'thief-takers' detecting criminals for bounties or payment. The presence of such men was recorded as early as the Elizabethan period, and grew in the early seventeenth century, the term being expressly used by a magistrate in 1609. They expanded again after 1660, especially in the Metropolis. Thus, Captain Bew, a notorious Restoration highwayman (and brother to another), was killed at Knightsbridge by "one Figg and some thief-takers".[124] However, the heyday of the thief-taker occurred after 1692, with the advent of

---

123. E. Melling (Ed.), *Crime and Punishment, Kentish Sources VI*, Maidstone, Kent County Council, 1969, pp.57-58.
124. Johnson, *A General History of the Lives and Adventures of the Most Famous Highwaymen*, p.322.

large-scale government funded rewards. Unfortunately, such men necessarily had to cultivate underworld contacts for information. This occasioned problems, as it encouraged thief-takers to become directly involved in negotiations between criminals and victims for the return (at a price) of stolen goods. It was then sometimes only a short step to combining the arrest of felons with becoming personally involved in organizing thefts and commercial receiving, as occurred with John Whitwood in the early 1690s.[125]

Vulnerability of Strangers

The role accorded to private individuals in investigating and pursuing crime meant that strangers could be vulnerable, especially in cases of homicide. There would often be no one to inquire into their disappearance and encourage investigation, particularly if a body was not discovered to prompt the local coroner into action. This was evidenced by a murder, in Chelmsford, in April 1654, which lay undetected for over a decade, being discovered in part due to good fortune (or the providential 'Finger of God'). The dead man, Thomas Kidderminster, a wealthy gentleman, had sold property in Ely and converted the proceeds, between £500 and £600, from silver into gold, at Cambridge, to ensure easier carriage. Well aware of the risks that he was running from robbers, he took an indirect

---

125. J.M. Beattie, *Policing and Punishment in London, 1660-1750*, Oxford, OUP, 2001, pp.228-235.

route to London, presumably believing that this would lessen the dangers inherent in taking a major highway into the capital. When he got to Chelmsford he spent the night at the White Horse Inn there. Unfortunately, the landlord, a man named Sewall, became aware of his gold. During the small hours of the night, Sewall together with his wife, eldest daughter and ostler entered Kidderminster's room and killed him, with a pole-axe blow to the head, after a brief struggle. His body was buried in the back garden of the tavern. Almost immediately, however, rumours as to what had occurred began to circulate in the town. The dead man's horse was seen in the inn's stables. A maid, not involved in the murder, noticed that the victim's clothes were still there, although she was told he had left. She swiftly suspected foul play. The landlord also sealed up the murder room, presumably to conceal obvious blood stains. Other traces of the dead man were gradually cleared up. His clothes were given to one of the inn servants, who had them dyed brown, despite the dyer noting that they would then look markedly inferior to their original green colour (years later he would be called to give evidence on this point). A much later investigation quickly produced two neighbours who remembered hearing, and inquiring about, nocturnal shouts of 'murder', and accepting implausible explanations from the landlord. Despite such apparently ample grounds for suspicion, no one pursued the matter. Perhaps the local JPs never even heard the rumours. Meanwhile, the dead man's widow made a "most diligent and exact search" for him when he failed to return, even following up leads that linked him to Cork, Amsterdam, Barbados and Jamaica, all to no avail.

However, in due course, the murderer sold the tavern to one Turner, who found that he was 'much prejudiced' in getting custom because of a widespread rumour that the "People of that Inn did use to murder Travellers, and bury them in the Dunghill". Some years later, while doing routine maintenance work in the garden, Turner's men came across a skeleton 'crammed in double' in the ground; the skull had a major puncture wound to its side. At last, the local coroner "sate upon the bones, and the Jury found it a murder, and that a blow upon the side of the Head was the cause of the person's death". There was not enough evidence at this point to pursue the matter further. Nevertheless, to clear his own name, Turner applied to the local JPs to issue warrants against Sewall and his wife. However, Sewall died two weeks before the assizes (the murder appears to have weighed heavily on his conscience, he had to be silenced by his wife on his death bed), and his spouse was remanded in custody to the next sessions, dying herself of the plague shortly beforehand. Sir Orlando Bridgeman, the Lord Chief Justice presiding at the assizes, ordered that details of the body be given to a 'News-Pamphlet' in the hope of identifying the victim. This publication asked that any who could give evidence about the missing man contact the constable of Chelmsford or a specified man in London. It was this advertisement that came to the widow's attention when her sister noticed it. The problems attendant on pursuing the matter were enormous and, not surprisingly, the widow's London friends urged her against it, pointing out the "Uncertainty, the Trouble, and the expense" involved, something which would be especially great given "how destitute she was both of [powerful] friends and money at that time". At first she followed their advice. However, being troubled by visions of her murdered husband 'looking very sternly upon her', and being a faithful wife, she at length decided to pursue the matter and enlisted the support of a male friend. They set off to walk to Chelmsford from London (about 20 miles) but became lost immediately after passing Stratford on the Essex road. Here, 'divine providence' once more intervened. Accidentally going to Romford, they sought rest in the Black Bull there and fell into conversation with a woman who hailed, originally, from Chelmsford and who told them that the inn-keeper: "... if he had had his Deserts, had been hanged long ago, for there was certainly a Gentleman murder'd in the house." This woman gave them details of the rumours and also informed them of a former ostler from the inn, who now lived locally in Romford. The landlord's daughter was also implicated in the crime, but fortunately for her there was little concrete evidence and the Grand jury subsequently returned the indictment against her 'ignoramus'. For the ostler, Moses Drayne, justice was waiting. Despite the belated nature of the investigation, the case against him was carefully prepared for trial. The dyer was called to testify to his strange request, and the neighbours were called to give evidence of the shouts. An errand boy was produced who remembered being whipped so hard by the defendant that he shouted: "What will you rob me of my money, and murder me too?" Drayne was duly convicted and executed. It is clear that without the efforts of the dead man's widow his involvement would not have been brought to light, despite the persistent rumours circulating in the town.[126]

This murder was by no means unusual. In many early modern cases of sudden death, even where there was a body available for examination, the dead person's neighbours appear to have harboured misgivings about the cause of death, but lacked the evidence, will or ability to take any formal action. Without a professional police force, and with basic forensic techniques, people might mutter to each other, but often went no further. In such circumstances, however, gossip and suspicion might linger for years. Thus, it was noted that John Lewes, a dissolute Lancashire clergyman defrocked in the 1630s for sexual offences and fighting, had had four young wives who all "died soon after their portions were spent". His neighbours suspected that these advantageous deaths were no coincidence, but did nothing. Similarly, after John Cupper of Bitterley, in Shropshire, was hanged for poisoning his wife to live with his house maid, his neighbours immediately voiced their suspicions that he had also earlier killed his two young children and murdered a Scotsman whose body had been found on the Clee Hills several years before (though Cupper denied these charges).[127] Of course, such gossip was not always accurate. At John Owen's execution in late seventeenth century Shropshire he made a lengthy gallows

126. Anon, *A true relation to the horrid murder committed upon the person of Thomas Kidderminster*, London, 1688, pp.1-10.
127. B. Capp, "Serial killers in 17th-century England," *History Today*, 1996, vol.46, issue 3, pp.21-31.

confession, which "discovered all the villenyes that he could remember that ever he had done". An indication that local rumour was not infallible was that among them were "several fellonyes that other persons had been blamed or suspected for".[128]

Arrest

As today, an arrest was the: "... apprehending & first restreining of a mans person, depriving it of his own will and liberty."[129] If a suspect was not detained red-handed, a warrant for his arrest could be issued by a JP. It would then often be enforced by the victim, albeit with the support of a parish officer. Thus, in 1721, Nicholas Leader, having been homosexually assaulted, and advised to prosecute his assailant by friends: "... procured a Warrant from Justice Tiller, and, taking a Constable with me, went on Sunday Morning to the same Meeting as before, where we found the Prisoner." As they moved in on him, the suspect attempted to flee, but was pursued and caught, at which: "He cry'd for Mercy, and begg'd that we would not expose him to public Shame."[130] Any warrant of arrest had to be in writing, not merely issued orally. JPs could not "command by word to arrest another being out of their presence". It was also not

---

128. R. Gough, *The History of Myddle*, D. Hey (Ed.), Harmondsworth, Penguin, 1981, 1701, p.150.
129. Dalton, *The Country Justice*, 1655, p.405.
130. Anon, *Select Trials for murder, robbery, &c. at the Sessions House in the Old Bailey*, 1742, vol.1, pp.105-8.

enough for a magistrate to issue a written warrant with a blank space where he "neither knew the parties name, nor the matter". One JP was fined by the Star Chamber for doing just this. Parish officers might themselves insist on the presence of a warrant if they were unsure of the legality of detaining someone, as it would provide protection for them against a civil suit for false arrest. Thus, George Fox recorded that when one Colonel Kirby attempted to seize Quakers, the local constable warned the Colonel that he could not keep them without a warrant. However, although all commoners could be arrested pursuant to such a warrant, magistrates could not issue them against noblemen. Nevertheless, they could enforce an order against a Peer of the Realm that came from the royal judges sitting at Westminster.[131] Notions of communal policing also meant that, in theory, and as today, if constables attempted to make an arrest: "If the accused threatens them and refuses to allow himself to be made prisoner, all those persons who by chance are present are obliged, if the constables desire it, to come to their aid."[132]

Additionally, constables could detain generally suspicious individuals who might "walke in the night, and sleepe in the day" or haunt houses of ill-repute. It was particularly important that "strange persons" found wandering at night in the warmer period between Ascension Day and Michaelmas, be stopped and arrested. The following morning, if nothing appeared untoward, they

---

131. Dalton, *The Country Justice*, 1655, p.406.
132. Muyden, *A Foreign View of England*, p.117.

could be released; if they still appeared suspicious, they might be produced before the JPs to provide recognisances for their future good behaviour.[133] This fear of nocturnal criminals appears to have been well founded in a world of very limited artificial light; dark brought real dangers and was frequently used by criminals for cover. Thus, according to Gough, one of his neighbours in seventeenth century Myddle, John Owen was the worst thief ever seen in the parish. This hardcore felon's habit was to: "... sleep in the day time, and to walke abroad in the night; sometimes near home, and sometimes further off, and whatsoever was found loose was a prize for him."[134]

Once a suspect was detained he would have to be secured pending examination. In London and large towns this was relatively easy, magistrates were readily to hand and there was often purpose built secure accommodation available in the Watch houses. Smaller communities might have recourse to any lockable premises that were available. If the constable and his neighbours were unwilling or unable to put a suspect in their own cellars, they might use the village stocks, which served a vital function as short term holding and pacifying units (as well as being punishments in their own right).[135] A suspect could be held there for a "reasonable time" until enough men could be found to "convey him safelie" to the local prison or a JP.[136] Indeed, sometimes, public nuisances could spend

---

133. W. Lambarde, *The Duties of Constables*, pp.12-13.
134. Gough, *The History of Myddle*, p.149.
135. Smith, *De Republica Angolorum*, p.109.
136. Lambarde, *The Duties of Constables*, p.18.

substantial periods in the stocks, especially during the summer months, in lieu of being committed to jail. Thus, at Warwick, in August 1587, a pedlar named Thomas Nicolson, "overladen with drink", sought to free his wife, Elizabeth, from the town's stocks. He was prevented in this by the area's constable, Edmund Yardley, as a result of which he: "... fought with the constable & tore his band and vilely abused him theruppon he was comyttid to the stocks for three dayes. And afterwards upon the constables request & the said Nicholson's submission he was sent away."[137] (Another illustration of negotiated justice.) If a community was of any size, it might have a small, purpose-built, 'lock-up', cage or clink, to hold those arrested before their being taken before a JP. Their designs varied. That at Westbury on Trym, near Bristol, which survives to this day, and which was built in the early eighteenth century, was an eight-foot-square, windowless cell, dug into a hill side, with a studded oak door and a small iron framed ventilator. Other communities might use an iron cage, largely open to the elements.

Preserving the Peace and Binding Over

Ideally, constables' duties were as much proactive as reactive, being: "... first in foreseeing that nothing be done that tendeth, either directlye, or by meanes, to the breach of

---

137. T. Kempt (Ed.), *The Book of John Fisher, Town Clerk and Deputy Recorder of Warwick 1580-1581,* Warwick, Henry Cooke & Son, Publishers, 1909, pp.183.

the peace: secondly, in quieting or pacifying those that are occupied in the breach of the peace: thirdly, in punishing such as have alreadie broken the peace."[138] A good constable would anticipate the potential causes of friction in his community, so keeping the peace. In its broadest sense, this was close to the early modern notion of being in 'charity' with one's neighbours, being a state of "amity, confidence, and quiet". However, legally, keeping the peace was more tightly defined, usually being seen as an abstinence from the use of threat of violence, making it "rather a restraining of hands, then an uniting of mindes".[139]

The recognisance played an essential role in the criminal litigation process, ensuring that prosecutors and their witnesses attended trial to give evidence, and allowing those accused of crimes to secure bail. However, it also served an important policing function in preventing potential violence and disorder by 'binding over' individuals who were likely to become involved in conflict, to be of good behaviour, on pain of forfeiting a sum of money.[140] This ancient power dated back to the Statute of 1361, which provided that: "Any one Justice of peace may compel such as are between the age of 15 years and threescore, to be sworn to keep the peace."[141] Likely candidates for such a constraint included common barreters,

---

138. Lambarde, *The Duties of Constables*, p.11.
139. Dalton, *The Country Justice*, 1661, p.10.
140. J. Samaha, "The Recognizance in Elizabethan Law Enforcement," *American Journal of Legal History*, vol.25, 1981, pp.189-204.
141. Dalton, *The Country Justice*, 1661, p.98.

'riotous' people and 'suspicious or suspected' individuals.[142] Frequently, if an actual affray produced no serious injuries, binding over would be considered a sufficient legal response (if 'dangerous hurt' was inflicted a felony trial might be necessary).[143] If an individual was 14 years of age or less, a friend would be bound over on his behalf. Such bindings over could be "for ever, or untill a certain day".[144] They could be sought by private individuals who were "in fear of another" as well as by the authorities.[145] Thus, anyone accused of a crime and at risk of revenge attacks could seek to bind over any man that he feared. Provision was expressly made for the physically handicapped to seek it: "One that is dumb may demand Surety of Peace by signes and tokens." Not everyone could ask for the protection afforded by the binding-over process. Aliens, lunatics any "condemned in a praemunere, ne ideots, may [not] require the Peace of any man".[146]

If a breach of the peace were subsequently committed, the specified sum would be forfeit, in addition to any new charges that might be brought. According to Dalton, a breach of the peace was any: "... injurious force or violence moved against the person of another, his goods, lands or other possessions, whether it be by threatening words, or by

---

142. W. Fleetwood, *The Office of a Justice of Peace*, London, Ralph Wood for W. Lee, 1657, p.30.
143. Lambarde, *The Duties of Constables*, p.16.
144. Fleetwood, *The Office of a Justice of Peace*, pp.30-1.
145. Bacon, Sir Francis (1841) "The Use of the Law," in Montagu, Basil (Ed.), *The Works of Francis Bacon*, vol.3, Philadelphia: Carey and Hart, at p.247.
146. Fleetwood, *The Office of a Justice of Peace*, pp.30-33.

furious gesture, or force of the body."[147] Lambarde went further and argued that it included: "... not only that fighting which we commonly cal the breach of the peace, but also that every murder, rape, manslaughter & felony whatsoever."[148] However, many observers took a narrower view. Most felt that it was something that violated an individual's 'corporal person' and that even menaces or threats to assault were not necessarily enough.[149] Additionally, it was thought that a constable could not arrest for heated words alone, unless they involved threats to kill, beat, or hurt another.[150] Numerous commentators also stressed that crimes such as theft, unlike robbery, assault or rape, were not *per se* breaches of the peace, because they were not "done to the person". Inevitably, the provision could be abused for reasons that were not entirely laudable. It was feared that some JPs, having more regard to friendship and private considerations than allowed by the: "... true meaning of their Commission, meddle with such Breaches further than good Equity would they should."[151] However, and perhaps indicative of the era's greater distribution of violence, the most socially elevated men could be, and regularly were, bound over. Thus, on June 9, 1582, William Lambarde: "... bound John Atkin of Horton, vicar, in 20 li.s to keep the peace against Walter Hemming of Dartford, yeoman."

---

147. Dalton, *The Country Justice*, 1661, p.10.
148. Lambarde, *The Duties of Constables*, p.12.
149. Fleetwood, *The Office of a Justice of Peace*, p.42.
150. Dalton, *The Country Justice*, 1661, p.36.
151. Fleetwood, *The Office of a Justice of Peace*, pp.41-42

The two main types of recognisance, to ensure attendance at trial and subsequent good behaviour, were often combined. Typically, in October 1644, John Payne, a labourer from Bredhurst in Kent, was bound over to appear at the following quarter sessions in Maidstone, in the sum of £40, following an incident with another villager. In the meantime, he was ordered to be of good behaviour towards all men and to: "... keep the peace towards our Sovereign Lord the King, all his people and especially against Nicholas Fosture of Bredhurst." As was common in minor cases, it also provided that he would not actually have to attend court, the order to do so becoming 'void', provided that he did not violate the terms of his bind-over.[152] Those who were bound over to keep the peace until the following sessions, without this provision, would appear together with the complainant and the: "... cause of binding to the peace examined, and both parties being heard, the whole bench is to determine as they see cause, either to continue the party so bound, or else to discharge him."[153] Finally, if all of their precautions to prevent disturbances failed, constables could use reasonable force to quell them and "both use his owne weapon, and may also cal others to assiste him". As this suggests, in an emergency, constables could carry bills (a broad bladed pole arm) or short pikes. If a brawler was injured during such disturbances "such a hurt person hath no [legal] remedie at al for it". But, if a constable was hurt

---

152. Howle, *Henry Howle's Notebook*, p.57.
153. Sir F. Bacon, "The Use of the Law," in Montagu, Basil (Ed.), *The Works of Francis Bacon*, vol.3, Philadelphia, Carey and Hart, 1841, p.250.

in the execution of his duties, he could bring a civil action against the perpetrator.[154]

Role of the Coroner

Coroners were normally drawn from the fringes of the political nation, or, in Sir Thomas Smith's words "chosen by the Prince of the meaner sort of gentlemen". They could spend many years in office. In seventeenth century Sussex one man served 47 years, another 41 years, and several exceeded 20 years service. Most counties had two designated coroners. Towns, cities and many local jurisdictions also often had their own independent coroners. Some men held two or more such positions simultaneously. Early modern coroners had similar functions to their present day counterparts. They had to "make inquireye of treasure found".[155] (A role they still possess.) Additionally, coroners had an important role in the sanctuary and abjuration procedures before the effective demise of these privileges at the Reformation. They were also involved in the outlawry process, attending the ancient county courts every four weeks to legalise what, by the 1500s, was merely a mechanism to ensure court attendance.[156] Nevertheless, by far their most important duty was to "enquire of such as

---

154. Lambarde, *The Duties of Constables*, p.15.
155. W. Harrison, "A description of England," in R. Holinshed, *The First Volume of the Chronicles of England, Scotland and Ireland*, London, John Harrison, 1577, p.75.
156. R.F. Hunnisett, *Sussex Coroners' Inquests 1603-1688*, London, PRO, 1988, p.11.

come to their death by violence".[157] This meant investigating all suspicious deaths, including suicides, and all deaths, however occasioned, that occurred in the county jails. A statute of 1487 (3 Henry VII c. 2), which remained in force until 1752, required coroners to produce accounts of their inquests on sudden deaths to the assizes judges. Many inquests that resulted in verdicts of murder or manslaughter would be used to found indictments (and kept with the files of the relevant circuit), coroners having the power to indict directly to the assizes for either homicide without the intervention of a grand jury.

It was vital that the coroner and his jury be able to physically examine the corpse of anyone who died in suspicious circumstances: "But if anie man, or child, be violently slaine, the murtherer not knowen, no man ought or dare buriethe bodie before the Coroner hath seene it." Anyone buried before such an examination would be dug up (early modern burial normally took place speedily after death).[158] Nevertheless, in the sixteenth and seventeenth centuries there were no death certificates and a coroner's inquest was held only when there were strong grounds for suspicion.[159] Sometimes, an inquest might be specifically requested to lay to rest local rumours. Thus, to deal with malicious allegations by the Duke of Newcastle that he had killed his negro servant, by having him castrated, Sir John Reresby asked that a coroner come from Sheffield to conduct

---

157. Harrison, "A description of England," p.75.
158. Smith, *De Republica Anglorum*, p.108.
159. Capp, "Serial killers in 17th-century England," pp.21-31.

an inquest on the dead boy, which was duly held in an Inn at Reresby's village. To modern eyes, there were some apparent 'irregularities' in its conduct. In particular, Reresby appears to have provided sustenance for the jurors, his accounts recording that he paid 14s 10d "for meete and wine for ye jury", though this may have been because he, himself, had (most unusually) initiated the process. Nevertheless, the inquest was conducted extremely thoroughly and carefully. The body was partially exhumed, but seemed to have decayed too far to justify removing it further (as was common with interments for the poor, it had been buried in a shroud without a coffin, six weeks earlier). However, all of Reresby's servants and the village women who laid the body out, were called to give evidence and confirmed that the boy had experienced what appears to have been a stroke, shortly after dancing with the other servants, and died two days later, having been ministered to by the local clergyman. The servant who shared the deceased's bed and the village women who laid him out all confirmed that his testicles were quite unscathed at death. Indeed, the women candidly admitted that because of the 'outlandish' nature of the boy (negroes being a rarity) they had closely examined his body. The jury returned a verdict of 'Act of God'. However, the saga did not end there, the Lord Chief Justice was apparently pressured into issuing a warrant requiring the coroner to re-examine the boy's body. The coroner, answerable only to the Crown, and a man of sturdy independence, refused. Despite this, lawyers connected with the Duke of Newcastle exhumed the corpse themselves, under the close supervision of Reresby's men, who feared that they would use their penknives to emasculate it. Amazingly, given the advanced state of putrefaction in most of the body (by then it was two months since the death), this revealed that the 'cod' had not corrupted, and that all was clearly intact, bringing an end to the allegations.[160]

Such post-mortem exhumations were quite common. In 1699, the body of Sarah Stout was dug up and examined six weeks after her death, after rumours circulated in Hertford that she had been murdered. This was despite an initial coroner's finding of suicide.[161] In a like case, Sir John Maynard, a King's Serjeant, also recorded a criminal investigation and trial in 1629, in which one Joan Norcott had been exhumed after burial. Norcott had been found dead in her bed, with her throat cut, the only means of access and egress to her room being through another chamber that was occupied. At the coroner's inquest, the jury, on viewing the body and hearing evidence from those in the adjacent room, were inclined to return a verdict of suicide. However, subsequently, worrying rumours in the neighbourhood surfaced, while disturbing features to the case suggested "that she did not, nor, according to those circumstances, could not possibly, murder herself". As a result, the jurors asked the coroner to have her body exhumed before they returned a final verdict. A month after her death, Joan was dug up: "... in the presence of the jury and a great number of people; whereupon the jury changed

---

160. A.F. Oakley, "Sir John Reresby and the Moor - A 17th century Coroner's Inquest," *History of Medicine*, 1971, vol.3, pp.27-31.
161. The Earl of Birkenhead, *Famous Trials of History*, vol.1, New York, Doubleday, Doran and Co., 1926, p.93.

their verdict."[162]

In some respects, forensic medicine in England lagged behind that in much of the Continent. Thus, the Carolina Code of 1631 provided detailed rules for conducting autopsies to protect the body being examined from damage, and valuable evidence being destroyed. In 1689, Bohne's classic work *De Renuncatore Vulnerum*, published in Leipzig, set out many basic principles for conducting a modern medico-legal autopsy, for example by insisting that all of the body cavities be opened, something that was frequently ignored in England. No major work specifically on forensic medicine was published in English until 1787, and then it was merely the translation of a mainstream European text on the subject.[163] Nevertheless, standards of medical examination were sometimes very high, even in England. Thus, in May 1613, the coroner for Rye (also the town's mayor) and jury sat at an inquest on the death of a local man during an argument over cards in a tavern. The dead man had been struck on the head by a stone beer pot. Four surgeons gave evidence, three from Rye and a very elderly Londoner. All gave evidence that having opened the dead man's skull they found it to be cracked and opined that the large amount of "bruised blood" that "lay in great abundance upon the brain" had killed him.[164]

However, the office of coroner was only as effective as the individual who held it. Negligence, laziness or

---

162. Rayner and Crook, *The Complete Newgate Calendar*, 1926, vol.I, pp.46-50.
163. J.D. Havard, *The Detection of Secret Homicide*, London, MacMillan, 1960, p.4.
164. Hunnisett, *Sussex Coroners' Inquests 1603-1688*, pp.29-30.

corruption in the performance of their duties was a real risk. This led to an early sixteenth century statute (Anno. 1. H 8. Cap.7) to punish misconduct (albeit very modestly), which provided that a fine of 40 shillings would be imposed: "... if the coroner uppon request to hym made to come and enquere upon the viewe of any person slayne, drouned, or other wyse dead by misadventur, do not diligently his office upon the view of the sayd body of every such person or persons." Receiving corrupt payments in office were to be punished in similar fashion.[165] Nevertheless, despite occasional failings, most coroners appear to have been conscientious men possessed of considerable amounts of common sense. The inquisitorial process that they employed could be surprisingly effective and independent, with jurors frequently making constructive suggestions about investigations. Unlike a criminal trial, the jury was not confined to a specific time or place to produce its verdict, but could take several days, if necessary, to make enquiries, so that by the: "... viewe of the bodie, and by such informations as they can take, [they] must search howe the person slaine came to his death, and by whome as the doer or causer thereof."[166] Thus, in 1514, a coroner's jury was empanelled immediately after the discovery of the apparent suicide of Richard Hunne, while he was imprisoned in the Bishop of London's prison near St Paul's and awaiting trial for heresy. The 24 jurymen, having carefully examined the body and the dead man's cell, dismissed any suggestion of

---

165. W. Middleton, *The Boke for a Justyce of Peace*, London, 1545, p.30.
166. Sir T. Smith, *De Republica Anglorum*, p.108.

suicide, and after a lengthy inquiry into the circumstances of the case, found a verdict of wilful murder against Doctor Horsey, the Bishop's chancellor, and his assistants. (Although these men were indicted, political influence was used to ensure that they were never brought to trial.)[167] Similarly, it was the foreman of the coroner's jury examining Fussell's body, in 1658, who suggested that local gunsmiths be questioned about the murder weapon.[168] A few years later, when a suspect in a Shropshire killing denied that it was physically possible for a maid to have identified him from a window. The "whoale jury came from Eyton to Marton" to test the claim. They concluded that it was possible, and the suspect was found to have committed murder, for which he was sent for trial at the Shrewsbury assizes, convicted and executed.[169] As these cases suggest, the deliberations of coroners and their juries were usually both thorough and rational. Thus, when, in 1684, Lady Phillips, a wealthy woman, estranged from her poorer and younger second husband, was found strangled in her bedroom by a cord attached to the chimney piece her spouse was swiftly suspected and "confined in his own house" pending the inquest. However, the coroner's jury, which sat two days after her death, returned a verdict of suicide, "having well inquired into the circumstances". They decided that her husband had probably been away when the incident occurred, that the couple were on the cusp of

---

167. A. Ogle, *The Tragedy of the Lollard's Tower*, Oxford, 1949, p.12.
168. Anon, *The Unhappy Marksman*, London, T.N., 1659, p.15.
169. R. Gough, *The History of Myddle, 1701*, D. Hey (Ed.), Harmondsworth, Penguin, 1981, p.121.

reconciliation, and, perhaps most importantly, that her death did not benefit him financially, as he would then lose a large part of the revenue from her estate.[170]

Occasionally, coroners would work closely with JPs to investigate obvious and sophisticated murders. When a Somerset curate named Trat was murdered in 1624, as a result of local antipathy occasioned by a dispute over an incumbency and his intemperate criticism of the moral life of some of his parishioners, great steps were taken to conceal the murder. The body was returned to the cleric's own house, where his killers dismembered it and then "burne[d] his head and privy member", to prevent identification. The remains were parboiled and salted to reduce the odour occasioned by putrefaction. An imposter then pretended to be the curate, claiming to inhabitants of another village to have killed and boiled an unknown traveller before disappearing. Ultimately, however, a coroner and two JPs investigating the murder concluded that the dismembered body was Trat's, after questioning neighbours, there "being one of his fingers knowne by a secret marke unto them". These neighbours also speedily provided a list of the deceased cleric's local enemies, all of whom were subsequently prosecuted for the murder.[171]

---

170. Anon, *Sad and dreadful news from Kings-street in Westminster*, London, L.C., 1684, p.1.
171. Anon, *The Crying Murther*, London, 1624, f.B2.

303

Chapter 10

Coming to Trial

A 'Private' System of Prosecution

Early modern England possessed weak policing and prosecuting agencies. Although the notion that the wider community had a legitimate interest in insisting on the prosecution of serious offences had been developing for several centuries before 1500, being most obviously manifest in the work of coroners and presentments by grand juries, the role of the individual in pursuing crime remained paramount. Even in 1750, the process of replacing private with public prosecution had barely started, and England still lacked public bodies corresponding to the modern police force and Crown Prosecution Service. In this, it was already slightly different to many continental European countries, where the imperatives of government finance and centralisation had encouraged more innovation. Thus, in the sixteenth century Italian states, the inquisitorial process *ex abrupto*, inherited from Roman law, allowed the executive to initiate criminal investigations and trials wherever it saw fit. There was no need for the state to wait for a formal complaint.[1] By contrast, as late as the 1820s, the Frenchman Charles Cottu was astonished by the lack of state involvement in the English investigation and prosecution of

---

1.   J.K. Brackett, *Criminal Justice and Crime: In Late Renaissance Florence, 1537-1609*, Cambridge, CUP, 1992, p.3.

crime, and at the manner in which it was largely dependent on the "hatred or resentment of the injured party".[2] Private involvement extended to the most serious offences. Thus, when, in 1682, Captain Bartholomew Sharpe and two of his crew were indicted on charges of piracy and murder in the High Court of the Admiralty, for crimes allegedly committed against the Spanish vessel *Rosario*, a year earlier, the Spanish Ambassador, Don Pedro Ronquillo, was chief prosecutor (Sharpe was acquitted on a technicality).[3] This often made the decision to prosecute a very personal matter, so that an indication of the robber Benjamin Child's magnanimity, at his execution in 1721, was that he found it in his heart to thank his prosecutor "whose evidence has taken away my life".[4]

However, even in England, state involvement was not entirely absent. Most importantly, unlike the appeal of felony, which had been a genuine private action in both theory and practice, its (virtual) replacement, prosecution on indictment, at least took the 'form' of a public action. Strictly speaking, if an action was brought against a suspect by: "... appeale, that is mine accusation against him. If I begun first to pursue him by information or denunciation to enditement, I am nowe no partie but the Prince."[5] Nevertheless, in

2.   D. Hay (Ed.), "Property, authority and the criminal law," in *Albion's Fatal Tree, Crime and Society in 18th Century England*, New York, Pantheon Books, 1975, p.43.
3.   J. Kelly, "The pirate, the ambassador and the map-maker. (Captain Bartholomew Sharpe)," *History Today*, 1998, vol. 48, issue 7, pp.49-55.
4.   Anon, *The Whole Life History of Benjamin Child*, 1722, p.31.
5.   Sir T. Smith, *De Republica Anglorum*, London, Henri Midleton for Gregorie Seton, 1583, p.123.

reality, this often meant little more than that the formal title of criminal process against a felon named Brown, whose victim was called Black, would read *Rex/Regina v. Brown* rather than *Black v. Brown*. Much of the practice of a private action remained unchanged. To a large extent, an ordinary individual (usually the victim), not a public prosecutor, still initiated the process, found witnesses, arranged for them to be examined and, subsequently, to appear at trial. Such a system inevitably produced numerous problems. Those pertaining to pursuit and arrest have already been addressed. However, even where there was a detained suspect, and apparently good evidence available to secure a conviction, prosecution was not certain.

Criticism of Popular Unwillingness to Prosecute

Perhaps surprisingly, the problems inherent to the country's prosecution process only started to be seen as politically 'unacceptable' towards the end of the period, and then primarily in London, prompting a variety of government initiatives to encourage recourse to the courts. However, throughout the early modern era, numerous observers complained that, even if English substantive law was largely sound, a lack of enforcement meant that "most of our Lawes are but dead and breathless carcases".[6] Thus, in the 1530s, Sir Thomas Elyot was appalled at an apparently widespread

---

6.   W. Sheppard, *The Whole Office of the County Justice of Peace*, 3rd. edn., London, W. Lee, 1656, pp.8-9.

willingness to ignore crime and disorder. He felt that this was sometimes motivated by misplaced sympathy for its perpetrators and 'false' pity. It was also often prompted by fear of the opprobrium that was the lot of anyone who sought to enforce the letter of the law. Such condemnation came not just from the: "... vulgare or commune people, but moche rather by them whiche have autoritie to them committed concernyng the effectuell execution of lawes."[7] Over a century later, in the 1650s, William Sheppard was also persuaded that one of the primary reasons for the lack of order in English society was a "want of information" to prosecute crimes.[8] At the end of the period, in 1751, Dr Johnson was *still* arguing that all laws against wickedness were ineffectual unless "some will inform and some will prosecute". He was convinced that a national reluctance to do this, if only to avoid having a man's death on potential prosecutors' consciences, meant that almost every thief would admit to having been "more than once seized and dismissed".[9]

As Johnson's remark indicates, numerous felons, even if caught red-handed, did not come to trial. By their very nature it is impossible to establish the proportion of such cases, although, when writing to Lord Burghley in 1596, the Somerset JP Edward Hext suggested it might be over 80 per cent: "... in the experience of my service here, that the fifth

7. Sir T. Elyot, *The Boke named The Governour*, London, J. M. Dent & Co., 1962, p.120.
8. Sheppard, *The Whole Office*, pp.8-9
9. S. Johnson, "Crime and Punishment," April 23, 1751, in *The Rambler*, London, Everyman's Library, 1953, p.186.

person that committeth a felony is not brought to this trial."[10] This was certainly not a new problem in the Elizabethan era. Indeed, by then, the situation had probably improved considerably from the 1300s, when the average value of goods stolen by those tried at gaol delivery (£3-4s) suggests that many fairly serious crimes did not go to royal courts.[11] Despite inflation, the value of a typical theft indictment had fallen substantially by the latter sixteenth century. Even so, numerous early modern lawyers, politicians and clerics urged the public to be more active in prosecuting offenders. Thus, in the early 1700s, the Bishop of St David's warned that even the best magistrates could not act against the most serious criminals without the assistance of others. Hence, it was the: "... Duty of private Persons to act subordinately to the Magistrates, and to render them capable of doing Justice effectually in the Way of Information and Testimony."[12] Of course, arguments that JPs were necessarily entirely 'passive' can be exaggerated. Daniel Defoe pointed out that if they bothered to acquaint themselves with their neighbourhoods they would "soon hear of the immoralities of the parish". Proactive magistrates were much more likely to encourage prosecution.

---

10. E. Hext,"Letter written by Edward Hext, a Somerset JP, to Lord Burghley on September 25, 1596," in *Tudor Economic Documents*,vol.2, R.H. Tawney and E. Power (Eds.), London, Longmans, 1951, p.340.
11. B.A. Hanawalt, "Fur Collar Crime: the Pattern of Crime amongst the Fourteenth-Century English Nobles," *Journal of Social History*, 1975, vol. 8, p.4.
12. R. Smalbroke, *Reformation necessary to prevent Our Ruine: A Sermon Preached to the Societies for Reformation of Manners, at St Mary-le-Bow, on Wednesday, January 10, 1727*, London: Joseph Downing, 1728, p.6.

Additionally, a JP was empowered to punish minor crimes that he personally witnessed and to "enquire into any he hears of casually". In reality, many turned a 'blind eye' to such things, especially when committed by their own associates.[13]

Nevertheless, such magisterial powers notwithstanding, and obvious exceptions such as treason, murder and 'victimless' moral offences apart, prosecution was largely private. The importance of the victim's role is exemplified by the case of Francis Godelard, who was robbed when only carrying a shilling, so that almost nothing was taken before his attacker was held by a passing group of soldiers, alerted by the victim's shouts of 'murder'. There was some confusion as to the correct charge, and it was left to Godelard to decide on it: "An Attorney advis'd me to prosecute him only for an Assault; but I was afterwards advis'd by another Attorney to charge him with the Robbery."[14] Indeed, although only very occasionally used, a prosecutor's power to choose an indictment for misdemeanour, for what was legally a felony, was affirmed by a meeting of judges summoned by Richard III in the Inner Star Chamber in 1484. It was reaffirmed as late as 1724 by the Court of King's Bench, which held that a prosecutor might, at his election, proceed against receivers of stolen goods for felony or misdemeanour despite an earlier statute

---

13. D. Defoe, "The Poor Man's Plea," in *The Shortest Way with the Dissenters*, Oxford, Basil Blackwell, 1927, pp.13-14.

14. Anon, *Select Trials at the Sessions-House in the Old Bailey, From the Year 1720-1742*, Dublin, S. Powell, for G. Ewing, and W. Smith in Dame-street, and G. Faulkner, in Essex-street, 1742, vol. 1, pp.153-4.

(3 W. & M. c.9, s.4.) making the crime felony.[15]

Although the prosecution was carried out in the name of the Crown (apart from the very rare appeal of felony), the more time, money and energy prosecutors were willing to spend in preparing and presenting a case, the more likely it was that a conviction would ensue. This was widely appreciated. In 1641, a Yorkshire miser, who had been robbed of a fortune, could only vent his fury on two labourers who had found and kept a bag containing a small portion of the stolen proceeds, which had been dropped by the robbers. Even so, the victim "swore he would hang them if it cost him half his estate".[16] As this suggests, the victims of a crime or their close kin usually carried out such preparation. However, this was not invariably the case. In 1721, William Casey, a soldier convicted of two robberies in London complained about a corporal who had been: "... very busy in managing the Evidence against him. And this he did, says Casey, not from any knowledge of my guilt, but merely on Account of an old grudge."[17] Such pre-trial efforts and 'vigorous' prosecutions could be crucial in difficult cases. Thus, Sir John Reresby observed in 1682 that convictions in a notorious murder case that year had followed a "very strict prosecution" by the victim's relatives. This phrase recurs regularly in contemporary accounts as the precursor to a finding of guilt. Thus, in some ways, early

---

15. P.R. Glazebrook, "The Merging of Misdemeanours," *Law Quarterly Review*, 1962, vol. 78, pp.565-566.
16. Anon, *Newes from the North*, London, 1641, p.5.
17. Anon, *Select Trials, for Murders, Robberies, Rapes, Sodomy, Coining, Frauds*, London, J. Wilford, 1734, vol. 1, pp.61-66.

modern England's system of criminal prosecution was not dissimilar to its current system of civil litigation. Under both, it was/is the victim who usually initiates and controls the process by which an offender (whether criminal or tort feasor) is brought to justice.

However, although, for most offences, the initial decision to invoke formal prosecution was largely the responsibility of the victim, once state involvement had been secured it became progressively more difficult for complainants to withdraw, and there might be penalties for doing so (not least a forfeiture of recognisances). Even so, such withdrawals occurred on a regular basis, and there were "numerous acquitalls", even at the Old Bailey, due to a "want of evidence" when witnesses failed to turn up or, if they did appear "for their not speaking home to the matter". In the latter case, their physical presence would usually allow them to keep their recognisance even though they had deliberately moderated their evidence.[18]

Prosecution a Last Resort

Invoking formal legal controls was often very much a last option. Thus, many crimes, especially incidents of violence, in which no one individual was obviously more culpable than any other, and in which there was no fatality, might simply be ignored. Even Sir John Reresby (admittedly a confrontational man), while travelling in Yorkshire, in

---

18. Anon, *Hanging, not Punishment Enough*, London, A. Baldwin, 1701, pp.11-13.

September 1660, recorded a violent dispute between his party and another over which would have precedence in taking a river boat: "I was struck over the head with a cudgel, which provoked me to wound one or two with my sword." A pitched battle appears to have ensued, in which only Sir John's Moorish servant saved him from serious injury, after which he noted: "I defended myself till I got into the house of an honest man, that gave us protection till the rabble was appeased."[19] The authorities and courts were not involved in this incident. Much violence might be ignored before formal action was taken. Most of the more than 300 cases that came before the late Elizabethan Star Chamber involved allegations of serious crimes, such as assault and arson, stretching back over several years, and yet which had never been previously prosecuted.[20]

Even where offences could not be entirely disregarded the village had a considerable capacity to police itself. It is an anthropological platitude that the institutions of 'law' do for societies with government what other forms of social control do elsewhere. Formal law enforcement is merely one form of social control, and its existence often varies inversely with the presence of others.[21] These were still readily available in the early modern English village. In

19.   Sir J. Reresby, *Memoirs of Sir John Reresby*, London, 1734, pp.33-34.
20.   B. Lenman and G. Parker, "The State, the Community and the Criminal Law in Early Modern Europe," *Crime and The Law: The Social History of Crime in Western Europe since 1500*, V.A.C. Gatrell *et al* (Eds), London, Europa, 1980, p.15.
21.   M. Strathern, "Discovering 'Social Control'," *Journal of Law and Society*, 1985, vol. 12, Number 2, p.111.

some cases, villagers, acting communally, might take it upon themselves to punish those considered guilty of anti-social or immoral conduct. This might be done by administering beatings or subjecting them to 'rough music', 'charivaris', 'skimmingtons', carting, stang-riding or ducking in the cucking stool. However, large numbers of people who had infringed community moral standards appear to have escaped even summary punishment. Other factors often seem to have been behind community action. For example, particularly glaring, flagrant and overt behaviour or individuals who were personally unpopular, newcomers or suspected of other forms of deviance. Thus, in a case from Burton-on-Trent in 1618, a couple, William and Margaret Cripple, complained about their treatment at the hands of their fellow townsmen to the Star Chamber. Significantly, the Cripples were strangers to the town, having only arrived to live there a month or so earlier. They appear to have been comparatively marginal individuals, alleged to entertain strangers, 'lusty yonge men', in their home. From the abuse heaped on them, 'theefe', 'knave' and 'whore', they may have been suspected of larceny; certainly, William was a suspicious figure who was reputed to make his living by playing the bagpipes. They were also strongly suspected of not being married, despite cohabiting, and thus guilty of fornication. The couple were abducted from the house in which they resided, forcibly lead through the town, to the sound of discordant music, and paraded in front of 400 people, being insulted and pelted with rubbish all the while. They were then placed in the stocks for over an hour, during which the townspeople "pissed on their heads", dragged by their feet through the streets for another hour, and left lying "amased and hurte". When they returned to their house, they found it ransacked. Many of those actively involved in the incident were disguised and masked, though this did not prevent the Cripples recognising 18 of them, including the local constable.[22]

Social solidarity meant that such communal activities could be very hard for the authorities to penetrate. Thus, at Frome in Somerset, in January 1731, after a local child was seized with strange fits, an elderly woman was dragged from her house as a suspected witch. Although ill, she was 'swum' in a millpond by the mob, in front of 200 cheering spectators. Having ingested a large amount of water, she was pulled out and given some brandy to revive her, before being left in a stable, where she died within an hour. However, the coroner's inquest: "... cou'd make no discovery of the ring-leaders, altho' above 40 persons assisted in the fact, yet none of them could be persuaded to accuse his neighbour: so that they were able to charge only three of them with Man-slaughter."[23] Sometimes, magistrates or other gentlemen would intercede and stop such proceedings, but legal action rarely followed, unless a death resulted.

Indeed, the realms of popular action and that of the authorities were not hermetically sealed. In moderation, each took cognisance of the other. Thus, the Cripples' local

---

22. J.R. Kent, "'Folk Justice' and Royal Justice in Early Seventeenth-Century England: A 'Charivari' in the Midlands," *Midland History*, 1983, vol. 8, pp.70-85.
23. *The Gentleman's Magazine*, 1731, vol. 1, p.30.

JPs were not interested in their complaints, necessitating recourse to Star Chamber. Similarly, the Quaker George Fox's experiences at Mansfield-Woodhouse, in 1648, are indicative of a tacit magisterial acceptance of such action. Fox could not resist attending the parish church there and preaching his uncompromising message to its priest and people. He generated such fury that the villagers attacked him and Fox was beaten with fists, Bibles and sticks. His assailants then dragged him to the stocks, where he was left for several hours and threatened with horsewhips. After some time, they unfastened him and took him before a local JP. This magistrate: "... seeing how evilly I had been used, after much threatening, set me at liberty." He was then stoned out of the town.[24]

Along with dramatic manifestations of informal parish discipline, such as communal beatings, there were more subtle means by which offenders could be punished. In small rural communities a general principle of reciprocity encouraged co-operative behaviour and reduced the benefits of dishonesty. These were often outweighed by the cost of losing the trust of other villagers. Employment, credit, and collaboration in communal ventures, such as harvesting, might all be affected. Thus, a man with a reputation as a knave or, more commonly, his wife, might be excluded from the gleaning field and would not be allowed to borrow tools or domestic implements. Life could be made 'uncomfortable' without any formal agencies being

---

24. G. Fox, *The Journal of George Fox*, London, Religious Society of Friends, 1975, at p.45.

involved. The poor law and the burgeoning early modern local charities, which were largely discretionary and often limited to the 'respectable' poor, ultimately also greatly enhanced the scope for punishing offenders without recourse to the courts.

As with village communities, many organisations were also likely to use alternative means to punish their criminal members. Thus, Dr Philip Nicols, a clerical Fellow of Trinity Hall, Cambridge, who stole and then sold large numbers of valuable library books from nearby St John's College and a town bookseller, escaped the full rigour of the law. This was despite employing considerable cunning in effecting the thefts, a large amount of media coverage and the Recorder of Cambridge having been informed of his crime. Depriving him of his fellowship, after a long and laborious hearing in his absence, appears to have been enough for Trinity Hall, something that may have been assisted by Nicols's sending several contrite letters of apology to those concerned, promising to reimburse them as soon as he could. (In old age he signed correspondence, referring to the "great injuries" he had done to the university, as "a poor penitent thief".)[25] A reluctance to have recourse to formal prosecution was not confined to the secular courts. Ideally, even a parson's punishing of sin and vice was, at least initially, informal, effected by: "... withdrawing his bounty and courtesie from the parties offending, or by private, or

---

25. O. Chadwick, "The Case of Philip Nichols, 1731," in *Transactions of the Cambridge Bibliographical Society*, 1953, vol. 1, part 5, pp.424-30. I am grateful to Dr Elisabeth Leedham-Green, Cambridge University Archives, for this reference.

publick re-proof, as the case requires, than by causing them to be presented [to the ecclesiastical courts], or otherwise complained of."[26]

Thus, except for the gravest offences, the decision to prosecute was rarely determined purely by legal guilt, or even the availability of evidence, but was normally founded on careful assessments of the actions and characters of the accused, and their immediate social background.[27] Something that quickly becomes apparent is a degree of bias against strangers accused of crimes, or at least in favour of local people in a similar situation. There were several reasons for this, natural human compassion for those with whom one is familiar being one. It also appears that potential prosecutors and other law enforcement agents could be subjected to considerable pressure from a suspect, his kinsmen, neighbours or other villagers to exercise mercy. This could be manifest by not prosecuting or by prosecuting for a lesser offence than that actually committed. Thus, in early seventeenth century Wiltshire, a man accused of sexually assaulting a girl approached one of the witnesses and urged him to "use him like a neighbour". Similarly, when a sack of stolen corn was found in the house of one Thomas Morris in the same county, he urged the searchers to think of his children's plight. As a result, a constable "moved with pity, sought his neighbours that this business might be concealed". In the same manner, when Charles

---

26. G. Herbert, *A Priest to the Temple*, London, T. Maxey for T. Garthwait, 1652, p.26.
27. C.B. Herrup, "Law and Morality in Seventeenth-Century England," *Past & Present*, 1985, Number 105, pp.102-105.

Gunter caused an indictment to be made against two men for theft, an intermediary tried to persuade him to reduce the charge to merely one of 'cozening', arguing that "in doing so you shall be well thought of, otherwise some people will speak evil of you".[28] Likewise, when, in 1636, John King was detained by a local constable after he stole eight hens in his Essex village, King begged the officer not to cast him away for a few chickens, claiming it was his first ever offence. The constable discussed the matter with the victim of the theft, and, having done so, ultimately released King uncharged, as the lesser of two evils.[29] The mass-murderer and highwayman, Thomas Austin, executed at Exeter in August 1694 for killing seven children (two of them his own), his wife and aunt had also experienced such initial forbearance. Although born to prosperous parents he squandered his inheritance and, not knowing how to earn a livelihood, resorted to crime to support himself and his family: "Several frauds he was detected in, which his neighbours were so good as to forgive, out of respect to his family and to what he had once been."[30] Sir Edward Coke recalled a case from Suffolk in which an attorney had advised the friends of a felon not to appear to give evidence

---

28. M.J. Ingram, "Communities and Courts: Law and Disorder in early-Seventeenth-Century Wiltshire," in J.S. Cockburn (Ed.), *Crime in England 1550-1800*, 1977, pp.128-129.

29. K. Wrightson, "Two concepts of order: justices constables and jurymen in seventeenth century England," in J. Brewer and J. Styles (Eds.), *An ungovernable people: the English and their law in the 17th and 18th centuries*, London, Hutchinson, 1980, p.31.

30. C. Johnson, *A General History of the Lives and Adventures of the Most Famous Highwaymen, Murderers, Street-Robbers*, London: J. Janeway, 1734, p.348.

against him, which was done (though viewed as contempt of court).[31] Where the prosecutor was wealthy or powerful, such acts of mercy also helped promote a popular faith in the 'paternalism' of local elements of the political nation.[32] It was inherently much less likely that such indulgence would be shown to strangers.

Additionally, local people could sometimes take advantage of defences that were not available to outsiders. For example, that 'stolen' animals had merely 'strayed' into their premises.[33] Furthermore, for as long as they continued to function, local men could be dealt with in forums, such as the manorial leet and church courts, that were inherently less likely (or even forbidden) to impose draconian punishments, and might merely sentence the accused to a modest fiscal penalty or public penance. These forums were often effectively denied to strangers. Thus, most local felons, unless they committed a very serious crime, had a long record of previous offending behind them, or were personally very unpopular were not prosecuted for felony in a court.

The Limits of Tolerance

Nevertheless, serious and persistent sins had to be punished

---

31. Sir E. Coke, *Institutes of the Lawes of England, Part Three, Concerning High Treason, and other Pleas of the Crown and Criminall causes*, London, 1644, p.139.
32. D. Hay, "Property, authority and the criminal law," *Albions Fatal Tree*, D. Hay *et al* (eds.), 1975, p.44.
33. Ingram, "Communities and Courts: Law and Disorder in early-Seventeenth-Century Wiltshire," pp.128-129.

appropriately and, eventually, even a clergyman would have no alternative but to: "... call in Authority, and to do such things of legall opposition either in the presenting, or punishing of any, as the vulgar ever consters for signes of ill will."[34] Similarly, in secular matters, ultimately the limits of tolerance or community action would be reached and formal sanctions invoked. The accusation that was eventually brought against an individual, who had become a thorough nuisance to his neighbours, might be 'incidental', a final offence which prompted the long-suffering local community into action.[35] Thus, in 1608, the inhabitants of Burnham sent a petition to the Norfolk JPs complaining about a local troublemaker who had exhausted their patience:

"... having longe tyme endured ye misdemenors and badd cariage of Henry Hopkins (dwelling amongst us) uppon hoope of his amendment, yett still fyndinge him worse, contynuinge in his bad corse of lyfe without reformacon, being a disturber of his Majesty's peace, a common makelate, an ydle lyver, a notorious raylor, and one gyven unto all lewdnes, wherefore we thought it our dutye to certife yor worships herin, as also to crave yor warrant of the good as well for example unto others, as also that by ye ordinary corse of lawe in tyme he may be brought under obedience."

---

34. Herbert, A *Priest to the Temple*, p.26.
35. A. Soman, "Deviance and Criminal Justice in Western Europe, 1300-1800: An Essay in Structure," *Criminal Justice History*, 1980, vol. 1, p.11.

It was signed by 14 local men and marked by six.[36] A few decades later, the experiences of John Aston of Myddle, in Shropshire, provide another typical example of community patience for a longstanding, albeit minor, local nuisance being exhausted. Aston was a physically disadvantaged man, with a "deformed countenance and mis-shapen body", and, it seems, somewhat backward, a "sort of a silly fellow very idle and much given to stealing of poultry and small things". There had been numerous informal attempts at curbing his anti-social behaviour: "He was many times catched in the fact and sometimes well cojeled [beaten] by those that would trouble themselves no further with him." Nevertheless, there were limits to how far such informal sanctions could be repeated and, at length, recourse was made to the criminal law: "But at last he grew insufferable and made it his common practice to steal hens in the night and bring them to Shrewsbury where he had confederates to receive them at any time of night." He was arrested and indicted for stealing 24 chickens. Fortunately for Aston, the Assizes judge clearly appreciated that he was dealing with a troublesome social inadequate rather than a serious menace, and expressly encouraged 'pious perjury' on the part of the jury, so that he would escape the death penalty: "... seeing him a silly man [the judge] told the jury that the matter of fact was so fully proved that they must find the prisoner guilty but they would do well to consider of the

---

36.   Sir N. Bacon, "The official papers of Sir Nathaniel Bacon of Stiffkey, Norfolk as Justice of the Peace 1580/1620," H.W. Saunders (Ed.), London, Royal History Society, *Camden Third Series*, 1915, vol. 26, p.23.

value of 11 pence." This would mean a conviction for non-capital petty larceny (being less than a shilling). When the jury followed his advice, the judge "laughed heartily and [said] he was glad to hear cocks and hens were so cheap in this county". Aston's conviction and ensuing non-capital punishment had the desired effect of moderating, if not ending, his anti-social behaviour; he became: "... more careful butt he left not his old trade whoolly."[37] A widespread reluctance to prosecute also meant that, when a decision was finally made to take formal action against an individual, a multiplicity of allegations might be forthcoming. Thus, in 1621, Robert Godfrey, an Essex alehouse keeper, was reported to the local quarter sessions for blasphemy, quarrelling, gambling, breaking the peace, theft, receiving stolen goods, harbouring suspicious persons, attending church infrequently, fathering a bastard on his maidservant, drunkenness, and running a disorderly alehouse that had been closed down and illegally reopened on three occasions.[38]

Inherent Problems in Private Prosecution

The problem with any system of private prosecution is that crime victims might be too busy, lazy, poor (or avaricious), intimidated, bribed or compassionate to take, or continue

---

37. R. Gough, *The History of Myddle*, D. Hey (Ed.), Penguin 1981, (originally written 1701), p.146.
38. T.C. Curtis and J.A. Sharpe, "Crime in Tudor and Stuart England," *History Today*, 1988, vol. 38, issue 2, pp.23-33.

with, proceedings against a suspect. All of these factors posed permanent problems for the authorities. If a thief had been apprehended red handed, or while trying to sell on his booty, his victim would normally recover anything that had been lost. If he did not catch the perpetrator in these circumstances, his losses were often irrecoverable. Either way, criminal proceedings would involve him in considerable trouble and expense for little tangible benefit. At the end of a prosecution, he might get the satisfaction of seeing the perpetrator punished, but usually there would be no compensation. In 1701, an anonymous writer alluded to these problems, claiming that English law did not take: "... sufficient care to make Restitution to the injured Party, and by that means many Prosecutions are hindred, since a Man's own goods or money taken from him by violence, are not easily (if at all) to be recovered, even tho the Thief be apprehended and convicted."[39] As a result, throughout the period, suspects might be released if they were captured by a: "... simple man that hath lost his goods, because he will not be bound to give evidence at the Assize to his trouble and charge."[40]

Prosecuting could be an expensive and troublesome business. Court and recognisance fees would have to be paid, and could sometimes amount to several guineas. A popular reluctance to incur such costs occasioned regular complaints about a decline in public spiritedness and the

---

39.   Anon, *Hanging, not Punishment Enough, for Murtherers, High-way Men, and House-Breakers*, London, A. Baldwin, 1701, pp.11-13.
40.   Hext, "Extract from a letter written by Edward Hext," p.341.

number of people who appeared too mean to enforce the law.[41] Additionally, outside London and other major towns and cities, prosecution might entail arduous journeys to find an examining JP and subsequently to attend trial. Although the responsibility of JPs for conducting pre-trial examinations was limited by geographical area, they were not evenly distributed. Thus, in Kent, in 1596, the great majority of parishes did not have a resident magistrate (though a few had two or more). All villages were clustered within a hundred, many, but still not all, of which did have a JP (these being gathered in their turn into larger 'Baylywikes' which always had at least one magistrate). As a result, the very active Kentish JP, Michael Sondes, in Throwley, was the only magistrate in the 17 parishes of the Faversham hundred.[42] Those in awkwardly situated parishes might have to walk up to 10 miles to find a JP. The journey to testify at the Assizes or quarter sessions could be more than 30 miles in large counties. This undoubtedly had a significant impact on crime reporting. Indeed, it was claimed that some victims refused to 'recognise' their stolen goods when taken before a magistrate and shown them: "... for fear of forfeiting their Recognizance, and of long journies, that may sometimes more than double the loss."[43] Additionally, then as now, giving evidence in court was traumatic. Even Bernard De Mandeville had some sympathy

---

41. A Citizen in London, *The Vices of the cities of London and Westminster trac'd from their original* ..., G.Faulkner, Dublin, 1751, p.11.
42. W. Lambarde, *A Perambulation of Kent* (written 1570), Baldwin, Cradock, Joy & Co., London, 1826, pp.23-24.
43. Anon, *Hanging, not Punishment Enough*, pp.11-13.

for the: "... backwardness of a meek home-bred person, who should complain, that to appear in open court, and speak before a judge, are terrible things to him."[44] Finally, if the defendant was a local man (as he often would be) and acquitted, the victim would have made an enemy and risked reprisals.

Conscience and moral scruples also discouraged action if a criminal was likely to be sentenced to death on conviction, particularly for a non-violent offence of dishonesty. Even in the late sixteenth century, observers such as Sir Edward Hext were pointing out that the draconian nature of the penalty for relatively minor thefts meant that victims, especially those who had recovered their property, were reluctant to prosecute: "... for most commonly the simple countryman and woman, looking no further than unto the loss of their own goods, are of opinion that they would not procure a man's death for all the goods in the world." Even if forced to attend trial, many would "gyve feynt evidence" so that the accused person was acquitted.[45] Indeed, in some situations, the courts themselves appear to have connived in this process, taking the opportunity to impose a minor penalty instead of initiating the full proceedings available, if the victim was amenable. Thus, in August 1581, John Keighley from Yorkshire, who had travelled to Warwickshire to work in the harvest there, was accused of stealing two jerkins, which he claimed he

---

44. B. De Mandeville, *An Enquiry into the Causes of the Frequent Executions at Tyburn*, London, 1725, p.3.
45. Hext, "Extract from a letter written by Edward Hext," p.341.

had found on the ground at Warwick fair. Given that their value was almost certainly over 12 pence this was potentially a capital felony. The owner of the jerkins identified them, and they were returned to him. However, Keighley was merely: "... punished till the next day & then let goo uppon informacion made by Humfrey Crane that the party was satisfied."[46] Such scruples about prosecuting a felon to conviction survived to the end of the period. Thus, in the 1650s, John Evelyn, summonsed to appear at the trial of a footpad who had robbed him, noted in his diary that "not being bound over (nor willing to hang the fellow) I did not appear". (Somewhat strangely, it seems the footpad was still convicted, again perhaps an indication of the periodic absence of 'trial by book'.)[47] There was a particularly widespread reluctance to pursue actions against the more pathetic types of criminal, such as former prostitutes reduced by illness to picking pockets. Such a woman normally rotted in Newgate "'till she is discharged because the plaintiff will not appear to prosecute her".[48] The authorities regularly and publicly deprecated this type of: "... vayne pitie; wherin is contayned neither iustice nor yet commendable charitie, but rather therby ensueth negligence, contempte, dissobedience."[49] Nevertheless, their criticisms seem to have had little effect.

---

46. T. Kempt (Ed.), *The Book of John Fisher, Town Clerk and Deputy Recorder of Warwick 1580-1581*, Warwick, Henry Cooke & Son, Pubs., 1909, p.51.
47. J. Evelyn, *The Diary of John Evelyn*, E.S. De Beer (Ed.), Oxford, Clarendon Press, 1955, vol. III, pp.69-71.
48. *The Gentleman's Magazine*, 1749, vol. 19, p.126.
49. Elyot, *The Boke named The Governour*, p.120.

Of course, occasionally, a reluctance to take legal action could be misadvised, as illustrated by a case from Gloucestershire in 1673. There, a prosperous yeoman's servant, of very "obscure birth" and extremely bad temper, developed a hopeless passion for his master's daughter. Her disdainful spurning of him eventually led him to desire revenge. Shortly after being rejected, he went berserk with a scythe, wounding the yeoman's wife. However, despite the gravity of the offence, after the servant claimed to be very sorry for what he had done, blaming his emotional turmoil, the yeoman's family "took no further course to punish him but only dismist him their service". He left, promising never to trouble them again. Some years later, he chanced upon the daughter milking cows in a field, and hacked her to death with a hedge-bill. A child accompanying her only narrowly escaped.[50]

Spawning Private Arrangements

Throughout the period, the royal courts were selective about trying to monopolize the determination of crimes. As a result, minor and intermediate level offences, even when detected, were frequently settled by private arrangements. England was not unusual in this. Indeed, compared to many European countries, it was early in removing heinous crimes from the private domain. Medieval royal justice had

---

50. Anon, *The Bloody Lover: or, Barbarous News from Gloucester*, London, P. Browesby, 1673, pp.3-5.

speedily monopolized homicide, relying on local coroners to ensure that suspicious deaths came to the Crown's attention. As a result, the blood-feud was eliminated by the thirteenth century.[51] By contrast, the private payment of compensation to the kin of murdered men, along with the settlement of many other serious crimes, lingered in parts of Northern Europe well into the early modern period. Within the British Isles it was at the root of the Gaelic *Brehon* law in Ireland, the influence of which only started to wane after the 1540s. Even in the 1590s, Sir Edmund Spenser was shocked by how, at variance to the common law, in a murder: "The Brehon that is ther judg, will compound betwene the murtherer, and the frends of the party murthered, which prosecute the action, that the malefactor shall give unto them, or to the child, or wife of him that is slaine, a recompence, which they call an Iriach; by which vile law of thers, many murders are amongst them made up and smothered." This seemed sheer wickedness.[52] Similarly, in parts of Wales, it lingered until the start of the early modern era as the law of *Galanas*. Even in lowland Scotland it was a reality until the end of the sixteenth century, with many homicides being settled by agreed payments of compensation without state involvement. Only after the turn of the century did such agreements have no effect in preventing the involvement of royal justice in punishing

---

51. J. Wormald, "Bloodfeud, Kindred and Government in Early Modern Scotland," *Past and Present*, 1980, vol. 87, pp.54-97.
52. E. Spenser, "A Veue of the Present State of Ireland," (1596), in A.B. Grosart (Ed.), *The Complete Works in Verse and Prose of Edmund Spenser*, London, privately published 1884, vol. 9, pp.18-19.

those guilty of murder. A similar situation prevailed in much of continental Europe. Thus, in 1582, the widow of a man slain in Seville agreed to pardon the killer of her husband upon payment of 200 ducats. (Though by then, even in Spain, this personal pardon required approval by the secular authorities, and the condemned man had to proceed to the gallows until a messenger brought notice of their agreement to commutation.)[53]

Nevertheless, at the lowest end of the English criminal spectrum there was little attempt by the Crown to involve itself in misdemeanours, such as assaults, in which private composition was normal, recognized and even encouraged by the courts. Thus, in November 1580, the Bailiff of Warwick (effectively both a Recorder and magistrate) noted that the constable of the market area and a clearly injured shopkeeper, William Sharples, "comying with bloody face", had brought one Richard Donghill before him. Apparently, Donghill, an unflatteringly named and habitual trouble-maker, had walked into Sharples's shop and, without provocation, "sudenly struke him". In the light of the evidence, it was decided that he should be committed to jail as a "Roge and comon barretter". However, Donghill asked for an adjournment for a day or two before this proposal was effected. This allowed informal negotiations and arrangements between criminal and victim. As a result, William Sharples: "... being the partie offendid and Thomas Saunders came and desired that he [Donghill] might be re-

---

53. M.E. Perry, *Crime and Society in Early Modern Seville*, Hanover (N.H.), University of New England Press, 1980, p.60.

leased in hope of a new lief." At this, Donghill played his allotted part in the drama, fell down on his knees and begged Sharples's forgiveness. Additionally, he promised to behave himself in future. Sharples, in turn, magnanimously undertook to be his friend, and, more practically, announced that he would send the defendant to London, to place him in work there "so as he should never agayn trouble the toune". (London appears to have been the natural receptacle for much of the criminal detritus of provincial society.) Donghill was set free with the warning that he would be "punished without favor" if he misbehaved again. However, this appears not to have had any effect as, within a few days, and having failed to depart for the Metropolis, he was arrested again for rowdy and violent drunken antics. This time, the authorities' patience was exhausted: "The balief sent him to the gaole as a roge".[54]

Compounding a misdemeanor was entirely legal in early modern England. A victim compounded an offence if s/he accepted a financial benefit as consideration for not seeking its prosecution. For example, by not reporting it to the authorities or, having reported it, by failing to proceed with it, in exchange for money. The legality of such a practise was significant. Given that it often needed considerable encouragement to induce people to prosecute felonies, it might be wondered why they would ever bother about lesser offences such as misdemeanours. One answer is that many such prosecutions were specifically aimed at obtaining personal benefit, whether in the form of a

---

54. Kempt, *The Book of John Fisher*, pp.9-10.

monetary payment or the personal satisfaction of a profuse (often public) apology, rather than the punishment of an offender. The threat of court action was frequently merely the 'stick' that brought about the accord. This was often explicitly recognised and connived at by the courts themselves. Thus, it has been suggested that the moderate average level of fines for common assaults determined at the Surrey quarter sessions in the late seventeenth century (only three shillings six pence if a few exceptional cases are excluded) indicates that these were often nominal sums imposed where the two parties had reached a satisfactory settlement out of court, rather than punishments aimed at deterring such conduct in the future. Many fines were as small as six pence or a shilling. However, a larger fine might be awarded by the court when such an agreement was not forthcoming, and the threat of such a penalty, along with that of imprisonment if it was not paid, was used by the courts as a way of persuading reluctant defendants to come to terms with complainants. Thus, when discussing assault and battery in 1729, the Recorder of London noted that it was: "... usual in these cases for the Defendant to make satisfaction to the Prosecutor for his wounds, and costs and charges before the Court sets the fine ... which is usually greater if a Defendant won't make a Prosecutor easy as the Court directs."[55] Later in the eighteenth century, William Blackstone deprecated the frequent practice whereby, even if a prosecution to conviction for a misdemeanour, such as

---

55. J. Beattie, *Crime and the Courts in England 1660-1800*, Oxford, OUP, 1986, pp.457-458.

battery, had been obtained, the court would: "... permit the defendant to *speak with the prosecutor*, before any judgement is pronounced; and if the prosecutor declares himself satisfied, to inflict but a trivial punishment." As Blackstone noted, this was done to reimburse the prosecutor for his expenses and provide some amends for his injury, without making him go to the trouble of taking a civil action. He strongly disapproved of the practice, as it meant that prosecutions for assault were: "... too frequently commenced rather for private lucre than for the great ends of public justice."[56] Nevertheless, such actions appear to have been endemic. It has been asserted that in eighteenth century Middlesex most common assault prosecutions were aimed not at punishing a defendant, but at obtaining compensation, making them quasi-civil suits.[57]

Indeed, JPs would often actively encourage complainants and suspects to reach an accord without formal charges even being brought. It was well recognised that for many lesser misdemeanours, especially those which did not involve dishonesty, a cardinal role of the magistrate was to effect a non-judicial settlement. This allowed the parties to return to harmonious co-existence and avoided the severity, trouble and expense of court proceedings. In 1594, even the legalistic Lambarde noted that a JP should be as much a "Compounder as a Commissioner of the Peace".[58]

---

56. W. Blackstone, *Commentaries on the Laws of England*, Oxford, Clarendon Press, 1769, vol. 4, pp.356-357.
57. N. Landau, "Indictment for Fun and Profit: A Prosecutor's Reward at Eighteenth-Century Quarter Sessions," *Law and History Review*, 1999, p.508.
58. W. Lambarde, *Eirenarcha*, London, Company of Stationers, 1594, p.10.

Almost 140 years later, similar views were still being expressed, it being claimed that the great majority of: "... Strifes and Dissentions which come before Justices of Peace, are such as are determinable by them no otherwise than as Mediators and Reconcilers of Differences, and not as Magistrates in which they can act by any authority of Law."[59] Of course, such a paternalistic role normally required that JPs be held in esteem. Unsurprisingly, it was not always successful, especially in those areas where their social status did not automatically command respect (as in suburban and Metropolitan areas in the eighteenth century).

Between murder and misdemeanour were numerous non-lethal felonies. Here, the Crown was keen to extend its domain, but constantly limited by its lack of royal officials. As a result, privately negotiated justice, between criminal and victim, remained a feature of such offences throughout the period, despite it being illegal to compound felonies (18 Eliz. c. 5 and 27 Eliz. c. 10). Even the angriest man who found that lost money or possessions were recoverable might cool down, so that the "business is generally made up (as they call it) among themselves, and 'tis never brought before a magistrate". Human nature meant that many men would "have an eye to their own interest, more than to the Publick". The dubious (and uncertain) personal satisfaction of seeing a felon hanged was often not enough.[60] This was especially likely if reparation was accompanied by an informal punishment, such as a beating.

---

59. *The Gentleman's Magazine*, 1732, vol. 2, p.910.
60. Anon, *Hanging, not Punishment Enough*, pp.11-13.

Consequently, if a criminal was caught red-handed he might offer immediate financial compensation to prevent a constable or watchman being summoned or being marched before a JP. If cash was short, some other tangible benefit might be proposed. Thus, in one case, when a thief was caught stealing from his employer, he begged him: "... repeatedly not to prosecute, and entered into negotiations to work on one of his master's houses in return for forgiveness."[61] After the authorities had become actively involved, and recognisances taken, such negotiations would be less likely. Nevertheless, they were still common. Thus, the victim and prosecutor of an arrested child thief, accused of having stolen and pawned a lace waistcoat, approached the girl's father, one Joseph Watkins and "wanted money to stop the proceedings, he having been at great expense ... He said, would I give nothing to save my child?" (Watkins' refusal proved justified when the girl was acquitted, apparently because she was deemed too young, at 11 years of age, to have sufficient discretion to be held guilty of the felony.)[62] Similarly, in 1745, John Twyford sexually assaulted his inebriated drinking partner, a soldier named John Mullins, while they shared a bed in a London tavern (a common sleeping arrangement at the time). The two men fell to blows and were carried to the watch-house. In the morning, Twyford, alarmed that he might face a charge of sodomy, approached Mullins: "Brother soldier, you had

---

61. Hay (Ed.), *Albions Fatal Tree,* p.41.
62. J.H. Langbein, "Historical Foundations of the Law of Evidence: A View From the Ryder Sources," *Columbia Law Review,* 1996, vol. 96, p.53.

better make this up: he said he had not much money about him, but he would give me half a crown, and he told me I must say that I was in liquor, and did not know what I said." This was a reference to Mullins's earlier complaint to the constable.[63] At a more elevated level, it was claimed that Mary Frith ('Moll Cutpurse'), facing execution, but having accumulated enormous wealth through her lengthy criminal career: "... procured her pardon by giving her adversary two thousand pounds."[64] Indeed, it has been argued that some lower class women brought rape allegations in the criminal courts as part of an informal process aimed at achieving a negotiation and 'settlement'. Their aim was not to produce a guilty verdict but to prompt the accused man into 'making up', and so to receive public acknowledgment of their (genuine) injury and, perhaps, some modest degree of financial compensation. This process, being misunderstood by the courts, may have occasioned the widespread seventeenth and eighteenth century fear of blackmail being behind rape allegations, which in turn encouraged judicial caution about such complaints. (Other modern observers have strongly challenged such an analysis.)[65] Thus, in 1678, a defendant accused of child rape argued in his defence that the victim's family had offered a composition. This received the sharp response from the court that if the "parents were

---

63. Anon, *The Proceedings on the King's Commissions*, London, 1745, pp.186-7.
64. J.L. Rayner and G.T. Crook (Eds.), *The Complete Newgate Calendar*, Privately printed for the Navarre Society, vol. I, p.172.
65. L. Edelstein, "An Accusation Easily to be Made? Rape and Malicious Prosecution in Eighteenth-Century England," *The American Journal of Legal History*, 1998, vol. 42, No. 4, p.353.

so wicked, as to offer a Composition, yet that made him not innocent".[66]

Agreements Between Thieves and Victims over Property

The ineffectualness of the criminal justice system also encouraged victims to enter into private arrangements with thieves for the recovery of their stolen property, at a mutually acceptable price. The spread of literacy facilitated such settlements, allowing the publication of newspaper advertisements offering money for the return of stolen items with 'no questions asked', and subsequently permitting contact via an exchange of letters. Thus, after Horatio Walpole was robbed by two men in Hyde Park, in November 1749, a pistol ball passing through his coach and burning his face, he received a letter from the highwaymen, intimating concern about the incident and offering to return his stolen watch and sword as well as his coachman's timepiece, if he would immediately send 40 pounds to a specific location. When he failed to do so, they reduced their claim to 20 pounds, threatening to destroy the items if he did not send the money.[67] Bernard De Mandeville (1670-1733) thought such negotiations shameful, feeling that it made the victims 'aiders and abetters' in the felony. The 'criminal selfishness' of such people had a disastrous impact

---

66. Anon, *An exact account of the trials of the several persons arraigned at the sessions-house in the Old-Bailey for London and Middlesex*, London, Gilham Hills, 1678, p.15.
67. *The Gentleman's Magazine*, 1749, vol. 19, p.522.

on crime levels, especially in London.[68]

De Mandeville was writing shortly before the exposure and prosecution of the 'Thief Taker General', Jonathan Wild, who arranged such settlements on a commercial basis. However, Wild had merely developed the system established by Mary Frith ('Moll Cutpurse') in the previous century. Seeking a safer and more profitable criminal career than that provided by theft, Frith had opened a shop in Fleet Street, and, for many years, fenced stolen articles she received from thieves, many of them virtually in her employ. Effectively, she became a commercial go-between between thieves and their wealthier victims. Of course, there were risks in her system. On one occasion, a countryman who had had his watch stolen repaired to her office to see if she could recover it, only to notice that the self same watch was already in her possession behind the counter. He summoned a constable and she was arrested and prosecuted for theft. However, she disputed the identity of the watch and arranged for one of her pick-pockets to steal it from court so that, despite warnings to her from the Bench, the: "Jury could not but acquit me for the present".[69]

---

68. B. De Mandeville, *An Enquiry into the Causes of the Frequent Executions at Tyburn*, 1725, London, p.3.

69. Anon, *The Life and Death of Mrs Mary Frith*, London, W.G. Ilberton, 1662, pp.64-67.

Unspoken Understandings between Criminals and Victims

In theory, as robbers and burglars were committing a serious felony, they had little to lose by killing their victims. In practice, however, this seems to have been relatively rare, except where resistance was shown. Part of the explanation for such restraint undoubtedly rests in a humane reluctance, on the part of many criminals, to shed innocent blood if they could avoid it. As James Maclane noted in a letter to one of his erstwhile victims, although he and his colleague had been obliged by misfortune to have recourse to robbery: "Yet we have Humanity Enough not to take any bodys life where there is Not a Nessecety for it."[70] However, there were also other factors at work. Generally speaking, instrumental crime that resulted in death was more likely to produce a concerted and effective hue and cry. Most importantly of all, there appears to have been a widespread realisation that forbearance and courtesy where possible *might* pay dividends in a criminal justice system in which prosecution was largely in the control of the victim. Thus, in the early 1650s, the footpad who had successfully robbed John Evelyn petitioned him to support his reprieve. Evelyn appears to have concurred with this request, the man being spared and (apparently) eventually executed for another crime, some years later.[71] The precise reasons for Evelyn's

---

70. Letter in the Evening Post 1749, in *Supplement to the Letters of Horace Walpole*, Paget Toynbee (Ed.), Oxford, Clarendon Press, 1925, vol.III, pp.132-135.
71. J. Evelyn, *The Diary of John Evelyn*, E.S. de Beer (Ed.), vol.III, Oxford, Clarendon Press, 1955, pp.69-71.

humanity are hard to establish; however, it may have been linked to a realisation that the accused man could easily have killed him, and had forborne to do so. This phenomenon had been noted by Thomas More in 1516, and was reiterated by Samuel Johnson in 1751, when he observed that a good man would often recoil at the thought of punishing a: "... slight injury with death, especially when he remembers that the thief might have procured safety by another crime from which he was restrained only by his remaining virtue."[72]

Sadly, some crime victims appear to have misjudged the extent to which such unspoken "rules of the game" applied, and antagonised their attackers by alluding to them. Thus, in 1692, Jocelin Harwood, with two accomplices, robbed the house of Sir Nehemiah Burroughs in Shropshire, binding the knight and his wife and servants, and then tying up his daughters. At this, one of the young women rashly alluded to such 'understandings': "Pray, sir, use us civilly; which if you do, we will use you in the same manner, in case you and your companions should be taken; for I am sure we shall know you again." This prompted the enraged Harwood to stab both daughters to death, along with their parents. Nevertheless, his behaviour was considered so unacceptable that his shocked colleagues, who had been unable to stop the murderous attack, subsequently tied him up and left him by the highway with part of the proceeds of the robbery, as a result of which he was captured, identified

---

72. *Samuel Johnson*, "Crime and Punishment, 23rd April 1751," *The Rambler*, London, Everyman's Library, 1953, p.186.

and hanged.[73]

Extortion via Threatened and Malicious Prosecution

A private system of prosecution meant that, along with legally justified actions not being brought, there were dangers that unjustified proceedings could be threatened or initiated with a view to personal gain. The dividing line between compensation for victims and extortion could be quite thin. Embarrassing allegations could easily be fabricated and potential prosecutors, whether the victims or witnesses of real or imaginary crimes, could extort money in lieu of proceedings. This appears to have been one of the principal motives behind malicious prosecution. As a result, the post-1690 Societies for the Reformation of Manners were acutely sensitive to allegations that their aim was not reform but the 'getting of money'. They stressed that reward motivated informers were not members of their organisations, although accepting that there were wicked people about who "extorted Money from Offenders, and *sometimes from honest Men*".[74] Blatantly malicious and unfounded prosecutions might also be brought because of personal hostility towards the defendant, as the Reverend Hawkins discovered in 1669, when 'framed' for theft after a dispute about tithes and churchmanship. However, the

---

73. C. Johnson, *A General History of the Lives and Adventures of the Most Famous Highwaymen, Murderers, Street-Robbers*, London: J. Janeway, 1734, pp.345-346.
74. Anon, *The Three and Thirtieth account of the progress made in the Cities of London and Westminster*, 1727, pp.39-40.

judiciary were alive to such possibilities. Thus, when, in 1678, George Hunt was found not guilty of felony at the Old Bailey: "... the Court taking notice of the malicious prosecution, gave him leave to take a Copy of the Indictment." This would facilitate a later civil action. Similarly, Lord Chief Baron Hale assisted Hawkins to sue his accusers, after he was acquitted. (He ultimately secured between £12 and £44 from each solvent defendant in a settlement of the action.)[75] As this case suggests, occasionally, a maliciously prosecuted man could secure "large amendes" from his accuser by such an action. As today, this required proof that malice rather than genuine mistake occasioned the prosecution, so that an award of substantial damages "chaunceth seldome".[76]

Governmental and Private Encouragement to Prosecute

By the latter decades of the period, longstanding concerns about the adequacy of existing law enforcement agencies and the prosecution process were becoming more acute, especially in London. This prompted government action aimed at encouraging the public to 'police' itself via financial and other rewards. The latter included saleable 'Tyburn tickets' excusing parish service as a constable etc. They were first introduced on an organised basis in 1692, by

---

75. Bernard, *The Case of John Atherton*, London, Luke Stokoe, 1710, pp.21-25 and p.44.
76. Sir T. Smith, *De Republica Anglorum*, London, 1583, p.116

the Highwayman Act (4 & 5 William & Mary c.8), which offered a £40 reward for the capture and conviction (by giving evidence) of robbers. Further Acts were passed in 1699 and 1706. Sometimes, special extra government funded rewards were also offered for specific and serious crimes. Additionally, there were local and private reward schemes, instituted by parishes and commercial organisations. Thus, in 1749, St Paul's Covent Garden offered 20 guineas to anyone apprehending a robber or detecting a gaming house, to be paid upon conviction. (Convicting the owner of a bawdy house secured the lesser sum of 10 pounds.)[77] Rewards might also be offered for individual criminals. In 1683, after William Nevison's crimes became notorious, a substantial sum was offered for his capture, which prompted many attempts to take him. Amongst them was that of two brothers named Fletcher, one of whom Nevison shot dead, before being captured by a Captain Hardcastle and sent to York jail. (He was tried and executed within a week.)[78] Rewards could be a serious financial business by the early 1700s. In August 1731, £600 was paid to several people for apprehending and prosecuting five highwaymen to conviction, at the Old Bailey.[79] In March of the following year, £400 was paid out of the Treasury to those concerned in arresting another gang, who were executed at Tyburn the same month.[80] In 1741, a cashier to the Bank of England who

---

77.   *The Gentleman's Magazine*, 1749, vol. 19, p.522.
78.   Johnson, *A General History of the Lives and Adventures of the Most Famous Highwaymen*, p.103.
79.   *The Gentleman's Magazine*, 1731, vol. 1, p.351.
80.   *The Gentleman's Magazine*, 1732, vol. 2, p.673.

withdrew East India bonds worth £10,000 and immediately disappeared, and the clerk to a City Alderman who stole £5,000 of Bank Bills and took the packet boat to Calais, attracted rewards of £200 from their erstwhile employers.[81] A logical development was to extend this system to the high seas, and, in the early 1700s, rewards of £200 were offered for those who succeeded in bringing notorious pirate leaders to justice.[82]The rapidly increasing scale of these inducements ultimately produced a series of scandals involving 'thief-takers' which would bring the whole system into disrepute in the eighteenth century. However, even ordinary people could be malignly influenced by the substantial sums available. In 1716, a Mr Jackson prosecuted two men to conviction and execution at York, for being the accessories of a 'robber' who, it was claimed, had received a penny ha'penny from Jackson's companion, in what many considered to be no more than a case of 'aggressive' begging on a public road. One of the condemned men, at the scaffold, accused Jackson of "down right perjury, insisting that he never demanded any money of them, or offered the least abuse". Thomas Gent, along with many others, was convinced that in this case the: "... temptation of the reward for taking highwaymen, proved the grand inducement to swear away the poor creatures' lives."[83]

81.   *The Gentleman's Magazine*, 1741, vol. 11, p.277.
82.   S. Smith, "Piracy in early British America," *History Today*, 1996, vol. 26, issue 5, p.29.
83.   T. Gent. *The Life of Mr Thomas Gent, Printer of York*, London, Thomas Thorpe, 1832, pp.56-57.

Informers

The existence of informers was closely linked to the reward system, playing a central role in many early modern English prosecutions, especially those of a variety of unpopular or 'victimless' crimes that would otherwise not have attracted a prosecutor. Thus, from the late medieval period, informers were heavily involved in the prosecution of economic and regulatory offences. In the ensuing three centuries their operations gradually expanded. By the early 1700s there was a plethora of small rewards, often for economic or regulatory offences, such as the 10 shillings paid to an informer who incriminated anyone riding on a cart or drey without "another on foot to guide it" (I Geo. c.57), the £5 paid to those who informed on anyone wearing printed calicos (except for blue ones), or the 20 shillings per dozen paid for informing on those who imported foreign buttons. (Such matters were often dealt with at petty sessions with an appeal lying to quarter sessions.)[84] Sometimes, such informers received their rewards directly from those whom they successfully convicted; at others, they came from the state. Typical of such men, Griffin Flood made a career as an informer in London in the early 1620s. He was a debauched man of "meane birth, [and] rude bringing up" who would haunt ale-houses to acquire useful information. Flood secured money from the rewards available for informing, or,

---

84. J. Shaw, *The Practical Justice of Peace: or a Treatise shewing the power and authority of that office in all its branches, etc.*, London, Thomas Ward, 1728, vol.1, pp.24-27.

where they were not offered, by using the threat of prosecution to exact blackmail. Thus, he would identify breaches of the Statute of Buildings and threaten to lay informations against the structures' owners, setting out the defects. On one occasion, he found a shopkeeper whose premises were not "sufficiently plastered with lime and haire". Ultimately, for "quitenesse sake", the shopkeeper was forced to provide "some satisfaction to be rid of him". Another time, he fetched churchwardens to a tavern that was open during divine service on a Sunday. There "finding certaine good fellows taking their morning draught, [Flood] fought to have him [the innkeeper] presented". He offered not to proceed if paid money.[85] Informing for gain was not only an urban phenomenon. Thomas Warie brought informations against dozens of people at the Somerset quarter sessions in the years between 1628 and 1631.[86] However, London was its epicentre. Thus, between 1682 and 1686 the notorious Hilton brothers led a large gang of informers targeting Protestant dissenters, such as Baptists and Quakers, who worshipped in illegal Metropolitan conventicles. The gang secretly infiltrated their meetings, laid informations with JPs against them, secured warrants for their arrest, gave evidence in court, and, when fines were not paid, seized and sold their goods. Many members of this gang had dubious pasts; the Hilton brothers themselves had become involved in forgery, coining and running an ale-

---

85. Anon, *The Life and Death of Griffin Flood*, London, 1623, ff.B1, B3 and C1.
86. P. Rawlings, *Policing: A Short History*, Cullompton, Willan Publishing, 2002, p.44.

house after settling in London in the 1670s. (Amid mounting popular resistance to their campaign, James II's abandonment of religious intolerance ended their operations.) Despite the hostility engendered by the Hiltons, informing continued to be an essential part of the criminal justice system, although some restrictions on the evidence of informers were imposed by statute, in 1692. Thus, an Act of 1700 offered £100 to those who secured the conviction of Catholic priests, and the Game Act of 1722 allowed them half of the fines incurred by those convicted for poaching.[87] In the last decade of the seventeenth, and the first three decades of the eighteenth, centuries, they were also used by the Societies for the Reformation of Manners (though without becoming members of these organisations). Within three weeks of the Gin Act of 1736 becoming law, it was reported that there were already more than 20 informers in London who made it their "sole Business to give Informations against Persons who presume to sell spirituous Liquors contrary to the late Act". Given that there was a five pound reward for securing a conviction, this is not, perhaps, surprising. A case could have as many as three informers (perhaps to bolster testimony), though most operated alone or in pairs. Informers using the 1736 Gin Act were active wherever spirits were distilled and distributed. Thus, two women in Norwich, described as "very expert in their Business", entrapped "several Top-Distillers, and a great

---

87. M. Goldie, "The Hilton gang: terrorising dissent in 1680s London," *History Today*, 1997, vol. 47, issue 10, p.26.

number more of petty Traders in Spirituous Liquors".[88]
Nevertheless, there had always been an awareness of the
risks involved in rewarding informers. A statute of 1548,
amending the 1533 Act on bestiality, and introduced,
presumably, to protect against malicious accusations made
for gain, added an additional clause to the earlier statute
advising that: "No person be received for witness or to lay
or give evidence against the said offendor ... [who] should
take any profit or commodity by the death of the said
offendor if he were attained or convicted of the said crime
and offence."[89] Additionally, the general public usually
hated informers, because they undermined social solidarity
and offended local mores. As a cleric observed, many held
informers in "great Detestation".[90] Indeed, according to
Defoe informing against a man, even for the "most open
Breach of the Laws of Morality, is enough to denominate a
Man unfit for Society".[91] The general opprobrium was such
that the Societies for the Reformation of Manners stressed
that their leaders had always insisted to members, who had:
"... given Informations against Vice or Prophaneness, that
they should never receive that Part of the Penalty which the
Law allows the Informer."[92] Several informers were

88. J. Warner, "Damn you, you informing Bitch," *Journal of Social History*, 1999, vol. 33, no. 2, p.299.
89. E. Fudge, "Monstrous acts. Bestiality in Early Modern England." *History Today*, 2000, vol. 50, issue 8, p.20.
90. Dr. Barton, *Dr Barton's Sermon Preached at St. Mary-le-Bow*, London, 1700, p.40.
91. D. Defoe, *The Poor Man's Plea*, Oxford, Basil Blackwell, 1927, p.13.
92. Anon, *The Three and Thirtieth Account of the progress made in the Cities of London and Westminster*, pp.39-40.

murdered, and even a bare allegation of informing could result in a man being pursued by a furious mob, so threatening that no man "durst afford him Shelter".[93] One informer in Bristol was set in the stocks and while he was there the mob brought a kettle of tar and "pitch'd him all over, and afterwards roll'd him in Feathers".[94] During the short-lived operation of the 1736 Act, informers who operated in greater London were attacked on at least 57 occasions, with four of them being killed as a result.[95]

Despite their unpopularity, informers were often effective in producing prosecutions, leading some eighteenth century commentators to argue that there was actually a need for more of them, not less, at least in London.[96] As a result, in March 1738, the Privy Council directed local magistrates to protect both informers and constables involved in prosecutions under the 1736 Gin Act from attacks by "disorderly and Malicious Persons". However, gradually, instances of informer perjury and public hostility undermined even judicial confidence. By March 1739, the *London Evening-Post* could report that the prevalence of perjury and criminal elements amongst informers meant that: "The Trade of informing against Persons for retailing spirituous Liquors against law, seems

---

93. *The Gentleman's Magazine*, 1743, vol. 13, p.636.
94. Warner, "Damn You, you informing Bitch," p.299.
95. J. Warner, F. Ivis and A. Demers, "A Predatory Social Structure: Informers in Westminster, 1737-1741," *Journal of Interdisciplinary History*, 2000, vol 30.4, pp.617-622.
96. A Citizen of London, *The Vices of the Cities of London and Westminster trac'd from their original*, Dublin, G.Faulkner, 1751, p.15.

almost at an end, few Magistrates caring to trouble themselves about it."[97]

Society for the Reformation of Manners

The creation of societies for the reformation of manners was one response to the general question: "... what are lawes without execution of them, & what execution is there without zeale?"[98] The first society was established in 1690 in the East London suburb of Tower Hamlets. By 1701, there were nearly 20 similar associations in London, and others had formed in the provinces. Many more followed in the early eighteenth century; they operated within a very loose confederation. Their swift growth was considerably assisted by royal support. Indeed, some prominent clerics, such as Gilbert Burnet, the Bishop of Salisbury, argued that, in this, William III was an instrument of God, reforming the national life. Although religiously 'orthodox' organisations, they included many dissenters amongst their members. As a result, although some Anglican clerics were enthusiastic supporters, others were more cautious or even hostile, blaming the new societies for further undermining the already moribund church courts (their prosecutions were all conducted in the secular courts) and alarmed at their ecumenism.

---

97. Warner, Ivis and Demers, "A Predatory Social Structure: Informers in Westminster, 1737-1741," pp.617-622.
98. Anon, A *true Report of the horrible Murther, which was committed in the house of Sir Jerome Bowes*, London, H.L. for Mathew Lownes, 1607, f.F4.

Many members of the societies appear to have feared that Satan had launched a counter-attack in England in the years after 1660, and claimed that without their work an allegedly 'prodigious' post-Restoration rate of moral deterioration would have continued unabated until England became "one of the most profligate Nations in the World".[99] Most importantly, they deprecated quietism, having a profound commitment to being their brothers' keepers (irrespective of their brothers' wishes). This inevitably meant active intervention in the lives of others.[100] As one cleric preaching to the Society asked: "... how can magistrates come to the knowledge of notorious offendors, if some will not generously inspect the manners and Behaviour of those about them?"[101] Rather than relying only on moral exhortation, the societies had an unprecedented willingness to use the secular criminal justice system to suppress public manifestations of immorality, such as bawdy houses, street prostitution, homosexuality and profanity.

Pursuant to this aim, networks of moral guardians were established. In the Metropolis, four stewards in each ward of the City were appointed, two for each parish, and a committee set up, whose business it was to record the names and addresses of those guilty of immorality and their transgressions. Individual members gathered information,

---

99. Anon, *The Three and Thirtieth Account of the progress made in the Cities of London and Westminster*, p.38.
100. M.G. Smith, "Pastoral Discipline and the Church Courts: the Hexham Court 1680-1730," York, *Borthwick Papers*, 1982, No.62, pp.9-10.
101. B.A. Atkinson, *A sermon preach'd to the Societies for the reformation of manners at Salter's-Hall*, London, 1726, p.17.

which was then passed on to JPs, the societies also providing funds to pay for prosecutions, or bringing prosecutions in their own right. Many members of the societies became highly interventionist local constables, and even some judges joined. Their activism was considerable, so that in the 1720s it could be observed that: "Multitudes, for more than 30 years last past, have been prosecuted, and punished according to Law, for lewd and scandalous Practices. Great Numbers of Bawdy-Houses, and other disorderly Houses, have been suppressed and shut up, and the Streets very much purged from the wretched Tribe of Night-walking Prostitutes, and most detestable Sodomites."[102] According to one account, in the year after December 1, 1726 the societies had prosecuted or were assisting in the prosecution of 1,363 offenders for "lewd and disorderly practices", drunkenness, gaming, swearing, cursing and exercising their trades on the Sabbath. Even more extraordinary, it was claimed that in the 36 years since the initial foundation, the societies in and about London alone had prosecuted 94,322 cases of immorality. Unsurprisingly, then, supporters were enthusiastic about their work, feeling that, since their establishment, a 'great check' had been given to the prevalence of vice.[103]

Not everyone shared such confidence. Many felt that the societies' success was exaggerated. According to Defoe, in the 1720s, the: "... conversation of our lower rank of people

102. Anon, *Reformation necessary to prevent Our Ruine*, London, Joseph Downing, 1728, p.38.
103. Anon, *The Three and Thirtieth account of the progress made in the Cities of London and Westminster*, p.38.

runs only upon bawdy and blasphemy, notwithstanding our societies for reformation, and our laws in force against profaneness."[104] Similarly, in 1729, a dystopian vision of London was provided by an anonymous author who claimed that the city was "one continued hurry of Vice". Its streets abounded with whores, thieves, sodomists, drunks and rioters. Immorality affected both rich and poor and all professions in the Metropolis.[105] The campaigns launched by the societies also occasioned considerable and widespread public hostility, from all social classes. Many 'gentlemen' found the activism and manner in which reforming constables exercised their powers extremely 'insolent', and did not understand how it was possible for a: "... set of Ruffians to break into private Companies, and hurry Gentlemen before a Magistrate on a bare suspicion of being criminal; to be committed to Prison over night, at discretion, only to be discharg'd [by the JP] in the Morning."[106] Perhaps not surprisingly, the societies swiftly became relatively cautious about pursuing upper class miscreants, though, as Defoe observed, this itself became a constant grievance for the poor.

As these complaints also indicate, moral campaigns could be highly authoritarian and have unpleasant consequences. Thus, in 1742, the High Constable of Westminster, while making a: "... general Search, did not scruple to commit to the Roundhouse any Person they found

---

104. A. Moreton (D.Defoe), *Every-Body's Business*, 2nd edn., 1725, p.27.
105. Anon, *Hell upon Earth: or the Town in an Uproar*, London, J. Roberts, 1729, p.B1 and p.12.
106. *The Gentleman's Magazine*, 1731, vol. 1, p.61.

in the Streets, tho' not offering the least Disturbance." He sent 28 women to St Martin's Roundhouse, many of whom were not soliciting, but were going about their lawful business (returning home from work etc.). Tragedy struck, when the prison's notorious keeper, William Bird, crammed them into the 'Hole', a six-foot-square cell, which had its window 'close shut'. Despite their cries of 'murder', he left them there, so that four women were suffocated. The coroner's jury returned a verdict of wilful murder against Bird and he was committed to Newgate.[107]

The impetus behind the societies appears to have petered out to virtual non-existence in the 1740s, leading to the need for their refounding in 1757. As John Wesley, preaching to the new Society for the Reformation of Manners in 1763, noted of its history: "... a few persons in London, towards the close of the last century, united together, and after a while, were termed, The Society for Reformation of Manners; and incredible good was done by them for near 40 years. But then, most of the original members being gone to their reward, those who succeeded them grew faint in their mind, and departed from the work: So that a few years ago the Society ceased; nor did any of the kind remain in the kingdom."[108]

---

107. *The Gentleman's Magazine*, 1742, vol. 12, p.386.
108. Rev. J. Wesley, "Sermon 52 preached before the Society for Reformation of Manners On Sunday, January 30, 1763," in *The Works of the Rev. J. Wesley*, London, Wesleyan Conference Office, 1872.

Prosecution Associations

One way of reducing the considerable cost of prosecuting, and also providing a public indication of a willingness to prosecute (to deter criminals from victimising specific individuals), was to share the burden by creating or joining an association for the prosecution of felons. These normally consisted of up to 100 members, living in roughly the same locality, whether borough, town or county, or engaged in the same trade. Each member contributed a fixed payment to a common fund. This money was then made available to pay the costs of prosecuting crimes committed against any individual member. Potential criminals would often be made aware of who was in the association as a list of members might be published in local newspapers or periodicals. Hundreds of such prosecution associations were established in the eighteenth century. However, most were founded after 1750.

Magisterial Activism

Very roughly, there were two extremes in attitudes to law enforcement to be found amongst early modern JPs and, to a lesser extent, parish constables. Some adopted a strict 'letter of the law' approach, attempting to fulfil directives issued from above (whether the Privy Council or visiting assizes judges etc.) in their entirety. Others were more flexible, preferring to secure community harmony and quiet rather than officiously enforcing regulations, especially where they involved apparently 'victimless' crimes. Such men would turn a 'blind eye' to many offences, unless grave. Inevitably, perhaps, most JPs fell between the extremes of rigidity and laxity in enforcement.

Despite the rapid growth in the magistracy, the sheer number of new statutes that they had to administer created major problems. As Edmund Bohun noted in the 1690s, the century that had passed since Lambarde had first complained about the quantity of legislation, far from bringing relief, had seen a further rapid expansion, so that the "number is now perhaps double to what it was then". Not surprisingly, he felt that a JP needed a "strong memory" for statutes if he was to perform effectively.[109] In reality, many were unaware of the full extent of their powers and duties, something that encouraged numerous informative manuals aimed at instructing them. Even where they were not openly ignored, the plethora of theoretical crimes could often only be addressed by tacitly allowing some to fall into desuetude. This was widely recognised, and sometimes even approved, by eminent lawyers and statesmen, who often encouraged magisterial restraint in initiating criminal litigation. In the early 1600s, Francis Bacon urged that: "Specially in case of laws penal, they ought to have care, that that was meant for terror, be not turned into rigor ... for penal laws pressed, are a shower of snares upon the people." Bacon suggested that if such laws had: "... been sleepers of long, or if they be grown unfit for the present time, [they should] be by wise judges confined in the

---

109. E. Bohun, *The Justice of Peace His Calling and Qualifications*, London, 1693, p.13.

execution."[110] Senior judicial figures might actively discourage officiousness amongst JPs. Thus, in 1693, a Middlesex magistrate who had insisted that one John Foster be imprisoned at Newgate and prosecuted at the Old Bailey for stealing a magpie worth two pence and its cage, worth four pence, not even allowing the victim an element of choice in the matter, came in for scathing criticism from the trial judge, who mocked the "foolish man [JP] for his pains to commit a poor fellow to gaol for such a silly trifling business". The court suggested that it should have been dealt with in an alternative manner. The presiding judge then blatantly encouraged the jury to acquit, telling them that the accused man's defence was convincing. They returned a swift not guilty verdict.[111]

Numerous ordinary magistrates willingly endorsed such views. It was not simple laziness that encouraged magisterial circumspection. Implementing all statutes and government directives could be counter-productive. As a result, some were quietly ignored by JPs who felt that laws became a "burthen when they are too many, and their very number is a cause that few are executed". Many argued that it was better to have a sound grasp of a handful of important statutes, and to enforce them properly.[112] For the same reason, in the 1650s, William Sheppard was strongly in favour of repealing all obsolete and 'useless' laws, something that would strengthen the authority of the

---

110. F. Bacon, "On Judicature," *The Essays*, London, Everyman edn., J.M. Dent, 1906, pp.162-165.
111. Anon, *The Tryal of John Foster*, London, 1693, pp.1-2.
112. Anon, *Foure Statutes*, London, Robert Barker, 1609, f.A3.

remainder, as "to take away the weeds will not hurt the wheat".[113] Even where proceedings were initiated, and a conviction secured, the full penalties available might not be implemented. JPs sitting at quarter sessions in Sussex regularly departed from the statutory minimums appointed for certain offences when imposing punishment, albeit without legal authority to do so.[114]

However, throughout the era, there were some JPs who felt that such a *laisser faire* approach actually engendered lawlessness. As early as the 1530s, Sir Thomas Elyot had lamented that opprobrium was the lot of any zealous magistrate who "accordyng to his duetie do execute duely and frequently the lawe or good ordinaunce, wherein is any sharpe punisshement". He claimed that such a JP's colleagues would accuse him of being devoid of charity and personally ambitious. After the Reformation, in the latter sixteenth and seventeenth centuries, the conflict between pragmatists and interventionists was often reflected in a clash between Puritan magistrates and others. From the 1690s, it was frequently manifest in the struggle between 'reforming' JPs (sometimes associated with the Societies for the Reformation of Manners) and more latitudinarian justices. A longstanding complaint of 'strict' enforcers was that although there was no shortage of laws to regulate society, the political 'will' to implement them at a local level was often absent. Thus, Elyot noted that numerous carefully

---

113. N.L. Mathews, *William Sheppard, Cromwell's Law Reformer*, Cambridge, CUP, 1984, p.175.
114. B.C. Redwood (Ed.), *Quarter Sessions Order Book 1642-1649*, Lewes: Sussex Record Society, 1954, p.31.

drafted and thought out statutes, ordinances, and orders in council had been enacted to punish crime, vagrancy and disorder, yet negligent implementation frustrated their aims: "Howe many proclamations therof haue ben divulgate and nat obayed? Howe many commissions directed and nat executed?"[115] Over 200 years later, a Metropolitan observer reiterated Elyot's complaint, believing that England already had the "best Laws, but the worst executed" of any country in the world. It was an inability to enforce them that was the problem, making it pointless to pass any more "useless scarecrow statutes".[116] Nevertheless, those urging rigid enforcement were rarely in a majority.

The Marian Examination

The pre-trial examination of suspected criminals and their accusers, the taking of depositions from them and the making of attendant interlocutory decisions, was a vital part of a JP's duties. He largely determined whether a case should be sent for indictment, in which forum it should be tried, and the evidence that would be adduced at the subsequent trial. He would often also make decisions on bail and take recognisances for the attendance of potential witnesses. This function was first formally regulated by the Marian statutes of 1555 (1 & 2 Philip & Mary c. 13) and 1556 (2 & 3 Philip & Mary c. 10). However, it is apparent that

---

115. Elyot, *The Boke named The Governour*, pp.119-120.
116. A Citizen of London, *The Vices of the Cities of London ...*, 1751, p.9.

these Acts merely formalised what was already a longstanding practice for many good JPs. Thus, in the 1530s, Sir John Gaynesford had carefully examined and taken statements from witnesses and potential defendants to a murder case in Surrey. Indeed, in conducting his examinations, Gaynesford appears to have anticipated many of the investigative techniques that William Lambarde was to urge on JPs three quarters of a century later in his *Eirenarcha*.[117] Michael Dalton was clearly wrong in believing, in the following century, that 1556 marked a new beginning in this respect: "Neither was a mans fault to be wrung out of himself (no not by examination only) but to be proved by others, untill the Stat. of 2 & 3 Philip & Mary cap. 10. gave authority to the Justices of peace to examine the Felon himself." Strictly speaking, the Marian statutes only required the justices to make examinations in suspected cases of felony, and neither Lambarde nor Dalton instructed their readers to examine those suspected of misdemeanour. In reality, however, it soon became widespread practice to examine for the more serious of even these lesser offences.[118] The suspect was not sworn before being questioned: "The offender himself shall not be examined upon oath, for by the Common Law, *Nullus tenetur seipsum prodere*."[119] Potential witnesses, other than the defendant, would normally be

---

117. W.B. Robison, "Murder at Crowhurst: A Case Study in Early Tudor Law Enforcement," *Criminal Justice History*, 1988, vol. 9, pp.44-45.
118. T. Barnes, "Examination Before A Justice in the Seventeenth Century," *Notes and Queries for Somerset and Dorset*, 1955, vol.27, pp.39-42.
119. M. Dalton, *The Country Justice, Containing the practise of the Justices of the Peace out of their Sessions ...*, London, Company of Stationers, 1655, p.369.

examined on oath (though this was not always the case in the sixteenth century). This preliminary examination helped to prevent complainants who lost interest in the proceedings, between arrest and trial, resiling from their allegations.

Throughout the period, except in the clearest cases, successful prosecutions were often founded on an effective initial examination of a suspect by a JP. However, its robustness and the ability with which it was conducted varied enormously. With some JPs, it could be a penetrating process, amongst others, cursory or superficial. This was widely appreciated by contemporary observers, who also recognised that subtlety was legitimate when questioning, so that it was: "... lawful and fit for magistrates to use many means to wind out the truth of facts from delinquents, which malefactors are not bound, upon such questions or inquisition, to reveal against their own lives."[120] Thus, the influential and very active magistrate, Sir Thomas De Veil, who served on the Commission of the Peace for Middlesex between 1729 and his death in 1746, owed much of his considerable success against Metropolitan and suburban criminals to his mastery of the techniques of interrogation. He was painstaking and: "... indefatigable in tracing out remarkable villainies, thro' long and tedious examinations." Additionally, he demonstrated 'uncommon skill' in cross-examining those brought before him. In particular, he knew how to: "... improve the slightest circumstance, to confound those he examined, to catch up their unguarded

---

120. J. Sym, *Life's Preservative Against Self-Killing*, London, 1637, p.104.

expressions, to piece together broken hints, and compel them to detect themselves." As a result, he secured evidence and convictions against numerous important criminals, including notorious murderers such as Charles Drew and James Hall.[121] Similarly, in 1753, towards the close of his life, and with his health rapidly failing, one of De Veil's successors, the Bow Street magistrate Henry Fielding, stressed the importance of a well-conducted examination. Fielding's sense of duty in pursuing Metropolitan felons meant that when examining and taking depositions he had "often spent whole days, nay, sometimes whole nights". He considered that this was especially important when there was any difficulty in procuring sufficient evidence to convict suspects, as was commonly the situation for street-robberies.[122] However, not all JPs had the forensic ability, time or inclination to go to such lengths. In 1596, Edward Hext complained about the lack of interrogative experience and energy of many magistrates fearing that numerous criminals were: "... brought before some Justice that either wanteth [lacks] experience to examine a cunning thief or will not take the pains that ought to be taken in sifting him upon every circumstance and presumption."[123]

Of course, robust or devious questioning could also occasion injustice, especially where the suspect was ignorant or intimidated. The malign power of magisterial suggestion can be seen in the case of John Perry, a servant who was

---

121. *The Gentleman's Magazine*, 1747, vol.17, pp.562-565.
122. H. Fielding, *Journal of a Voyage to Lisbon*, London, A. Millar, 1755, p.20.
123. Hext, "Extract from a letter written by Edward Hext," pp.340-341.

suspected of murdering William Harrison, the elderly steward to Lady Cambden, in Gloucestershire, in 1660. Harrison had disappeared while collecting rent and when Perry was questioned: "... after several Examinations, [he] confes'd, that his mother and Brother had murther'd and thrown him into the great sink by Wallington's Mill, with several other probable Circumstances." Despite his mother and brother vigorously denying the charge, all were tried, convicted and executed. Two years later, the missing, supposedly murdered, steward, turned up alive and well with a bizarre story about being abducted to Turkey.[124] Although ingenious, some of De Veil's investigative techniques would also certainly not be considered correct today. Thus, faced by a suspect accused of burglary from an eating-house in Covent Garden he offered an inducement: "... upon a promise that he should be prosecuted only for a simple felony, the fellow confessed the fact."[125]

These problems were aggravated because those being questioned had few legal rights. Even in the 1840s, there was no entitlement to legal representation at the pre-trial examination, though magistrates could allow it if they thought fit, and a few did so. The same situation seems to have prevailed in the late seventeenth century. Thomas De Veil cautioned against the dangers posed to magistrates by corrupt "Newgate Solicitors" who would "skip into Justices Houses with a crowd", while felons and witnesses were

124. Sir T. Overbury, *A True and Perfect Account of the Examination, Confession, Tryal, Condemnation, andExecution of Joan Perry*, London, 1676, p.6.
125. Sir T. De Veil, *Memoirs of the Life and Times of Sir Thomas De Veil*, London, 1748, p.55.

being examined, searching for a technical defect in proceedings.[126] This suggests that such examinations in the Metropolis were open to the public. Nevertheless, the vast majority of defendants were not represented, either because the examining JP did not allow it, or because they could not afford it. Other aspects of the pre-trial examination were also largely unregulated, at least until some clarity was brought to the matter by Sir John Jervis's Act in 1848. Thus, examinations might be conducted with or without cautions to the suspect, there might be a hostile cross-examination or not, etc.[127] Many might subsequently regret what they had said in the intimacy of the examination room, perhaps not appreciating its legal implications. Nevertheless, confessing crimes early could also have some advantages, as it often had a significant affect on the gravity with which an offence was charged and on any decision to reprieve from execution after conviction. Only one defendant in Colchester in the years 1577-1579 who made a full confession received the death penalty (and that man had been caught *in flagrante* committing bestiality).[128]

The frequency with which allegations of felony made to a JP might be dismissed out of hand because of a lack of evidence is difficult to assess. Such cases produced few, if any, records. Nevertheless, it appears that, like the granting

---

126. Sir T. De Veil, *Observations on the Practice of a Justice of the Peace*, London, Edward Withers, 1747, p.2.
127. W. Wesley Pue, "The Criminal Twilight Zone: Pre-Trial Procedures in the 1840s," *Alberta Law Review*, vol.21, 1983, pp.335-364.
128. J. Samaha, "Hanging for Felony: The Rule of Law in Elizabethan Colchester," *Historical Journal*, 1978, vol.21, p.778.

of bail, it was slightly more common than is sometimes suggested, whatever the theory might have been before the late 1700s. Thus, William Mitchell, a poor sailor, who had made his way along the Eastern coast from Lowestoft, where he was put ashore in the winter of 1576-7, was released after confessing that he stole a shirt only to keep warm, and protesting that he left behind a number of other valuable items which he could easily have taken as well.[129] Similarly, when a curate named Trat was suspected of murdering his wife by pushing her over a cliff into the Severn estuary, in c.1620, the rumours eventually reached the authorities, and he was called in for an examination before the JPs. However, the allegations were dismissed by the magistrates, and he was "clear'd without any further triall".[130]

Absence of Torture

Although the JPs' examination might not meet modern standards of fairness, torture was almost never used to exact confessions or information. Indeed, in theory, if a jailer put unlawful pressure on a prisoner to turn evidence against himself, or if they "torment[ed] any prisoner committed to their custody for the revealing of his accomplices", they were committing a long-standing statutory felony, sometimes termed "duress of imprisonment" (14 Edw. 111,

---

129. Samaha, "Hanging for Felony," p.778.
130. Anon, *The Crying Murther*, London, 1624, f.A1.

c.10).[131] Englishmen were very aware of the unusual nature of their society in this respect. Even in the fifteenth century, Sir John Fortescue had been shocked by the "inhumanity of such exquisite tortures" as were found in France and other foreign countries. Describing the regular employment of the rack and water tortures (forced ingestion of fluid through an oscular funnel) on the continent, he averred that their use was entirely pointless because no man was: "... so stout or resolute, who has once gone through this horrid trial by torture, be he never so innocent, who will not rather confess himself guilty of all kinds of wickedness, than undergo the like tortures a second time?"[132] English observers regularly reiterated this point, feeling that their own nation's legal system was both merciful and rational in comparison. Torture was cruel and its fruits often worthless: "... being rather Trials of the Strength and Hardiness of the Sufferer, than any Proof of the Truth."[133] As a result, it was feared that many innocent people would be "sacrificed were this barbarous custom adopted".[134] Additionally, some observers, such as Sir Thomas Smith and William Harrison, argued that torture was inherently inimical to the

---

131. Harrison, *Elizabethan England*, p.238, see also W. Blackstone, *Commentaries on the Laws of England*, vol.4, Oxford, Clarendon Press, 1769, p.129.

132. F. Grigor, *Sir John Fortescue's Commendation of the Laws of England*, London, Sweet and Maxwell, 1917 (written c.1461-5, Ist published in Latin c.1537), p.37.

133. T. Barlow, *The Justice of Peace: A Treatise Containing the Power and Duty of that Magistrate*, London, Lintot, 1745, p.190.

134. M. Van Muyden (Trans. and Ed.), *A foreign View of England in the reigns of George I and George II; The letters of Monsieur Cesar de Saussure, to his Family*, London, John Murray, 1902, p.119.

Anglo-Saxon character. They felt that Englishmen despised death but could not bear to be tormented, preferring to make admissions rather than: "... to yield our bodies unto such servile haulings and tearings as are used in other countries."[135] Smith was also concerned that if a man who had been tortured were subsequently to be acquitted, no adequate amends could be made to him.[136]

It should, perhaps, be noted that many Englishmen who deprecated torture appear to have been rather ignorant of the finer details surrounding its use in the civil law tradition. In particular, they seem to have been unaware that theory required that there should always be a strong *prima facie* case before it could be used, and that any resulting confession should be repeated in the absence of torture. Thus, in early modern Germany, the *peinliche Befragung* (painful questioning) was supposed to be applied to suspects against whom there was circumstantial evidence or other good grounds for suspicion and was finely graded. Normally, it would start with threats and then gradually progress to ever more painful forms of torture. Even so, the absence of torture in England was something that also always impressed foreign observers: "A Rack is not known among them; and their Examination of criminals is not at all severe."[137]

Nevertheless, some Englishmen in positions of authority

---

135. W. Harrison, *Elizabethan England*, London, Camelot Series, E. Rhys (Ed.), 1889, p.237.

136. Smith, *De Republica Anglorum*, pp.117-118.

137. M. Misson, *Memoirs and Observations in his Travels over England*, M. Ozell (Trans.), London, 1719, p.67.

were well aware of the efficacy of torture, and its need in the contemporary Roman law tradition (with its mechanistic rules on evidential proof). As the 1536 Act for the punishment of pirates and robbers of the sea (28 Henry viii, c.15) ruefully noted, the problem of judging piracy "after the course of the civil laws", as was done in England before 1536, was that in the absence of the appropriate number and type of witnesses the only way to secure a conviction was for the defendants to "plainly confess their offences (which they will never do without torture or pains)".[138] However, although torture was virtually absent for those accused of conventional felony before the normal criminal courts, the practice of beating confessions out of young inmates at Bridewell was only curtailed in the seventeenth century. Additionally, although interrogations using "pain and torture in these common cases with us is greatlie abhored", as the limitation to 'common cases' suggests, there were a small number of situations, usually involving treason or quasi-political offences, in which torture was used by special order of the Privy Council, at least until the Civil War.[139]

Recognisance to give Evidence

It is apparent that by the late medieval period it was vital that prosecution witnesses appear at the assizes and quarter

---

138. G.R. Elton, *The Tudor Constitution*, 2nd edn., Cambridge, CUP, 1982, pp.158-159.
139. T.C., *The Glory of England*, London, 1618, p.221.

sessions if a conviction was to be obtained (still normally the position today). In their absence, in the words of Sir Thomas Smith, a defendant was "without difficultie acquited". An important development in encouraging such attendance (as well as recourse to the criminal courts generally) was the statute of 1529 (21 Henry VIII c.11) which offered restitution of lost property to a victim who gave evidence against the accused and helped secure a conviction. This also reduced the motivation for making private 'deals' between criminal and victim.[140] However, it was the power to bind over witnesses that arrived with the Marian statute of 1555 that appears to have been crucial in encouraging successful prosecutions. Potential witnesses could be compelled to attend trial to give evidence for the Crown on pain of forfeiting a predetermined sum of money if they failed to do so. Thus, in the 1560s, Smith noted that JPs might bind witnesses and prosecutors in: "... recognisance of x.l xx.l. xxx.l xl.l. or C.1 [£10-£100] according to his discretion, and the qualities of the crime ... which certified under his hande, is levied upon the recognisance if they faile of beinge there."[141] This was sufficient to provide a real incentive to appear at trial, and also to deter people from making allegations that would not be pressed. At the least, it would concentrate their minds. Thus, when Mary Carleton was forcibly carried from her lodgings and put before a JP, on suspicion of bigamy (primarily, she claimed, to intimidate

---

140. J.G. Bellamy, *The Criminal Trial in Later Medieval England Felony Before the Courts From Edward I to the Sixteenth Century*, Toronto, University of Toronto Press, 1998, p.119.
141. Smith, *De Republica Anglorum*, pp.107-108.

her), the examining justice, having heard the allegations, refused to commit her for trial: "... unless they would be bound to prosecute me; which my husband being unwilling to, the Justice demanded of his Father whether he would prosecute me, saying, they must not make a fool of him; and so after some whisperings, the Father and his Son were both bound to prosecute; and thereupon I was committed to prison."[142] Typically, between 1644 and 1650, George Howle, an active Kentish JP (and son or grandson of Henry Howle JP, whose legal notebook he added to) took numerous recognisances for attendance at the following quarter sessions, interspersed with more serious, unusual or difficult crimes that were reserved for the assizes. Thus, in June 1647, a potential witness to a serious offence was bound over in the sum of £40: "The Condition is that he shall appear at the next Assizes or Gaol Delivery to prefer a bill of Indictment against Robert Payne now prisoner in the Gaol for buggering a cow and likewise give evidence to the Jury that shall pass upon life for the same."[143]

Bail

The examining magistrate would also have to make a decision about bail. Bail and maineprize (the latter was similar to the former in effect but subtly different legally)

---

142. Anon, *The Case of Madam Mary Carleton*, London, 1663, pp.93-94.
143. H. Howle, *Henry Howle's Notebook*, F. Hull (Ed.), Kent Records, New Series, vol. 1, Parts 1-3, Kent Archaeology Society, 1990, p.69.

was a complicated and uncertain area of the law, based on a mass of historic, and sometimes conflicting, statutes and legal precedents. Granting bail meant that an accused person could be freed pending trial and "upon sufficent surety found for his appearance and yealding of his body, delivered out of prison".[144] (Unsurprisingly, in the 1500s, those who had abjured the realm on an earlier occasion were not allowed bail; similarly, it was not to be granted after conviction for felony, pending punishment.) The early modern provisions for bail before trial were still largely based on the system established by the Statute of Westminster in 1275, passed after Edward I had become concerned that corrupt sheriffs were taking bribes to release heinous felons and refusing bail to deserving men. This Act codified procedure and formally listed bailable and non-bailable offences. It remained the bedrock of the English system, though substantially modified by statute in 1554 (1 & 2 Philip & Mary c.13), the Petition of Rights in 1627, the Habeas Corpus Act of 1679 (which ensured a bail hearing), and the Bill of Rights of 1688 (which forbade the imposition of excessive recognisances for bail).[145]

For misdemeanours, granting bail was usually a straightforward process. Provided that a suspect could produce the appropriate, normally modest, recognisance, it would usually be allowed. However, very occasionally, magistrates might be reluctant to grant it in apparently

---

144. E. Coke, A *Little Treatise of Baile and Maineprize*, 2nd edn., London, William Cooke, 1637, p.2.
145. K.X. Metzmeier, "Preventative Detention," *Pace International Law Review*, 1996, vol. 8, p.401.

deserving cases, if there were political undertones. Thus, in 1661, after John Bunyan had been in custody for five or six days for misdemeanour, his associates sought to secure his release by providing bondsmen "for so ran my *mittimus*, that I should lie there till I could find sureties". They went to a JP at Elstow asking him to take surety for Bunyan's appearance at the next quarter sessions. Fearing that there might be more against Bunyan than appeared in his *mittimus*, he declared that as he was "but a young man, therefore he durst not do it".[146]

For felonies, the situation was very different, at least in theory. In some respects, the early modern English law on bail was not entirely dissimilar to its modern English counterpart (the 1976 Bail Act), seeking to take into account many of the same factors. Some very grave offences were not bailable. How far these extended was uncertain. In the fourteenth century, Bracton had claimed that all suspected felons except murderers could be bailed. Nevertheless, as Coke noted, this position had been qualified in the ensuing centuries. By the 1500s, non-bailable offences included, for example, treason, petty treason, being the principal in some types of murder, committing arson against buildings or conspiring to falsely indict others. The number of crimes in which bail was supposed to be denied increased steadily. By the early 1600s, on some counts, there were dozens, though many were quite arcane.[147] However, for most of the period

---

146. J. Bunyan, *A Relation of the Imprisonment of Mr John Bunyan, Minister of the Gospel at Bedford ... in November 1660*, London, James Buckland, 1765, p.79.
147. Metzmeier, "Preventative Detention," p.401.

the majority of felonies *could* be bailed in appropriate circumstances. These included burglary, robbery, and even cases where men were indicted for "putting out of Eyes, cutting out of tongues, may be bailed". Indeed, although William Sheppard felt that murderers were "not to be bailed at all", he qualified this by noting that some commentators thought a man was "bailable in case of manslaughter". In reality, bail was also possible if there was a plausible defence to a murder allegation, such as self-defence.

In these situations, other factors might affect the decision to grant or withhold bail. As in the modern era, the strength of the evidence was of prime importance. This meant that if a man was caught red-handed committing a felony, "taken in the manner, he ought not to be bailed".[148] Similarly, William Sheppard considered that bail should not be granted to any man that: "... confesseth the felony, is taken in the maner, or known to have done the felony, especially if it be the killing of a man, and the *mittimus* expresse the commitment to be for felony confessed." By contrast, according to Sir Francis Bacon: "In felony, baile may be admitted where the fact is not notorious, and the person not of ill name."[149] As today, a defendant with a bad criminal record, reputed to be a "notorious Thiefe", might be denied bail, as might a man who had failed to answer to his bail on a previous occasion or who had attempted to escape from jail while in custody.[150] Much would also depend on the

---

148. Coke, *A Little Treatise of Baile and Maineprize*, pp.22-24.
149. Sir F. Bacon, *Cases of Treason*, London, 1641, p.13.
150. Coke, *A Little Treatise of Baile and Maineprize*, pp.2-11.

gravity of the offence. Thus, in 1733, John Hobson noted that when Roger Woumbel from Barnsley was detained for stabbing Richard Oates with a pen-knife as they was quarrelling in an ale-house at Horbury: "It was thought the stabb had been mortall, and Mr Woumbel was secured; but there being hopes of Mr Oates's recovery, he is admitted to bail."[151]

If not bailed by an examining magistrate, prisoners could be granted bail at a sessions of the peace, provided that one JP present (of at least two) was taken from the quorum. If these magistrates refused to grant bail, the prisoner could then appeal to the sheriff of the county concerned on a "Writ de Manucaptione".[152] Additionally, the higher courts had a general power to bail in special circumstances. Thus, in August 1679, a group of scholars from Westminster school, accused of killing a bailiff, had their trial deferred while the authorities sought several of their accomplices. The judges at the Old Bailey, mindful of their age, education and genteel backgrounds, admitted them to "Extraordinary Bail", rather than see them continue to be held in the corrupting conditions of Newgate.[153]

In theory, the ability of a single JP to grant bail outside sessions was limited (in part this was the result of the Marian legislation). Even where it was legally permissible, they were encouraged to be cautious about allowing it (and

151. J. Hobson, "John Hobson's Diary," in *The Making of Barnsley*, B. Elliott, Barnsley, Wharncliffe Publishing Ltd., 1988, p.115.
152. Coke, *A Little Treatise of Baile and Maineprize*, pp.22-24.
153. Anon, *The Proceedings of the Sessions at the Old-Bailey*, August 27-28, 1679, London, 1679, p.3.

also about dismissing charges out of hand). Michael Dalton was satisfied that it was better, and normal, to temporarily imprison an innocent man than to let a felon go. He felt it was the: "... common practice at this day, and it seemeth to be very serviceable; and of two evils the lesse is to be chosen, fc. that an offender, or suspected person, should be imprisoned for a time (though sometimes wrongfully) than that one which hath committed Felony should escape unpunished."[154] Most other legal writers agreed that, even if the prosecution evidence appeared weak, the testimony of one credible witness was enough to provide a sufficient *prima facie* case to justify imprisonment pending trial. Nevertheless, an examination of court records would suggest that Dalton and his colleagues were overstating the 'common practice' of their era and that even 'non-bailable' offences were frequently bailed in reality. This was a longstanding problem. In 1485, the newly crowned Henry VII had demanded that JPs refuse bail to any man "knowing and deeming him to be felon".[155] Similarly, in 1663, Sir Orlando Bridgeman, the Lord Chief Justice of Common Pleas, investigating Newgate and the Old Bailey at the behest of Lord Clarendon, complained that "some notorious Felons [were] bayled for offences not baleable".[156] In particular, despite claims that it was only in the eighteenth century that individual examining JPs became confident

---

154. Dalton, *The Country Justice*, 1655, p.374.
155. C. Williams (Ed.), *English Historical Documents, 1485-1588*, vol 5, London, Eyre and Spottiswoode, 1967, pp.532-534.
156. Sir O. Bridgeman, "Newgate, 1663-A Letter of Sir Orlando Bridgeman, Chief Justice," *American Journal of Legal History*, vol.13, p.386.

enough to bail those accused on apparently tenuous evidence, it appears to have been periodically granted, throughout the era, where the evidence was thin but slightly too substantial to justify dismissing an allegation out of hand. Thus, in the early 1600s it was noted that if an examining JP found the "suspicion but light, then he taketh bond, with sureties of the accused, to appear [at trial]".[157] Not surprisingly, those who had been bailed were much more likely to be acquitted at the assizes than those kept in prison.

Bills of Indictment

From the list of prisoners in jail the clerks of the court prepared a 'calendar' of the prisoners to be tried at each assizes, together with the names of all those who were bringing charges and everyone who would be required to give evidence. From this, the clerks then drew up bills of indictment to go to the grand jury. John Bunyan provides an insight into some of the administrative manoeuvring behind this process. After he was incarcerated at Bedford, in 1662, Bunyan was ignored by the quarter sessions. When the assizes approached, and wanting to come before a judge: "I desired my jailor to put my name into the calendar among the felons, and made friends of the judge and high-sheriff, who promised that I should be called." However, all was in

---

157. Sir F. Bacon (1841) "The Use Of The Law," in Montagu, Basil (Ed.),*The Works of Francis Bacon*, vol. 3, Philadelphia, Carey and Hart, p.250.

vain, as the JPs and their clerk of the peace (i.e. the clerk to the justices) arranged matters so that he was not allowed to appear. Bunyan believed that the magistrates' clerk had approached the jailer and asked him to remove his name from the list, despite the calendar already having gone to the judge and sheriff. Additionally, he also "took the calendar and blotted out my accusation, as my jailor had written it". The clerk of the peace then approached his counterpart, the clerk of the assizes, and threatened that if Bunyan went before the judge and was released, he would complain about the jailer at the next quarter sessions for making "false calendars". Bunyan was left in prison.[158]

---

158. Bunyan, *A Relation of the Imprisonment of Mr John Bunyan*, pp.51-52.

Chapter 11

The English Courts with 'Criminal' Jurisdiction

Classification of Crimes

It is necessary to classify the main types of offence that could be prosecuted by the secular common law courts, as this had an important bearing on the forums that would try them. There were three: treason, felony and misdemeanour. Many aspects of high treason (coining excepted) are outside the parameters of this book, though the crime will be referred to as it casts a light on aspects of the wider criminal justice system. Cases of treason were normally highly political and, in Michael Dalton's words, were: "... alwayes esteemed a grievous offence, done or attempted against the estate legall, viz. against the King (the head, life, and ruler of the Commonwealth) in his person."[1] By contrast, all normal crimes could be divided into felonies and misdemeanours. (Though some commentators listed murder separately to other felonies.)

Felony encompassed the most serious offences. According to William Harrison: "The word felon is derived of the Saxon words fell and one, that is to say, an evil and wicked one, a one of untameable nature and lewdness not to be suffered for fear of evil example and the corruption of

---

1.   M. Dalton, *The Country Justice, Containing The Practice of the Justices of the Peace out of their Sessions ...*, London, Company of Stationers, 1655, p.283.

others."[2] Death was the appointed punishment for felony, even if avoided for some reason. The only exception was petty larceny (theft of goods worth less than 12 pence), the one felony which was not capital. The exact 'cut-off' point for this crime was in dispute in the sixteenth century. A treatise from the 1530s suggested that petty larceny included any sum less than 13 pence: "... for the which he shal not dye, but make a fyne to the kyng."[3] Others (the majority) argued that a full shilling was capital, though because of 'pious perjury' such precision was usually academic. Not surprisingly, where a crime was initially charged as petty felony, it was often prosecuted at quarter sessions (sometimes termed 'county' sessions). However, even if not charged *per se*, it was a regular alternative verdict for grand larceny indictments at the assizes.

The number of medieval felonies had been quite limited, largely being confined to longstanding common law offences such as homicide, arson, rape, robbery, larceny and burglary.[4] During the early modern period, their range was considerably extended by statute, such as that which made bigamy a felony in 1603 (1 Ja. 1, c.11) and ultimately included such diverse crimes as grievous and intentional wounding, such as putting out eyes, taking 20 shillings' worth of government military stores in breach of trust,

---

2.   Canon W. Harrison, *Elizabethan England, Edited from the Description of England*, E. Rhys (Ed.), London, Camelot Series, 1889, p.242.
3.   W. Middleton, *The Boke For a Justyce of Peace*, London, 1545, p.10.
4.   B.A. Hanawalt, "Fur Collar Crime: the Pattern of Crime amongst the Fourteenth-Century English Nobles," *Journal of Social History*, 1975, vol. 8, p.2.

knowingly receiving a Catholic seminary priest, buggery, conjuring spirits, witchcraft, desertion by an embodied and paid soldier, stealing "certaine kinds of hawkes" and a second conviction for forgery.[5] Additionally, despite its name "under the word Felony, is included Petty treason".[6] By contrast, misdemeanours were an ill-defined series of less serious crimes, whether common law or statutory. Thus, they included most minor assaults and offences of criminal damage. Such crimes did not carry the death penalty and the courts viewed them with much less gravity, sometimes treating them almost as quasi-civil matters. The normal punishments for committing misdemeanours were corporal (being whipped or stocked) or fiscal; more rarely, a sentence of imprisonment might be imposed.

Criminal Forums

Serious crimes could be tried in an enormous range of tribunals. As Lambarde noted: "Criminall Causes belong yet still either generally to the King's Bench; or specially to the Court of Star-chamber, or else particularly to the Constables Court, to the Marshalsey, Admiralthie, Gaol-deliverie, Oyer and Terminer, and sessions of Peace for our own Subjects, or to the Wardens Court in the Marches."[7] Lesser offences could be dealt with in a further, and almost as extensive,

---

5.   Sir F. Bacon, *Cases of Treason*, London, John More, 1641, p.8.
6.   Dalton, *The Country Justice*, 1655, p.295.
7.   W. Lambarde, *Archeion*, London, 1635, p.23.

range of minor courts. Despite this, it is possible to identify a 'typical' structure for England, one that was found throughout much of the land. It must be remembered that there were numerous and major regional exceptions to the pattern, and that no local system approximated entirely with such an ideal-typical model.

By the close of the period there were three main levels of secular criminal jurisdiction. Two of them, assizes and quarter sessions, were present throughout the 250 years and had their roots deep in the medieval era. The third, petty sessions, had emerged during this period, gradually replacing a number of other forums for determining minor matters. Most serious felonies were tried at the assizes courts or their Metropolitan equivalents, with a few being dealt with by the JPs sitting at quarter sessions, so that a contemporary observer could note: "In felony, the proceedings are in the Kings Bench, or before Commissioners of Oyer and Terminer, or of Gaol delivery, and in some case before Justices of the Peace."[8] Despite placing the court of King's Bench first, as behoved its superior status, it dealt with relatively few cases from outside Middlesex. By contrast, misdemeanours, with some less serious felonies, were primarily the province of the quarter sessions.

However, there was no rigid dividing line between the jurisdictions of assizes and quarter sessions, the distribution of cases being partly based on local custom. As a result, the allocation of crimes between the two courts varied greatly

8. Sir F. Bacon, *Cases of Treason*, p.14.

with both time and place, at least until 1842, when some statutory clarification was given.[9] (It was only then that quarter sessions formally lost the by then long abandoned power to try murder cases.) Some assizes courts continued to hear a considerable number of misdemeanours, though it was general practice that they should only be tried in these forums after the felony hearings had been completed.[10] Potentially more serious, quarter sessions continued to preside over a significant number of serious crimes in the late sixteenth and early seventeenth centuries. Thus, in Yorkshire, a large number of felonies (17 per cent of their cases) were dealt with at the county's sessions in the first half of the 1600s. Some of these continued to be for serious matters that attracted a death sentence. This does not appear to have been simply the result of an excessive case-load at the assizes, as these courts also dealt with numerous misdemeanours; indeed, they made up a majority of their cases (54.4 per cent).[11] Yorkshire was unusual, but not unique. Thus, in the years between 1629 and 1640, the Somerset quarter sessions convicted and executed eight thieves.[12] In West Kent, in theory, serious (i.e. capital) cases were reserved for the higher court, an entry in the calendar of prisoners for Easter 1634 noting that: "These are indicted

---

9.   E. Melling (Ed.), *Crime and Punishment*, Kentish Sources VI, Maidstone, Kent County Council, 1969, p.2.
10. H. Twyford, *The Office of the Clerk of Assize*, London, 1676, p.18.
11. S. Mercer, "Crime in Late-Seventeenth-Century Yorkshire: an Exception to a National Pattern?," *Northern History*, 1991, vol. 27, p.111.
12. T. Barnes (Ed.), *Somerset Assize Orders 1629-1640*, Frome, Somerset Record Society, 1959, vol. 65, p.8.

and bills found against them without clergy and therefore to remain in gaol until next assize." Nevertheless, in practice the provision was often ignored. The Kentish quarter sessions continued to try murder, armed robbery and other serious felonies on a regular basis and to pass death sentences until the Restoration. Thus, a death sentence for robbery was passed in 1627, and another in 1635.

However, after 1660, England's lower courts became increasingly reluctant to pass death sentences or to deal with very serious crimes. No death sentence was passed at Kent's quarter sessions after the Restoration, though, for the remainder of the seventeenth century, offenders who were expected to claim benefit of clergy successfully if convicted were tried and sentenced there, and, in 1696, a full (un-clergyable) murder trial was conducted, albeit resulting in an acquittal (possibly envisaged in advance). This appears to match the pattern for most of the country. By the eighteenth century, the judicial work of Kent's quarter sessions was concerned almost entirely with misdemeanours and petty larceny. Indeed, in correspondence from the mid eighteenth century, the Recorder of Deal argued that JPs sitting at quarter sessions should not try any case of capital felony, even if it was within the ambit of benefit of clergy.[13]

Nevertheless, despite a degree of obfuscation between the jurisdiction of the two courts, especially in the years before 1660, a rough division was normally readily identifiable. Indeed, as early as 1537, Fitzherbert had suggested, completely erroneously, that JPs had *"non*

---

13. Melling, *Crime and Punishment*, p.3.

auctoritie" to inquire into full murder cases (unlike manslaughters). Occasionally, if the examining magistrate had made a clearly unsuitable decision as to forum, sending to quarter sessions a felony that should properly have gone to the Westminster judges, the JPs themselves would refuse jurisdiction and refer the matter back to the assizes. Thus, at the Hilary quarter sessions held in Wiltshire in 1642, the order book recorded that, having looked at a complex case, the magistrates decided that: "... because it is a case of difficulty this Court doth order that the Judges of Assizes shall be attended with the plea at the next assizes."[14] This division in gravity of cases was also manifest in the imposition of punishment. The proportion of convicted defendants who were hanged at the Kent assizes in the early 1600s was much higher than that at county sessions, 36 per cent compared to one per cent. Almost half of those convicted at county sessions were fined; none of those convicted at the assizes received this disposal.[15] By 1559, the earliest year from which the Home Circuit records survive in numbers, it seems that the assizes in the south-east were mainly dealing with the more serious felonies: murder, manslaughter, infanticide, horse theft, robbery, rape and coining. More generally, three broad types of case were particularly likely to be reserved for the Westminster judges: publicly dangerous crimes that required the "theatrics of condemnation" that characterised the higher court; those

---

14. J. Hurstfield, *Freedom, Corruption and Government in Elizabethan England*, London, Jonathan Cape, 1973, pp.257-9.
15. L.A. Knafla, *Kent at Law 1602. The County Jurisdiction: Assizes and sessions of the Peace*, London, HMSO and PRO, 1994, p.29.

committed by repeat offenders, who had exhausted the patience of JPs by committing further serious crimes after earlier indulgences; and, especially after the reformed commissions of the peace of 1590, difficult cases requiring legal expertise. It was not a simple matter of the 'value' of goods stolen; certain crimes were seen as direct threats to the Commonwealth in a way that others were not. Interestingly, despite some modern claims to the contrary, grand larceny did not *necessarily* come into this category, in the way that robbery and homicide did. The separation provided major benefits for JPs. Their legal knowledge was less likely to be tested, and they did not incur responsibility or local opprobrium for mistaken or unpopular capital cases. Thus, an analysis of the cases allocated between the assizes and quarter sessions in Kent, in 1602, reveals that all cases of murder (seven of them) were tried before the assizes, and all but one of the 15 cases of manslaughter. Similarly, eight of the nine cases of robbery were determined at the higher court, along with two-thirds of the cases of horse theft (normally viewed as a socially injurious crime). More instances of grand larceny were tried at the county sessions than at the assizes (51 cases compared to 42). Perhaps surprisingly, there were also more really large cases amongst the quarter sessions' larcenies, seven being over 10 pounds in value, compared to only five at the assizes. Also surprisingly, all four cases of counterfeiting were determined at the quarter sessions, though these were probably very minor examples, such as 'clipping'. More predictably, all cases of poaching and unlawful shooting were heard at the inferior court. However, and indicative of the lack of neat division between the forums, the Kent assizes determined more cases of petty larceny than did the county sessions.[16] (It is possible that this was to use up available forensic time, as occasionally happens today when a High Court judge finishes a serious case earlier than expected on circuit.)

Quarter Sessions

The quarter (county) sessions were the lowest criminal courts administering the common law that also determined trials on indictment before a jury. At them, local JPs would "inquyre of the common annoyances of the king's leege people".[17] An Act of 1361 provided that they were to be held, as the name suggests, every three months, and it remained the rule that: "Justyces of Peas shall holde theyr Cessyons iiii [four] tymes of the yere." These were usually at Epiphany, Easter, Michaelmas and the Feast of St Thomas. Additionally, if pressure of business made it convenient, they could hold "more cessyons if nede be after theyr dyscrecyon".[18] Towards the end of the period, increased numbers of sittings became common throughout the country. This did not necessarily mean that each part of a county would witness four sessions. Large counties were often subdivided. Thus, in Kent, although there was only

---

16. Knafla, *Kent at Law 1602*, pp.21-22.
17. W. Harrison, "Description of England," R. Holinshed, *The First Volume of the Chronicles of England, Scotland and Ireland*, London, John Harrison, 1577, p.75.
18. Middleton, *The Boke of Justices of Peas*, f.Aiii.

one commission of the peace from the mid-fifteenth century onwards, the justices acted in two divisions. The eastern division would normally hold their quarter sessions at Canterbury, the western at Maidstone. Justices mainly (though not invariably) acted in their own division and officials only attended the divisions in which their area lay. As a result, during the sixteenth and seventeenth centuries, quarter sessions were only held twice in each part: at Epiphany and mid-Summer in East Kent and Easter and Michaelmas in West Kent. This practice was deplored by William Lambarde in his *Eirenarcha*, as it meant that each division effectively only had a bi-annual court.[19] There were some other regional variations. Although Yorkshire was the country's largest county, it was divided into three ridings, each of which had much of the administrative status of a county in their own right, though they shared a high sheriff. Each riding had its own court of quarter sessions. In Cheshire, there were four locations for the county sessions, each being held in a different and well spaced-apart town, allowing convenient forums for trials at Epiphany (Chester), Easter (Knutsford), Midsummer (Nantwich) and Michaelmas (Northwich or Middlewich).[20]

There was persistent concern at the legal competence of many of the JPs who presided over quarter sessions. This regularly led the Privy Council to reiterate the importance of reserving serious matters to the assizes. This was also

---

19. Melling, *Crime and Punishment*, pp.9 and 44.
20. J.C. Morrill, *The Cheshire Grand Jury 1625-1659, A Social and Administrative Study*, Leicester, Leicester University Press, 1976, p.9.

stressed by the reformed commission of the peace of 1590, which, although still permitting quarter sessions to determine felonies, qualified this with a *casus difficultatis* clause, inserted at the instigation of Lord Chief Justice Wray, and insisting that difficult cases be sent to the higher courts. This was often understood to mean that those felonies likely to result in actual, not commuted, death sentences if proved should be left for the superior court: "The jurisdiction of this court by statute 34 Edw. III c. 1. extends to the trying and determining all felonies and trespasses whatsoever: though they seldom, if ever, try any greater offence than small felonies within the benefit of clergy."[21] However, this was already common practice well before 1590, and one of the reasons that JPs were ordered to examine felony suspects in 1555. Thus, even in 1581, Lambarde had noted (with some exaggeration) that JPs were "not now adaies much occupied" with the trial of felonies. He claimed that if faced by a felony, they would normally "deferre it til the coming of the Justices of asizes".[22] The bulk of their judicial work at the end of the Elizabethan period (they also had a major administrative function in county society) was a mixture of prosecutions arising out of interpersonal disputes, such as petty theft, assault, poaching and trespass; regulative prosecutions, such as drunkenness, vagrancy, swearing, gaming, non-attendance at church, Sabbath-breaking, harbouring rogues; and prosecutions relating to the

---

21. W. Blackstone, *Commentaries on the Laws of England*, vol. 4, Oxford, Clarendon Press, 1769, p.268.
22. P.C. Lawson, "Property Crime and Hard Times in England, 1559-1624," *Law and History Review*, 1986, vol. 4, p.101.

enforcement of obligations on those who had abused or neglected an appointed office, such as constables.

In theory, when felonies were heard at such forums there were additional safeguards in place. According to a statute dating from the reign of Richard II: "Two men of lawe shoulde be in any comyssion of peas to procede to delyverence of felons."[23] This was not a moribund requirement in the early modern period. In 1657, William Fleetwood was adamant that when JPs were trying felons at quarter sessions there should always be two qualified barristers or serjeants at law amongst the magistrates present: "... then must there be in the same Commission of the Peace, two learned men in the Law, in which case the Justices of Peace may proceed to the Goal-delivery by their discretions, as after they see cause."[24] Indeed, in 1663, the judge Sir Robert Hide urged legally unqualified JPs to "acquiesce" in the judgment of lawyer magistrates sitting on the bench when it came to deciding points of law (as opposed to fact). He was concerned that, frequently, they were putting such matters to a general vote in which "ignorant Justices" on the bench might find according to their "fancy and opinion".[25] Of course this safeguard did not necessarily extend to misdemeanours. It was also sometimes overlooked in practice even for felonies.

Attendance rates for JPs at sessions varied with time and

---

23. Middleton, *The Boke of Justices of Peas*, f.Aii.
24. W. Fleetwood, *The Office of a Justice of Peace*, London, Ralph Wood for W. Lee, 1657, p.96.
25. H. Townshend, *Notes of the Office of a Justice of Peace, 1661-3*, R.D. Hunt (Ed.), Worcester, Worcestershire Historical Society, 1967, p.101.

place, but were never close to being the great majority of magistrates on a local commission. In Wiltshire, in the late sixteenth century, quarter sessions would normally attract between eight and 11 JPs. Sometimes, there were far fewer. Thus, at the sessions held at Devizes, in July 1576, there were only three men present. Fifteen months later, the Michaelmas sessions in the same town attracted only two. Less surprisingly, it was not unusual for special sessions to attract only a pair of JPs (the legal minimum). There was a similar degree of variation in the following century, although the increased number of magistrates appointed meant that more were usually in attendance; at the Easter sessions of 1620, 29 magistrates attended. Even so, numbers were still sometimes in single figures. Individual attendance also varied greatly. Many JPs went to only one sessions a year, some two, and a few, three. In some years, half of the members of the commission did not appear at all.[26] At sessions, the JPs were supposed be attended by the constables of all the hundreds and liberties within the county, and by the sheriff or his deputy.[27]

Special Sessions

The JPs' special sessions (sometimes called statute sessions) were, effectively, localised and *ad hoc* 'general' or quarter

---

26. Hurstfield, *Freedom, Corruption* .., p.259.
27. Sir F. Bacon, "The Use of the Law," in Montagu, Basil (Ed.), *The Works of Francis Bacon*, vol.3, Philadelphia: Carey and Hart, 1841, at pp.247-253, p.250.

sessions, often limited to a specific hundred, presided over by a minimum of two magistrates, at least one of whom was of the quorum, but still employing a jury (unlike petty sessions). Sheppard, a great supporter of such tribunals, felt that they were: "... of speciall use to deliever Gaols of unruly servants, petty thieves and others which get no good by lying there." The extent of their jurisdiction was not entirely clear. Some argued that it overlapped entirely with that of quarter sessions so that as long as there was: "... one Justice of the Quorum present, they may hear and determine any article within the Commission of the Peace at this sessions as well as at the Quarter-sessions." Others were slightly more circumspect. However, most accepted that they could determine offences where a statute specifically allowed it, and this could be by inference, extending to: "Statutes that do use the word sessions, indifferently, without adding, general or special."[28] Sheppard was particularly keen that JPs keep special sessions to deal with specific and localised forms of disorder. Significantly, he felt that such sessions should use a 'choice jury', individually named by the JPs to the sheriff (who had the responsibility of summoning them), rather than men chosen at random. Sheppard also believed that their jurisdictional area should be confined to one or two hundreds, and that special sessions ought to be specialised, dealing with discreet facets of disorder, such as vagrancy and ale-house offences, at each sitting.[29] Special

---

28. W. Sheppard, *The Whole Office of the County Justice of Peace*, 3rd edn., London, W. Lee, 1656, Book 2, pp.1-3.
29. Sheppard, *The Whole Office of the County Justice of Peace*, 3rd edn., Book 1, p.2.

sessions were a regular feature of the administration of justice in some counties, such as Kent, less common in others.

Clerk of the Peace

As today, the clerk of the peace and his clerical staff provided the professional element in the system of lay magistracy, and many of their functions would be familiar to their modern equivalents. Thus, the office of *Custos Rotulorum* having become an honorary position by the sixteenth century (usually held by the most senior of the JPs or the lord lieutenant) the clerk had responsibility for preserving the documents used in and out of quarter sessions. He would have drafted many of these himself. The clerk also recorded the decisions of the court in the order book, dealt with much general correspondence and liaised with the bench.[30] He might also be entrusted by the magistrates with delicate "behind the scenes" tasks. Thus, in April 1661, after his first imprisonment, John Bunyan was visited by the Bedfordshire clerk of the peace. The clerk was blunt about who had sent him and why. He asked that Bunyan abandon his private religious meetings as contrary to statute law and warned that he was: "... sent to you by the justices to tell you that they do intend to prosecute the law against you if you submit not." In the lengthy ensuing

---

30. J.A. Sharpe, *Crime in Seventeenth Century England*, Cambridge, CUP, 1983, p.31.

argument, he used all his powers of persuasion to urge Bunyan, to be 'ruled', albeit unavailingly. Nevertheless, the clerk remained polite throughout, prompting Bunyan to thank him for his "civil and meek discoursing".[31] In seventeenth century Essex, such clerks of the peace were usually drawn from the ranks of the petty gentry. It was a secure and modestly profitable office, but not normally a stepping-stone to higher advancement. This social pattern seems to have been replicated in other counties. The office was sometimes held by the same men who took other minor legal positions, such as associate clerk to the assizes. It was a position that was more likely to appeal to an attorney than a barrister.[32]

Borough Courts

The county commissions of the peace did not have a monopoly of quarter sessions. As Blackstone noted: "In most corporation towns there are quarter sessions kept before justices of their own, within their respective limits: which have exactly the same authority as the general quarter sessions of the county."[33] These were usually heard before the town's mayor and jurats or legates, acting as *ex officio* magistrates by dint of their position. Some towns also had a part-time professional judge, a Recorder, sitting on the

---

31. J. Bunyan, *A Relation of my Imprisonment*, 1765, pp.20-23.
32. Sharpe, *Crime in Seventeenth-Century England*, p.31.
33. Blackstone, *Commentaries on the Laws of England*, vol. 4, p.269.

Bench and providing legal expertise. Such individuals were usually barristers engaged in normal legal practice for most of the year. Thus, in Essex, the county quarter sessions did not have sole jurisdiction throughout the shire. The boroughs of Maldon, Harwich, Saffron Walden and Thaxted, along with the liberty of Havering, all held their own sessions.[34] (Additionally, the bishops of Durham and Ely, and the Archbishop of York, were empowered by statute to hold sessions within their liberties.)

Some borough courts, usually those of major chartered towns and cities, also had the power of gaol delivery, allowing them to determine serious felonies and execute those found guilty, if appropriate. Thus, Queen Elizabeth I gave Newcastle a charter which empowered the city's mayor, Recorder and aldermen: "... three or more of them, whereof the Mayor or Recorder to be one; from time to time ever hereafter, to be Justices at the gaol delievery, and to deliver out of prison in the same, committed to the same Gaol for what cause soever." Furthermore, they were authorised to erect gallows within the liberty of Newcastle to execute felons.[35] Similarly, Rye, a Sussex port of about 4,000 people in the mid-sixteenth century, also enjoyed power of gaol delivery. It witnessed nine executions in the 45 years between 1558 and 1603.[36] In Essex, only Colchester had the ability to punish serious felonies, putting it on a par with the county quarter sessions in theory, and the assizes

34. Sharpe, *Crime in Seventeenth-Century England*, p.20.
35. R. Gardner, *England's Grievance Discovered*, London, p.11.
36. J.S. Cockburn, "Punishment and Brutalization in the English Enlightenment," *Law and History Review*, vol. 12, Number 1, 1994, p.159.

in practice.[37]

By itself, the extra power allowed to these boroughs would not have been hugely significant if they had been willing to remit their potentially capital cases to the assizes, in the same way that the county quarter sessions normally did. However, before 1660, many borough sessions with power of gaol delivery were willing to exercise their jurisdiction over even the most serious cases. Thus, Alice Arden and her associates were tried, convicted and sentenced to death for murder by the Faversham sessions in 1551. Richard Skeete and Lydia Downes were hanged for murder by the Colchester sessions in 1639.[38] After the Restoration, such chartered boroughs became increasingly reluctant to use their powers if it would mean passing an unreprieved or unclergied death penalty. According to Defoe, Yarmouth became noteworthy in the 1670s precisely because it exercised its right to "try, condemn, and execute in especial cases without waiting for a warrant from above". A naval captain was hanged there for a murder committed in the town's streets. Generally, although some towns where the borough court of sessions had power to determine capital offences continued to hear such cases into the eighteenth century, they almost invariably recommended that pardons be granted to those convicted.

---

37. Sharpe, *Crime in Seventeenth-Century England*, p.20.
38. D. Cressey, *Travesties and Transgressions in Tudor and Stuart England*, Oxford, OUP, 2000, p.76.

The Assizes

The assizes did not sit in permanent session, but were temporary courts presided over twice a year during the Lent and long vacations (usually July and August) by judges sent from London. As Paul Hentzner noted in the 1590s: "... the greater [matters] are tried by the judges, formerly called travelling judges of assize; these go their circuits through the counties twice every year to hear causes, and pronounce sentence upon prisoners."[39] The times of these circuits might be varied in emergency. Thus, in 1690, the threat from French warships to the south coast meant that the Home Circuit 'summer' assizes, presided over by Mr Justice Rokeby and Lord Chief Justice Holt, was put back from July to early September.[40] Some foreigners felt that the delays attendant on the English system of occasional and centrally controlled courts, even for the most serious offences, were not conducive to efficient felony control. Thus, in c.1500, an Italian visitor suggested that the nation's: "... great prevalence of crime might have been better prevented, had not former kings condensed the criminal jurisdiction under one head, called the Chief Justice, who has the supreme power over punishment by death."[41] Perhaps significantly, London was excluded from the national system, having much more frequent sittings at the Old Bailey.

---

39. P. Hentzner, *Travels in England during the reign of Queen Elizabeth*, 1889, p.80.
40. Mr Justice Rokeby, *The Diary of Mr Justice Rokeby printed from a manuscript in the Possession of Sir Henry Peek*, London, Wyman and Sons, 1887, p.11.
41. Anon, *A Relation, or Rather a True Account of the Island of England ... About the Year 1500*, C. Sneyd (Trans.), London, Camden Society, 1847, p.33.

Although the assizes had a civil jurisdiction (that of *nisi prius*), most of their work was criminal. The criminal and civil matters would usually be heard simultaneously in adjacent courts. Judges would often alternate between presiding over the *nisi prius* cases and the Crown side (criminal) matters, swapping with their co-adjutors from location to location as they progressed around their circuit. Although civil matters were considered to be intellectually more demanding, if only because of the frequent presence of counsel, the case load was much more modest than that on the Crown side. One of the benefits of the circuit system was that the pairs of judges might consult each other over difficult points of law.

From the reign of Henry II, England had been divided into six circuits, each of them made up of groups of adjoining counties. Thus, after 1558, the Western Circuit covered the counties of Devon, Cornwall, Dorset, Somerset, Hampshire and Wiltshire. The Home Circuit covered the counties around London, the misleadingly named Norfolk Circuit included Bedfordshire, Buckinghamshire and the East Anglian counties, the Midland Circuit held the central counties, such as Rutland and Leicestershire, the Oxford Circuit included Monmouthshire, while the Northern Circuit contained Cumberland, Westmoreland, Northumberland, Yorkshire and Lancashire. Wales was *sui generis*. Although Henrician statutes of 1536 and 1543 had incorporated the Principality into the realm, giving it substantial uniformity with England in the administration of justice, and applying common law to its courts, it was granted its own courts of Great Sessions. These were the equivalent of the English assizes. They were modelled on the practice already used in the three northern Welsh counties of Anglesey, Caernarfon and Merioneth, but with 12 counties now grouped into four judicial circuits. In each county there would be at least one and usually two or more assizes towns, where the judges might sit, though only one would be used on any single judicial circuit. Some were occasional venues, others regularly employed. Thus, in March 1694, on the Norfolk Circuit, Stowmarket was unexpectedly used for the Suffolk assizes, despite never having served in that capacity before, because there was smallpox at Bury, the normal choice, and "ye Country was afraid of comeing there". It was held in a specially improvised courtroom.[42] Similarly, in 1608, the Derbyshire assizes were held at Chesterfield, owing to the prevalence of plague in Derby. Normally, such assizes towns were *le principal et chieefe villes de les counties*, to employ Richard Crompton's tortuous law French.[43] However, occasionally, a smaller town might become a major assizes location because it was convenient for transportation and the movements of the circulating judges. Thus, Little Brickhill in Buckinghamshire, which bordered its fellow circuit county of Bedfordshire, and was less than two miles from the London road, although little more than a large village, was sometimes used for the Buckinghamshire assizes, especially during the Elizabethan

---

42. Rokeby, *The Diary of Mr Justice Rokeby*, p.39.
43. R. Crompton, *L'Authoritie et Jurisdiction Des Courts de la Maiestie de la Roygne*, London, 1594, p.226.

and Jacobean period (it was referred to as the county's assizes town in Saxton's map of 1574). Between 1561 and 1620, the names of 42 executed criminals appear among the burials in the parish register. (The gallows were less than half a mile from the town.) The assizes were last held there in 1638. So important were they to the town's economy that the borough appears to have fallen into decay after their removal.[44]

The assizes judges were primarily drawn from the judiciary of the courts of Common Pleas, King's Bench, and Exchequer based in Westminster, where they sat for most of the year. Thus, they included the nation's most eminent legal figures. Six pairs of judges were needed for the circuits, and there were only four judges in each court. Assizes work and its attendant travelling were taxing. Judges who were sick, frail or engaged on other state duties could not attempt it. As a result, their numbers would be supplemented, on an ad hoc basis, by experienced serjeants at law (senior lawyers) who were used to make up the necessary numbers.[45] Normally, such temporary appointments would be paired with the more experienced Westminster judges when on circuit. The two men would travel together around the circuit, moving from one assizes town to another, spending two or three days in each, dispensing justice on the way. The length of an assizes circuit varied with time, location and caseload. Thus, the

---

44. D. and S. Lysons, *Magna Britannia*, vol. 1, London: T. Kadell and W. Davies, 1806, at p.521.
45. Cockburn, *A History of English Assizes, 1558-1714*, Cambridge, CUP, pp.120-127.

summer assizes on the Northern Circuit usually lasted 17 days in the 1580s. However, by 1690, if an assizes was held in Hull, it could go on for as much as 35 days during the long vacation.[46] Until 1820, for reasons of distance and (to a lesser extent) security, the four most northern and distant counties, Cumberland, Westmoreland, Northumberland and Durham, had to make do with one assizes a year, held in the summer.[47] This meant that the winter assizes on that circuit, normally held only in York and Lancaster, might be completed in seven days.[48] Judges could travel over 200 miles when on circuit. Thus, the (considerably delayed) Home Circuit for the summer of 1690, began at Hertford on September 1, moved on to Chelmsford in Essex on the 3rd of that month, to Kingston on Thames in Surrey on the 8th and then Horsham, Sussex on the 11th. The final stop was Maidstone, Kent, reached on September 16, the hearings presumably finishing a few days afterwards and allowing the judges to make the fairly short return journey to London.[49] Travelling anywhere in England was arduous and slow. Lawyers journeying to and from the north of England to London, during the Elizabethan and Jacobean periods, might allow up to six days for the journey.[50] In July 1696, the road from Oxford to Gloucester was so bad that Rokeby and

---

46. Cockburn, "The Northern Assize Circuit," *Northern History*, 1968, vol. 3, p.122.
47. D.R. Bentley (Ed.), *Select cases from the twelve Judges notebooks*, London, John Rees, 1997, p.2.
48. Cockburn, "The Northern Assize Circuit," p.122.
49. Rokeby, *The Diary of Mr Justice Rokeby*, p.11.
50. W. Prest, *The Rise of the Barristers: A Social History of the English Bar 1590-1640*, Oxford, Clarendon Press, 1986, p.46.

his fellow assizes' judges did not arrive before 9.30 pm, having left the University City at 7.30 am. This was despite the judiciary making careful preparations for their travels. Typically, Rokeby hired a carriage and four horses as transport, often adding a pair of his own animals to the team to bolster its traction power. His chamber clerk from Westminster Hall was allowed to travel in the carriage with him (and, presumably, the other judge and his clerk), while he hired a horse for his personal servant to ride alongside.[51]

Unexpected emergencies could arise while on circuit and would have to be dealt with as best they could. Thus, during Lent 1698, Rokeby was called back suddenly to London from Oxford, after completing the assizes held there and (earlier) at Reading, leaving his fellow judge, Mr Justice Eyre, to go on alone for the remainder of the circuit. Presumably, he dealt with the most pressing cases and adjourned the remainder to the next circuit. Rokeby took their rented carriage to make the return journey, leaving Eyre to continue on horseback, something that occasioned a dispute between the two judges as to the apportionment of payment between them for the transport. This was referred to Mr Justice Powell and another judge for informal 'arbitration'. (They found against Rokeby.)[52]

Judges were empowered by several temporary commissions, the most important of which, for criminal matters, were those of oyer and terminer and gaol delivery. Thus, the assizes circuit was usually initiated by a

---

51.   Rokeby, *The Diary of Mr Justice Rokeby*, pp.40 and 46.
52.   Rokeby, *The Diary of Mr Justice Rokeby*, p.11.

commission of gaol delivery, issued by the Crown, addressed to five judges and authorising any two of them to hold the assizes in a specified county at a set time. This commission allowed the judges to deal with every prisoner in the county jail "for what offence soever he be ther". Ideally, by the end of each assizes, the local prison should have been completely cleared (in practice this rarely happened).[53] In the 1560s, according to Sir Thomas Smith, at the end of the law term immediately before the judges going on circuit, details of their itinerary were written up and displayed in the Exchequer, stating "on what day and in what place" they would be. Those selected for the duty would also write to the sheriff of each county, requesting them to make the necessary arrangements. The sheriffs would initially bear many of the judges' charges personally, subsequently seeking "allowance for it in the Exchequer".

The assizes were conducted with considerable ceremony, something that reinforced the authority of central government and its law. Before beginning their lists, the scarlet and ermine robed judges would attend a service at the local parish church or cathedral, with their trumpeters, javelin-men, court officers, and the sheriff and under-sheriff of the county, in attendance. There, they would listen to a special assizes sermon, delivered by a prominent clergyman. It was one of the High Sheriff's duties to make arrangements for this preacher. Such sermons normally emphasised a legal-religious theme, and were indicative of contemporary

---

53. Sir F. Bacon, (1841) "The Use of the Law," pp.247-253.

(establishment) attitudes towards justice.[54] Thus, William Cole, the High Sheriff of Bedfordshire, arranged for John Wesley to preach on Friday, March 10, 1758, before Sir Edward Clive, a judge of the Court of Common Pleas, in St Paul's Church, Bedford, where Clive was due to hold the Lent assizes. Wesley had expected to preach a day earlier; however, the service was postponed, probably because cases at the previous assizes town had overrun. His theme was the Great Assize when all would stand before Christ's judgement-seat; he compared the role of the trial judges to this final event. In his journal, he noted that the congregation was both large and very attentive. As was customary, after the sermon, the judge sent Wesley an invitation to dine with him.[55] His sermon was a fairly standard one for such occasions, numerous other preachers also warned their legal congregations to fear the: "... generalle sessions of the great Judgement of the world, When we shall all appear before the Judgement-Seat of Christ."[56] Other regular themes included stressing the need for obedience and condemning perjury.

Outside London there was rarely a purpose built court available for criminal hearings, and the assizes might be held in a "towne House, or in some open or common place".[57] The county shire hall was a frequent location. Thus,

---

54. J.M. Beattie, *Crime and the Courts in England 1660-1800*, Oxford, OUP, p.316.
55. Rev. J. Wesley, "Sermon 15," in The Works of the Rev. J. Wesley, London, Wesleyan Conference Office, 1872.
56. W. Thomas, *The regulation of Law-Suits, Evidence, and Pleadings-An Assize-Sermon, Preached at Caernarvon, 16th March 1657*, London, 1657, p.37.
57. Sir T. Smith, *De Republica Anglorum*, London, 1583, p.111.

from 1229, the Rutland assizes were held in the great hall of Oakham castle, which was also the seat of the town's lord of the manor. The county jail was conveniently close, also being inside the castle grounds. When the other castle buildings were allowed to fall into ruin, in the late medieval period, basic maintenance was carried out on this unusual piece of twelfth century domestic architecture, because, as was noted in 1521, it was "convenient to be kept upholden" as a seat for a variety of local courts. Along with the assizes, the Rutland quarter sessions, coroners' inquests, and, in the seventeenth century, local petty sessions, were all held there. Additionally, it was the forum for the manorial courts leet and baron until their abolition.[58] The judge, usually sitting on a raised platform, would be flanked by senior JPs, with other magistrates sitting on a bench below them, along with the minor dignitaries. Beneath these was a table where sat the *Custos Rotulorum* or keeper of writs, the under-sheriff and "such clarkes as doe write".[59]

The assizes were great social occasions for the county gentry, far more so than the quarter sessions (though these were not insignificant events). Much commerce was done and gossip shared. Many men of quality, resident in the county, made an effort to be there, it being "an honor which they owe to the Reverend Judges and Magistrates, to attend them".[60] The judges would entertain local notables to dinner

---

58. T.H. Mackenzie, *Oakham Castle: A Guide and History*, Clough, Oakham, Rutland County Council, 1999, pp.14-17.
59. Smith, *De Republica Anglorum*, p.111.
60. G. Herbert, *A Priest to the Temple*, London, T. Maxey for T. Garthwait, 1652, p.39.

in the evening. At least the occasion meant that they could expect to dine well, as the county sheriff usually made a special effort to indulge them. Thus, in Shropshire, after 1660, a local chef, Richard Hunt, was: "... very famouse for his skill in the art of cookery, and therefore was much imployed by the Sheriffs of this county, for dressing of theire dinners att the Assizes."[61]

The Clerks to the Assizes

Clerks of assizes supported the judges, and were responsible for most of the circuit administration. It appears that these men had originated as private clerks to the judges, the position becoming a barristers' monopoly in the late fourteenth century, though, for obvious reasons, its holders were forbidden by statute to practise law on their own circuits (33 Hen.viii c.24). By the mid-seventeenth century it had developed into an almost full-time office, responsible for the administration of a small department and the smooth running of each assizes circuit. Although it was not usually a highly prestigious position, it was a very responsible one.[62] Thus, typically, the two men who served as clerks to the Somerset assizes in the years between 1629 and 1640 were members of the Middle Temple and had been called to the

---

61. R. Gough, *The History of Myddle*, D. Hey (Ed.) 1981, Harmondsworth, Penguin, 1701, p.175.
62. Cockburn, "Seventeenth-Century Clerks of Assize-Some Anonymous Members of the Legal Profession," *The American Journal of Legal History*, vol. 13, p.317.

Bar. Their social backgrounds were similar, both being minor gentlemen, one with very recent yeoman ancestry, rather than the more socially prominent members of their professions. In the sixteenth century, however, a few clerks had been quite distinguished; Sir Thomas Elyot was clerk to the Western Circuit between 1511 and 1526. The extensive fees available, for both criminal and civil matters, meant that the position was well remunerated. (They also meant that it occasioned periodic allegations of corruption.) Clerks would be based in a circuit assizes town, though some, like the Northern Circuit's Thomas Potts, with his lodgings in Chancery Lane in the winter of 1612 to 1613, spent a considerable amount of time in the capital.

The clerks' pre-trial role was primarily a co-ordinating one as they would usually be supported by several associates, 'inferior' lawyers, normally attorneys rather than barristers, who would draw up many of the formal documents, under the clerk's direction.[63] This was alluded to by Henry Twyford when he stressed that many of the tasks that he had identified as incidental to their office were actually performed by others: "Note also, that where it is said the Clerk of Assize must do such and such things, they are usually done by the associate."[64] Below the associates were several, legally less qualified, clerks to assist with administration. Illustrative of a typical court complement, in 1650, the Oxford Circuit staff consisted of two associates and four clerks in addition to the clerk of assize. One associate

---

63. Barnes, *Somerset Assize Orders 1629-1640*, vol. 65, p.34.
64. Twyford, *The Office of the Clerk of Assize*, p.27.

took each (criminal) Crown side and one each (civil) *nisi prius* hearing. The four inferior clerks were mainly concentrated on the pressured Crown side rather than the less busy *nisi prius* work, being heavily engaged in drafting indictments and other documents.[65] Associates were remunerated much more modestly than their superiors, something that frequently prompted them to seek supplemental offices. Typically, the legal author and court associate Zachary Babbington was also steward of the manor court of Yoxall in Staffordshire. Others combined associateship with a clerkship or deputy clerkship of the peace. Thus, Thomas Audley, a Norfolk Circuit associate was clerk for Bedfordshire between 1619 and 1627. Some served as coroners.

The clerk's personal role at trial was often significant. Assizes judges, especially those not drawn from the court of King's Bench, spent most of their lives in London dealing with civil not criminal matters. As a result, they were often heavily dependent on the clerk's expertise in criminal law and procedure when on circuit. In Bacon's words, an: "... ancient clerk, skilful in precedents, wary in proceeding, and understanding in the business of the court, is an excellent finger of a court; and doth many times point the way to the judge himself."[66] It is *possible* that, in an emergency, such as judicial sickness, they may even have carried out some lesser judicial functions. In any event, their specialist

---

65. Cockburn, "Seventeenth-Century Clerks of Assize," pp.317-327.
66. Sir F. Bacon, "On Judicature," *The Essays*, London, Everyman edn., J.M. Dent, 1906, pp.162-165.

knowledge meant that the judges would often be dependent on them for advice, especially on procedure. Thus, in 1754, Jerome Knapp, a barrister who was the Clerk for the Home Circuit, gave tips to the neophyte assizes judge Sir Dudley Ryder on practice matters (as did Ryder's coadjutor, the very experienced Sir Michael Foster, who told him how to pass criminal sentences and the mechanics of reprieving convicts).[67]

Special Jurisdictions

Over most of England the royal courts had reduced private jurisdictions for felony to relative insignificance by the fourteenth century. However, some parts of the country escaped the centralised system that developed. The largest exceptions were the three counties palatine. Two of these, Chester and Durham, had enjoyed their special status from time immemorial, something that may have been linked to their strategic position in the North. Edward III had expressly granted Lancaster's privilege to Henry Plantagenet. As a result, at one time, the Earl of Chester, the Bishop of Durham, and the Duke of Lancaster, had had the same legal powers as the Crown when it came to doing justice in their dominions, being able to pardon felonies, appoint judges and JPs, having writs and indictments issued in their names and all offences being said to be done against

---

67.   J. H. Langbein, "Shaping the Eighteenth-Century Criminal Trial: A View from the Ryder Sources," *University of Chicago Law Review*, 1983, vol. 50, p.28.

their peace rather than *contra pacem domini Regis*. However, only Durham had survived in the hands of a subject (the bishop), the earldom of Chester being united to the Crown by Henry III, and, during the reign of Edward IV, the Duchy of Lancaster being forfeited to the Crown. In any event, under a Henrician statute of 1536 (27 Hen. VIII), the powers of the counties palatine were considerably reduced.[68] Thus, the 1536 Act provided that in Cheshire JPs should sit at quarter sessions, which replaced part of the criminal function of the ancient Cheshire county court. However, the special character of the palatinates survived; parliament kept Lancaster "distinct and separate from other inheritances of the crown". In Cheshire, rather than abolishing all the county's ancient privileges, the position of the county was redefined by asserting the king's direct sovereignty, so that the palatinate was still not subject to the control of Westminster institutions like most other shires.[69] It remained outside the assizes system, its court of Great Sessions having exclusive cognizance of all Crown pleas with regard to crime. It also had its own chief justice and an assistant puisne judge, recruited from outside the Westminster courts (the regicide John Bradshaw was chief justice of Chester in 1647), together with a permanent administrative staff. Twice a year it sat as a court of assize to determine felonies.[70] Of course, such local courts were modest in scale. Even the chief justiceship of Chester,

---

68. Blackstone, *Commentaries on the Laws of England*, vol. 1, p.113.
69. T. Thornton, "Cardinal Wolsey and the Abbot of Chester," *History Today*, 1995, vol. 45, issue 8, p.12.
70. Morrill, *The Cheshire Grand Jury 1625-1659*, p.6.

though it had considerable status, was only a part-time office, carrying a salary of 500 pounds a year. Thus, on his appointment to the position in 1680, another of its notorious occupants, Sir George Jeffreys, retained both the Recordership of London and his extensive practice at the Bar.[71] The assizes jurisdiction of the palatinates was finally abolished in Chester in 1830, and in Durham and Lancaster in 1876.

Although in some ways similar to the three northern counties, the Isle of Ely was not a county palatine, though sometimes mistakenly called one. It was a royal franchise, the bishop having: "... by grant of king Henry the first, jura regalia within the isle of Ely, and thereby he exercises a jurisdiction over all causes, as well criminal, as civil."[72] The bishop's jurisdiction was not abolished until 1836. The Cinque Ports and their subsidiaries, in Kent and Sussex, provided another important local exception to the national pattern. The five ancient ports of Sandwich, Hythe, Romsey, Hastings and Dover and their associated towns had numerous privileges, due to their importance to national defence. Among them was the right to "do justice upon criminall offendors".[73] They had their own courts, which were able to try all felonies. Thus, Thomas Arden's murderers were convicted and sentenced to death at an 'assizes' held in Faversham. This was a borough sessions, in

---

71. G.W. Keeton, "Judge Jeffreys as Chief Justice of Chester 1680-1683," *Law Quarterly Review*, vol. 77, p.38.
72. Blackstone, *Commentaries on the Laws of England*, vol. 1, p.115.
73. W. Lambarde, *A Perambulation of Kent* (written 1570), London, Baldwin, Cradock, Joy and Co, 1828, p.126.

a town which, as a limb of the Cinque Ports, was empowered to try capital felonies independently from the national system.[74]

London and Middlesex

Criminal courts in the Metropolis differed markedly from those outside London and Middlesex (a substantially, and increasingly, suburban county). London had a unique legal and governmental system, Hentzner noting that the control of the city was lodged, by ancient right, in 24 aldermen who annually elected: "... out of their own body a mayor and two sheriffs, who determine causes according to municipal laws." Misdemeanours in the square mile, such as fraud, riot and assault were normally determined at the sessions of the peace for the City of London. After 1411, these were usually held at the imposing Guildhall, which was partly built for the "session of the several courts". (It was also sometimes the setting for famous state trials, such as that of Lady Jane Grey in 1553.) By charter, the Lord Mayor and senior aldermen were also JPs for the borough of Southwark, south of the river, and held regular sessions of the peace there. The equivalent sessions for most of the county of Middlesex were held at the Castle Inn, in St John Street, Clerkenwell, until 1613, when a purpose built court, Hick's Hall, was opened nearby. By this time, such sessions

---

74. Anon, *The History of the Most Remarkable Tryals in Great Britain and Ireland*, London, A. Bell, 1715, pp.248-262.

were normally being held eight times a year, as they were at the Old Bailey.[75] The separate Westminster quarter sessions continued to be held in a tavern, near Westminster Hall, until the eighteenth century.[76]

More serious Metropolitan crimes would be heard at the sessions house situated at the Old Bailey in the City. This was opened in 1539, replacing an earlier open-air hustings. It was a joint court (for both London and Middlesex) and returned two separate juries to conduct trials for each location. The adjacent Newgate prison was used for the detention of criminals from both the City and Middlesex, pending trial. As a result, many people held in custody elsewhere in the Metropolis would be transferred to Newgate to await their hearings shortly before each session at the Old Bailey. These gaol delivery sessions (and the general sessions of oyer and terminer that were normally held at the same time) usually dealt with counterfeiting and felonies such as murder, burglary and larceny. Occasionally, like the assizes, they also tried serious misdemeanours. However, a practice developed during the 1600s of diverting many minor felonies from the mainstream system by committing suspects to the Bridewell as vagrants, rather than sending them for prosecution on indictment.[77] The Old Bailey sat eight times a year, four times as frequently as the

75. E.D. Mercer and K. Goodacre, *Guide to the Middlesex sessions Records, 1549-1884*, London, GLRO, 1965, p.14.
76. A. Babington, *A House in Bow Street*, 2nd edn., Chichester, Barry Rose, 1999, p.51.
77. J. Beattie, *Policing and Punishment in London, 1660-1750*, Oxford, OUP, 2001, pp.24-33.

provincial assizes (of which it was roughly the equivalent), though, before the 1660s, this number was not precisely adhered to.

The Court of King's Bench was the highest court of common law in England and Wales, and the only Westminster court to have a criminal as well as civil jurisdiction. Originally, it had not determined criminal matters. However, in 1323, in the aftermath of the lawlessness that followed the civil war between Edward II and Thomas of Lancaster, it was ordered to hear felonies from some northern counties. This jurisdiction was expanded over the following decade, so that its involvement in criminal justice came to distinguish it from the Court of Common Pleas and that of the Exchequer.[78] At King's Bench, civil cases were heard on the 'Plea Side' and criminal cases on the 'Crown Side'. The Crown Side contained three separate criminal jurisdictions. It had an original jurisdiction over all matters of a criminal and public nature, in its capacity as the *custos morum* of the monarch's subjects. This meant that it regularly heard cases with political overtones, such as treason, from anywhere in the nation, and cases where the defendant was of an elevated or special status. Gentlemen accused of murder were more likely to be tried there (rather than at provincial assizes or the Old Bailey) than were commoners. Typically, in 1612, the Scottish Lord Sanquire was arraigned at the King's Bench bar as an accessory to murder, while his hired assassins were tried at

---

78. G.O. Sayles, *The Court of King's Bench in Law and History*, London, Selden Society, 1959, pp.12-14.

the Old Bailey.[79] The court also possessed supervisory powers over inferior courts, with the ability to transfer indictments to its jurisdiction from all lesser courts. As was noted in 1526, its judges: "... *ont aussi poier de proceder et termyner inditements presentementes prises en alcun counte deins le royalme.*"[80] Thus, it could hear felonies initiated in the provinces, though this power was rarely exercised without special cause. Finally, it had a local jurisdiction, in that its presence within any county allowed it to hear and try criminal cases. As the court had become fixed at Westminster by the fifteenth century, its local criminal jurisdiction was limited to Middlesex and its subordinate jurisdictions (principally Westminster and the Tower Hamlets), though the Old Bailey remained a much more common forum for cases from these areas. Because of this multiplicity of jurisdictions, the criminal cases determined by the court could range from the gravest cases of high treason to relatively petty matters.

Court of Star Chamber

The Court of Star Chamber, named after the star-spangled ceiling of the room in the old palace of Westminster where it normally sat, was the most important of the prerogative courts (those basing their authority on sovereign power) that

---

79. J.L Rayner and G.T. Crook (Eds.), *The Complete Newgate Calendar* (vols. 1-5). London, Privately printed for the Navarre Society, 1926, vol. I, p.36.
80. Pyson, *Diversite de Courts et leur Jurisdictions*, London, 1526, f.Aiii.

also exercised a criminal jurisdiction.[81] (Its original civil jurisdiction had become largely unimportant by the 1560s.) It was not the novel institution sometimes portrayed by 'Whig' historians, being the judicial arm of the King's Council, and having developed out of that body in the years after 1485.[82] In its judicial role, Star Chamber was responsible for administering justice directly to the public and also for supervising other courts and officials. Thus, it investigated corruption amongst juries and in the wider justice system, and was an important forum for making complaints about the conduct of individual JPs, such as allegations of bias and abuse of position.[83] By the first years of Henry VIII's reign the council met almost daily during term time. However, it was not until the 1530s that there was a definite administrative distinction between its executive and judicial functions, roles that had previously been combined. While Star Chamber retained its legal function, the executive role of the council, as the King's private or 'privy' council, moved to Whitehall in 1540.[84]

As a court, Star Chamber was openly inquisitorial. It was made up of a mixture of senior judges taken from common law forums, great officers of state and ordinary privy counsellors. However, it sat without juries, either grand or

---

81.   W. Hudson, *A Treatise on the Court of Star-Chamber*, London, 1792, p.8.
82.   Lambarde, *Archeion*, p.156, see also T.G Barnes, "Due Process and Slow Process in the Late Elizabethan-Early Stuart Star Chamber," *The American Journal of Legal History*, 1962, vol. 6, pp.225-6.
83.   Hudson, *A Treatise on the Court of Star-Chamber*, p.64.
84.   S. Thurley, "The Lost Palace of Whitehall," *History Today*, 1998, vol. 48, issue 1, pp.47-52.

trial. Additionally, although it applied the substantive law of the realm, Star Chamber was not bound by the normal procedural rules of the common law, something that made it much more flexible than, for example, the assizes. Thus, court officials examined witnesses and defendants in camera and under oath. Against this, defendants could have the assistance of counsel and their witnesses could give sworn evidence, the advent of which to the common law courts would wait until the 1700s. Cases began on petition from individual complainants or information otherwise received. Individual petitions would normally be addressed to the monarch, set out the crimes alleged to have been committed, describe the circumstances surrounding their commission, and ask that the defendant be subpoenaed to answer the allegations in the Star Chamber. The court could take depositions, make an accused person answer the petitioner's bill and reply to detailed interrogatories. It reached a verdict by a simple majority of its members, each man giving his verdict (and sentence) in ascending order of seniority. The Lord Chancellor had a casting vote if there was an equal division.[85] Most Star Chamber cases in which a defendant was convicted resulted in a fine, even if accompanied by another sentence. The court's punishments also included imprisonment, the pillory, whipping, branding and, the most serious, mutilation (cutting off ears or slitting noses). However, as the crimes prosecuted were, in theory, only "gross misdemeanours", rather than felonies, its penal repertoire did not include execution.

---

85. Barnes, "Due Process and Slow Process ...," pp.225-8.

Star Chamber became increasingly popular as a forum during the reign of Henry VIII, especially under the Chancellorship of Thomas Wolsey (1515-1529). This was largely because of its ability to enforce the law when local jurisdictions failed to do so because of corruption or external pressure and influence. It was particularly effective in dealing with magnates who could intimidate ordinary JPs. Thus, Sir Thomas Smith noted in the Elizabethan period that Star Chamber had been necessary to deal with men of "power and force", especially those from the distant North, who could not be controlled by "meane Gentlemen".[86] Arguably, it played an important role in re-establishing the 'rule of law' in magnate dominated provincial England in the early 1500s. In addition to being a forum for prosecuting riot and similar crimes, it determined numerous cases of slander, forgery, conspiracy, sedition and, in the early 1500s, various statutory offences and violations of royal proclamations. Star Chamber was also a very important forum for punishing perjury (a "lye confirmed by oath"). It shared this function with the church courts, the division between the two jurisdictions appears to have been premised on the forum in which the initial perjury occurred. Normally, the Star Chamber dealt with lies told in courts of record. Perjury committed in inferior courts (or out of court) was "rather punishable by ecclesiastical penance".[87]

Very controversially, however, Cardinal Wolsey had encouraged plaintiffs to appeal to Star Chamber at first

---

86. Smith, *De Republica Anglorum*, pp.125-126.
87. Anon, *Star-Chamber Cases*, London, 1630, p.7

instance, rather than waiting to see if they could achieve an efficient remedy in the ordinary forums. As a result, the court grew in importance throughout the sixteenth century, so that its caseload increased from c.150 p.a. in the 1530s to considerably over 300 p.a. by the 1590s. There were 8,228 actions brought during the reign of James I alone. However, during the 1630s, Star Chamber attracted increasing opposition from a combination of common law courts, elements in Parliament and Puritans (who were sometimes on the receiving end of punishment imposed by the court). This hostility was aggravated when Star Chamber was used to enforce the growing number of royal proclamations, such as those against enclosures and sheriffs who refused to collect ship money. As a result, in 1641, one of the first acts of the Long Parliament was to abolish it along with some of the other prerogative courts. However, although political events led the House of Commons to condemn Star Chamber, it had been an important legal institution for much of its history. The Court of King's Bench subsequently adopted much of the criminal law fashioned in it, suggesting that it was not simply a 'kangaroo' court.[88]

---

88.   Barnes, "Due Process and Slow Process ...," p.225.

Chapter 12

Courts of Minor Jurisdiction

Petty Sessions

Summary jurisdiction, exercised without a jury by one or more JPs, was almost unknown to common law, largely being the creation of a series of statutes passed from the sixteenth century onwards. A reflection of this was that fines paid for summary offences were not usually returnable to the Crown, but went instead to local purposes. JPs had first regularly divided themselves into localised groups to conduct lesser business in the sixteenth century. In Wiltshire, for example, petty sessions appear to have emerged from a tradition of private meetings held by small numbers of JPs to settle urgent matters (petty sessions were initially often termed 'private' sessions). Sometimes, these were conducted at the express order of the quarter sessions. Thus, the practice of holding such meetings in Calne went back to at least 1565.[1] By 1577, William Harrison could note that "Petie sessions" were responsible for both administrative issues and minor criminal matters, so that in them "roges and runnagates are often reformed for their excesses".[2] In 1605, the Privy Council expressly encouraged

---

1. J. Hurstfield, *Freedom, Corruption and Government in Elizabethan England*, London, Jonathan Cape, 1973, p.261.
2. W. Harrison, *Description of England*, R. Holinshed's *The First Volume of the Chronicles of England, Scotland and Ireland*, London, J. Harrison, 1577, p.75.

the establishment of local sessions for the dispatch of urgent business not requiring a jury. However, the real impetus to the growth of the criminal (as opposed to administrative) function of petty sessions seems to have come after 1631. Although the aims of the Caroline Book of Orders, issued that year, had many precedents, it prescribed innovative administrative procedures to effect them. All active JPs were ordered to split themselves into small groups and their counties into divisions. They were also directed to meet once a month, so establishing regular petty sessions.[3] As a result, the use of such sessions swiftly became more widespread, frequent and less *ad hoc*. Thus, in December 1633, some Devon JPs recorded that they had met every month since receiving the Book of Orders. This process seems to have occurred in other counties as well.[4] Perhaps significantly, it was only in 1828 that petty sessions were formally established by statute.

These forums gradually assumed responsibility for a variety of minor offences, ranging from poaching (one of the most important areas for summary justice), drunkenness and selling light-weight bread to throwing squibs in the street and breaking excise regulations.[5] The use of 'sessions' conducted by two or more JPs (one of whom was normally

---

3. H. Langeluddecke, "Patchy and Spasmodic?: The Response of Justices of the Peace to Charles I's Book of Orders," *English Historical Review*, 1998, vol. 113, no. 454, p.1231.
4. H. Langeluddecke, "Law and order in seventeenth-century England: the organisation of local administration during the personal rule of Charles I," *Law and History Review*, 1997, vol. 15, pp.57-59.
5. E. Melling (Ed.), *Crime and Punishment, Kentish Sources VI*, Maidstone, Kent County Council, 1969, p.44.

of the quorum), without a jury, to determine minor matters that were nevertheless beyond the jurisdiction of a single magistrate, increased after 1660. Thus, a statute from Charles II's reign empowered three magistrates sitting together without a jury to convict and sentence a person accused of burning a hayrick to seven years transportation.[6] This process accelerated towards the end of the period as such forums were increasingly employed by the post-1690 campaigns for the Reformation of Manners. Although petty sessions would usually be held every month, they could meet more frequently and were often convened on an ad hoc basis. Their arrangements were usually very informal; typically, they were held in a tavern or private house. Thus, when, on June 2, 1687, Anne Watts, an unusually literate itinerant, appeared before the Essex petty sessions, accused of pretending to be a fortune-teller, they were held in a tavern at Stratford (a suburban part of the county). The JPs, including the local magistrate, William Holcroft, did not even bind her over to appear at a subsequent quarter sessions, or insist that those arrested with her by the constable be produced (presumably they were her clients), but merely ordered that her seized magic books "be burnt, & she was [then] discharged".[7]

In the early 1740s, De Veil appears to have become the first English magistrate to arrange his office in a recognizably 'modern' style, for a summary court, with the

---

6.   A. Babington, *A House in Bow Street*, 2nd edn., Chichester, Barry Rose Law Publishing, 1999, pp.32-33.

7.   W. Holcroft, *'William Holcroft His Booke'*, Local Office-holding in Late Stuart Essex, J.A. Sharpe (Ed.), Chelmsford, Essex Record Office, 1986, pp.86-87.

magistrate sitting on a raised dais at one end of the room, his clerk seated at a desk immediately below him, rows of seats on either side and a raised gallery for spectators. (Eventually, this would become the pattern for most petty sessional courts.)[8] In the City of London, magistrates had enhanced powers, and often could act alone to deal with minor offences which elsewhere required two JPs. By ancient charter, the Lord Mayor and senior aldermen (from 1741 all aldermen) were *ex officio* JPs. London petty sessions were held before the Lord Mayor, originally at the Guildhall, but, from the mid-eighteenth century in the Justice Room at the new Mansion House. In 1737 a second Justice Room was set up at Guildhall where regular sittings were also held before one of the aldermen. Nevertheless, despite their speed, simplicity and the normally modest penalties imposed by petty sessions, the expansion of summary jurisdiction was often unpopular. Blackstone blamed its growth for the decline in significance of the manorial courts. He felt that leets should be revived to deal with lesser matters, as these employed juries.[9]

Manorial Leet Courts

In the thirteenth and early fourteenth centuries, those guilty of serious crimes were as likely to be executed by local

---

8.   A. Babington, *A House in Bow Street*, p.51.
9.   W. Blackstone, *Commentaries on the Laws of England*, vol. 4, Oxford, Clarendon Press, 1769, p.407.

jurisdictions as they were by the King's courts. Thus, the Bishop of Ely had Liberty of Gallows, and, under Edward I, had both scaffold and pillory at his manor at Feltwell in Norfolk. However, in the later medieval period, state or 'royal' law gradually replaced local or customary law throughout Europe. England was no exception, albeit that, for obvious reasons, royal common law was more likely to accord with historic custom than continental civil law. The state's courts often had greater coercive power than local tribunals, and, most importantly, could restrict competition by 'monopolising' offences. By the fifteenth century, the royal courts had gained effective control over all cases that might affect life or member.[10] However, even as local jurisdictions for serious crime declined, those for petty offences flourished. In the centuries after 1250, manorial courts thrived, developing both trial and presentment by jury, their procedures increasingly aping those of the higher royal courts, and their records being written down in a compressed form of Latin.[11]

The manorial system covered much, but not all, of England. Manors were estates that were administered as a single unit. They varied greatly in size, ranging from a few acres within a parish to manors covering many square miles and several entire parishes. Thus, there were seven manors in the parish of Feltwell in Norfolk. The standard late

---

10. J.B. Post, "Local Jurisdictions and Judgment of Death in Later Medieval England," *Criminal Justice History*, 1983, vol. 4, p.1.
11. J.S. Beckerman, "Procedural Innovation and Institutional change in Medieval English Manorial Courts," *Law and History Review*, 1992, vol. 10, Number 2, pp.197-198.

sixteenth century work of reference on their courts was John Kitchin's *Le Court Leete et Courte Baron*, which was first published in French and Latin in 1579, and became a model for later English manuals. Most of these distinguished the court leet, which was viewed as a petty police and criminal court, held by the lord of a manor from the king, and the court baron, the lord's court for his freehold tenants, which was essentially a civil court, primarily concerned with land holding and administration.[12] Virtually all manors had a court baron (sometimes referred to as the *curia baronis, curia parva* or *halmote court*). It dealt with transfers of land, the management of common fields and pastures, agricultural practices, the repair of defective hedges, clearing blocked paths, etc.[13] A steward normally presided over the court, on behalf of the manorial lord, and ensured that his employer's interests were not ignored. All tenants of the manor were supposed to attend and, if absent, could be fined. However, courts baron did not have a petty criminal jurisdiction, so that crimes, even broadly defined, were not usually mentioned in their court rolls.

Local criminal jurisdiction was, historically, a function of the hundred courts. These were survivors of the ancient Saxon system of law enforcement.[14] Every county in England was sub-divided into smaller units called hundreds: "... where the Hundredut or Aldermanus Lord of

---

12. M. Griffiths, "Kirtlington Manor, 1500-1650," *Oxoniensia*, 1980, p.265.
13. J.L. and B. Hammond, *The Village Labourer 1760-1832*, London, Longmans, 1920, p.30.
14. G.J. Edwards, *The Grand Jury, An Essay*, Philadelphia, George T. Bisel Company, 1906, pp.4-7.

the Hundred, with the chiefe Lord of each Townshippe within their lymits judged."[15] Twice a year the sheriff would preside over such courts to deal with offences. The hundred courts were made up of representatives from all the manors within their boundaries. After the Norman Conquest, as royal courts assumed responsibility for serious crimes, their jurisdiction gradually became confined to lesser criminal offences and minor forms of anti-social conduct. Thus, the court roll for the hundred of Berkeley and Wotton Foreign in 1534 recorded presentments made by the respective decennarii or tithing men of all its manors, as well as the appointment of new constables and tithing men. Among the criminal matters heard were: "That Richard Phelippes committed an assault upon William Mallett, with a stick of no value [valuing the offensive weapon was a traditional part of such indictments for legal reasons], against the peace of the lord the king; he is amerced [fined] 12d." Several other men and women were presented for assaults committed "with a stick" or "with his fist".[16]

The criminal function of the hundred courts waned rapidly during the sixteenth century. However, traditionally, individual manorial lords could apply to the Crown to have the jurisdiction of the hundred court transferred to them, for use within their own manors. This allowed them to exercise the peace keeping and criminal jurisdiction of the sheriff's twice-yearly tourn. Effectively, it

---

15. J. Selden, *A Briefe Discourse Concerning the Powers of the Peeres and Comons of Parliament*, London, 1640, at p.2.
16. W.P.W. Phillimore, *Gloucestershire Notes and Queries*, vol.v, 1891-1893, London, 1894, pp.85-88.

meant contracting out of the latter in favour of a smaller scale, more local, court.[17] Such a manorial court, with a criminal jurisdiction, was usually called a 'court leet'.[18] Thus, leet court powers were: "... at the first derived and taken out of the Tourn."[19] This made them the most common franchise courts in the land. Nevertheless, not all manorial lords applied for, or were granted, such a privilege. Leets were not: "... incident to everie mannor, but to those onely which by special graunt, or long prescription have such libertie."[20] Many manors continued to possess only courts baron, leaving minor criminal jurisdiction to the hundred courts for as long as the latter operated, and to the JPs afterwards. Thus, in Warwickshire, the Alcester court leet dated back to at least 1272. However, the parishes around Alcester, mostly held by the Throckmortons of Coughton, had only received leets for their manors during the reign of Henry VIII. By contrast, the three nearby manors of Kinwarton, Arrow and Haselor continued to possess only courts baron until the end of the period. Their inhabitants attended the Hundred Court for the determination of minor criminal matters, or sought it from other forums.

A jury of tenants would 'present' matters that were to be

---

17. Griffiths, "Kirtlington Manor Court 1500-1650," p.265.
18. The term was not always used, and, confusing matters further, by the eighteenth century the various different manorial courts had often been merged into a single tribunal, variously called the View of Frankpledge, the Court Leet, the Court Baron, the Great Court or the Little Court.
19. Sir E. Coke, *The Fourth Part of the Institutes of the Laws of England*, New York, Gryphon editions, 1644, p.261.
20. Sir T. Smith, *De Republica Anglorum*, 1st edn. London 1583, (written 1565), p.103.

heard at the leet. After the fourteenth century, such presentments were usually confined to petty crimes committed within the manor, for example, batteries and brawls that did not amount to felonies. Legally, early modern leets could hear most common law misdemeanours, but not statutory offences. A rare illustration of the highest courts with criminal jurisdiction taking cognisance of the lowest was that JPs could bind over common drunkards to be of good behaviour if they had first been tried for such a crime: "... at the Assises, Quarter Sessions of the peace, or in the Court Leet, and thereupon a due proceeding to conviction."[21] Leets normally met twice a year under the presidency of the manorial lord's steward (the same individual who presided over the court baron), though by the eighteenth century such meetings had often declined to annual events. By the late medieval period the steward was usually a lawyer of some description, if only an attorney, though sometimes barristers and even serjeants were employed. As with the court baron, all adult male villagers (whether freeholders or cottagers) were supposed to attend. The constitution of the leet jury seems to have varied between different manors. In some, tenants were chosen in rotation, in others, the steward or his nominee controlled the choice, sometimes with the assistance of a nominee provided by the villagers.[22] Whatever the system, the advantages of leet courts were obvious; they were cheap and (because

---

21. M. Dalton, *The Country Justice, Containing The practise of the Justices of the Peace out of their Sessions ...,* London, Company of Stationers, 1655, p.215.
22. Hammond, *The Village Labourer 1760-1832,* p.30.

local) very convenient. They were also flexible, although there has been some debate as to the extent to which they applied substantive legal rules, or were, instead, *ad hoc* determinations based on local societal norms and shared values. It was recognised as early as 1268 that a defendant might challenge leet jurors for partiality, as he could in the royal courts (though this was rare and often impractical). This suggests that the manorial hearing was not, primarily, an informal adjudication.[23] Nevertheless, even allowing for the presence of a legally qualified steward, a considerable amount of fact-based equity was probably applied to decisions.

Leet courts had a dual criminal function, to: "... enquire of all offences against the peace, and for those that are against the Crowne and Peace both, to enquire onely, and certifie to the Justices of Gaole delivery; but those that are against the peace simply, they are to enquire and punish."[24] Thus, treason and felonies were to be presented at the court leet, but, as serious offences, were outside their trial jurisdiction. The details of such crimes were supposed to be 'set down in writing' and delivered to the judges sitting at the next county assizes, who would determine them at their general gaol delivery.[25] Typically, the manor court of the Liberty of Havering in Essex prepared felony indictments

---

23. J.S. Beckerman, "Toward a Theory of Medieval Manorial Adjudication: The Nature of communal Judgments in a System of Customary Law," *Law and History Review*, 1995, vol. 13, No. 1, pp.1-23.
24. Sir F. Bacon, *Cases of Treason*, London, John More, 1641, p.24.
25. Anon, *The Order of Keeping A Court Leet and Court Baron*, London, William Lee, 1650, p.10.

for the assizes in serious cases. Thus, in 1507, they presented a female servant of Roger Sabern for feloniously stealing wool, yarn and money in her master's house.[26]

Two types of case could be both presented and punished at courts leet. Obviously, there were a large number of regulatory offences pertaining to the manor, for example, breaking hedges, cleaning hemp in ponds and rivers that were also used to water cattle, etc. These were usually dealt with by a fine and, sometimes, an award of compensation. Additionally, sellers of "Corrupt Victuals" were punished and steps taken to enforce the 'moral economy' by holding the Assizes of Bread and Ale. This would regulate prices for necessities, and ensure that ostlers sold hay and oats at reasonable cost. There was also a more general policing jurisdiction for minor conventional criminal offences. Many of these were specifically designed to preserve village harmony. Thus, those who broke the peace or created affrays, 'brawlers' and 'scoulders', were presented and, if the case was proved, punished. Those who spread strife in more insidious forms, 'common barratours' and 'evesdroppers' who listened in on conversations so that they could create "debate between their neighbours", were also punished. Village morality was preserved by presenting "keepers of bawdry", vagabonds, any who might "walk by night" and sleep in the day, haunt taverns or who lacked a legitimate source of income, for investigation.[27]

---

26. M. McIntosh, *A community transformed: The manor and Liberty of Havering, 1500-1620*, Cambridge, CUP, 1991, p.310.
27. Anon, *The Order of Keeping a Court Leet and Court Baron*, p.10.

Additionally, some allegations of petty theft would be determined. These would usually involve the stealing of farm implements, poultry or small domestic items. Thus, a legal guide of 1556 suggested that leet courts deal with: "... any small theves amonge you that steal geese, capons, hennes, chickens, sheeves of corne in harvest, or ani other geare in menes windows pryvely that passeth not the value of 3d."[28]

Typically, in the early 1500s, the manor court at Havering in Essex fined petty thieves and dealt with cases of gaming, drunkenness and sexual misbehaviour. Thus, in 1530, the wife of one Thomas Hache, said to be "badly governed in her body", was banned from Havering, never to return, on penalty of spending three days in the stocks and being fined. However, the court also sought to prevent potentially dangerous situations from escalating by catching them early and imposing fines and warnings on those involved, something that its 'local' nature facilitated.[29] Very occasionally, a much more serious crime, outside the theoretical jurisdiction of a leet court, would be dealt with, perhaps to limit its legal consequences. Thus, at Cannock and Rugeley, a case involving the theft of four horses was heard in 1551 and, in 1583, that of a gelding worth four pounds. In 1554, a local man was also tried for robbing a woman of 10 shillings.[30] All were serious felonies, and had they gone before the royal courts, the punishment would

---

28. Anon, *Booke for a Justice of Peace*, 1556, p.85.
29. McIntosh, *A community transformed*, p.310.
30. A. Barrett and C. Harrison, *Crime and punishment in England*, London, UCL Press, 1999, p.40.

have been capital if proved.

However, after 1600, leet courts increasingly became restricted to trying the smallest types of misdemeanour. This was partly because their ability to punish was progressively limited to amercement. In the seventeenth century, Sir Edward Coke held that a court leet had no legal power to imprison, but could only impose fiscal penalties. By then, his views reflected what was probably already a widely recognised restriction. Indeed, as time went on, the leets' capacity to enforce even fines became progressively weaker. By contrast, in the fifteenth century such courts had used the stocks, the tumbrel or cucking stool, eviction from the community and at least the threat of whipping or imprisonment (even if rarely employed).[31] Banishment was a particularly important weapon in the court's armoury, though it was much more likely to be used against recent arrivals than long term residents. Thus, those at the Southampton leet in 1603 presented: "... an idle and suspected woeman Lyenge at the house of John frayston in Caneshot Lane for the riddance of whome out of the Towne we desier under may be taken." She was warned to "avoyde the Towne" by a designated date "or else to be carted".[32] Such non-fiscal penalties were vital to the leet courts' penal armoury, as some of those who appeared before them were too poor to pay even modest fines.

In many areas, the courts' criminal jurisdiction had

---

31. McIntosh, *A community transformed*, pp.63-65.
32. F.J.C. Hearnshaw (Ed.), *Court Leet Records, vol.1, Part III, 1603-1624*, Southampton, Southampton Record Society Publications, 1907, p.383.

begun a process of relentless decline as early as the 1520s. Analysis of records from manorial and hundred courts in East Anglia, Southeast England and the southern Midlands suggest that most of them were carrying out little or no leet business by 1600. Indeed, these parts of England included few local courts that were dealing 'aggressively' with misconduct after c.1560.[33] After the sixteenth century, their duties were increasingly transferred to the local JPs, Blackstone mournfully noting that: "... both the tourn and the leet have been for a long time in a declining way ... their business hath for the most part gradually devolved upon the quarter sessions."[34] Thus, in 1603, amid a plethora of cases involving broken fences, boundary disputes, overgrown ditches, inaccurate measures, broken pavements and dangerous chimneys, the Southampton leet court witnessed very few cases that would amount to 'conventional' crime. A man was presented for selling beer in a quart pot with a false bottom, another for an assault. Even then, the assault appears to have ultimately been referred to the JPs.[35] The leets' abandonment of criminal jurisdiction was not primarily the result of new restrictions imposed from above, the courts preserved their historic powers to punish anti-social conduct. However, in practice, they appear to have been prepared to let the sessions of the peace, and, sometimes, the church courts deal with any misbehaviour that arose within their areas. Thus, in Havering such matters

---

33. M.K. McIntosh, *Controlling Misbehaviour in England, 1370-1600*, Cambridge, CUP, 1998, pp.43-45.
34. Blackstone, *Commentaries on the Laws of England*, vol.4, p.271.
35. Hearnshaw, *Court Leet Records*, pp.379-383.

gradually became the province of the borough's JPs or outside bodies, though the manor court continued to appoint the constables.[36] In its decline, it mirrored the national position, as courts with a leet function declined into exercising the same powers that their neighbours that had only ever been courts baron employed (land matters etc.) even if they preserved their different title. This process was accelerated by the growth in significance of petty sessions, which took away many small cases that would previously have been eminently suitable for leets. Thus, the taking of wood from hedgerows to the prejudice of the hedge - because, for example, live wood or inordinate amounts of material were taken - had been an important leet jurisdiction in those manors where over-population, poverty and a shortage of common woodland had made the local authorities nervous about timber gathering. This sort of case became the sole province of petty sessions.

Sometimes, the end for effective manorial leet courts came quite suddenly, being connected to a particular external event. Thus, at Earls Colne in Essex, the local leet dealt with almost as many offenders in the 30 years before to 1590 as it had between 1531 and 1560. However, on the sale of the manor to the Harlakendens by the De Vere family in 1592, it immediately ceased to deal with any petty offences other than a failure to scour ditches. The Harlakendens were JPs and may have preferred to see

---

36. McIntosh, *A community transformed*, p.310.

offendors prosecuted before the quarter sessions.[37] The leets' willingness to investigate and present felonies to the royal courts also declined, a formal answer frequently being given when asked if there was any matter to indict. Thus, typically, the Southampton leet noted in 1611: "Itm we present the like concerninge Treasons, peteet Treasons and felonies we have heere of non neither of there accessories."[38]

However, even in the areas mentioned above, a few leet courts were active until well into the sixteenth century, and in northern and western parts of England, in counties such as Cumberland, Yorkshire, Westmorland, Somerset, Devon, Wiltshire, Gloucestershire, Herefordshire, Staffordshire and Shropshire, many were dealing vigorously with local misconduct until at least 1600, if not later, and regularly passing byelaws. In some areas, the activity of leet courts actually increased during the Elizabethan period.[39] Thus, in the joint manor Court of Cannock and Rugeley, in Staffordshire, there were hundreds of prosecutions for non-felonious crime between 1584 and 1602. By contrast, the same area produced only 18 cases of theft and nine of assault that went to the JPs at quarter sessions in the same period. A similar picture pertains to the Lancashire manor of Prescott, as late as the years between 1615 and 1660.[40]

---

37. R. Von Friedeburg, "Reformation of Manners and the Social Composition of Offenders in an East Anglian Cloth Village: Earls Colne, Essex, 1531-1642," *Journal of British Studies*, 1990, vol.28, Number 4, pp.358-9.
38. Hearnshaw, *Court Leet Records*, p.436.
39. McIntosh, *Controlling Misbehaviour*, pp.43-45.
40. C. Harrison, "Manor Courts and the Governance of Tudor England," C. Brooks (Ed.), *Communities and Courts in Britain 1150-1900*, London, Hambledon, 1997, p.43.

Given the limited number of working JPs available in the sixteenth century, the leets were probably still necessary if justice was to be effectively administered. Even after their decline, such traditional courts often continued to sit, co-existing with the new methods of low-level social control, with their duties becoming increasingly nominal. As late as the 1840s, in the remote village of Alston in Cumberland, it was noted that: "Courts Leet and Baron for the manor of Alston Moor, are held here twice a year, within a month after Easter and Michaelmass. Petty sessions are held at the Blue Bell Inn, once a month."[41]

Ecclesiastical Courts

In the medieval period, the church courts had dealt with a significant number of 'mainstream' felonies, even where neither victim nor perpetrator had any clerical connection. This was despite common law rules forbidding them jurisdiction in such cases. Occasionally, even people accused of murder, rape and burglary, were prosecuted in these forums; cases of theft were determined more frequently. Thus, as late as 1503, Richard Swale was tried at York for stealing linen belonging to one John Tramell. The ecclesiastical courts (like Star Chamber) fulfilled a particularly valuable function in punishing inchoate offences, such as attempt, an area where the common law

---

41. Mannix and W. Whellan, *History, Gazetteer and Directory of Cumberland*, Beverley, printed for the authors, 1847, pp.236-237.

criminal tribunals were often reluctant to intervene, preferring to wait for a completed crime to be identified.[42] The rudimentary development of the criminal law of attempt at this period partly explains their hesitation.[43] As Sir Thomas Smith noted in the 1560s, an: "Attempt to impoison a man, or laying await to kill a man, though he wound him daungerously if death followe not, is no felony by the lawe of Englande, for the Prince hath lost no man, and life ought to be given we say, but for life only."[44]

In the sixteenth century, however, serious conventional crimes committed by laymen rapidly became the exclusive province of the secular courts. Nevertheless, the ecclesiastical courts continued to possess a quasi-criminal (or 'correction') jurisdiction, albeit one that increasingly dealt with offences against 'morality', though Mathew Hale was adamant that the distribution of work between secular and ecclesiastical courts merely reflected administrative convenience, the "Law of the Land has indulged unto that [church] jurisdiction the Cognizance of some Crimes and not of others." As a result, while early modern church courts obviously dealt with the professional failings of clerics, such as leaving a body unburied, and lapses in the religious observance of the laity, such as not taking communion, they also dealt with numerous offences against morality as well as some more 'mainstream' criminal matters. Thus, under

---

42. R.H. Helmholz, *Canon Law and the Law of England*, London, Hambledon, 1987, pp.119-144.
43. Sir E. Coke, *The Fourth Part of the Institutes of the Laws of England*, New York, Gryphon editions, 1823, p.69.
44. Smith, *De Republica Anglorum*, p.117.

Archbishop Laud's visitation articles of 1635, churchwardens were asked whether their parish contained, to their knowledge, any guilty of adultery or fornication. Additionally, they were asked to seek out common drunkards, blasphemers, swearers, slanderers, sowers of discord, "lascivious talkers", usurers, bawds and harbourers of unmarried pregnant women, along with those who used types of witchcraft "not made felony by the statutes of this realm" (i.e. serious malefic witchcraft that was to be left to the common law courts) and perjurors (a primary concern of the church courts, even where the offence had been committed in a secular forum).[45] Sometimes, spiritual and personal failings would be grouped together, identifying general anti-social elements. Thus, at Warbleton, Sussex, in 1676, John Turner was presented at the Church Court: "... for being a common rayler and filthy talker, a sower of strife, debate and discord between neighbours, and he hath forsaken the church."[46] The church was especially concerned with the dignity and reputation of its own officers, and those connected to the administration of the parish could expect particularly close scrutiny. In 1599, John Wilkins of Whitstable in Kent was cited before the local Archdeaconry court "for going about the street in woman's apparel, being the parish clerk at that time". (The court accepted his explanation that, while at a marriage, he "did disguise himself in his wife's apparel to make some mirth to the

---

45. W. Laud, "Visitation Articles, 1635," *Anglicanism*, E. More (Ed.), Harrisburg, PA, Morehouse Publishing, 1935, pp.702-705.
46. P. Hair (Ed.), *Before the Bawdy Court ...*, London, Elek Books Ltd, 1972, p.177.

company".)[47] There was nothing very novel about the presence of such ecclesiastical discipline in England. In Scotland offences such as adultery and fornication were also often dealt with by the Kirk sessions.[48]

However, ecclesiastical courts also determined matters that, even today, would be considered 'criminal', under any definition. These included lesser 'conventional' crimes that had a church connection, such as assault on a minister or other church officials, vandalism of church property and fighting and disorder in the churchyard or during divine service. Thus, in 1595, Joan Madyson of Buttesbury in Essex was reported to the church courts for striking the local minister on his head, as a result of which "she brake the same & made the blood run down". She was ex-communicated. In 1597, John Stud of Mawdon was cited for throwing stones at the parish church, breaking several roof tiles.[49] The previous year, in Southend, Essex, a butcher named John Sowthen had been presented for "beastly & lewdly" defiling a stile leading to his parish church. A few criminal areas of special concern had a less obvious ecclesiastical connection, especially wife-beating, an important jurisdiction for the church courts. Typically, in 1592, William Hylls of Sandon was reported for being a "very lewd and uncharitable man with his wife, and hath used her most ungodly, not only by refusing her company,

---

47. D. Cressey, "Gender Trouble and Cross-Dressing in Early Modern England," *Journal of British Studies*, 1996, vol.35, p.463.
48. Anon, *Punishment and Crime in East Lothian 1600-1800*, Haddington, East Lothian District Library: Local History Publications, 1982, pp.1-2.
49. Hair, *Before the Bawdy Court*, p.177.

but also by beating her most cruelly". He admitted the allegation, and promised to reform. As this case suggests, church courts were particularly active in protecting women, and attracted a proportionately greater number of female complainants than secular courts. Similarly, with the exception of the Interregnum, incest was entirely an ecclesiastical matter in England. Thus, in 1596, William Foster of Barking was presented on suspicion of having sexual relations with his daughter. This was not solely on the basis of 'common report' but also on the assertion of women who had physically examined the girl.[50]

Ecclesiastical Court Structure

The basic church court for administering justice was usually that of the archdeacon, though decisions could be appealed to higher ecclesiastical courts at a diocesan and provincial level. Thus, each bishopric had a consistory court, presided over by the bishop's chancellor, and located in his cathedral. There was also a commissary court that could conduct hearings in remote parts of the diocese, distant from the chancellor's court, in circumstances in which it would cause excessive vexation to call witnesses and parties to appear before the chancellor. Its existence reflected the need for compurgators to be local to the accused person and apprised

---

50. W. Hale (Ed.), *A series of precedents and proceedings in criminal causes 1475-1640, Extracted from Act-Books of Ecclesiastical Courts in the Diocese of London,* London, 1847, pp.211-212.

of the background to defendants.[51]

Cases would often be presented to the church courts after the periodic episcopal and archdiaconal visitations held in each area every few years. Thus, the episcopal visitation to Wiltshire in 1587 produced 686 presentments.[52] The clergy could present on suspicion, something that placed them at an advantage to the secular courts. However, this normally had to be based on pre-existing public fame, i.e. openly disseminated rumour, that the accused person had committed a crime or religious offence. Usually, such suspicion had to be held by reliable, respectable and substantial people.[53] Additionally, the courts would try to identify exactly on what they had based their opinions, whether 'known' and specific facts, or mere rumour.[54] Those in charge of the church courts were well aware that unfavourable general reputations could be unfounded or based on human malice. Even so, the normal method of proceeding still put a premium on village 'gossip'. This posed problems for the clergy, as malicious gossip was itself often punishable in both secular and religious courts, especially if untrue. Nevertheless, without it the wheels of justice might not operate. This occasioned considerable tension, because if a minister was to: "... forbid all disclosing of faults, many an evil may not only be, but also spread in

---

51. H. Consett, *The Practice of the Spiritual or Ecclesiastical Courts*, London, 1685, p.338.
52. M.J. Ingram, *Church Courts, Sex and Marriage in England 1570-1640*, Cambridge, CUP, 1987, p.68.
53. Helmholz, *Canon Law and the Law of England*, pp.132-133.
54. Consett, *The Practice of the Spiritual or Ecclesiastical Courts*, London, p.396.

his Parish, without any remedy ... On the other side, if it be unlawful to open faults, no benefit or advantage can make it lawfull." George Herbert felt that the motivation prompting individuals to reveal 'common fame' was crucial in providing a distinction. Were informants moved by "rancour" or public service?[55]

Once presented, the church courts employed inquisition, with defendants having to answer questions on oath without a prima facie case being first established. (This also occurred in the prerogative courts like Star Chamber.) The *ex officio* oath, usually called the oath *de veritate dicenda* in canon law, was administered by the judge of an ecclesiastical court at the start of proceedings. It required parties to answer truthfully any questions put to them, even though they did not necessarily know precisely what the questions would be when they took the oath. Critics claimed that this forced respondents to prove their innocence and permitted ecclesiastical courts to embark on 'fishing expeditions' for evidence of immorality, religious or personal laxity and dissent. In 1607, it was even claimed, in a case heard at King's Bench, that the *ex officio* oath inevitably encouraged perjury.[56] The normal method of trial was by canonical purgation. This required an accused person to take a formal oath that he was innocent of the offence alleged against him and to find a number of compurgators who would support his oath by swearing that

---

55. Herbert, *A Priest to the Temple*, p.42.
56. R.H. Helmholz, "Origins of the privilege against self-incrimination: The role of the European Jus Commune," *New York University Law Review*, 1990, pp.965 and 989.

they believed he had sworn truly. If the requisite number were adduced, and, after examination, found to be satisfactory, the charge would be dismissed.[57] Very importantly, the compurgators were not swearing to the truth (or lack of it) of the underlying allegations, of which they could be entirely ignorant, but to their faith in the trustworthiness of the accused person's oath. Compurgators would normally be of the same gender as the accused. Additionally, the courts sought to ensure that they were people of some status. In theory, their opinion was only to be received if they were unrelated to the accused, not "Parents, Kinsfolk or Tenants of the Party producing them". Ideally, they would also not be "poor and needy" people who might be bribed or suborned to give a favourable result for the accused. In particular, poor people were not to be called from a parish that was well populated, though it was recognised that it might be necessary in small villages, in the absence of other potential compurgators. People who had previously been convicted, were of "stained reputation", or notorious for committing the same offence as that with which the defendant was charged were also not to be called as compurgators.[58]

During the seventeenth century, a cumulatively fatal blow was dealt to the church courts by the increased willingness of Parliament to pass legislation giving the secular courts, especially those presided over by JPs, authority to deal with Sabbath breaking and other matters

---

57. Ingram, *Church Courts, Sex and Marriage in England*, pp.51-52.
58. Consett, *The Practice of the Spiritual or Ecclesiastical Courts*, p.396.

involving 'morality' that had long been the province of the ecclesiastical forums. Additionally, magistrates became increasingly active in local initiatives to control morality. Thus, in August 1616, the JPs of Lancashire, while attending the assizes judges, decided that anyone selling goods (other than necessities) during divine service or on Sunday afternoons would be presented by constables to be bound over to the next assizes. Householders were also forbidden to entertain people in their homes at such times (family members excepted) so that "all persons within the sayd howse may goe to the Church". Ale-houses that were patronised during religious services were to lose their licences, and ale-house keepers were required to attend church on Sunday with their families "upon payne to loose and forfeite xij d. as to bee discharged from brewinge". Anyone found loitering in churchyards or market places during services was also to be fined 12 pence and Sabbath recreations were restricted.[59] (One probable explanation for the magisterial activism in this heavily Catholic county is that the sanctions of the church courts were of limited practical effect for many people.) However, despite much criticism, the ecclesiastical courts survived until the Civil War, when they ceased to operate in the confused situation that followed the assembling of the Long Parliament in November 1640. This prompted some popular celebration, manifest in numerous satirical prints and pamphlets. Typically, one portrayal had a church lawyer boasting: "I

---

59.   B.W. Quintrell (Ed.), *Lancashire JPs at the Sheriff's Table 1578-1694*, Lancashire, The Record Society of Lancashire and Cheshire, 1981, pp.72-73.

got very well by a wench that has beene undone in a darke entry. Sir John would commit her penance into 10 pounds, towards the repaire of Pauls, and then we would share it."[60] Puritans generally appear to have considered that the ecclesiastical courts were encumbered by abuses and archaic Papist practices, were ineffective, corrupt in their willingness to remit penalties for money payment, used excommunication excessively, and were partisan in their treatment of 'Godley' (i.e. Puritan) ministers.[61] Thus, the Root and Branch Petition submitted in December 1640 to the House of Commons, with 15,000 signatories, blamed a supposed increase in prostitution and adultery on the "prelates' corrupt administration of justice in such cases". It alleged that clergymen used their punitive powers as a way of securing money, rather than combating vice, and alleged that the *ex officio* oath was used to extort cash from men who worked on saints' days. Additionally, the petition claimed that ecclesiastical courts had encouraged ministers to "despise the temporal magistracy" and demanded their total abolition.[62] Nevertheless, such criticisms did not prevent many Puritans from presenting cases to the church courts to advance their own moral agenda.

The post-1640 absence of the church courts left a void in the armoury of social control, one that was filled by

60. Anon, *The Spirituall Courts Epitomized*, London, 1641, p.3.
61. R.L. Greaves, *Society and Religion in Elizabethan England*, Minneapolis, University of Minnesota Press, 1981, p.677.
62. H. Gee and W.J. Hardy (Eds.), "The Root and Branch Petition (1640)," in *Documents Illustrative of English Church History*, New York, Macmillan, 1896, pp.544-547.

attempts to make secular offences out of matters previously dealt with by the Church. The drastic nature and intrusiveness of some of these new criminal statutes contributed to a revision in perspective, so that the ecclesiastical courts were restored in 1660. Even so, they did not recover from their enforced absence and declined inexorably after the Restoration.[63] However, the speed with which this occurred varied significantly throughout the country. In Middlesex, by 1700, their control of even the most minor types of 'conventional' crime was of almost no significance, the field having been left to the JPs.[64] In some other, remoter, parts of the country, the process was slightly slower. Nevertheless, by the end of the seventeenth century, magisterial involvement was the 'normal' response to many moral 'crimes'. Thus, when, in 1680, a number of men from suburban Essex were arrested for "tiplinge at the bowling green at Layton on Sunday the 16 January, in church time" they were taken before William Holcroft, a JP. They immediately "confessed the fact" and were ordered to pay 3 shillings 4 pence each into the local churchwarden's hands.[65] Significantly, the Campaign for the Reformation of Manners, which started in 1690, ignored the church courts, and brought all their prosecutions in front of the JPs, despite having an explicitly religious orientation. The reformers felt

---

63. M. Dean, *Law-Making and Society in Late Elizabethan England*, Cambridge, CUP, 1996, pp.116-120.
64. R.B. Shoemaker, *Prosecution and Punishment*, Cambridge, CUP, 1991, pp.19-23.
65. Holcroft, *William Holcroft His Booke' Local Office-holding in Late Stuart Essex*, p.69.

that the church court procedures were 'long and tedious' compared to quarter and petty sessions and that their punishments for offences like fornication were "in no sort adequate to the crime".[66] Despite this, and although they received a 'bad press' from Victorian historians, many of whom were influenced by earlier Puritan criticism, modern research suggests that the ecclesiastical courts were not invariably inefficient, slow, corrupt and devoid of popular support amongst those they policed. Nor were their proceedings as arcane as is sometimes suggested. Thus, although the formal documents might be in Latin, the hearings were normally conducted in English.[67]

Ecclesiastical Punishment

If a person admitted an offence before the ecclesiastical courts, or could not produce the requisite number of neighbours to support their denial, a public penance would normally be ordered, often combined with the payment of a substantial court fee. Other punishments included fines and excommunication. Penance would usually be carried out in the parish church on a Sunday, with the accused person (whether man or woman), wearing a white sheet, carrying a white wand, publicly admitting their offence and asking for forgiveness.[68] Typically, the churchwardens'

---

66. Shoemaker, *Prosecution and Punishment*, pp.19-23.
67. Ingram, *Church Courts, Sex and Marriage in England*, pp.40-47.
68. A. Macfarlane, *Witchcraft in Tudor and Stuart Essex*, London, p.72.

accounts for Wakefield Cathedral record many instances of sheets being loaned to both men and women "to do penance in". Excommunication was the most draconian penalty available to such courts, depriving the transgressor of the Church's sacraments and services (it also carried some adverse civil consequences). Many excommunicates were appalled by their punishment. Thus, in 1633, in Buckinghamshire, Francis Page was presented to the church court for: "... pressing in amongst the communicants of Wootten and receiving the Communion unawares to the minister being excommunicated the same time."[69] Indeed, sometimes the denial of sacraments would have to be physically enforced by the parish constables, if they noticed an excommunicant in church.

To those who were geographically mobile, irreligious, recusant or dissenter the Church's sanctions had fewer terrors. Even some of those who did not fall within these categories appear not to have been unduly concerned by excommunication. Penance occasioned even less fear. As a result, by the Elizabethan period, many shared William Harrison's belief that the penalty for adultery and fornication was nugatory, "standing in a sheet, though the weather be never so cold", for half an hour, was a minor matter.[70] Mary Frith certainly agreed. Her habit of wearing "manly apparel" eventually resulted in her being brought before the Court of Arches (an ecclesiastical court in London). Dispensing with the services of a proctor (the

69. Hair, *Before the Bawdy Court*, p.224.
70. Harrison, *Elizabethan England*, p.242.

church courts' equivalent of a solicitor) she was sentenced to do penance in a white sheet, standing near St Pauls Cross. However, to a woman of her stamp this was nothing: "They might as soon have shamed a Black Dog as me, with any kind of such punishment." She arranged for her pick-pocketing colleagues to 'work' the crowd that assembled to watch the proceedings.[71] (According to the Consistory of London Correction Book, Mary Frith appeared before that court on January 27, 1612.) England was not unique in such punishments. In Scotland, many of the punishments imposed by the Kirk sessions, such as sitting on the 'penitence stool' in church on Sundays, exposed to public view wearing sackcloth, were similar to those south of the Border. However, they also had greater powers than their English counterparts. More serious cases might be dealt with by a period in the stocks or the 'jougs' - the Scottish equivalent of the pillory - an iron collar mounted five feet up a wall by a chain.[72]

---

71. Anon, *The Life and Death of Mrs Mary Frith, Commonly Called Mal Cutpurse*, London, W.G. Ilberton, 1662, p.69.
72. Anon, *Punishment and Crime in East Lothian 1600-1800*, East Lothian District Library: Local History Publications, pp.1-2.

Chapter 13

The Magistracy, Shrievalty and Judiciary

The principal duty of a judge, is to suppress force and fraud; whereof force is the more pernicious, when it is open, and fraud, when it is close and disguised.

Francis Bacon, On Judicature

England's judges, in the broadest sense of the word, were a mixture of lay amateurs and highly experienced professional lawyers, most with many years of practice behind them. Despite this, none of its professional judges were specialists in criminal law or procedure, with the partial exception of the Recorder of London.

The JPs

An Act of 1327, building on earlier, informal, initiatives, first provided for the appointment of "good and lawful men" in each county to help keep the peace, the title 'Justices of the Peace' being granted in 1361. Their primary criminal function was to "determyne felonies and trespasses committed and done agaynste the peace, and doo reasonable punyshement, accordying to lawe and reason."[1] Unlike some of the other fourteenth century ventures aimed

---

1. Anon, *The Boke for a Justyce of Peace*, London, Thomas Berthel, 1534, p.1.

'The Raw'

A small Northumberland Bastle House now used as a barn. Note the raised entrance for human occupation on the first floor, and that for animals in the undercroft. Both are covered by an arrowslit. This provided the most basic protection against Border Reivers.

(Author's photograph)

'The Raw'

Entrance to the undercroft giving an indication of the thickness of its walls.

(Author's photograph)

Woodhouses Bastle

A late (1602) fortified house. Note the surviving slit windows. The slate roof is a later addition. (Author's photograph)

Elsdon Tower
A Northumberland Pele tower. Its walls are 8 feet thick.
(Author's photograph)

Oakham Castle
The venue for Rutland's assizes and quarter sessions in the early modern period.
(Author's photograph)

Dacre Castle
Despite its name, this is an imposing Cumberland Pele tower. Originally built in the 14th Century, it provided protection against both Scots and Border Reivers. A decline in reiving in the 17th Century allowed the addition of large windows.
(Author's photograph)

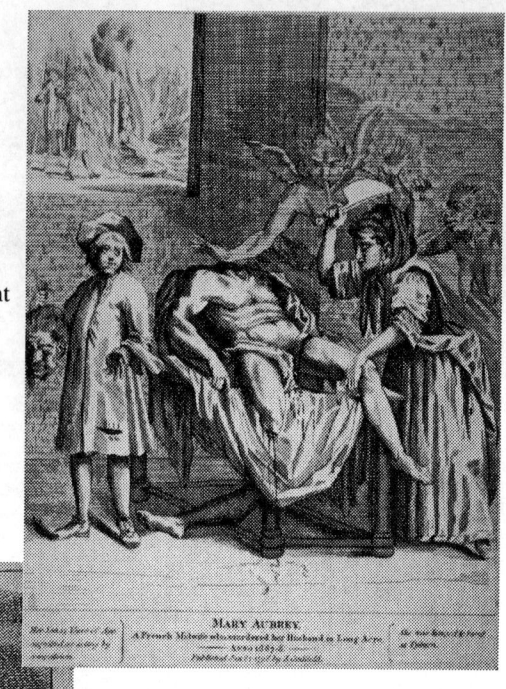

Mary Aubrey murdering her husband in
1687. For this 'petty treason' she was burnt
at the stake (Inset)
(Picture courtesy Corporation of London)

A pickpocket at work at St. Bartholomew
Fair in Smithfield c 1715
(Picture courtesy Corporation of London)

17th Century statue of a wounded soldier from St. Bartholomew's Hospital.
Such discharged servicemen faced many problems in adjusting to civilian life - some returned to crime.
(Author's photograph)

Tomb Effigy of Sir Michael Sondes, J.P.
A conscientious Jacobean magistrate in Kent.
(Author's photograph)

**Francis Bacon,
Viscount St.Albans (1561-1621)**
Lord Chancellor and an important jurist.
(Picture courtesy of The Picture Library NPG
London)

This portrait of the infamous Titus Oates in 1685
illustrates the mechanics of several early modern punishments
(Picture courtesy of British Museum)

James Nailor Quaker, set 2 howers on the Pillory at Westminster whiped by the Hang
man to the old Exchainge London, Som dayes after, Stood too howers more on the Pillory
at the Exchainge, and there had his Tongue Bored throug with a hot Iron, &
Stigmatized in the Forehead with the Letter:B: Decem' 17: anno Dom: 1 6 5 6:

An illustration of whipping at the cart's tail and the pillory
(Picture courtesy Corporation of London)

A German print of The 'Triple Tree' at Tyburn in 1696
(Picture courtesy Corporation of London)

There was little segregation in early modern prisons, as this illustration from 1691 shows. (Picture courtesy Corporation of London)

An example of prison brutality from 1691 (Picture courtesy Corporation of London)

at enhancing local order, JPs flourished. Most importantly, the office meant that central authority could be exercised through local elites, something that had a major impact on English society. Although they were almost two centuries old by 1500, the willingness of Tudor governments to continually add to the JPs' responsibilities substantially changed the nature of the office during the sixteenth century, something that led to a major Elizabethan revision of the commission of the peace in 1590. It also prompted William Lambarde to produce a large handbook, *Eirenarcha*, in 1582, to explain the "growth of duties" which had occurred. The sixteenth century also witnessed an improvement in the average quality of JPs, albeit that this was not very difficult, given the poor state of the fifteenth century magistracy. In the 1400s, quite notorious men were sometimes found on the bench, individuals, like Sir Gilbert Debenham, who were given to riot, corruption, disorder, perjury and even piracy.[2]

JPs held their positions for life, or until removed from their commissions. They were appointed by the Lord Chancellor, his decision being based on advice to the Crown from the Lord Lieutenant of the County concerned and visiting assizes judges, who acted as conduits for provincial opinion as well as being active agents of the Crown. Central government also received information about prospective magistrates from *inter alia* peers, bishops and heralds'

---

2.   J.R. Lander, *English Justices of the Peace, 1461-1509*, London, Alan Sutton, 1989, p.157.

449

visitations.[3] However, despite the formalities of appointment, selection was primarily a local process, vulnerable to factionalism and 'interests'. This became even more significant with the emergence of 'party' loyalties after 1660, which meant that appointments to the commission became increasingly politicised. This could result in the periodic removal of individuals from magisterial office, if they were thought to oppose government policies, even if their replacements were less well qualified. Thus, on one occasion in 1700, 74 Middlesex justices were removed from the local commission.[4]

In theory, JPs were the cream of county society, being required by a law of 1439 to have an income of at least 20 pounds a year from their lands, an amount set with a view to excluding those "whose povertie made them both covetous and contemptible and who sought the office for profit".[5] In 1732, the property qualification for appointment was raised, again because it was considered to be of the "utmost consequence to provide against persons of mean estates".[6] Such qualifications reflected a widespread belief that unless JPs had a "competent Estate" carrying out the office properly would prove personally too costly. Additionally, it was feared that impecunious magistrates were more susceptible to corruption, bribery and intimidation: "Men of small Estates are very often meen

---

3. Lander, *English Justices of the Peace, 146-1509*, p.157.
4. A. Babington, *A House in Bow Street*, 2nd edn, Chichester, Barry Rose Law Publishers, 1999, p.35.
5. W. Lambarde, *Eirenarcha*, London, Companies of Stationers, 1619, pp.30-31.
6. Babington, *A House in Bow Street*, p.35.

spirits, and dare not do their Duties where they Expect Opposition, and have great and rich men to deal with." It was all too apparent in such situations how much power a "rich clown" could exert on a magistrate. Many also shared Edmund Bohun's belief that the prevailing culture of social deference meant that many Englishmen preferred to have their justice meted out by men of 'quality'.[7]

The number of JPs appointed for each county varied, depending on a combination of factors. These included the size and population of the shire in question, the number of men willing and able to carry out the office, and the area's judicial needs. The more influential gentlemen there were who were desirous of being appointed to the commission, the more JPs the King and Lord Chancellor were likely to appoint. However, there was also a bare minimum of magistrates required in each county. If insufficient men of appropriate quality came forward, less well-qualified and poorer men might have to be accepted. Initially, the number of JPs appointed had been quite limited. Even in 1506, it was only necessary that "In every countye shall be assygned viii Justyces of peas."[8] (Though by then this figure was already manifestly anachronistic.) There was a rapid expansion in numbers after 1530. As William Lambarde observed, this was mainly due to the growth in legal work and the enhanced social prestige of the office: "... together with the like ambitious desire of bearing rule in some the growing

---

7. E. Bohun, *The Justice of Peace His Calling and Qualifications*, London, 1693, pp.15-16 and 19.
8. Anon, *The Boke of Justices of Peas*, London, 1506, reprinted New Jersey, Walter J. Johnson, Inc., 1976, p.1.

number of the statute lawes, committed from time to time to the charge of the Justices of the peace, hath bene the cause that they also are now againe increased to the overflowing of each Shire at this day."[9] By Sir Thomas Smith's time, in the 1560s, their ranks had expanded to "xxx or xl in every shire".[10] At the end of the sixteenth century, an average of over 40 per county was common, and set to rise still further during the ensuing 100 years.[11] Thus, in Wiltshire, the Commission of the Peace, omitting honourary JPs and eminent judicial members, had been made up of 25 local men in 1562, 46 in 1600, and 65 in the last years of the Interregnum.[12] By 1660, Kent had 83 JPs (49 of them of the quorum).[13] In the same year, Bedfordshire had 44 magistrates (28 of the quorum). However, remote, large but relatively lawless Northumberland managed with only 25 JPs (19 of the quorum).[14] Nevertheless, even with this major expansion, their numbers often appeared relatively limited for the judicial and administrative duties that they were entrusted with. This was partly because of widespread magisterial indolence.

It has been remarked that the present-day notion of the overworked early modern JP appears to be something of a

---

9. Lambarde, *Eirenarcha*, p.32.
10. Sir T. Smith, *De Republica Anglorum*, London, 1583, p.104.
11. C.B. Herrup, *The Common Peace*, Cambridge, CUP, 1987, p.44.
12. J. Hurstfield, *Freedom, Corruption and Government in Elizabethan England*, London, Jonathan Cape, 1973, p.253.
13. Anon, *A Perfect List of all such Persons as by Commission under the Great Seal of England are now Confirmed to be Custos Rotulorum ...*, London, 1660, pp.23-24.
14. Anon, *A Perfect List of all such Persons*, pp.1-2 and 41-2.

myth.[15] Certainly, Edmund Bohun was following an already long tradition when, in the 1690s, he lambasted the chronic absenteeism and laziness found amongst many magistrates. Such men took their oath of office and then would: "... never appear at any Sessions by the Space of many years together, without any lawful excuse, or hindrance, or [alternatively, were] those who come and take the Kinges, and before half the business is done betake themselves to the Tavern, leaving two or three to finish."[16] Many of the JPs appointed to each commission seem to have engaged in fairly minimal duties. Of course, some of these had been appointed on an honourary basis, with no expectation that active service would ensue. Local aristocrats and national statesmen had traditionally been included in "most of the commissions of all the shires of England".[17] Thus, in 1562, the Wiltshire commission included Sir Nicholas Bacon, the Lord Keeper, the Marquess of Winchester, the Lord Treasurer, and the Earl of Arundel, the Lord Steward.[18] However, many ordinary JPs, though supposedly 'active', were also relatively modest in their contributions, both out of court and at sessions. Most magistrates spent fewer than 40 days a year on their duties, many considerably less.[19] Only a third of the roughly 90 JPs appointed to the Kentish commission were heavily engaged in their duties between 1598 and

---

15. J.A. Sharpe, *Crime in Seventeenth Century England*, Cambridge, CUP, 1983, p.30.
16. Bohun, *The Justice of Peace His Calling and Qualifications*, p.156.
17. Smith, *De Republica Anglorum*, p.103.
18. Hurstfield, *Freedom, Corruption*, p.252.
19. Sharpe, *Crime in Seventeenth Century England*, p.30.

1602. Similarly, in the North Riding of Yorkshire, in the years between 1603 and 1625, only between 10 and 18 magistrates normally attended quarter sessions out of a total of 59.[20]

Nevertheless, in each county, there was normally a small coterie of hard-working and able men who went to considerable personal trouble in fulfilling their obligations, and who carried out a quite disproportionate amount of legal work. These magistrates, men such as Sir Michael Sondes in Kent and Sir Nathaniel Bacon in Norfolk, dedicated a large amount of time to the office and acquired considerable legal expertise (albeit over a confined area) as a result. Such a level of dedication required wealthy individuals who could spare the time involved. It would have been difficult for anyone to match it whose presence on his own estates was indispensable because he could not afford a steward to manage his affairs. The personal motivations of these hard-working men are not always easy to fathom. The price paid by the very best sort of JP was well recognised: "His nights, his meals are short and interrupted; all which he bears well, because be knows himself made for a public servant of peace and justice."[21] Similarly, as was observed in the 1690s: "The Justice of the Peace enters upon an imployment that will occasion him much loss of Time, some Expense, and many Enemies." In exchange, all he could expect was a "little unprofitable

---

20. Lander, *English Justices of the Peace, 1461-1509*, p.157.
21. J. Hall, *Characters of virtues and vices*, London, Melch. Bradwood, 1608, Book 1, p.58.

Honour attended with much envy".[22] Presumably, much of the prestige of the office would still have accrued to them if they had been a little less active. Suspending cynicism, a genuine dedication to public service combined with an interest in the work appears to have been an important motivation.

It should, perhaps, be noted that there was nothing new in this early modern magisterial division between 'work-horses' and 'absentees'. It had existed in Kent in the fifteenth century and in Gloucestershire in the 1390s.[23] An interesting further division is also apparent amongst the 'active' magistrates. Some seem to have concentrated their efforts on attending court hearings, others on conducting the pre-trial examinations of suspected offenders and administrative matters. Yet others were 'all rounders', making a major contribution to both areas, though generally the lowest performing magistrates were the same in both categories. Even amongst the court attenders, some concentrated on the quarter sessions, others on the assizes, and some divided their attendance proportionately between the two forums. Thus, in Kent, Thomas Wilford only attended 10 per cent of the assizes hearings but managed 75 per cent of the quarter sessions. By contrast, Edward Filmer managed to get to 70 per cent of the assizes but none of the county sessions. Thomas Fludd, however, was remarkably diligent, attending all the sessions of both courts.[24]

---

22. Bohun, *The Justices of Peace His Calling and Qualifications*, p.14.
23. Lander, *English Justices of the Peace, 1461-1509*, p.64.
24. L.A. Knafla, *Kent at Law 1602. The County Jurisdiction: Assizes and Sessions of the Peace*, London, HMSO and PRO, 1994, pp.21-22.

Nevertheless, despite the presence of a small number of highly committed and able JPs there were permanent problems with the ability of the commissions of the peace to accommodate their workloads. Along with a lack of enthusiasm amongst individual members, this could be due to the presence of elderly and infirm magistrates, a failure by the Privy Council to recruit replacements for deceased JPs, or magisterial absence, especially amongst those who preferred the Metropolitan social life or conducting litigation in London, to a quieter country existence. The neglect and carelessness shown by JPs towards their responsibilities regularly led the Privy Council to admonish them. Individual magistrates, left without assistance, also frequently stated their dissatisfaction. Thus, in 1630, two JPs in Derbyshire complained that they had been left to conduct all of their local work because: "... one of us was at London at the first coming down of the proclamacon and came not down to the country untill about three weekes since, and Sir William Kinreton one other Justice of peace in this division is olde, and not able to travill, and Sir John Fferrers hath (as he saith) business that he cannot come."[25]

As the period advanced such problems became more serious. After 1660, changing social fashions meant that more and more gentlemen left their estates for large parts of the year and gravitated towards London and other cities, such as Bath, there to live in "perfect idleness, and luxury".

---

25. H. Langeluddecke, "Law and order in seventeenth-century England: the organisation of local administration during the personal rule of Charles I," *Law and History Review*, 1997, vol.15, pp.49-76, at pp.60-62.

Even worse, it was felt that there was a new spirit abroad that meant that upper class men would "not take the pains their Ancestors did" over magisterial matters. Sadly, as Bohun presciently noted in the 1690s, there was little reason to think that this situation would improve. His pessimism was well founded; matters became significantly worse in the following century. Bohun recognized that one solution to such problems would be to secure the services of suitable men of "Smaller Estates and greater Industry".[26] This had occurred, to some extent, under the Commonwealth, when the social profile of appointments to the bench had widened, with fewer noblemen and more esquires being made JPs. Initially, this trend was reversed at the Restoration. However, an acceptance of men of smaller means became common in the eighteenth century. As individuals like Bacon and Sondes became a rarity, their absence was partly filled by the appointment of minor gentry and of clerical magistrates (a rarity in the 1600s). The presence of 'men of the cloth' on the active bench had mixed results. Although they were, by definition, educated and stipened, their presence necessarily changed the face of the magistracy, as they lacked the local 'standing' of their more active squire forbears. Where even clerics could not be found who were willing to take the office, as occurred in areas such as the Metropolis, it was inevitable that increased numbers of men would emerge to make a business of the position, relying on its remuneration to survive.

---

26.   Bohun, *The Justice of Peace His Calling and Qualifications*, pp.18-19.

Magisterial Rewards, Trading Justices, the Character and Quality of JPs

By an Act of 1389, commoner JPs had received a 'subsistence allowance' of four shillings a day. This appears to have largely lapsed in the ensuing centuries, presumably because most were well-to-do landowners who were not concerned about such small sums. As Lambarde observed, Parliament had always stipulated that: "Choice should bee made of such person for this office of the Peace, as need not reward for their travell in that behalfe."[27] However, in Wiltshire and some other counties, the 4 shillings a day payment to lesser members of the Commission (those below the rank of 'banneret') continued to be made, not to individuals but commuted to a common fund that was used to: "... provide for all the justices' dinners the first day of every [Quarter] sessions in lieu of wages allowed them by his majesty." On one occasion, in 1630, after receiving a particularly disgusting meal from an innkeeper in Devizes, the JPs demanded to receive their payment in cash![28]

Nevertheless, despite the frequent loss of the daily payment, JPs did receive some direct remuneration from their office. As was noted, to encourage magistrates to serve with "more alacrite and cheerefulnesse ... the laws do now and then cast them a trifle". These were not always totally insignificant. Thus, when sitting in execution of the Statute of Labourers, JPs were entitled to 5 shillings a day. They

---

27. Lambarde, *Eirenarcha*, pp.30-31.
28. Hurstfield, *Freedom, Corruption*, p.255.

could also keep a proportion of some administrative fines, such as half of the 40 shillings that would be levied on a man who refused to be made an overseer to ensure that the Statute of Clothmaking was kept. Additionally, every JP or sheriff could seize the goods of any gypsies that came into the realm within a month of their arrival. They would divide and share these with the Crown.[29] Most importantly, a JP could retain 12 pence for every recognisance provided by those licensed to keep ale-houses.

To many JPs, such rewards truly were 'trifles' of little consequence.[30] Nevertheless, there was already enough remuneration available that it was predictable that entrepreneurial magistrates would develop, should the social profile of the bench decline. This phenomenon is particularly associated with urban areas and the eighteenth century. However, the JP who was motivated by financial considerations was not a new phenomenon even then, having been noted periodically from the 1500s. One reason for parliamentary resistance to the granting of extra powers to the late Elizabethan and Stuart magistracy was a fear that the inferior origins of many that held the office meant that they would abuse their positions to make a personal profit. Thus, George More referred to the "meanness of many [justices] in these days". His concerns were by no means eccentric. A parliamentary allegation of widespread corruption on the part of the "inferior sort of Justices" was

---

29. Dalton, Michael, *The Country Justice,* London, Company of Stationers, 1661, p.56.
30. Lambarde, *Eirenarcha*, Book 3, p.355.

made in the House of Commons in 1601. The MP involved, Edward Glascock, claimed that many were known as 'basket justices' because of the container they carried for the reception of gifts. In a lengthy diatribe to the House, he, too, complained about the humble origins and general poverty of many magistrates.[31] He might have been referring to men like Maurice Gilbert of Wincanton, who, it was alleged in 1603, was a man of "small living" and heavily in debt. There were claims that he took bribes and sold ale-house licences.[32] Similarly, in the 1660s, the corrupt magistrate Sir John Croke: "... tho' a Justice of Peace in Bucks, was a Prisoner of the Kings Bench for Debt, and was as usual, [with] their Mr Brown for his keeper." This individual had Croke under a form of arrest while he was away from the prison. Brown had eavesdropped on Croke, fearing that he planned to escape. He overheard Croke and another man conspiring to falsely indict and convict the Reverend Robert Hawkins. After this was exposed, Croke was dismissed from the Commission of the Peace.[33] Although Gilbert and Croke were not 'typical' of most English JPs, they had enough equivalents not to be dismissed as 'bad apples' in an otherwise healthy barrel. In 1693, Bohun reiterated Glascock's fears about magistrates who brought the office

---

31. J.R. Kent, "Attitudes of Members of the House of Commons to the Regulation of 'Personal Conduct' in Late Elizabethan and Early Stuart England," *British Institute of Historical Research*, 1973, vol.46, pp.52-53.
32. D. Underdown, *Revel, Riot & Rebellion, Popular Politics and Culture in England 1603-1660*, Oxford, OUP, 1985, p.23.
33. N. Bernard, Dean of Ardagh, *The Case of John Atherton*, London, Luke Stokoe, 1710, p.21.

into disrepute, and who: "... for half a Dozen of Chickens will dispense with a whole Dozen of penal Statutes: these are Basket Justices ... If he grants a Warrant against a Felon, you must put 2 shillings in his Pocket as his Clerk's Fee." Thoughtful observers in the eighteenth century were aware that their era's mercenary JPs were following an already old tradition: "Basket Justices have only changed their style, and are now distinguish'd by the Title of trading Justices."[34]

Nevertheless, though not novel, such magistrates became particularly widespread in the 1700s, especially in London. It was feared that they took bribes to overlook the transgressions of bawdy and gaming houses. Even worse, it was claimed that they would deliberately inflame quarrels between neighbours with a view to binding them over to keep the peace and then releasing the disputants from their bonds, for both of which services JPs were entitled to a fee.[35] Even laudatory obituaries of the influential eighteenth century Metropolitan magistrate Thomas De Veil freely acknowledged that he possessed "little virtue", loved money, opulence and pleasure. He was a rapacious philanderer who grossly abused his legal position and "served himself by means of his office with a variety of women", even constructing a "private closet for the examination of the fair sex".[36]

However, such magistrates, though unpopular, provided vital legal services that would otherwise not have

---

34. *The Gentleman's Magazine*, 1732, vol.2, p.892.
35. N. Landau, *The Justices of the Peace 1679-1760*, Berkeley, University of California Press, p.185.
36. *The Gentleman's Magazine*, 1747, vol.17, p.563.

been available. Although despised by their superiors as: "...
needy, mercenary tools; and hated by their inferiors, as
instruments of oppression, yet [they were] absolutely
necessary to keep the common people within due bounds,
as well in regard to their superiors as to one another, and
the less dangerous, as their conduct is inspected by superior
authority."[37] The office hours and work of a quasi-
professional magistrate in London could be arduous. In the
early 1750s, Henry Fielding noted that his clerk sometimes
sat almost 16 hours a day, in the most: "... nauseous air in
the universe, and which hath in his case corrupted a good
constitution without contaminating his morals."[38]
Unsurprisingly, gentlemen were increasingly unwilling to
serve in the Metropolis as JPs. In April 1666, John Evelyn
was personally pressed by King Charles II to serve for his
part of London (he was already a non-active member of the
commission of the peace), with a view to "preventing some
disorder" in his parish. He replied that he was too busily
engaged on other royal duties and begged to be excused
from the office, something that the King allowed when
Evelyn was able to recommend an alternative. Evelyn was
appalled at the idea of being a Metropolitan Justice: "... the
thing in the world, I had most industriously avoided to act
in hitherto, in reguard of the perpetual trouble theroff in this
numerous Parish &c."[39]

Along with specific concerns about trading justices,

---

37. *The Gentleman's Magazine*, 1747, vol.17, p.562.
38. H. Fielding, *A Voyage to Lisbon*, London, 1755, A. Millar, p.24.
39. J. Evelyn, *The Diary of John Evelyn*, E.S. De Beer (Ed.), Oxford, Clarendon
     Press, 1955, vol.III, p.434.

there were more general questions about magisterial quality. In theory, the Lord Chancellor was supposed to appoint to the Commission those who were "good men and laufull, that ben no maynteiners of yuell".[40] All observers agreed that it was desirable that magistrates have sterling characters, if only to deal with the temptations that the office brought. Thus, in 1608, a bishop noted that a JP might face: "A bribe in his closet, or a letter on the bench, or the whispering and winks of a great neighbour." In theory, these would be dealt with by an "angry and courageous repulse". Ideally, once a JP was on the bench, he became devoid of personal feelings, so that private allegiances of: "... blood, alliance, amity, are forgotten; and if his own son come under trial, he knows him not."[41] Indeed, as Lambarde noted, under their appointment oath magistrates were required to swear that they would "do equal right to the poor and to the rich". In reality, of course, and even ignoring the trading justices, this was often easier said than done. Significantly, Michael Dalton thought it necessary to warn JPs of the need to avoid common human failings including a fear of the "power or countenance of another", a desire to seek favour by attempting to please an important neighbour and acting out of personal malice towards a litigant. This still left simple bribery and corruption, when JPs might receive a "fee, gift, or reward."[42]

JP were not usually professional lawyers, and often

---

40. Anon, *The Boke for a Justyce of Peace*, London, Thomas Berthel, 1534, p.1.
41. Hall, *Characters of virtues and vices*, pp.58-59.
42. Dalton, *The Country Justice*, 1655, pp.7-9.

suffered from a lack of legal expertise, a problem that became more serious as their duties increased. As Dalton noted, numerous difficulties were engendered by magisterial "ignorance or want of true understanding". In particular, a lack of legal knowledge combined with arrogance could lead JPs to proceed according to their own 'affections' rather than proper legal authority. Shakespeare's Master Shallow had real life counterparts. Sir Humphrey Gilbert lamented that many aristocrats who sat as JPs (and sheriffs) were so ignorant of the law that the "best are often tymes subjecte to the direction of farre their Inferiors". The widespread social practice of gentlemen joining and spending time at the Inns of Court when young, especially in the century after 1550, ought slightly to have ameliorated this situation as, before the Civil War, they provided a legal education of sorts. Until 1640, students were expected to keep the two annual learning vacations (Lent and Summer), when courses of lectures were provided. In term time, they attended Westminster Hall, where seats were set aside so that students could watch the law in action. Throughout the year, they participated in lengthy moots (debates on points of law) in hall. However, arguably, even the Elizabethan and early Stuart Inns were educationally moribund. The Inns were almost shut down for four years during the Civil War, and their educational role was irreversibly damaged. Legal readings were discontinued, and their half-hearted revival following the Interregnum was short lived, petering out after 1678.[43] The erosion of collegiality and education swiftly became apparent, leading to periodic complaints that the societies: "... were instituted, to serve as Colleges for students and professors of the Law, tho' now inhabited by such as have no business at all."[44]

Nevertheless, long before this sad state of affairs developed, many of the numerous gentlemen students who frequented the Inns without intending to enter practice failed to take their studies seriously. They were more interested in the fencing and dancing schools nearby, and in the entertainments and political 'networking' associated with the Inns, rather than any legal training that was available. Paul Hentzner was deeply sceptical about the level of legal studies carried out by most English bar students, though satisfied that they pursued other academic interests as well as having an enjoyable time: "In these colleges numbers of young nobility, gentry, and others, are educated, and chiefly in the study of physic, for very few apply themselves to that of the law."[45] In so far as they did seek to equip themselves with legal knowledge, many would have concentrated on the more arcane aspects of English land law - useful to men who would inherit estates - rather than on criminal law.

Most JPs learnt their criminal law on the bench or from the numerous manuals that were available from the latter

---

43. J.H. Baker, *The Inner Temple: A Brief Historical Description*, London, The Honorable Society of the Inner Temple, 1991, p.8.
44. *The Gentleman's Magazine*, 1731, vol.1, p.59.
45. P. Hentzner, *Travels in England during the reign of Queen Elizabeth*, London, Cassell & Co., 1889, p.43.

sixteenth century, rather than from any time they had spent in legal London.[46] These treatises included Lambarde's *Eirenarcha*, the publication of which, in 1581, was partly motivated by the author's service as a JP in Kent, and a consequent realization that there was an acute lack of standardised procedures regulating the office.[47] It was immediately viewed as authoritative, the fifteenth and final printing occurring in 1619, after which Michael Dalton's *The Country Justice* gradually ousted it. Dalton was to be the magistrates' primary *vade mecum* for the rest of the seventeenth century, before being superseded, in turn, by other manuals, such as that published by Edmund Bohun in 1693.

A variety of expedients were adopted to remedy the lack of legal knowledge amongst JPs. One was to bifurcate the commission into ordinary magistrates and a special group, the quorum, of proven experience or competence, entrusted with extra judicial responsibilities: "... the least skilful in the lawe are of the peace, the other both of the peace and quorum otherwise called of Oyer & Determiner, so that the first have authoritie onlly to heare, the other to heare & determine such matters as are brought into her presence."[48] According to William Lambarde, members of the quorum were "chosen specially for their knowledge in the laws of

---

46. W. Prest, "Legal Education of the Gentry at the Inns of Court, 1560-1640," *Past and Present*, 1967, Number 38, pp.20-39.
47. R.J. Terill, "William Lambarde: Elizabethan Humanist and Legal Historian," *The Journal of Legal History*, 1985, vol.6, pp.157-176.
48. W. Harrison, *Description of England*, R. Holinshed's *The First Volume of the Chronicles of England, Scotland and Ireland*, London, J. Harrison, 1577, p.75.

the land". Most Tudor Acts expressly specified when the presence of members of the quorum was necessary for the execution of statutory powers and duties. Their presence was also required at all quarter sessions. However, as the period advanced, membership was granted more and more freely, so that by the mid-eighteenth century it was the practice to advance almost all JPs to that status, except, perhaps "one inconsiderable perfon for the sake of propriety".[49]

Additionally, from the late fourteenth century, statute also required that all commissions of the peace include at least two "men of the law" in the quorum (i.e. qualified lawyers, not simply former law students). However, if willing and available, many more such men could be appointed to the bench. According to one Elizabethan observer: "The policy of this government hath made a special choice of lawyers to be justices of the peace." An examination of six counties suggests that the proportion of barrister JPs increased from 14 per cent in the mid-sixteenth century to 21 per cent by 1636. Much would depend on the shire involved, especially on how remote and prosperous it was. Thus, in Worcestershire, in 1636, only two JPs out of 35 were barristers or serjeants (the minimum possible). By contrast, in Norfolk at the same period the figure was 16 out of 62.[50]

That the JPs attracted many contemporary admirers is

---

49. W. Blackstone, *Commentaries on the Laws of England*, Oxford, Clarendon Press, 1765, vol.I, p.340.
50. W. Prest, *The Rise of the Barrister: A Social History of the English Bar 1590-1640*, Oxford, Clarendon Press, 1986, pp.8 and 237.

well known. Sir Edward Coke publicly described the office as "such a form of subordinate government for security and quiet of the realm as no part of the Christian world hath the like". Whether all such plaudits were justified is open to question. There was also a groundswell of informed criticism of the magistracy for much of the period, and, from the later 1500s, concern about their abilities became increasingly widespread. It was periodically alleged that many were unwilling or incapable of carrying out their duties properly. Some claimed that this was especially manifest in the administration of criminal law. Thus, Queen Elizabeth I's Lord Keeper warned that this meant that professional judges might have to be appointed in their place: "Her Majesty may be driven, clean contrary to her most gracious nature and inclination, to appoint and assign private men for profit and gain sake to see her penal laws to be executed." His views were not surprising, given some of the available evidence. Typically, in 1587, Lord Burghley received a letter from Edwin Sandys, the Archbishop of York, in which the cleric complained about local JPs who deserved to be removed from the Commission. They included men such as Robert Lee, a notorious adulterer, who abused his magisterial position "to work private displeasure a[nd] to serve other men's turns". Another, Peter Stanley, was a "great fornicator", who possessed "small wisdom, and less skill". Yet others lived "much in London" (a complaint that would become more frequent a century later), were of "no countenance", lacked ability or were of small estates. In Yorkshire, at least, it was apparently "very hard to choose fit men" to be JPs.[51] Concern about the quality of the active magistracy continued throughout the seventeenth century. In the 1690s, Edmund Bohun lamented that too many upper class men entrusted with the magistracy were degenerate in their own lifestyles and consequently devoid of moral authority: "For how can a Justice of Peace send a man to the stock for Drunkenness, when he is hardly well recovered of his last Debauch."[52] His views were reiterated in the early 1700s, when Defoe also complained that many JPs cursed, swore and were habitual drunkards.[53]

The High Sheriff

Historically, the high sheriff had played a vital role in criminal law enforcement, being, in Sir Edward Coke's words, the "principalis conservator pacis, within the countie". However, by the sixteenth century, the office had declined in status from its medieval heyday, losing many of its judicial duties and gradually being marginalised in county society. The reduction in the sheriff's power, which occurred at the same time as those of the JPs were being enhanced, appears to have been partly based on the reputation for disloyalty and corruption that the office acquired during the internecine conflicts of the fifteenth

---

51. T.A. Morris, *Tudor Government*, London, Routledge, 1999, p.69.
52. Bohun, *The Justice of Peace His Calling and Qualifications*, p.21.
53. D. Defoe, *The Poor Man's Plea*, Oxford, Basil Blackwell, 1927, pp.6-7.

century, when many sheriffs sided with local magnates against the Crown. Ultimately, JPs were even given some supervisory powers over the work of the sheriff.[54] However, the office preserved a number of significant responsibilities, even after 1500. The sheriff, or his under-officers (who did most of the work in practice), was still responsible for the collection of debts and royal revenues, the service of writs and the enforcement of civil judgments.[55] Most importantly for the criminal justice system, his duties included summoning jurors for service, making some of the arrangements for the assizes, supervising prisoners, jails and the gallows, raising fines, seizing convicted felons' estates and accounting for them to the Treasury: "... to attend upon the judges, and put their sentence in execution; to empanel the jury ... to convey the condemned to execution."[56] The Privy Council appointed sheriffs for a one year term in office. Unfortunately, the position required them to reside in their county, rather than London, and uphold the office at their own expense (though sums expended on visiting judges could be recovered from the Exchequer). Since this usually cost considerably more than the position paid, by the seventeenth century increasingly few men were seeking the honour. The office also carried potentially onerous legal liabilities for negligence or misconduct, so that it was necessary that a sheriff be a: "Person of Worth and Value,

---

54. I. Gladwin, *The Sheriff: The Man and his Office*, London, Victor Gollancz, 1974, p.269.
55. Coke, *The Institutes of the Laws of England*, Section 168a.
56. P. Hentzner, *Travels in England during the reign of Queen Elizabeth*, London, Cassell & Co., 1889, p.80.

that so he may be responsible for any Defaults, either of himself or his Officers."[57] By the eighteenth century, its unpopularity was such that relatively minor gentlemen, like the prison reformer John Howard, could be selected.

The Judiciary

England's professional judges sat over cases tried at assizes and their urban equivalents. At the highest level they were largely recruited from the twelve puisne judges of the three Westminster courts (Common Pleas, King's Bench and Exchequer). Although not specialists in criminal law these men were usually competent, and sometimes outstanding, lawyers. There was also a plethora of lesser salaried judicial offices, a few of which, such as the Recorder and Sheriff of London, were full-time. However, many were part-time, such as the numerous Recorders who bolstered borough sessions.

The judicial 'ideal' was well established by the early modern period. Thus, Dalton approvingly quoted the charge of James I to his judges, in which the King required: "That they do justice uprightly and indifferently, without delay, partiality, fear, or bribery, with stout and upright hearts, with clean and uncorrupt hands."[58] Similarly, if surprisingly for a man who had been dismissed from office for

---

57. M. Hale, *The History of the Common Law of England*, London, J. Walthoe, 1713, p.252.
58. Dalton, *The Country Justice*, 1661, p.8.

471

corruption, Francis Bacon held an equally idealistic view of the position, considering that judges ought to be: "... more learned, than witty, more reverend, than plausible, and more advised, than confident. Above all things, integrity is their portion and proper virtue."[59] In reality there was endemic judicial corruption and politicisation until quite late in the period. Thus, in 1592, Sir Roger Manwood appears to have offered Lord Burghley 500 marks for the vacant Chief Justiceship of the Court of King's Bench.[60]

Nevertheless, the era saw a gradual improvement in judicial probity. By 1631, an elderly lawyer, although believing that there was still much impropriety, thought that the judiciary was of a "most reformed and unimpeachable condition" when compared to the judges of his early manhood, since which time there had been a "happy alteration".[61] In 1667, Sir Mathew Hale, Lord Chief Baron, presiding at the Buckinghamshire assizes, appears to have been genuinely shocked that anyone could think to influence a judge in a criminal case by offering gifts: "Sir John Croke sent me this morning two sugar loaves, to excuse his absence yesterday, but I sent them back again I did not then so well know what he meant by them as I do now. Surely Sir John does not think the King's justices will take

---

59. Bacon, "Of Judicature," pp.162-165.
60. J.G. Bellamy, *The Criminal Trial in Later Medieval England, Felony Before the Courts From Edward I to the Sixteenth Century*, Toronto, University of Toronto Press, 1998, p.10.
61. Anon, *The just Lawyer: His Conscionable Complaint against Auricular or Private Informing and Soliciting of Judges*, London, George Purslowe, 1631, f. A3.

bribes?"[62] By the early eighteenth century, the judiciary had also become legally more secure in their positions. In 1600, judges held office at the pleasure of the Crown, *durante bene placito*, something that led to regular dismissals under the Stuarts. In 1701, however, the Act of Settlement recognised the principle of security of judicial tenure during good behaviour, and provided a safer mechanism for removing a judge who behaved badly in office (resolution of parliament).

Nevertheless, momentous though these changes were, for ordinary 'run of the mill' criminal trials held at the assizes, their direct impact was probably quite modest. Even in the earlier period, judicial corruption usually pertained to civil suits, rather than routine criminal matters. Most accused men were too poor to offer worthwhile douceurs, though the ability to grant a reprieve and recommend a pardon may have been susceptible to gifts from occasional wealthy defendants. A habitual chicken thief in the provinces could offer little in this regard. However, such changes may have had an important indirect effect by promoting notions of judicial professionalism, ideals that were less susceptible to abusive judging, even in criminal matters.

---

62. J.L Rayner and G.T. Crook (Eds.), *The Complete Newgate Calendar* (Vols. 1-5). London, Privately printed for the Navarre Society, 1926, vol. I, pp.213-214, see also Bernard, *The Case of John Atherton*, p.44.

Chapter 14

The Criminal Trial: Introduction

"Let us consider the reason of the case. For nothing is law that is not reason" - Sir John Powell: *Coggs vs. Bernard*, 2 Ld. Raym. Rep. p. 911.

Introduction

In the modern era, many well informed but non-specialist observers have based their knowledge of early modern criminal procedure on causes célèbres, frequently treason or (less commonly) witchcraft trials. In particular, their views are heavily influenced by the cases recorded in the State Trials series of reports, although, as was observed as early as 1850 (with considerable exaggeration) "taken in the mass, [they] are of no authority whatsoever". In some cases, the identities of the authors of the reports, the circumstances under which they were written and the location of the original documents are unknown.[1] Most importantly, the great majority of the cases reported are not representative of 'ordinary' crime. They were exceptional offences, dealt with using extraordinary methods which may, frequently, have been conducted in an overtly unfair, arbitrary and even despotic manner.[2] The uniquely savage punishment visited

---

1. *Notes and Queries*, vol.4, 2nd series, 1857, p.427.
2. W.B. Robison, "Murder at Crowhurst: A Case Study in Early Tudor Law Enforcement," *Criminal Justice History*, 1988, vol.9, p.52.

on traitors, so much at variance to normal English penal practice, is indicative of its status as a 'crime apart'. As the Recusant writer Martin Aray ruefully acknowledged in 1599, if the authorities wished to take away men's lives they did not have to do so blatantly: "... they can do it by sleight, deceit and coosinage, and yet stil with exterior face and show of Justice."[3] Similarly, Paul Hentzner noted that when noblemen were sent to the Elizabethan Tower of London, accused of serious crimes or treason, they would "seldom or never recover their liberty".[4] However, an examination of routine criminal hearings reveals how dangerous it is to take such trials, especially those from the Tudor era, as an archetypal model for ordinary felony hearings conducted at the Old Bailey, assizes and quarter sessions. This is not to say that such everyday hearings were 'fair' by modern standards. Many aspects of what would pass today for due process were missing. However, they were certainly not a ritual preceding 'judicial murder' in the way that the trials of Thomas More and Walter Raleigh undoubtedly were.

Sir John Fortescue's *De Laudibus Legum Angliae*, written (in Latin) in the years between 1468 and 1470, while the author, a former Lord Chief Justice, was living in France as an exile in the court of Henry VI, provides a useful insight into English criminal law and procedure at the very end of the medieval period. It was partly produced to provide

---

3. M. Aray, The *Discoverie and Confutation of a Tragical Fiction, Devysed and Played by Edward Squyor, yeoman soldier, hanged at Tyburne the 23.November, 1598*, London, 1599, p.14.
4. P. Hentzner, *Travels in England during the reign of Queen Elizabeth*, London, Cassell & Co, 1889, p.39.

instruction for the young Prince Edward in the unique laws and legal traditions of the country, taking the form of a dialogue between the author and the prince. It vigorously praised the superiority of English common law over the civil law found in France and other continental countries, something that would later make it popular in the constitutional debates of the 1620s. The structure it portrays was the bedrock of the early modern English system of justice. However, in the decades immediately after Fortescue was writing there were some significant developments in the criminal trial process. Most of these late medieval changes were complete by the early to middle decades of the sixteenth century. Limited change was underway again by the 1730s, in a process that, when completed in the early nineteenth century, would have transformed the English criminal trial into its modern adversarial form. Thus, the manner of trial that held sway between c.1550 and c.1700 can be considered to be the early modern 'model', and will be the main focus of attention here. Nevertheless, even these years were not entirely static. Criminal trials were slightly more formal in 1700 than they had been in 1550, with the prosecution completing its case more clearly before the defendant gave his version of events.[5] Such changes were relatively modest, and Sir Thomas Smith's account of the Elizabethan criminal trial of the 1560s is strikingly similar to the picture provided by an examination of Old Bailey trials in the 1680s, despite the

---

5.   T.A. Green, *Verdict According to Conscience*, Chicago, University of Chicago Press, 1985, p.270.

passage of over a century.[6]

According to Sir Thomas, the prosecution case was usually opened, after the arraignment, by the JP who had examined the defendant. This magistrate would either read a verbatim account or (more commonly) a précis of his examination to the court, there being no requirement for it to be a strictly contemporaneous record. Individual witnesses were then called, to provide a narrative account of their experiences. As they did so, both prosecution witnesses and the prisoner were subject to 'disputatious' questioning by the judge, jury and each other, producing a wide-ranging and informal enquiry, though, as the period advanced, judges became stricter about 'relevance'. Once all available and relevant evidence had been put before the court, the judge called a halt to proceedings, gave a brief closing address to the jury (often little more than a few sentences) and charged them to decide the case. Jurors frequently heard evidence from a number of trials before considering their verdicts on all of them together. To modern common law lawyers, this seems crude, and many might agree with Professor Cockburn that Tudor and Stuart criminal trials were "nasty, brutish, and essentially short". Certainly, counsel were usually absent, rules of evidence minimal, judges routinely questioned witnesses and defendants in a robust and even brutal manner, only prosecution witnesses were allowed to enhance their testimony by giving evidence on oath, jurors might employ

6. S. Landsman, "The rise of the contentious spirit: Adversary procedure in Eighteenth Century England," *Cornell Law Review*, 1990, vol.75, p.505.

private knowledge, gained outside the courtroom, and there was almost no appeal from their decisions.[7] However, the cumulative impression can be misleading, ignoring the fundamentally different 'model' for the criminal trial that dominated the era.

Cases of treason notwithstanding, normal felonies were usually dealt with by a careful concern for correctness of adjudication, if not procedural fairness, albeit one that was subject to the inherent limitations of the era.[8] Thus, in 1530, St Germain stressed that though a defendant might be considered a: "... comon offendor or that he be [manifestly] gyltye yet he ought to have that the lawe gyveth hym."[9] This was not mere wishful thinking. According to Professor Samaha, criminal cases tried in Elizabethan Colchester manifest a scrupulous adherence to the requirements of legal proof.[10] Examples of such care, from other parts of the country, are also easy to find. Thus, in London, the judge presiding over the trials of a group of riotous apprentices in 1668, warned the jury that in cases where the constables could not provide a firm identification it was better that the guilty walked free than that the innocent suffered, and that in his view: "I cannot see how you can find them guilty, God forbid." The men he identified as being in this category

---

7. Landsman, "The rise of the contentious spirit," pp.498 and 505.
8. Robison, "Murder at Crowhurst," pp.42 and 52.
9. T.C. Plucknett and J.C. Barton (Eds.), *2nd Dialogue, 1530, St Germain's Doctor and Student*, London, Selden Society, 1974, p.285.
10. J. Samaha, "Hanging for Felony: The Rule of Law in Elizabethan Colchester," *Historical Journal*, 1978, vol. 21, p.769.

were acquitted.[11] Similarly, a decade later, when James Smith was accused of stealing three white hogs (two large, one small) from Leonard Sanders, his defence was simply to deny ever being in possession of such animals. However, a reliable eyewitness had clearly seen him with three pale pigs of the appropriate sizes. Nevertheless, and unsurprisingly, the loser of the hogs had not seen him with them, and the eyewitness did not remember precise details as to the animals' appearance (markings etc.), again creating a problem as to identification. Although it was apparent that Smith was lying about a key issue, the: "Evidence being uncertain as to the particulars charged, the Court left [it] to the discretion of the Jury". They, too, acquitted.[12]

To a considerable extent, judges and jurors in early modern felony cases were trying the 'whole man'. Although legal guilt of the crime alleged was the paramount consideration, the huge amount of discretion in the system provided by 'pious perjury', reprieves and the other mechanisms available for escaping post-conviction execution, meant that for all but the most serious crimes, trials were almost as much about establishing whether a felon deserved death as they were about establishing his guilt or innocence of the charge indicted. For example, did he appear to be a recidivist or a professional criminal?

---

11. Anon, *The Tryals of such Persons (Peter Messenger, Richard Beasley .. as under the Notion of London-Apprentices were tumultuously assembled in Moorfields 1668)*, London, Robert Pawlet, at pp.1-10.

12. Anon, *An exact account of the trials of the several persons arraigned at the sessions-house in the Old-Bailey for London and Middlesex*, London, Gilham Hills, 1678, p.28.

Conversely, was he normally a hard working and valuable member of the community who was 'down on his luck' or subject to sudden temptation, and for whom reputable people would speak?

Forensic Atmosphere

By modern standards, a typical felony trial was not necessarily a grave, dignified and sombre occasion. Noise from spectators was common, even at the most serious trials, and, in 1588, a man was murdered in open court. The judiciary could be as bad as the general public. Sir Edmund Anderson, an Elizabethan Lord Chief Justice, was notorious for his "many oaths and reproachful revilings on the bench". A robust judge, at the age of seventy-two, while on circuit in Somerville, and confronted with public disorder Anderson seized a sword from a man-at-arms and personally quelled it.[13] A century later, according to a (admittedly antagonistic) Cheshire MP, who complained in Parliament, George Jeffreys lacked gravity when conducting the office of Chief Justice of Chester: "He was witty upon the prisoners at the bar. He was full of his jokes upon people that came to give evidence, not suffering them to declare what they had to say in their own way and method, but would interrupt them because they behaved themselves with more gravity than he." Additionally, it was rumoured that he was a heavy drinker, and often turned up at the

---

13. A.L. Rowse, The *England of Elizabeth - The Structure of Society*, 1961, p.374.

assizes showing the symptoms of a man "that overnight had taken a large cup".[14] George Fox, when tried at the assizes in the early 1660s, was also shocked to see "so much lightness in a court, where such solemn matters are handled".[15] Things were as bad, if not worse, in the lower courts. According to Edward Hext, there were even cases of outright intimidation at Elizabethan quarter sessions, with some defendants openly threatening the Bench. In one case, he alleged, a defendant: "... in the face and hearynge of the whole bench, swore a great othe that yf he weere whipped yt shold be the deerest whipping to some that ever was."[16]

Lack of Legal Representation in Felony Trials

One of the most important characteristics of the early modern English criminal trial was the dearth of legal expertise from sources other than the Bench. The audience rights of defence counsel in criminal and treason cases were heavily circumscribed by law. Prosecution counsel, though not formally banned, were usually absent in practice. As a result, in most early modern felony trials the judge and his clerks were the only trained lawyers present. By contrast, in

---

14. G.W. Keeton, "Judge Jeffreys as Chief Justice of Chester 1680-1683," *Law Quarterly Review*, 1961, vol. 77, p.43.

15. G. Fox, *George Fox - an Autobiography*, R.M. Jones (Ed.), 1908 edn., Reprint Richmond Indiana, Friends United Press, 1976, p.177.

16. E. Hext, "Letter written by E. Hext to Lord Burghley," *Tudor Economic Documents*, R.H. Tawney and E.Power (Eds.), London, Longmans, 1951, vol.2, p.341.

civil cases, lawyers had the right both to examine witnesses and to address the jury. The absence of criminal lawyers had enormous ramifications for the whole felony trial process. Although to modern observers it appears unfair, it was premised on a radically different view of the function of the trial process.

Justifications for the Absence of Counsel

Many contemporary observers believed that the absence of defence counsel encouraged spontaneity in an accused's response to allegations, something that was also facilitated by the near absence of pre-trial discovery, which gave them little chance to ascertain, in advance, the precise details of the allegations against them. The truth, it was believed, spoke for itself. As Serjeant William Hawkins noted in his influential treatise of 1721, *Pleas of the Crown*, an innocent defendant had no need of counsel because: "Every one of Common Understanding may as properly speak to a Matter of Fact, as if he were the best Lawyer." By contrast, the "very Speech, Gesture and Countenance, and Manner of Defense of those who are Guilty, when they speak for themselves, may often help to disclose the Truth, which probably would not so well be discovered from the artificial Defense of others speaking for them."[17] His views were received judicial opinion. Thus, when a foreign defendant,

---

17. J.H. Langbein, "The historical origins of the privilege against self-incrimination at Common Law," *Michigan Law Review*, vol. 92, p.1053.

being tried at the Old Bailey in February 1681, asked for an adjournment because he did not understand English law and had not had an opportunity to instruct counsel for an out of court conference, his motion was swiftly rejected; Lord Chief Justice North pointed out that he was accused of a: "... matter of fact, that none can instruct him in but himself, Council can do him no good in such a case as this."[18]

Additionally, at least in theory, even if the Crown was represented by counsel, the trial judge was required to intervene to ensure a generally 'level playing field'. Thus, Bacon urged that whenever there was a: "... violent prosecution, cunning advantages taken, combination, power, great counsel, then is the virtue of a judge seen, to make inequality equal; that he may plant his judgment as upon an even ground."[19] As early as 1530, when St. Germain had rhetorically asked how the prohibition on defence counsel could be justified, he had concluded that it was exactly because the judiciary replaced the need for counsel in such cases. Trial judges would prevent technicalities prejudicing a defendant and: "... so instructe hym & so ordre hym that he shall reme into noo Jeopardye by hys myspleadyngeas."[20]

In reality, such an analysis normally meant little more than that judges would protect defendants against blatant

---

18. Anon, *The Tryal and Condemnation of George Brosky*, London, Thomas Basset, 1682, pp.4-5.
19. Sir F. Bacon, "On Judicature," *The Essays*, London, Everyman edn., J.M. Dent, 1906, pp.162-165.
20. Plucknett and Barton, *2nd Dialogue*, p.284-285.

misunderstandings of court procedure and from clearly and fundamentally illegal indictments, not that they would help formulate their defences, act as their advocates, or take issue with subtle procedural defects.[21] Most judges were reluctant to probe deeply into prosecution cases or the veracity of the Crown's witnesses, if only because of pressure of time. Indeed, in many treason and 'political' cases the bench did not even pretend to act as counsel for the accused and could be quite blatant about rejecting such a notion. Thus, when the Reverend John Udall asked Serjeant Pickering, the presiding judge at his trial at the Southwark assizes, in 1590, to explain his right to challenge jurors, he received the terse response: "Nay, I am not to tell you that; I sit to judge and not to give you counsel." Even worse, some judges actively sought to advance the prosecution case in such hearings. Thus, the presiding judge at Nicholas Throckmorton's treason trial in 1554 repeatedly urged him to confess the charges, telling him "it will be best for you".

Although this does not reflect normal practice in routine felony cases, unless, perhaps, the judge was utterly convinced of an accused's guilt, the defendant's supposed entitlement to have the trial judge serve as his counsel was, even in theory, limited to matters of law, not fact. As Chief Justice Hyde noted in 1663, when explaining the limits of the court's duty to be counsel to a defendant, his function was to ensure that "you suffer nothing for your want of

---

21. J.M. Beattie, "Scales of Justice: Defence Counsel and the English Criminal Trial in the Eighteenth and Nineteenth Centuries," *Law and History Review*, 1991, vol.9, Number 2, 1991, p.223.

knowledge in matter of law". Nevertheless, judges did sometimes go beyond this in assisting felony defendants, doing their limited best to aid the accused, subject to their heavy caseloads.[22] For example, they might help by focusing a defendant's mind on the important issues in the prosecution case that he had to address (as a modern magistrate's clerk will sometimes do with an unrepresented defendant). Thus, at the completion of the prosecution's case at his trial at the Old Bailey, for being an accessory to murder, in 1681, Count Coningsmarke was told by the presiding judge: "Now you must come to your defence; I will put you in mind of some things my Lord, which things it will concern you to give some Account of."[23] Perhaps as a result of such cases, there was a real and widespread faith amongst many ordinary defendants in the judge's role as 'prisoner's friend'. Thus, at his trial for regicide at the Old Bailey, in 1660, Colonel Daniel Axtell declared that he had heard that it was the: "... duty of your Lordships and the Judges to be of Counsel for the Prisoner in things wherein he is ignorant in matters of law, to make his just defence ... by his Oath he is also to be Counsellor to the Prisoner, and stands as a Mediator between the King and Prisoner." He also asked (rather optimistically given the context) that the judge prevent legal niceties prejudicing him during the

---

22. Langbein, "The Historical Origins of the Privilege Against Self-Incrimination at Common Law," pp.1048-1054.
23. Anon, *The Tryal and Condemnation of George Brosky*, p.41.

hearing.[24] Similarly, in 1663, the burglar James Turner was sufficiently concerned about exaggerated reports of his own legal abilities to caution the trial judge not to treat him differently to a legally ignorant prisoner: "I beg of your Honour and the Bench to be Counsell for me, for though the world looks on me as a Solicitor, it is a mistake my Lord."[25] However, in 1699, when Spencer Cowper also alluded to his unrepresented status, the presiding judge, Baron Hatfell, could not resist pointing out that he was "not under such disadvantage as men usually are that stand where you do". (Cowper was well regarded as a lawyer).[26] Even in the 1760s, after procedural change was underway, William Blackstone could still maintain that it was one of a trial judge's obligations to: "... be counsel for the prisoner; that is, [he] shall see that the proceedings against him are legal and strictly regular."

There was also considerable concern about the extra delay that would be occasioned by admitting counsel to the trial process, in an already 'pressured' system. Thus, even in the 1550s, Sir William Staunford (1509-1558), a judge of the Court of Common Pleas, and author of *Pleas of the Crown*, had feared that "Trials will take too long if men of law were

---

24. H. Finch, *An Exact and Impartial Account Of the Indictment, Arraignment, Tryal, and Judgment (according to Law) of Twenty Nine Regicides ...*; London, Andrew Crook & Edward Powel, 1660, p.190. Heneage Finch (1621-82) was Solicitor General, serving as prosecutor at the trial of the regicides. He subsequently became Attorney General, in 1670, and Lord Chancellor in 1675.
25. Anon, *A True and Impartial Account of the Arraignment, Tryal, Examination, Confession and Condemnation of Col. James Turner*, London, 1663, p.10.
26. Anon, *The Tryal of Spencer Cowper*, London, 1699, p.3.

allowed".[27] Over 140 years later, prosecuting counsel could warn a trial judge that if some of the legal points taken by the lawyer defendant were fully argued out "we should keep you here while to morrow morning".[28] Even more importantly, however, the absence of trial lawyers facilitated a process in which legal theory in criminal trials frequently parted company with reality. Although a disregard for legal niceties is commonly associated with political trials, there was also an imaginative approach to procedural matters in ordinary criminal hearings, one that is alien to modern forensic usage. In theory, for example, the contents of an assizes indictment had been settled by c.1400. To be valid they had to be extremely precise and accurate, stipulating the occupation and place of residence of the accused and the correct date of the alleged crime. In practice, these entries were often largely fallacious. Nevertheless, usually, this does not appear to have presented any problems in court. It was the accuracy of the substance, not the form, of the indictment that concerned trial jurors, rather than the truth of every detail contained in it.

Even in the absence of counsel, where out of court legal advice was more freely available, such technicalities could become real problems. Despite cases in the seventeenth century that often required that a writ of error have the fiat of the attorney general, in the early 1700s Thomas De Veil claimed that Metropolitan 'Newgate Solicitors' were "constantly employed to extricate notorious offendors out of

---

27. Sir W. Staunford, *Please of the Crown*, London, 1607, p.105.
28. Anon, *The Tryal of Spencer Cowper*, p.3.

their difficulties".[29] In those (rare) cases where an accused person did have access to legal advice, they were often successful in seeking the removal of indictments to the Court of King's Bench. Most defendants probably did not appreciate that they could object to the indictments on which they were being tried. One modern observer, having made an intensive study, concluded that competent lawyers could have made 'mincemeat' of up to half of the criminal indictments heard at early modern assizes.[30] This could even occur in 'political' cases. At his trial in 1533, Thomas More initially amused himself by pointing out deficiencies that invalidated his own indictment, the trial only proceeding when he had "taken as many exceptions as he thought meet".[31] Indeed, sometimes, even intelligent laymen could do this, as can be seen in the ease with which George Fox wrought confusion on the Lancashire assizes in 1664. Fox warned the judge, Mr Justice Turner, that, although not a lawyer, he had "much to say". He then pointed out numerous failings in the indictment on which he was to be tried. For example, the specified day on which he was supposed to have refused to take an oath was incorrect and the year of the King's reign set out in his co-defendant's Margaret Fell's indictment was also wrong. Turner

---

29. Sir T. De Veil, *Observations on the Practice of a Justice of the Peace*, London, Edward Withers, 1747, p.4.
30. J.S. Cockburn, "Trial by the Book? Fact and Theory in the Criminal Process 1558-1625," *Legal Records and the Historian*, Royal Historical Society, London, J.H. Baker (Ed.), pp.62-64.
31. W. Roper: "The Life of Sir Thomas More," in *Lives of Sir Thomas More*, E.G. Reynolds (Ed.), London, Everyman edn., J.M. Dent, 1963, p.46.

acknowledged that these were "great errors".[32] One inference that has been drawn from this is that the grand jury cannot have been very effective as a scrutinising body, if it failed to detect that up to 50 per cent of the bills it considered were fundamentally flawed. According to this analysis, it largely confined itself to endorsing earlier bureaucratic decisions.

Nonetheless, the significance of some of these flaws is also open to challenge. Many discrepancies as to the jobs held by defendants are explicable on the basis of multiple occupations, a distinction between employment and 'status' and occupational changes. Discrepancies about dates or valuations, provided they were correctly over or under cardinal 'cut off' points, such as 12 pence, were often of less legal significance than might at first appear.[33] It *is* likely that both the grand jury and judiciary were not overly concerned with legal or descriptive technicalities (most grand jurors were not lawyers). However, this does not mean that they failed to establish the commission of an offence and insist on the presence of some tangible evidence to connect an accused person to that crime. The evidence suggests that, normally, there was clearly a case to answer if a finding of *billa verra* was returned.

Even so, the absence of 'trial by book', combined with an imaginative approach to the law, might, occasionally, have meant that some stages of the criminal process were

---

32. Fox, *George Fox: An Autobiography*, p.170.
33. A. MacFarlane, "Review Essay on 'Calendar of Assize Records Essex Indictments Elizabeth I' by J.S. Cockburn," *American Journal of Legal History*, 1980, vol. 21, pp.171-177.

deliberately simplified or even completely ignored. There are a few indications of this happening. Thus, in 1568, two men were convicted at an assizes of raping an 'unknown' woman. Presumably, this indicates that the victim did not give evidence at trial, though still alive, something that would be fatal to most modern prosecutions. At the Hertford assizes in 1616, the trial of an adulterous wife who arranged with the man who was her lover, neighbour and co-defendant to murder her husband, by shooting him through a hole bored in the partition wall separating their two houses, occasioned difficulties. Her spouse was only slightly wounded, precluding a murder indictment. However, the rudimentary nature of the law of attempt meant that it would be very hard to punish the guilty parties to their deserts by prosecuting the inchoate offence. Ultimately, the adulterous couple were executed for the substantive offence of burglary (the neighbour) and as an accessory to that crime (the wife). Although the decision by Mr Justice Houghton was legally dubious, given the lack of personal physical entry into premises normally required for the crime, King James I commended it as the "most rational of any that he had heard in the common law".[34] Similarly, when, in 1631, the dissolute Lord Mervyn Touchet, Earl of Castlehaven, was accused of aiding the rape of his own wife and committing sodomy with his servants, and tried before his peers, there was a concerted attempt not to allow technicalities, however vital, to stand in the way of a conviction. Arguably, the case was as much about his

---

34.   Cockburn, *Trial by the Book?* pp.65-68.

general misconduct and inappropriate behaviour towards his 'inferiors' as his sexual irregularities, the legal case against both the earl and his servants being weak. Despite the already well established importance of sexual penetration in both rape and sodomy, the evidence for this in both counts was thin or nonexistent. On the charge of sodomy, a servant clearly testified that Castlehaven had "spent his seed but did not penetrate his body", and the Earl denied any sodomitical activity. During his defence he asked the court whether "buggery was within the statute without penetration". When the judges told him that it was, he was "much amazed". This is not surprising, as it went against existing case law. Not surprisingly, the decision was later declared to be applicable "only upon this case". Within a few years of his execution, reservations were being expressed about the trial.[35]

To an extent, the 'robust' approach to existing law seen in such cases was also facilitated by the doctrine of legally binding precedent (*stare decisis*) not yet having assumed its modern form. In theory, judges did not have a free hand in applying the law. James I warned that they were: "... not to utter their own conceits, but the true meaning of the Law, not making Lawes, but interpreting the Law."[36] Similarly,

---

35. Sir R. Hutton, *The Reports of That Reverend and Learned Judge ...*, London: H. Twyford and T. Dring, 1656, p.116, quoted C.B. Herrup, "Finding the Bodies," *GLQ: A Journal of Lesbian and Gay Studies*, 1999, vol. 5.3, pp.255-265, see also C.B. Herrup, *A House in Gross Disorder: Sex, Law, and the Second Earl of Castlehaven*, New York, Oxford University Press, 1999, pp.122-123.
36. M. Dalton, *The Country Justice, Containing The practise of the Justices of the Peace out of their Sessions ...*, London, Company of Stationers, 1655, p.8..

Francis Bacon was adamant that judges should remember that their office was: *"... jus dicere*, and not *jus dare;* to interpret law, and not to make law." Otherwise, he felt, they would be behaving like the Church of Rome, which altered scripture under the pretext of interpreting it.[37] Nevertheless, for much of the period, earlier case law provided important guidance, rather than rigidly fixed rules. Some judges, such as Lord Chief Justice Anderson, were notorious for ignoring precedents they considered to be foolish. However, in the early-seventeenth century, legal argument from precedent began to assume greater significance, acquiring constitutional implications. This process was facilitated by the importance placed by Sir Edward Coke on the authority of rules previously enunciated by common law courts. Even so, Coke's Reports were only advanced as 'examples' of the correct rule and not in themselves authoritative sources. (Coke also distorted many older cases to support his own legal opinions.) It was not until 1673 that Lord Chief Justice Vaughan clearly distinguished between *obiter dicta* and *ratio decidendi*, providing the legal tools for a fully precedent based system.[38] This lack of rigidity was greatly assisted in felony trials by the near absence of lawyers to challenge the trial judge's decision, and the dearth of appellate review to condemn or give enhanced value to earlier decisions. Nevertheless, it seems to have been very rare for the law to be stretched in ordinary criminal trials to the lengths seen in

---

37. Sir F. Bacon, "On Judicature," *The Essays*, London, Everyman edn., J.M. Dent, 1906, pp.162-165.
38. H.J. Berman, "The transformation of English Legal Science: from Hale to Blackstone," *Emory Law Journal*, 1996, vol. 45, pp.446-448.

Lord Audley's case.

Personal Representation Amongst Defendants

Prisoners were substantially responsible for their own defences, though in exceptional circumstances a 'next friend' might be allowed to assist a defendant who would otherwise have trouble following the evidence. Thus, at the notorious trial of Alice Lisle, for High Treason, before Lord Chief Justice Jeffreys, on a Special Commission of Oyer and Terminer, held at Winchester in August 1685, the defendant: "... being old and Infirm, and thick of Hearing, one Matthew Brown, at her Request, was permitted by the Court, to stand by her, to inform her what pass'd in Court, and to give her his Assistance."[39] Educated defendants were sometimes forceful advocates in their own causes. Thus, at his trial, Sir Walter Raleigh repeatedly spoke to the jury directly about salient evidence. Similarly, in 1554, Nicholas Throckmorton addressed the jurors by name at least six times.[40] His skill and eloquence achieved the remarkable result, for a Tudor treason trial, of a 'not guilty' verdict. Of course, such cases were not typical. However, even some of those accused in routine felonies took steps to enhance their forensic expertise in preparation for trial. In 1725, Bernard

---

39. T. Salmon, *Tryals for High-Treason, and other Crimes. With proceedings on bills of attainder, and impeachments. For three hundred years past ...*, vol. 4, London, D. Brown etc., 1720, pp.384-402
40. R.L. Marcus, "English Common Law," *University of Illinois Law Review*, 1984, p.684.

Mandeville was convinced that Newgate inmates honed their courtroom skills while awaiting their hearings: "... in mock Tryals, and instructing one another in cross Questions, to confound Witnesses."[41] Even in provincial jails, it is likely that prisoners would often have become familiar with basic court procedure and strategy by associating with 'old hands'.

Although articulate defendants could sometimes seize their opportunity, and make a good fist of defending themselves, many ordinary people accused of serious crimes found running their own defences very difficult. Inevitably, a few went 'too far' in the process, while many others were excessively taciturn. Thus, Lord Chief Justice Sir John Holt, presiding at the trial of Henry Harrison in 1692, was forced to warn him not to: "... fall into a Passion, it may be more to your Advantage, in the making your Defence, if you keep your temper."[42] Similarly, in 1664, the notorious burglar Colonel Turner was found guilty at the Old Bailey sessions after showing great "confidence at the barr, but yet great indiscretion in his argueing". According to Pepys, this amounted to outright 'impudence'.[43] However, most defendants were unused to speaking in public, frequently being tongue-tied, intimidated, naturally inarticulate and

---

41. B. De Mandeville, *An Enquiry into the Causes of the Frequent Executions at Tyburn*, London, 1725, p.17.
42. Anon, *The Arraignment, Tryal, Conviction and Condemnation of Henry Harrison*, London, 1692, p.17.
43. S. Pepys, *The Diary of Samuel Pepys*, R. Latham and W. Matthews (Eds.), London, Bell and Hyman, 1971, vol. 5, p.20.

often unwell from the effects of their incarceration.[44] Defendants in the Tudor treason trials repeatedly attributed their poor memory of events to the effects of their pre-trial imprisonment. Thomas More claimed that custody had so impaired his intelligence that he could "scarce remember the third part" of the allegations in his indictment. Similarly, Nicholas Throckmorton claimed his "memory is not good, and the same much decayed since my grievous imprisonment". Although being interned in the Tower was arduous, it was still probably preferable to the ordinary county jails that suspected felons would be detained in.[45]

Mary Goodenough, convicted of infanticide at the Oxfordshire assizes in February 1691, can be considered a classic example of a multiply disadvantaged defendant. She seemed: "... never to have had any great Faculty or Freedom of Speech; and Farther, the Fatigue and hard fare of a Prison, to one that kept Two Thirds of her Lying-in-month there, had mightily weakened her, and impaired her spirits." Goodenough received sentence of death and was executed, although the case against her was more complex than normal, being premised on the basis that her newborn illegitimate baby had died for want of "suitable Help and due Attendance".[46] Goodenough was certainly not alone in finding it difficult to defend herself in what was, otherwise,

---

44. Langbein, "The Historical Origins of the Privilege Against Self-Incrimination at Common Law," pp.1053-1054.
45. Marcus, "English Common Law," p.694.
46. Anon, *Fair warnings to murderers of infants being an account of the tryal, codemnation [sic] and execution of Mary Goodenough*, London, J. Robinson, 1692, p.3.

495

an 'arguable' case. Francis Newland was convicted of murder in 1695 and sentenced to death, despite most neutral observers entertaining the gravest doubts as to his guilt and believing that his conviction was primarily due to a lack of forensic ability: "... by rason of his immature Age, and want of experience, [so that he was] unable to make his Defence as he should." Like many falsely accused people, he was not properly prepared for trial, "presuming too much on his innocence". In particular, his ability to cross-examine prosecution witnesses was lamentably deficient and he was: "... at a great Loss, in not knowing how to manage his Tryal; and in not asking the witnesses for the King questions proper to this; to which their Answers would certainly have cleared what was said against him."[47]

Exceptions to the Prohibition on Defence Counsel

Ironically, the common law had always allowed representation for defendants in cases involving allegations of misdemeanour. Indeed, the inferior courts in which they were normally tried appear to have provided important work for the junior Bar and an early forum for barristers attempting to gain an advocacy monopoly. Thus, at Hereford assizes in March 1663, Sir Robert Hide told the assembled JPs for the county that "none but councell learned

---

47. R. Smith, *Mistaken Justice: or, Innocence condemn'd, in the person of Francis Newland*, London, 1695, p.27.

ought to move at [quarter sessions], and not attorneys".[48]

Counsel regularly attended quarter sessions when the parties were rich enough to pay their fees (not a very frequent event). Thus, in October 1681, Slingsby Bethel was tried for assaulting a waterman during a political fracas. Three lawyers represented the prosecution, including two eminent barristers (one of them John Holt). A barrister also represented the defendant.[49]

Counsel were allowed to argue points of pure law at felony trials, in open court, a right that dated back to the fifteenth century. As a result, in 1664, the Quaker, Margaret Fell, indicted at the Lancaster assizes had counsel to plead, who "found many errors in her indictment and so she was put by".[50] Similarly, in 1729, Major John Oneby, who had been tried for murdering a man in a 'duel' and received a special verdict, referable to the opinion of the 12 judges, had counsel to argue his case at the court of King's Bench, two barristers, a solicitor and a clerk being assigned to him.[51] Nevertheless, this exception was quite restrictively interpreted. At his trial for treason, before his peers, in 1680, Lord Stafford had the assistance of "what Counsel he would to direct him in his plea, that stood by him". However, there were quickly objections that they were 'overstepping the

---

48. H. Townshend, *Notes of the Office of a Justice of Peace 1661-3*, R.D. Hunt (Ed.), Worcester, Worcestershire Historical Society, 1967, p.114.
49. Anon, *The Tryal of Slingsby Bethel*, London, R. Harbottle, 1681, pp.1-9.
50. G. Fox, *The Journal of George Fox*, London, Religious Society of Friends, 1975, at p.477.
51. J.L Rayner and G.T. Crook (Eds.), *The Complete Newgate Calendar* (vols. 1-5), London, Privately printed for the Navarre Society, 1926, vol. III, p.54.

mark' by prompting him on points of fact.

Prosecuting Counsel

There was never a formal bar on prosecuting counsel in felony trials. They could be briefed by the victim of the felony, his relatives or the state. Thus, in the prosecution of the killers of Anthony Thynne, the dead man's brother had "counsel instructed and wait[ing] here to go on". He had paid for a barrister, Sir Francis Withins, to prosecute the case.[52] Obviously, the government would fund prosecution counsel in treason cases (at Stafford's trial in 1680 four eminent lawyers appeared for the Crown).[53] Serious non-political crimes, which lacked an obvious prosecutor, perhaps because the victim had been murdered, might also occasionally attract state funded counsel, especially in London and the Home counties. Thus, the wife of George Saunders, tried for his murder in 1583, was prosecuted by "master Geffrey, the Queene's maiesties Serjeant".[54] If, as in the case of Spencer Cowper and his co-defendants at the Hertford assizes in 1699, the accused were lawyers it also made sense to have the Crown represented by counsel.[55]

---

52. Anon, *The Tryal and Condemnation of George Brosky*, p.4.
53. J. Evelyn, *The Diary of John Evelyn*, E.S. De Beer (Ed.), Oxford, Clarendon Press, 1955, vol. IV, p.229.
54. Anon, A *briefe discourse of the late murther of Master George Saunders*, London, Henry Bynnemen, 1573, f.B3.
55. Earl of Birkenhead, *Famous Trials of History*, vol. 1, New York, Doubleday, Doran and Co., 1926, p.92.

In the early eighteenth century, the number of lawyers appearing for the prosecution increased significantly, and the government became more willing to pay for such counsel, at least in grave crimes. Thus, in the 1720s, under Sir Robert Walpole's administration, the Crown hired lawyers to ensure that some cases of murder, rape and gang robbery were prosecuted effectively. At the trial of Richard ('Dick') Turpin, for horse theft, at the York assizes, in 1739, the Crown was represented by the distinguished lawyer, Thomas Place (also Recorder of the City of York) and another barrister, Richard Crowle.[56] Private individuals, especially thief takers seeking rewards, may also have contributed to this process by hiring counsel to boost their chances of securing a conviction (and thus a reward). Nevertheless, the presence of prosecuting counsel was rare. Most cases were prosecuted by victims, not lawyers, if only for reasons of expense. Like defendants, prosecutors might find this difficult, and excessive zeal or timidity by an unrepresented victim could be counterproductive, if less disastrously so than for the accused. Thus, in 1727, when Margaret Brown stood trial at the Old Bailey for theft, it was recorded that the prosecutor: "... charged the Prisoner with more heat than became her in a Court of Justice; it being the Prosecutor's Place only to swear to the best of their Knowledge, and that too, with Decorum, Caution, and a calm undisturbed Disposition of Mind." She failed to show

---

56. T. Kyll, *The Trial of the notorious Highwayman Richard Turpin*, York, 1739, pp.1-3.

sufficient restraint and Brown was acquitted.[57]

Advent of Defence Counsel for Treason and Felonies

A breach was made in the general rule excluding defence counsel by the 1696 *Act for Regulating of Trials in Cases of Treason*, which allowed those accused of treason legal representation on both legal *and* factual matters for the first time. This provision was a reflection of unease at the conduct of earlier Stuart treason cases, lengthy hearings in which distinguished lawyers appeared for the Crown against unrepresented defendants. Although confined to treason trials, the 1696 Act set an important precedent for the introduction of defence counsel into felony trials in the following century. The growth in the use of prosecution counsel in felony trials in the early 1700s, which appeared to shift the balance in favour of the Crown, may also have led to a general feeling that it was unfair to leave defendants unrepresented. Some judges probably sympathised with men like one Power, who, in 1731, at his trial for being an incendiary, complained to the court about the unfairness of being faced by counsel: "I did not expect so vigorous a Prosecution; here is Counsel speaks against me; I am a naked person, and no advantages of this kind allow'd me."[58] This may have encouraged judges to attempt to 'level' the situation. Whatever the motivation, and without there being

---

57. Landsman, "The rise of the contentious spirit," p.519.
58. *The Gentlemen's Magazine*, 1731, vol. 1, p.397.

any formal change in the law, defence counsel started to appear in felony trials at the assizes and Old Bailey in the early 1730s, albeit in very small numbers. The previous rule against representation appears to have been tacitly abandoned.[59] By 1736, Henry Justice, although himself a (fortuitously named) barrister, was willing to employ counsel at his trial at the Old Bailey for stealing books (though his deafness, and the fact that the Crown was legally represented, may also have encouraged representation). Similarly, Amy Hutchinson, who was executed at Ely, in November 1750, for the murder of her husband, had defence counsel at her trial, albeit to no avail.[60]

However, initially, counsel began by strengthening the defence side, rather than by taking it over (a development that would not occur until the end of the eighteenth century).[61] Thus, although Justice's lawyer argued numerous points of law on his client's behalf, and asked many questions, his interjections were matched by those made personally by the defendant. Lawyers still did not dominate the hearing, even when employed.[62] Ultimately, the advent of counsel was to be enormously significant to the development of the common law criminal trial. Their

59. Beattie, "Scales of Justice," pp.221-225.
60. Rayner and Crook, *The Complete Newgate Calendar*, vol. III, pp.185-186.
61. C. Allen, *The Law of Evidence in Victorian England*, Cambridge, CUP, 1997, p.146.
62. P. Gaskell, "Henry Justice, a Cambridge Book Thief," *Transactions of the Cambridge Bibliographical Society*, 1952, pp.348-357, I am grateful to Dr Jonathan Smith, Librarian, Trinity College Library, Cambridge, for this reference.

presence increased the number of witnesses likely to be called, led to closer cross-examination of those witnesses, and the development of increasingly defined rules of evidence, producing a far more adversarial trial than had traditionally been the case in England.[63] Nevertheless, these changes are largely outside the time frame of this book; even in the 1750s, Sir Dudley Ryder's judicial notebooks suggest that there was still only a trickle of lawyers appearing for either the prosecution or the defence.[64]

---

63. J.D. Rice, "The criminal trial Before and After the Lawyers: Authority, Law and Culture in Maryland Jury Trials, 1681-1837," *American Journal of Legal History*, 1996, vol. 40, no. 4, p.459.
64. Langbein, "Historical Foundations of the Law of Evidence: A View From the Ryder Sources," *Columbia Law Review*, 1996, vol.96, p.1197.

Chapter 15

The Course of the Trial

Who finds the heifer dead and bleeding fresh,
And sees fast by a butcher with an axe,
But will suspect 'twas he that made the slaughter,
William Shakespeare, Henry V1, Part 2, Act iii, Scene 2

The trial process normally began with those accused who were in custody, being brought to court "by the gaoler all chained one to another".[1] If not in prison they would answer to their bail, when summoned at the start of proceedings, so as not to forfeit their recognisances. The first stage would be for the grand jury to consider the validity of their bills of indictment.

The Grand Jury

The grand jury was established by a series of twelfth century ordinances intended to improve procedures for prosecuting crime. Its original duty was to inform the itinerant royal judges of the most serious offences committed in each locality, and to name any man "accused or notoriously suspect of being a robber or murderer or thief". Thus, it began life primarily as a jury of presentment. Arguably, it was older than the criminal petty jury as those

---

1.   Sir T. Smith, *De Republica Anglorum*, London, 1583, p.112.

presented were normally tried by ordeal until after 1215.[2] However, in the ensuing centuries it acquired another judicial function, the scrutiny of indictments, so that by the early modern period it had, in theory, a dual role, either to: "... receive the indictments, or of their own knowledge to present any offenders against his Majesties lawes; and the like course hath hitherto ben used at the Assizes, for that such persons are better acquainted with the Comon grievance of the Countrie, then Justices are."[3] Despite the theory, in practice, by then, very few felonies were being presented at assizes by the grand jury on its own initiative. Its scrutinising function had become paramount. Nevertheless, the (near) fiction of presentment lived on, being alluded to in an 'exhortation to the jury' by assizes judges in 1606. In it, they claimed that as they could not deal with crimes without information, they had summoned the grand jurors from: "... all parts of this Shire, as men which by common intendment, in respect of your intercourses, cannot be altogether ignorant of such offences, as we have power to deale withall, committed within the severall divisions and places of your habitation."[4]

At quarter sessions, it was slightly more common for the grand jury to present cases, and in some counties, such as Sussex, this ought to have been facilitated by the practice of

---

2. J.C. Oldham, "The Origins of the Special Jury," *University of Chicago Law Review*, 1983, vol. 50, p.613..

3. J.C. Morrill, *The Cheshire Grand Jury 1625-1659*, Leicester, Leicester University Press, 1976, p.5

4. R. Crompton, *L'office et auctority de justices de Peace*, London, The Company of Stationers, 1606, p.2.

using constables as sessions grand jurors. However, regular admonitions from JPs and judges make it clear that even in this forum relatively few cases were being initiated in this way. Thus, William Lambarde regularly exhorted the quarter sessions grand jury for Kent to be more active in presenting offences. In 1587, he stressed to them that: "Your oath and duty is not only to hear and receive what others shall bring but also to inquire and present what yourselves do know." He, too, reminded them that they were: "... gathered of diverse parts, dispersed throughout the shire (if it were so many eyes put into one head) that nothing might escape your sight and knowledge." In another address to this body, in the same year, he complained that some of its members would not present their social superiors for fear that they would be angry and might seek revenge. Others allegedly protected their personal friends.[5] Even at quarter sessions the grand jury's scrutinising role had become far more important than its presenting function.

Although the property qualification varied, it was usually much greater for membership of the grand jury than for the petit jury, especially at the assizes. Thus, in the early 1700s, it was £80 a year freehold for the former and only £10 a year freehold or copyhold for the latter.[6] This meant that, in theory, the majority of even the 'middling sort' failed to qualify as assizes grand jurors, an office which was supposed to be reserved for gentlemen and prosperous

---

5.   C. Read (Ed.), *William Lambarde and Local Government*, New York, Cornell University Press, Ithaca, 1962, (written in 1580-1588), p.88.
6.   G. Jacob, *The Compleat Parish Officer*, 7th edn., p.24.

merchants. Indeed, the grand jury was partly so called because its social status was higher than that of the trial jury (its larger size also partly explained the title). However, this social superiority was not always manifest in reality. In 1652, Leach felt that, unlike earlier periods: "... in these latter times Sheriffs have been more carelesse and negligent in returning honest and able men for Grand Jury-men." There were, apparently, fewer knights, esquires and gentlemen sitting than formerly. He also complained that sheriffs were doing favours for personal acquaintances, relieving them of the onerous duty by not summoning them (itself indicative of the office's popularity), although it should have been viewed as a prestigious form of public service. Leach favoured a system of public nomination and lottery to ensure that only the best men, selected for their estates and personal qualities, were chosen.[7] Also indicative of a fairly wide social composition, the grand jury that returned a *billa vera* against John Selman, before to his trial at King's Bench in 1611, included only one gentleman and two esquires, but had 15 yeomen.[8]

Normally, there was a social distinction between those who sat on the more prestigious assizes grand jury and the slightly humbler men who filled the equivalent body at quarter sessions, though a neat social distinction between the two was not always found, and even the inferior court's grand jury was supposed to be of special status and ability.

---

7.   W. Leach, *The Bribe-Takers of Jury-Men, partiall, Dishonest, and Ignorant Discovered and Abolished*, London, 1652, pp.5 and 12.
8.   Anon, *The Arraignment of John Selman ...*, London, 1612, p.7.

Thus, according to an undated order of the Jacobean Privy Council: "For the great Inquest at the Quarter Sessions, the sherife of the Countie returneth by warrant, two, or three out of every hundred, of the most discreet, able and sufficent persons, both for their estates and understanding." In Cheshire and some other shires, the same men normally sat on both grand juries. By contrast, in some counties, such as Oxfordshire, JPs could frequently be found sitting on the assizes grand jury, and in Sussex they were expected to serve in this capacity. In others, such as Essex, Somerset or Staffordshire, such a practice was rare.[9]

After its members were sworn, the grand jury went through the bills of indictment in private (to prevent external influence and pressure), usually in a chamber close to the main courtrooms. Secrecy of proceedings was a vital part of the grand jurors' oath. According to John Somers, confidentiality about evidence, any witnesses heard, and the jury's deliberations, helped to prevent the escape of criminals still at liberty by leaked 'intelligence'. It also established whether witnesses were biased, preserved independence of decision-making and protected the innocent from the work of "false accusers and malicious Conspirators".[10] If the grand jury found a bill to be: "... true they do nothing but write on the backe of it, *billa vera* ... Then he who is there named is called indicted." However, if they did not find a case to answer they would write

---

9.   Morrill, *The Cheshire Grand Jury 1625-1659*, pp.5 and 41.

10. J. Somers, *The Security of Inglish-Mens Lives, or the Trust, Power, and Duty of the Grand Jurys of England*, London, Benj. Alsop, 1682, pp.21-23 and 44.

ignoramus on it and return it to the JPs by whom it was "rent in peeces immediately". Once a man was indicted, he would be treated more strictly, perhaps losing his liberty pending the outcome of the trial if he was on bail.[11] Grand jurors normally considered only prosecution evidence, usually the depositions and examinations submitted by JPs and the testimony of live witnesses. The proportion of oral evidence that would be heard varied. It was normally provided that those who had appeared at assizes with information that they wished to present should be sent to the grand jury, accompanied by a bailiff, to "give their evidence".[12] This might allow proceedings to be initiated by presentment, or, if they had already been commenced via a JP, increase the prospects of a *billa vera* being found. Similarly, at the start of quarter sessions, an accuser was often called into court and asked to prepare a bill of indictment against the prisoner, and then to go with it to the grand jury, and "give evidence upon their oaths, he and the witnesses".[13] However, evidence or information, other than that provided by live witnesses, or contained in formal depositions, appears not to have been received, especially if not requested. Thus, in 1662, one Edward Pitt, an apothecary in Worcester, was, by Sir Robert Hide: "... severly chekt for writing to the [assizes] Grand Jury his judgment in a case of indictment, not being desired, of a woman supposed to be

---

11. Sir T. Smith, *De Republica Anglorum*, p.105.
12. H. Twyford, *The Office of the Clerk of Assize*, London, 1676, p.7.
13. Sir F. Bacon, "The Use Of The Law," *The Works of Francis Bacon*, vol. 3, B. Montagu (Ed.), Philadelphia, Carey and Hart, 1841, p.250.

with child, and afterwards either miscarried or mistaken."[14] Like a modern magistrates' committal hearing (which serves much the same purpose), the grand jury did not need to hear evidence beyond that which indicated a clear prima facie case, shortage of time often not allowing for more. If they wished to dismiss a bill of indictment, it was considered correct to hear or read all of the potential evidence: "It is very safe for Grand Jurors, before they find a Ignoramus, to examine every witness produced, but if they have many witnesses in Murder or Felony, if any one witness induce a strong and pregnant presumption it is enough, without perplexing themselves, in hast of business, they need not examine any more, but put *billa vera* unto it."[15] Unlike the trial jury, their numbers were not limited to a dozen men and decisions were reached by simple majority rather than unanimously, though at least 12 men had to be agreed that there was a case to answer before they could indict.[16] At the assizes, bodies of up to 27 men were sometimes found, an odd number preventing 'hung' juries.[17] At the quarter sessions, the grand jury was often made up of 16 'discreet' freeholders chosen from a panel of 24 men summoned by the sheriff.[18] If caseloads permitted, the grand jury would spend the first morning of the assizes

---

14. H. Townshend, *Notes of the Office of a Justice of Peace 1661-3*, R.D. Hunt (Ed.), Worcester, Worcestershire Historical Society, 1967, p.100.
15. Z. Babington, *Advice to Grand Jurors in Cases of Blood*, London, John Amery, 1677, p.130.
16. J. Somers, *The Security of Inglish-Mens Lives, or the Trust, Power, and Duty of the Grand Jurys of England*, London, Benj. Alsop, 1682, p.9
17. Morrill, *The Cheshire Grand Jury 1625-1659*, p.5.
18. Bacon, "The Use Of The Law," p.250.

considering bills of indictment with the trials of those they found *billa vera* running from the same afternoon.[19] Not infrequently, however, pressure of time meant that trials would convene as soon as the first bills certified *billa vera* arrived from the grand jury room. In passing, it should be noted that as well as scrutinising indictments, grand jurors, especially those at assizes, had an important role in speaking as the 'body of the county' when their local community wished to complain to higher authority.

Plea

Assuming that an indictment was passed *billa vera*, the arraignment took place in open court. The defendants were called to the bar and the first to face trial would be ordered by the court clerk to "hold up thy hand". This ensured that the correct prisoner was tried for the right offence. Although the indictment was in Latin until Lady-day 1733 (apart from a brief period during the Interregnum), the details were also read to the jury in English.[20] The need for this ended when the 1731 Act for 'Englishing' the law came into force, and the vernacular replaced the legal languages of Latin and Law French on all legal documents, including indictments. The Act also stipulated that such documents must be written in a clearly 'legible' hand, rather than traditional 'court

19. Twyford, *The Office of the clerk of Assize*, p.7.
20. F. Grigor, *Sir John Fortescue's Commendation of the Laws of England: The Translation into English of De Laudibus Legum Angliae*, London, Sweet and Maxwell, 1917, (written c.1461-5, first published in Latin c.1537), p.41.

hand'.[21] By then, some 200 years had passed since Thomas Starkey had called for the replacement of Law French, so that Englishmen could readily understand the laws that they were required to obey, assuming that the existing situation was "a thing that no man may well defend".[22] Over a century had passed since James I had made a similar request.

Although the indictment would normally only specify offences committed within the county in which it was being tried, a Henrician statute (H.8.ca.14) provided that a defendant indicted in one county could be tried at the same time for offences committed in neighbouring shires.[23] After the clerk had read out the indictment in English he asked: "How sayest thou ... [name] art thou guilty of this felony as it is laid in the indictment whereof thou standest indicted or not guilty?" At this point, the accused man (or woman) had three options: "... either he doth confesse the offence, and the Indictment to bee true: or he estrangeth himself from the offence, and pleadeth, Not guiltea: or else hee doth answere indirectly, and so in effect hee standeth mute, and maketh no answere."[24] As will be seen, the last option, deliberately standing mute, had drastic consequences and rarely occurred.

A defendant always had the option of pleading guilty.

---

21. *The Gentleman's Magazine*, 1731, vol. 1, p.213, and 1733, vol. 3, p.65.
22. K.M. Burton (Ed.), *A Dialogue between Reginal Pole and Thomas Lupset*, London, Chatto and Windus, 1948, p.117.
23. Sir W. Staunford, *Les Plees Del Corone*, London, 1607, p.154.
24. F. Pulton, *De Pace Regis et Regni; Viz. A Treatise Declaring Which Be The Great And General Offences of the Realme*, London, 1623, p.177.

However, the law required that such a plea must be "free and without menace". If it appeared to have been coerced, it was the duty of the judge to "cause the prisoner to pleade to the offence, not guiltea". Thus, Pulton cited a case in which a woman had tried to plead guilty to the theft of two shillings worth of bread, after apparent pressure to do so from her husband. Detecting this, the trial judges "for Pitie would not record the offence" and insisted she change her plea. Their decision was justified when the jury acquitted her on the basis that she had acted under her spouse's duress. As this case suggests, it was especially important that a not guilty plea be entered where it was apparent that legal ignorance might make the defendant "confesse the offence in mistaking of the law". For example, an accused person might not appreciate that a vital element of an offence was not made out. Judicial alertness to such possibilities was vital given the absence of defence counsel in felony trials.[25] Thus, in 1530, St Germain stressed that if a defendant: "... wyll pleade that he never knewe the man that was slayne or that he never had a peny worthe of the goods that is supposed that he sholde steele in these cases the Judges are bounde in consyence to enforme hym that he muste take the generall yssue and plede that he is not gyltye."[26] How frequent such judicial care was in reality, is harder to establish.

Although the courts usually accepted a guilty plea, if properly entered, for convenience and correctness of

---

25. Pulton, *De Pace Regis et Regni*, London, 1623, p.177.
26. Plucknett and Barton, *2nd Dialogue*, pp.284-285.

adjudication, it was widely felt that there was no moral or legal requirement on a defendant to acknowledge the truth of the indictment against him. As the Reverend John Sym noted in 1637, the law: "... doth permit and accept of such an affirmative answer but neither commands nor commends it because the law takes notice of things and censures them politically and not theologically considered." Sym was convinced that even where a defendant was guilty of a felony he could quite morally put the prosecution to strict proof of their case, although, if convicted, he should admit the offence prior to execution. It was axiomatic that "no man is bound to betray himself". In many situations, by pleading not guilty, a defendant was not lying, but merely putting the issue: "... to a *legall triall*, whether his fact shall bee found against him in that sense and forme, as in those *Law termes*."[27]

Unsurprisingly, by modern standards, guilty pleas were exceptionally rare in felony cases. The normal brevity of criminal trials meant there was little necessity for the state to provide encouragement for them, and, given the limited number and fixed nature of the punishments available for most crimes (usually death for felonies), there was little incentive for the defendant to plead guilty. Additionally, for one reason or another, there was always the possibility that prosecution witnesses would not attend court to give evidence or might falter in their testimony. Even if they did not, a trial might throw up mitigating circumstances that would encourage a post-conviction reprieve or, more

---

27. Sym, *Life's Preservative Against Self-Killing*, London, 1637, p.102.

commonly, the trial jury might commit 'pious perjury' and acquit or convict for a lesser offence. As a result, numerous contemporary observers noted that guilty pleas were unusual, and frequently discouraged, even by the judiciary. In 1680, Mathew Hale was convinced that many judges would actively advise a defendant who wished to plead guilty to "put himself upon his trial". The rarity of such pleas, even where there had been extensive pre-trial admissions during a magistrate's examination, was reflected in Sir Thomas Smith's introductory remarks on contested trials in the 1560s: "If he plead not guiltie, as commonly all theeves, robbers, and murderers doe, though they have confessed the fact before the Justice of the peace that examined them." Little had changed a century later, when Henri Misson observed that at arraignment if a defendant: "... answers Guilty, (*which very seldom happens*) he is sent back to Prison till the Time comes for pronouncing sentence upon him."[28] Similarly, in the 1720s, Cesar de Saussure also noted that a plea of guilty: "... rarely occurs, for every criminal prefers trying to escape by pleading 'Not Guilty'."[29] Even two of the four highwaymen caught red-handed, in front of up to 200 witnesses, after a ferocious battle at Hampstead in 1674, sought to contest their trials after they

---

28. M. Misson, *Memoirs and Observations in his Travels over England*, J. Ozell (Trans.), London, 1719, p.326.
29. M. Van Muyden (Ed. and Trans.), A *foreign View of England in the reigns of George I and George II; The letters of Monsieur Cesar de Saussure, to his Family*, London, John Murray, 1902, p.120.

were sent from Newgate to the Sessions House.[30]
Nevertheless, care must be taken with generalisations
based on Old Bailey experience, and even at that court, a
number of defendants *did* plead guilty if they thought their
situation was hopeless. In other courts, it was slightly more
common. King's Bench, in particular, seems to have
witnessed a somewhat higher number of guilty pleas than
was typical elsewhere. Thus, the pickpocket John Selman,
having been caught red-handed, "answered guilty" when
arraigned there in 1611.[31] The following year, when the
Scottish Lord Sanquire was arraigned at the same court as
an accessory to murder, he too "confessed the indictment",
and was thereupon condemned and executed in Palace
Yard.[32] Although the assizes showed *relatively* few guilty
pleas, according closely to Old Bailey practice in this
respect, there were exceptions in these forums as well. Thus,
in Kent, in 1602, a significant number of defendants
'confessed' at their arraignment at the county assizes. Pleas
of guilty to felony where the consequences of conviction
were not expected to be severe were also more common.
Hence, in 1678, William Shakesby: "... confess'd himself
guilty of that [bullock theft] and all other offences within the
benefit of clergy."[33] For similar reasons, guilty pleas were

---

30. Anon, *The Confession Of the Four High-Way-Men; As it was Written by One of
    them, and Allowed by the Rest*, London, 1674, pp.3-4.
31. Anon, *The arraignment of John Selman ...*, London, 1612, p.13.
32. Rayner and Crook, *The Complete Newgate Calendar*, vol. I, p.36.
33. Anon, *An exact account of the trials of the several persons arraigned at the
    sessions-house in the Old-Bailey for London and Middlesex*, London, Gilham
    Hills, 1678, p.4.

also more frequent at misdemeanour trials, the stakes being comparatively small.

Peine Forte et Dure

Deliberately refusing to enter a plea had dire consequences: "Such felons as stand mute, and speak not at their arraignment, are pressed to death by huge weights laid upon a board, that lieth over their breast, and a sharp stone under their backs."[34] This assumes, of course, that they were 'mute of malice'. If "mute by the visitation of God", because, for example, they were dumb, a not guilty plea would be entered on their behalf. Pressing, and the strange dietary regime that traditionally accompanied it, was a relic of the situation before 1215 in which a defendant had to 'choose' jury trial rather than that by ordeal. If he was reluctant to choose he had to be 'encouraged' to do so. Under the Statute of Westminster of 1275, the peine was imposed solely by imprisoning and starving defendants into submission. In 1406, however, pressing to death was added to the regime, perhaps as a result of the growing need for expeditiousness in the trial process. The combination of the two produced the hybrid version described by Henri Misson in the 1690s:

"He is stretchd'd out naked upon his Back, and his Arms and Legs drawn out by Cords, and fasten'd to the

---

34. Canon W. Harrison, *Elizabethan England, edited from the Description of England*, London, Camelot Series, E. Rhys (Ed.), 1889, p.244.

four Corners of the Dungeon, A Board or Plate of Iron is laid upon his stomach, and this is heep'd up with stones to a certain weight. The next Day they give him, at three different Times, three little Morsels of Barly Bread, and nothing to drink. The next day three little Glasses of water, and nothing to eat: And if he continues in his obstinacy, they leave him in that condition 'till he dies."[35]

It would normally be conducted in the local prison; at Newgate, it took place in the appropriately named Press Yard. Noblemen were subject to the regime in the same way as commoners. Thus, on February 28, 1556, when Lord Stourton was arraigned at Westminster Hall for murder, he initially would not answer the charge made against him: "... till at last the Lord Chief Justice declared to him that he must be pressed to death, according to the laws of the land, if he would not answer; after which he made answer."[36] Nor was the rule confined to men. In 1616, Arthur Turnour recorded being told by Mr Long, the Clerk of the Peace for Middlesex, that if a woman stood mute and refused to plead: "... she shall have judgment of *peine forte et dure* as well as a man. Which thing he affirmed that he had seene in experience often at Newgate." Even worse, and unlike females facing execution, according to Long, a woman who faced pressing would: "... not have the benefit of her belly. The reason is, because of her wilfull contempt of her

---

35.   Misson, *Memoirs and Observations in his Travels over England*, p.218.
36.   Rayner and Crook, *The Complete Newgate Calendar*, vol. I, p.24.

tryall."[37] However, as Henri Misson noted, pressing was not necessary in cases of high treason, as opposed to felony and petty treason, because in these cases "their silence would condemn them".[38] (Perhaps given the draconian punishment for treason more traitors might otherwise have been willing to face pressing.) Similarly, silence in the face of misdemeanour indictments was considered to be tantamount to a guilty plea, precluding the need for pressing in minor cases. In the 1650s, in his reforming legal work *England's balme*, William Sheppard recommended that pressing be replaced by the automatic entry of a plea of 'not guilty'.[39] However, this suggestion was not followed. The simple expedient of treating those who were 'mute of malice' as pleading guilty was left until 1772, and the better, modern, approach of treating such behaviour as tantamount to a plea of 'not guilty' waited until 1827. The *peine* appears to have been used as late as 1742, at the Cambridge assizes.

Not surprisingly, Sir Thomas Smith could describe the *peine* as one of the 'cruellest deaths' possible. It might seem strange that anyone would submit to it. There were sound reasons for doing so. Most importantly: "In felony, the death of the party before conviction dischargeth all proceedings and forfeitures."[40] This was important as the penalty for being convicted of a felony was not limited to execution;

---

37. J.H. Baker, "Criminal Justice at Newgate 1616-1627," *The Irish Jurist*, 1973, vol. 8, p.316.
38. Misson, *Memoirs and Observations in his Travels over England*, p.218.
39. N.L. Mathews, *William Sheppard, Cromwell's Law Reformer*, Cambridge, CUP, 1984, p.73.
40. Sir F. Bacon, *Cases of Treason*, London, John More, 1641, p.13.

generally, there also followed: "... corruption of bloud, except it bee in cases made felony by speciall statutes, with a proviso that there shall be no corruption of blood."[41] This had major legal consequences; most importantly, a convicted felon would forfeit to the Crown all his lands, tenements and goods and chattels. Thus, in theory, most of a convict's property was lost to his family. Those who died before conviction avoided this. However, suicide was shameful and a special felony potentially resulting in forfeiture in its own right. As a result, pressing was chosen by some "strong and stout hearted" individuals, because, not being convicted "his blood is not corrupted, his lands nor goods confiscate to the Prince, which in all cases of felonie are commonly lost from him and his heires".[42] Between 1607 and 1616 it has been estimated that Middlesex and the City of London alone witnessed 32 cases of people being pressed to death for refusing to enter a plea.[43]

There was some legal confusion, and local variations, as to the extent of the property that would be forfeit to the Crown. Thus, the provision does not appear to have extended to "lands intailed". Additionally, in Kent, even fee simple lands were exempt as the county's unusual system of succession on death, 'gavelkind', whereby there was no free alienation of property, meant that any heir to property secured his inheritance "notwithstanding the offence of his ancestors". However, this indulgence did not extend to

---

41. Bacon, *Cases of Treason*, p.12.
42. Smith, *De Republica Anglorum*, p.112.
43. P. Jenkins, "From Gallows to Prison? The Execution Rate in Early Modern England," *Criminal Justice History*, 1996, vol. 17, pp.56-60.

treason, and, according to Lambarde, might not even have covered new statute created felonies.[44] Many commentators felt that pressing meant that although the accused man saved his lands, he still forfeited his goods.[45] In practice, though, they often seem to have saved their chattels as well and "save[d] their goods unto their wives and children".[46]

Unsurprisingly, very few poor men refused to enter a plea, having little to save that was of interest to the Crown. This gradually extended higher up the social scale as juries increasingly returned a formalised answer, irrespective of the truth, when asked what property a convict possessed, "their common answer is, none to our knowledge".[47] In the 1560s, the sheriff would still sometimes make enquiries about a convict's property, despite such a verdict. This level of care became increasingly infrequent. Some deprecated the almost ritual jury verdict on a prisoner's estates, given "according to form" and with no proper enquiry about its accuracy, believing that it encouraged criminals. A thief would know that it was likely that his money and chattels would go to "his whore, or his Bastard" rather than the Crown, after his execution.[48] Nevertheless, even the Court of King's Bench was sympathetic to the pick-pocket John Selman's request that, after he was executed, his body might

---

44. W. Lambarde, A *Perambulation of Kent*, London, Baldwin, Cradock Joy & Co., 1570, p.616.
45. Bacon, *Cases of Treason*, p.13.
46. Canon W. Harrison, *A Description of England*, (2nd book, 2nd edn., 1587), London, New Shakespeare Society, 1877, p.228.
47. T.W., *The Clerk of Assize*, London, Timothy Twyford, 1660, p.16.
48. Anon, *Hanging, not Punishment Enough, for Murtherers, High-way Men, and House-Breakers*, London, A. Baldwin, 1701, pp.12-13.

be delivered to his wife for a Christian burial, and the "goods which he had, (part of which was welgotten, some otherwise) might not bee taken from her". The judges acceded to this, provided that he was forthcoming in revealing the identities of other London cutpurses to the authorities.[49] Similarly, although citing the wish to avoid loss of property as a reason for undergoing pressing, Cesar de Saussure also noted that it was very rare for the King to make use of this privilege. Instead the monarch: "... almost always gives up these possessions in favour of the families of the criminals."[50] By the mid-eighteenth century, only a few thousand pounds a year were being recovered for the Crown via this mechanism.

Nevertheless, although most of the low to middle income defendants coming before the courts produced such 'routine' verdicts when convicted, forfeiture for felony was not formally abolished until 1871.[51] Additionally, where the hanged man was obviously rich it was harder for the jury to return such a customary verdict, and the Crown was much more likely to take an interest in the felon's estate. Thus, for the few defendants with substantial assets, confiscation remained a concern. As a result, in 1659, Major Strangeways, accused of shooting dead a lawyer named Fussell who was intimate with the officer's sister, resolved not to plead to save his estates. This also explains why, in 1676, Sir John Reresby, a Yorkshire magnate, believed that the Duke of

49.   Anon, *The arraignment of John Selman ...*, 1612, p.13
50.   Muyden, *A foreign View of England in the reigns of George I and George II*, p.119.
51.   E. Melling (Ed.), *Crime and Punishment, Kentish Sources VI*, Maidstone, Kent County Council, 1969, p.7.

Newcastle, with whom he had earlier had a legal dispute and other differences, was behind malicious gossip accusing him of causing the death of John Black, his (Reresby's) negro servant boy, by 'gelding' him. Reresby thought this was done with a view to getting him accused and convicted and that Newcastle: "... had waited upon the King to beg my estate in case it proved forfeited by this felony."[52] However, for reasons that are not always entirely clear, a few brave but relatively poor individuals also refused to enter a plea. Sometimes, this may have been done to avoid the stigma of a conviction for shameful offences and the infamy of public hanging, so sparing their families extra distress. They also escaped being humiliated at trial by prosecutors and witnesses they considered to be their bitter enemies.[53]

Some defendants entered pleas when threatened by such draconian treatment, and, if a change of heart appeared likely, an accused person's thumbs might first be tied with whipcord, a milder form of torture that could make pressing unnecessary. Others were resolute to the end. Thus, in 1659, Major Strangeways did not flinch when Lord Chief Justice Glynn ordered that he be loaded with "as much iron and stone as he can bear".[54] In Strangeway's case, however, the sometimes drawn-out process was surprisingly quick, perhaps because it was accepted that the ex-soldier would show fortitude and refuse to change his mind. The major was draped in a mourning cloak, and accompanied to his

---

52. A.F. Oakley, "Sir John Reresby and the Moor - A 17th century Coroner's Inquest," *History of Medicine*, 1971, vol. 3, p.27.
53. J. Sym, *Life's Preservative Against Self-Killing*, London, 1637, p.96.
54. Anon, *The unhappy marksman*, London, TN, 1659, p.22.

death by his friends, who, like the intimates of condemned men at Tyburn, also assisted in expediting the process. Despite stones and lumps of iron being rapidly piled upon Strangeways, the weight remained insufficient to kill him and he stayed alive until they hastened death by standing on the weights.[55] This killed him within 10 minutes, even though he was "prohibited that usuall favour in that kind, to have a sharp piece of timber lodged under his back". Some observers believed that this accelerated death.[56] (Others felt that the victim's pains were actually enhanced by placing a "sharpe stone under their backs".)[57] Not surprisingly, however, witnesses heard Major Strangeway's "dying groans filling the uncouth dungeon with the Voyce of Terrour".[58]

A 'not guilty' plea was, as Ferdinando Pulton noted in 1609, the "most common and usual plea" in a felony trial, and also one that "receiveth great favour in the Law". After a defendant had entered such a plea he would be asked "How will you be tried?" To which the prisoner had to reply "By God and my country". (A formal legacy of the use of alternative methods of trial: ordeal, battle etc., in the medieval period.)[59] The clerk would then say "God send you a good deliverance" and a contested trial would ensue.

---

55. W. Andrews, *Bygone Punishments*, London, W. Andrews & Co., 1899, p.93.
56. Anon, *The unhappy marksman*, p.30.
57. Harrison, *A Description of England*, p.228.
58. Anon, *The unhappy marksman*, p.29.
59. Sir J.F. Stephen, *A history of the Criminal Law of England*, 3 vols, London, Macmillan, 1883, vol. 1, pp.298-299.

Brevity of Criminal Trials

Criminal trials were normally very brief. This was a matter of necessity, as there might be over 50 of them set down for trial at each town on an assizes circuit, especially in the earlier part of our period. Thus, in 1694, during the Oxford Circuit assizes, Mr. Justice Rokeby was listed to preside over 225 trials, of which 198 actually took place, the remainder presumably 'folding' due to witnesses not turning up or defendants escaping or failing to answer to their bail. Most of these would have been criminal matters (civil hearings taking considerably longer).[60] Exigencies of time and heavy case loads meant that the sitting hours kept by courts were often much greater than they are today, producing long working days, 12 hours not being unusual. Thus, Fleetwood, writing to Lord Burghley in 1585, noted that at one Friday sessions at the Old Bailey, the court had sat from 7 a.m. to 7 p.m.[61] At provincial assizes, pressures to extend the day could be even greater, as there was always another venue to move on to. Nevertheless, even allowing for longer sittings, most trials lasted less than 30 minutes, sometimes significantly so. Over 20 trials a day might be heard, and at least 15 was normal. The acute pressure of legal business can be seen in the drastic steps taken by John Bunyan to draw the alleged illegality of his (first) imprisonment, imposed at an earlier quarter sessions, to the attention of the assizes

---

60. Rokeby, *The Diary of Mr Justice Rokeby*, London, Wyman & Sons, 1887, p.40.
61. E. Hext, "Letter written by E. Hext to Lord Burghley," *Tudor Economic Documents*, R.H. Tawney and E. Power (Eds.), London, Longmans, 1951, vol. 2, p.337.

judges sitting at Bedford, in August 1661. He initially sent his wife to deliver a written petition to Sir Mathew Hale and his co-adjutor, Sir Thomas Twisden, when they were dining with local JPs and gentry at the Swan Inn. Fearing this would not be enough, and that they might: "... through the multitude of business, forget me, we did throw another petition into the coach to Judge Twisdon."[62] It should also be remembered that a combination of judicial expeditiousness and the early modern lack of technicality, legal representation, exclusionary rules of evidence and voir dire proceedings (held in the absence of the jury), along with the greater level of experience manifest by many jurors when compared to their present-day counterparts, all meant that far more material could be covered within the allotted time than would be the case today. An hour of Tudor forensic time would be worth several in the modern era.

There were also occasional exceptions to the general pattern of high-speed justice. Difficult individual cases might take up to a day, although adjournment overnight, apart from treason hearings, seems virtually unheard of until late in the eighteenth century. Thus, Sir John Reresby noted that the trial of Thomas Thynne's three killers at the Old Bailey on February 28, 1682 "lasted from nine in the morning till five in the afternoon".[63] Even worse, the trial of Mrs Dorothy Longley, for murdering her husband, lasted 13

---

62. J. Bunyan, A *Relation of the Imprisonment of Mr. John Bunyan, Minister of the Gospel at Bedford ... in November 1660*, London, James Buckland, 1765, p.41.
63. Sir J. Reresby, *The Memoirs of Sir John Reresby*, London, 1734, p.82.

hours at the Guildford assizes in 1732.[64] Similarly, the trial of Spencer Cowper and his legal colleagues, also for murder, took an entire day at the Hertford assizes in 1699. So unusual was this that independent observers were concerned that important aspects of the case might have been overlooked because of its exceptional length: "The Tryal lasted many hours, and many witnesses were examined and both judge and jury were so fatigued with the tediousness therof, that it was impossible to think of everything."[65] Despite the very tight confines of the court's timetable, a certain amount of flexibility might still be allowed in scheduling. At the trial of Mary Carleton for bigamy, in the early 1660s, she "prayed time till the morrow, my witnesses not being ready". This was granted, and the matter put back until 9 a.m. the following morning. On the next day, the prosecution was not fully ready to proceed and also requested a short adjournment. One of her husbands came into court (in his wedding-suit for dramatic effect) and asked that, as his own witnesses were not yet ready, the trial "might be deferred for halfe an hour". However, by then the court's patience was exhausted and the presiding judge insisted that the matter go on immediately, declaring that they were "not bound to wait on him or his witnesses".[66]

---

64. *The Gentleman's Magazine*, 1731, vol. 1, pp.454 and 492, and 1732, vol. 2, p.676.
65. Anon, *A dialogue between a Quaker and his neighbour in Hertford, about the murder of Mrs Sarah Stout*, London, Society of Friends, 1699, pp.1-2.
66. Anon, *The Case of Madam Mary Carleton*, London, Sam Speed, 1663, pp.74-75 and p.128.

The Judicial Role and Trial Informality

According to Bacon, a judge normally had four functions at trial: "... to direct the evidence; to moderate length, repetition, or impertinency of speech; to recapitulate, select, and collate the material points, of that which hath been said; and to give the rule or sentence." However, in the case of unrepresented (i.e. most) parties in criminal trials their responsibilities could be more extensive. The absence of counsel produced a dramatic difference between felony trials and those for important civil cases. In the latter, excessive judicial interventionism was discouraged, even in the 1600s, as there would be advocates available to conduct the case so that: "It is no grace to a judge, first to find that, which he might have heard in due time from the bar; or to show quickness of conceit, in cutting off evidence or counsel too short; or to prevent information by questions - though pertinent."[67] By contrast, in felony hearings, if the court was to run efficiently, the trial judge necessarily had to dominate proceedings and conduct much of the questioning of witnesses, a role he shared with the parties themselves and, to a lesser extent, the jurors. Thus, in 1680, even the barrister Sir John Hawles accepted that, because of their experience, judges were presumed to be: "... best qualified to ask pertinent questions. And in the most perspicuous manner soonest to sift out truth from amongst the tedious impertinent circumstances and Tautologies; they therefore

---

67. Sir F. Bacon, "On Judicature," *The Essays*, London, Everyman edn., J.M. Dent, 1906, pp.162-165.

commonly *examine the witnesses* in the Court, yet not *excluding the Jury.*" (Hawles considered that jurors could ask questions of witnesses as of right and without asking judicial leave, albeit that they should do so with "modesty and discretion").[68] As a result, although trials were primarily adversarial - inevitable with victim prosecution - the judicial contribution was substantially inquisitorial. Such proofs as were adduced were as likely to be the fruits of the judge's questioning as of the parties' efforts.[69] This questioning could be searching and, at times, both aggressive and devious. Thus, when the Lord Chief Justice was questioning rioting apprentices, in 1668, he informed one defendant, who could not produce a witness to support his defence of duress, that "all that you say is of little use: for it is no great thing to make a lye to save ones life". Another prisoner, William Green, was tricked into incriminating himself. Having initially denied being at the crime scene, the judge suggested that Green might have been there, but was knocked down. When the defendant agreed with this, possibly mitigating version of events, the judge immediately responded by asking: "How could you be knockt down if you were not amongst them?"[70]

The absence of lawyers also meant that trials were

---

68. Sir J. Hawles, *The Englishmans Right*, London, 1680, p.4.
69. S. Landsman, "The rise of the contentious spirit: Adversary procedure in Eighteenth Century England," *Cornell Law Review*, 1990, vol. 75, p.505-506.
70. Anon, *The Tryals of such Persons (Peter Messenger, Richard Beasley ...) as under the Notion of London-Apprentices were tumultuously assembled in Moorfields*, 1668, London, Robert Pawlet, at pp.1-10.

usually very informal, by modern standards; there might be direct, unmediated, confrontation between prosecution witnesses and defendants. Thus, Sir Thomas Smith noted that when a trial judge was trying to establish the identity of a defendant to the satisfaction of the court:

"The partie pursuivaunt giveth good ensignes *verbi gratia*, I know thee well ynough, thou robbest me in such a place, thou beatest mee, thou tookest my horse from mee, and my purse, thou hadfst then such a coate and such a man in thy companie: the theefe will say no, and so they stand a while in altercation."[71]

Smith depicted a trial in which the defendant engaged in a 'confrontational dialogue' with the accusing witnesses, including, normally, the alleged victim, responding to each item of prosecution evidence as it came up.[72] His description accords with other contemporary portrayals, though the procedure became a little more formal in the following century, and it was never a complete 'free for all'. Thus, when, at his trial at the Old Bailey in 1660, Colonel Daniel Axtell became too "disputatious", preventing the orderly adduction of prosecution evidence by interspersing his own account of what had occurred with his questioning of the Crown's witnesses, the Lord Chief Baron urged that he: "Take the Old and Antient course, let the Witnesses that are

---

71. Smith, *De Republica Anglorum*, p.114.
72. J.H. Langbein, "The historical origins of the privilege against self-incrimination at Common Law," *Michigan Law Review*, vol. 92, p.1049.

produced for the king be all heard, then give your answer to all of them together."[73] However, the questioning of prosecution witnesses by a defendant was often done directly by him/her; alternatively, it might be done using the Bench as an intermediary. Sometimes, the informality of trials allowed dramatic forensic tests. At the trial of Moses Drayne for (an old) murder, in 1664, the Crown, possessed of the victim's skeleton, brought the dead man's skull into court, where: "... by their Direction Moses Drayne the prisoner was bid to take it up; but he trembled so much, that he could hardly hold it in his hand."[74] Unsurprisingly, in such an unstructured process, modern notions of 'closing' the prosecution case, after which fresh evidence could not be added, were largely absent. Thus, if the court or jurors were in: "... doubt of any thing that is saide, or would heare againe some of them that give evidence to interrogate them more at full, or if any that can give evidence come late: it is permitted that any that is sworn to say trueth, may be interrogated of them to enforme their consciences."[75]

Lack of Exclusionary Rules of Evidence

At no time during the period did the modern common law rules of evidence - essentially a series of exclusionary rules

---

73. H. Finch, *An Exact and Impartial Accompt Of the Indictment, Arraignment, Tryal, and Judgment (according to Law) of Twenty Nine Regicides ...*, London, Andrew Crook & Edward Powel, 1660, p.188.
74. Anon, *A True Relation of a Horrid Murder Committed upon the Person of Thomas Kidderminster of Topley ...*, p.8.
75. Smith, *De Republica Anglorum*, p.114.

preventing the adduction of certain types of information - fully exist. However, before the period ended, there were signs as to likely future developments, though these largely came to fruition in the ensuing 70 years. Professor Langbein has distinguished a pre-modern law of evidence that operated until the middle of the eighteenth century, one that was primarily concerned about the competence of a witness to give evidence and the authenticity of documents, and a modern law that emerged after the 1750s, replete with exclusionary rules governing witness testimony. An examination of the court shorthand notes of criminal trials presided over by Sir Dudley Ryder suggests that these were still largely absent, even in the 1750s.[76]

Thus, hearsay frequently went unregulated, so that witnesses might repeat what they had learned from 'a man'. Only occasionally, did judges show acute concern about its admissibility, and, when they did so, it was usually over particularly blatant examples. Hence, at the Old Bailey, in the early 1660s, during the trial of the bigamist Mary Carleton, a prosecution witness claimed to have seen one of Carleton's husbands who "did say that *James Knot* was the man that gave her in marriage to him". At this, the presiding judge (Howel) interjected: "Where is this man her husband? Hearsays must condemn no man: what do you know of your own knowledge?"[77] That this was at the Old Bailey may have been significant. The frequent use there of

---

76. J.H. Langbein, "Historical Foundations of the Law of Evidence: A View From the Ryder Sources," *Columbia Law Review*, 1996, vol. 96, p.1172.
77. Anon, *The Case of Madam Mary Carleton*, p.84.

communal benches, with several judges sitting together, its proximity to the Inns of Court and the high level of publicity accorded to hearings all probably gave a presiding judge less discretion and freedom than he would have enjoyed at a provincial assizes. Nevertheless, even in this forum, such strictness was not typical. Although hearsay was seen as an evidentiary problem, especially when tendered for the Crown, the courts were inconsistent and generally permissive in their attitudes towards it. In many cases, the hearsay provenance of evidence merely affected its weight rather than admissibility (as it does today in non-criminal cases in England). Thus, in 1678, when Richard Bradshaw was indicted for high treason (clipping the King's coin) an important prosecution witness: "... a Goldsmiths Boy shew'd some Ingots, which he had from that *Jolliffe* [who was not called], who said he had them from the Prisoner, but he was not to be found."[78] Additionally, even in the early 1700s, trial judges still willingly received testimony about defendants' prior misconduct. The general exclusion of such evidence was still many decades away. Confessions induced by duress or inducements were frequently (though not invariably) received. Opinion evidence still sometimes came from ordinary witnesses rather than experts, so that at the Old Bailey psychiatric testimony was received from a prisoner's employer and medical evidence from a publican who "cured bruises".[79]

---

78. Anon, *An exact account of the trials of the several persons arraigned at the sessions-house in the Old-Bailey for London and Middlesex*, p.23.
79. T.P. Gallanis, "The Rise of Modern Evidence Law," *Iowa Law Review*, 1999, vol. 84, p.515.

Evidential Practice

To modern eyes the evidence adduced in a criminal trial before the eighteenth century appears to be a strange combination of highly probative and equally bizarre material. Illustrative of this juxtaposition are the 'facts' of an unusual murder case from 1629, which was at first thought to have been suicide. Serjeant Maynard, present in court, carefully recorded the subsequent criminal hearing, partly because some of the evidence was so peculiar. The elderly minister of the parish where the crime was committed deposed that the victim's body had been exhumed a month after death, and four suspects (the victim's relatives) required to touch it. The results were remarkable; the: "... brow of the dead began to have a dew, or gentle sweat, arise on it, which increased by degrees, till the sweat ran down by drops on her face. The brow changed to a lively colour, and the dead opened one of her eyes and shut it again; and this opening of the eye was done three several times." Perhaps not surprisingly, even in the 1620s, many educated people, especially lawyers, were not very credulous of such matters. The presiding judge, Lord Chief Justice Nicholas Hyde, "seeming to doubt the evidence", asked the minister whether anyone else had witnessed the change. He was told that all present had observed it, and the cleric assured the judge that if anyone had suggested that this might be in issue, other witnesses could have been called to support his account. Nevertheless, the minister, observing "some admiration" in the court, stressed that it had seemed "wonderful" to him as well, and that he had no personal interest in the matter. He called his brother, another graveside witness, and also a cleric, to support his version of events.

Nonetheless, the rest of the evidence adduced at the same hearing, and its interpretation, would have been considered highly cogent and rational in any modern trial. It was a mixture of circumstantial and forensic evidence. In essence, it seemed that if the victim "did not murder herself, they [the defendants] must be the murderers", as no one else had had access to her room that night. To prove that she did not commit suicide, evidence was adduced that she lay in a "composed manner", without the bedclothes being disturbed, that her neck was broken, and that she could "not possibly break her neck in the bed if she first cut her throat, nor contra". Additionally, there was hardly any blood on the bed, but there were two streams of blood on the floor, suggesting that that was where the wounds were inflicted so that she "bled in two places severally". There was also blood *under* the mat. The knife with which she was supposed to have killed herself was found sticking in the floor, at a "good distance" from the bed, with its point towards her, and bearing the "print of a thumb and four fingers of a left hand". When Hyde demanded that the witness explain how he could distinguish the print of a left hand from that of a right hand, he provided a scientific explanation that was "tried and approved" by the court. The jury acquitted one defendant and convicted the grandmother and husband, who were executed, and the aunt, who (being pregnant) pleaded her belly.[80] As this case indicates, most early modern forensic reasoning was entirely logical. Similarly, it was argued that Sarah Stout had not been murdered in 1699 as she was found with six pounds in her pocket, indicating that she was not the victim of a violent robbery, nor was she pregnant according to the post mortem examination, suggesting that she was not killed so that "shame might have been prevented."[81]

Dislike of Circumstantial Evidence

In practice, in normal felony trials, juries were reluctant to convict, and grand juries to indict, on vague circumstantial evidence that was unsupported by either direct testimony or confessions. This is partly explained by the speed and superficiality of the era's criminal trials. There was simply not enough time, or a thorough enough pre-trial investigation, to properly explore alternative and legitimate explanations for such evidence. Thus, although the case against Dorothy Longley for murder, in 1731, was pregnant with suspicion, the trial jury, having retired for an hour to consider their verdict (a long time for the era) returned a verdict of 'Not guilty', the "Evidence to prove the Fact only

---

80. C. Johnson, *A General History of the Lives and Adventures of the Most Famous Highwaymen, Murderers, Street-Robbers*, London: J. Janeway, 1734, pp.156-157, see also Sir J. Maynard, *The case of Murther in Hertfordshire*, London, 1699.
81. Anon, *A dialogue between a Quaker and his neighbour in Hertford, about the murder of Mrs. Sarah Stout*, London, Society of Friends, 1699, p.1.

being circumstantial".[82] Without a confession to support it, such evidence rarely resulted in a conviction if the accused could also produce a 'good' character. In a case reported in the *Old Bailey Sessions Papers* in 1715, one Jane Thomas was accused of pick-pocketing; the reporter noted that although: "The Fact was prov'd very presumptuous [i.e. on a strong circumstantial basis] on the Prisoner; but the Evidence not being positive; some Persons whom she call'd to her Reputation, giving her a good Character; and that she got an honest Livelihood, she was acquitted." However, the presence of a confession made an enormous difference to an otherwise circumstantial case. In 1715, it reduced the likelihood of acquittal from 37 per cent to five per cent.[83] This was well known to examining JPs, who would be chary about allowing charges unsupported by proven bad character, direct evidence or admissions to go to trial, even if personally persuaded of a person's guilt. In the early 1600s, magistrates questioned a married couple closely and repeatedly, on suspicion of murdering two small children, who were last seen in their company. However, the pair always denied any involvement in the crime. The magistrates did not have sufficient evidence to justify bringing a case against them, despite being convinced of their guilt. As a result, they were remanded on bail, from assizes to assizes, for four years, until tangible evidence

---

82. *The Gentleman's Magazine*, 1731, vol. 1, pp.454 and 492, and 1732, vol. 2, p.676.
83. G. Fisher, "The Jury's Rise as Law Detector," *Yale Law Review*, 1997, vol. 107, p.575.

became available that led to their conviction.[84] Indeed, despite having a (false) confession by an accused man implicating two other co-defendants in a (non-existent) murder, the judge presiding over criminal cases at the Gloucester assizes in the summer of 1660 would not try the three accused for the crime "because the body was not found". Unfortunately, a different judge on the same circuit the following spring was less fastidious, and agreed to proceed with the hearing.[85]

Contemporary observers were well aware of the desirability of 'direct' evidence. In the 1670s, a vicious burglar was convicted at the Sussex assizes held at East Grinstead, on the evidence of his own daughter, who was the maid in one of the houses that he robbed. Crucially, and unlike the owner of the house, she was able to be specific about identity, having secretly peeped at the intruders when their faces were illuminated by candlelight. As a result, although her master: "... swore only to circumstances, and that to the best of his knowledge, they were the men; but the Daughter swore it directly and positively, that they were the very same."[86] The importance of direct evidence was also appreciated by felons, and, occasionally, even exaggerated. In 1641, Peter Moore, an Exeter apprentice who poisoned his master, was convinced that although suspected, imprisoned

---

84. Anon, *The Horrible Murther of a young Boy of three yeres of age, whose sister had her tongue cut out ...*, London, 1606, p.2.
85. Sir T. Overbury, *A true and Perfect Account of the Examination, Confession, Tryal, Condemnation, and execution of Joan Perry*, London, 1676, pp.1-23 and p.12.
86. Anon, *News from Sussex, Or the Barbarous Robber*, London, 1676, pp.1-7.

and tried for the murder, he would ultimately be acquitted provided he maintained his innocence throughout: "I thought my selfe to be secure from being found out, because I did the act unseen." However, he was convicted and executed.[87]

Expert Testimony

By the last quarter of the era, ordinary witnesses were slowly being discouraged from providing the court with opinion, as opposed to evidence of facts, as evidential rules gradually became stricter. Thus, witnesses were told to state: "... not what they believe, for they are to swear nothing but what they have heard or seen."[88] Nevertheless, such opinion was not firmly excluded until after 1750. However, the calling of partisan expert witnesses, as opposed to experts appointed by the court to sit on special juries or to assist the judge, occurred in the seventeenth century, with medical experts - surgeons, physicians and apothecaries - most commonly being employed in criminal trials. The amount of 'expert' (even if expert *ad hoc*) testimony adduced at the trial of the barrister, Spencer Cowper, in 1699, was enormous, a tribute to his social pre-eminence and wealth. The key issue was whether a young woman had been murdered by Cowper or, as he claimed, had committed suicide by drowning herself. Numerous physicians, some eminent

---

87. Anon, *The Apprentices Warning-Piece* ..., London, 1641, f.A3.
88. W. Nelson, *The Law of evidence*, London, R. Gosling, 1717, p.7.

others local, were called by both the Crown and defence. They included Sir Hans Sloane, two Royal Navy sailors who had witnessed men drowned at sea and others killed out of the water and then thrown or fallen into it (apparently the former sank, the latter floated) and a woman, Sarah Kimpton, who had seen both the deceased's body and that of a boy who had indisputably drowned some months earlier, also allowing her to draw comparisons. In a step that would become common practice for forensic experts, the doctors retained for the defence were allowed to stay in court to hear the evidence of those called by the Crown.[89] Similarly, in 1730, when Gilbert Laurence was accused of buggering Paul Oliver, his 14-year-old apprentice, the examining JP immediately sent for a surgeon, Jean Barbat, to conduct an intimate examination of the boy. Barbat subsequently gave evidence at the Old Bailey stating:

"That upon examining the Lad, he found his Fundament quite open; that it had been penetrated above an Inch, and much lacerated; that there was a Hole, in which a Finger and Thumb might be put, and that the Fundament was Black all round, and appear'd like that of a Hen after laying an Egg."[90]

The trial of Mrs Dorothy Longley for poisoning her

---

89. Anon, *The Tryal of Spencer Cowper, Esq. ... upon an indictment for the murther of Mrs Sarah Stout*, London, 1699, p.13.
90. Anon, *The Proceedings at the Sessions of the Peace, and Oyer and Terminer, for the City of London, and County of Middlesex*, London, T. Payne, 1730, pp.6-7.

husband, held at the Lent assizes for Surrey in 1732, also involved the presentation of exceptionally detailed forensic evidence. The dead man had been married 'uneasily' to the accused woman for only six weeks. It was claimed that: "She was vex'd to find his circumstances not agreeable; and he, that she kept Company with another Man, whom he found in her Chamber; for which she said she would give him a Pill." He then suffered a very sudden and 'unaccountable' death. An apothecary attending the dying man believed that he had been poisoned with liquid laudanum, and claimed that when he tried to smell the dead man's vomit for tell-tale signs, his wife "snatch'd the Porringer away" and threw it out of the window, to prevent him from doing so. Even more suspiciously, she would not readmit him when he came to visit again. On his deathbed, the husband was heard to say, somewhat ambiguously, "Now you have your Ends, I'm a dead Man". The prosecution case was supported by two surgeons and a physician, who claimed that a dog that had been fed the contents of the dead man's stomach had fallen into a coma for seven hours, then convulsed and died. It was also proved that the accused had sent for two ounces of laudanum. Even worse, she had tried to bribe another witness to say that he had heard her apprentice, the youth sent to purchase the drug, threatening to "be reveng'd on her for not giving him his indentures", suggesting that if her husband had been poisoned, he (the apprentice) was behind it. There were clearly very strong grounds for suspicion. However, in her defence, Mrs Longley was able to establish that her husband was a hard drinker, who had had occasional fits, and was "generally very drowsy". She was able to call evidence to indicate that she was herself a regular user of laudanum, for medicinal purposes (nose bleeds), giving a legitimate explanation for ordering the drug. She also called a defence 'expert', a surgeon, to suggest, as a possibility, that it was the putrefaction of the deceased's stomach contents, rather than ingested poison, that killed the dog. This witness also attributed marks on the husband's stomach to earlier, recreational, use of opium. Mrs Longley, who had made no incriminating admissions when questioned, was acquitted.[91]

Even so, the use of experts in criminal trials remained rare to the end of the period. This is not surprising, given the cost, lack of legal advice and limited education of most litigants. Even at the Old Bailey, between 1717 and 1817, cases in which expert medical testimony was presented averaged little more than a dozen a year (out of between three hundred and over six hundred cases heard annually). As with the general trend in witness production, medical experts appeared far more often for the prosecution (164 times) than for the defence (26 times). Medical witnesses were most commonly called in murder cases (75 per cent of cases in which an expert was called). The remainder were divided among rape cases (9 per cent), infanticides (10 per cent), and various assault and attempted murder proceedings (5 per cent). There were 49 cases in which one side called more than a single medical witness to support its

---

91. *The Gentleman's Magazine*, 1731, vol. 1, pp.454 and 492, and 1732, vol. 2, p.676.

case.[92]

Witness Testimony

Unlike most continental civil law systems, English criminal process stressed the importance of oral evidence, given in public, by 'live' witnesses. This was something that always struck European observers, used to a procedure that was often held in camera, and which emphasised the use of written depositions. Thus, a Venetian visitor noted in 1500: "Nor are proceedings carried on in this country by the deposition of any one, or by writing, but by opinion of men, both in criminal and civil causes."[93] Almost 200 years later, in the 1690s, a visiting Frenchman shared his surprise: "... all this [criminal] Proceeding passes in an open Court, and every thing spoken with a loud Voice. This is one of the Privileges of the English Nation."[94] Englishmen, familiar with continental legal practice, also thought the lack of documentary evidence in their own country was noteworthy (and laudable). In the 1560s, Sir Thomas Smith, contrasting the orality of the English criminal trial with the written procedure found in Europe, observed that: "It will seem strange to all nations that do use the civil Law of the Roman Emperors, that for life and death there is nothing put in

---

92. S. Landsman, "One Hundred Years of Rectitude: Medical Witnesses at the Old Bailey, 1717-1817," *Law and History Review*, 1998, vol. 16, p.445.

93. Anon, *A relation, or Rather A True Account of The Island of England ... About the Year 1500*, C. Sneyd (Trans.), London, Camden Society, 1847, p.32.

94. Misson, Memoirs and Observations in his Travels over England, p.124.

writing but the indictment only." The emphasis on oral testimony meant that having a strong case and establishing it forensically were not necessarily the same thing; as Henry Fielding complained in 1754, law courts knew "nothing of a cause more than what is told them on oath by a witness". The normal course of prosecution testimony was identified by Sir Thomas Smith in the 1560s; if those who had been bound by the JPs to give evidence for the Crown turned up at court: "... first is read the examination, which the Justice of peace doeth give in: then is heard (if he be there) the man robbed what he can say, being first sworne to say trueth, and after the Constable, and as many as were at the apprehension of the malefactor: and so many as can say anything being sworn one after an other to say truth."[95] As today, it was normal for the victim to give evidence first, a situation that still applied at the end of the period: "The person who has been the cause of his arrest appears and proceeds to give a detailed account of the circumstances which have led to the prisoner's arrest."[96] Other witnesses could then support the prosecution case against the prisoner unless, as Misson noted, their testimony could "lawfully be rejected".[97] By this, he was alluding to two main possibilities. Either the witness might be of a type whose evidence could not be received, or, alternatively, the evidence itself might be of a type that was legally inadmissible. Of the two, the former case was easily the

---

95. Smith, *De Republica Anglorum*, pp.113-114.
96. Muyden, *A foreign View of England in the reigns of George I and George II*, p.120.
97. Misson, *Memoirs and Observations in his Travels over England*, p.327.

most important during the period, and encompassed classes of witness who were excluded from giving testimony. For example, there was normally strict enforcement of the provision that a: "... person ones perjured is repelled from bearyng wytnesse againe, because the law presumeth that he setteth not so much by an othe."[98] Such limitations apart, anyone could testify. Usually, prosecution witnesses would have to be sworn for their evidence to be received. This could have serious consequences for those unwilling to take an oath on principle. Thus, in 1678, William Brayn was accused of stealing a gelding from Ambrose Galloway. A witness confirmed that it was Galloway's animal. However, the loser, being a Quaker, would not: "... for conscience-sake, as he said, swear, and so could give no testimony about his losing him. Upon which the court directed the jury to find the prisoner not guilty for want of evidence, and committed the Quaker, as a concealer of felony, for refusing an Oath to Witness for the King."[99]

An exception to the general rule requiring sworn evidence for the Crown was made in the case of a few special types of offence and witness. Most importantly, these included crimes in which children were victims and where there were strong policy grounds for such an indulgence, for example, offences involving the rape of minors. Thus, a girl of between nine and 10 years of age gave testimony in 1678: "... without being Sworn. That she saw in a Room, the

---

98. Sir T. More, "The Deballaryon of Salem and Bizance, 1533," *Works of Sir Thomas More*, London, (Scholar Press facsimile), 1577, p.987.
99. Anon, *An exact account of the trials of the several persons ...*, p.27.

Prisoner lying a top of the little Girl [the victim], but what they did she knew not, but the Girls Petticoats were up." The victim, a year younger still, also testified that the defendant had abused her. Even so, and significantly, the jury were extremely nervous about her unsworn evidence. This prompted the court to question her about her fitness to take an oath, and subsequently to allow her to testify again on a sworn basis.[100] Additionally, although most people could give evidence, a hierarchical society inevitably produced a hierarchy of evidential weight; not everyone's testimony was of equal significance. As William Sheppard noted, although: "... any men how meen soever, may be allowed as a competent witnesse, yet some heed is to be given to the witnesses [social status]."[101] It was common for courts to examine witnesses and defendants about their 'quality and estate'. For similar reasons, infanticide and witchcraft apart, a substantial majority of witnesses in criminal cases were male.

Defendants' Evidence

Defendants were expected to address the court personally. The modern privilege against self-incrimination was largely the result of the advent of defence counsel after 1750. It was (and is) almost impossible to sustain a defence without a

---

100. Anon, *An exact account of the trials of the several persons ...*, pp.14-15.
101. W. Sheppard, *The Whole Office of the County Justice of Peace*, 3rd. edn., London, W. Lee, 1656, p.35.

'proxy' to conduct the case if an accused refuses to testify.[102] However, defendants (and, until 1702, their witnesses) could not give sworn evidence. Considerable emphasis has been placed on this in the modern era, and much work has been done into the theoretical implications of the absence of an oath to bolster defence testimony. Giving judgment in the 1970s, a future Lord Chancellor, describing the defects of the eighteenth century justice system, noted that: "... the accused was unable to give evidence on his own behalf and was therefore largely at the mercy of any evidence, either perjured or oppressively obtained, that might be brought against him."[103] According to one academic analysis, the reluctance to allow the calling of defence witnesses in the sixteenth century, the refusal to allow them to be sworn until the start of the eighteenth century, and the failure to allow a defendant to give sworn evidence until the nineteenth century (1898 for most offences) was designed to avoid creating a 'conflict' between oaths. It is claimed that this permitted an evidentiary presumption that all sworn evidence was truthful, the oath being its source of legitimacy. This allegedly contrasts with the modern view that it is the jury, acting as 'lie detector', and not the oath, that screens out unreliable evidence.[104]

Such a distinction *may* have been significant in a few high profile criminal and treason cases, especially in the early part of the period. Sometimes it made a defendant's

---

102. Langbein, "The Historical Origins of the Privilege Against Self-Incrimination at Common Law," p.1054.
103. *DPP v. Ping Lin* [1976] AC 574.
104. Fisher, "The Jury's Rise as Lie Detector," p.580.

testimony, and that of his witnesses, manifestly inferior to sworn evidence. Occasionally, even in ordinary criminal cases, if the evidence appeared overwhelming, and came from independent and very reputable sources, the court might stress the inferior status of unsworn testimony. Thus, in 1678, when Mary Read was tried at the Old Bailey for stealing a gold ring, both the goldsmith who owned the ring, and an independent female witness of genteel status, were called to give sworn, and highly incriminating, evidence for the Crown. In her defence, the prisoner, after a "great deal of whining [merely] denied the thing". Virtually directing a conviction, the presiding judge told the jury that the "Witnesses Othes were to outway her bare Allegations".[105]

However, even in state trials, such an approach to sworn testimony was not always taken. When Richard Rich, the Solicitor General, was called by the Crown to give evidence of a conversation he had had with Thomas More in the Tower of London, before the latter's trial in 1535, More was not at all intimidated simply because Rich gave evidence "upon his oath". He responded by attacking his credibility and invited the jury to disbelieve his testimony: "I am sorrier for your perjury than for mine own peril, and you shall understand that neither I, nor no man else to my knowledge ever took you to be a man of such credit as in any matter of importance." He also claimed that, since childhood, Rich had had a reputation as a liar and was

---

105. Anon, *An exact account of the trials of the several persons...*, p.8.

"always reputed for one of so little truth".[106]

More importantly, whatever the situation in treason trials, the practical consequences of witnesses not being sworn in the 'rough and tumble' of most assizes and quarter sessions was probably very limited. The high incidence of acquittals after contested trials, throughout the early modern period, indicates that jurors must regularly have preferred unsworn accounts to evidence on oath, or at least have been undecided between the two. Thus, in 1680, the barrister, John Hawles, was convinced that: "When any matter is sworn, Deed read, or offered whether it shall be believed or not, or whether it be *true or false* in point of Fact, the jurors are proper judges."[107] It is likely that they normally made little distinction between sworn and unsworn testimony, not least because of the frequent judicial directions to unsworn witnesses to tell the truth: "The judges usualy heare evidence on the behalf of the prisoner, but not upon oath, yet with a chardg to speake the truth before God as upon oath; so Sir Robert Hide at Worcester Assizes August 22, 1661 in Hurdman's case, and Sir Windham March 5, 1662; and then leave the same to the Jury."[108] It must also be remembered that it was only in 1563 that perjury became a (rarely prosecuted) common law offence (as opposed to one punishable in the ecclesiastical courts). Many men did not place much significance on oaths because of the apparently widespread presence of untruthful, but sworn, testimony.

---

106. W. Roper, *The Life of Sir Thomas More, in Lives of Sir Thomas More*, E.G. Reynolds (Ed.), London, Everyman/J.M. Dent, 1963, pp.42-43.

107. Hawles, *The English-mans right*, p.8.

108. Townshend, *Notes of the Office of a Justice of Peace*, p.95.

Thus, in 1653, Henry Robinson was distinctly unimpressed by the value of an oath in bolstering witness credibility: "At Sessions and at Assizes, all up and downe the land, nothing but Oathing of it, swearing and forswearing, though not so often yet as publicke, and as unpunished, and the parties as remedilesse, though perhaps most Causes are lost by the perjurie of one or other." He wanted perjury to be punished much more effectively, with heavy penalties invariably applied to those found to have lied when giving sworn testimony.[109] Tellingly, a few years later, in 1657, a cleric observed in an assizes sermon, that, *unlike* human tribunals, God was omniscient and would not be swayed by "corrupt evidences".[110] Similarly, in the 1690s, Edmund Bohun felt that although oaths might be of some value when sworn by grave and collected witnesses, they were of very limited worth with angry ones, albeit that the temper of such witnesses could itself be very revealing: "Men who are in passion one against another, do little regard the religion of an Oath, and yet their very Passion will discover the Truth without one, if a magistrate will take but a little patience." Bohun praised the practice found (he believed) amongst Turkish country magistrates, of not using oaths at all but instead employing forensic skills and the demeanour of the witnesses involved to "pick out the truth". He felt that although such an approach was "troublesome, and will take time, but it will discover the Truth sometimes, when oaths

---

109. H. Robinson, *Certaine proposals in order to a new modelling of the lawes, and law-proceedings*, London, Mathew Simmons, 1653, pp.8-9.
110. T. William, *The regulation of Law-Suits, Evidence, and Pleadings - An Assize-Sermon*, London, 1657, p.37.

would not, and save the Perjury too". Bohun demanded that magistrates ensure that 'ignorant' people who committed proven perjury in their courts, by resiling on matters, even if minor, that they had earlier sworn to be true, should receive a "sharp reproof". He also asked that the significance of the oath and its religious sanctions be carefully explained to potential witnesses before they were sworn.[111] By the Restoration period, Mathew Hale had a recognisably modern view of the evidential process and the jury's part within it. He was convinced that jurors "weigh the Credibility of Witnesses, and the Force and Efficacy of their Testimonies". They were not required to accept evidence from a source with 'blemished' credibility, or even believe the testimony of two witnesses if the: "Probability of the Fact does upon other Circumstances reasonably encounter them."[112]

Defence Witnesses

According to some assessments, at the start of the early modern period, not only was the defendant unsworn when giving testimony but there does not appear to have been a regularized practice of allowing him to call others to speak to facts on his behalf. However, caution is needed in accepting this as the general model for the early 1500s. In

---

111. E. Bohun, *The Justice of Peace His Calling and Qualifications*, London, 1693, pp.168-170.
112. M. Hale, *The History of the Common Law of England*, London, J. Walthoe, 1713, pp.259-260.

1533, Thomas More, discussing the widespread use of false alibis by suspected felons observed: "I cannot tel how often, that in the excuse of a theefe some have taken an oath, that ye felon was with him in his owne house, at such tyme as the felony should be done in another place." By 'taking an oath' he could be referring to a witness examined by a JP before trial, or evidence at the trial itself. Although it is not entirely clear, More appears to have been referring to sworn evidence at a felony trial as he also asserts that jurors were not required to follow witnesses who "first testified upon theyr othe" that the defendant was not guilty, if they knew this to be untrue. Additionally, More subsequently discusses a situation in which: "... two or thre wytnesses would at the barre excuse upon their othes, some one man of felony, and afterward when they were stepped from the bar happed to be heard rowne and rejoyce together, that thei had given evidence for acquitayle of theyr felow, who with them self had been at the same robbery."[113] This suggests that defence witnesses were being received, on oath, at felony trials in the 1530s, contrary to some portrayals of the situation after c.1550. Nevertheless, there may have been a general practice of discouraging the calling of defence witnesses. Certainly, later in the century, there were prominent trials in which courts refused to hear defence witnesses who were present and willing to testify. A Marian decree made it clear that this was not a rule of law, indicating that refusing such evidence may have become common. The decree does not appear to have been closely followed. Thus, at his trial for

---

113. Sir T. More, "The Deballaryon of Salem and Bizance," pp.996-998.

treason in 1554, Nicholas Throckmorton pointed out that the Queen had instructed the courts to ignore their "old error" of not allowing witnesses to speak against the Crown, and that: "... her highness's pleasure was, that whatsoever could be brought in favour of the subject, should be admitted to be heard." Even so, the presiding Chief Justice refused to allow him to call any witnesses in his support, telling Throckmorton that he had no reason to complain because he had been allowed to say as much as he wished in his own defence. Nevertheless, as ever, it is dangerous to generalise from the position at state trials to that at an ordinary assizes felony hearing, where a general informality probably did sometimes allow witnesses to be called for a defendant, even in the 1550s.

Whatever the situation at mid-century, by the late 1500s defence witnesses were frequently being called to testify, and were a regular feature of early seventeenth century criminal trials.[114] Indeed, by the eighteenth century, Blackstone was highly critical of the situation in France, where he considered that the courts "admit witnesses to be heard only on the side of the prosecution".[115] Even when an accused person was legally permitted to call defence witnesses, his position was made difficult because it was difficult to subpoena reluctant witnesses who could give potentially favourable evidence on his behalf (a situation

---

114. Fisher, "The Jury's Rise as Lie Detector," pp.603-604.
115. W. Blackstone, *Commentaries on the Laws of England*, Oxford, Clarendon Press, 1769, vol.4, p.138.

that prevailed until 1867).[116] As a result, an examination of the *Old Bailey Sessions Papers* for 1715 reveals that only seven per cent of case reports mention defence witnesses, other than character witnesses or the defendant himself, being called.[117] Additionally, whatever the situation in More's era, it was swiftly established that defence witnesses, like the defendant, had to testify unsworn: "In felony, no witnesse shall bee received upon oath for the parties Justification no more than in treason."[118] This situation prevailed until legislation in 1702 allowed them to give their evidence on oath, cases of treason apart (1 Anne, stat.2, ch.9).

Corroboration

At common law a defendant could normally be convicted on the evidence of a single witness (still the case today). This meant that unlike civil law countries, English jurors did not sometimes need the evidence of two or more witnesses to prove a case, nor were they compelled to reject the evidence of an unsupported witness.[119] However, civil law had influenced English criminal procedure in a few areas. Most importantly, although the requirement for two witnesses to found a conviction in cases of treason was only finally settled in 1696, its existence had been mooted for centuries,

---

116. Langbein, "The Historical Origins of the Privilege Against Self-Incrimination at Common Law," p.1055.
117. Fisher, "The Jury's Rise as Lie Detector," pp.604-605.
118. Bacon, *Cases of Treason*, p.13.
119. Hale, *The History of the Common Law of England*, p.260.

being incorporated into the Elizabethan Treason Act of 1571, and several even older statutes. More interestingly, it seems to have emerged from an ancient notion that two witnesses were necessary in trials at common law generally, one that had been enunciated by commentators such as Henry de Bracton in the thirteenth century. This may have been the result of the influence of Roman and canon law on the early common law (along with biblical injunctions). Treason cases apart, such a rule did not survive into the early modern era, though a Henrician statute may have alluded to it.[120] Nevertheless, by the early 1700s, a number of minor regulatory or economic offences had been added to treason in requiring two witnesses to secure a conviction. This is unsurprising, given that they were often proved by informers.[121]

For most crimes common law was devoid of technical rules on evidential quantity. English lawyers were acutely aware of this. Michael Dalton freely accepted that in this respect England not only differed to the civil law tradition but also appeared to ignore Biblical injunctions "By Gods law one witnesse shall not be sufficient against an offender". He was able to reconcile the Bible with common law, albeit with some difficulty, by arguing that a single witness was sufficient where the trial was by a jury, because its members

---

120. L.M. Hill, "The Two-witness Rule in English Treason Trials: Some comments on the Emergence of Procedural Law," *American Journal of Legal History*, 1996, vol. 40, pp.95-112.
121. J. Shaw, *The Practical Justice of Peace: or a Treatise shewing the power and authority of that office in all its branches, etc.*, London, Thomas Ward, 1728, pp.24-27.

were "all sworn to try the particular matter wherewith the defendant is charged".[122] The Reverend John Udall was not convinced by such arguments. However, his desire to have two reputable witnesses brought against him at the Surrey assizes in 1590, according to Biblical precepts, brought a terse response from the presiding judge: "That was according to Moses' law which we are not tied unto."[123] Not everyone approved of the common law position. One of the first demands that the Levellers made in their 'Large Petition' of March 1647, was that no man be executed without having been convicted on the "testimony of two witnesses at least, of honest conversation".[124]

Evidential Status of an Examination/Deposition

A distinction must be drawn between the examination of a suspect by a JP, and the deposition of a potential prosecution witness given to the same magistrate. (The different terminology provides a common, though not certain, distinction.) Examinations and depositions usually had a different evidential status. A defendant's out-of-court and adverse admissions to a JP could normally be produced as evidence against him. Thus, at trial, the court clerk would look out examinations made by each defendant "as his cause

---

122. M. Dalton, *The Country Justice, Containing The practise of the Justices of the Peace out of their Sessions ...*, London, Company of Stationers, 1655, p.367.
123. Cobbett, *State Trials*, vol. 1, pp.1278-1302.
124. R. Zaller, "The Debate on Capital Punishment During the English Revolution," *American Journal of Legal History*, vol. 31, 1987, p.128.

is in hearing, and if it be evidence for the King he readeth it to the Jury".[125] Despite this, in 1699, John Bellingham, although himself the son of a JP, sought to argue at his Old Bailey trial for forgery that it was an old legal maxim that: "... what a prisoner should confess before a justice should not be given in evidence against him." Not surprisingly, this novel and unfounded argument produced a negative response from the judge, who declared that "if there was such a maxim, it was so old it was forgotten". When asked if he could produce any record of such a ruling Bellingham was forced to answer 'No'. He was convicted and executed.[126] Nevertheless, like modern confessions to the police, such out of court admissions, even if damning, did not preclude a 'not guilty' plea at trial, being: "... no conviction of the offendor, except he shal after confesse the same againe upon his triall or arraignment."[127] Indeed, in 1530, St Germain had stressed that full legal proprieties should be followed even where a defendant had earlier confessed his guilt on examination by a magistrate. This was especially important as "somtyme a man by examanyacon and by wytnes may appeare gylty that is not gylty".[128] If a defendant was not willing to reiterate his admissions to the court, or at least accept that those read out by the court clerk had been made by him on an earlier occasion (even if he

---

125. T.W., *The Clerk of Assize*, p.14.
126. C. Johnson, *A General History of the Lives and Adventures of the Most Famous Highwaymen, Murderers, Street-Robbers*, London: J. Janeway, 1734, pp.358-359.
127. Dalton, *The Country Justice*, 1661, pp.269-277.
128. T.F. Plucknett and J.C. Barton (Eds.), *2nd Dialogue, 1530, St Germain's Doctor and Student*, London, Selden Society, 1974, p.285.

denied their truth at trial), they would have to be formally proved. This could be done by calling the examining JP, his clerk (if he had one) or anyone else who had been present; many examinations were not held in private. Thus, in the case of one of the Perry brothers, falsely accused of murder in 1661: "... John's Confession, before the Justice was proved, viva voce, by several witnesses who heard the same, [in response] he told them, he was then mad, and knew not what he said."[129] Similarly, in 1678, John Baltee, accused of stealing a tankard belonging to a cook named Thomas Browning, pleaded not guilty, despite earlier confessing the matter before Sir William Turner, whose: "Clerk witnessed his Confession before Sir William, and that he said, he was a poor fellow and in distress, and so took it to relieve his Wants."[130]

Although a confession made to an examining JP was admissible against its maker, prosecutions in which there was no other evidence, whether direct or circumstantial, apart from the admission, were rarely successful, and usually not even brought: "A negative answer at triall is as strong to save a man, as his former affirmative in confession before a Justice can be to condemne him; except either he publickly at his triall acknowledge the same; or that there be some other proofe, or evidence against him."[131] Significantly, in the sixteenth century, some even thought that an out of court confession that was unsupported by prosecution

---

129. Sir T. Overbury, *A true and Perfect Account of the Examination, Confession, Tryal, Condemnation, and execution of Joan Perry*, London, 1676, p.12.
130. Anon, *An exact account of the trials of the several persons ...*, p.6.
131. Sym, *Life's Preservative Against Self-Killing*, pp.108-109.

witnesses could not found a conviction in normal felony cases: "If none come in to give evidence although the malefactor hath confessed the crime to the Justice of the peace, and that appear by his hande and confirmation, the xii. men will acquite the prisoner."[132] Such a view was reiterated in the early 1700s by Henri Misson, who was convinced that if no prosecution witnesses were to appear, the: "... Prisoner would be acquitted by the jury, even tho' he had confessed his Crime upon his first Examination before the Justice of the Peace."[133]

The evidential status of prosecution witness depositions was different to that of defendants' examinations. However, like the latter, during the sixteenth century at least, they were often formally proved to the court at the outset of a trial, usually by the JP who took them. Thus, William Lambarde noted that at the Rochester assizes of 1585: "I certified all the recognizances and examinations [in this case depositions] thereto belonging."[134] At some point in the early modern era, but long before 1700, the practice of reading depositions at the start of a trial was abandoned, at both the Old Bailey and assizes. The reasons for this are not apparent, but it may have been linked to their being superfluous; the original deponents were necessarily in court to give evidence, making duplication pointless in an already pressured system. However, the depositions

---

132. Smith, *De Republica Anglorum*, p.113.
133. Misson, *Memoirs and Observations in his Travels over England*, p.27.
134. W. Lambarde, "Ephemeris," *William Lambarde and Local Government*, Conyers Read (Ed.), New York, Cornell University Press, Ithaca, 1962, (written in 1580-1588), p.29.

remained available to inform the judge, refresh memory and impeach witnesses.[135] Crucially, unlike confessions, the depositions, on their own, even if proved, were not normally evidence. Throughout the period, it was vital that prosecution witnesses appear in person at both the assizes and quarter sessions if a conviction was to be secured. In their absence, in the words of Sir Thomas Smith, a defendant was usually "without difficultie acquited". Normally, anything contained in the prosecution depositions would have to be repeated orally as sworn evidence. This could occasion problems if key witnesses failed to appear at court to prosecute, without a covering affidavit providing a legitimate explanation for their absence (such as sickness). If such affidavits were forthcoming the accused person might be remanded to the next sessions, whether on bail or in custody. In their absence, the defendant would normally be released by proclamation at the end of the assizes along with those found "not guilty". Thus, in the late 1570s, although John Bull confessed to stealing wool in Suffolk and bringing it to Colchester for sale, he was not tried (and was subsequently released) because the prosecutors lived in Suffolk and had not been able to make the journey to court.[136] Similarly, in 1695, John Oliver, a Frenchman (he had interpreters at the Old Bailey), who was arrested above a coffee shop in Charing Cross, claimed that he had gone into the building

---

135. J.H. Langbein, "Shaping the Eighteenth-Century Criminal Trial: A View from the Ryder Sources," *University of Chicago Law Review*, 1983, vol. 50, p.83.

136. J. Samaha, "Hanging for Felony: The Rule of Law in Elizabethan Colchester," *Historical Journal*, 1978, vol. 21, p.769.

to sleep. However, stolen items, including a ring, were found on him. Nevertheless, despite the implausibility of his defence: "... for want of the Constables Evidence, who searched him, he was found not guilty, by reason none gave Evidence against him in court."[137] For the same reasons, difficulties could be occasioned if, for some reason, the defendants failed to appear on time at court. In 1663, Lord Chief Justice Bridgeman complained that some recognisances for suspected felons granted bail were administered so loosely that they were turning up late for their trials at the Old Bailey sessions, by which time the "prosecutors were gone or weary with attendance."[138]

Very occasionally, especially before 1660, it seems that the statement of an absent witness *was* simply read out. At his trial in 1590, at the Surrey assizes in Southwark (albeit for a quasi-political matter), the Reverend John Udall argued that most of the evidence against him, being in the form of depositions, would not be permitted in many civil cases "much less to be allowed in a case of life". His reaction indicates that it was normal in criminal matters for "full living witnesses" to testify, not merely read out statements. However, Serjeant Puckering, the presiding judge, robustly rejected his arguments against adducing ecclesiastical depositions: "You are deceived if that you think the witnesses against you the less lawful, because the parties

---

137. Anon (1695) *The True Relation of the tryals at the Sessions of Oyer and Terminer, ... as particularly of E. Wigenton for whipping a girl to death ...*, London, pp.1-2.
138. Sir O. Bridgeman, "Newgate, 1663, A Letter of Sir Orlando Bridgeman, Chief Justice," *American Journal of Legal History*, vol. 13, pp.384-386.

were not present."[139] Nevertheless, after the middle of the seventeenth century the circumstances in which this could occur were very limited, usually being confined to situations in which illness, death, abduction or intimidation kept the witness from reiterating their evidence at trial, and in which the earlier deposition had been sworn.[140] An unexplained absence was not enough. Thus, when the Crown at Henry Harrison's trial in 1692 wished to adduce the evidence of an apprentice named Andrew Bowfell, who had made an earlier deposition to a coroner and then failed to appear at court, the prosecuting counsel was required to argue that the youth had been deliberately kept out of the way. Having adduced evidence that the boy had been approached in the street, offered a bribe, and then suddenly disappeared, leaving his clothes behind, he was allowed to call the coroner to prove the making of the deposition. This was then produced as evidence in its own right, the trial judge advising the jurors that: "There was another piece of Evidence, viz. That of the Boy's, who does not appear, he was examined before the coroner. There has been Evidence given of ill practice to take him out of the way, and therefore his Affidavit is read for evidence."[141]

The need to call live witnesses, combined with the normal brevity of criminal trials, meant that, where a lot of depositions had been taken before trial, constraints of time

---

139. Cobbett, *State trials*, vol. 1, pp.1278-1302.
140. Sir J. Kelyng, *A Report of Divers Cases in Pleas of the Crown, From the original manuscript*, London, Isaac Cleave, 1708, 3rd. edn., pp.54-55.
141. Anon, *The Arraignment, Tryal, Conviction and Condemnation of Henry Harrison*, London, 1692, pp.16 and 30.

might mean that not all the witnesses examined and summoned to court could be called to testify. Thus, in a notorious Suffolk multiple murder case from 1620, the very conscientious examining JP took 28 witness depositions: "... all of great moment, by way of circumstance and consequence to prove the same; whereof, though no more than 18 were produced at the Barre, because time (which there is precious) would have been otherwise taken up, and those that were produced in the judgment of the honourable judge, were sufficient, yea, more than enough."[142]

Summing up to the Jury

Unlike the modern situation, a judge's end-of-trial summing up to the jury was usually very brief, often only a few sentences, such as a reminder to jurors to remember their oath, with little attempt to recapitulate the salient evidence; this was normally unnecessary, given the speed of most hearings. Thus, in the 1560s it might entail simply telling the jury: "... ye have heard what these men say against the prisoner, you have also heard what the prisoner can say for himselfe, have an eye to your othe, and to your duetie, to God and the Prince and doe that which God shall put in your mindes to the discharge of your consciences, and marke well what is saide."[143] By this stage, in any event, a judge would often have made his opinion on the merits of

---

142. T. Cooper, *The Cry and Revenge of Blood*, London, Nicholas Okes, 1620, p.47.
143. Smith, *De Republica Anglorum*, p.114.

the case clear. Occasionally, however, in difficult cases, they might discuss the evidence in more detail. Judges did not view themselves as disinterested referees. Some observers thought that trial judges attempted to be fair to defendants, erring in favour of the accused when summing up if he discussed the evidence: "He weighs in general more upon the good than upon the bad."[144] Thus, at the trial of Henry Harrison in 1692, it was expressly noted that the Lord Chief Justice had summed up "very impartially". Others did not share such confidence, and complained of judicial bias, though this is common amongst unsuccessful litigants of all types. In 1722, after his conviction for robbery, John Hawkins "upbraided the Judge as partial"; equally unsurprisingly, a former accomplice who had turned King's evidence thought this was unfair. He claimed that Hawkins had been treated with leniency, though the trial judge had openly remarked that his fine attire seemed excessive given his claimed profession as a footman.[145] Much must have turned on the individual judge and his views on the case in question.

It is clear that, where they thought it to be appropriate, the judiciary would often give tell-tale and well recognised hints encouraging an acquittal, so that jurors would: "... perceive the Judge would have the prisoner escape, and in repeating the evidence doe give them thereof some watchworde."[146] Thus, Mr Justice Howel, presiding over the

---

144. Muyden, A *foreign View of England in the reigns of George I and George II*; p.15.
145. R.Wilson, *A Full and Impartial Account of all the Robberies Committed by John Hawkins* ..., 3rd edn., London, J. Peele, 1722, pp.25-26.
146. Smith, *De Republica Anglorum*, p.120.

trial of Mary Carleton for bigamy in the early 1660s, clearly encouraged a 'not guilty' verdict in a fairly lengthy closing address. He pointed out to the jury that all the evidence of the disputed marriage depended on only one witness, who was very vague about the 'particulars' of the wedding. He also stressed that the circumstances were such as would have led most people to expect more evidence of the nuptials to be available. Howel then pointedly warned the jury that it was a capital offence. Not surprisingly, given the tenor of his comments, the jury, after a "short consultation" in private, acquitted.[147] However, judges could also be brutal, blatantly encouraging a conviction and openly ridiculing defences. This was most clearly manifest in political cases. At John Lilburne's trial in 1649, the presiding judge, Mr Justice Keble, at the close of the prosecution case, and without even having heard the defendant's account, announced: "I hope the Jury hath seen the Evidence so plain and so fully, that it doth confirm them to do their duty, and to find the Prisoner guilty of what is charged upon him."[148] Nevertheless, judicial directions in ordinary trials could be almost as robust, though they were usually slightly less blatant. In 1678, at the Old Bailey sessions, the presiding judge instructed jurors to convict an elderly defendant, accused of theft, who had put forward a particularly feeble defence: "... which poor excuse was not accepted by the Court, but they directed the Jury to find him Guilty, upon so

---

147. Anon, *The Case of Madam Mary Carleton*, pp.103-4.
148. Langbein, "The Historical Origins of the Privilege Against Self-Incrimination at Common Law," pp.1048-1054.

plain an Evidence." A similar direction awaited Hannah Henman, accused of stealing silk from a mercer, albeit that it was accompanied by a tacit invitation to the jury to commit pious perjury. The judge: "... directed the Jury to find it according to so plain an Evidence; but because the man had his Goods again, left the Value to their Consideration." The jury, without even retiring, found her guilty of the theft of nine pence worth of goods (a non-capital amount).[149] Some judges were sufficiently open-minded to change their opinions during the course of a hearing. Thus, in 1669, Lord Chief Baron Hale, presiding over the assizes trial of the falsely accused Reverend Robert Hawkins, announced to the jury after hearing the prosecution case "Here is evidence enough to hang 20 men". However, by the end of the trial, when summing up, he declared that the Crown's case appeared to be based on a "most foul and malicious conspiracy". The jury acquitted without leaving court.

Legal Arguments as Defences

Highly technical legal defences were sometimes taken, especially in circumstances in which the evidence appeared strong and where the accused had access to legal advice, was himself a lawyer, a man of strong native intelligence or merely wished to avoid having the facts of the case aired in

---

149. Anon, *An exact account of the trials of the several persons arraigned at the sessions-house in the Old-Bailey for London and Middlesex*, p.6

public. Not all such arguments succeeded. In 1736, the barrister, Henry Justice, accused of stealing books from the library of his alma mater, Trinity College, Cambridge, argued that as he had been admitted a Fellow Commoner there two years earlier he had a "Property in the Books", and so could not be guilty of felony. He read the college's charter to the court to prove it, but after "several hours debate", the trial judge resolved that he was only a "Boarder or Lodger", leading to the jury convicting him. (He was transported to the Americas, having pleaded in vain merely to be "burnt in the Hand" so that he could continue his legal work and compensate the college!)[150] At his trial, Justice and his defence counsel had also sought to argue (unavailingly) that the 60 books named in the indictment had not been properly identified.[151] Similarly, in 1698, the notorious Captain Rigby, accused of indecently assaulting a man: "... being sensible of his Guilt, and unwilling the same should be disclosed to the World, would not therefore Plead 'Not Guilty' to his Inditment; neither would he confess the same [plead guilty], but Demurr'd to the Indictment, in hopes, as his council alledged, that they might find some Fault therein." To 'demur' meant to found a defence on a point of law, while refusing to plead to the facts alleged. Unfortunately for Rigby, after debating the issue, the court decided the indictment was good, and therefore judgment was given against him. Affidavits giving the salient details

---

150. *The Gentleman's Magazine*, 1742, vol. 12, p.290.
151. P. Gaskell, "Henry Justice, a Cambridge Book Thief," *Transactions of the Cambridge Bibliographical Society*, 1952, pp.348-357.

of his crime were then read before sentence was passed. Regretting his course of action, Rigby insisted on his innocence and asserted that he was "misadvised by his Council in Demurring to the Inditment". This being a misdemeanour accusation, a failure to plead did not lead to pressing, but was treated as a plea of guilty, and Rigby could be legally represented.[152] Others met with more success. Thus, three of the four counts against Sir Thomas More at his trial in 1535 appear to have been dismissed after he chose to demur, admitting the facts of the first three averments but submitting that they were not sufficient in law to constitute offences (on the fourth count he was forced to enter a 'not guilty' plea, on which he was ultimately convicted and executed).[153]

The Criminal Trial for Noblemen

As Cesare Beccaria noted, until late in the eighteenth century, continental Europe abounded with nobles whose legal privileges made up "so great a part of the laws of nations."[154] England was different. Although its peers had special rights with regard to arrest, execution and mode of trial, very few men qualified for these privileges. Unlike most continental countries, the great majority of upper class

---

152. Anon, *An Account of the Proceedings against Capt Edward Rigby*, London, F. Collins, 1698, pp.1-2.
153. H. Schulte Herbruggen, "The Process against Sir Thomas More," *Law Quarterly Review*, 1983, vol. 99, p.130.
154. C. Beccaria, *An Essay on Crimes and Punishments*, London, J. Almon, p.80.

Englishmen were not members of the aristocracy. The peerage was confined to those who could sit in the House of Lords: dukes, marquises, earls, viscounts, and barons, often referred to collectively as "noblemen". Knights and esquires were "simply called gentlemen".[155] Such gentlemen had no extra legal privileges. As Sir Edward Coke noted in his *Institutes*: "The true [legal] division of persons is, that everie man is either of nobilitie, that is, a lord of parliament of the upper house, or under the degree of nobilitie, amongst the commons."[156] Misson put it more succinctly by observing that commoners were "the People, not noble".[157] Whether a defendant was a baronet, knight, gentleman, yeoman, husbandman or vagabond (i.e. 99.9 per cent of the population) criminal procedure was, theoretically, the same.[158] Despite the widespread existence of courtesy titles for the younger sons of noblemen, even these had no legal implications, in a country where normally only the eldest male child inherited nobility: "The rest of the sons of the nobility by the rigour of the law be but esquires."[159]

Only those of the same status could try a nobleman. This meant that if accused of a capital crime or treason he was: "... judged by his peers and equals: that is, the yeomanrie [i.e. those who made up the trial jury at assizes] doth not go

---

155. W. Harrison, "Description of England," R. Holinshed, *The First Volume of the Chronicles of England, Scotland and Ireland*, London, John Harrison, 1577, The Thirde Book, pp.103-104.
156. See also Blackstone, *Commentaries on the laws of England*, vol. 1, pp.397-406.
157. Misson, *Memoirs and Observations in his Travels over England*, p.161.
158. Smith, *De Republica Anglorum*, p.119.
159. Harrison, "Description of England," pp.103-104.

upon him." In such cases, each available peer would normally take part in the hearing (sometimes a selection would be used instead), and give an individual verdict on the accused man, starting with the most junior, finishing with the most senior, and with one prominent nobleman presiding in the judicial role: "And for Judge one Lord sitteth, who is Constable of England for that day."[160] Trials of aristocrats for conventional felony, as opposed to treason, were very rare, usually being *causes célèbres*, such as that of Mervyn Touchet for rape in 1631. However, Touchet was not unique. Thus, in 1678, Philip, Earl of Pembroke and Montgomery, was tried before his fellow peers for the murder of a man named Nathaniel Cony, whom he had struck and kicked during a drink fuelled argument over which of them was the better 'gentleman'. The trial took place in a specially appointed court in Westminster Hall. The defendant was prosecuted by the Attorney and Solicitor General, as appears to have been common in cases involving the peerage, and warned to be cautious in his defence, but also encouraged that, as with commoners: "... their Lordships thought themselves bound in honour to be counsel for him in matters of law; and that, though there were counsel to plead against him, no skill or arguments could pervert their Lordships' justice. He should not fall by the charms of eloquence." Much of the mechanics of the trial were similar to other criminal matters heard on indictment. The prisoner was arraigned, and "held up his hand". When the Crown's sworn evidence was complete he was given the

---

160. Smith, *De Republica Anglorum*, p.119.

opportunity to speak (unsworn) in his own defence but declined to do so. The Lords retired to their own chamber and after two hours' debate returned to court to give their verdicts, individually and in reverse order of seniority, the Lord High Steward (presiding over the trial) keeping a record of the numbers. Six found him guilty of murder (for which he would have been executed), 18 favoured a complete acquittal and 40 convicted of the lesser crime of manslaughter. Unlike a (unanimous) jury verdict in a normal trial on indictment, peers decided by a simple majority, so that a finding of manslaughter was returned.[161] Similarly, Lord Charles Mohun was acquitted by a majority when he stood trial in 1693, for murdering the actor William Mountfort. It was claimed that he had been an accessory to one Captain Hill, a personal friend, who actually stabbed Mountfort. In his defence he claimed to have been an innocent bystander to the incident. Unlike normal felony hearings, the trial took place over several days. Like Pembroke, he was tried at Westminster Hall, also being prosecuted by the Crown's law officers, again with the Lord High Steward presiding. Of the peers present, 67 declared, with their hands on their breasts according to custom, "Not Guilty, upon my honour", while 14 found him guilty, so he was acquitted. (Seven years later he was again prosecuted for murder committed in the course of a duel. At this trial his acquittal was unanimous.)[162]

---

161. Rayner and Crook, *The Complete Newgate Calendar*, vol.I, at pp.271-273.
162. Birkenhead, *Famous Trials of History*, vol.1, pp.86-87.

Chapter 16

Juries, Verdicts, Appeals and Sentence

The Trial Jury

Then as now, the bifurcation of tribunal between law and fact was noteworthy for foreign visitors from civil law countries, where the two were normally combined. Thus, a German traveller in the 1590s carefully recorded that the jury: "... sit upon facts, and return their verdict to the judges (who in England are only such of the law, and not of the fact)."[1] The sheriff had responsibility for returning the trial jury. This would be taken from a panel that was, in theory, twice its size, a necessary precaution because many who were summoned avoided the duty or accepted the fine for non-attendance, and others might (less frequently) be challenged: "... only Twelve are sworn, yet Twenty-four are to be returned to supply the Defects or Want of Appearance of those that are challenged off, or make Default."[2] In 1731, in a statutory attempt to ensure random selection, it was provided that the names of those summoned for service on a jury panel were to be written on "distinct pieces of parchment", placed in a box, and then drawn at random until there was the complement of 12.[3] Broadly speaking, as

---

1. P. Hentzner, *Travels in England during the reign of Queen Elizabeth*, London, Cassell & Co. 1889, p.80.
2. M. Hale, *The History of the Common Law of England*, London, J. Walthoe, 1713, p.253.
3. *The Gentleman's Magazine*, 1731, vol. 1, p.28.

Mathew Hale noted, jurors were to be appointed, "Without the Nomination of either Party", from those of appropriate estates and quality who came from the "Neighbourhood of the Fact to be inquired, or at least of the County or Bailywick". Thus, there were personal, economic and geographic preconditions for service, though, as Hale's comment makes clear, the last of these had become very loose by the later seventeenth century.

Jury service was confined to men between the age of 21 and 70 years (it was unusual to summon jurors in their 60s if they were decrepit). There were special exemptions from service for clerics and a few government office holders. In theory, jurors were men of good character. Thus, Hale noted that they should not be: "Convict of any notorious Crime that may render them unfit for that Employment."[4] What this meant, according to Sir Edward Coke's *Institutes*, was that any juror could be challenged if he was attainted or convicted of treason, felony, returning a false verdict, perjury, or had suffered any "corporall punishment whereby he becommeth infamous". Coke suggested that the list of those excluded might extend to debtors and excommunicants. In reality, however, screening was not as strictly enforced as his remarks suggest. Nevertheless, the county sheriff, responsible for jury selection, was expressly warned against accepting 'notorious' characters for service. None of the jurors in Hertfordshire in the late sixteenth and early seventeenth century appear to have been convicted of a felony. This did not necessarily make them of 'spotless'

---

4.   Hale, *The History of the Common Law of England*, p.254.

reputation. Several had been indicted for lesser offences, including riot and assault. Thomas Kent, a grand juror, had also been the subject of several complaints by women who claimed that he had molested them.[5] Given the difficulties involved in finding appropriate numbers of suitable men, it is likely that convictions were often ignored unless for grave matters.

Trial jurors were normally members of the middling social orders.[6] Theoretically, over three-quarters of adult males were not qualified to sit on even a quarter sessions petty jury. Typically, rural jurors would include a large admixture of small yeoman or tenant farmers and the more skilled type of craftsman. Urban jurors often consisted of "Tradesmen, merchants, or [minor] Gentlemen".[7] In many counties there was a modest social difference between those who sat as trial jurors at quarter sessions and those summoned for the more exalted assizes. This was not invariably the case. Thus, in Cheshire, there was a considerable overlap between the jury composition of the two courts; 66 per cent who served in the assizes also sat as jurors at quarter sessions, and another 12 per cent were

---

5. P.C. Lawson, "Lawless Juries? The Composition and Behaviour of Hertfordshire Juries, 1573-1624," J.S.Cockburn and Green (eds.) *Twelve Good Men and True: The Criminal Trial Jury in England 1200-1800*, Princeton, Princeton University Press, 1988, p.121.
6. F. Grigor, *Sir John Fortescue's Commendation of the Laws of England: The Translation into English of De Laudibus Legum Angliae*, London, Sweet and Maxwell, 1917, (written c.1461-5, first published in Latin c.1537), p.48.
7. M. Misson, *Memoirs and Observations in his Travels over England*, J.Ozell (Trans.), London, 1719, p.161.

empanelled for those courts, although not ultimately called.[8]

Over the years, Parliament experimented with different property requirements for trial jurors. A 40 shilling requirement (lands or revenues to at least that value a year) was the general rule in royal courts for the late medieval period and much of the sixteenth century. A frequent justification for this restriction, was a fear that in its absence: "... by reason of their meanness and poverty, they [jurors] may be liable to be easily bribed or subborned."[9] To early modern notions, the property qualification ensured the presence of higher quality jurors: "The general course of the world being to esteem men according to their estates." Additionally, some thought that there were other practical benefits, not least because: "Jurors that have estates to lose, will be afraid to commit perjury [by returning verdicts against the evidence]."[10] Others stressed that such men would also be reluctant to bring shame on their families by returning a perverse verdict.

Linked to such beliefs were longstanding claims that the 40 shillings qualification was too modest. Even in the fifteenth century, Fortescue had suggested that for serious felonies it was desirable to have men with annual lands and revenues "to the value of a 100 shillings". As a result of such arguments, an Elizabethan statute of 1585 (27 Eliz., ch. 6) eventually raised it to £4 a year of lands, rent or tenements.[11]

---

8.   J.C. Morrill, *The Cheshire Grand Jury 1625-1659, A Social and Administrative Study*, Leicester, Leicester University Press, 1976, p.12.

9.   Grigor, *Sir John Fortescue's Commendation of the Laws of England*, p.40.

10. Sir F. Bacon, *Cases of Treason*, London, John More, 1641, p.13.

11. Grigor, *Sir John Fortescue's Commendation of the Laws of England*, pp.24 and 48.

By the seventeenth century, inflation meant that the property qualification was lower in real terms than it had been in 1558, embracing minor freeholders as well as 'substantial' men. As a result, in 1652, William Leach could complain that one reason for an apparent decline in the quality of jurors, both personal and intellectual, was: "The Estates of Jury Men in these modern times, being far lesse in value ... then they have been in ancient times." He considered that inferior men were increasingly carrying out the duty. Even worse, such men were often "not onley indigant, but [also] keepers of Ale-houses, and other places of Tipling, and the newer and worser sort."[12] Such fears led to ambitious suggestions during the Barebones parliament that jury service should be confined to men with an income of 600 pounds a year.[13] More modestly, and realistically, Leach felt that the financial qualification should be enforced more strictly, proper allowance being made for a potential juror's debts, and that ideally jurors should always have 40 pounds of disposable assets before being chosen.[14] However, the four pound figure was retained until 1664, when Parliament raised the requirement to 20 pounds so as not to "returne the poorer and simpler Freeholders lesse able to descerne the Causes in question". This provision was limited in duration to 13 years, after which the earlier four pound requirement revived. However, in 1692, parliament

---

12. W. Leach, *The Bribe-Takers of Jury-Men*, London, E. Cotes, 1652, p.3.
13. S. Roberts, "Jury Vetting in the 17th Century," *History Today*, 1982, vol. 33, issue 2, p.26.
14. Leach, *The Bribe-Takers of Jury-Men*, p.6.

introduced a 10 pound freehold for jurors in all royal courts, such as the assizes, and also for gaol delivery if conducted at quarter sessions (though borough courts were excepted from the provision).

Although the aim of such statutes was to secure judgment by the most educated and least corruptible social elements, the "ablest and sufficientist" in the words of the 1664 Act, in practice they often failed woefully in this task. Quite frequently, the qualifications were simply ignored.[15] Indeed, one risk in setting the property requirement for jurors too high was that any semblance of following the prescribed statute might be abandoned. For much of the early modern period, petty jurors, for both quarter sessions and assizes, were in short supply. Even in the 1560s, Sir Thomas Smith had noted that in many towns and cities, the lack of yeomen allowed the poor, who normally had "no voice nor authoritie" in society, to sit on inferior juries.[16] This reality must be remembered when considering claims that a more 'democratically' recruited jury would have been less likely to sanction customs deemed criminal by the authorities.

Service on trial juries was often highly unpopular. It lacked social prestige (unlike the grand jury) involved an interruption to the juror's own business, a sometimes lengthy and arduous journey, and an absence from regular recreations. This encouraged many who were eligible to risk

---

15. J. C. Oldham, "The Origins of the Special Jury," *University of Chicago Law Review*, 1983, vol. 50, p.146.
16. Sir T. Smith, *De Republica Anglorum*, London, 1565, pp.76-77.

a small fine to avoid it. Others might resort to bribery. It was claimed that the well-to-do could usually avoid jury service by "giving a Shilling or Half a Crown to the Sheriff's Officer".[17] Such practices produced periodic statutes designed to deal with the "grete extorcions and oppressions" caused by the "subtilie and untrue demanor of Sherevis and their ministers".[18] These normally met only limited success, such practices rarely being severely punished. Thus, in 1731, at the Monmouth assizes, a bailiff (i.e. one of the sheriff's men) who was convicted of taking money to excuse freeholders from attendance was merely fined.[19]

In the few cases where a gentleman was accused of a felony it appears that informal steps were often taken to enhance the social complexion of the trial jury from its usual mixture of small freeholders, lesser merchants and tradesmen. William Harrison, as well as noting that a jury of yeomen could not, legally, try noblemen also observed that if a gentleman was tried it was: "... by gentlemen and an inferior, by God and by the country, to wit, the yeomanry."[20] Thus, when the aristocratic continentals accused of murdering Anthony Thynne were tried at the Old Bailey, in 1681, it was reported to the presiding judge, Lord Chief Justice North, that one of the defendants had asked that his jurors might be "Persons of some Quality, as

---

17. *The Gentleman's Magazine*, 1737, vol. 7, p.808.
18. Oldham, "The Origins of the Special Jury," pp.142-144.
19. *The Gentleman's Magazine*, 1731, vol. 1, p.125.
20. Canon W. Harrison, *Elizabethan England edited from the Description of England*, E. Rhys (Ed.), London, Camelot Series, 1889, p.242.

they use to treat Persons of his Quality". Rather than being annoyed at this request, North immediately checked with the under-sheriff: "You have merchants of good Account, I suppose, upon this Pannel?" He was assured that they were all drawn from such backgrounds.[21] Similarly, at Alice Lisle's trial at Winchester, in 1685, the case being a "Cause of some Expectation, the Lord Chief Justice order'd the Sheriff to return a Jury of Good Quality".[22] Of course, not all requests that jurors of a higher than normal standard be returned were successful, especially when the defendants were themselves of marginal status. Thus, at his felony trial at the Croydon assizes in 1590, the Puritan Minister John Udall was philosophical when denied trial by an: "... inquest of learned men; but seeing I shall not, I am contented to be tried by the ordinary course."[23] Conversely, middle ranking jurors might occasionally show sympathy towards members of their own class who were accused of crimes against men from the upper social strata. Thus, a victualler named John Peetly, living in Holborn, was roused one night in 1695 by a group of roistering gentlemen who threw lighted tapers into his house, setting fire to a pile of linen. He pursued them, carrying a carbine loaded with buckshot. When he eventually caught up with the group, they had already been stopped and disarmed by several watchmen. Nevertheless, after being "pushed by a Watchman", his gun went off,

---

21. Anon, *The Tryal and Condemnation of George Brosky*, London, Thomas Basset, 1682, p.6.
22. T. Salmon, *Tryals for High-Treason, and other Crimes* ..., vol.4, London, D. Brown,1720, pp.384-402.
23. Oldham, "The Origins of the Special Jury," p.157.

mortally wounding the nephew of a peer. Peetly was acquitted as the jury accepted that the gun discharged "without his knowledge".[24]

Whatever the theory, in cases involving ordinary defendants at least, the quality of the jury could be very 'mixed' in practice. At the trial of one Crosby, a constable, for murdering a man involved in an illegal gathering at St Albans in 1662, the dead man's supporters complained that the petty jury was grossly unqualified, doubting whether even three of its members met the 40 shillings per annum freehold requirement. The jurors were allegedly made up of two innkeepers, four ale-house keepers, a fiddler, a tapster, a grocer, a barber, a chandler and a blacksmith. Even worse, though less reliably, they claimed that these individuals were of doubtful probity, and thus likely to be sympathetic to defendants and acquittals, being a: "... company of ignorant, inconsiderate, heady, wicked, ungodly, vicious, debauched, prophane, drunken and swearing fellows."[25] The erosion of the rules on jury qualification could extend to the most important cases. Thus, the Bill of Rights of 1689 complained that in recent years "partial, corrupt, and unqualified persons" had served on juries, some of them not even freeholders.

Indicative of the problems attendant on finding even 12 appropriate men is the regularity with which talesmen, "men of all sorts", were taken up by bailiffs in many areas.

---

24. Anon, *The True Relation of the tryals at the Sessions of Oyer and Terminer, ... as particularly of E.Wigenton for whipping a girl to death ...*, London, 1695, pp.1-2.
25. Anon, *Murther will Out*, London, 1662, pp.8-9.

These were jurors enlisted from the close vicinity of the assizes or sessions court, immediately prior to the trials going on, to make up the requisite numbers on jury panels. By the 1620s, and "contrary to the ancient writs and forms of law", more Western Circuit causes were being tried by talesmen than by properly empanelled jurymen.[26] Talesmen were not required to have the property qualifications of jurors summoned in the normal manner by the sheriff. Indeed, it was only in 1692 that they had to meet any property requirement at all, and then it was realistically set at only half the normal level provided for by statute (4 W. & M. C.24), making it five pounds in England and three pounds in Wales. In practice, many talesmen were actually witnesses, constables or sureties attending the assizes on other business. Sometimes, even grand jurors might be asked to sit on a trial jury to boost numbers.

Significantly, however, in many counties, the use of talesmen began to decline after c. 1650. This may have been linked to an apparent increase in the use of a 'hard core' of jurors who repeatedly attended assizes and sessions. The employment of very experienced jurors was not an entirely new phenomenon, even then. Although of the 6,408 men sworn to jury service on the Home Circuit between 1559 and 1603 only 22 per cent sat more than twice, a small number sat extremely frequently, perhaps 30 to 40 times. This became much more marked after 1650, by which time, for example, all Kent jury panels contained several very experienced men, one of whom nearly always served as the

---

26.   Oldham, "The Origins of the Special Jury," pp.142-144.

jury foreman.[27] In Cheshire, one in six juries had no new members at all, though, on average, there were two or three novice jurors in most of them.[28] This may have been a deliberate policy, aimed at allowing a quota of frequently called men to gain an intimate familiarity with the office and a basic knowledge of criminal law and procedure. Their experience must have assisted the speed and smooth running of the courts. It might also explain the growing concern of many observers that one or two "antient jurymen" (the foreman usually amongst them) were dominating discussions on verdicts.[29] Whether 'old hands' or not, the speed, brevity and lack of technicality in criminal trials were also conducive to jurors acquiring a better understanding of their role than their modern counterparts.

Attitudes to the Jury

Jurors had a huge responsibility, as their service involved the: "... Suppressing of Sathan and his kingdome, the securite of his Maiestie, [and] the preservation of the common Peace of this Countie."[30] Could they measure up to

27. J.S. Cockburn, "Twelve Silly Men? The trial Jury at Assizes, 1560-1670," J.S.Cockburn and T.A. Green (Eds.), *Twelve Good Men and True: The Criminal Trial Jury in England 1200-1800*, Princeton, Princeton University Press, 1988, pp.161 and 165.
28. Morrill, *The Cheshire Grand Jury 1625-1659*, p.12.
29. Sir J.Hawles, *The Englishmans Right*, London, 1680, p.36.
30. R. Crompton, *L'office et auctority de justices de Peace*, London, The Company of Stationers, 1606, p.3.

such onerous demands? Here, contemporary opinion differed. Some jurists, such as Mathew Hale and William Blackstone, were enormously impressed by this 'palladium' of English justice, seeing it as an: "... admirable criterion of truth, and most important guardian both of public and private liberty."[31] Such views were not confined to lawyers. By the sixteenth century, there was an element of national pride in the institution, a desire to avoid "Frenchified and Italianated inventions", and a fear that its abandonment would reduce Englishmen to the "like depth of bondage with our neighbours". This was a theme that would become hackneyed in the following century. According to William Walwin, many English travellers, familiar with 'abroad', such as Colonel Henry Marten, developed a "zealous affection" and respect for juries. So strong was this that when Marten sat as a judge at Reading he insisted the grand jury wear their hats in his presence."[32]

Nevertheless, even patriotic Englishmen were some-times troubled by the apparent absence of the institution from most of continental Europe, and sought to explain it. To Fortescue, the reason for England being almost alone in using the jury, despite its inherent superiority, was simple: unlike continentals, the: "... common people of England are better inclined and qualified to discern into such causes, which require a nice examination." The reason for this, he (ingeniously) claimed, was that the country was so fertile

---

31. W. Blackstone, *Commentaries on the Laws of England*, Oxford, Clarendon Press, 1769, vol. 4, p.407.
32. W. Walwin, *Juries justified*, London, Robert Wood, 1651, pp.2-3.

and productive that it could support large numbers of yeomen in any given locality, men whose minds were refined and not excessively fatigued by hard labour. Given that jurors were supposed to come from the immediate vicinity of a criminal or civil allegation (about to change even in England) this was vital. European countries could not produce sufficient men of the appropriate standard.[33] Even in England, and interspersing outbursts of national pride and the periodic encomiums of legal writers, there was also a steady groundswell of concern about the use of juries.

Praise for the institution was contingent on juries attracting men of an appropriate calibre. The problems attendant on finding individuals of sufficient estates to fill the office have been noted. Linked to them, was a wider concern about the personal quality of many jurymen. This was found at the highest levels. Thus, in 1607, a 'Proclamation for Jurors' issued by James I frankly acknowledged that jury service: "... oftentimes resteth upon such as are either simple and ignorant, and almost at a gaze in any cause of difficultie, or else upon those that are so accustomed and inured to passe and serve upon Juries, and they have almost lost that tendernesse of Conscience, which in such cases is to bee wished, and make the service, as it were an occupation and practice."[34] The King's fears were not new, and were to be regularly reiterated in subsequent decades. Thus, at the trial of the Earl of Essex in 1600,

---

33. Grigor, *Sir John Fortescue's Commendation of the Laws of England*, pp.47-8.
34. Oldham, "The Origins of the Special Jury," pp.142-144.

Francis Bacon observed to the peers who would judge him: "I speak not to any ordinary Jury, but to prudent, grave and wise peers."[35] His inference was that such qualities were often missing amongst normal jurors. Similarly, in 1654, William Sheppard lamented that jurors were "generally very corrupt". By this he meant they were in some way defective, whether ignorant, illiterate, unqualified, or subject to external influences and bribes.[36] In particular, there was frequent concern about their impartiality, some complaining that it was "hard to get an unbiased Jury".[37] It was feared that intimidation, bribery and false verdicts were widespread. Thus, in 1682, John Evelyn was convinced that Count Coningsmark, an alleged principal in a murder, was acquitted by a "corrupt jury, and so got away".[38] There was also concern that some jurymen were motivated by mercenary considerations. Jurors, though not formally paid, were normally granted eight pence per day in expenses. Although, in theory, the money was granted to cover the cost of meals, there were periodic suggestions that it was the primary motivation behind some men's service, and that there were jurors serving who: "... had more need to be relieved by the 8d. than discretion to sift out the truth of the fact."[39]

---

35. R.L. Marcus, "English Common Law ...," *University of Illinois Law Review*, 1984, p.687.
36. Roberts, "Jury Vetting in the 17th Century," p.26.
37. Bacon, *Cases of Treason*, p.12.
38. J. Evelyn, *The Diary of John Evelyn*, vol.III, E.S. De Beer (Ed.), Oxford, Clarendon Press, 1955, p.273.
39. Bacon, *Cases of Treason*, p.12.

The two contending schools of thought about the value of juries were manifest in the published dispute between William Walwin and Henry Robinson (who were also personal friends). In 1651, Robinson, "emboldened" by Cromwellian legal reforms, such as the introduction of the vernacular to the indictment and other documents and the avoidance of unnecessary court fees, suggested that juries might usefully be replaced. He advanced seven specific objections to the institution, though some overlapped. In particular, he asserted that there were "not a competent number of understanding and fit men to be had in the lesser Divisions of a county". Those that were summoned, frequently resented the office because of the work involved and only served to avoid being fined, not out of choice. Additionally, and like Hawles, he thought that a number of clever individual jurors had a disproportionate influence on the jury's deliberations. This was aggravated by the practice of:

"... keeping the Jury without Fire-light, Bread, or Drink, as the Law requires, [which] may possibly make the major part of them, if not all, agree upon a verdict contrary to their Consciences, to be freed from any of these exigencies; at least, some of them to strike up with the rest in a Joint-Verdict, since it is well near impossible for twelve men, all circumstances considered, much more in a doubtful case, to be of one opinion; and though the case were never so clear, yet one peremptory man of a strong constitution, whether his judgment be right or wrong, may starve all the rest, unless they will give verdict as he will have them."

Robinson proposed an alternative system of professional, salaried, judges, sitting alone who would determine all matters, criminal and civil, without juries (essentially, the system already found in much of continental Europe, though many European countries used panels of judges).[40]

By contrast, Walwin denied that England had any shortage of men clever enough to "Judge between right and wrong". To Walwin, objections that jurors resented the loss of time involved, because it led them to neglect their own affairs, were absurd. The entire English justice system was reliant on unpaid part-timers; those serving as constables and headboroughs had much more onerous (and unpopular) duties than jurors. Complaints that men were 'wearied' into giving their verdicts by being deprived of food, drink or light until they reached a decision were also stoutly rejected, if only because a "true English conscience is of more solid stuff". Similarly, he dismissed allegations that a few assertive jurors frequently dominated deliberations and would "over-sway all the rest of the Jury". According to Walwin, the stolid national character meant that in England such overtly opinionated and 'clever' men aroused suspicion rather than respect: "... our nimble-pated men are not in so great credit, as possibly they are in other parts." Finally, he saw no reason why even those who only

---

40.   H. Robinson, *Certain Consideration In Order to a more Speedy, Cheap, and Equall Distribution of Justice throughout the Nation*, London, Mathew Simmons, 1651, pp.2-3.

served to avoid being fined would still not act conscientiously in reaching a verdict.[41]

Alien Jurors

In urban areas, with significant immigrant populations, it was normal to allow a foreign defendant to be tried *per medietatem linguae* ("by half tongue"), that is, to find six of his fellow-countrymen on the trial jury. This tradition had originated in Norman times, and stemmed from the novel presence of Jews in the country, and the Crown's desire (largely for mercenary reasons) not to see them treated unfairly in civil litigation with Christians. It subsequently expanded to cover Italian and German merchants. In 1353, the Statute of the Staple codified the common law customary right, and the following year another statute extended it to all aliens in any civil or criminal case. The right was only formally ended in 1870, although it was withdrawn from treason cases in 1554.[42] Thus, throughout the early modern period foreign defendants could ask for a special jury of six "denizens" and six aliens. Although originally used for mercantile disputes, the provision became most significant in criminal matters, and aimed at preventing nationalistic bias on the part of native jurors from prejudicing

41. Walwin, *Juries justified*, pp.5-12.
42. D.A. Ramirez, "The Mixed Jury And The Ancient Custom Of Trial By Jury De Medietate Linguae: A History And A Proposal For Change," *Boston University Law Review*, 1994, vol. 74, pp.784-786.

foreigners.[43] In 1681, the translator at the murder trial of a German reported that his client asked to be tried by "half his own country and half English".[44] Similarly, in 1700, a jury whose members were divided between Englishmen and foreigners convicted three Dutch Metropolitan publicans of murdering a patron.[45] Where the defendants were French, German or from the low-countries, six fellow countrymen could often be secured quite easily, especially in London. Where they were from a more exotic location, it might be necessary to offer them men from other (albeit sympathetic rather than hostile) continental states, rather than their own nationals. Interestingly, even before 1603, Scotsmen were not deemed to be aliens, as one W.D. found to his cost after he asked for such a jury in 1571, when tried for rape at the Court of Queen's Bench. As well as leaving his request too late (he should have asked before the petty jurymen were sworn) the judges held, rather dubiously, that a Scotsman was "never here accounted an alien" and that the "Scottish [lowland] language is not a strange tongue, but mere English". This suggests that some observers thought that linguistic considerations were as much behind the privilege as a fear of national sympathies.[46]

---

43. J.M. Cornett, "Hoodwink'd by custom ...," *William and Mary Journal of Women and the Law*, 1997, vol. 4, pp.16-17.
44. Anon, *The Tryal and Condemnation of George Brosky*, p.3.
45. J.L Rayner and G.T. Crook (Eds.), *The Complete Newgate Calendar* (Vols. 1-5). London, Privately printed for the Navarre Society, 1926, vol. II, pp.127-128.
46. L. Mortimer, "A More than Ordinary Case of 'Rape'," 13 and 14 Elizabeth 1, *The American Journal of Legal History*, 1969, vol. 7, p.159.

Challenges to Jurors

There were 35 peremptory challenges available to each defendant throughout the early modern period (i.e. challenges which allowed them to reject potential jurors without the need to show cause).[47] The limitation prevented a defendant rejecting three entire juries (36 men) without stated reasons. However he could challenge "as many as he hath cause of chalenge to if he can prove it".[48] This meant that if, for example, he could show the likelihood of bias through personal animosity he could request the removal of any number of jurors. Then as now, any challenges had to be made before the jurors were sworn. Thus, a group of Quakers indicted for failing to take the oath of allegiance in 1663, belatedly attempted to challenge jurors that they recognized as openly hostile to them, *after* they had taken the oath. This was rejected by the assizes judge, who, when they complained that they had been ignorant of their right to do so earlier, gave the terse retort "That was your own fault."[49]

Despite these impressive theoretical rights, challenges of either type were only rarely exercised in practice. As the young Cesar de Saussure stressed in 1726: "You must not think, however, that the jury is changed for every criminal, for as these habitually come from the scum of the people,

---

47. Grigor, *Sir John Fortescue's Commendation of the Laws of England*, p.44.
48. T.F.Plucknett and J.C.Barton (Eds.), 1st *Dialogue, 1523, St Germain's Doctor and Student*, London, Selden Society, 1974, p.63.
49. Anon, *A Cry Against Oppression and Cruelty*, London, 1663, p.13.

honest artisans are usually chosen for the whole assizes."[50] Mary Carleton, facing trial for bigamy at the Old Bailey in the 1660s, was probably typical of most defendants in her reaction to the empanelling of the jury and her dependence, in the absence of a lawyer, on friendly advice: "I pleaded Not guilty: and, as instructed by my friends ... put my self for my Triall upon God and the Country, without making any exception, or ever so much as examining what my Jury were."[51] The normality of such a reaction was fortunate, given the relatively small jury panel available. Occasionally, special circumstances meant that these 'theoretical' rights were actively invoked. Thus, when the barrister Spencer Cowper and three other lawyers were tried for murder at Hertford assizes on July 16, 1699, the prisoners and the Crown's counsel challenged so many men that they were unable, initially, to produce a full jury, others having to be added to the panel. This was despite the defendants 'pooling' their challenges, rather than exercising the full quota individually.[52] Similarly, in the *cause célèbre* arising out of the murder of Anthony Thynne in 1680, the foreign defendants, who had had their rights carefully explained by a translator, set about challenging members of the jury panel with gusto. Their objections ranged from suspicions that the proposed jurors were acquainted with Thynne, via disliking the country of origin of some of the six foreign jurors

50. M. Van Muyden (Trans. and Ed.), *A foreign View of England in the reigns of George I and George II; The letters of Monsieur Cesar de Saussure, to his Family*, London, John Murray, 1902, p.118.
51. Anon, *The Case of Madam Mary Carleton*, London, Sam Speed, pp.74-75.
52. Rayner and Crook, *The Complete Newgate Calendar*, vol. II, p.109.

tendered, to simply not liking the appearance of individual men.[53]

No longer a Self-Informing Jury

It appears that early fourteenth-century criminal trial jurors were usually drawn from at least the hundred, and often the immediate neighbourhood, of the crimes they tried. As a result, they frequently came to court already cognisant of many of the facts of a case. However, in the ensuing two centuries, the trial jury went from being a self-informing body, which attended court as much to speak as to hear, to being largely passive triers of fact, coming to court to listen to evidence on which they then based their verdicts. This process was complete well before the end of the sixteenth century. Thus, in the 1560s, it was noted that a prisoner would not usually challenge a juror because, for the most part, they were "unknowen to him, nor they know not him". (If only because social differences between middling order jurors and the "idle men" frequently accused of commiting felonies meant that they were inherently unlikely to be acquainted.)[54] By the eighteenth century, any expectation of jury knowledge was gone. As a result, Giles Duncombe, in his *Trials per Pais*, could suggest that jurors should step out of the jury box and take the witness stand to testify if it transpired that they had information relevant to a dispute.

---

53. Anon, *The Tryal and Condemnation of George Brosky*, p.6.
54. Smith, *De Republica Anglorum*, p.113.

He cited a case where this had happened in 1656 (and asserted that there was no need to swear the 'witness' as he was already covered by his jury oath).[55] This policy had been judicially suggested as early as 1650 and very cautiously approved by the distinguished judge Sir John Holt in 1698.

Nonetheless, although it is apparent that the Angevin system of self-informing juries was breaking down by the late middle ages, the exact speed at which this occurred is difficult to assess. Some have argued for a relatively sudden and revolutionary change in the late fifteenth century. Others have suggested a much more gradual development, lasting several centuries. Either way, it would appear that by the beginning of the early modern period the process was already well advanced. Indeed, some recent research suggests that medieval jurors were never quite as self-informing as has sometimes been thought. Thus, in civil matters, a partial separation between witnesses and jurors can occasionally be found as early as the beginning of the thirteenth century, at least for complicated matters. In criminal cases, the process clearly started later and took longer to complete. Nevertheless, even in the thirteenth century witnesses were being summoned to appear before the General Eyre, the (indirect) ancestor of the assizes, and, by the end of that century, it appears that some juries lacked the local knowledge to be properly self-informing. Arguably, by 1400, the criminal trial jury was already fairly

---

55.   J. Oldham, "Truth-Telling in the Eighteenth-Century English Courtroom," *Law and History Review*, 1994, vol. 12, Number 1, p.106.

similar to that of the late 1500s, the active 'medieval' jury having substantially yielded to the passive triers of fact of the modern era.[56] By the 1500s, it was normal for jurors to be largely ignorant before trial of the matters that they were to determine.[57] Indeed, there was an implicit acceptance that jurors could only act on evidence received in a Henrician Statute of 1536 (28 Henry VIII, c.15). This provided that the trial of pirates should be by "12 lawful men inhabited in the shire" rather than, as had previously been the case, "judged and determined before the admiral or his lieutenant or commissary, after the course of the civil laws". Such jurors could not possibly have any personal knowledge of the defendant or his alleged crimes, which would often have been committed hundreds of miles away at sea.[58] This had major implications for the trial process, as jurors were likely to be swayed less by ancient custom and their own social norms, rather than judicial directions, when reaching their verdicts.

Nevertheless, change was gradual, so that some relics of the medieval approach to jury knowledge survived well into the early modern period. In the transitional stage, between c.1400 and c.1700, jurors, though not partial or intimately familiar with the details of a case before trial, were also not

---

56. E. Powell, "Jury Trial at Gaol Delivery in the Late Middle Ages: The Midland Circuit, 1400-1429," J.S. Cockburn and T.A. Green (Eds.), *Twelve Good Men and True*, Princeton, Princeton University Press, 1988, at pp.78-116.
57. J. Langbein, "The Origins of Public Prosecution at Common Law," *The American Journal of Legal History*, 1973, vol. 17, pp.314-315.
58. G.R. Elton, *The Tudor Constitution: Documents and Commentary*, 2nd edn., Cambridge, CUP, 1982, pp.158-159.

necessarily completely ignorant of them. Thus, in the 1460s, Fortescue was convinced that a guilty defendant's "life and conversation would be restraint and terror sufficent to those who should have any inclination to [perversely] acquit him". He could still suggest that the English felony jury merged witnesses with triers of fact, being made up of: "... good and lawful men of the neighbourhood to the Vill where the fact was done, who are in no wise allied to the person accused."[59] Fortescue clearly envisaged men without an axe to grind but who also knew the reputations of the parties and the general background to the allegation. Indeed, it has been argued that one reason that England lacked a statute dealing with witness perjury (as opposed to that of jurors) until the Elizabethan Perjury Statute of 1563, was an anachronistic view of the informative role of the jury and that of evidence providing witnesses at trial. (Others have argued that the Act simply enhanced the punishment available for an existing common law offence.)[60] Indicative of at least some jurors still having significant personal knowledge, in 1531, St Germain considered the position of a juror who knew details about a case but whose colleagues insisted on ignoring his information: "Yf one of the xii men of an enquest know the very trouth of his own knowledge and instructed his felowes thereof; and they wyll in no wyse

---

59. Grigor, *Sir John Fortescue's Commendation of the Laws of England*, pp.24 and 45.
60. M.D. Gordon, "The Invention of a Common Law Crime: Perjury and the Elizabethan Courts," *American Journal of Legal History*, 1980, vol. 24, pp.145-170.

gyve credence to hym."[61] Even in the 1600s, some (by then anachronistic) observers were still asserting that the petty jury should come from the "very neighbourhood *de vicinetto*, where the offence was committed". This was necessary, it was claimed, as they were: "... presumed to know something experimentally (besides what they have by testimony) both of the quality of the person, truth, and nature of the offence, with all its circumstances, and happily the credit of the accuser and his witnesses."[62] In 1679, Sir Francis North (wrongly) rejected an attempt to challenge a juror who, it was claimed, knew the prosecutor, on the grounds that jurors "should not be wholly strangers to the fact".[63] The following year, Sir John Hawles also suggested that it was not improper for jurors to have background knowledge when he observed that the trial judge heard only the evidence given in court "for he can regularly know no other, *though the Jury may*".[64] As late as 1698, Sir John Holt accepted that a jury could, theoretically, "give a verdict upon their own knowledge, [though if they did] they ought to tell the Courts so."[65]

Such relics of the older tradition gradually died out. In

---

61. T.F.Plucknett and J.C.Barton (Eds.), *2nd Dialogue, 1530, St Germain's Doctor and Student*, London, Selden Society, 1974, p.292. Christopher St Germain, who died in 1540, at the age of 80, was a native Londoner and a successful lawyer, being a member of the Middle Temple and sometime Master of Requests.
62. Powell, "Jury Trial at Gaol Delivery in the Late Middle Ages: The Midland Circuit, 1400-1429," at pp.78-116.
63. Roberts, "Jury Vetting in the 17th Century," p.26.
64. Hawles, *The English-man's Right*, pp.10-11. My italics.
65. 90 Eng. Rep. 112 (1698).

the 1670s, Mathew Hale was satisfied that not only were jurors not to be "Kindred or Alliance" to any of the parties, but also that they were: "Not to be such as are prepossed or prejudiced before they hear their Evidence."[66] Indeed, Sir John Johnston, executed in December 1690 for assisting in the abduction of an heiress who was subjected to a forced marriage to one of his associates (the union was later dissolved by Parliament), clearly thought that the notoriety and publicity the case had attracted prejudiced his jury trial. At Tyburn, he claimed that he had been greatly wronged by printed papers in which he was charged with another rape at Chester and a similar crime at Utrecht in Holland.[67]

The change in attitudes and practice was closely linked to a change in jury recruitment. The traditional approach for criminal matters, as restated by Sir William Staunford in 1557, was that trial should be *"per 12 homes del vicinet ou le treason ou felonye fuist fait."*[68] In theory, until the 1670s, at least four jurors had to be from the hundred where the crime had been committed (the number was subsequently reduced to two). However, in reality, as Mathew Hale stressed, such a requirement had long been modified in many cases.[69] There was a gradual acceptance during the Elizabethan period that it was often not practical to secure local (to the defendant) men as jurors. Increasingly, jurors drawn from the same shire as the defendant, and in which the assizes was being held, were deemed to be sufficiently

---

66. Hale, *The History of the Common Law of England*, p.253.
67. Rayner and Crook, *The Complete Newgate Calendar*, vol. II, p.59.
68. Sir W. Staunford, *Les Plees Del Corone*, London, 1607, p.154.
69. Hale, *The History of the Common Law of England*, p.253.

'local' to form the jury (though this raises problems of cause and effect). This custom was only belatedly recognised by statute in 1705. There was a growing tendency to recruit jurors from within a small radius of the assizes town. Thus, in Devonshire, although the defendants at the assizes and quarter sessions were drawn from everywhere within that large county, the jurors that tried them were taken almost exclusively from the areas closest to the trial venues, such as Exeter and its environs. This meant that they would have little or no knowledge of cases taken from distant parishes.[70] Similarly, in Kent, jurors from Maidstone presiding over that town's assizes would be unaware of much of the 'background' to defendants from Ashford. This fundamental change appears to have been linked to a general growth in judicial business, making it increasingly impractical to assemble jurors who were local to defendants.

Defences

In many trials, a simple denial by a defendant of the allegations against him would not be sufficient to secure an acquittal, as a *prima facie* case would normally have been established before his being called on to give his account of events. However, even vaguely plausible alternative explanations for suspicious circumstances were often accepted, if the accused was of good character. Thus, Jonathon Telcoat was acquitted in 1695 of murdering a

---

70.   Roberts, "Jury Vetting in the 17th Century," p.27.

woman found dead in a room with him, after it was proved that she was an epileptic and might have hit her head on a nearby flat-iron, and that the defendant could have been standing on the other side of the room.[71] Where identity was in issue, false alibis could be readily procured, at least in urban areas, and were a popular line of defence for anyone who had not been caught red-handed. According to Sir Thomas More, this was common even in the 1530s.[72] The risks of giving such perjured testimony appear to have been quite modest, or at least not so serious as to discourage their use. At his trial for robbery, in 1721, William Casey, a soldier: "... deny'd that he was present when Mr Stone [the victim] was assaulted, and brought five Witnesses to swear, that he was in another Place at that time." At the gallows he admitted the truth of the allegation.[73] Nevertheless, the general suspicion of such alibis also meant that special care might be taken in testing them during cross-examination. When Henry Harrison called alibi witnesses in 1692 they were "Examined apart", at the request of the prosecuting counsel.[74] Schemes for calling false alibis did not always work. In August 1731, Thomas Willar, accused of stealing horses in Essex, faced the Chelmsford assizes with misplaced confidence having approached fellow inmates in the

---

71. Anon, *The True Relation of the tryals at the Sessions of Oyer and Terminer, ... as particularly of E.Wigenton for whipping a girl to death* ..., London, 1695, pp.1-2.
72. Sir T. More, "The Deballaryon of Salem and Bizance 1533," *Works of Sir Thomas More*, London, 1577, pp.996-998.
73. Anon, *Select Trials, for Murders, Robberies, Rapes, Sodomy, Coining, Frauds, And other Offences*, London, J. Wilford, 1734, vol. 1, pp.61-66.
74. Anon, *The Arraignment, Tryal, Conviction and Condemnation of Henry Harrison*, p.17.

county jail and: "... persuaded another Felon to take his Fact upon him, but at the Bar he disown'd it, and left Willar in the Lurch."[75] Why this man should, initially, have agreed to provide Willar with a defence, at the cost of his own neck, is difficult to assess. He may already have been in a hopeless situation, and hoped to profit financially by the service.

An alternative and innocent explanation for apparently incriminating conduct was favoured where the evidence of the witnesses making an allegation could not be dismissed out of hand. Thus, in June 1656, John Sweedale of Easby informed a JP that, while out walking, he had seen a labourer named William Clarke committing bestiality, with a horse, to the "best of his judgment". When Clarke himself was questioned he admitted being near the animal at the relevant time but denied buggery and claimed that he was looking at the mare's hindquarters to see whether an ox had: "... gored her behind or not, for as his master's draught was going down a hill that same day in the afternoon he saw one of the oxen hip at the said mare which was then in the draught."[76] John Deacon and Thomas Blair took a similar approach when they were indicted for committing sodomy at Farringdon in 1743. One of the chief prosecution witnesses, a constable named Robert Pert, was doing his rounds when he heard whispering in a small court that was known as a popular Metropolitan location for homosexual liaisons. Pert crept in and witnessed the two men in an apparently compromising position. Deacon, the younger

---

75. *The Gentleman's Magazine*, 1731, vol. 1, p.351.
76. E. Fudge, "Monstrous Acts," *History Today*, 2000, vol. 50, issue 8, p.20.

man, was clinging to the other: "... his Breeches were down, and his Shirt appeared: I then thought it was a Man and a Woman, for the youngest was in the same Motion as a Man is when he is embracing a Woman." Challenged, the two men pulled up their trousers and claimed to have been, respectively, defecating and urinating, a defence they repeated at trial. However, no excrement was found at the scene when a watchman with a lantern examined it. Blair claimed that the reason for this was that the constable had pulled him away prematurely, so that he fouled his trousers. Pert's response to this suggestion, when it was put to him in cross-examination, was devastating: "I should have smelt him in the Watch-house, if any such Thing as that had been done, for he set close to me a great while."[77]

The explanations given for being found in possession of incriminating items are readily familiar to anyone who has practised in modern criminal courts. The case of John White, a Worcestershire butcher, was typical. He was examined by a JP in 1651, after being suspected of stealing and slaughtering a local gentleman's sheep. White accounted for his possession of a large leg and sirloin of mutton by saying that one evening, a few days earlier, he had been to a house in Evesham that was owned by a local carrier. There, he had, quite fortuitously, met another country butcher, who had sold him the meat for two shillings, eight pence: "But where the country butcher dwells or what is his name John White knoweth not." He claimed that he bought the meat in

---

77.   Anon, *Select Trials for murder, robbery, burglary ... at the Sessions House in the Old-Bailey, from ... 1741 to the present year, etc.*, London, 1764, vol. 1, pp.67-70.

such an irregular manner because his daughter was sick and craved mutton.[78] The case of Hannah Henman was similar. She was accused of stealing silk from a mercer in Lombard-Street in London, in 1678. Two neighbours of the victim saw Henman and another woman snatch the silk from the mercer's shop and attempt to escape. They followed the pair and caught Henman but: "... the other slipt from them and ran for it; but they found the Silk about her [Henman]; upon which they carried her before the Magistrate." Henman's rather feeble defence was that the other woman told her she had bought the silk, and gave it to her to carry away. Unfortunately, she "could not produce the Woman, nor would tell the Name".[79] Allegations of malicious prosecution, sometimes linked to blackmail, were also regularly used as a defence.

The Role of Reputation

Reputation was a vital commodity in the trial process, perhaps not surprisingly, given the speed of most hearings. Juries appear to have been unwilling to convict men of good character unless the evidence was especially clear, sometimes accepting quite far-fetched defences. Men of bad character were less likely to get the benefit of any doubt.

---

78. Anon, *Crime in the Vale of Evesham 1651-1670*, WEA Evesham History Workshop, Hereford and Worcester County Libraries, p.1.
79. Anon, *An exact account of the trials of the several persons arraigned at the sessions-house in the Old-Bailey for London and Middlesex*, London, Gilham Hills, 1678, p.6

Men of previous good character were also more likely to benefit from pious perjury or post-conviction reprieve. According to Cesar de Saussure, writing in the 1720s, witnesses could be called to establish both good and bad character. Unlike a modern trial: "... should any person be able to declare on his oath that the accused is a person of bad antecedents, and suspected of such and such a bad action, he will be listened to with attention." Although this may not have been a regular occurrence it is clear that the rule that developed after 1800, forbidding the adduction of bad character evidence, apart from exceptional circumstances (termed 'similar fact' evidence by modern lawyers), did not apply. It was not even to be hinted at until the first edition of Sir Michael Foster's treatise on *Crown Law* was published in 1762. Thus, the case against Margaret Ferne-Seede for murdering her husband in 1608 appears to have relied heavily on her general bad reputation (along with compelling circumstantial evidence). At trial, several witnesses were called by the Crown to give evidence about the "incontinentnes of her life past". Additionally, evidence was given of an alleged earlier attempt on her husband's life by poisoning.[80] Similarly, at John Owen's trial for horse-theft at the Shrewsbury assizes, in the late 1600s, his antecedents were made apparent and a "list of articles of many of his villenyes was presented to the Judge, who, upon reading of them said it was a great shame that such a man should

---

80. Anon, The *Arraignement and burning of Margaret Ferne-Seede*, London, Henry Gusson, 1608, f.B1.

live."[81] Establishing good character was always important, and the ability to call witnesses to attest to it could be crucial to a defence. Thus, a foreign visitor stressed that a: "... prisoner's good reputation is of great value. If several persons take the oath and say that he has always been an honest man, his case will be considered in quite a different light to what it would have been had he been suspected on other occasions of villainy."[82] Not surprisingly, some were tempted to invent characters to which they were not entitled.

As today, reputation was also important in ascribing weight to general testimony. For example, Henry Harrison, at his trial at the Old Bailey in April 1692, called several witnesses to support his version of events. However, the case was being prosecuted by a barrister who somehow appears to have been prepared for the evidence that the defendant would call, and was ready to challenge the moral standing of his references. He produced a record to prove that one of the prisoner's character witnesses had been convicted of cheating the parish of St Giles's out of excessive payments when he worked there as a scavenger, and he called two other witnesses who testified that another of Harrison's witnesses kept a "very disorderly house, where thieves and housebreakers and lewd women resorted". This was clearly both significant and effective; although the jury withdrew for half an hour to consider their verdict on the

---

81. R. Gough, *The History of Myddle*, (originally written 1701), D. Hey (Ed.), Harmondsworth, Penguin, 1981, p.150.

82. Muyden, *A foreign View of England in the reigns of George I and George II*, p.121.

case (not common in this period) they convicted Harrison of murder and he was sentenced of death.[83]

Judicial Control of Juries

Despite the very low medieval conviction rate for felonies, judges do not appear to have pressured juries to return guilty verdicts, apparently accepting the role of conscience amongst them.[84] However, throughout the Tudor and Stuart era judicial pressure on juries to return desired verdicts could be robust. Thus, jurors might be sent out again to reconsider a verdict with which the judge did not agree, in the hope (often justified) that they would change their minds. According to Sir Thomas Smith, jurors who refused to convict against the evidence were not merely: "... rebuked by the Judges, but also threatned of punishment, and many times commaunded to appeare in the starrechamber, or before the privie counsell for the matter." In practice, juries who failed to succumb to such pressure were not necessarily penalized.[85] Even in the 1560s, Smith was adamant that cases where jurymen were actually bound over to appear at the Star Chamber or fined for returning the 'wrong' verdict,

---

83. Rayner and Crook, *The Complete Newgate Calendar*, vol. II, pp.81-82, see also Anon, *The arraignment, tryal, and condemnation of Henry Harrison for the murther of A. Clenche, to which is also added, the tryal of J. Cole, for the murther of the said Doctor Clenche*, London, 1692. p.24.
84. J.G. Bellamy, *The Criminal Trial in Later Medieval England Felony Before the Courts From Edward I to the Sixteenth Century*, Toronto, University of Toronto Press, 1998, p.14.
85. Cockburn, "Twelve Silly Men? The trial Jury at Assizes, 1560-1670," p.158.

were rare and thought to be contrary to the "liberty and custome" of England. Judicial threats were often more bark than bite: "But this threatning chaunceth oftener than the execution thereof, and the xii answere with most gentle wordes, they did according to their consciences, and pray the Judges to be good unto them ... and so it passeth away for the most part."[86]

Nevertheless, juries that 'perversely' returned verdicts that did not find favour with the judiciary or government, usually by acquitting, *were* sometimes punished. They could be disciplined by a variety of methods. At the start of the period, the grand jury, which had reviewed the evidence before trial, often had a role in this process: "And then yf it apere unto the graund jurye in theyr conscience, that the petty jury wylfully of som corrupt mynde regarded not the wytnesses, and therefore in the gyvyng of theyr verdict passed against theyr owne conscience everye man well wotten that they shall be attaynted." Alternatively, and more commonly as the sixteenth century advanced, the judge could take action personally: "If the Jury likewise regard ye witnesses so sleightly, that the Judges think they quyt the felon against their owne conscience they bind them sometime to apere before ye King's Counsel."[87] This body could then punish them. Thus, in February 1528, grand jurors who returned a murder indictment *ignoramus* in a case the Crown considered to be clearly suitable for *billa vera*, ignoring the prosecution's allegedly "pregnant and

---

86. Smith, *De Republica Anglorum*, p.120
87. More, "The Deballaryon of Salem and Bizance," p.998.

manifest" evidence, were presented by the King's solicitor (hence the Crown's interest) and committed to the Fleet prison on the orders of the Council. New bills and a new jury were commanded (a grand jury finding of *ignoramus* did not constitute an acquittal).[88] Similarly, when Sir Nicholas Throckmorton was charged with high treason, for his role in Sir Thomas Wyatt's conspiracy, in October 1554, the London jurors who unexpectedly acquitted him, *"pur ceo que le matter fuit tenus dettre prove sufficement vers luy"*, were called to the Court of Star Chamber and fined heavily (*"graund summes"*), of at least £500 each, and imprisoned.

Many of these cases had political overtones. Indeed, frequently, the need for dealing with recalcitrant jurors in such cases could be avoided by packing the jury in advance with men who were already sympathetic to the Crown. Thus, two of the jurors who convicted Thomas More in 1535 were subsequently assigned to sit on the jury that convicted Bishop John Fisher six weeks later. This was well known to defendants, such as Nicholas Throckmorton, who, in 1544, expressed the hope that his petty jury was not made up of "picked fellows for the nonce".[89] Similarly, in 1655 (during the Interregnum), Colonel John Penruddock announced that he was doomed after a quick view of the selected, and pressured, jury that would try him. Nevertheless, punishment of jurors also occasionally occurred in mainstream felony cases. Thus, Sir Roger Manwood, the Chief Baron of the Exchequer, punished a jury when presiding on the

---

88. Bellamy, *The Criminal Trial in Later Medieval England Felony*, p.33.
89. Marcus, "English Common Law ...," p.687.

Western Circuit in 1589. Why he did so is unclear, he may have thought that their finding against his direction was not based on a disagreement about the forensic evidence but reflected a prejudiced refusal to even consider the facts presented to them in court. In Crompton's tortuous law French (and abbreviations): "*Vide rj. dun jurie que acquite un Hodie de felony, avant Sir Roger Manwood cheefe Baron in son circuite in comit Somerset, cont apparant evidence, fueront fined in Starre Chamber, et did were papers in le sale de Westm, circa 22.Eliz. que ieo vie.*"[90] Before too much significance is placed on this case, it should be noted that Manwood had a volatile temperament, and, although the author of many good works in his native Kent, his judicial career was marred by frequent controversy and allegations of corruption. In 1592, he was subjected to house arrest, dying the following year.[91] Such punishment of jurors for verdicts 'against' the evidence was rare in normal felony cases. Usually, a trial judge would accept their refusal to follow his view of a case with reasonably good grace. If the jury convicted after he had encouraged them to acquit, he could always recommend a reprieve (something that also discouraged jurors from following such a course). If they acquitted after he had encouraged a conviction, he could make a few scathing comments from the Bench.

Nevertheless, it was only after the Restoration that the

---

90. R. Crompton, *L'Authoritie et Jurisdiction Des Courts de la Maiestie de la Roygne: Nouelment collect & compose*, London, 1594, p.32.

91. Crompton, *L'Authoritie et Jurisdiction Des Courts de la Maiestie de la Roygne*, p.32.

first steps were taken to legally safeguard jury independence. In *Hood's* case (1666), Lord Chief Justice Kelyng fined jurors five pounds apiece after they brought in a manslaughter verdict against his direction.[92] The following year, however, he was called before the Bar of the House of Commons to answer allegations of oppressing jurors.[93] John Milward recorded Kelyng's appearance before Parliament. Although his treatment of juries presiding over the trial of Quakers has attracted most attention, Kelyng was also summoned because of his conduct in several more conventional cases, and an analysis of them encourages a measure of sympathy for the unpopular judge. Thus, in one case, an angry smith had struck his apprentice over the head with an iron bar, fracturing his skull, as a result of which the youth died three days later. However: "The Jury could not find this murder at the first, wherupon he [Kelyng] threatened them and made them go out againe, and told them that they ought to find it murder, which accordingly they did." The smith was condemned to death but because he was "very well spoke of (and for) by his neighbours" he procured a pardon from the King. Kelyng's annoyance with their initial verdict appears to have been legally well founded, and, to modern eyes, not unreasonable. After a four-hour debate, Parliament censured the Lord Chief Justice's conduct, but accepted that he was a man of integrity and resolved to take no further action against

---

92. J.M. Kaye, "The Early History of Murder and Manslaughter (part 2)," *The Law Quarterly Review*, 1967, vol. 83, p.601.
93. E. Stockdale, *A Study of Bedford Prison*, Chichester, Philimore, 1977, p.5.

him.[94] It was Parliament, as much as Kelyng, which was being innovative in this case.

The principle of jury independence was only firmly established by *Bushell's* case in 1670. This arose from the arrest of two Quakers, William Penn and William Mead, for violating the Conventicle Act while preaching in the City of London. They were subsequently charged with sedition. As a 'political' trial a high degree of judicial partiality was predictable. At his hearing, Penn insisted that, as the government refused to present a formal indictment, the jury could not reach a guilty verdict. The jury, led by Edward Bushell, seems to have accepted this argument, and repeatedly ignored acute judicial pressure to convict. Thus, the Lord Mayor, sitting on the Bench with the Recorder of London (judicial panels were common at the Old Bailey) hectored them: "What will you be led by such a silly Fellow as *Bushell?* an impudent canting Fellow? I warrant you, you shall come [serve] no more upon Juries in haste." Turning to the foreman he made his understanding of the man's function clear "I thought you had understood your Place better". After they returned 'not guilty' verdicts, the Recorder of London fined them, and added his own view of the jury's proper role: "I am sorry, Gentlemen, you have followed your own Judgments and Opinions, rather than the good and wholsome Advice, which was given you."[95]

---

94. J. Milward, *The Diary of John Milward September 1666 to May 1668*, C. Robbins (Ed.), Cambridge, CUP, 1938, pp.167-168.

95. W. Penn, and W. Mead, "The Trial of William Penn and William Mead, at The Old-Baily, September, 1670," *A Complete Collection of State-Trials, Proceedings upon High Treason and other Crimes and Misdemeanors, from the*

The jurors refused to pay and were committed to the adjacent Newgate prison. There, four of them, including Bushell, remained obdurate, retaining lawyers to argue their case. Eventually, after two months, the Court of Common Pleas issued a writ of *habeas corpus* and granted them bail. A year later, Lord Chief Justice Sir John Vaughan and 11 other judges concluded that a jury could not be punished for its verdict.

Bushell's case did nothing to stop judges pressuring juries to return certain verdicts; it merely prevented the few juries that resisted such pressure from being punished. Thus, eight years later, in 1678, when Stephen Arrowsmith was found 'not guilty' of rape at the Old Bailey, the presiding judge, again the Recorder of London: "... not conceiving it to be according to their Evidence, would not take from them without further deliberation, and labour'd to satisfie them of the Manifestness of the Proof." The jury retired again and, accepting the judge's guidance, subsequently found that Arrowsmith was guilty of the rape.[96] Nevertheless, *Bushell's* case meant that, in the 1690s, although the trial judge normally made his view as to the 'correct' verdict clear to the jury in his summing up, telling them that they "ought to bring it in so or so", this was without their being "under the least Restraint to keep to the Conclusions of the Judge that has harangu'd them".[97] Some

---

Reign of King Richard II to the End of the Reign of King George I, vol. 2, 2nd edn., London, 1730, pp.606-607 and p.612.

96. Anon, *An exact account of the trials of the several persons arraigned at the sessions-house in the Old-Bailey for London and Middlesex,* pp.15-16.

97. Misson, *Memoirs and Observations in his Travels over England,* p.124.

observers, such as the barrister Sir John Hawles, stressed that jurors should not automatically follow the direction given to them by the judiciary, which would make their function pointless, a: "... troublesome *Delay*, of great *Charge*, much *Formality*, and no real use in determining right and wrong, but meer *Ecchos* to sound back the pleasure of the Court." In making their decisions as to culpability, he also thought that jurors could have regard to all the circumstances of the case and its consequences, and not merely the substantive law and bare 'facts' established by the evidence. Although not committed to a general theory of jury nullification - the power of a trial jury to acquit a defendant simply because they consider that applying the substantive law is not reasonable - in the way that the Levellers had been, Hawles was convinced that English law had not instituted juries to: "... so little purpose as to Pronounce men *Guilty*, without regard to the nature of the Offence, or to what is to be Inflicted thereupon."[98]

Reaching a Verdict

Once they retired (if they did so) jurors were isolated in a special room and encouraged to produce a speedy verdict, it being provided that they must agree "before they shall either eat or drink".[99] In theory, heating and lighting would

---

98. Hawles, *The English-man's Right*, pp.29-39. Hawles became Solicitor-General during the reign of William III.
99. Walwin, "Juries justified," p.11.

also be withheld, and a bailiff appointed to ensure that: "... no man doe speake with them, and that they have neither bread, drinke, meate, ne fire brought to them, but there to remaine in a chamber together till they agree."[100] How strictly these provisions were enforced is debatable. In 1530, St Germain argued that their generality and rigidity was exaggerated, claiming that the rule merely prevented jurors eating and drinking without the permission of the judge. He believed this was done to avoid them being entertained by litigants, defendants or prosecutors and so subject to bribery. St Germain felt that courts could allow refreshment to be taken, provided it was not at the expense of a party to the proceedings.[101] However, it is clear that it was *not* normally permitted, and that the primary reason for this was to prevent excessive delay in the trial process.

The principle of orality meant that jurors were not allowed to receive evidence in private while deliberating (anymore than they are today). In 1678, during a rape trial at the Old Bailey, information was given to the court that, contrary to law, the jury had two children with them in their retiring room (one was the victim the other also a prosecution witness): "Whereupon the Officer appointed to keep them, was sent for, and it being sworn against him, that he had admitted them in, he was sent to Newgate." The jurors denied being involved in summoning the children to

---

100. Smith, *De Republica Anglorum,* p.114.
101. Plucknett and Barton (Eds.), *2nd Dialogue, 1530, St Germain's Doctor and Student,* p.293.

their chamber.[102] It only needed one man to prevent a verdict being returned (a situation that prevailed in England until 1967). Not surprisingly, in these circumstances, there were periodic cases of embracery, the offence of attempting to influence a jury corruptly by bribes or threats. William Leach feared that "honest jurymen (being weak, and sickly men)" were being starved and frozen into agreeing with a few biased or corrupt jurors. Why honest men should also often be sickly, and so susceptible to being pressured against their true inclinations, is not clear. More plausibly, Leach felt that the difficulties attendant on proving embracery meant that prosecutions for such crimes were virtually impossible to bring successfully.[103] Cesar de Saussure claimed to be aware of cases where one man, wishing to save a defendant, had held out against a majority in favour of convicting, exploiting the need for unanimity. More realistically, however, he appreciated that it was very unusual that a juror: "... insisted on declaring him [a defendant] innocent, and after remaining an entire day and even two without food, forcing the others to come round to his opinion: but such a case is extremely rare."[104] The great majority of juries swiftly produced unanimous verdicts. Where there were difficulties in this direction, the presiding judge could always give them some robust encouragement towards reaching unanimity. This can be seen in the case of

---

102. Anon, *An exact account of the trials of the several persons arraigned at the sessions-house in the Old-Bailey for London and Middlesex*, p.16
103. Leach, *The Bribe-Takers of Jury-Men*, pp.4-5.
104. Muyden, *A foreign View of England in the reigns of George I and George II*, p.122.

Elizabeth Ridgway, who was burned at Leicester in 1684 for poisoning her husband three weeks into their marriage. She vigorously denied the crime at her trial (though she appears to have confessed to it on the day of her execution). The initial evidence against her was not overwhelming; it included 'cruenation' (the dead man's corpse bleeding after she touched it), a forensic technique that was already going out of fashion, the testimony of a very young apprentice and circumstantial evidence. At her trial at the Leicester assizes the jury was initially 'hung', dividing eight votes to four. However, they quickly found her guilty after a further direction from the trial judge, Sir Thomas Street.[105] Nevertheless, if even a single man disagreed with his colleagues, they could, theoretically, be forcibly kept together until he or the other 11 changed their minds "by strength of Reason or Argument". Such mavericks were not to be "Hecktor'd, much less punisht by the Court into a Compliance". Hawles cited an ancient case in which it had been suggested that the way to deal with such juries was to carry them around the circuit in carts until they reached unanimity.[106] In reality, there are no recorded cases of this occurring. Indeed, *Bushell's* jury was exceptional in being kept overnight with a view to forcing a change of verdict. Much more practically, as St Germain observed in the 1530s, if a jury could not agree, the judge could order a retrial.[107]

---

105. B. Capp, "Serial killers in 17th-century England," *History Today*, 1996, vol. 46, issue 3, at pp.21-31.
106. Hawles, *The English-mans right*, p.39.
107. Plucknett and Barton (Eds.), *2nd Dialogue, 1530, St Germain's Doctor and Student*, p.293.

Burden and Standard of Proof

A standard of proof that was 'beyond reasonable doubt' was not formally enunciated until the final quarter of the eighteenth century, when, in 1777, Lord Mansfield directed a jury that the evidence should irresistibly prove the crime, and that if "not perfectly convinced you must find the accused not guilty". However, a belief that doubts should be resolved in favour of the accused was much older, though a lack of precise formulation may have reduced its impact.[108] There are numerous intimations from the late medieval period onwards that any uncertainty would normally work in a defendant's favour.[109] Thus, although the standard of proof was often still vague in the 1460s, in serious conventional felonies at least it was generally accepted that it was much better that: "... 20 guilty persons should escape the punishment of death, than that one innocent person should be condemned and suffer capitally."[110] Similarly, in 1603, Coke assured Walter Raleigh's trial jury that a just person would "condemn no man, but upon plain Evidence". His views were matched in the 1760s, when Blackstone demanded especially clear proof in cases of rape and buggery, citing Mathew Hale, and also argued that forensic evidence "ought to be the more clear in proportion as the

---

108. B.J. Shapiro, "To A Moral Certainty: Theories of Knowledge and Anglo-American Juries 1600-1850," *Hastings Law Journal*, University of California, 1986, p.156.
109. J.H. Langbein, "The historical origins of the privilege against self-incrimination at Common Law," *Michigan Law Review*, vol.92, p.1057.
110. Grigor, *Sir John Fortescue's Commendation of the Laws of England*, p.45.

crime is the more detestable".[111] Such notions impressed foreigners. In the early 1700s, Cesar de Saussure clearly believed that Englishmen had a different, and higher, standard of proof to that found in many continental jurisdictions, feeling that it was: "... better that 12 culprits should escape human justice rather than that one innocent man should perish."[112] However, there was also a notable absence of many modern common law notions of 'due process'. In practice, once a *prima facie* case had been made, it was often for the defendant to establish his innocence. Indeed, until the 1930s, there was widespread and overt judicial acceptance of the validity of the doctrine, laid down by Mr Justice Forster, that in every charge of murder, once a killing was established, defences of accident, necessity or infirmity were to be: "... satisfactorily proved by the prisoner, unless they arise out of the evidence produced against him; for the law presumes the fact to be founded on malice until the contrary appears."[113]

Verdict

Practice in delivering verdicts varied over time and with location. For much of the seventeenth century, at the Old

---

111. Blackstone, *Commentaries on the Laws of England*, vol. 4, p.214.
112. Muyden, *A foreign View of England in the reigns of George I and George II*, p.119.
113. Rayner and Crook, *The Complete Newgate Calendar*, vol. IV, p.184. The doctrine was formally rejected by Lord Sankey in the case of *Woolmington v. DPP* [1935] AC 462, which placed the legal burden for rebutting such defences on the Crown.

Bailey at least, juries were being asked to consider their verdicts on up to a dozen felons at a time. Although this was probably the upper practical limit, and seven or eight was more normal, a similar pattern seems to have been found at the assizes conducted elsewhere in the country. Such a practice was not necessarily universal, and, if a case was exceptionally grave or complicated, or involved someone of note, it would often merit individual consideration. Many criminal cases heard in front of a jury at the Court of King's Bench fell into this category. Similarly, in 1699, the assizes jury that sat in judgment on Spencer Cowper and his colleagues, during a day long trial, withdrew for half-an-hour to consider the evidence against the four men unencumbered by the need to reach verdicts in other cases.[114] Even in ordinary cases, Sir Thomas Smith was adamant that trial jurors in the mid-sixteenth century would sometimes complain if asked to consider more than two or three verdicts at a time: "For if they [jurors] should be charged with more, the inquest will say, my Lorde, we pray you charge us with no more, it is ynough for our memorie." Indeed, often, he claimed, juries were charged "but with one or two" defendants.[115] This does not appear to accord with normal practice in most of the country (though it may have done in the medieval era). Thus, on the Home Circuit, between 1559 and 1625, the average number of defendants each jury was charged with was 6.7, rising to almost eight in

---

114. Rayner and Crook, *The Complete Newgate Calendar*, vol. II, p.113.
115. Smith, *De Republica Anglorum*, p.114.

the period between 1625 and 1670.[116] The heavy caseloads on the other circuits probably produced a similar result, for most of the time.

The 'modern' system of discussing each and every case individually was a creature of the eighteenth century. The precise point at which this occurred at the Old Bailey, probably a little in advance of most provincial assizes, can be identified. At the sessions opening at the Bailey on the 6th December 1738, the Lord Mayor informed the jury that:

> "... having taken notice of the Inconvenience in the usual Method of trying Prisoners, in which the Jurors sat as commonly to give Verdicts on 12 or more Tryals together, depending on their memories, or Assistance of Notes, has thought fit to Alter the method of proceeding; and accordingly their seats are now so placed that they might consult one another and give in their verdict immediately, or in case of any Difficulty, withdraw for Consideration."

As a result, the juries returned verdicts "on each Tryal before they were charged with another". Three days later, as the sessions ended, it was agreed that the new system, far from being attended by any inconvenience "as was apprehended", was a major improvement, the court lasting only a day longer than the previous sessions despite handling twice as many prisoners.[117]

---

116. Cockburn, "Twelve Silly Men? The Trial Jury at Assizes, 1560-1670," p.178.
117. *The Gentleman's Magazine*, 1738, vol. 8, p.659.

The practical results of determining numerous cases together would have been significant, as jurors would have to remember the evidence from several trials simultaneously. This was made more difficult because, unlike civil law jurisdictions, with their numerous depositions placed in front of the tribunal, jurors, when retiring to consider their verdicts, "have in writing nothing given them, but the enditement".[118] The indictment helped to remind them, at least, of the names of the defendants and the offences with which they were charged. By the latter part of the period, the situation was slightly improved because literacy amongst the social groups from which jurors were normally drawn had become sufficiently widespread that they could, if they wished, take a personal note of the evidence, and this sometimes seems to have occurred. In 1680, the barrister John Hawles urged jurors to "write down the evidence or the Heads thereof that you may the better Recall it to memory". A few years later, an admiring foreign observer claimed that while evidence was given, the jury were: "... all the while attentive, and setting down upon Paper every Thing that is alled'd upon both sides."[119] The judiciary usually had no objection to this; when Spencer Cowper's jury asked for pen and ink in 1699, the judge decreed "Let as many have it as will".[120]

Nevertheless, many jurors may well have been unable to discuss individual cases very thoroughly, perhaps

---

118. Smith, *De Republica Anglorum*, p.114.
119. Misson, *Memoirs and Observations in his Travels over England*, p.327.
120. Anon, *The Tryal of Spencer Cowper*, p.3.

encouraging them to rely on the opinions provided by the foreman and more experienced jurymen, or the indication given by the judge.[121] Certainly, in a number of cases, jurors did not even retire, but briefly put their heads together where they sat and produced their verdict[s]. Thus, in several trials held at the Old Bailey in 1678, juries returned verdicts "without coming from the Bar". Similarly, at James Maclane's hearing for highway robbery, in 1750, the evidence was so overwhelming that the jury convicted "without going out of court".[122] In simple cases, the judiciary would support such a practice. Thus, a judge at the Old Bailey, encouraging the acquittal of a man accused of stealing a magpie, observed to the jurors: "You need not give your selves the trouble to go out of the Court about such a small indifferent matter as this."

The lack of formal justification for a jury verdict surprised continentals such as Misson (as it does to this day): "Then they return into Court, and he that speaks for the rest, the Foreman, without making any set speech, or giving any Train of reasons, merely says 'Guilty', or 'Not Guilty'." The only, partial, exception to this rule that he identified was the brief explanation that might accompany the returning of a verdict of guilty to a lesser offence, such as manslaughter in a murder case.[123] These exceptions were probably slightly more extensive than Misson appreciated. During the seventeenth and early eighteenth centuries,

---

121. Cockburn, "Twelve Silly Men? The trial Jury at Assizes, 1560-1670," p.178.
122. Rayner and Crook, *The Complete Newgate Calendar*, vol. III, p.183.
123. Misson, *Memoirs and Observations in his Travels over England*, p.162.

Surrey juries would sometimes be asked to explain (briefly), in writing, not guilty verdicts in homicide cases, where their decision was based on the death being occasioned by misfortune or self-defence. Thus, a 1654 jury signed a statement declaring: "We finde that Will Draper did by chance accidentally kill Isaacke Axtell with a pronge as they were playing together."[124] Another exception was where the jury returned a 'special verdict'.

Special Verdicts

Special verdicts were returned in trials in which neither the judge nor jury knew how to apply the law to the facts of a particularly difficult case. They consisted of a resumé of the facts found by the jury to have been proved. This was then referred to the combined panel of judges sitting at Westminster for consideration as to an appropriate verdict. Thus, in 1721, the evidence indicated that George Dufus, although accused of sodomy, had not achieved full penetration or ejaculation. According to his victim he had inserted "about an inch" before being thrown off, and then "emitted in his own hand". Perhaps because the full offence was capital, and unlike Lord Audley's trial a century earlier, the court was scrupulous about the law: "The Spermatic Injection not being prov'd, the Court directed the Jury to bring in their Verdict Special." This was subsequently

---

124. J. Beattie, *Crime and the Courts in England 1660-1800*, Oxford, OUP, 1986, p.81, n.18.

considered by a meeting of the 12 Westminster judges, who concluded that the prisoner had not committed a complete felony. (However, he was reindicted and convicted of *attempted* sodomy, being fined, pilloried and sentenced to two months' imprisonment.)[125]

Pious Perjury

The willingness of early modern trial juries at assizes to convict for lesser offences, or the less serious charges on an indictment, while acquitting on the graver counts, has been well documented. In some cases, jurors may have been reluctant to have a particular man's death on their consciences for an instrumental crime committed without violence, or have held reservations about the evidence adduced. Age and necessity amongst defendants also appear to have been factors that were often taken into account by juries. Thus, in the 1570s, Ann Clark, a 13-year-old Colchester market cut-purse, was acquitted of all charges against her, except one minor offence, for which she was whipped.[126] In many situations, 'pious perjury' seems to have been almost institutionalised, with verdicts to lesser offences being routinely returned in certain well-established situations. Thus, an examination of the value of goods in cases of felonious theft during the

---

125. Anon, "The Trial of George Dufus, 1721," *Select Trials*, 1742, vol. 1, pp.105-8.
126. J. Samaha, "Hanging for Felony: The Rule of Law in Elizabethan Colchester," *Historical Journal*, 1978, vol. 21, p.778.

Elizabethan period, in the South East of England, indicates that few people were found guilty of stealing goods worth between 12 pence and 10 shillings. Those cases where juries did convict for such a (capital) sum usually involved defendants who could plead benefit of clergy, or instances in which the crime had involved an aggravating feature such as an assault.[127] Clearly, juries were methodically downgrading small sums that, nevertheless, were above the 12 pence (non-capital petty larceny) threshold. This could produce bizarre results. When a youth named William Booth stood trial at the Old Bailey in 1731, accused of picking a pocket of cash worth two shillings and six pence the jury found him guilty "to the value of 10 pence".[128] As this case indicates, benefit of clergy also seems to have been factored into the equation. Thus, in trials for house-breaking, examples included theft of 23 guineas from a house, lace valued at more than a 100 pounds in the indictment, gold rings and jewellery valued by their owners at more than 300 pounds, all of which were "found by the jury to be 39 shillings worth" (i.e. below the non-clergyable 40 shillings cut-off for this crime).[129] In many cases, judges openly connived at or encouraged such verdicts, which provided one way of moderating the death for felony rule. Nevertheless, pious perjury was not always necessarily motivated by compassion; sometimes, it might have been

---

127. Bellamy, *The Criminal Trial in Later Medieval England Felony Before the Courts From Edward I to the Sixteenth Century*, p.125.
128. *The Gentleman's Magazine*, 1731, vol. 1, p.401.
129. Beattie, *Crime and the Courts in England 1660-1800*, p.424.

the result of a desire to see a defendant whipped for petty larceny rather than simply being clergied and released for grand larceny.

Acquittals

Early modern trials were certainly not formalities. Acquittal was a real possibility, though less likely than in the medieval era. The Kent gaol delivery records for 1559-1572 provide a conviction rate of only 56.5 per cent, itself a rise of between 50 per cent and 80 per cent on the very low conviction levels pertaining in the middle years of the fifteenth century. In Essex, the conviction rate by trial juries almost doubled in the same period, but was still only 63.6 per cent. It has been argued that this increase amounted to a virtual revolution in criminal law administration and is one of the few features to distinguish the era's criminal justice from that of the late medieval period.[130] Nevertheless, compared to Victorian conviction rates, the early modern percentage was still relatively modest. Thus, the highwayman, Thomas Cox, executed in 1691, had been "three times tried for his life before the last fatal trial".[131] Even during the highly untypical Civil War witch panic in East Anglia, in the 1640s, when there were several mass trials, acquittals continued to be frequent. At the assizes held

---

130. Bellamy, *The Criminal Trial in Later Medieval England Felony Before the Courts From Edward I to the Sixteenth Century*, p.95.
131. C. Johnson, *A General History of the Lives and Adventures of the Most Famous Highwaymen, Murderers, Street-Robbers*, London: J. Janeway, 1734, p.341.

in Norfolk and Suffolk in 1645, although 40 alleged witches were "arraigned for their lives" only half were executed.[132]

Given that, in many cases, crimes had only been brought to court as a last resort, with earlier offences being ignored, and that they had always been (loosely) scrutinised by a JP, and (more closely) by the grand jury, an acquittal rate that was usually over a third, throughout the early modern period, might appear surprising. One inference that can be drawn from this is that the courts took a relatively strict approach to the evidence. That reputable local men were convinced of a defendant's guilt, as a result of experience, personal knowledge and 'hunches', was not usually enough. Having a good case and proving it in court were two very different things, so that, according to some observers, on a daily basis: "... for want of a positive, strong, clear, and full Evidence, even the guilty are acquitted, and for a while escape the Hands of Justice."[133] Ripped out of context, apparently strong evidence could be explained or appear flimsy in the context of a 30 minute trial.

The risk of mistaken convictions in capital offences was well known and made popular reading throughout the era, possibly encouraging acquittals. A few thoughtful observers were worried that not enough effort was made to prevent such miscarriages of justice. According to Richard Smith, writing in 1695, they illustrated how it was "notorious, that

---

132. Anon, *Signes and Wonders from Heaven* ..., London, I.H., 1645, p.4.
133. Anon, *Select Trials, for Murders, Robberies, Rapes, Sodomy, Coining, Frauds, And other Offences*, pp.61-66.

Justice is often very ill administered in this nation".[134] However, the authorities were usually sanguine about such mistakes feeling that: "'Tis true, it has now and then happen'd, that, by means of some unlucky and unaccountable Circumstances, a Man has been condemn'd undeservedly; but such Cases are far from being common."[135] Additionally, there was a strong belief that it was: "... not in all the wittes of the worlde, for punyshment of mischevous wretches, to devise a law in such wyse, that men may be sure that none innocent can take harme thereby." It was feared that the nation's criminal justice system would collapse with appalling consequences for public safety if all the conceivable steps possible to prevent mistaken convictions were taken.[136] Indeed, some were more concerned with the effect that such errors had on jurors' future readiness to return a guilty verdict than with the inherent injustice of the decisions.

Sentence

After a guilty verdict was returned, defendants would be asked whether they had anything to say before sentence being passed. When Thomas More was convicted after his trial at the Court of King's Bench, in 1535, the Lord

---

134. R. Smith, *Mistaken Justice: or, Innocence condemn'd, in the person of Francis Newland*, London, 1695, p.36.
135. Anon, *Select Trials, for Murders, Robberies, Rapes, Sodomy, Coining, Frauds*, pp.61-6.
136. More, "The Deballaryon of Salem and Bizance," p.995.

Chancellor, presiding over the case, appears to have been peremptory ("incontinent upon the verdict"), and initially omitted this stage until, after beginning his judgment, he was reminded of it by the defendant: "'My Lord, when I was towards the law, the manner in such case was to ask the prisoner before judgment, why judgment should not be given against him?' Whereupon the Lord Chancellor staying his judgment, wherein he had partly proceeded, demanded of him what he was able to say to the contrary."[137] In ordinary felony cases, such pre-sentence addresses were not purely academic. They allowed convicts to ask for clergy or to plead their bellies. Additionally, where this was not possible, they might allow a convict to provide mitigating information that would encourage the recommendation or granting of a reprieve or the substitution of transportation for execution. Not everyone who received sentence of death accepted it with equanimity. In 1690, the highwayman James Smith had to be tied up to hear his sentence being passed and "exceedingly misbehav'd in court". He cursed and swore at the judges, calling them "most opprobrious names", and continued to do so until hanged.[138]

Appeals

Historically, common law lacked a mechanism allowing an

---

137. W. Roper, "The Life of Sir Thomas More," *Lives of Sir Thomas More*, E.G. Reynolds (Ed.), London, Everyman edn., J.M. Dent, 1963, p.45.
138. A. Smith, A *Compleat history of the lives and robberies of the most notorious highwaymen, ... for above an hundred years past*, London, Briscoe, 1719, vol. 2, p.136.

already adjudicated case to be appealed to a higher tribunal in the hope of obtaining a more favourable verdict or sentence. It was very difficult to go behind a jury decision (as it still is today): "This short sentence is irrevocable and without appeal, unless the King's mercy interposes."[139] Formal provision for appeal was largely a creature of the nineteenth century. Indeed, a specialist Criminal Court of Appeal was only established in 1908. This was in marked contrast to the hierarchical civil law tradition established after the thirteenth century in continental Europe. The common law knew only two processes that even roughly approximated to modern appeals. One was where the original trial was declared null and void for a serious technical fault. The other was where the presiding judge in a criminal trial held at the assizes or Old Bailey reserved a relevant point of law from the case, about which he was personally uncertain, for later consideration by all 12 puisne judges from the Westminster Courts. (Special verdicts would also be sent to this forum for determination.) For this, the puisne judges would normally sit together at Serjeants' Inn or the Exchequer Chamber in London, although one or two of them might be absent through illness. This procedure had started with civil cases in the fourteenth century, but extended to criminal ones by the 1500s. However, it did not apply to convictions at quarter sessions. The 12 judges would meet about three times a year. If they decided that a conviction was wrong as a matter of law, they could recommend that the defendant be pardoned. Where an

---

139. Misson, *Memoirs and Observations in his Travels over England*, p.164.

indictment was defective, they could also recommend that judgment be arrested.[140] In 1848, this informal tribunal became the Court for Crown Cases Reserved.

The principal reason for the difference between common law and civil law in this respect was political. In France, the increasing subjection of regional rulers to royal control meant that their courts also became subject to Parisian supervision. In England, from early on, the assizes judges that presided over serious trials, outside London, came from, and spent most of their time at, the central royal courts at Westminster, preventing the development of hierarchy.[141] Nevertheless, the differences between Europe and England should not be exaggerated. For most ordinary criminals, sentenced to death on the continent, appeals were a rarity. Indeed, according to Cesar de Saussure, England was relatively slow in carrying out its executions: "Criminals are not executed immediately after their trial, as they are abroad, but are given several days to prepare for death." (He was greatly impressed that during this intervening time they would have the ministrations of a prison chaplain.)[142]

There was normally no appeal by the Crown against a jury acquittal on indictment (any more than there is today): "In felony, if the party bee once acquit, or in peril of judgement of life lawfully, hee shall never be brought in

---

140. D.R. Bentley QC (Ed.), *Select cases from the twelve Judges' notebooks*, London, John Rees, 1997, p.9.
141. R.C. Van Caenegam, *Judges, Legislators & Professors: Chapters in European Legal History*, Cambridge, C.U.P., 1987, p.2.
142. Muyden, *A foreign View of England in the reigns of George I and George II*, p.124.

Question againe [on indictment] for the same fact."[143] Additionally, although notions of *autrefois acquit* or *convict*, preventing a previously acquitted or convicted defendant from being reindicted, were not as precise as they are today, they usually prevented blatant reprosecution on indictment. Thus, in March 1661, at the Worcester assizes, Sir Robert Hide held that Mary Robinson, earlier acquitted of murdering Elizabeth Robinson 'per incantacionem', like any other prisoner who had been found not guilty, could not be "reendited or arrayned for the same offence ever after".[144] Similarly, in 1678, James Turner, accused of stealing a brown mare was released for the same reason: "Upon whose trial, it appearing that he had been Auterfoits acquit, the Jury were discharged of him."[145]

Appeal of Felony

However, in cases of murder, an appeal of felony could, very occasionally, provide an opportunity to retry a case that had produced an acquittal on indictment. Such appeals were a medieval form of *private* prosecution, having almost no relationship to modern appeals aimed at correcting trial errors. They were similar, in some respects, to civil suits, being commenced by a writ or bill issued by the wife, heir

---

143. Bacon, *Cases of Treason*, p.13.
144. H. Townshend, *Notes of the Office of a Justice of Peace 1661-3*, R.D. Hunt (Ed.), Worcester, Worcestershire Historical Society, 1967, p.94.
145. Anon, *An exact account of the trials of the several persons arraigned at the sessions-house in the Old-Bailey for London and Middlesex*, p.28

or closest kin of the deceased person, within a year and a day of the latter's death.[146] Unlike murderers found guilty on indictment, the Crown could not pardon those convicted on appeal. The use of such actions peaked in the late twelfth century, declining sharply thereafter. By the end of the thirteenth century, relatively few criminals were being prosecuted in this way. This was probably due to judicial hostility to the process and because out of court settlements between felons and appellors ceased to preclude appellees being sent for trial on indictment.[147] Additionally, appeal was an uncertain, expensive and potentially hazardous way of bringing someone suspected of a serious crime to trial, when compared to prosecution on indictment, encouraging use of the latter mechanism. This was exacerbated because appellees were permitted counsel at trial, unlike felony defendants tried on indictment. It became even more unpopular in the years after 1529, when restitution, traditionally only allowed in an appeal of robbery, was extended to proceedings for the same crime when prosecuted on indictment. As a result, appeals were moribund by 1550, with the sole exception of the appeal of murder. The main advantage of this particular appeal was that it allowed the next of kin of a slain man a remedy if a grand jury refused to indict for murder, or a trial jury appeared to acquit perversely. Indeed, a statute of 1487

---

146. G. Jacob, *The Laws of Appeals and Murder*, London, 1709, pp.3-6.
147. D. Klerman, "Settlement and the Decline of Private Prosecution in Thirteenth-Century England," *Law and History Review*, 2001, vol. 19, Rev. 1, p.3.

specifically excluded an earlier acquittal on a murder indictment from being a bar to an appeal of murder, as it was to an appeal for any other type of felony at common law.[148] Thus: "... *si le murderer soit acquyte deins lan all sute le roy, il sera autre foitz en appele arrayn deis mesme lan al sute de party.*"[149]

Nevertheless, despite its continued existence, it was rarely used, even for murder, and was disliked by many judges. However, even the judiciary occasionally saw merits in the process. Thus, in 1629, after Joan Norcott's husband and mother-in-law were tried on indictment and acquitted for her murder at Hertford assizes, it was: "...so much against the evidence, that judge Harvey let fall his opinion that it were better an appeal were brought than so foul a murder escape un-punished." As a result, they were subsequently tried, convicted and executed on an appeal brought by Joan's son (her next of kin).[150] There was also an attempt to use the appeal of murder after the jury acquittal of Spencer Cowper and three other barristers for the murder of Sarah Stout at Hertford assizes, in 1699, albeit that it was unsuccessful for technical reasons (a frequent occurrence with such actions).[151] However, in 1709, Henry Young successfully brought an appeal against Christopher

---

148. J.H. Baker, "Criminal Courts and Procedure at Common Law 1550-1800," J.S. Cockburn (Ed.), *Crime in England 1550-1800*, London, Methuen, 1977, pp.17-18.

149. Pyson, *Diversite de Courts et leur Jurisdictions*, London, 1526, f.Bv.

150. C. Johnson, *A General History of the Lives and Adventures of the Most Famous Highwaymen, Murderers, Street-Robbers*, London: J. Janeway, 1734, p.156

151. Earl of Birkenhead, *Famous Trials of History*, vol. 1, New York, Doubleday, Doran and Co., 1926, p.101.

Slaughterford, in the Court of Queen's Bench, for killing his sister. Slaughterford had earlier been acquitted of the murder at the Kingston Assizes, something that infuriated the dead woman's neighbours, who subsequently banded together to fund the appeal. He was found guilty by a Surrey jury at a trial presided over by Sir John Holt (a rare judicial supporter of the appeal mechanism), and executed at Guildford on July 9, maintaining his innocence until the end. As late as 1817, when the alleged rapist and murderer Abraham Thornton was acquitted at the Warwick assizes, apparently against the evidence, the Secretary of State authorised the county sheriff to detain Thornton on an appeal of murder, to be prosecuted by William Ashford, the brother and heir-at-law of the dead woman. However, the Court of King's Bench discharged him when insufficient cause was shown to justify further proceedings (also conveniently obviating the need for Thornton to pursue his unexpected but legal request for trial by battle, rather than jury, on an appeal of felony).[152] Such appeals were abolished shortly afterwards.

---

152. Rayner and Crook, *The Complete Newgate Calendar*, vol. IV, p.169.

PART THREE:
EARLY MODERN PUNISHMENT

Chapter 17

The Death Penalty

There are inferior Gallows which bear
(According to the season) twice a year:
And there's a kind of watrish Tree at Wapping,
Whereas Sea-thieves or Pirates are catched napping:
But Tyburn doth deserve before them all
The title and addition capital,
Of Arch or great Grand Gallows of our Land,
Whilst all the rest like ragged Lackeys stand.

John Taylor (the Water-Poet) The Description of Tyburn
(Extract)

Centrality of the Death Penalty

England's courts and modes of trial were not the only aspects of the country's criminal justice system that were unusual by continental standards; its penal system was also remarkable. As Cesar de Saussure observed in the early 1700s, the punishment of criminals in England was "done in quite a different way to what it is in other countries".[1] Most

---

1. M. Van Muyden (Trans. and Ed.), *A foreign View of England in the reigns of George I and George II; The letters of Monsieur Cesar de Saussure, to his Family*, London, John Murray, 1902, p.116.

continental visitors were particularly struck by the country's relative paucity of punishments and its lack of fine gradations within the penal repertoire, something that, for much of the period, frequently produced a 'noose or loose' approach to punishment to employ a modern American phrase. They were also astonished by some arcane, indeed apparently irrational, practices, such as 'benefit of clergy', as well as being impressed by the apparent stoicism of those 'going west' to execution at Tyburn. Such views were not confined to foreigners, many Englishmen also found their nation's penal policies strange. Even in Thomas More's time, the modern notion of 'justice' as a rational, bureaucratic decision, with gradations of sentence consistently, indifferently and uniformly administered, had been slowly gaining ground, at the expense of highly individualised and personalised medieval concepts. Legal reformers, such as William Sheppard in the 1650s, had sought to remove some of the 'irrationality' of the nation's criminal justice system. However, progress in this direction, though manifest, remained limited until after the period.[2] Remnants of a highly personalised system survived beyond 1750. Thus, in 1760, it was noted that had Patrick McCarty's execution for a heinous murder, carried out on October 24 of that year, been deferred by a single day, he might, in all probability, have been reprieved and released, King George II having died, and his successor, marking his accession according to ancient custom, "granted a general amnesty and pardon to

---

2.   D. Hay, "Property, authority and the criminal law," Albion's Fatal Tree, D. Hay *et al* (eds.), 1975, p.40.

criminals".[3]

Almost all felonies, i.e. all significant crimes, carried the death penalty, so that Henri Misson could claim that: "Hanging is the most Common Punishment in England." Execution had a markedly greater importance than it had in the penal systems of many other European jurisdictions. Thus, even in the late 1460s, according to Sir John Fortescue (then resident in France), more men were hanged in England each year for robbery than were hanged in France for the same crime in seven years. As Fortescue appreciated, the English punishment for thefts valued at more than 12 pence was more draconian than that normally found on the continent, where a guilty party would sometimes merely have to make restitution to a multiple (perhaps four times if Biblical injunctions were followed) of the value of goods taken.[4]

Continental visitors were sometimes shocked by this difference. Typically, in the early 1600s, the Venetian chaplain, Horatio Busino, observed, albeit slightly inaccurately, that in England: "The slightest theft is punished with death, even a youth of 15 for his first crime or theft is hanged, unless he chances to know how to read and write [allowing him his clergy]."[5] He was appalled at how petty some of these capital crimes could be, noting a

---

3. Rayner and Crook, *The Complete Newgate Calendar*, vol. III, p.311.
4. F. Grigor (Ed.), *Sir John Fortescue's Commendation of the Laws of England*, London, Sweet and Maxwell, 1917, (written c.1461-5, first published in Latin c.1537), p.78.
5. T. Platter and H. Busino, *Journals of two travellers in Elizabethan and early Stuart England*, P. Razzell (Ed.), London, Caliban, 1995, p.148.

case in which: "... a lad was seen on his way to the gallows merely for having stolen a bag of currants."[6] Many Englishmen shared his concern at the lack of proportionality in the system. They agreed with Thomas More that there ought to be a difference between killing a man and merely stealing his purse. Such observers believed that simple theft was not so great a crime that it ought to cost a man his life.[7] In the 1530s, Thomas Starkey, the chaplain to Henry VIII, also suggested that the punishment for theft that was "privily committed" (i.e. without the use or threat of force) was excessively draconian, especially as many such crimes were committed out of necessity. He thought that execution should be reserved for homicides and major robberies.[8] Over a century later, in the 1650s, William Sheppard advocated that capital punishment should be confined to murder, treason, and, Puritan that he was, "horrid blasphemies". He, too, felt that many felonies that carried the death penalty, such as forgery, theft and arcane crimes like taking sheep out of the realm, were "extreme and oppressive to the people". Even Sir Mathew Hale conceded that the English punishment for theft was "possibly more severe than other Nations, yea, and than the Offence in itself simply considered deserves."[9] Significantly, in the legal codes of the various seventeenth century American colonies

6. Platter and Busino, *Journals of two travellers*, p.148.
7. Sir T. More, *Utopia*, R. Robinson Ware, Wordsworth Classics, 1997, p.37.
8. T. Starkey, *A Dialogue between Reginal Pole and Thomas Lupset*, K.M. Burton (Ed.), London, Chatto & Windus, 1948, pp.114 and 177.
9. Sir M. Hale, *A Discourse touching Provision for the Poor*, London, William Shrowsbery, 1683, Preface, pp.1-4.

(some of which were Biblically influenced in this respect), the punishment of property offences was generally less bloody than in England. Theft was not usually a capital offence.[10]

Concern about the use of capital punishment was not confined to lawyers and educated men. There was also a groundswell of popular feeling that, in the words of an Interregnum petition, hanging a man for stealing meant punishing "his iniquity beyond the rule of equity". It seemed to contravene the Biblical commands in the book of *Exodus*, which normally provided for restitution in the case of theft and so ensured that the remedy was not "worse than the disease". Some even felt that it was a moral sin to execute anyone "merely for stealing".[11] Given such criticisms, it might be wondered why the country persisted in prescribing the death penalty for a multitude of (often petty) crimes, so that in 1725, Bernard De Mandeville could still ask why, amongst the vulgar, "such great numbers are yearly lavish'd away for Trifles"?[12]

Flexibility in Appointing Death

One answer is that many convicted felons were not actually executed. Despite its centrality to the system, the criminal

---

10. B. Chapin, "Criminal Justice In Colonial America, 1606-1660," *The University of Georgia Press*, 1983, p.147.
11. Anon, *A cry against a crying Sinne*, London, Samuel Chidley, 1652, pp.3-4.
12. B. De Mandeville, *An Enquiry into the Course of the Frequent Executions at Tyburn*, London, 1725, p.4.

justice system allowed for enormous flexibility in passing death sentences, and this prevented the number of hangings from being far greater than would otherwise have been the case. Even after a conviction for felony a prisoner could still escape the scaffold by a plethora of entirely legal mechanisms. As a result, a town such as Colchester, which had power of gaol delivery, saw only two death sentences that were not commuted passed in the two years between 1577 and 1579 (and one of these may not have been carried out). Most felony prosecutions either did not result in a conviction, or, if they did, did not produce an execution.[13] This allowed a crude refinement within the generality of the punishment (death) appointed for felonies other than petty larceny. Frequently, crimes of blood and robbery appear to have been distinguished from other forms of instrumental crime, at least in normal times. Thus, when Mr Justice Kelyng was petitioned to reprieve a servant convicted of beating an apprentice to death, he refused on principle: "I do acknowledge I am very strict and severe against highway robbers, and in cases of blood."[14] However, the distinction, and many of the safeguards against execution, *could* be circumvented if there was a will to do so. Examining JPs might fail to down charge offences, juries could refuse to commit pious perjury by convicting for lesser crimes, the test for clergy could be administered strictly, excluding all but the genuinely literate, and post-conviction reprieves

---

13. J. Samaha, "Hanging for Felony: The Rule of Law in Elizabethan Colchester," *Historical Journal*, 1978, vol. 21, p.769.
14. J. Milward, *The Diary of John Milward Esq., September 1666 to May 1668*, C. Robbins (Ed.), Cambridge, CUP, 1938, pp.167-168.

could be refused. Thus, in Elizabethan Colchester, the general practice of distinguishing between property offences and violent crimes became attenuated during periods when the community was particularly concerned about crime. These included the national crisis of 1588 and the economically harsh late 1590s, when a perceived 'crime wave' in Colchester hardened the attitudes of all participants in the criminal process. As a result, at least three ordinary thieves went to the gallows in that period.[15] Yet another crucial explanation for the centrality of execution in England was the country's dearth of penal alternatives.

Lack of Intermediate Punishments

As Horatio Busino observed, one of the principal reasons for the frequent English recourse to execution was the country's lack of intermediate punishments. England was less willing to use fiscal penalties for moderately severe crimes and, most importantly, had: "... no mitigation such as banishment or the galleys, this [their punishment] invariably involves life or death."[16] By contrast, many countries used convicts for compulsory labour. Thus, in France, in the 1690s, there were 40 galleys based at Marseilles alone, containing 10,000 galley slaves, many of whom had been condemned to serve on them by the royal courts after being convicted. It was a

---

15. Samaha, "Hanging for Felony," p.770.
16. Platter and Busino, *Journals of two travellers*, p.148.

tradition that was already centuries old by then.[17]
Unsurprisingly, Englishmen openly speculated about
the value of introducing such penalties to their own country,
not always, perhaps, from the best of motives. The use of
felons to power galleys was seriously considered several
times during Henry VIII's reign. In More's *Utopia* (1516)
slavery was the main punishment for even the most serious
crimes. It was considered to be as terrible to the criminals
themselves as death, while being more in the interests of the
commonwealth since: "... as their labour is a greater benefit
to the public than their death could be, so the sight of their
misery is a more lasting terror to other men." In *Utopia*,
death was reserved for those who rebelled from such
servitude; the penitent had the prospect of eventual release.
In the 1530s, Thomas Starkey supported such plans,
thinking it: "... good that the felon should be take and put in
some common work, as to labour in building the walls of
cities and towns."[18] A few decades later, William Harrison
added his own voice to the debate, urging that those
convicted be: "... made bond or slaves unto those that
received the injury, to sell and give where they listed, or to
be condemned to the galleys: for that punishment would
prove more bitter to them."[19] Others, however, rejected such
proposals as impractical and even potentially hazardous.
Trading felons as "slaves to barbary" risked their returning

---

17. A. Zysberg, "*Galeres et galerians en France a la fin du xviiE sièle: une image du pouvoir royal a l'age classique,*" *Criminal Justice History*, 1980, vol. 1, pp.51-55.
18. Starkey, *A dialogue between Reginal Pole and Thomas Lupset*, p.177.
19. Canon W. Harrison, *Elizabethan England edited from the Description of England*, E. Rhys (Ed.), London, Camelot Series, 1889, p.242.

as Moslem warriors, while making them "perpetual slaves at home" would risk their escaping, so that they would require constant supervision. It was also feared that it would be ineffective due to the innate humanity of Englishmen.[20] This lack of intermediate punishments would, eventually, be substantially remedied by the growth in transportation after the 1650s (and especially after 1718), the development of which closely parallels a decline in executions.

However, the lack of penal refinement does not entirely explain why the execution rate was so high in the sixteenth and early seventeenth centuries, when compared with the period after c.1635 and, even more so, to the early 1700s. To an extent, this difference probably reflects a lag between medieval notions of jurisprudence and 'modern' notions of enforcement. Because medieval provision for formal law enforcement was haphazardly organised and administered, being thinly distributed and sometimes almost absent, with numerous points at which felons could escape justice, punishment necessarily had to be draconian to deter. This was especially so in a world already hardened to extremes of violence. It took time for a more ordered society to recognise that the increased numbers of felons that came into its law enforcement net merited less savagery. Even so, the Tudor execution rate appears to have been higher than that for late medieval England.[21] In part, this may have reflected the effects of inflation, which meant that between

---

20. Anon, *Hanging, not Punishment Enough*, London, A. Baldwin, 1701, p.16.
21. J.G. Bellamy, *The Criminal Trial in Later Medieval England Felony Before the Courts From Edward I to the Sixteenth Century*, Toronto, University of Toronto Press, 1998, pp.155-156.

1500 and 1650 the real value of a shilling (from the twelfth century the boundary for capital offences) fell six-fold. However, 'pious perjury' by juries greatly reduced the significance of this decline; virtually no one was executed for theft of goods worth only a few pence over the limit. More realistically, huge population growth combined with cycles of poor harvests and economic crisis in the sixteenth century may have occasioned a real increase in both criminality and penality.[22]

Ineffectiveness of Execution

Whatever the reasons for the high incidence of execution in the sixteenth century, it was apparent to many thoughtful Englishmen, even then, that extensive recourse to the gallows was not effective in preventing crime. As Thomas Starkey observed in the 1530s: "...it availeth not so to the repressing of the fault, as by long time and many years we have had proof sufficient."[23] Inevitably, some, such as Fortescue, writing 70 years earlier, argued that this indicated that any moderation of the existing regime would be disastrous: "For though in England felons of all sorts are everywhere punished with death; yet they still go on in defiance of all laws to the contrary: and, how much less would they abstain, if only a gentler punishment were

---

22. P. Jenkins, "From Gallows to Prison? The Execution Rate in Early Modern England," *Criminal Justice History*, 1986, vol. 7, pp.61-63.
23. Starkey, *A Dialogue between Reginal Pole and Thomas Lupset*, p.115.

threatened and inflicted."[24] Others concluded that draconian punishments were ineffective on their own. Amongst them were important judicial figures. Thus, in 1516, when Thomas More's fictional English lawyer took occasion to praise the severe punishment meted out to thieves in England, so that that there were sometimes "20 hanged together" ón a single gibbet, Raphael was moved to reply that he could only wonder by what: "... evil luck it should come to pass, that thieves nevertheless were in every place so rife and so rank."[25] Over a century later, Sir Edward Coke, despite his faith in the general excellence of English criminal law, could not fail to notice that "Those offences are often committed that are often punished". He feared that the frequency of capital punishment made it "so familiar as it is not feared". He was also appalled at the huge annual English total of people "strangled on that cursed tree".[26] A few decades further on again, Sir Mathew Hale reiterated concern that, despite England's harsh laws against theft, the country's prisons were "never the emptier".[27] Many legislators shared such concerns. The preface to the 1718 Transportation Act (4 Geo. I, c. 11) candidly acknowledged

---

24. Grigor (Ed.), *Sir John Fortescue's Commendation of the Laws of England*, p.78.
25. More, *Utopia*, p.31.
26. Sir E. Coke, *The Institutes of the Lawes of England, Part Three, Concerning High Treason, and other Pleas of the Crown and Criminall causes*, London, 1644, pp.245-246. Nevertheless, Coke's solutions were fairly anodyne; good moral education of the young, and their early instruction in a practical trade combined with the provision of firm laws against idleness, so that more did not start on the slippery path towards felony.
27. Sir M. Hale, *A Discourse touching Provision for the Poor*, London, William Shrowsbery, 1683, Preface, pp.1-4.

failure in the nation's penal policy, asserting that it was found by experience: "That the Punishments inflicted by the Laws now in Force against the Offences of Robbery, Larceny and other felonious Taking and Stealing of Money and Goods, have not proved effectual to deter wicked and evil-disposed Persons." Such concerns survived to the very end of the early modern period, so that in March 1735 a Metropolitan observer lamented that in London, which had an especially high execution rate: "Notwithstanding the Number of Criminals condemn'd at the Old-Bailey, Street Robbers and Housebreakers abound and are very barbarous."[28]

Variation in Execution Rates in Early Modern England

Although, in 1751, Samuel Johnson was still expressly associating himself with Thomas More's criticism of the frequency of English execution, delivered almost 250 years earlier, the two men's penal environments differed greatly, as did the proportion of felons executed in their respective eras.[29] Modern scholarship has frequently stressed the apparent late eighteenth and early nineteenth century penal 'transformation', in which prisons replaced the gallows as the 'dominant' form of punishment. This has readily accommodated a Marxist analysis in which modern penal

---

28. *The Gentleman's Magazine*, 1735, vol. 5, p.162.
29. S. Johnson, "Crime and Punishment," *The Rambler*, London, Everyman's Library, 1953, p.186.

practices are seen to stem from late eighteenth century bourgeois revolutions. Such an analysis has also served to engender confusion, especially in an English context. Most importantly, it has obscured the manner in which, even as the growth of capital offences under the notorious 'bloody code' got underway, the actual use of execution was declining rapidly, increasingly being replaced by alternative punishments, particularly transportation. Most of the prisoners transported after 1660 would have been executed if their crimes had been committed under the Tudors.[30] Indeed, in 1663, Sir Orlando Bridgeman, the Lord Chief Justice, complained that at the Old Bailey administration was so loose that some felons convicted of non-clergyable felonies were being mistakenly transported to the Americas rather than executed.[31] As Blackstone noted, the *ad hoc* passing of little scrutinised capital offences during the eighteenth century, such as that which provided death for breaking down the dams of fish-ponds so that their occupants escaped (9 Geo. I c.22), was 'absurd'. However, as he also pointed out, they were largely empty statutes; such: "... outrageous penalties, being seldom or never inflicted, are hardly known to be law by the public."[32] (Nevertheless, in August 1731, at the Lewes assizes, two people were capitally convicted under the Black Act for cutting down the head of a fishpond, though they may have been reprieved

30. Jenkins, "From Gallows to Prison?," pp.51 and 66.
31. Sir O. Bridgeman, "Newgate, 1663, A Letter of Sir Orlando Bridgeman, Chief Justice," *American Journal of Legal History*, vol. 13, pp.384 and 386.
32. W. Blackstone, *Commentaries on the Laws of England*, vol. 4, Oxford, Clarendon Press, 1769, p.4.

subsequently.)[33] The passing of such statutes was often the little scrutinised work of small political pressure groups.

Decline in Execution Rates

The beginning of the early modern period witnessed an especially large-scale use of capital punishment, the incidence of which appears to have gradually declined as the era advanced. Thus, in the 1580s, William Harrison estimated that 300-400 'rogues' were hanged each year in England, and his figure appears to have been an underestimate unless confined to legally defined vagabonds. In the late 1590s, Paul Hentzner, a German visitor, noted "above 300 are said to be hanged annually at London". Some estimates suggest that as many as 6,000 people were executed in the Metropolis during the reign of Elizabeth I alone. Allowing for population growth, this would represent about 4,000 hangings annually in the modern capital.[34] Harrison also believed that Henry VIII had executed 72,000 criminals during his reign (though this was undoubtedly a very major exaggeration).[35] On a less impressionistic basis, between 1607 and 1616 it has been estimated that Middlesex and the City of London witnessed at least 1,400 executions. This must be compared to 1,696

33. *The Gentleman's Magazine*, 1731, vol. 1, p.351.
34. J.A. Sharpe, "Lessons of History: Hard times revive law and order panic," *The Independent*, London, April 12, 1993, p.2.
35. Canon W. Harrison, *A Description of England*, (The 2nd book, 2nd edn., 1587), London, New Shakespeare Society, 1877, p.231.

offenders executed there between 1749 and 1799, even though the period also witnessed a major growth in the Metropolis's population from its level in the early 1600s. This development was matched in the provinces. In Devonshire, between 1598 and 1639, 620 people were executed. However, 53 per cent of these cases occurred in the 11 years prior to 1609, with a steep decline occurring thereafter. In the 1630s, the average execution rate was only 13, compared to 28 in the early years of the seventeenth century. Nationally, the number of executions appears to have fallen from c.800 per year in 1600, to between 80 and 100 a year in 1750. Allowing for a significant expansion in population, this means that the rate by then may have been little more than six per cent of the 1600 level.[36] Thus, the real incidence of executions was declining rapidly. Abolitionism in the decades after 1780 was, in reality, the logical continuation of this early modern process. The fall in execution rates after the early 1600s was probably partly linked to a real decline in criminality (both recorded and actual). However, the emergence of secondary punishments as alternatives, combined with greater notions of 'humanity' (already alluded to) also explains much of the decline.

The Executioner

Hanging was the normal English method of executing felons. William Dugdale traced its use as the primary

---

36. Jenkins, "From Gallows to Prison?" pp.52-60.

method of execution back to King Ina's reign in the Dark Ages, though the Normans had briefly used blinding and mutilation of the genitals for some grave offences.[37] In London, the office of common hangman was a full-time position, something justified by the city's high number and frequency of executions. One London hangman, Jack Ketch, who died in 1686, lent his name to the office for the following two centuries. In most provincial areas it was a part-time employment, though a few individuals held the position in several neighbouring counties simultaneously. They were often men of the worst character, and a few had taken the position to secure a reprieve from their own executions. Thus, in 1684, each of two young brothers, sentenced to be hanged at Ibstock for robbery, were told that one of them could save his own life if he agreed to hang the other and also burn a woman sentenced to death for poisoning her husband. In this case, family loyalty survived, and they both refused.[38] However, this was not always the case. In c.1660, a father and two sons named Crossland were tried at the Derby assizes, and condemned to death for horse theft. The court, after sentence, and noting the lack of a town hangman, entertained the cruel whim of extending mercy to one of the criminals on condition that the pardoned man should hang the other two. The father and eldest son refused. The younger, John, accepted immediately, and: "... performed the fatal work without remorse upon his father

---

37. W. Dugdale, *Origines Juridicales*, London, F. and T. Warren, 1666, p.88.
38. B. Capp, "Serial killers in 17th century England," *History Today*, 1996, vol.46, issue 3, pp.21-31.

and brother, and acquitted himself with such dexterity, that he was appointed to the office of hangman in Derby, and two or three neighbouring counties." He continued in the office until extreme old age, dying in 1705, allegedly so void of feeling that he "rejoiced at a murder because it brought the prospect of a guinea". He was so reviled in the town that even children pelted him in the streets when he passed by.[39] Other hangmen were themselves executed for crimes committed while in office. Thus, John Price was hanged in chains in Bunhill Fields in May 1718, for brutally murdering an elderly woman who had resisted his drunken sexual advances. In the process, he almost knocked one of her eyes "out of her head". He went to his execution with a bottle of gin.[40] In 1736, one of his successors: "Jack Catch [sic] on his Return from doing his Office at Tyburn, robb'd a Woman of three shillings and six pence for which he was committed to Newgate."[41] A hangman's work was not confined to executions, as he would normally also be responsible, *inter alia*, for branding clergied felons, and conducting whippings for petty larceny and other minor offences. He might also burn obscene and confiscated books.

As John Crossland's reaction indicates, by ancient custom, a hangman claimed the dead man's clothes, a tradition reaching back far into the medieval period. If the executed man was wealthy, the profits could be substantial.

---

39. W. Hutton, *The History of Derby*, London, 1791, pp.239-243.
40. A. Smith, *A Compleat history of the lives and robberies of the most notorious highwaymen, ... for above an hundred years past*, London, Briscoe, 1719, vol. 2, pp.329-330.
41. *The Gentleman's Magazine*, 1736, vol. 6, p.291.

John Ketch made 10 guineas by selling Lord Russell's "coat, hat, and periwig". Some of the condemned, aware that the executioner would claim their clothes afterwards, wore something cheap and simple, like a nightshirt, to deny him any substantial profit. Thus, in 1535, Sir Thomas More, prior to his execution: "... as one that had been invited to a solemn feast, changed himself into his best apparel; which Mr. Lieutenant [of the Tower] espying, advised him to put it off, saying, That he that should have it was but a javel [low fellow]." Although he eventually yielded to the Lieutenant's entreaties, More did not forget the axeman: "... he altered his apparel, yet, after the example of that holy martyr St Cyprian, did he of that little money that was left him, send one angel of gold to his executioner."[42] Others made private arrangements with the hangman prior to their deaths. Thus, Colonel Turner summoned the executioner and told him that his friends were: "... desirous of all his Clothes, and that in Consideration thereof, he gave him 50 shillings and 2 shillings, six pence to drink and about 15 shillings to the Serjeants and Yeomen attending to see his Body and clothes delivered to one Mrs Smith there."[43]

Tyburn

Because of the city's size and the high incidence of death

---

42. W. Roper, *The Life of Sir Thomas More*, in *Lives of Sir Thomas More*, E.G. Reynolds (Ed.), London, Everyman edn., Dent, 1963, p.49.
43. Anon, *The Speech and Deportment of Colonel James Turner at his execution in Leaden-Hall-Street, January 21, 1663*, London, 1663, p.3.

sentences passed, London executions, held at Tyburn, were spectacular, so that an observer could record that the attendant "noise and confusion is unbelievable".[44] They were held eight times a year (before the 1660s sometimes less or more frequently), a few days after the Newgate sessions, when, in the words of Thomas Platter in 1599, there ensued a:

"... slaughtering and a hanging, and from all the prisons (of which there are several scattered about the town where) people are taken and tried; when the trial is over, those condemned to the rope are placed on a cart, each one with a rope about his neck, and the hangman drives with them out of the town to the gallows, called Tyburn, almost an hour away from the city, there he fastens them up one after another by the rope and drives the cart off under the gallows which is not very high off the ground; then the criminal's friends come and draw them down by their feet, that they may die all the sooner."

It was rare that fewer than 20 to 30 people, both men and women, were executed at such six weekly events during the Elizabethan period.

Foreigners were struck by the stoicism, indeed raw bravery, of those facing execution in England. This was

---

44. M. Van Muyden (Trans. and Ed.), *A foreign View of England in the reigns of George I and George II; The letters of Monsieur Cesar de Saussure, to his Family*, London, John Murray, 1902, p.126.

reiterated so frequently that it must have borne some correspondence to reality, albeit that their views were mainly based on observation of Tyburn, rather than provincial gallows. Thus, Horatio Busino was astonished by the *sang froid* of the condemned, riding six to a cart, on their way to Tyburn: "They go along quite jollily, holding their sprigs of Rosemary and singing songs."[45] Similarly, a century later, according to Cesar de Saussure, it was still common to see criminals going to their deaths "perfectly unconcerned". This convinced him that Englishmen looked on death in a different light to men from other nations, and were not afraid of it: "... most criminals may be seen going with wonderful courage and fortitude to the gallows."[46] Although not a committed Anglophile, even Henri Misson was struck by this quality amongst those destined for Tyburn, feeling that their "extraordinary courage looks upon it as a trifle". Some went to their deaths in their best clothes or shrouds, laughing and joking.[47] Doubtless, such observers had been struck by the executions of men like the 18-year-old former soldier, James Leonard, hanged for robbery in 1693. Leonard was so little concerned at his end that he tried to cut the gallows' rope with a knife he had concealed about his person, purely to give the hangman the "trouble of buying a new rope". Leaning against his coffin he boasted, laughed and jested with the crowd. He also complained about the cold, which meant he would be

---

45. Platter and Busino, *Journals of two travellers*, pp.36 and 148.
46. Muyden, *A foreign View of England in the reigns of George I and George II*, p.198.
47. M. Misson, *Memoirs and Observations in his Travels over England*, J. Ozell (Trans.), London, 1719, p.124.

hanged in the sort of weather that would "freeze a body before the job's over".[48] Why those about to be executed in England, especially London, should show more phlegm than their continental counterparts is hard to explain, though the absence of aggravated forms of death may have contributed to it, as might the lack of pre-conviction torture; this was an explanation that William Harrison subscribed to feeling that it was "one cause wherefore our condemned persons do go so cheerfully to their deaths".[49] The social support provided by the assembled crowd to ordinary felons might also have had something to do with it, as both Doctor Johnson and Bernard De Mandeville were to suggest in the eighteenth century. However, alcohol also probably played a major part, at least in London. Cesar de Saussure noted that many condemned men were intoxicated on their way to the scaffold. Indeed, Mandeville was convinced that their apparent bravery was not true courage at all, but primarily due to the prisoners' inebriation, a state of affairs that was kept permanent by up to six stops at taverns on the way to Tyburn.[50]

Additionally, as even foreign observers appreciated, there were many exceptions to the general pattern of stoicism. Thus, Misson noted that although presenting a brave countenance was deemed to be 'correct' behaviour, it was certainly not universal: "I must needs own that if a pretty many of these People dress thus gayly, and go to it

48. Rayner and Crook, *The Complete Newgate Calendar*, vol. II, pp.89-90.
49. Harrison, *Elizabethan England*, p.237.
50. Mandeville, *An Enquiry into the Course of the Frequent Executions at Tyburn*, p.23.

with such an Air of Indifference, there are many others that go slovenly enough, and with very dismal Phizzes [faces]."[51] Similarly, in the 1650s, it was observed that although condemned 'Hectors' went to Tyburn with "much seeming cheerfulnesse" there were numerous others who failed to put on a good show.[52] Many of the condemned must have shared the murderer Thomas Savage's dismay, when confronted with the coffin that he would carry to the gallows and which would receive his corpse: "Is it not a terrible thing to see one's own coffin and burial clothes, when at the same time (as to my bodily health) I am every whit as well as you?"[53] Additionally, not everyone was impressed by the general bravura. Mandeville was horrified at the lack of contrition evidenced by many of the condemned, and the carnival atmosphere amongst the spectators. He was particularly shocked by the manner in which prisoners awaiting execution jested and swore.[54]

The Mechanics of Death

Although the English death penalty may not have been deliberately aggravated, to Horatio Busino at least, the

---

51. Misson, *Memoirs and Observations in his Travels over England*, p.124.

52. Anon, *Notable and pleasant History of the Famous renowned Knights of the Blade*, London, Richard Harper, 1652, p.2.

53. C. Johnson, *A General History of the Lives and Adventures of the Most Famous Highwaymen, Murderers, Street-Robbers*, London, J. Janeway, 1734, p.137.

54. Mandeville, *An Enquiry into the Causes of the Frequent Executions at Tyburn*, pp.19-23.

proceedings at Tyburn were still "really barbarous". One reason for their horror was that early modern gallows, lacking a 'drop', effected death through strangulation rather than the broken neck of Victorian and later times. Thus, Busino watched the executioner apply his whip to horses pulling the convicts' carts, after their passengers had been noosed, so that they remained "dangling in the air precisely like a bunch of fat thrushes". Like Platter, he witnessed up to 25 people at a time being hanged, and friends and relatives pulling on their legs or throwing brickbats at their chests to speed up death, without which they found it "hard to die of themselves".[55] Nothing had changed over a century later, Misson recording that as men swung kicking in the air: "The Hangman does not give himself the Trouble to put them out of their Pain, but some of their Friends or relations do it for them. They pull the dying Person by the legs, and beat his Breast, to dispatch him as soon as possible."[56]

The sheer inefficiency of the gallows procedure was evidenced by periodic cases of post-execution survival, as can be seen in the gruesome events surrounding the hanging of Thomas Savage at Ratcliff Cross in October 1668, an improvised gallows having been raised near where he had murdered a servant maid. When turned off the cart he "struggled for a while". A kindly friend, noticing this: "... struck him several blows upon his breast with all his strength, to put him out of his pain, till no motion could be perceived in him." After Savage had hung for some time in

---

55.   Platter and Busino, *Journals of two travellers*, p.148.
56.   Misson, *Memoirs and Observations in his Travels over England*, p.123.

this condition, he was cut down and his body was taken to a tavern, the *Sign of the Rose*, to be laid out.[57] There, however, signs of life were noticed. Seamen drinking in the public house lit a fire to warm him, and bathed his body with spirits, so that he began to move his arms and legs. Unfortunately for Savage, the sheriff was informed and arrived with peace officers to secure him. Although unable to speak, Savage kicked out as he was taken from the bed in which he had been placed. Within four hours of his original execution he was hanged again, this time until completely dead.[58] Some survivors did rather better. Anne Green was hanged at Oxford in 1649 for infanticide (the evidence was tenuous). She, too, was given numerous "blowes on the breast" with the musket butts of attendant soldiers. After her body was cut down for anatomising by the barber surgeons in the University City, she, too, started to recover, in her case on the dissection table! Some wished to have her re-hanged, others, however, rejected this course as morally wrong and possibly illegal.[59] Similarly, William Duell, who was hanged at Tyburn in 1740 for raping, robbing and murdering a woman at Acton, also benefited from his extraordinary escape. His body was brought to the Surgeon's Hall to be anatomised but: "... after it was stripp'd and laid on the Board, and one of the Servants was washing him in order to be cut, he perceived Life in him, and found his Breath to come quicker and quicker; on which a Surgeon

---

57. Johnson, *A General History of the Lives and Adventures of the Most Famous Highwaymen ...*, p.137.
58. T. Savage, *Gods Justice against Murther*, London, 1668, pp.10-11.
59. A. Green, *A wonder of wonders ...*, London, 1650, at pp.1-6.

took some Ounces of Blood from him; in two Hours he was able to sit up in his Chair." That evening he was committed again to Newgate. In Duell's case, execution was then commuted to transportation.[60] The notorious Derbyshire executioner, John Crossland, having charge of the bodies of those executed as one of the 'perquisites' of his job (to remove clothing etc.), avoided such problems by summary action: "... signs of life have been known to return after execution, in which case he prevented their growing existence by violence."[61] Those who revived had normally survived a considerable period dangling from the hemp noose of the era (its inflexibility aided their escape). When Colonel Turner, anxious about the shame of being publicly exhibited after his death, asked the Sheriff of London "must I hang all day?" Sir Richard Ford reassured him he would be cut down as soon as he was dead, and that at the most he would not hang for more than half an hour."[62] This appears to have been a fairly standard time, 70 years earlier, Harrison talked of "half-an-hour's hanging".[63] Anne Green, too, had been hanged for 30 minutes.

The Execution of Pirates at Wapping

Pirates and maritime felons executed in London escaped a trip to Tyburn and had their own ancient procession and

---

60. *The Gentleman's Magazine*, 1740, vol. 10, p.570.
61. Hutton, *The History of Derby*, pp.239-243.
62. Anon, *The Speech and Deportment of Colonel James Turner*, pp.6-13, 20.
63. Harrison, *Elizabethan England*, p.242.

ritual instead, one that was followed for almost 400 years. Those convicted, usually at a special Admiralty Sessions at the Old Bailey, were brought from the Marshalsea Prison in Southwark, or Newgate prison in the City, past the Tower, to Execution Dock, a few yards below Wapping Old Stairs, where there were permanent gallows. The Admiralty Marshal, or his deputy, carrying a silver oar (representing the jurisdiction of the Admiralty court over maritime crimes) led the procession on horseback. Like the Tyburn ritual, the prisoner travelled on a cart with a chaplain by his side. With St Mary's Church in the background, and a crowd assembled on the riverbank or on nearby boats, he was given the same opportunity to make a last dying speech. However, unlike those executed at Tyburn, felons would not be cut down promptly after execution. By ancient tradition: "Pirates and robbers by sea are condemned in the Court of the Admiralty, and hanged on the shore at low-water mark, where they are left till three tides have overwashed them."[64] Stow had alluded to this punishment (albeit in slightly different terms) in the sixteenth century, noting that such a convict was: "... tied to a post in the Thames at a good wharfe where boates are fastened, [for] two ebbings and two flowings of the water."[65] Thus, on May 23, 1701 (Captain) William Kidd was taken to Wapping with three other pirates in two horse-drawn carts. By then, Kidd was partially intoxicated. At the scaffold, however, he

---

64. Harrison, *A Description of England*, p.229.
65. J. Stow, *A survey of London reprinted from the text of 1603*, vol. 1, Oxford, Clarendon, 1603, p.65.

managed to address the large crowd present, warning other captains to learn from his fate. The four men were then 'turned off', but Kidd's rope snapped and he fell to the ground, dazed but still alive. The chaplain said more prayers and Kidd was rehoisted.[66] Pirates who preyed on their own country's ships in wartime, while operating from an enemy privateer, might expect to be executed for high treason. In 1743, Thomas Rounce, an English sailor from Yarmouth who had been convicted at the Admiralty Sessions, in December 1742, for voluntarily fighting against his own country on Spanish vessels, was sentenced to the aggravated punishment reserved for that offence. This was carried out the following month, Rounce being conveyed on a hurdle to execution dock, accompanied by an executioner, publicly carrying the scimitar with which he would quarter him: "... soon after he was hung up, the Executioner cut him down, and immediately sever'd his Head from his Body, ripped up his stomach, and took out his Heart, &c. exposing them for some time to the croud, which was so very great that many were hurt." Gruesome though his end was, the executioner appears to have slightly modified the original sentence, beheading him before his 'privities' were cut off.[67]

Improvised Gallows

Conviction in an especially notorious crime, particularly

---

66. R. Cavendish, "Execution of Captain Kidd," *History Today*, 2001, vol. 51, issue 5, p.53.

67. *The Gentleman's Magazine*, 1742, vol. 12, p.657, and *The Gentleman's Magazine*, 1743, vol. 13, p.49.

murder, would often encourage the authorities to set a special example by hanging the guilty man near to where his offence was committed, rather than at Tyburn or the normal county gallows. This was as common in London as the provinces and would necessitate the use of an improvised and temporary scaffold. Thus, Colonel James Turner, a Civil War veteran who had gagged and robbed an elderly merchant of £5,000 in money and jewels, in his home, was hanged in January 1664 at the end of Lyme Street, where the crime occurred. (Samuel Pepys paid a shilling to stand in "great pain" on a cartwheel to observe proceedings.)[68] Similarly, Arnold Cosbie, executed for murder in 1591, was conveyed in a cart from the Marshalsea prison, where he had been detained, to Wandsworth, where a special gibbet was set up on a local hill. Nevertheless, despite the *ad hoc* arrangements, the normal spiritual support was also provided, so that he found Doctor Fletcher, the Lord Bishop of Bristol waiting to "comfort him against the fear of death, who persuaded him to defy murder and to acknowledge his offence".[69]

Provincial Executions

The smaller numbers executed in the provinces, a handful twice a year after each assizes, with occasional hangings in

68. S. Pepys, *The Diary of Samuel Pepys*, R. Latham and W. Matthews (Eds.), London, Bell and Hyman, vol. 5, 1971, p.23.
69. Anon, *The manner of the death and execution of Arnold Cosbie*, London, William Wright, 1591, f.A4.

the early part of the period after quarter and borough sessions, meant that provincial executions were less 'spectacular' and frequent than those in London. Such executions were often ad hoc affairs, using specially constructed gallows, and normally conducted by a part-time hangman of little skill. The numbers executed at any one time were usually few enough for them to be 'turned off' individually from a ladder, suddenly twisted around, rather than a cart. The attendant crowds were also not so large, making the process more seemly. Nevertheless, the procedure was broadly similar to that conducted at Tyburn. The county sheriff was usually present, religious ministrations were always provided, and the scaffold ritual was roughly the same.

Scaffold Ritual

However it came about, execution was supposed to provide a total severance of social solidarity (though by the 1700s this did not always occur at Tyburn). As the pick-pocket John Selman lamented, before his hanging in 1612: "I stand here as shames example, ready to bee spewed out of the Common wealth."[70] Those to be executed could go some way to being reconciled to society by following approved procedures. These included assisting the authorities, showing forgiveness to the hangman for his necessary service, repentance for their crimes, and an acceptance of the

---

70. Anon, *The arraignment of John Selman*, London, T. Archer, 1612, p.16.

justice of their sentence. To encourage this, condemned men were "well prepared for heaven [so that] many times a man may gather thence Remorse, devotion, and true penitence."[71] In a large-scale hanging of commoners, as at Tyburn, pressure of time meant that one man might be appointed as spokesman, to make a short speech for the whole group.[72] In an era that was more accustomed to death than our own, many convicts played their designated parts. Thus, Benjamin Child, executed in 1721 for highway robbery, was well aware of normal protocol in such situations: "... It being customary for men, under my unhappy circumstances, to declare what religion they die of, or whether they suffer wrongfully or justly, at the place of execution." He went on to declare that he was an Anglican, was entirely guilty of the crime for which he was to be hanged, and commended the judge and jury for their righteous verdicts and sentence (though regretting that he was to be gibbeted and denied a Christian burial). He then asked forgiveness for his crimes and dissolute life.[73] As this case suggests, gallows' confessions were considered important as they publicly demonstrated the correctness of the trial adjudication. Joan Perry, wrongly executed with her two sons at the Spring assizes in Gloucestershire in 1661, for a non-existent murder, was hanged first because she was "reputed a witch" and, it was feared, might be using her power to prevent her

---

71. J. Taylor (the Water-Poet), *The Description of Tyburn*.
72. Platter and Busino, *Journals of two travellers*, p.148.
73. Anon, *The Whole Life History of Benjamin Child*, London, 1722, at pp.31-32.

children from making appropriate scaffold admissions.[74] Another important 'standardised' service, commonly performed at or before execution, was to provide information that would aid the authorities in their fight against crime. Thus, in 1612, when Selman was asked at the gallows if he would: "... discover any of his fraternity, for the good of the Common wealth or not: [He] Answered, that he had already left the names of divers notorious malefactors in writing behind him, which hee thought sufficient."[75] Stereotyped explanations for a convict's fall were also often offered in gallows' speeches, no doubt, in part, the result of clerical prompting. In time-honoured fashion, the murderer John Owen blamed a lewd, wicked, woman for his downfall. Showing a softer side to his character, he also admitted that he had planned to murder his wife with a hammer, but could not find the heart to do it.[76]

Some gallows' speeches could be quite lengthy. When a large crowd gathered for the execution of Colonel James Turner (he was a relatively distinguished man) in 1664, he made the most of his time in the spotlight. His dying speech ranged across a huge spectrum of matters, often to the annoyance of the attending officials. Thus, as well as saying prayers, he gallantly attempted to exonerate his sons from the crime (two were then in custody) and to diminish the role of his 'hirelings'. Additionally, he discussed his

---

74. Sir T. Overbury, *A true and Perfect Account of the Examination, Confession, Tryal, Condemnation, and execution of Joan Perry*, London, 1676, p.12.
75. Anon, *The arraignment of John Selman*, pp.16-17.
76. R. Gough, *The History of Myddle*, D. Hey (Ed.), Harmondsworth, Penguin, 1981, (originally written 1701), p.150.

eminently respectable parentage (his father had been a parson and JP near London), his successful military career and the need for penal reform! This was despite Sir Richard Ford, the sheriff, advising him that they were not "proper work for a dying man". Turner, however, continued in this vein, so that Ford interjected again urging him to "put that little time that you have to spend here to better use". Finally, the exasperated sheriff suspected an ulterior motive in Turner's delay and told him that he was not expecting a gallows' reprieve. The Ordinary from Newgate prison then attempted to clear up some serious outstanding crimes, one of his traditional functions, asking if Turner knew anything about a "glass jewel, delivered to the Countess of Devonshire in the room of another?" (He denied any knowledge.) The cleric also exhorted the condemned man to make a more detailed confession, disliking the generalised terms in which Turner was couching his contrition. Endeavouring to ensure that other traditional parts of the execution speech were also present, the Ordinary later prompted the condemned man to "Express your Charity as to the world", which he duly did.[77]

Not everyone was willing to 'play the game' at the scaffold. Sawney Douglas, a 53 year old Scottish highwayman who was hanged at Tyburn on the 10th of September 1664, behaved indecently, ignoring the available religious ministrations, telling spectators that it was hard that a man could not go to the gallows in peace, and

---

77. Anon, *A True and Impartial Account of the Arraignment, Tryal, Examination, Confession and Condemnation of Col. James Turner*, London, 1663, pp.85-90.

declaring that he would prefer to be hanged twice without ceremony, than once in such a "superstitious" manner. At the scaffold, he took no notice of the Ordinary's prayers and urged the hangman to be quick about his work.[78] William Alcock, executed at Northampton in 1733 for murdering his wife, was defiant to the end: "He never own'd the Fact, nor was at all concern'd at his approaching Death." Additionally, he kicked and swore at spectators, struck a bible to the ground, ignored the psalms and prayers at the gallows and, although already somewhat intoxicated, repeatedly called for more drink.[79] Similarly, at his execution in 1691, Tom Cox was "resolute to the last" and when the Ordinary invited him to pray, kicked him off the scaffold cart.[80] Sometimes, if the authorities feared that the scaffold ritual would be abused, they might take precautionary steps, especially in 'political' cases. Thus, at the execution in 1662, of Sir Henry Vane (the younger) a Puritan Statesman during the Commonwealth, convicted of treason by the Restoration government, the authorities endeavoured to stymie his lengthy address, which was "many times interrupted by the Sheriffe". Trumpets were also played under the scaffold, so that he was drowned out.[81]

---

78. A. Smith, *A Compleat history of the lives and robberies of the most notorious highwaymen, ... for above an hundred years past*, London, Briscoe, 1719, vol. 2, p.194.
79. *The Gentleman's Magazine*, 1733, vol. 3, p.154.
80. A. Smith, *A Compleat history of the lives and robberies of the most notorious highwaymen*, 1719, vol. 1, p.51.
81. Pepys, *The Diary of Samuel Pepys*, vol. 4, p.108.

Anatomising and Gibbeting

Although there were few aggravated forms of death in England, once dead, a felon's corpse might have further punishment visited on it, via anatomising and being gibbeted. In 1540, Henry VIII granted the Barber Surgeons Company the right to use the corpses of four executed felons a year for anatomical study (32 Hen. VIII, c.42). This was the beginning of a practice that would be greatly expanded in the eighteenth century. Nevertheless, for much of the period, the modest number of cadavers involved, compared to those executed, meant that it could be confined to friendless or unpopular felons, limiting resistance by the attendant crowds to the practice.[82] Thus, after her execution in 1635, the corpse of the murderer Elizabeth Evans was: "... conveied to Barber Surgions Hall for a skeleton having her bones reserved in a perfect forme of her body which is to be seene, and now remaines in the aforesaid Hall." After appropriate treatment it produced a "dryed Carkase or Skeleton of Bones and Gristles".[83] A similar fate awaited Jack Bird's body after his execution for robbery in March 1690. In an era when medical knowledge was expanding, providing bodies for dissection was one of the most valuable functions of the gallows. As John Taylor acknowledged, the: "... fruit which it produces, doth seldom serve for profitable uses: except the skillful surgeons

---

82. J.S. Cockburn, "Punishment and Brutalization in the English Enlightenment," *Law and History Review*, 1994, vol. 12, no. 1, p.170.

83. H. Goodcole, *Heavens Speedie Hue and Cry sent after Lust and Murther*, London, N. and I. Okes, 1635, ff.C3 and D1.

industry do make dissection of anatomy." As the early modern era progressed, and medical training improved, there was a greatly increased demand for corpses. The need for bodies occasioned less discrimination in their selection at the gallows. By the early 1700s, Cesar de Saussure noted that after execution any "unclaimed bodies are sold to surgeons to be dissected".[84] Ultimately, a shortage of cadavers would spawn the eighteenth century 'Resurrectionists' who would dig up recently buried corpses for sale to medical schools.

As well as providing an essential service for medical students, it was argued that anatomising enhanced the deterrent value of execution, because of the: "... superstitious Reverence of the Vulgar for a Corpse, even of a Malefactour, and the strong Aversion they have against dissecting them." Certainly, there was a widespread popular belief in the need for Christian burial, something that periodically occasioned riots as onlookers at Tyburn sought to recover the corpses of the hanged, as they were being taken by the surgeons. Mandeville felt that everyone who was executed should be at risk of this disposal, to increase the exemplary effect of the gallows.[85] Such views (and the need for more bodies) lay behind an Act of 1751, passed for the "more effectual prevention" of murder, which decreed that convicted murderers should either be hanged in chains or anatomised.

The most serious offenders might be gibbeted after

---

84. Muyden, *A foreign View of England in the reigns of George I and George II*, p.123.
85. Mandeville, *An Enquiry into the causes of the frequent executions at Tyburn*, p.26.

death. Although, legally, gibbeting only became a formal part of the punishment for grave offences in the eighteenth century, it was common practice in heinous cases long before this. As was noted in the Elizabethan period, if a man was: "... convicted of wilful murder, done either upon pretended malice or in any notable robbery, he is either hanged alive in chains near the place where the fact was committed (or else upon compassion taken, first strangled with a rope), and so continueth till his bones consume to nothing."[86] This situation still prevailed over a century later. Henri Misson noted in the 1690s that highwaymen who killed their victims were the most likely type of criminal to be gibbeted, it being the only difference to the punishment normally meted out to their more humane (i.e. non-lethal) colleagues. Many continental observers thought it was unfair that murdering robbers did: "... not suffer any greater Punishment than the others, but their Bodies must be expose'd upon the very Road where they committed the Crime." It was considered that their presence, near a crime scene, might have an extra deterrent effect. Thus, the body of Thomas Sherwood, a notorious Metropolitan robber and murderer, executed in 1635, was initially "hangeth in Chaines" near St Pancras Church. It does not appear to have had a very salutary effect; one passerby was robbed by a gang of roughs and tied up to the very same gibbet from which Sherwood dangled. Eventually, local farmers - St Pancras was on the fringes of London's built up area - complaining about the crowds that came to gawp at the

---

86. Harrison, *Elizabethan England*, p.242.

corpse, trampelling their crops in the process, prompted its move further out of London, to North Islington.[87] To firmly attach the displayed corpse: "They [would] fasten the Body with several Iron Hoops, which form a kind of sack, and hang it upon the gibbet."[88] Bodies would remain on display until 'consumed by the weather'. Thus, in 1661, Samuel Pepys, riding with a companion at Shooters Hill, eight miles out of London, witnessed such a gruesome spectacle: "Mrs Arn and I rode under the man that hangs upon Shooters hill; and a filthy sight it was to see too how his flesh is shrunk to his bones." Its location was not mere coincidence. Shooters Hill was one of the most dangerous points on the Dover to London road, as the highway narrowed there, and ready cover was provided for highwaymen and footpads by adjacent woods and copses.[89] Similarly, although the corpses of maritime felons executed at Wapping could be removed after the customary three tides had passed over them, the bodies of the most notorious were likely to be tarred and then suspended from a gibbet beside the Thames, as a warning to sailors on passing ships. Thus, Captain Kidd's body was hanged in chains at Tilbury Point.[90]

Alternative Forms of Death

William Dugdale noted that in the distant past there had

---

87. Goodcole, *Heavens Speedie Hue and Cry*, p.C1.
88. Misson, *Memoirs and Observations in his Travels over England*, p.78.
89. Pepys, *The Diary of Samuel Pepys*, vol. 2, pp.72-73.
90. Cavendish, "Execution of Captain Kidd," p.53.

been some local variations on the normal English mode of execution. Thus, in one hundred in Kent, drowning had been employed in lieu of hanging, and the County Palatine of Cheshire had used beheading until quite late in the medieval period.[91] However, the only significant local variation that survived into the early modern period appears to have been that employed at Halifax. As Harrison noted in the Elizabethan period, all English felons were hanged "saving in Halifax where they are beheaded after a strange manner". The Halifax gibbet was actually a primitive guillotine, similar to the type that would emerge in Paris centuries later. It was used to behead thieves who had stolen goods worth the peculiar sum of 13 and a half pence or more (in the estimation of four local constables), as well as other felons. According to Daniel Defoe, writing in the 1720s, the emergence of the town's special punishment (and also its unusual criminal procedure) was linked to the vulnerability of the area's principal industry: "... it was first erected purely, or at least principally, for such thieves as were apprehended stealing cloth from the tenters." Between 1541 and 1650, the records suggest that the gibbet executed 53 people, the last recorded deaths being those of Anthony Mitchell and John Wilkinson, convicted of horse theft and stealing cloth from tenters' frames. After these executions, its use appears to have fallen into desuetude and the machine into ruin. (There has been speculation that its demise was influenced by public reaction to the decapitation of King Charles I in 1649.) The apparatus provided a swift

---

91. Dugdale, *Origines Juridicales*, p.88.

and humane, if gory, death, and certainly seems to have been preferable to the slow strangulation of hanging. The machine's power meant that even: "... if the necke of the trangressor were so big as that of a bull, it should be cut in sunder at a stroke, and roll from the bodie by an huge distance." This is not surprising; the remains of the device were still visible when Defoe visited the town in the 1720s, and recorded that the axe was loaded with so much lead that it removed any "possibility of its failing to cut off the head". According to Harrison, to make the lesson that crime did not pay even clearer, where a condemned man was executed for stealing a sheep, cow, ox or horse, the animal involved would initiate the operation of the guillotine: "... the self beast or other of the same kind shall have the end of the rope tied somewhere unto them, so that they, being driven, do draw out the pin, whereby the offender is executed."[92] The gibbet's origins appear to have lain deep in the medieval period, though, perhaps, even more of a deterrent than the special manner of execution at Halifax, was the swift local hearing that normally preceded it.

Decapitation of Nobles

Nobles who were executed did rather better than commoners as usually: "... this meanes of their death [hanging] is converted into the losse of their heads onelie."[93]

---

92. Harrison, *Elizabethan England*, p.243.
93. Harrison, *A Description of England*, pp.222 and 227.

Dugdale traced the practice of beheading peers, instead of hanging them, to the execution of Waltheof, the Earl of Northumberland, in 1075.[94] According to Hentzner, the reason for the indulgence was that such men viewed beheading as "less infamous than hanging". Its use amongst noblemen was not confined to treason (aristocrats were always disproportionately represented amongst traitors' ranks) but extended to well-born felons. Thus, in May 1631, the minor peer, Mervin Touchet, Lord Audley and Earl of Castlehaven, was beheaded on Tower Hill after being convicted by a jury of 27 of his peers of rape and sodomy (possibly becoming the only peer executed solely for sexual crimes).[95] The legal basis for this commutation was uncertain. Bacon claimed that given that the 'normal' punishment for felony was hanging, some thought it "doubtfull whether the King may turn it into beheading in the case of a Peer, or other person of dignity". Nevertheless, even he accepted that, on this issue, precedents went "both wayes".[96] In reality, until 1747, it was normal practice. However, it was a boon to the codemned peer, and not a right. Thus, during the reign of Philip and Mary, Lord Stourton was refused such an indulgence. Stourton had murdered his family agents, a father and son named Hartgill, for dissuading his widowed mother from signing a bond promising that she would not marry again. After being convicted by his peers he was sentenced to death, the

94. Dugdale, *Origines Juridicales*, p.88.
95. C.B. Herrup, "Finding the Bodies," *GLQ: A Journal of Lesbian and Gay Studies*, 1999, vol. 5.3, pp.255-256.
96. Sir F. Bacon, *Cases of Treason*, London, John More, 1641, p.11.

execution being held in the marketplace at Salisbury on March 6, 1556. Because the murder was "aggravated with very bad circumstances, [he] could not obtain the usual grace of the Crown (viz., to be beheaded), but Queen Mary positively ordered that, like a common malefactor, he should die at the gallows". Even worse, after being hanged, his friends could only obtain the Bishop's permission to have him buried in Salisbury Cathedral if, as a further mark of infamy, the silken halter with which he was hanged was erected over his grave in the church as a monument to his crime. (A wire noose, exhibited over his now demolished grave as late as 1773, is still in the possession of the cathedral library.)[97] Because it was a privilege, not a right, Lord Audley was moved to thank the King for allowing him the axe at his execution in 1632. Similarly, when, Alice Lisle was sentenced to be burnt, as was "usual where a Woman is Convicted of Treason", she sent a petition to James II, asking that he alter the manner of execution to beheading. Several precedents were produced to the King, including those of Lord Audley and Catherine Howard: "Whereupon the King sign'd a Warrant for her being Beheaded, and directed therein, that the Head and Body should be deliver'd to her Relatives, to be Interr'd as they saw fit."[98]

The beheading of aristocrats was often conducted close

---

97.   Defoe, *A Tour thro' the Whole Island of Great Britain.* Letter to present author dated 2nd November 2000 from Miss S.E. Edward, Librarian and Keeper of the Muniments, Salisbury Cathedral.

98.   T. Salmon, *Tryals for High-Treason, and other Crimes. With proceedings on bills of attainder, and impeachments. For three hundred years past ...*, vol. 4, London, D. Brown etc., 1720, pp.384-402.

to the Tower of London in: "... a large open space; on the highest part of it is erected a wooden scaffold, for the execution of noble criminals."[99] However, like most English gallows outside Tyburn, it was a flimsy and impermanent affair, as Thomas More humorously appreciated when facing his own death after being fetched there by the Lord Lieutenant of the Tower: "... going up the scaffold, which was so weak that it was ready to fall, he said to Master Lieutenant, 'I pray you, I pray you, Master Lieutenant, see me safe up, and for my coming down let me shift for myself'."[100] The octogenarian Lord Lovat, beheaded for High Treason as a Jacobite in April 1747, was the last man to undergo such punishment. Encouraged by a gift of ten guineas, and after Lovat had personally checked that the axe was suitably sharp, the executioner took his head off with a single stroke, the two parts of his body then being reunited and buried in the Tower.[101] However, Lovat was fortunate. Thomas More's last advice to the axeman, in 1535, was understandable: "... my neck is very short. Take heed therefore thou shoot not awaa thine honesty."[102] Executioners did not get enough practice in decapitation to ensure a clean and swift severance. John ('Jack') Ketch was reported to have beheaded Lord William Russell (1683) in a gruesomely inept manner, taking numerous strokes. He was subsequently forced into print to defend his bungled decapitation, and to protest against the "hard usage" Russell

---

99. Hentzner, *Travels in England during the reign of Queen Elizabeth*, p.40.
100. Roper, *The Life of Sir Thomas More*, p.50.
101. Rayner and Crook, *The Complete Newgate Calendar*, vol. III, pp.140-141.
102. Roper, *The Life of Sir Thomas More*, p.50.

was said to have had in the "severing of his head". According to Ketch, such allegations were simply scurrilous. Contrary to popular rumour, he claimed that he had not gone to bed intoxicated the previous night, and was not 'hung-over' the following morning, nor had he accidentally hit Lord Russell's shoulder with his axe. In any event, it was largely Russell's own fault that he did not have a "quicker dispatch out of this world". He had adopted an unsuitable posture at the execution block, and, because he did not wear a blindfold, have his cap pulled over his eyes or give a signal that he was ready for the blow, flinched when it fell. Additionally, Ketch claimed to have been distracted by the crowd "just as I was taking Aim and going to give the blow".[103] Despite this, only two years later, he took at least eight strokes to behead the Duke of Monmouth.

Aggravated Forms of the Death Penalty

As a general rule, as Cesar de Saussure observed, in England: "There is no other form of execution but hanging; it is thought that the taking of life is sufficient punishment for any crime without worse torture." (Though he noted that after death, murderers were likely to be gibbetted.)[104] With the exception of treason, petty treason, heresy until well into the seventeenth century (heretics were burnt alive, as two Elizabethan Anabaptists and a pair of Jacobean Arians

---

103. J. Ketch, *The Apologie of John Ketch Esq*, London, John Brown, 1683, pp.1-2.
104. Muyden, *A foreign View of England in the reigns of George I and George II*, p.126.

discovered), and, briefly, poisoning, aggravated forms of the death penalty were absent in early modern England. No matter how serious the felony, in all "capital crimes as are not reputed for treason or hurt of the estate, our sentence pronounced upon the offender is, to hang till he be dead". This made the country distinct in Europe, as it put people to death with use neither of the "wheel nor of the bar, as in other countries".[105] More graphically, Sir Thomas Smith noted that: "Heading, tormenting, demembring, either arme or legge, breaking upon the wheele, empailing, and such cruell torments, as be used in other nations by the order of their law, we have not."[106] This, like the country's absence of torture, was as striking to visiting foreigners to England as to English travellers abroad. Thus, Henri Misson was still remarking in the 1690s that the country's punishments had "nothing terrible in them but death". Unlike France, breaking upon the wheel: "... tearing of the Flesh with red hot Pincers and pulling to pieces with four Horses, are not known in England, no more than the strappado and the Rack." (Though he noted that military deserters were shot.)[107]

Continental civil law jurisdictions showed more variety and viciousness in their methods of execution. Thus, there were numerous different lethal punishments found amongst the scores of German jurisdictions. These combined hangings and decapitation by a sword (by far their most

---

105. Harrison, *Elizabethan England*, pp.237 and 242.
106. Sir T. Smith, *De Republica Anglorum*, London, 1583, p.117.
107. Misson, *Memoirs and Observations in his Travels over England*, pp.67 and 226.

common forms of execution) for ordinary crimes with more esoteric forms of death. Normally, the most draconian, such as breaking on the wheel and quartering were reserved for men convicted of aggravated murder. Common murderers, robbers, arsonists and forgers were often simply beheaded, and ordinary thieves, if executed, merely hanged. However, those convicted of infanticide or rape might be buried alive. Heretics could be drowned or boiled and witches were burnt (in England they were hanged like everyone else). Some of these punishments were concentrated amongst a specific sex. German women were much more likely to be interred alive, men to be broken on the wheel.[108] (It should, perhaps, be noted that the use of the more gruesome forms of continental execution declined gradually throughout the period.)

Many Englishmen argued that such cruelties were unnecessary in their own country. In 1618, 'T.C.' asserted that although of aggravated punishments "used in other countries we have no knowledge or use; and yet so few greevous crimes committed with us as else where in the world."[109] Some visitors shared this view. Nevertheless, such sentiments were not universal, even amongst Englishmen, who sometimes looked enviously at the execution repertoire found in the rest of Europe. Thus, Sir William Petty, although advocating "simple death" for solitary killings,

---

108. R. Van Dulmen, *Theatre of Horror: Crime and Punishment in Early Modern Germany*, Cambridge, Polity Press, 1990, p.101.

109. T.C., *The Glory of England*, London, 1618, p.221.

favoured "Torture & death-for repeated murthers".[110] Similarly, in 1701, an anonymous pamphleteer published a strongly argued case for introducing continental style aggravated executions. He complained that despite few pardons and reprieves being granted to convicted highwaymen there had been a lamentable increase in their numbers, along with those of other criminals. To this observer, it was clear that the traditional form of execution, founded on longstanding English "Clemency and Mildness", was woefully inadequate and that the noose alone was not a sufficient deterrant. It was necessary to be ruthless. If the normal form of execution would not restrain criminals: "Hanging them in Chains, and Starving them, or (if Murtherers and Robbers at the same time, or night incendiaries) breaking them on the wheel, or whipping them to Death, a Roman Punishment should." Such felons could not be reasoned with, having no hopes of salvation after death, so that no argument would be "so cogent, as pain in an intense degree". Like some foreigners, he felt that denying some men an "easie death" was also necessary to differentiate properly between minor and major capital crimes, for example, between simple theft and murder.[111] Such views never gained widespread support. Nevertheless, even in England there was a limited category of exceptions to the general rule eschewing aggravated forms of execution.

---

110. Sir W. Petty, *The Petty Papers: Some Unpublished Writings of Sir William Petty*, Edited from the Bowood Papers by the Marquis of Lansdowne, New York, Augustus M. Kelley Publishers, 1967, vol. 2, p.213.
111. Anon, *Hanging, not Punishment Enough*, pp.A2 and 1-5.

High Treason

The most prominent of these was the punishment for high treason. This offence included any attack on the Sovereign, his family or his immediate representatives, whether the great officers of state or senior members of the judiciary as "every Judge so fitting by the King's Authority, representeth the Majesty and Person of the King".[112] The full punishment for the crime was horrific. At a symbolic level, to distinguish them from ordinary felons, traitors were forbidden to use a cart, instead being drawn to the gallows from prison "upon an hurdle or sled".[113] Much worse was to follow. The guilty party, if male, would then be hanged, but taken down while still alive and his: "... bowels taken out and burned before his face, then to be beheaded, and quartered, and those set up in diverse places."[114] As with normal executions, improvised gallows might be erected near a notorious crime scene. In 1570, John Felton, who had attached a Papal Bull to the Bishop of London's gates, was found guilty of high treason. He was hanged in St Paul's yard, on a specially constructed gallows erected on the morning of his execution, and "being cut down alive, he was bowelled and quartered".[115]

However, in less serious cases, this punishment might be mitigated; Harrison noted that mutilation was sometimes

---

112. Anon, *A Complete Collection of State-Trials, And Proceedings for High Treason, and other Crimes and Misdemeanours*, London, T. Wright, 1776, vol. 1, pp.v-vi.
113. Harrison, *Elizabethan England*, pp.238-239.
114. Smith, *De Republica Anglorum*, p.118.
115. J. Stow, *The Annales of England*, London, Ralfe Nebery, 1592, p.1139.

delayed until life had passed: "... if the trespass be not the more heinous, they are suffered to hang till they be quite dead."[116] Not surprisingly, it was considered a genuine mercy for the King to commute "all but the beheading" for noblemen convicted of treason.[117] Whether simply beheaded, or also quartered, it was then customary to display the dead man's separated parts to the public, though, as Lovat's case shows, this was not invariably done. Thus, on October 17, 1662, John Evelyn, who kept a detailed journal for most of his long life (1620-1706), recorded the aftermath of the death of some of the regicides at Charing Cross, seeing: "... their quarters mangld & cutt & reaking as they were brought from the Gallows in baskets on the hurdle."[118] London Bridge was a frequent site for severed heads, as it caught riverine, vehicular and pedestrian traffic. Typically, in the Elizabethan period, after John Story was drawn from the Tower of London to Tyburn and there "hanged, bowelled and quarterd, his head [was] set on London bridge, and his quarters on the gates of the citie".[119] Paul Hentzner calculated the number of heads displayed there in the 1590s: "Upon this is built a tower, on whose top the heads of such as have been executed for high treason are placed on iron spikes: we counted above 30."[120] However, women who were guilty of high treason would normally be

---

116. Harrison, *Elizabethan England*, pp.238-239.
117. Blackstone, *Commentaries on the Laws of England*, vol. 4, p.179.
118. J. Evelyn, The *Diary of John Evelyn*, vol. III, E.S. De Beer (Ed.), Oxford, Clarendon Press, 1955, p.259.
119. Stow, *The Annales of England*, p.1141.
120. P. Hentzner, *Travels in England during the reign of Queen Elizabeth*, p.30.

burnt alive as the "natural modesty of the sex forbids the exposing and publicly mangling their bodies". (Again, the Crown might limit the sentence to beheading in appropriate cases.)[121]

In theory, coining and clipping were high treason, not felony, and so subject to the full regime of punishment for that crime, the only time that ordinary criminals would normally encounter it. In the Tudor period, this often occurred in practice. Thus, on May 30, 1576, a goldsmith named Thomas Greene was: "... drawn from Newgate of London to Tyburne and there hanged, headed, and quartered, for clipping of coine both gold and silver."[122] However, by the latter half of the seventeenth century, those convicted of coining (a "treason of a different complexion from the rest") were usually subject to a more merciful execution, with only a symbolic difference differentiating them from executed felons, the: "... punishment is milder for male offenders; being only to be drawn, and hanged by the neck till dead."[123]

Petty Treason

Sir Francis Bacon defined "petie Treason" as occurring: "Where a servant killeth his Master, the wife, the Husband, the Spirituall man his prelate, to whom hee is subordinate,

---

121. Blackstone, *Commentaries on the Laws of England*, vol. 4, p.93.
122. Stow, *The Annales of England*, p.1163.
123. Blackstone, *Commentaries on the Laws of England*, vol. 4, p.93.

and oweth faith and obedience." In domestic situations, the protection afforded to employers was also extended to their spouses, so that: "... if the servant kill the wife of his master, it is Petit treason, for he is servant both to the husband and wife."[124] However, perhaps strangely, the legal position when children killed their parents was uncertain. Bacon believed (rightly) that the bulk of "experience and opinion" held that it was not petty treason, though he personally thought this was contrary to "law and reason". Interestingly, according to Bacon, discharged servants who killed their former masters still committed petty treason (perhaps aimed at discouraging dismissed servants from taking revenge against their erstwhile employers). Nevertheless, those who assisted people to carry out such crimes did not commit the same offence, unless in a similar relationship to the victim as the principal, but were guilty only of simple murder: "In petie Treason, all Accessories are but in case of Felonie."[125]

By ancient tradition, petty treason had its own execution regime, though few would agree with Blackstone's view that it was "handed down to us from the laws of the ancient Druids".[126] For men, the punishment was much less draconian than that for high treason, and almost the same as for normal felony, merely involving a symbolic modicum of extra shame and the discomfort of being taken to the gallows on a flimsy sledge rather than in the normal cart. There was no drawing and quartering. Thus, when the

---

124. Coke, *Institutes of the Lawes of England, Part Three, Concerning High Treason, and other Pleas of the Crown and Criminall causes*, London, 1644, p.20.
125. Bacon, *Cases of Treason*, pp.7-8.
126. Blackstone, *Commentaries on the Laws of England*, Book 4, p.204.

Reverend Lowe, a murderous curate who had killed his employing vicar, was sentenced to death, it was merely ordered that he was "upon a hurdle to be drawne to the place of execution, and there to be hanged".[127] For women, however, there was no difference between the punishment for the two forms of treason: "In petie Treason, the corporall punishment [for men] is by drawing on an hurdle, and hanging, and in a woman burning."[128] Even to some contemporary observers, the aggravation for female spouse killers was unfair, given that it was not reciprocated: "Women who have murdered their husbands are put to death in what I consider to be an unjust way: they are condemned to be burnt alive. Men who murder their wives are only hanged."[129] In theory at least, it was not simply a manifestation of misogyny; the rule applied to anyone who killed his or her immediate 'lord'. Its aim was to preserve hierarchy, respect and deference within the 'great chain of being', though this may not have been of much comfort to the women involved.

The distinction from normal murder meant that while Alice Arden and the female servants involved in the killing of Thomas Arden were burnt at the stake at Canterbury for their 'petty treason' in killing a husband and master, the rest of those involved in the murder (not being employees of Mr

---

127. Anon, *A True Relation of the most inhumane and bloody murther of Master James Minister and Preacher of the word of God at Rockland in Norfolk*, London, R. Bowan, 1609, f.B4.
128. Bacon, *Cases of Treason*, pp.7-8.
129. Muyden, *A foreign View of England in the reigns of George I and George II*, p.127.

Arden) were hanged and then hung in chains.[130] Similarly, the wife of the Norfolk clergyman who had assisted Lowe (her lover) to murder her husband was burnt in the presence of her paramour, while the latter awaited his own hanging: "... on the side of a high hill called castle hill in Thetford was a fire kindled where in the very sight of Lowe she was consumed to ashes."[131] As this suggests, the bonfire would often be placed as close as possible to the normal gallows. However, this was not always the case. Some towns had special locations for such forms of execution. In London, burnings were traditionally conducted at Smithfield, not Tyburn. Thus, in April 1652, Evelyn could laconically record that "passing by Smithfield there was a miserable Creature burning who had murder'd her husband".

Much of the attendant ceremony was the same as for a hanging, with a ministering Ordinary etc. However, some of the practical details differed. Thus, as was common in such cases, Margaret Ferne-Seede, convicted of murdering her husband in 1608, was "stripped of her ordinary wearing apparell", and, before being dressed in a white sheet, covered in a "kirtle of canvass-pitched clean through" to facilitate combustion. Subsequently, at the place of execution, while she was being fastened to a stake, an attendant chaplain urged that she: "... confesse that fact for which she was now ready to suffer, which she denying the reeds were planted about, unto which fire being given she

---

130. Anon, *The History of the Most Remarkable Tryals in Great Britain and Ireland in Capital Cases*, London, A. Bell, 1715, pp.261-262.
131. Anon, *A True Relation of the most inhumane and bloody murther of Master James Minister*, p.B4.

was presently dead."[132] Mercifully, after 1660, it became normal for the executioner to strangle the accused woman so that she was dead, or at least unconscious, by the time the flames reached her. Thus, in 1722, Eleanor Elsom was burnt at Lincoln for murdering her husband. Like Ferne-Seede she was draped in cloth impregnated with tar, her limbs also being smeared with the inflammable substance, and a tarred bonnet put on her head. She was then taken from prison on a hurdle, her bonfire being situated near the normal gallows. After appropriate religious ministrations, the executioner placed her on top of a tar barrel and against a stake, where her body was fixed with three irons. However, a rope was also placed around her neck, she herself helping to fasten it. This was connected to a pulley fastened onto the stake and the executioner tugged upon the rope. Although a dry timber fire was then lit, it was thought that Elsom was quite dead before the flames reached her, although her body could be seen amid the fire for almost half-an-hour.[133] The process of strangulation was conducted quite separately in 1750, when Amy Hutchinson was executed for the murder of her husband in Ely, avoiding the risk of mistakes: "... the executioner strangled her, and 20 minutes after the fire was kindled, and burned half-an-hour."[134] The burning of women for petty treason was only ended in 1790, cases

---

132. Anon, *The Arraignement and burning of Margaret Ferne-Seede,* London, Henry Gusson, 1608, p.B3.
133. W. Andrews, *Bygone Punishments*, London, W. Andrews & Co., 1899, p.100.
134. Rayner and Crook, *The Complete Newgate Calendar*, vol. III, p.190. .

occurring until just before abolition.[135]

Boiling of Poisoners

One of the few other forms of aggravated death found in early modern England was that imposed on poisoners, who under a short-lived "new lawe made in King Henrie the eights time shalbe boyled to death". Perhaps fortunately, the Act was not often invoked, if only because poisoning was "rare and almost unknowen in England".[136] According to Harrison, this 1531 statute extended to the inchoate offence, so that "he that poisoneth a man is to be boiled to death in water or lead, although the partie die not of the practice".[137] (However, this had not been contemplated in the Act's original draft.) The Henrician statute was specifically passed to deal with Richard Rouse, a cook who had attempted to poison John Fisher, the Bishop of Rochester, several other people (but not the cleric) dying after ingesting the tainted food. It was feared that such an insidious and 'detestable' form of crime might spread if there was not condign punishment.[138] As a result, Rouse was: "... boylyd in a caulderne in Smythfield ... locked in a chayne and pullyd up and downe with a gybbyt at dyvers tymes tyll he was

---

135. R. Campbell, "Sentence of Death by Burning for Women," *Journal of Legal History*, 1984, vol. 5, pp.44-48
136. Smith, *De Republica Anglorum*, p.117.
137. Harrison, *A Description of England*, p.225.
138. K. Kesselring, "A Draft for the 1531 'Acte for Poysoning'," *English Historical Review*, 2001, vol. 116, at pp.894-899

ded."[139] It seems that only two other people, both women, definitely met their deaths in this way (it needed an extremely large cauldron), one in 1531 and the other in 1542. The last, Margaret Davey, was also boiled at Smithfield for poisoning the family for whom she worked in London. The Act appears to have been repealed, along with several others, in 1547, during the brief reign of Edward VI, though some, such as Harrison, were unaware of this, and there was an unavailing attempt to restore it in 1563. As a result, women like Alice Clarke, who poisoned her husband in 1635, merely suffered burning for their petty treason.[140]

Felons who had used Violence in the Precincts of a Court

In cases of "wilful manslaughter", i.e. murder, Harrison claimed that there was still, occasionally, some aggravation, during the Elizabethan era, in the manner of execution: "... beside hanging, the offender hath his right hand commonly stricken off before or near unto the place where the act was done, after which he is led forth to the place of execution."[141] Nevertheless, this does not appear to have been a common occurrence, even for murder. However, it was normal practise in the Tudor era to cut off the offending hand of a felon, prior to execution, who had also assaulted a witness, juror, judge or law officer in open court. Thus, in December

---

139. J. Gough Nichols (Ed.), *Chronicle of the Grey Friars of London*, London, Camden Society, 1852, p.35.
140. H. Goodcole, *The Adultresses Funerall Day*, London, N. and I. Okes, 1635, p.1.
141. Harrison, *Elizabethan England*, p.242.

1556, Gregorie Carpenter tried to stab his co-defendant, who had turned Queen's evidence and "given witnesse against him" in the Old Bailey court, though the wound did not prove fatal. As punishment, Carpenter had his hand cut off and was then hanged from a gibbet next to the Justice Hall.[142] This custom seems to have reached back to at least the fourteenth century and continued until the 1630s.[143] In 1631, a convicted felon, Henry Gillingham, who, in the execrable law-French of the case report *"ject un brickbat ... que narrowly mist"*, at Lord Chief Justice Richardson, presiding at the Salisbury assizes, experienced this punishment in the city's market place: *"... son dexter manus ampute et fix a gibbet, sur que luy mesme immediatement hange in presence de court."* The last case in which it was meted out appears to have occurred at Chester in 1633 (the dead man's hand being nailed to the City gate), though such a sentence was passed and then pardoned as late as 1664. The provision appears never to have been formally repealed.[144]

Exposure to Judicial Violence

Exposure to acute 'judicial violence' was disproportionately concentrated in London, with its high execution rate (sometimes almost half the national total), large population, confined geographic area, and early development of complicated execution rituals, such as the very public

---

142. Stow, *The Annales of England*, p.1066.
143. Bellamy, *The Criminal Trial in Later Medieval England*, p.154.
144. J.H. Baker, "Le brickbat que narrowly mist," *Law Quarterly Review*, 1984, vol. 100, pp.544-548.

procession to Tyburn from Newgate. Although most famously recorded by several prominent eighteenth century writers and engravers, the Metropolitan execution spectacle was not a new phenomenon in the 1700s. Thus, when the killers of a London merchant, George Saunders, were driven to Tyburn from Newgate, in 1583: "... almost the whole fielde, and all the way from Newgate, was as full of folke as coulde well stande one by another." All adjacent chambers were packed, windows and walls were broken down by the mob, and rooftops were crowded with observers.[145] However, London was not typical of the country as a whole; in the provinces it would often require some effort to witness an execution, unless one lived in an assizes town. Additionally, the relative infrequency of provincial gibbeting before the eighteenth century (only one example being recorded on the Home Circuit between 1559 and 1625) meant that even the aftermath of an execution might not be witnessed. Exposure to the particularly gruesome death reserved for male traitors, and the attendant displaying of dismembered body parts, would be exceptionally rare outside London. Limited publicity and the difficulties of travel made drawing large crowds relatively difficult in the provinces, at least until the mid-seventeenth century. Of course, lower level brutality, the public whipping of both men and women, at the "cart's arse", until they were bloody, was much more widespread.[146]

---

145. Anon, *A briefe discourse of the late murther of Master George Saunders*, London, Henry Bynnemen, 1573, p.B3.
146. Cockburn, "Punishment and Brutalization," pp.157-161.

Chapter 18

Mitigating the Death Penalty for Felony

Every felony (i.e. all serious crimes) with the exception of petty larceny carried a potential death penalty. However, despite the huge number of executions carried out in sixteenth and early seventeenth century England, and the relatively high number, compared with many other European countries, executed in the remainder of the early modern period, a large number of felons against whom process was brought, or would have been brought if the opportunity had presented itself, escaped death by a variety of legal mechanisms. Foremost amongst these were benefit of clergy, pleading the belly, pardon and reprieve. In the early part of our period these were accompanied by abjuration following a claim to temporary religious sanctuary, or es-cape to a permanent sanctuary. Together, these provisions probably meant that, by the late sixteenth century, only a minority of those guilty of felony faced execution, a minority that became progressively smaller as the era advanced.

Benefit of Clergy

Benefit of clergy was one of the three historic privileges, originally associated with the English medieval church, which allowed felons to evade execution for their offences. It mitigated the harshness of English criminal law, which imposed the death penalty for many offences that today would be considered trivial. So vital was it in reducing the number of hangings that trial juries were sometimes expressly informed where it was not available, as it could affect their weighing of evidence and eventual verdict. Thus, an Old Bailey judge, directing the jury presiding over the trial of a female bigamist in the 1660s, warned them: "You see what the circumstances are, it is penal; if guilty, she must die; a Woman hath no Clergy, she is to die by the Law, if guilty."[1] As it commuted execution, it obviously did not apply to misdemeanours; nor did it apply to treason. The privilege was a relic of the Church-State struggles of the medieval period, whereby offending clerics could escape temporal punishment by insisting on being handed over to more lenient ecclesiastical courts. Whatever its origins, by the early 1530s, men such as Christopher St Germain (admittedly an individual with strong anti-clerical inclinations), were adamant that: "... where a man shall have his clergie, and where not, be under the power and auctorities of the parlyament." He firmly rejected any suggestion that the privilege was granted by the spiritual authority. Instead, he claimed that it was based on the "olde customes and maximes of the law of the realme". Ultimately, it was for the royal judges to decide who would have sanctuary or clergy.[2] Such an analysis, even if historically inaccurate, allowed clergy (and sanctuary) to survive the Reformation.

---

1. Anon, *The Case of Madam Mary Carleton*, London, 1663, p.103.
2. T.F. Plucknett and J.C. Barton (Eds.), 2nd *Dialogue, 1531, St Germain's Doctor and Student*, London, Selden Society, 1974, p.322.

The early modern history of benefit of clergy is the story of two, simultaneous, developments. On the one hand, it was progressively extended by a series of legal fictions to include most men, and, by seventeenth century statute, women. However, even as more and more people could claim the privilege, the number of offences for which it was available was steadily reduced. Thus, as early as the fourteenth century, the King's courts were prepared to accept that any man able to read must be a clergyman. This was *almost* true in the 1300s, increasingly less so subsequently. As reading became the sole test for clerical status, numerous laymen were able to claim it. Determining literacy was usually a matter for the court chaplain, who was normally a local clergyman appointed by the diocesan bishop to attend provincial assizes: "If the Ordinary say legit, then must the prisoner be burned in the hand: but if the Ordinary *Saith non legit ut Clericus,* the prisoner must be executed."[3] Originally, and unsurprisingly given that the notion of female clerics was anathema, women could not claim the privilege. They were allowed clergy by statute for lesser cases of theft in 1623. As a result, it was recorded that Mary Frith ('Moll Cutpurse' 1589-1663), the seventeenth century female master criminal, had "been burnt in the hand four times".[4] In 1693, women were allowed clergy on the same basis as men (3 and 4 Will. and M. c. 9).

In the medieval era, clergy had been allowed for all

---

3. Anon, *The Office of the Clerk of Assize,* London, 1671, p.24.
4. J.L Rayner and G.T. Crook (Eds.), *The Complete Newgate Calendar* (vols. 1-5), London, Privately printed for the Navarre Society, 1926, vol. I, p.172.

offences except treason and theft from churches. However, by the early seventeenth century a wave of Tudor legislation meant that clergy was "taken away for murder, burglary, robbery, purse-cutting, horse-stealing, and divers other felonies particularized by the statutes".[5] Thus, a late fifteenth century statute (12 Henry VII, c. 7), the introduction of which was apparently prompted by the murder of a gentleman by his literate servant, deprived the felon of his clergy, so that he could be adequately punished, and provided that in future those who committed petty treason, like anyone who was guilty of high treason, should not be entitled to the privilege. Benefit of clergy was denied to ordinary murderers in 1512 (4 Henry VIII c.2), and, in 1530, it was abolished for deliberate acts of poisoning (22 Henry VIII, c. 9). In 1533, it was withdrawn from buggery, committed with either man or beast (25 Henry VIII c.6). Under Edward VI, burglary, highway robbery and several other offences were withdrawn from the privilege (I Edw.VI c.12). As a result, by the mid-sixteenth century, no "open robberies" or nocturnal burglaries could be clergied. Most other aggravated forms of theft had been withdrawn from its ambit by the 1580s. An underlying rationale appears to have been that most of these offences involved the use, threat or (in burglary) potential for violence. As a result, many clergied Elizabethan offenders had been convicted of a first offence of simple theft in which aggravating features were absent. Typically, it was claimed by men who had

---

5.   Sir F. Bacon, "The Use Of The Law," B. Montagu (Ed.), *The Works of Francis Bacon*, vol. 3, Philadelphia, Carey and Hart, 1841, p.251.

"stolen nothing else but oxen, sheep, money, or such like". Thus, Thomas Halden, a sailor from East Greenwich, who was convicted of stealing broadcloth from a shop worth £10, pleaded his clergy and was branded.[6] The early seventeenth century saw yet more offences added to the list of excepted felonies, and new felonies were expressly created without clergy, so that Bacon could note, albeit with considerable exaggeration: "In felony, at the common law, the benefit of Clergie or Sanctuary was allowed, but now by Statute it is taken away in most cases."[7]

Some years after the Restoration, there was another wave of statutory withdrawal, as the advent of transportation allowed alternative, non-lethal, punishment. Offences removed included taking goods from a house when occupied by someone who was put in fear, breaking into houses, shops and warehouses and stealing goods to the value of five shillings (1691); shoplifting and thefts from warehouses and stables to the value of five shillings (1699), and theft from a house or out-house to the value of 40 shillings, even when empty and where there was no break-in (1713). Sheep stealing (1741), cattle theft (1742), theft from a bleaching ground of linen or cotton cloth worth 10 shillings or more (1731 and 1745), theft from a ship in a navigable river or from a wharf, of goods valued at 40 shillings or more (1751) and theft from the mail (1765) all

---

6.   E. Melling (Ed.), *Crime and Punishment, Kentish Sources VI*, Maidstone, Kent County Council, 1969, p.47.

7.   Sir F. Bacon, *Cases of Treason*, London, 1641, p.13.

gradually followed.[8] Not everyone approved of such developments, which affected offenders who by no stretch of the imagination threatened the person, and eventually meant that in theory (though not in practice): "For, as the Benefit of the Clergy is of late taken from Pick-pockets, so they are now in the Eye of the Law upon the same foot with Murthers, Highway Men, and housebreakers."[9] Clergy was only finally abolished in England in 1827, although by then its residual significance was minimal.

In 1487, Henry VII also reduced its scope by limiting laymen (i.e. those not in holy orders) to claiming the privilege on just one occasion. This prompted the introduction of branding for clergied laymen, who were "burned in the left hand, upon the brawn of the thumb, with a hot iron". In theory, this prevented them claiming their clergy a second time, so that if they were: "... apprehended again, that mark betrayeth them to have been arraigned of felony before, whereby they are sure at that time to have no mercy."[10] For the short period between 1699 and 1706 branding on the cheek replaced branding on the brawn of the thumb. As a result, in 1700, the keeper of the Kent county jail, at Maidstone, purchased an "engine according to Act of Parliament for burning in the left cheek". (The £3 five shillings involved was reimbursed to him from county

---

8.   J. Beattie, *Crime and the Courts in England 1660-1800*, Oxford, OUP, 1986, pp.144-145.
9.   Anon, *Hanging, not Punishment Enough*, p.5.
10. W. Harrison, *Elizabethan England*, London, Camelot Series, E. Rhys (Ed.), 1889, p.244.

funds.)[11] The change in bodily position appears to have been aimed at enhancing the deterrent value of making even a successful plea of clergy.[12] However, 'genuine' clergymen, able to produce valid orders, were expressly allowed by the 1487 Act (4 Henry VII. c.13) to claim it as often as they needed. Before the Reformation, but after 1487, it was alleged that this created problems with criminals who took up minor clerical orders, such as psalmists, lectors and acolytes, where the necessary qualifications were slender, with a view to deliberately circumventing the limitation. According to Pope Leo X, this meant that in England, sometimes the "crimes of ne'er-do-wells remain[ed] unpunished".[13] Even after the Reformation Parliament clerics were theoretically able to claim clergy a second time and escaped branding in the hand, though the number of men who were defined as clergymen fell greatly.[14] In 1518, the central courts also began to supervise the granting of clergy to those tried in the provinces more strictly. Lists of men to whom it had been granted were solicited by writ, this practice being regularised by statute in 1543 (34 & 35 Henry VIII c. 14). This Act cited the abuses occasioned by the absence of a formal record of claimants. Thenceforth 'clergy rolls' were kept at the Court of King's Bench.[15]

---

11. Melling, *Crime and Punishment*, p.181.
12. Beattie, *Crime and the Courts*, p.144.
13. A. Ogle, *The Tragedy of the Lollard's Tower*, Oxford, 1949, pp.167-168.
14. Sir E. Coke, *The Second Part of the Institutes of the Laws of England*, London, M. Fletcher, 1642, at p.637.
15. J.S. Cockburn, *Calendar of Assize Records, Home Circuit Indictments, Elizabeth and James 1: Introduction*, London, HMSO, 1985, pp.118-119.

Nevertheless, in reality, the theory and the custom of limiting laymen to a single claim regularly appear to have parted company. By the Elizabethan period restrictions on repeated use of the privilege were sometimes not being enforced, adding to the courts' already enormous discretion.[16] Even in the 1590s, Edward Hext was concerned that the attendant branding was carried out in such a perfunctory manner that it was often useless as a record: "... others havinge byn burnt in the hand more tymes than once, for after a month or too there wilbe no syne in the worlde." As a result, those allowed their clergy could easily circumvent any adverse consequences to their convictions by simple expedients: "... they will change both name and habytt and commonly go ynto other shires so as no man shall knowe them."[17] Many claimed clergy two or more times. By the early 1700s, the ineffectualness of branding had been further increased by the development of a practice whereby on: "... paying thirteen and a half pence he has a right to have the iron dipped in cold water before being touched with it."[18] Finally, in 1706 (5 Anne c.5) branding was abolished altogether and it was provided that offenders could be committed to a house of correction for up to two years in lieu for some cases. Nevertheless, adding to the

---

16. Beattie, *Crime and the Courts*, p.142.
17. E. Hext, "Letter written by Edward Hext, a Somerset JP, to Lord Burghley on September 25, 1596," *Tudor Economic Documents*, R.H. Tawney and E. Power (Eds.), London, Longmans, 1951, vol. 2, p.340
18. M. Van Muyden (Trans. and Ed.), *A foreign View of England in the reigns of George I and George II; The letters of Monsieur Cesar de Saussure, to his Family*, London, John Murray, 1902, p.125.

uncertainty, the law was sometimes strictly applied, even quite late in the period, and the consequences of previous branding could be drastic. Thus, in 1679, John Maccarty was convicted of stealing 10 shillings worth of ribbon (clearly a clergyable matter). However, the: "... Executioner going to search his Hand, found that he had formerly been burned, so that he being an incorrigable offendor, the court passed sentence of Death upon him." He was subsequently hanged.[19]

Of course, the need to brand only arose if the test for clergy (literacy) was satisfied. As the seventeenth century advanced this occurred increasingly frequently. There were several reasons for this. More people genuinely were literate. Thus, in the early 1690s, Edmund Bohun observed that reading had increased so much from former times that it extended to tradesmen, ladies and mere 'mechanicks'.[20] In the same decade, Henri Misson could note, with some exaggeration, that the spread of literacy had made the test for clergy indiscriminate as: "... tho' at present there is hardly the meanest Peasant in England but what can read, yet the Law is still in Force." However, even more important than the spread of literacy was a greatly increased practical willingness to grant clergy via laxity in conducting the reading test. The mechanics of this test were straight-forward. After the customary request to a convicted felon: "... what hast thou to demand in Favour of thy selfe to

---

19. Anon, *The Narrative of the Confession and Execution of the three Prisoners at Tyburn*, London, 1679, p.3.
20. E. Bohun, *The Justice of Peace His Calling and Qualifications*, London, 1693, p.23.

hinder sentence of Death being pass'd upon thee? The Criminal answer, I demand the benefit of the Clergy." A Bible or Psalter would be handed to the felon, and the court chaplain then asked the convict to read a passage before making his decision. At the Old Bailey, the Newgate Ordinary was usually able to make up his mind after "a few words".[21] The passages customarily used for the test were either verses taken from St Mathew's gospel or (most commonly) the first verse of the 51st psalm "Have mercy on me, O God, according to Thy steadfast love ...". Because the same passages were usually employed, they were called the 'neck verses'. This predictability also meant that memorising them in advance was often feasible, even for complete illiterates. On other occasions, someone in the court itself might prompt the reader, sotto voce, with the court's connivance. Even in the Elizabethan period, Edward Hext was concerned that some JPs at quarter sessions were so lax about granting clergy that some convicts were "havynge their books by intreatye of the Justices themselves that cannot reade a word".[22]

However, there was no rule allowing such prompting, or confining the chaplain to the traditional passages, and if the court wished the test could be made stricter. Arthur Turnour's reports from Newgate cast some light on this. In 1616, he witnessed a defendant convicted of manslaughter ask for his clergy, before the judge, Thomas Coventry

---

21.   T. Platter and H. Busino, *Journals of two travellers in Elizabethan and early Stuart England*, P. Razzell (Ed.), London, Caliban, 1995, p.148.
22.   Hext, "Letter written by Edward Hext," p.340.

(1578-1640). Because it was a "case of blood", Coventry appears to have been reluctant to make it easy for the defendant. He took the Bible and selected the passage that the Ordinary was to give the convicted man, to avoid him being given the predictable 'neck verse'. Not content with this, the judge also ordered that the defendant be "set apart from other the standers by, to the ende no man might prompte him". More controversially (in Turnour's opinion), when the accused man successfully read the passage initially given to him, Coventry selected another passage for him to read, although this was contrary to normal custom. (The defendant was genuinely literate and passed the test with no difficulty, gaining his clergy.)[23] Similarly, in 1674, a defendant at the Old Bailey accused of murder was convicted of manslaughter after the Lord Mayor, presiding at the trial, asked the jurors to reconsider their initial outright acquittal. Apparently convinced of the man's guilt of the heinous offence originally charged, the Lord Mayor was also reluctant to see him clergied for the lesser offence. Initially, the accused man passed the cursory test provided by the court chaplain, probably having been asked to recite the 'neck verse'. The Lord Mayor then called for the Bible and stuck a pin in it at random, asking the convict to read the selected passage, which he could not do. He only escaped death by agreeing to transportation, rather than being branded and discharged, as he would have been had

---

23. J.H. Baker, "Criminal Justice at Newgate 1616-1627: Some Manuscript Reports in the Harvard Law School," *The Irish Jurist*, 1973, vol. 8, p.315.

he gained his clergy.[24]

Nevertheless, this level of judicial care was increasingly unusual after the early seventeenth century. By the 1690s, any pretence to it being a real test rather than a legal fiction appears to have been largely abandoned, so that when a criminal had the right to ask for clergy the courts would: "... seldom give themselves the Trouble to examine whether they can read or no, be he the greatest scholar in the world, or the greatest Blockhead, 'tis all a case, so he gives but a little spill of money to the Ordinary, who tells him in a low voice (which the whole Court may hear) three or four words which he pronounces, and there's an End of the matter."[25] When the by then almost pointless test was finally abolished in 1706, everyone became entitled to its benefit, literate or not, where it still existed. Throughout the early modern period, it was assumed that peers could read for the purposes of claiming clergy, so that no test was administered to them. Nor were they branded after claiming the privilege.[26] Thus, in 1678, after being convicted of manslaughter by his fellow peers, the Earl of Pembroke immediately asked for his clergy; the Lord High Steward (presiding over the trial) agreed that he must have it: "... for as by the Act clergy was allowed to a commoner by reading and burning in the hand, a peer convicted of such felony was to be delivered without either." He also reminded him

---

24. J. Beattie, *Policing and Punishment in London, 1660-1750*, Oxford, OUP, 2001, p.304.
25. M. Misson, *Memoirs and Observations in his Travels over England*, M. Ozell (Trans.), London, 1719, pp.17-18.
26. Misson, *Memoirs and Observations in his Travels over England*, p.18.

that no layman, even a peer, could have clergy more than once.[27]

As a result of such laxity, the use of clergy to escape the gallows showed a major increase between the late medieval and late Tudor periods. In the fourteenth and fifteenth centuries, an average of only three per cent of convicts made successful claims (with another two to three per cent receiving a pardon). During Elizabeth's reign, c. 30 per cent of those arraigned for felony on the Home Circuit successfully claimed benefit of clergy (another five per cent pleaded a pardon, so that more than a third of convicts escaped execution). Nevertheless, given the almost doubling of the felony conviction rate in the same period, it would be a mistake to view this as a simple expression of increased humanity. Some research suggests that the percentage of arraigned felons actually executed at the end of the sixteenth century was higher than in the late medieval period (26 per cent compared to only 14 per cent), though the dearth of fifteenth century evidence makes such assessments very difficult.[28] It is possible that the two processes, increased conviction rates and a growth in the use of clergy, were closely linked.

Rationale

Benefit of clergy was hard to justify intellectually, though

---

27.   Rayner and Crook, *The Complete Newgate Calendar*, vol. I, p.273.
28.   Bellamy, *The Criminal Trial in Later Medieval England*, pp.155-156.

attempts were made to do so. Harrison considered that it was an ancient rule "devised to train the inhabitants of this land to the love of learning".[29] Similarly, Busino thought that it was allowed to a literate defendant "in consideration of his acquirements". Platter's confusing, and wholly inaccurate, explanation was that a literate felon was allowed his life "in the hope that he may yet perform some good".[30] However, its obvious absence from continental countries undermined such rationalisations: "I doo not read that this custome of saving by the booke is used aniewhere else than in England."[31] Many visiting foreigners thought that the system was ridiculous, and its consequences dangerous. Thus, in 1500, a Venetian noted that literate criminals were "liberated from the power of the law".[32] English observers were also often sceptical about the value of a system that frequently allowed serious crimes to go virtually unpunished, and could mean that those convicted of non-capital petty larceny (and whipped) might suffer more than those clergied for grand larceny. Edward Hext had no doubt that it should be abolished: "And happy were yt for England yf Clergy were taken awaye in case of felonye." In particular, he feared that it undermined the deterrent effect of the criminal justice system, as those that avoided death in this manner: "... infect great numbers, emboldening them by their escapes that cannot read a word."[33] Similarly, William

---

29. Harrison, *Elizabethan England*, p.244.
30. Platter and Busino, *Journals of two travellers*, pp.53 and 148.
31. Harrison, *A Description of England*, p.229.
32. Anon, *A relation, or rather a true account of the Island of England*, p.36.
33. Hext, "Letter written by Edward Hext," p.340.

Sheppard was keen to abolish clergy in parallel with reducing the extent of the death penalty (which it moderated).[34] Undoubtedly, such men were aware that in cases of homicide (for example) much the same result was achieved elsewhere in Europe, using different, and much more rational, legal mechanisms. Thus, in Picardy, an analysis of the court records for the years between 1523 and 1550 indicates that the great majority of the many killings in that province were classified as involuntary homicide, providing a means whereby the guilty party could escape execution and be reintegrated into society. Generally, Picardy's judicial system was very discriminating in its use of the death penalty.[35]

Before 1576, as the visiting Venetian noted, a convict who made a successful claim was "given as a clerk into the hands of the bishop".[36] After a clergied layman was burnt on the hand, a clerk discharged on reading, a peer without either burning or reading, they were delivered to the Ordinary (chaplain): "... to be kept in the Bishops prison, from whence after a certaine time by an other enquest of Clarkes he is delivered and let at large."[37] In theory, the clerical authorities instituted a kind of purgation. The party concerned was required to take an oath of innocence and 12

---

34. N.L. Mathews, *William Sheppard, Cromwell's Law Reformer*, Cambridge, CUP, 1984, p.171.
35. D. Potter, "Rigueur de justice: Crime, Murder and the Law in Picardy, Fifteenth-Sixteenth Centuries," *French History*, 1997, vol. 11, no. 3, pp.308-309.
36. Anon, *A relation, or rather a true account of the Island of England*, p.36.
37. Sir T. Smith, *De Republica Anglorum*, London, 1583, p.116.

compurgators were called to testify to their belief in the falsehood of the charges. Afterwards, he brought forward witnesses to establish his innocence. Everyone found guilty, whether laymen or clerics, was compelled to do penance. Genuine clergymen might be downgraded. In practice, many escaped even such modest penalties by perjury and leniency. As early as the 1530s, statutes (for example, 23 Henry VIII, 2 c. 1) complained about laxity in the process, claiming that "manifest thieves and murderers" were being set at large having been allowed to "make their purgations by such as nothing know of their misdeeds".[38] It was for this reason that the 1531 Poisoning Act, though still allowing genuine clerics, unlike laymen, to claim benefit of clergy if convicted under the new statute, required that after being handed over to the Church's custody they would "remayne and be in p[er]pertuall prisone during his lyfe w[ith]out any purgacon therof in any wise to be made".[39] By the Elizabethan period, purgation was purely a formality, being virtually synonymous with acquittal. This residual link with the ecclesiastical courts was finally abandoned by statute in 1576 (18 Elizabeth I, c. 7) when the requirement that clergied offenders be turned over to the Ordinary to undergo purgation was abolished. Instead, they were liable to be jailed for up to a year, at the discretion of the secular court, though in practice this very rarely occurred. Henceforth, a successful claim of clergy was normally followed by

---

38. Beattie, *Crime and the Courts*, p.142.
39. K. Kesselring, "A Draft for the 1531 'Acte for Poysoning'," in *English Historical Review*, vol. 116, pp.894-899.

immediate discharge after branding.[40]

Despite being a bizarre fiction, the restricted existence of clergy served a useful function, over and above mitigating the death penalty, by encouraging the technical development and refinement of the criminal law. Although death was the normal penalty for felony, some, but not all, felonies were clergyable. Thus, for much of the period, it was crucially important to distinguish murder (not clergyable) from manslaughter (clergyable), robbery from theft etc. This encouraged the development of English criminal jurisprudence.[41]

Abjuration and Sanctuary

Unlike benefit of clergy, the other two historic ecclesiastical privileges that allowed felons to evade potential execution for their offences, abjuration of the realm and sanctuary in a church, did not survive very far into the early modern period. Though still significant in the first 50 years of Tudor rule, they gradually disappeared after 1530. James I abolished the last remnants of criminal sanctuary (though some locations continued to preserve limited immunity from civil process). However, Henry VIII's reign had already witnessed the near demise of abjuration and seen sanctuary gravely damaged.

Abjuration, a uniquely English custom, and sanctuary

---

40. Beattie, *Crime and the Courts*, p.142.
41. Harrison, *A Description of England*, p.229.

(found in much of Europe), were closely linked. A suspected felon in medieval England could take refuge for up to 40 days in any church. After this time, if he refused to abjure or to submit to royal officials he could be starved out. It was forbidden to speak with overstayers or give them food or drink, on pain of death. However, the secular authorities were usually reluctant to secure such men with force, as shedding blood would mean violating holy ground, though a priest could force a sanctuary seeker out without committing sacrilege. Fugitives who were still in a non-chartered sanctuary after 40 days were also precluded from subsequently seeking abjuration and were deemed to be felons. Those resident near the church involved were supposed to prevent a fugitive's escape until a local coroner could be summoned to conduct the abjurement process. The privilege was only open to felons, not to those accused of misdemeanour, or, after 1534, treason, and was not allowed to convicted criminals who had subsequently escaped punishment.[42]

However, as well as there being a general right to short-term sanctuary in any church, there were also some 'special' sanctuaries, created by royal or papal grants or by immemorial custom. Felons who reached them were not limited in the length of time that they could remain within their confines, and the grounds of such sanctuaries sometimes extended considerably further than the church

---

42. J.L. Carro, "Sanctuary: The resurgence of an age-old right or a dangerous misinterpretation of an abandoned ancient privilege?," *University of Cincinnati Law Review*, vol. 54, pp.761-763.

precincts. Several monasteries, like Colchester and Glastonbury, had charters allowing them to provide indefinite sanctuary. Some, like Hexham and Beverly in the north of England, were large enough to afford sanctuary men an opportunity to practise their trades, if they had one, and to live an almost 'normal' life within the adjoining town or monastic environs. At Hexham, crosses were erected at a mile's distance around the abbey to indicate the substantial area of sanctuary. Others were more confined.

England's special sanctuaries were fiercely criticised. In 1528, Polydore Vergil singled them out as an example of the general abuse of sanctuary in Christendom, claiming that they harboured "all manner of criminals".[43] In some of the smaller ones, long-term survival was difficult, encouraging their occupants to break out when opportunity presented itself. This occasioned a widespread fear that felons were using them as secure bases for ongoing criminal activity: "Theues bryng thyther theyr stollen goodes, and there lyve thereon. There deuise thei newe roberies, nightlye they steale out, they robbe and reue, and kyll, and come in again as though those places gaue them not onely a safe garde for the harme they haue done, but a licence also to dooe more."[44] The Henrician statutes (26 & 28 H 8 c. 13 & 7) which ultimately limited the privilege also complained that the existence of special sanctuaries meant that "malefactors

---

43. J.H. Baker, "The English Law of Sanctuary," *Ecclesiastical Law Journal*, vol. 43, pp.9-10.
44. Sir T. More, "The History of King Richard the Thirde," in *The English Works of Sir Thomas More*, A.W. Reed *et al* (eds.), London: Eyre and Spottiswoode, 1931, vol. 1, p.47.

are partly instigated and moved, and the more bold and willing to offend."[45] The apparently undeserved and undiscriminating nature of the privilege was also widely condemned, with many noting how few sanctuary men there were "whome any fauourable necessitie compelled to gooe thither". Usually, it was claimed, they were a "rabble of theues, murtherers, and maliciuos heyghnous Traitours". Indeed, by the early 1500s, the very notion of sanctuary, particularly 'special' sanctuary, appeared absurd to many observers: "But as for theeves, of whiche these places bee full, and which neuer fall fro the crafte, after thei once falle thereto, it is pitie the saintuarye shoulde serue them. And muche more mannequellers whome Godde badde to take from the aulter and kyll them, yf theyr murther were wylfull."[46] The law was becoming more 'rational'.

Such concerns were exacerbated by the cause célèbre that ensued after a JP, John Pauncefote, was shot and mutilated while travelling to the Gloucestershire quarter sessions in 1516. Some of his killers, including a knight named Savage, fled to the sanctuary of St John's Priory, in Clerkenwell. The Court of Star Chamber considered the legitimacy of the protection afforded to them, hearing legal argument by canon lawyers. There was no final judgment, Savage eventually being pardoned. However, Henry VIII appears to have been outraged by the case, and claims to special sanctuary came under increasingly close scrutiny. A series of statutes limited the offences for which it could be

---

45. Sir W. Staunford, *Les Plees Del Corone*, London, 1607, pp.119.
46. Sir T. More, "The History of King Richard the Third," pp.47-49.

claimed and stiffened the conditions under which it was granted. Thus, in 1535 all permanent sanctuary men were required to wear badges and might forfeit their privilege if caught out at night or with weapons.

An offender in a general (40 day) sanctuary who wished to abjure rather than submit to trial was required to confess his crime to the coroner and swear to leave the country immediately, never to return. This effectively produced a public ceremony, in which the community expelled the felon from its midst. Abjurors were then required to travel by the most direct route to their designated embarkation port. The traditional oath included a promise not to spend more than one night at any town while en route. In theory, they would walk bareheaded, dressed in a long white or sackcloth robe, carrying a wooden cross in their right hand. Abjurors were legally protected from attack, as long as they remained on the royal highway (any found away from it could be executed immediately, though this was discouraged by the late medieval period).[47] On arrival at the coast, they had to seek the first passage abroad available, and were supposed to walk into the sea up to their knees every day as a token of their desire to sail. As with later transportees, abjurors faced execution if they returned (unless granted a special licence by the Crown) and could not claim the privilege a second time. Like convicted felons, their land was, in theory, escheated and their goods and chattels were forfeit to the Crown.

The coroner would specify a particular exit port;

---

47. Carro, "Sanctuary," p.761.

Portsmouth, Newcastle, Dover and Kingston on Hull were favoured, though many others were also used, and some abjurors were sent to the Scottish border. Thus, when Thomas Parker fled to a church in Leicester, in June 1527, he informed the two city coroners who attended: "I haue strykyn ... Thomas Otfield & gaff hym the wound wherof he died & therefor I, the seid Thomas Parker, clayme and aske this seyntuary for the saluacion of my lyff." Upon swearing to leave the realm, he was sent to the port of Boston in Lincolnshire. However, an abjuror was not always sent to his nearest port, especially if two or more men set out at the same time. Thus, Hertford coroner Gregory Waron assigned nine different ports to a group of men who abjured before him in November 1527.[48] As these examples suggest, abjuration was still being claimed by a significant number of felons in the late 1520s. A close examination indicates that the overwhelming majority were male, with a relatively high proportion coming from the middling social orders. This is understandable, exiles faced numerous difficulties abroad, and many people would have preferred to take their chances at trial.[49] Thus, the (very incomplete) coroners' records held at the Court of King's Bench, reveal that of 212 people who claimed the privilege between 1485 and 1545, only four were women, 75 per cent admitted to thefts or burglaries and 34 per cent to homicides (20 cases involved both murder and theft).[50] Many records reveal a significant

---

48. K. Kesselring, "Abjuration and its Demise," *Canadian Journal of History*, 1999, vol. 34, no. 3, p.350.
49. Carro, "Sanctuary," p.761.
50. Kesselring, "Abjuration and its Demise," pp.350-351.

gap between the date and place of the offence and that of the felon claiming sanctuary, suggesting an initial escape; others indicate an almost immediate fleeing to a local church after the commission of a felony.

A statute of 1529 (21 Henry VIII, c. 2) sought to discourage abjurors from absconding en route or returning illegally from abroad by ordering that coroners brand them. This was similar to the practice already employed in benefit of clergy cases; the: "... coroner immediately after his confession, and before his abjuration, shall cause every such felon or murderer to be marked with an hot iron upon the braune of the thumbe of the right hand, with the signe of an A to the intent he may bee the better known among the kings subjects."[51] More humanely, from at least the 1490s, some coroners preferred to ensure that abjurors reached their embarkation ports by ordering that they be passed from one parish constable to the next until they reached the sea-port designated, rather than leaving them to their own devices. However, even in the early 1520s, it was not considered fair to make such parish officers personally liable for any escapes by men under their supervision. As the: "... constables under the statute cannot keep him securely nor employ force or imprisonment for his safe custody, it would not be reasonable to charge them with the escape."[52] In reality, absconding en route must have been a very regular occurrence.

---

51. Staunford, *Les Plees Del Corone*, pp.108-9.
52. T.F. Plucknett and J.C. Barton (Eds.), 1st *Dialogue, 1523, St Germain's Doctor and Student*, London, Selden Society, 1974, p.37.

Radical change to the system came in 1531, when statute provided that those who claimed sanctuary and then abjured did not have to leave the country. Instead, they were to be led into one of nine designated permanent sanctuaries, usually large monasteries such as Rippon or Westminster, for internal exile. In the records surviving for the years that follow, 51 abjurors are mentioned as having been sent to such sanctuaries. (Commission of a further felony would forfeit the right to remain in these refuges.) The Act's preamble suggests that this change may have been motivated by a concern that abjuration encouraged the emigration of militarily useful men, including skilled archers, "very expert Maryners", and many other "apt men for the Warres and for defence of this realme". (This may also indicate plans to pardon abjurors at a future date in exchange for service.) However, within a decade, in 1540 (26 & 28 H 8 c. 13 & 7), the Reformation Parliament dismantled the chartered privileges of these great abbeys, and permanent ecclesiastical sanctuaries disappeared. Nevertheless, ordinary churches retained their ability to provide 40 days protection, and, in lieu of the nine permanent ecclesiastical sanctuaries, several towns and cities were appointed to which coroners could direct abjurers, including Westminster, York and Norwich, each being allowed to accommodate up to 20 such men at a time. However, and very significantly, the Henrician Statute of 1540 also decreed that sanctuary and abjuration no longer applied to a large number of serious felonies, mimicking the process that gradually removed benefit of clergy from grave offences. Thus, they ceased to be open to those who committed "wilfull murther", burglary, robbery, rape, or arson.[53] Although the Act of 1540 was aimed at preventing severe abuses while not completely ignoring the "law of mercy", it seems almost to have marked the end of abjuration.[54] Records of only two subsequent abjurations into the newly specified sanctuary towns survive. In one of them, in 1541, William Crypis, a Rye fisherman, abjured before coroner Robert Woodless for the theft of a horse; he was branded, handed a cross to carry and sent to Norwich. With these exceptions, abjuration died out in the early 1540s, no longer being an attractive option to felons who might claim their clergy, seek pardon from the King or risk flight or trial in lieu. Nevertheless, its existence lingered in legal theory, as it was never formally abolished. Even in 1556, leet court tythingmen were being advised to examine whether: "... there be any amonge you that hath taken the churchyarde and escaped withoute abjuration of the realme as the lawe wyll."[55] As late as the early 1600s, Francis Bacon appears to have been referring to the reformed system, and its limitations, when noting briefly that: "Where a man committeth any felony, for the which at this day hee may have priviledge of sanctuary, and confesseth the felony, he shall abjure the liberty of the Realme and chuse his sanctuary."[56] By then, however, it appears to have been a historical curiosity.

---

53. J. Wilkinson, A *Treatise Collected out of the Statutes of this Kingdom* ..., London, 1618, Book 1, p.24.
54. Staunford, *Les Plees Del Corone*, p.119.
55. B.L., *Booke for a Justice of Peace*, London, 1556 (or 1559), p.85.
56. Sir F. Bacon, *Cases of Treason*, London, John More, 1641, p.14.

Similarly, although the 1540 Act did not mark the complete demise of sanctuary in England, without anywhere permanent for sanctuary seekers to flee to, it became largely insignificant. There appear to be no extant records of it being claimed under Queen Elizabeth. Statutes abolishing nearly all privileges of sanctuary were enacted, under James I, in 1603 and 1623 (1 James I, c. 25; 21 James I, c.28). If there were any instances of its use in the decades immediately before 1603 they must have been exceptionally rare, although why going to the trouble of repealing a privilege that was otherwise never used was thought necessary is difficult to explain.

Although, today, these two privileges are often considered to have been archaic social evils and relics of medieval 'superstition', whose end was a welcome by-product of the Reformation, a close examination reveals a slightly more complex picture. Like benefit of clergy, they had originally served important social functions. Their end was as much linked to the emergence of new concepts of mercy and justice, as it was to their inherent defects, real though these undoubtedly were. Although Henry VII had refined the laws governing sanctuary and abjuration, there was, it seems, no inexorable drive to eradicate them in the late 1400s. As Christopher St Germain could note, even in 1531, sanctuary and clergy were: "... under the power of the parlyament, yet the parlyament hath not broken them, ne extended his fule power on them, to put them generalye awaye: but in particular cases some tyme hit hath."[57]

---

57.   Plucknett and Barton, *2nd Dialogue*, 1531, p.322.

Arguably, for medieval English people, justice was not purely concerned with abstract notions of logic and reason, but also with the practical values of forgiveness and a restoration of fractured relationships within communities. Reconciliation was sometimes as important as retribution in maintaining peace and order in society.[58] Thus, sanctuary's purpose was to "safeguard of the life of man, which hath offended the Law, and it is grounded upon the Law of mercie".[59] In theory, when combined with abjuration, it rid the realm of a felon and confiscated his property for the Crown almost as effectively as execution, while manifesting mercy. Historically, sanctuary had served some other practical functions. It allowed the deferral of judgment, permitting decisions to be reached in a calmer atmosphere, so helping to prevent summary revenge being enacted and blood feuds prolonged.[60]

By the early 1500s, England's legal mechanisms had become more sophisticated and no longer required a 'cooling off' period. There was also a growing perception, amongst many observers (including Sir Thomas More), that mercy was inappropriate for the more heinous felonies, and that granting it merely served to encourage other offenders. However, these factors alone do not explain the end of abjuration, especially given the survival of benefit of clergy, which also frequently allowed serious felons to go almost scot-free. It appears that there was an increased

---

58. P. McCune, "Justice, Mercy, and Late Medieval Governance," *Michigan Law Review*, 1991, vol. 89, p.1672.
59. Wilkinson, *A Treatise ... Book* 1, p.25.
60. Carro, "Sanctuary," p.769.

determination, on the part of the Crown, to be seen to administer all justice. Benefit of clergy had been adapted in the medieval period so that it was only claimed *after* conviction; defendants first had to face trial in the Crown's courts. Abjuration, however, had been a right, not an indulgence granted by a compassionate ruler. This may have contributed to its demise under the ever more interventionist Tudors, making its disappearance a manifestation of royal power.[61]

Unlike abjuration and benefit of clergy, sanctuary in a church was found in much of early modern Europe before the Reformation, and in Catholic countries for some time afterwards, though its terms and scope varied with each state. This ubiquity is unsurprising, given that it had an ancient scriptural basis (the Hebrews had six Levitical cities of refuge). Thus, in Spain, ordinary criminals could sometimes find asylum from the secular authorities in churches, despite attempts by the Spanish Crown to stamp out the practice. Although, in 1493, Ferdinand and Isabella had sent an ordinance to Seville prohibiting the harbouring of fugitives, as late as 1582, a killer was returned to the church where he had earlier sought refuge, before being forcibly removed, because, as the secular judges declared, his crime had not been 'perfidious' and so they did not have the right to detain him in a place of worship.[62]

---

61. Kesselring, "Abjuration and its Demise," p.358.
62. M.E. Perry, *Crime and Society in Early Modern Seville*, Hanover (NH), University of New England Press, 1980, pp.60-61.

Pleading the Belly

A female convicted of felony and liable to be sentenced to death could 'postpone' execution if pregnant. This was known as "pleading the Belly". Once a convict made such a claim the sheriff would have to return a jury of "matrons or discreet women" to consider the issue.[63] The judge would direct the assembled matrons to determine whether the convict was "quick with child" (carrying a dead child was not sufficient). The jury of matrons was an ancient body, mentioned by Bracton in the thirteenth century. The matrons were midwives or married and widowed women with personal experience of childbirth. Unlike the trial jury, they received their evidence in private, having been led by the bailiff to a closed chamber for the physical examination of the convicted woman. They acted publicly only when being sworn and announcing their verdict. In the seventeenth century, the normal oath required them to swear that they would: "... search and try the Prisoner at the Bar, whether she be quick with Child of a quick Child, and thereof a true Verdict shall return according to the best of [their] judgment." Their leader, known as a forematron, often took a more individualised oath. Courts used the all female jury for reasons of delicacy and, even more importantly, because they viewed the women concerned as experts in identifying the physical signs of pregnancy.[64] Although the jury of

---

63. Blackstone, *Commentaries on the Laws of England*, vol. 4, p.388.

64. J.M. Cornett, "Hoodwink'd by custom: The exclusion of women from juries in Eighteenth-Century English Law," *William and Mary Journal of Women and the Law*, 1997, vol. 4, pp.18-28.

matrons could be the same size as the trial jury (12), it was often smaller, sometimes being as few as three women.

In practice, pleading the belly was often a 'fiction', being claimed indiscriminately by many convicted women, whether pregnant or not. As Henri Misson observed: "The women or wenches that are condemned to death, never fail to plead that they are with child." Of course, as Misson also noted, in the largely unsegregated prisons of the era, even if a female entered a virgin, she was likely to be made aware of the advantages of getting pregnant, and "who would not hearken to such wholsum Advice?"[65] Nevertheless, most who claimed it had not even availed themselves of their male colleagues' services. As the privilege effectively mitigated the harshness of the criminal law, it gave women the same leeway that was available to men via benefit of clergy (females not being able to plead their clergy on fully equal terms with men until the late seventeenth century). As a result, the willingness of the matrons and the courts to grant it depended heavily on forum. At quarter sessions, which were usually reluctant to inflict a death sentence, the matrons were probably tacitly encouraged to return such a positive finding when a woman was capitally convicted. Indeed, it may have been on the understanding that this would happen that a case had initially been listed before that court and a 'guilty' verdict returned. Thus, three women convicted of felony at the special gaol delivery sessions conducted by JPs (including William Lambarde) at Maidstone, in January 1597, all claimed to be pregnant and

---

65. Misson, *Memoirs and Observations in his Travels over England*, p.329.

asked for the "benefit of their increased wombs". They were examined by the jury of matrons and granted a stay of judgment (which, presumably, eventually became permanent). This was despite two of them having husbands who had been incarcerated for some time in Maidstone jail, making it inherently unlikely that they had impregnated the women. Significantly, 12 men who were convicted with them were also "read as clerks and burnt on their left hands", despite the great improbability of them all being literate at this time. Thus, pleading the belly, like clergy, was a procedural device that allowed JPs to determine felonies while simultaneously only rarely passing the death penalty.[66]

In forums where a death sentence was more willingly passed and expected, such as the provincial assizes or the Newgate (Old Bailey) sessions in London, the matrons were likely to be more stringent, and were consequently more willing to produce a negative verdict. Nevertheless, even there, doubt would normally be decided in favour of the examined woman; according to Mathew Hale, the "compassion of their sex is gentle to them in their verdict, if there be any colour to support a sparing verdict". In theory, if the jury gave an affirmative answer, execution would be put back until after the delivery or until it became apparent that the woman was not pregnant. Legally, it was not cancelled, merely postponed. Nor did pregnancy put off the initial trial or even the formal passing of sentence: "... though she be quicke with child, yet Judgement shall not be

---

66. Melling, *Crime and Punishment*, pp.135-136.

delayed, but only execution deferred."[67] However, after a female felon had been temporarily reprieved by pleading her belly a warrant for her execution had to be issued by the sheriff before she could be hanged. In 1604, Elizabeth Caldwell had tried to murder her husband with a poisoned cake, which, unfortunately, was eaten by a child, the infant subsequently dying. She was questioned by three JPs, made full admissions, and pleaded guilty at the Chester assizes (where an accomplice of hers was pressed to death for refusing to enter a plea). At the time that she was convicted, Caldwell was genuinely, and heavily, pregnant and so execution was deferred. However, her fortunate husband had no wish to see her escape the noose. After giving birth to a boy, who joined his older brother in the keeping of their father: "... it was generally reported, hee made sute to the judge to precure a warrant to have his wife executed within a certain time after her deliverance." Despite intervention by Lady Cholmsley, who wished to petition the King for a permanent reprieve, the execution went ahead, albeit some months after the delivery.[68] Similarly, in December 1703, Moll Hawkins, a thief who had been sentenced to death in March of that year, was executed: "... having been reprieved for nine months, upon account of her being then alleged quick with child."[69]

In many cases, however, execution would not be

---

67. Anon, *The Laws Resolutions of Womens Rights: or, the Lawes Provision for Woemen*, London, John More, 1632, p.207.
68. G. Dougdale, *A true discourse of the practices of Elizabeth Cauldwell*, London, 1604, ff.B2-B4.
69. Rayner and Crook, *The Complete Newgate Calendar*, vol. II, p.172

authorised. After the child was born or (more commonly) the woman proved not to be pregnant, she would merely spend a few months in jail and then be reprieved and released. As a result, some escaped death several times via this mechanism. In December 1738, at the Old Bailey, Constantia James failed in her attempt to claim pregnancy to avoid being hanged for stealing over seven pounds in cash. This probably came as a surprise to her, as she had previously "got off nine times by pleading her belly". On this occasion she was executed at Tyburn.[70] Although the rationale behind the provision was to protect an innocent (if unborn) life, this reasoning was somewhat eroded because, in theory, the privilege could not be used indefinitely for the same offence (a harsh if realistic view of the nature of most early modern jails). Thus: "If after such respite when she is once delivered, she become great againe, and object to prolong her life, the judge ought to command execution presently, for this benefit shall be claimed but once." (There was also provision to fine the sheriff or marshal for their negligence in allowing the defendant to get impregnated again!)[71]

Amnesty/Reprieve

Special national occasions, such as a coronation or royal birth might produce a general amnesty, a "releasement of

---

70. *The Gentleman's Magazine*, 1738, vol. 8, p.659.
71. Anon, *The Laws Resolutions of Womens Rights*, p.207.

divers prisoners" awaiting trial or punishment. Thus, John Bunyan noted that on the coronation of Charles II in 1660 "they let out thousands"; sadly he was not amongst them.[72] However, at the Gloucester assizes in September 1660, the three members of the Perry family, mistakenly accused of murder, did plead guilty to a separate count, involving the theft of £140 the previous year, after being prompted by "some who were unwilling to lose time", given that it was covered by the new King's Act of Oblivion. The three were immediately pardoned for this crime.[73] Sometimes, the terms of such amnesties would be general; more commonly, they would be limited to certain offences. Thomas Wynne, an Elizabethan burglar who had stolen 400 pounds worth of plate from the royal lodgings at Whitehall Palace was a lucky beneficiary of such indulgence. Elizabeth's Act of Grace came out soon afterwards, granting a free pardon for all offences except treason, murder, and a few other notorious crimes. Wynne was allowed the benefit of the Act, and obtained his liberty, along with numerous other criminals.[74] Sadly, many released under these provisions did not reform as a result of their good fortune. In 1603, Jonathan Woodward and James Philpot, two notorious Metropolitan housebreakers detained at the Marshalsea prison pending execution, narrowly escaped death after

---

72. J. Bunyan, *A Relation of the Imprisonment of Mr John Bunyan, Minister of the Gospel at Bedford ... in November 1660*, London, 1765, p.41.
73. Sir T. Overbury, *A true and Perfect Account of the Examination, Confession, Tryal, Condemnation, and execution of Joan Perry*, London, 1676, p.12.
74. C. Johnson, *A General History of the Lives and Adventures of the Most Famous Highwaymen, Murderers, Street-Robbers*, London: J. Janeway, 1734, p.134.

King James I, on his accession to the English throne, pardoned all criminals, except those convicted of high treason and wilful murder. However, both men swiftly re-offended, and were eventually executed.[75]

Even more important than general amnesties were the individual reprieves granted to 'deserving' cases. These were in the gift of the Crown. At assizes, a judge could grant a temporary stay of execution after a capital conviction, pending such a reprieve being granted: "... and so declare the matter to the Prince, and obtaineth after a time for the prisoner his pardon."[76] Such temporary stays were not so necessary in London, given its normal proximity to the monarch, allowing easier petitioning. Thus, after his conviction for burglary, Colonel Turner asked the presiding judge at the Old Bailey to grant him a reprieve. He refused, pointing out: "That we cannot do, the court must give Judgement upon you: if you can by any means prevail with his Majesty to do it, you may use your interest but the Court cannot do it."[77] Reprieves were available throughout the early modern period, their roots lying deep in the medieval era. Thus, in the fifteenth century, Fortescue, who had seen a woman convicted and burnt at Salisbury assizes for the murder of her husband, on apparently weak evidence,

---

75. Rayner and Crook, *The Complete Newgate Calendar*, vol. I, p.42.
76. Smith, *De Republica Anglorum*, p.120.
77. Anon, *A True and Impartial Account of the Arraignment, Tryal, examination, Confession and Condemnation of Col. James Turner*, London, 1663, pp.84-85. Turner then sought to be transported, receiving a similar response, which prompted him to complain that others had received it; the judges denied this to be the case in burglary.

noted that the trial judge "after the whole proceedings were over, might have respited the execution of the woman". This could have been for a year or indefinitely. (Subsequently, one of her husband's servants was convicted before the same judge, for the same offence, and absolved his erstwhile mistress from any part in the murder.)[78] In the early 1500s, Thomas More felt that the existence of reprieves meant that sanctuaries were no longer necessary, as they permitted felons who committed their crimes in mitigating circumstances to avoid death: "For yf eyther necessitie, hys owne defence, or misfortune drawe hym to that dede, a pardon serueth which eyther the law graunteth of course, or the Kynge of pitie maye."[79]

Many judges appear to have taken seriously Francis Bacon's observation that in capital cases judges ought to remember mercy and to "cast a severe eye upon the example, but a merciful eye upon the person".[80] Cases of jurors acquitting, despite judicial pressure to convict, are widely celebrated. However, throughout the early modern period, judges could, and regularly did, 'second guess' a jury's guilty verdict in felonies by reprieving the sentence. Sometimes, pardons might even be secured in advance from the Chancery, before the case was heard. On other occasions, the trial judge would postpone execution and then apply for

---

78. Grigor, *Sir John Fortescue's Commendation of the Laws of England*, p.91.
79. More, *The History of King Richard the Third*, pp.47-49.
80. Sir F. Bacon, "On Judicature," *The Essays*, London, Everyman edn., J.M. Dent, 1906, pp.162-165.

a pardon.[81] Typically, judges might do this if they felt that the trial jury had convicted on unsatisfactory evidence or that the convict was not deserving of death though technically guilty. Thus, they reprieved where jurors had: "... gone too violently against the evidence given in matters criminall, either it is upon slender evidence they have pronounced him giltie, whom the Judges and most part of the Justices thinkes by the evidence not fullie prooved guiltie, or for some other cause, do thinke the person rather worthie to live than to die."[82] In making this decision it would appear that judges sometimes had regard to extra-forensic information. Accordingly, in one case, Mr Justice Rokeby noted: "I reprieved Jane Jones, wife of Wm. Jones, found guilty of clipping and coining, there being only one witness who swore the fact against her, and there was not any clipt money or tools found, nor any concurring circumstance to corroborate his testimony." Additionally, the key prosecution witness was a man of whom Rokeby had "received a very ill character".[83] In the 1750s, Sir Dudley Ryder, presiding over the Home Circuit Assizes, also reprieved convicts where he thought the evidence against them was unclear, or the accused person was deserving of clemency. However, he was likely to refuse such indulgence, even when pressed by others (in one case by the Lord Lieutenant of Surrey), where the crime was clear and

---

81. T. Barnes (Ed.), *Somerset Assize Orders 1629-1640*, Frome, Somerset Record Society, 1959, vol. 65, p.19.
82. Smith, *De Republica Anglorum*, p.120.
83. Mr Justice Rokeby, *The Diary of Mr Justice Rokeby printed from a manuscript in the Possession of Sir Henry Peek*, London, Wyman and Sons, 1887, p.53.

heinous or the convict was a multiple or repeat offender.[84] Nevertheless, even though an assizes judge might have personal doubts about the justice of a conviction, their discretion was not unfettered. A reprieve might not follow if the climate of local or national opinion was against it. Thus, in 1682, Lord Chief Justice North, though strongly disapproving of a Devon jury's conviction of three local 'witches', explained why they had not been recommended for reprieve. In a letter to Sir Leoline Jenkins, the Secretary of State, who possessed the formal power to authorise such a measure, he noted that although the women appeared depressed and unbalanced there was enormous local hostility towards them. They had made devastating admissions and the consequences of granting a reprieve would be severe, socially and legally: "... we cannot reprieve them without appearing to deny the very being of witches, which, as it is contrary to law, so I think it would be ill for his Majesty's service." In an account of the same trial, North's brother noted that the tumult surrounding it was such that: "... if these women had been acquitted, it was thought the country people would have committed some disorder." It was easier to let them hang.[85]

During the sixteenth century, the number of reprieves was quite small. Thus, of 10 cutpurses and horse thieves condemned at the Old Bailey one Friday in 1585, nine were executed the following (Saturday) morning "the tenthe

---

84. J. H. Langbein, "Shaping the Eighteenth-Century Criminal Trial: A View from the Ryder Sources," *University of Chicago Law Review*, 1983, vol. 50, pp.29-30.

85. F.J. Gent, *The Trial of the Bideford Witches*, Crediton, Privately Published, p.85.

[being] stayed by a meenes from the Courte".[86] However, their use subsequently expanded, and there developed periodic concern at the reduction in deterrence that this might occasion.[87] Thus, in 1663, Lord Chief Justice Sir Orlando Bridgeman protested that in London and Middlesex considerable numbers of felons were being reprieved after conviction "which reprieves for ought I perceive were made (at least some of them) *ad arbitrium*".[88] Such fears were to become widespread in the eighteenth century as the incidence of reprieves continued to increase. Adding drama to the process, reprieves would sometimes only be granted when a felon was at the gallows. Pepys was convinced that this explained Colonel Turner's filibustering at the scaffold: "... delaying the time by long discourses and prayers, one after another in hopes of a reprieve; but none come, and at last he was flung off the ladder in his cloak." (The attendant sheriff shared Pepys' view and warned Turner not to expect a pardon.)[89] Others had better outcomes. In 1650, one of George Fox's fellow prison inmates at Derby, a woman convicted of theft from her master, was sentenced to death, despite the Quaker writing to the court asking for mercy on her behalf. She was taken to the gallows on a cart, but when there, although: "... they

86. R.H. Tawney and E.Power (Eds.), "Fleetwood to Lord Burghley July 7, 1585," *Tudor Economic Documents*, London, Longmans, 1951, vol. 2, p.337.
87. Sir E. Coke, *Institutes of the Lawes of England, Part Three, Concerning High Treason, and other Pleas of the Crown and Criminall causes*, London, 1644, p.246.
88. Sir O. Bridgeman, "Newgate, 1663-A Letter of Sir Orlando Bridgeman, Chief Justice," *American Journal of Legal History*, vol. 13, pp.384 and 386.
89. S. Pepys, *The Diary of Samuel Pepys*, R. Latham and W. Matthews (Eds.), London, Bell and Hyman, 1971, vol. 5, pp.23-24.

had her upon the ladder, with a cloth bound over her face, ready to be turned off, yet they did not put her to death, but brought her back to prison." She was later formally reprieved. Mandeville deplored such gallows' escapes, as he believed they prevented condemned men focusing their minds properly on their solemn situations, encouraging them instead to think of: "... the Possibility of Pardons and Reprieves that often come very late, and which, with or without grounds, most criminals continue to hope for, 'till they are hanged." He favoured a requirement that any reprieves be invalid if received less than 24 hours before execution.[90]

Intervention on the part of respectable members of society to secure a reprieve or pardon became increasingly frequent, and successful, in the latter part of the period. As a result, by the late seventeenth century, some judges on circuit were apparently reluctant to grant temporary reprieves in serious cases, as even those guilty of barbarous murders could sometimes use the time provided to secure pardons, through corrupt ministers of justice and the "Prevalence of Greatmen".[91] That a man of 'quality' would go to the trouble of petitioning on behalf of a condemned man was often considered indicative of the convict being a potentially worthwhile member of society and deserving of clemency. Thus, in the 1690s, the young John Price, a notorious future Metropolitan hangman, was convicted at

---

90. B. De Mandeville, *An Enquiry into the Causes of the Frequent Executions at Tyburn*, London, 1725, p.25.
91. R. Smith, *Mistaken Justice: or, Innocence condemn'd, in the person of Francis Newland*, London, 1695, p.6.

the Chelmsford assizes for robbing a woman of 18 shillings and received sentence of death. However, a former employer, by then the High Sheriff of Essex, interceded on his behalf, despite having earlier dismissed Price from his own service.[92] Nevertheless, many other supplicants were unsuccessful. As soon as Arnold Coke was convicted of malicious wounding (a capital offence under a statute from Charles II's reign) at the Bury assizes, on Saturday March 31, 1721, he sought to avoid the death sentence that was passed and: "... diligently apply'd himself to the obtaining a Pardon; to which End Many Persons were employed to sollicite Mr Crispe [the victim] to a reconciliation." Crispe was also under pressure from others not to support a reprieve, and refused; Coke was executed.[93] In the same year, a condemned soldier, William Casey, recognised at the gallows the efforts that his commanding officers had made on his behalf, albeit unavailingly, and gave: "... hearty thanks to the Honourable Colonel Pitts, and Colonel Pagill, for their endeavours to save my Life."[94]

Such intercessions could be misplaced. In the early 1600s, two men, one of them a former servant of Sir Jerome Bowes, avoided the gallows for theft when Sir Jerome intervened on their behalf. Despite having such "lenitie, and clemencie extended to them", they repaid the knight, in 1606, by murdering his housemaid and then ransacking his

92. Rayner and Crook, *The Complete Newgate Calendar*, 1926, vol. II, p.266.
93. Anon, *An Account of the behaviour, Confession, and last Dying words of Arnold Coke Esq., and John Woodburne, Labourer*, London, 1722, p.3.
94. Anon, *Select Trials, for Murders, Robberies, Rapes, Sodomy, Coining, Frauds, And other Offences*, London, J. Wilford, 1734, vol. 1, pp.61-6.

London residence, stealing anything of value they could find. (Like any modern victim of crime, it was not the money but the personal violation of his home, and the atrocity committed within it, that exercised Bowes: "... howsoever he might make little reckoning of his losse, yet that his dwelling house should be made a slaughterhouse he could not but be grieved".)[95] After the 1650s, a reprieve might be accompanied by transportation, and, after 1718, 14 years transportation to the colonies became the usual alternative.

Enlistment in Lieu

Encouraging those accused or convicted of all but the most heinous crimes to join the army or navy in lieu of punishment was a regular feature of recruitment in many European countries, including England. It was, unsurprisingly, especially common in wartime. Of course, if already enlisted this option was not available, although a condemned man might ask for a dangerous assignment and credit for his previous service. In 1721, the disappointed soldier, William Casey, facing execution observed: "... I had some small hopes that his Majesty (in consideration of the Services of my whole Family, having all been faithful Soldiers, and Servants to the Crown of England) would have

---

95. Anon, *A true Report of the horrible Murther, which was committed in the house of Sir Jerome Bowes, Knight, on the 29 day of February, Anno Dom 1606*, London, Mathew Lownes, 1607, pp.B2-B3.

extended one branch of his Mercy to me, and have sent me
to have serv'd him in another Country."[96]

96.　Anon, *Select Trials, for Murders, Robberies, Rapes, Sodomy, Coining, Frauds,* vol.
　　1, pp.61-6.

Chapter 19

Transportation, Incarceration, Shaming and Corporal Punishments

"Why dost thou lash that whore? Strip thine own back;
Thou hotly lust'st to use her in that kind For which thou
whipp'st her."

William Shakespeare, King Lear, Act 4, Scene 6

Transportation

Penal transportation in England has a history going back to
1597 when courts of quarter sessions were empowered to
banish abroad vagabonds who would "not be reformed of
their roguish kind of life". However, this power appears to
have been very little used. Even so, the potential labour
resource provided by convicts remained attractive to some
of those in the colonies. Thus, one governor specifically
asked for convict labour in 1611. In the 1630s, Thomas
Verney, having settled in Barbados, and troubled by the
island's acute manpower shortage, wrote to his father
imploring him to send 100 men, to work in his cotton and
tobacco fields. Aware of his father's connection to the
Marshalsea prison, Thomas suggested that, if necessary,
they could be procured with the "great help of bridewell

and the prisons".[1]

The practice of reprieving prisoners from execution on condition that they agreed to transport themselves to the colonies, though present in the early 1600s, first became widespread during the Interregnum, and was further expanded after 1660. It was used for some offenders who had pleaded benefit of clergy and for others reprieved through the royal prerogative of mercy, as death was considered too harsh in their particular cases. Thus, in 1677, one man, accused, with his father, of murdering his sister-in-law and coining, mistakenly "pleaded guilty to both indictments and afterwards beg'd for Transportation". (When it was refused, he "alleged that he Pleaded guilty only to take off the crime from his father".) He was hanged.[2] Additionally, in the 1660s, transportation was made a punishment, in its own right, for a small selection of special offences such as rick burning.

Before 1718, however, transportation was plagued with problems of enforcement. As a result, an Act of that year could complain that: "... many Offenders to whom royal Mercy hath been extended, upon Condition of transporting themselves to the West-Indies, have often neglected to perform the said Condition, but returned to their former Wickedness." Typical of such people was Susan Banster, who pleaded guilty at the Old Bailey in 1678 to stealing goods to the value of £13. She "had been Convicted before

---

1. L. Gragg, "A vagabond in paradise: Thomas Verney in Barbados," *History Today*, 1995, vol. 45, issue 8, pp.40-47.
2. Anon, *Horrid News from St Martins*, London, 1677, p.9.

of Felony, and was to be Transported; but as she was going, committed this Theft". This time, she was executed.[3] Others who made the journey apparently came back prematurely. This was not surprising, the long-term prospects for poor whites in the West Indies, the most common transportation destination after 1660, were bad when compared to the American colonies favoured after 1718. Thus, Mary Carleton (the 'German Princess'), a notorious and polygamous thief from Kent, who was convicted at Newgate of stealing a silver tankard, condemned, reprieved and transported to Jamaica, returned home after less than two years. She was detected and executed in 1673.[4]

Two parliamentary attempts to stiffen the consequences of committing clergyable felony by replacing branding and discharge with transportation had been made, unsuccessfully, in 1663.[5] There was another unsuccessful parliamentary bill in 1702. Success was finally attained in 1717 when the Transportation Act (4 Geo. I, c. 11) received the royal assent, coming into force the following year. After this date, defendants convicted of clergyable offences, especially those involving dishonesty, were frequently

---

3. Anon, *An exact account of the trials of the several persons arraigned at the sessions-house in the Old-Bailey for London and Middlesex*, London, Gilham Hills, 1678, p.4.

4. Anon, *The Mary Carleton Narratives, 1663-1673. A missing chapter in the history of the English novel*, Cambridge (Mass.), Harvard University Press, 1914, p.106, see also Anon. (F. Kirkman?) *The case of Madam Mary Carleton*, London, Sam Speed, 1663, p.139, and Rayner and Crook, *The Complete Newgate Calendar*, 1926, vol. I, pp.264-268

5. J. Beattie, *Crime and the Courts in England 1660-1800*, Oxford, OUP, 1986, p.471.

sentenced to transportation for seven years, the Act providing that where any convicts were entitled to benefit of clergy, and so:

"... liable only to the Penalties of Burning in the hand or Whipping ... it shall and may be lawful for the Court before whom they were convicted ... if they think fit, instead, of ordering any such Offenders to be burnt in the Hand or whipt, to order and direct, That such Offenders ... shall be sent as soon as conveniently may be, to some of his Majesty's Colonies and Plantations in America for the Space of seven Years."

However, those clergied for manslaughter were still not normally transported, and could usually expect immediate release (perhaps a recognition that 'anyone' could become involved in a homicidal quarrel). Additionally, under the Act, those convicted of non-clergyable offences and sentenced to death could be pardoned on condition of transportation for 14 years or life. The impact of the new statute on the execution rate was swift, so that even in 1725 Mandeville could note that transportation: "... for some years last past, on many occasions, has been substituted, and inflicted in the room of capital punishment."[6] Typically, the August assizes of 1731, held at Maidstone, produced five sentences of death, two being of highwaymen, another a woman who had murdered her illegitimate child, a burglar

---

6. B. De Mandeville, *An Enquiry into the Causes of the Frequent Executions at Tyburn*, London, 1725, p.46.

and a horse thief; however, an equal number of sentences of transportation were passed.[7] In many courts the proportions of convicts being transported speedily exceeded those executed. Between 1718 and 1769, 69.5 per cent of those convicted of felony at the Old Bailey were transported to America. Only 15.5 per cent were sentenced to death.

The practical arrangements for transportation were also considerably improved, reducing absconding and post-conviction crimes. Thus, pursuant to the new statute, convicted felons remained in prison until their transportation, when they were handed over to merchant agents who could sell their services to landowners in the Americas on arrival. These contractors gave a bond to guarantee that transportation would take place and that the convict would not return until the end of his or her sentence. As a result, after 1718, those convicted on the Western Circuit were handed over to six different contractors by the judges and JPs. Ships' masters certified receipt of the convicts from jail and obtained landing certificates on arrival in America from the governor or chief customs house officer of the appropriate State (usually Virginia or Maryland). These certificates were returned to the courts as evidence that the sentence had been carried out. After 1718, the initial cost of transportation was borne by the state, not the contractor, also facilitating the removal of prisoners who were unlikely to secure a good price in America.

Even under the new system, there were periodic problems. In 1725, Mandeville was convinced that

---

7.   *The Gentleman's Magazine*, 1731, vol. 1, p.351.

transportees were still escaping en route to the Americas, or returning early from the colonies, having corrupted the black slaves there by: "... teaching the Africans, more villeny and mischief."[8] Certainly, there were numerous well documented cases of premature return. Thus, on March 31, 1732, William Warner, who had been transported for stealing deer, was hanged at Leicester for his early return (ironically on the same gibbet at which his own father's murderer had been hanged in chains a year earlier).[9] Nevertheless, such returnees only appear to have become a statistically significant problem later in the eighteenth century. Most of those who were transported chose to remain in the colonies, after their designated seven or 14 years were over.[10]

Prisons

There were numerous prisons in early modern England. The Metropolis, in particular, abounded with them, albeit that some were for debtors. Thus, John Taylour, noted that in 1630: "In London, and within a mile, I ween There are jails or prisons full fifteen." Additionally, each county would have a: "... Gaole or Prison appointed for the restraint of liberty of such persons as for their offences are there unto

---

8. Mandeville, *An Enquiry into the Course of the Frequent Executions at Tyburn* 1725, p.47.
9. *The Gentleman's Magazine*, 1732, vol. 2, p.722.
10. Beattie, *Crime and the Courts in England 1660-1800*, pp.540-541.

comitted until they shall be delievered by course of law."[11] Major boroughs also had their own prisons. Thus, if an offender committed a crime in Derbyshire, he would normally be confined within the county jail (which was situated in the town of Derby), if in Derby itself, he would go to the separate municipal prison.

However, the function of early modern prisons was very different to their modern counterparts. Today, imprisonment is the main form of punishment for serious (and often not so serious) offences. However, this type of incarceral prison is little more than two centuries old, being the lineal descendant of a rash of institutions constructed, largely independently, around England, after 1775.[12] In the medieval period, most prisoners were suspected felons awaiting trial, convicts awaiting the implementation of their sentences and civil debtors. The notion of confining convicts as a punishment in its own right was largely absent. Only a few offences carried even short sentences of imprisonment, and only a small number of (usually upper class) men, often accused of treason, who had had their death sentences commuted, were likely to be incarcerated for any length of time. Other forms of punishment, capital, corporal and fiscal were preferred, if only for economic reasons.

In 1500, serious punishment was primarily based around execution and other forms of bodily chastisement, such as whipping, these often being bolstered by symbolic

---

11. Sir F. Bacon, *Cases of Treason*, London, 1641, p.35.
12. G. Fisher, "The Birth of the Prison Retold," *Yale Law Journal*, 1995, vol. 104, pp.1236-1252

acts of shaming, sometimes conducted in an almost theatrical manner. The apparent trend away from capital and corporal punishment towards imprisonment in the eighteenth century has been variously attributed to human progress and the enlightenment. Other observers, such as Michel Foucault and Michael Ignatieff, have explained its development as part of a larger attempt by an emergent bourgeois society to discipline and control by imposing its own definition of normative behaviour. However, the recent emphasis by such academics on a supposed radical transformation from an execution and corporal punishment based system to one premised on imprisonment, in the late eighteenth century, has been exaggerated. It overstates the continuity in 'traditional' society and the speed of transition to a 'modern' one. In particular, it ignores the precursors of the modern prison.

Although *most* prisons in early modern England existed to keep men rather than to punish them, this was not *invariably* the case. The first significant use of incarceral prisons, the Houses of Correction (Bridewells), institutions specifically aimed at punishment and reform, came in the sixteenth century. As such, they were, arguably, Europe's first true 'prisons' and not merely 'jails' for holding defendants before other disposals. As the era advanced, incarceration also became increasingly significant, though still not dominant, in the penal repertoire. Thus, short periods of imprisonment, usually only months, were used as punishments for several offences and a little used Elizabethan Statute authorized judges to imprison clergied offenders for up to a year.[13] As a result, there was a significant co-existence between the scaffold and the prison prior to the late 1700s, even though incarceration as a punishment *per se* remained relatively rare.

Prison Conditions

Conditions in early modern jails were very different to those in the 'new' prisons, with high walls and individual cells, that slowly developed after the late eighteenth-century reform campaigns associated with men such as John Howard, and the ending of transportation to the Americas. These often had an avowedly reformist ethos, and the lives of their inmates were consequently closely monitored.[14] By contrast, in early modern incarceral institutions, the presence of authority on a day-to-day basis was often minimal. Additionally, the endemic system of paying fees for almost every kind of service, privilege and even some punishments meant that jails were in constant danger of becoming exploitative hostels. Thus, even the master criminal Mary Frith had to provide garnish of two shillings, six pence to the other prisoners, when detained in the 'hole' at the Counter prison, in lieu of being stripped of her clothes.[15] So lucrative were prisons for their managers that, in 1696, the Newgate Keeper paid £3,500 for his office.

---

13. Beattie, *Crime and the Courts in England 1660-1800*, p.492.
14. Fisher, "The Birth of the Prison Retold," pp.1236-1252.
15. Anon, *The Life and Death of Mrs Mary Frith, Commonly Called Mal Cutpurse*, London, W.G. Ilberton, 1662, p.64.

When combined with a lack of close supervision and regulation of inmates, and prevalent notions about prisoners' traditional 'rights', this could produce strange results. Thus, Joan Crumpton, the female keeper of Shrewsbury County Jail in 1716, complained that her inmates: "Frequently send for strong liquors out of the town into the gaol, sitt up late, gett drunk, and very often insult and abuse the said gaoler and her servants, and disturb other prisoners." Additionally, in some rooms they supplied their own beds, declining to pay for the prison issue ones, and even refused the jailer admittance to other chambers "pretending they have a right so to doe". Unsurprisingly, in these circumstances, inmates also freely admitted that exposure to their fellow prisoners could be one of the sorest trials of incarceration. In 1655, Edmund Gayton noted "our fellow prisoners lie heaviest upon us, and are to a new commoner worse than flies to a sore leg". Nevertheless, they also provided moral support and company; John Earle recorded a "great deal of good fellowship" amongst his incarcerated colleagues in 1629.[16]

Early modern felons would be supplied with a basic allowance of bread each day, a penny loaf being normal. Even in the 1770s, it was never more than two pence worth. The bread allowance was the only food supplied to the prisoners at public expense. Not surprisingly, it was of great importance to the inmates. However, bakers contracted to supply the bread might attempt to cut corners to maximise

---

16. R. Evans, *The Fabrication of virtue: English prison architecture, 1750-1840*, Cambridge, CUP, 1982, pp.22-23 and p.33.

their profits (and perhaps those of the wardens). Thus, in 1682, Derbyshire JPs sitting at county sessions received a petition from inmates at Derby jail. In it, they complained that Thomas Mee, the court appointed prison baker, produced bread that was: "... not soe wholesome and serviceable as that which former Bakers have delivered to them to their great injury, And therefore prayed that another Baker might be employed by this Court to joyne with the said Thomas Mee in bakeing of their bread for the future." Recognising its importance to the prisoners, the JPs agreed, and ordered that John Piggin take turns with Mee in supplying their bread.

Ironically, the bread allowance was not given to debtors, who were, in this regard, at a disadvantage compared to murderers and highwaymen. Nor was it given to inmates of the Houses of Correction, who were supposed to work for their livings at ascribed tasks.[17] As a result, in the 1590s, Edward Hext strongly urged that those in ordinary jails, where six pence a week was normally provided at public expense for the maintenance of inmates, also be made to work.[18] However, even prisoners found it hard to live by such bread alone. Those who could afford it had food and clothing sent in to them from outside, or purchased such items from the keeper at inflated prices, along with spirits, candles, and even water. Jailers also charged for many other

---

17.　J. Howard, *The State of the Prisons* (1st pub. 1777), London, Everyman edn., J.M. Dent, 1929, pp.2-3.
18.　E. Hext, "Letter written by Edward Hext, a Somerset JP, to Lord Burghley on September 25, 1596," in *Tudor Economic Documents*, vol. 2, R.H. Tawney and E. Power (Eds.), London, Longmans, 1951, p.342.

'privileges'. However, before being too hard on the wardens of England's early modern jails, it should be remembered that this exploitation was a common feature in the administration of many of the era's institutions. Thus, in 1632, the appropriately named Dr Hilkiah Crooke, the Master of the Bethlem lunatic asylum in London, was investigated after complaints were made to the hospital's governors that funds were finding their way into his pocket. He was dismissed, and accounting procedures improved.[19] In the absence of personal means or helpful friends outside, prisoners might have to beg to survive. According to a visiting Swiss medical student, Thomas Platter, writing in 1599, London prisoners (probably debtors in this case) would beg: "... alms of the passers by, and sometimes they collect so much by their begging that they can purchase their freedom."[20] The begging grate was so vital that in 1698 the inmates of Ludgate prison successfully petitioned the Mayor of London to be allowed to knock a second one into the prison walls so that they could solicit alms more effectively. Where there was no grate, an ordinary window might be pressed into service. At Exeter Southgate jail, a boot hung on a string was left dangling from an upper storey window to receive offerings. In some cases, fettered prisoners were even released into adjacent streets with a bowl or shackled to the prison walls.[21] Also indicative of the lack of state

---

19. R. Porter, "Bethlem/Bedlam: methods of madness?" *History Today*, 1997, vol. 47, issue 10, p.41.
20. T. Platter and H. Busino, *Journals of two travellers in Elizabethan and early Stuart England*, P. Razzell (Ed.), London, Caliban, 1995, p.38.
21. Evans, *The Fabrication of virtue*, p.28.

provision, when a collection that was normally made at the Southwark fair for debtors in the Marshalsea prison was cancelled, in 1743, due to the duration of the fair being reduced to three days, the disappointed inmates were so enraged that they gathered stones and threw them: "... over the Prison-wall upon the Bowling-Green, whereby a Child was kill'd in a Woman's Arms, and several People wounded and bruised."[22]

Prison conditions were always very harsh. In 1643, prisoners in the numerous London prisons, especially those in Newgate, and the Marshalsea, complained about their "cruell and implacable Jaylors, being for the most part, men of austere and inhumane conditions, such as are fitter to keepe wild Beasts in cages". These men apparently possessed "greedy humours with money, wine and the like presents".[23] According to an inmate, even in 1724, Newgate prison was paved with stone so that prisoners who could not afford beds lay on the floor and "endured great misery and hardship". Newgate was London's most important prison, holding a mixture of criminals awaiting trial or sentence, debtors, and even the occasional traitor. Founded in 1188, it had been re-edified in 1422 and again at the end of the sixteenth century. Unfortunately, it was burned down in the Great Fire of 1666, subsequent rebuilding being completed in 1672. Despite an impressive facade, its interior was squalid. The cells were dark and damp, the prison

---

22. *The Gentleman's Magazine*, 1743, vol. 13, p.495.
23. Anon, *The humble Remonstrance and Complaint of Many thousands of poore distressed Prisoners in the prisones in and about the Citie of London*, London, John Gibson, 1643, pp.5-6.

poorly ventilated and its smell quite noxious. As a result, Letitia Wigington, awaiting execution there in 1681, for killing her 11 year old female apprentice, declared: "... thrice welcome is that Rope which is to put a period to all my miseries and oppressions which have been very numerous and great, for I have been kept a prisoner now eight months, where I have lain upon the hard boards having nothing but bread and water, and no more than a penny-loaf a day neither; and my flesh black and blew with lying upon the boards for want of a bed."[24]

Gaol fever, a form of typhus brought about by a combination of overcrowding, poor sanitation and nutrition appears to have been widespread. It was probably behind the 'Black Assize' held at Oxford in 1577, in which the judges, jurors, witnesses and spectators present in court were killed by a: "... pestilent savour, whether arising from the noisome smell of the prisoners, or from the damp of the ground, is uncertain; but all that were present, within 40 hours died, except the prisoners." Presumably, the accused were spared because they had developed a degree of immunity from prolonged exposure. Amongst the dead were Lord Chief Baron Robert Bell, Robert De Olie, and Sir William Babington, the High Sheriff of Oxfordshire. Over 150 years later, gaol fever may have been responsible for the deaths of Lord Chief Baron Pengelly and Sir James Shepherd, along with several other court officers, during the Lent assizes at Blandford on the Western Circuit. The

---

24. L. Wigington, *The Confession and execution of Letitia Wigington of Ratclif ...*, London, Langley Curtiss, 1684, p.3.

disease was thought to have emanated from the "stench of some prisoners brought from Ilchester gaol". There were further large scale deaths in 1750, amongst those attending trials at the Old Bailey, prompting a doctor to urge that all houses of confinement be kept as "airy and clean" as possible. As a result, Newgate was washed with vinegar, as were its prisoners, while the numbers being sent for trial were also limited to 15 at a time for that period.[25] However, even in the 1770s, John Howard was convinced that more prisoners died from disease than were executed in England.[26]

There was little deliberate segregation within prisons. Such separation as did occur was often the product of financial resources. Prisoners with means could afford to rent superior accommodation. Thus, Newgate had a whole wing for paying prisoners at different levels of comfort and expense. In provincial prisons less developed arrangements existed for wealthier inmates. At Derby jail, prisoners who could afford the fees boarded in the jailer's own house. However, prices were always extortionate. In 1643, Metropolitan prisoners complained about the "extraordinary rent of our chambers in prison surpassing all the usury and brokerage in the world".[27] Most prisons had a 'dungeon', or 'hold', which provided both the most basic accommodation for felons and also enhanced security where necessary. The conditions there were normally especially

---

25. *The Gentleman's Magazine*, 1750, vol. 20, p.235.
26. J. Howard, *The State of the Prisons in England and Wales* (1st pub. 1777), London, Everyman edn., J.M. Dent, 1929, p.2.
27. Anon, *The humble Remonstrance*, pp.5-6.

bad. At his execution in 1664, Colonel Turner could not resist the temptation to demand changes at Newgate, and, in particular, to the 'Hole' where those awaiting execution were held: "... it is a most fearfull bad, deplorable, place, Hell it self in Comparison cannot be such a place, there is neither Bench, stool nor stick for any person there, they lye like swine upon the ground one upon another howling and roaring, it was more terrible to me than this Death." He asked that the Hole be provided with boards so that condemned men did not have to lie upon the ground. This request prompted an immediate reply from the keeper of Newgate prison, one Jackson, who was present at the scaffold, and who noted that in the past even basic furnishings there had been abused: "Seventeen out of nineteen made their escapes out of the Hole, they having only a Form there."[28]

Substantial reform did not come prior to 1750. Even in the 1770s, Howard claimed to have witnessed numerous prison inmates who were half starved. In many jails, and in most Bridewells, there was still no allowance of bedding or straw for prisoners to sleep on, so that many still slept on the bare floor or rags. Some inmates were quite evidently insane. At Knaresboro prison, Howard found an earth floor, no fire and an open sewer from the town running through the premises, which swarmed with rats. At Plymouth jail, he discovered that the 'clink' was only 15 feet by eight feet three inches and about six feet high, with a wicket in the door seven inches by five to admit light and air. To this

28. Anon, *The Speech and Deportment of Colonel James Turner*, pp.14-15.

"three men, who were confined near two months under sentence for transportation, came by turns for breath".[29]

Nevertheless, prisons were not entirely unregulated. In theory, they were subject to periodic inspection by the authorities, especially the sheriff and JPs. Indeed, on one occasion, when the authorities investigated George Fox's living conditions they found them so bad that they summoned the jailers into the dungeon, and required them to find sureties for their good behaviour. The under-jailer, who had been a particularly "cruel fellow, they put into the dungeon with me". However, such inspections were often fairly cursory. John Howard claimed that magistrates were sometimes dissuaded from investigating properly by prison wardens who "artfully dropped a hint" that there was fever in the prison. Even so, it is also mistaken to suggest that prior to Howard's work there was little high level knowledge or concern about the conditions prevalent in the country's prisons. The Society for the Promotion of Christian Knowledge (SPCK) had worked for prison reform since its foundation by the Reverend Thomas Bray in 1699. Subsequently, James Edward Oglethorpe persuaded the House of Commons to establish a Gaols Committee and to launch a series of inquiries into prison conditions. He recruited and chaired the meetings of a group of fellow MPs that carried out investigations between 1728 and 1737 (albeit with an emphasis on debtors). The committee produced three reports that exposed the endemic overcrowding, brutality and extortion found in the nation's prisons.

---

29. Howard, *The State of the Prisons*, p.222.

However, both the SPCK and Oglethorpe met only limited success in producing long lasting reforms, as John Howard subsequently found. His exposure (as High Sheriff) to the squalor of his local county prison, Bedford jail, prompted him to travel around England to establish whether it was typical of the country's prisons. He concluded that many were even worse. Largely as a result of the evidence that he provided, Parliament passed the 1774 Gaol Act, which abolished jailers' fees and suggested improvements to prison hygiene. Although some of its provisions were ignored, reform was underway.

As the 1774 Act indicates, during the early modern period, even if an inmate was acquitted and had not purchased special privileges it was axiomatic that a: "Prisoner of sufficent ability shall bear his own charges, and of them that shall be appointed to guard him to the gaol."[30] Thus, after the Reverend Hawkins was acquitted at the Lent assizes at Aylesbury, following his prosecution pursuant to a vicious conspiracy to 'frame' him, he asked that he might be discharged without paying his fees because he was "very poor". Sir Mathew Hale, the Lord Chief Baron presiding over the trial, answered that it was beyond his power to order this, as he: "... could not give away other people's rights: if they [the jailers] would not remit their fees, he must pay them."[31] Of course, if the acquitted inmate was

---

30. H. Townshend, *Notes of the Office of a Justice of Peace 1661-3*, R.D. Hunt (Ed.), Worcester, Worcestershire Historical Society, 1967, p.110.
31. Rayner and Crook, *The Complete Newgate Calendar*, vol. I, pp.209-214, see also N. Bernard, Dean of Ardagh, *The Case of John Atherton, Bishop of Waterford in Ireland*, London, Luke Stokoe, 1710, p.44.

hopelessly impoverished, it might be cheaper for the court or jailer to release them forthwith, rather than continue to waste resources, however meagre. Thus, in the case of a man acquitted at the Old Bailey in 1693 of stealing a magpie, the trial judge observed that: "...because you are a poor man, the court has considered of your Condition, and acquitted you of the Fees."[32] Even this might leave court fees to be paid. In 1680, Francis Gibson, a prisoner in Derby jail, petitioned the JPs at the quarter sessions held in the city on October 5, to order his release. In his pitiful appeal, he noted that he had been tried, convicted and pardoned at the assizes held in Derby weeks earlier. Although he had not paid all of his prison fees, the jailer was happy for him to be released immediately as he "knows my powverty soe well ... he saith he will forgive my fees which are deu to him". This still left the court fees to be paid, so that he remained confined at the "Cunteries charge and my own Reuin by the Clarke of the assizes". Although he had been in custody for 80 weeks, Gibson stressed that he had not received: "A grote from any Relation I Have in the world; nether have I any friends or Relations to help mee in the least if I was shure to perish." (The petition was granted.) It was this facet of the system that first prompted John Howard into action. As Sheriff of Bedfordshire, in the 1770s, he saw men who had been found not guilty returned to jail until they payed "sundry fees to the gaoler, the clerk of assize, etc." It was only after 1774 that acquitted prisoners were excused from paying such fees, the statute providing that they be immediately set at

---

32. Anon, *The Tryal of John Foster*, London, 1693, p.2.

liberty in open court.[33]

Prison Security

Security in the country's prisons and jails was often poor, with escapes regularly reported. Thus, in December 1556, Gregorie Carpenter, a French blacksmith: "... was arraigned for making counterfeite keys, wherewith to have opened the lockes of Newgate, to have slayne the keeper, and set forth the prisoners." Despite having been served with notice about Carpenter's danger, the authorities still failed to take sufficient care of their prisoner. In court, he tried to stab a co-defendant who had turned Queen's evidence. The Keeper of Newgate, who had custody of Carpenter while he was going to court (a jailer's customary responsibility), was arraigned for failing to search the prisoner properly, overlooking the concealed blade and leaving his hands unbound.[34] Such incidents continued throughout the period. In the seventeenth century, the thief Richard Preece was committed to Shrewsbury jail where he paid a: "... silly boy to procure him instruments to breake prison. The boy brought to him a bar of iron and a broken broome hooke, and with these he pulled out severall stones, and made through the stone wall of the dungeon, and soe escaped." Preece disappeared but the simple lad who had provided

33. Howard, *The State of the Prisons*, pp.14-15.
34. J. Stow, *The Annales of England*, London, Ralfe Nebery, 1592, p.1066.

the escape tools was executed.[35] Tom Cox, caught after a robbery in Somerset and confined to Ilchester jail, broke into the keeper's apartment there, while the latter slept off a drinking bout, and stole the prison keys, a horse and a silver tankard before escaping.[36] In 1736, Daniel Malden escaped the night before his execution was due, after he: "... took up a Board and got out of his Cell, and made his Escape from Newgate, by breaking an Hole into an Empty house adjoining to the prison." The same journal also reported that one Henry Fisher, a murderer, who had escaped from the same prison several years earlier, had recently been seen in Leghorn.[37] The Hallam brothers attempted to escape from Lincoln jail in classic style: "... by sawing off their Fetters with a Case Knife notch'd like a saw, and digging thro' the Wall with a large Nail."[38] More ambitious schemes of mass escape were also attempted, though these were usually less successful. In 1697, John Shorter, a highwayman incarcerated in Newgate, unavailingly conspired with others to revolt, planning to seize the prison officers' blunderbusses in the process. One of the prisoners, a former blacksmith, would remove the others' fetters, and the seized turnkeys would be bound and held in the 'dungeon', any who resisted having their throats cut. Once out, the escapees planned to steal horses on the highways around London and

---

35. R. Gough, *The History of Myddle*, D. Hey (Ed.), Penguin 1981, (originally written 1701), p.133.
36. J.L Rayner and G.T. Crook (Eds.), *The Complete Newgate Calendar* (Vols. 1-5), London. Privately printed for the Navarre Society, 1926, vol.II, p.71.
37. *The Gentleman's Magazine*, 1736, vol. 6, p.291.
38. *The Gentleman's Magazine*, 1733, vol. 3, p.154.

ride off.[39] Similarly, in 1743, the felons held in Norwich Castle jail seized the turnkeys, placing them in the prison's dungeon, and then bored a hole in the prison walls. The would-be escapees also managed to remove their leg irons, throwing them at members of the public. However, the jailer, aware of what was afoot, had summoned assistance and wounded the felons who tried to escape through the improvised hole. The prisoners were "glad to retire, and they were all soon secured".[40]

As these cases suggest, an absence of perimeter and internal security in a prison was partially remedied by: "Loading prisoners with heavy irons which make their walking, and even lying down to sleep, difficult and painful." Even women might be placed in leg irons.[41] The dangerous highwayman, William Nevison, having been captured and committed to Leicester jail was: "... so narrowly watched, and strongly ironed, that he could scarce stir."[42] Nevertheless, prison turnkeys could be vulnerable when desperate men were unsupervised. In 1690, Tom Kelsey, awaiting trial in Newgate, and expecting execution, resolved to do all the mischief he could before his death. He achieved this aim by stabbing to death one of the turnkeys. For this, he was hanged and then briefly gibbeted outside

39. Rayner and Crook, *The Complete Newgate Calendar*, vol. II, pp.107-108.
40. *The Gentleman's Magazine*, 1743, vol. 13, p.49.
41. Howard, *The State of the Prisons*, p.12.
42. C. Johnson, *A General History of the Lives and Adventures of the Most Famous Highwaymen, Murderers, Street-Robbers*, London: J. Janeway, 1734, p.104.

the prison as a warning to other inmates.[43]

Few of these problems were unique to English jails, and most were common throughout Europe. Pedro de Leon, a Jesuit chaplain to the huge royal prison at Seville provided a detailed account of jail life there in his *Compendio*. There was widespread disease as well as overcrowding and squalor for all but the rich. As in England, the prison was not normally a punishment in its own right, but used to hold criminals pending another disposal. Prisoners who could not pay for their board might literally starve to death, prompting monks and beggars to plead for alms on their behalf in the streets. However, for the jailers, and like their English counterparts, the prison was a lucrative business. Thus, the assistant warden had special cells and beds that he could rent out and prisoners were forced to buy their food and drink at extortionate prices from the prison's own stores and taverns. The warden sold the office of deputies to the highest bidders. As in England, some inmates became trustees or 'Porteros', being given special privileges in exchange for administrative duties within the prison. They were even given keys so they could distribute new prisoners among the cells. For this service they would charge each one four reales, keeping half for themselves and giving the rest to the inmates already in the designated cell, in a ritual that appears to have been very similar to English 'garnish'.[44] Additionally, it must be remembered that the standards of

43. C. Johnson, *A General History of the Lives and Adventures of the Most Famous Highwaymen*, p.326.
44. M.E. Perry, *Crime and Society in Early Modern Seville*, Hanover (N.H.), University of New England Press, 1980, pp.76-79.

the era were low. Not everyone was appalled by English prison conditions. In the 1630s, the translator of a Spanish book on crime, which referred to the "miseries which are endured in prison", added a footnote that: "The Author would not have beene so vehement, had he been in one of our English prisons, which for the most part are made rather places of ease and delight than punishment."[45]

Bridewells

At the heart of Foucault's influential analysis of social control is the notion that, in the middle ages and early modern period, punishment was, for the most part, a 'spectacle'. By contrast, from the later eighteenth century onwards, economic and attendant social changes meant that it was necessary for a new bourgeois ruling class to develop a more systematic form of control over individuals, with an emphasis on 'reform' rather than simple physical chastisement.[46] Unfortunately, in the English context at least, such an analysis appears unsatisfactory. In particular, it fails to take into account the development of institutional Houses of Correction, the first in Europe, starting with the London Bridewell (which gave its name to the type) in the 1550s. Perhaps significantly, in the mid-1570s, Bethlem, the London lunatic asylum, was placed under joint governance

---

45. W.M., *The Sonne of the Rogue, or the Politicke Theefe*, London, 1638, p.1.
46. M. Foucault, *Discipline and Punish: The Birth of the Prison*, Penguin, Harmondsworth, 1979, pp.305-308.

with Bridewell, sharing a president, treasurer and governing body. (The joint system lasted until at least 1619, when its Master, Dr Hilkiah Crooke, urged that Bethlem be made independent.)[47] Originally, Bridewells had a far more 'reformist' ethos than the jails, serving effectively as workhouses for vagrants.

Bridewell Palace, situated near the City on the western bank of the Fleet River, had been built during the reign of Henry VIII (it was rebuilt after being destroyed in the Great Fire of 1666), being mainly used to lodge foreign dignitaries. As one inmate wryly noted, it was "formerly a Palace for the best".[48] In 1555, it was given over to the relief of the poor, and became the first 'House of Correction'. The original purpose of such establishments was to remove beggars and vagrants from circulation, especially in urban areas. It was hoped that a mixture of enforced labour and punishment would then reform the lazy and immoral. By 1562, the London Bridewell had been followed by one at Oxford and in 1576 JPs were required to build houses of correction throughout England. As a result, numerous Bridewells were opened in cities and towns in the following decades. Another wave of Bridewells were established during the straitened 1690s, such as that at Bristol in 1696. It was followed by a dozen more before 1712. Whenever they were opened, some Bridewells were purpose built, others, like the original, converted buildings. Thus, in Norwich, a large

---

47. Porter, "Bethlem/Bedlam: methods of madness?" p.41.
48. W. Fuller, *Mr William Fuller's Trip to Bridewell: With A True Account of his Barbarous Usage in the Pillory*, London, 1703, p.9.

former merchant's house was converted into a Bridewell. Similarly, the Guildhall in Lavenham ultimately became the Suffolk Bridewell, operating as such until replaced in 1787. Such improvised buildings were not ideal. Although, at Lavenham, unruly offenders were held in the cellar of the building, security was poor and became worse as time progressed, alarming local both residents and the authorities. By 1784, it was so out of repair that "prisoners escaped through the walls" and magistrates were forced to send thumb-screws to secure the prisoners.[49]

The Governor or Master of a House of Correction was normally appointed by the JPs, sitting at quarter sessions, and was paid from the county rate. He was required to receive all rogues sent by county magistrates (accompanied by an appropriate *mittimus*) and ensure that they did not escape, his task being the "keeping, correcting, and setting to worke of Rogues, Vagabonds, sturdy beggars, and other idle and disorderly persons". Because Bridewells were originally established to provide work, magistrates had to ensure that they were equipped with "mills, tures, cards" and other tools so that inmates could be usefully employed. This was vital, as, during their incarceration, and unlike felons, they were to be "in no sort chargeable to the Country for any allowance".[50] Their very sustenance was (theoretically) contingent on work being available, as there was no free bread allowance. A typical *mittimus* required

---

49. A. Betterton, "The Guildhall, Lavenham (Suffolk, England)," *History Today*, 1995, vol. 45, issue 1, pp.22-26.
50. W. Sheppard, *The Whole Office of the County Justice of Peace*, first edn., London, 1641, pp.244-247.

that: "... during all the time, he [an inmate] shall continue with you, that you hold him to work, and labour." It enjoined that he only be given food according to his efforts.[51] Prisoners were put to a wide variety of individual and group tasks, which ranged from cleaning drains to spinning. To encourage inmates in their work, the Master could punish them as he saw cause by "putting on Fetters, or Gives upon them, and by a moderate whipping of them".[52] Additionally, prostitutes and vagrants were often whipped on arrival, as an inherent part of their punishment, with twelve lashes for adults and six for juveniles being common. Thus, Thomas Platter, from Basle, noted in 1599 that when the Metropolitan authorities came across a case of prostitution they punished the man with imprisonment and fine: "The woman is taken to Bridewell, the King's palace, situated near the river, where the executioner scourges her naked before the populace."

Felons were rarely admitted to Bridewells until the eighteenth century (by which time they were often as bad as the prisons).[53] However, an important exception to this general pattern was London, where a practice developed in the seventeenth century of decanting those guilty of thefts of small to medium value from the normal criminal justice system, centred on the Old Bailey, to the Bridewell, by

---

51. H. Twyford, T. Dring and F. Place, *Justice Restored: Or a Guide For His Majestie's Justices of Peace*, 2nd edn. London, T. Roycroft, 1660, p.5.
52. Sheppard, *The Whole Office of the County Justice of Peace*, first edn., London, 1641, pp.244-247.
53. P. Spierenburg, *The Prison Experience: Disciplinary Institutions and their Inmates in Early Modern Europe*, London, Rutgers University Press, 1991, p.264.

treating them as vagrants. As a result, William Fuller, an educated prisoner, witnessed a wide range of offenders in the London Bridewell in the early 1700s. In his cell were a 77-year-old man, committed for sleeping with prostitutes, an apprentice who had quarrelled with his master, while "The rest were Boys, all Thieves and Pick-pockets". Like Fuller, the pickpockets were all whipped and set to labour. The entrepreneurial nature of all English prisons (whether Bridewells or jails) meant that he was able to console himself with drink, having obtained half a quartern of brandy. He also arranged to have veal cutlets for his supper, being permitted to "eat what I pleas'd paying for it my self". Nevertheless, although Fuller could afford good food, he lacked the money to "Bribe the Beedles, as Thieves and Pick-pockets [could], so they did me all the spight they could". Additionally, he still had to face his whipping. After being secured by his wrists he was struck 39 times by a scourge with a dozen strings "notted at the end". Although he had given his flagellant half a crown in advance, to moderate the severity of the beating, Fuller could not forbear from "bawling". At the end, he was released and watched the seven pickpockets who were incarcerated with him receive the same treatment. Afterwards, he was set to work beating hemp, with a 12lb 'beatle'. This lasted from 6 a.m. to 6 p.m. with a break for lunch. By this period, the London Bridewell was also being used for some remand prisoners including a: "Thief, that was carried thence next morning to Newgate, in order to be Try'd the next Sessions for his Life."[54] Perhaps because of the presence of these mainstream criminals and remand prisoners, irons were frequently worn.

Despite their reformist origins, Bridewells were probably always fairly grim institutions. They deteriorated even further after 1660. Corruption was widespread. Women were only properly separated from male prisoners in the nineteenth century. In earlier periods, some governors of the London Bridewell had effectively forced female inmates into providing sexual services, almost turning the prison into a brothel.[55] Fuller was convinced that most thieves sent there were not brought before a JP if they could "procure a Guinea for a bribe". Taskmasters, supervising the compulsory work, were often brutal, regularly striking inmates and threatening "beat hard, lift up your Beatles, or I'll noint you".[56] Cesar de Saussure, visiting the Bridewell near Fleet Street (by the 1720s there were two in the London area) also witnessed "Captain whip 'em", the prison's Inspector, encourage inmates of both sexes who were beating flax to greater efforts by the judicious use of a stout cane.[57] Their hard labour meant that the Bridewells were certainly not an easy option. According to the Elizabethan Somerset JP, Edward Hext: "I sent dyvers wandrynge

---

54. Fuller, *Mr William Fuller's Trip to Bridewell*, pp.9-14.
55. Morris, N. and Rothman, D.J. (Eds.), *The Oxford History of the Prison*, Oxford, OUP, 1995, p.329
56. Fuller, *Mr William Fuller's Trip to Bridewell*, pp.14-24.
57. M. Van Muyden (Trans.) and (Ed.), *A foreign View of England in the reigns of George I and George II; The letters of Monsieur Cesar de Saussure, to his Family*, London, John Murray, 1902, pp.299-300.

suspycous persons to the house of Correction, and all in general would beseche me with bytter teares to send them rather to the gayle, and denyinge yt them, some confessed felonyes unto me by which they hazarded their lyves, to thend they would not be sent to the house of correction where they shold by ynforced to worke."[58] However, the food provided at the Bridewells may have been better than that found in prisons, if only to fuel the forced work. At the start of the eighteenth century, the mid-day "House-Allowance" consisted of a piece of bread, six ounces of poor quality beef and some milk-porridge.[59] Despite the strict discipline, some inmates could not abandon their former habits. Thus, shortly after foundation, in June 1556, there was a "yonge man hangged within Brydewelle for robery within the sayd howse".[60]

The Bridewells' original work ethos started to wane at the end of the seventeenth century, partly because of changes in the general mode of poor relief. Indeed, it is difficult to see how sufficient provision could ever have been made for constructive work for inmates in the cramped surroundings of many improvised houses of correction. Whatever the earlier situation, from the late 1600s, the emphasis on labour was increasingly abandoned. Instead, deserving individuals were given out-relief, or (after 1722) a place in a proper workhouse. By 1751, Henry Fielding could complain that Bridewells were "at present, in general,

---

58. Hext, "Letter written by Edward Hext," p.340.
59. Fuller, *Mr William Fuller's Trip to Bridewell*, pp.14-24.
60. J. Gough Nichols (Ed.), *Chronicle of the Grey Friars of London*, London, Camden Society, 1852, p.96.

no other than schools of vice". The power of whipping inmates, which a Jacobean Act had vested in the governor, was seldom used, and the compulsory labour was laughable: "Insomuch, that they must be very lazy persons indeed who can esteem the labour imposed in any of these houses as a punishment." In some, such as that at Middlesex, there was no provision made for labour at all. One alleged reason for this was that the advent of hardened felons to such institutions meant it was not safe to entrust them with heavy or sharp tools that could be converted into weapons.[61] In the 1770s, John Howard could record that there were: "... few bridewells in which any work is done, or can be done. The prisoners have neither tools, nor materials of any kind: but spend their time in sloth, profaness and debauchery."[62]

Bridewells were quickly followed by the (independent) foundation of similar establishments in Holland and other parts of Northern Europe.[63] Thus, Henri Misson compared them to the Dutch rasphouses, which served a similar purpose.[64] Nor was the use of brutal 'encouragement' to labour unique to England. In the early 1680s, Jack Bird, a deserter from the English army in the low countries, and a future highwayman, stole a piece of silk from a stall in Amsterdam, for which he was arrested and sentenced by a

---

61. H. Fielding, *An Enquiry into the causes of the Late Increase of Robbers*, London, 1751, Preface, p.63.
62. Howard, *The State of the Prisons*, p.1.
63. Spierenburg, *The Prison Experience*, pp.2-8.
64. M. Misson, *Memoirs and Observations in his Travels over England*, M. Ozell (Trans.), London, 1719, p.22.

magistrate to 12 months hard labour in the rasp-house. Appropriately, this included rasping logwood. Unaccustomed to strenuous work, he fainted, for which offence his taskmasters allegedly chained him to the bottom of a dry cistern and then flooded it, so that he was obliged to pump for his life for an hour. (Though it has been strongly argued that this oft-repeated story was apocryphal.)[65] Similarly, in Frankfurt, in the 1670s, Philipp Jacob Spener established a workhouse that stressed discipline and labour. Between 1700 and 1704, the city council of the Protestant German city of Leipzig, alarmed by an apparent growth in the numbers of urban poor and their dissolute lifestyles, also constructed a combined poor house, orphanage, lunatic asylum, and penitentiary named St George. It accommodated 100 inmates within a year and over 200 by the 1720s.[66]

Fiscal, Shaming and Corporal Punishments

Those convicted of any offence below felony were likely to be fined or suffer some form of corporal or shaming punishment. Thus, in the Elizabethan era, William Harrison noted that: "Rogues and vagabonds are often stocked and whipped; scolds are ducked upon cucking-stools in the

---

65. C. Johnson, *A General History of the Lives and Adventures of the Most Famous Highwaymen, Murderers, Street-Robbers*, London: J. Janeway, 1734, p.127.

66. T. Kevorkian, "The Rise of the Poor, Weak, and Wicked: Poor Care, Punishment, Religion, and Patriarchy in Leipzig 1700-1730," *Journal of Social History*, 2000, vol. 34, no. 1, p.163.

water". The punishment for petty larceny (technically a felony) also usually entailed being whipped, at the cart's tail or a post. Generally, attitudes to the body of an offender changed between 1500 and 1750, albeit only slowly and incompletely. Judges and magistrates became increasingly reluctant not only to impose death sentences but also penalties involving physical chastisement and mutilation. These were sometimes replaced by fiscal penalties or short periods of imprisonment. Not everyone welcomed the developing limitations on corporal punishment. In the 1690s Bohun argued that it was "a great pity the power of inflicting corporal punishment instead of Pecuniary, should not be extended further than it is". Really poor people were not able to pay the small fines imposed for minor offences, such as the 12 pence penalty for absence from church, and, as a result, they often went unpunished. Yet frequently, he considered, such small misdemeanours, if left unchecked, were the precursors of more serious crimes.[67] However, even in 1750, corporal and shaming punishments remained a vital part of the penal repertoire, and would be so for decades to come.

Shame via public exposure was an essential component of many punishments, including execution. Indeed, fines and incarceration apart, it was present in nearly all of them. For some minor matters it might be the only real punishment. In face-to-face communities, where most people knew each other, it could be highly effective. It promoted deterrence and, in some cases, especially in urban

---

67. E. Bohun, *The Justice of Peace His Calling and Qualifications*, London, 1693, p.53.

environments, by identifying criminals alerted others to the dangers posed by some individuals: "... infamy is a part of the sentence against malefactors, which the Law intends, as is evident by those, which are branded for rogues, that they may be known; or put into the stocks, that they may be looked upon."[68] Some localised shaming punishments appear to have had limited legal authority. Thus, in Newcastle, in the 1650s, drunkards might be forced to walk through the streets wearing a beer barrel like a cloak, with just their heads and arms exposed, though the normal statutory penalty was to be fined or placed in the stocks for five hours.[69] Such punishments were very widespread throughout Europe. Thus, in the separate (to England) legal jurisdiction of the Isle of Man, malicious slander was dealt with by making the defamatory individual stand in the market-place, on a special scaffold, with their tongue in a noose made of leather, called: "... a bridle, and having been thus exposed to the view of the people for some time, on the taking off this machine they are obliged to say three times, *Tongue thou hast lyed."* As well as being a personally humiliating experience, such exposure meant that future lies from the same source would gain little credit.[70] As this illustration suggests, a prerequisite for the effectiveness of shaming punishments was a relatively static and stable community where reputation was a vital commodity. For

68. G. Herbert, *A Priest to the Temple*, London, T. Garthwait, 1652, p.42.
69. R. Gardner, *England's Grievance Discovered in Relation to the Coal-Trade*, London, 1655, pp.110-111.
70. G. Waldron, *A description of the Isle of Man*, (1731) Douglas, Manx Society Publications, vol. 11, 1859, pp.40-46.

early modern England's growing number of transients, their value was greatly reduced.

Some of these punishments were associated with a specific gender. Thus, the cucking-stool had ancient roots, allowing the immersion in water of those punished. However, by the early modern period it was used almost exclusively for females. Typically, a leet court could note that their local stool, placed over a drainage ditch, was broken: "And we thincke it verie fitt there should be a new one forthwith made to punishe the manifold number of scoldinge woemen that be in this Towne & other evill livinge women."[71] Similarly, as late as 1688, the inhabitants of Deptford were ordered to provide a cucking-stool to punish "idle, lewd and disorderly scolding women". In particular, it was hoped that it would deal with the many "ill disposed contentious and brawling" females found in Deptford and Greenwich, who were disturbing their neighbours.[72] Henri Misson, who visited England in the late 1690s, left a detailed description of the operation of such a device:

"They fasten an arm chair to the end of two beams, twelve or fifteen feet long, and parallel to each other, so that these two pieces of wood, with their two ends, embrace the chair, which hangs between them upon a sort of axle, by which means it plays freely, and always

71. F.J.C. Hearnshaw, *Court Leet Records, vol. 1, part III, 1603-1624*, Southampton, Southampton Record Society Publications, 1907, p.381.
72. E. Melling (Ed.), *Crime and Punishment, Kentish Sources VI*, Maidstone, Kent County Council, 1969, p.193

remains in the natural horizontal position in which the chair should be, that a person may sit conveniently in it, whether you raise it or let it down. They set up a post on the bank of a pond or river, and over this post they lay, almost in equilibrio, the two pieces of wood, at one end of which the chair hangs just over the water. They place the woman in this chair, and so plunge her into the water, as often as the sentence directs, in order to cool her immoderate heat."[73]

The 'scold's bridle' (or 'branks') was also primarily a female punishment. It was an iron cage designed to cover the scold's head, and contained a flange of iron that was placed in the woman's mouth over the tongue. This made any attempt to speak - the very fault that had led to her punishment - acutely painful. Thus, in 1655, Ralph Gardiner witnessed one Anne Bridlestone being led through the streets of Newcastle-on-Tyne by a town officer holding a rope: "... fastened to an engine called the branks, which is like a crown, being of iron, which was musled over the head and face, with a great gag or tongue of iron forced into her mouth, which forced blood out; and that is the punishment which magistrates do inflict upon chiding and scolding women; and he hath often seen the like done to others." Nevertheless, the punishment was rare and of dubious legality in England; Ralph Gardiner described it as part of his assault on Newcastle's Magistrates and Corporation. It differed from the normal national situation in which scolds

---

73. Misson, *Memoirs and Observations of his Travels over England*, p.65

were "duckt over head and ears into the water in a Ducking-stool".[74]

The pillory and stocks were used for both sexes, though far more men than women were punished in them. They both involved detention in a public place, the first by the wrists and neck and the second by the ankles. As Henri Misson noted in the 1690s, the pillory was used, *inter alia*, for cheats, imposters, those who libelled the Crown and government, gave false testimony or blasphemed in public.[75] Such people often attracted popular hostility, something that became an inherent part of the punishment. It was normal to be exposed publicly on several (usually three) occasions, this being, commonly, for two hours at a time. Thus, in Shropshire, a wastrel named Clarke, who had moved from Quakerism to Catholicism as opportunity presented, having been made excessively confident by the accession of a co-religionist (James II), publicly announced in 1685 that his parish church should be returned to Rome and all Protestants fried. After being reported to a JP, Clarke was committed to prison and sentenced at the assizes to stand in the pillory in three market towns, Shrewsbury, Ellesmere and (Welsh) Oswaldstry. The consequences were severe, despite the precautions taken by the authorities: "He was sett on the pillory at Shrewsbury; butt the under-sheriff, (knowing how inraged the people were against him) suffered him to stand without fastening of his head through the penance-boards." Even so, he was pelted him with eggs,

---

74. Gardner, *England's Grievance Discovered*, pp.110-111.
75. Misson, *Memoirs and Observations in his Travels over England*, p.218.

turnips, carrots, stones and dirt, forcing the undersheriff to remove him early "for feare hee should bee killed outright". Clarke was pursued back to the jail door, being stoned all the way. Sick and bruised, he faced similar "hard usage" at Ellesmere. However, it was feared that the situation in Oswaldstry would be even worse. In consequence, the High Sheriff wrote to the sentencing judge warning that he: "... could not promise to bring him alive from amongst the inraged Welshmen; and thereupon the rest of the punishment was remitted."[76] At the Old Bailey, in 1698, Captain Rigby, convicted of attempted sodomy (the full offence carried the death penalty) was also sentenced to stand on "Three several Days in the Pillory, for the space of two Hours, from Eleven of the Clock to One". This was to be conducted in Pall Mall, Charing Cross and at Temple Bar. (Additionally, he was sentenced to a year's imprisonment, fined £1,000, and required to find sureties for good behaviour for seven years.)[77] Homosexuals could expect especially rough treatment from the public. Thus, in the early 1700s, Charles Hitchin, a former City Marshal who was also convicted of attempted sodomy, had to be removed from the pillory after only half an hour because he risked being pelted to death. Unsurprisingly, Captain Rigby preferred to escape abroad.

William Fuller, sentenced by the Court of King's Bench to Bridewell in 1703, and, like Rigby, three two-hour

---

76. Gough, *The History of Myddle*, p.174.
77. Anon, *An Account of the Proceedings against Capt Edward Rigby*, London, F. Collins in the Old Bailey, 1698, pp.1-2.

sessions in the pillory at various London locations (for libelling the late King William's ministers), gave a graphic account of his experiences. Already highly unpopular with the 'mob' he was: "... no sooner on the Pillory and my head thro' the Hole, but Dirt and rotten Eggs came about my Head, Body and Leggs, as thick and fast as Hail; amongst them came several stones and some of them struck me." Anticipating crowd trouble, many constables and watchmen were on duty, and some made ineffectual attempts to shield him. Others, however, encouraged the mob and even allowed some within the prohibited 'ring' so that they were closer to launch their missiles (one man apparently threw four shillings worth of eggs). At the end of his two hours, Fuller could not stand up when released and his head was "broke in several places". His next spell in the pillory, a day or so later, was even worse. It was set very low, so that he had to stoop painfully, and so savagely was he bombarded that he choked on his own blood. One stone that was thrown at him apparently weighed six pounds. The situation became so bad that the sheriff's officers went to a judge at Serjeant's Inn, and obtained an order that Fuller be released after only an hour. Had he stayed longer he might have died. Again, his exposed head and the small of his back were severely bruised.[78] If the punished offence did not attract public hostility there was little physical risk: "If the People think there is nothing very odious in the action that rais'd him to this Honour, they stand quietly by and only

---

78. Fuller, *Mr William Fuller's Trip to Bridewell*, pp.2-7.

look at him."[79] Sometimes, the crowd could discriminate between apparently similar defendants. Thus, on March 8, 1731, two solicitors, convicted of forgery, were pilloried at the Royal Exchange: "... the first was severely us'd by the Populace, but the other was very much favour'd and protected by six or seven Fellows who got upon the Pillory to screen him from the Insults of the mob."[80]

Whipping

Whipping, while attached to a post or the rear of a moving cart, was one of the most commonly used lesser punishments. Unlike fiscal penalties, it could always be levied, even on the indigent. As a result, it was used to punish a range of minor offences, including larceny, vagrancy and prostitution. Doubtless, as Shakespeare appreciated, there were sometimes salacious impulses behind the beadles' frequent scourging of whores. It was also regularly administered in the country's Bridewells. Under Henry VIII, the first Act had been passed by which all vagrants were to be flogged severely at the cart's-tail until "bloody by reason of such whipping". This enactment remained in force throughout the reign of Elizabeth. It was also the normal punishment for theft valued at less than 12 pence. Thus, in 1678, a group of pickpockets and other thieves convicted at the Old Bailey of petty larceny (often

---

79. Misson, *Memoirs and Observations in his Travels over England*, p.218.
80. *The Gentleman's Magazine*, 1731, vol. 1, p.124.

after pious perjury down valued the goods taken), including several women, received sentence: "That you be carried from hence to the place from whence you came, and from thence be dragg'd ti'd to a Carts-tail through the streets, your Bodies being stript from the Girdle upwards, and be Whipt till your Bodies bleed." The judge asked that two particularly fortunate women, who had stolen items which were, in reality, worth far above the 12 pence limit be thrashed especially robustly and warned that they could expect no indulgence in the future.[81] Similarly, it was ordered that four men and women convicted of stealing a sheet, at the Sussex quarter sessions held in Arundel at Epiphany 1647, were to be whipped from one end of the town to the other and back *"flagellari per villam de Arundell adversus et retorsus quousquo* etc".[82] However, gentlemen and women of 'quality' were not normally flogged. It was felt that their status would mean that the degradation attendant on whipping would be a more draconian punishment than the law intended.[83] It might also subvert the natural 'order'. Towards the end of the period there was also a growing reluctance to scourge women in public.

---

81. Anon, *An exact account of the trials of the several persons arraigned at the sessions-house in the Old-Bailey for London and Middlesex*, London, Gilham Hills, 1678, p.35.
82. B.C. Redwood (Ed.), *Quarter Sessions Order Book 1642-1649*, Lewes, Sussex Record Society, 1954, vol.54, p.145.
83. Beattie, *Crime and the Courts in England 1660-1800*, p.463.

Chapter 20

General Conclusion

Crime

What lessons, if any, can be drawn from the history of crime during the 250-year period? Obviously, it had changed significantly in this time. The small number of 'robber barons' who had lingered into the sixteenth century had long disappeared. By contrast, a report by a special committee of the House of Commons, published in November 1677, criticised the promoters of overpriced stock who had sold out at the peak of the market, on secret information; their concern presaged modern problems with insider trading. Similarly, well before the end of the period, in 1711, the South Sea Bubble crash provided the first instance of high level and large-scale white-collar crime. England's new commercial empire meant that fraud had become increasingly important in the canon of criminal offences. Attitudes towards crime had also changed. The increased amount of crime committed by 'outsiders' made it a more frightening phenomenon than it had been in earlier eras. At the same time, the number of educated men who saw it as a potentially remediable social pathology, rather than the sum of innate individual sins, had increased significantly (though they had never been entirely absent). Additionally, by the end of the period, a feeling that the state was failing to deliver adequate levels of security was becoming more prevalent, though it was still many decades away from becoming a politically dominant perspective. Other broad trends can be identified. By the 1700s, conventional crime was increasingly viewed as 'unacceptable' if committed by members of the middling and wealthy classes, though endemic corruption in the upper social orders of Hanoverian England should encourage caution before lauding 'progress'. The process by which criminal conduct would come to be largely associated with a stratum of the 'lower' class, rather than being distributed across the social spectrum, had advanced substantially, though there was still some way to go before the 'dangerous classes' of the Victorian era would be identified.

Society, generally, had become markedly less violent. Indeed, Englishmen surveying their history from the vantage point of 1950 would have been entitled to consider themselves as being at the latest stage of a story of almost continuous progress, one that reached back four centuries or more. Since then, however, society has changed, and, in this respect, not necessarily for the better. Although the burgeoning increase in instrumental crime in the last half of the twentieth century is partly explained by the plethora of stealable goods available in modern consumer culture, it is worrying that the number of homicides in England and Wales has also increased significantly from its low-point in the 1950s, despite an ongoing improvement in emergency medicine. Though murder rates are still modest by much international comparison, this process has reversed the broadly downward trend that had been evident from at least the mid-seventeenth century. It is still too early to draw firm conclusions, however, it appears that the widespread cultural resistance to potentially lethal violence that was slowly, and with difficulty, engendered after 1660 (if not before), and which made homicide a 'crime apart', is in retreat. It is possible that this is merely a temporary 'glitch', as appears to have occurred in the late Elizabethan period, that will be reversed in due course. If it is not, the long-term consequences may well be very unfortunate.

More generally, attempts are sometimes made to draw wider social lessons from the era's crime problems. Thus, the apparently crime plagued years between 1580 and 1630 are compared with the first half of the nineteenth century, also a crime-troubled era. The background to both was certainly one of social and economic dislocation. This allegedly created a large class of poor people for whom life was hard at the best of times, and who were reduced to desperate poverty by trade depressions and harvest failures: "Under such circumstances they turned to begging or stealing." As a result, it has been claimed that both periods demonstrate that levels of crime are closely connected to the degree of economic 'comfort' found amongst the poorest third or so of society.[1] Such views have threatened to become the orthodoxy of modern academia. Nevertheless, they are not entirely satisfactory. As has been noted, there is little evidence that universal (or even widespread) affluence prevents offending. The general upward trend in modern crime began during the 'never had it so good' years of the

---

1.　J. Sharpe, "Lessons of History: Hard times revive law and order panic," *The Independent Newspaper*, London, April 12, 1993, p.2.

late 1950s and 1960s. There were difficult economic times at several points in the eighteenth century, and, even before this period, the crime/need connection is often uncertain. The paradigm needs to be much subtler. The rate of indigence is certainly important. The apparent reduction in crime in the latter half of the seventeenth century undoubtedly reflects, in part, an improving economic climate. However, as much as poverty, it is social dislocation and upheaval, engendering social disorganisation and a loss of social control, which appears to be criminogenic. Poverty can be better endured in some situations than others. A cohesive and stable society, one that is relatively homogenous, possesses comparatively widely shared values, transmitted across the generations, and that has a high degree of social interdependence seems better able to resist the criminogenic effects of straitened (or even affluent) times. The reasons for this are not entirely clear but probably reflect the superior effectiveness of informal social control mechanisms, especially those that encourage a fear of shame and ostracism, in preventing misbehaviour. The static communities of medieval England had many of these qualities. Internecine conflict in the late medieval period, accompanied by rapid social change and increased mobility, encouraged a decline in communitarianism. The parish ceased to define the boundaries of early modern Englishmen's worlds. What have been termed the forces of disruption, factors which can prevent the operation of the 'civilizing process', whether the presence of large numbers of discharged veterans or migrants, created an unprecedented challenge. Unfortunately, acute social dislocation is sometimes the price of 'progress'. Modern, frenetic, multi-cultural England faces changes that have produced a similar loss of social cohesion, and that have, arguably, produced the same results. It must accept challenges every bit as great as those that beset its early modern predecessor.

Even as social disruption increased, late medieval society was on the cusp of changes, engendered by the process of state formation, which actually reduced its tolerance for disorder. As a result, England's criminal justice system moved to centre stage in the century following 1500, after a period of relative ineffectualness. More offences were criminalized and the courts, as a manifestation of state power, became increasingly assertive. They were more efficient in processing defendants, in larger numbers, and subjecting all social groups to their power. Indeed, this can be seen as part of a wider development in early modern Europe, which generally witnessed a move away from the imposition of local 'community' sanctions against those considered to be guilty of misconduct towards invoking state laws to deal with them. Informal communal sanctions, though still very significant, slowly declined in importance, yielding to those of the state. This *may* have been encouraged by their apparent ineffectiveness against transients. At the beginning of the period, much criminal law was still rooted in community custom and enforced on a local basis. By its end, it was overwhelmingly defined and imposed by the state. Interestingly, the process by which local justice is replaced by state justice has been noted, in a very attenuated form, in modern societies that have moved from being close-knit and separate communities to being fully integrated in their wider states.[2] Inevitably, the growth of centralised law, bringing standards that sometimes differed significantly from those found in the localities, also sometimes produces a culture conflict between local and governmental legal values.

However, a survey of the era's crime and criminal justice history also indicates the sheer ineffectualness of a *purely* penal approach to crime. The criminal justice system is merely one mechanism for controlling anti-social behaviour, and, in reality, often rather an inefficient one. It is subject to several severe limitations, being inherently slow and uncertain in its operation - early modern provincial felons might wait six months for the assizes or three months for quarter sessions and many felons were either not apprehended or not prosecuted - and frequently lacking in discrimination and flexibility. In a largely static society the localised and fairly sure, but normally mild, justice provided by leet and hundred courts may have been powerful instruments of social control. The more distant and much more infrequently exercised power of royal courts was no substitute, however draconian. Even then, however, the ineffectiveness of penality was apparent to thoughtful men, such as More, Hale and Coke, just as it has been to observers in the past 50 years. Acknowledging such a reality is easy; providing an alternative is not. The criminal law

---

2.   C.M. Turnbull, "The Individual, Community and Society: Rights and Responsibilities from an Anthropolgical Perspective," *Washington and Lee Law Review*, 1984, vol. 41, pp.101-103.

undergirds informal means for effecting social and cultural discipline. It reinforces social solidarity by setting the boundaries of 'acceptable' behaviour and by reassuring those that keep within such boundaries of their moral superiority, and is the logical 'next step' after informal sanctions, whether social ostracism, communal violence or expulsion from community have failed. Penality is usually adopted *faute de mieux* by societies that cannot adequately provide such alternative means to address the disorder borne of rapid social change. Just as the apparent failure of the welfare solutions to crime of the 1960s and 1970s encouraged a return to a more punitive approach in the following decades, the early modern English state experimented with more thorough and draconian law enforcement as a means of establishing 'order'. This initially encouraged a heavy reliance on coercive formal punishment, a stratagem that was largely unsuccessful. Perhaps in partial recognition of this, in the 90 years after 1660, the criminal justice system, with the possible (and significant) exception of London, appeared to become less central to the national life than had been the case in the previous 150 years. However, crime seems to have declined in these years. This reflected a reduction in social dislocation. It was also testament to the emergence of new methods of social control. There was an enormous increase in expenditure on poor relief, perhaps a tenfold growth between the beginning and end of the seventeenth century, far outstipping population increase. Discretionary charities also expanded rapidly. Arguably, this growth in selective charity and the poor law provided an alternative and more effective means of regulating the poorer and more criminogenic sections of society. Far more than the 'spectacle of the scaffold', this provided a powerful instrument for social control. Locally administered, and unfettered by requirements of strict proof, they were often more flexible than the criminal law. Selective distribution of public funds replaced the threat of prosecution as a means of controlling the vagabond, and increasingly shifted the problem of vagrancy from the criminal courts to the parish.[3]

Justice

It is a truism that the wider culture and legal ideology of a society and its criminal justice and policing systems are closely linked. Thus, as Henry Fielding observed at the end of the period, if the customs, manners, and habits of a nation altered it would also be necessary for its justice system to change. In England, as the importance of ancient and unquestioned legal tradition waned, new justifications for the role of the state in sanctioning certain forms of behaviour were developed. They included, *inter alia*, the various contractarian theories promulgated by Hobbes, Locke and others in the second half of the period. However, generally, a study of the early modern criminal justice system reveals that a 'modern', essentially pragmatic,

---

3. A.L. Beier, *Masterless Men: The Vagrancy Problem In England 1560-1640*, London, Methuen & Co, 1986, pp.173-174.

concept of law, as a practical and rational instrument designed to effect human ends advanced slowly (and incompletely) over the 250 year period, gradually replacing older, more personalised, traditions which accorded a binding status to historic, but inscrutable, custom. In England, the advance of 'rationalism' was particularly marked in the country's substantive criminal law, where offence parameters and distinctions, their essential elements and (most importantly) their requisite mental conditions were much more refined, settled and clearer in 1750 than had been the case in 1500. In this process, tort had become firmly distinguished from crime and moral culpability had developed into a prerequisite for most serious offences. As a result, it is at least arguable that the conscious aim of removing the illogicalities and unnecessary cruelties of the criminal justice system, manifest in the late eighteenth century work of the English disciples of Beccaria (such as Jeremy Bentham), was building on already established foundations. Nevertheless, the process of 'rationalisation' was still far from complete in 1750, particularly in the areas of policing, procedural law and punishment, where much of the impact of modernity lay in the future. Thus, English penal practices, though far more sophisticated than those in existence 250 years earlier, still had far to go in establishing a carefully graduated system of punishment, premised on proportionality. However, it is also clear that, in an English context, the notion of a sudden move from 'spectacular' to 'disciplinary' punishments in the late 1700s is mistaken. The change had roots going back far into the sixteenth century.

Some distinguished present-day observers have

questioned the manner in which such change was effected in England. In particular, it has been argued that it was a mistake to adapt a medieval system of criminal justice to deal with the changed circumstances of the modern era, rather than attempting a more radical restructuring. Certainly, there was a tendency towards minimalism and gradualism. Change was usually as modest as possible, introduced belatedly on a piece-meal, *ad hoc*, basis, and often not even acknowledged as such. As a result, by the 1700s, many observers shared Fielding's view that England's criminal justice system, which had been appropriate to the government of the lower orders in the Norman era, had failed to keep pace with the 'modern' world and was no longer capable of controlling the country's potential felons: "Hath this civil power kept equal pace with them in the increase of its force, or hath it not rather, by the remissness of the magistrate, lost much of its ancient energy?"[4] Fielding wanted to see drastic changes to England's policing and justice system. His impatience is partly understandable. In some areas, there had been little tangible progress in over 200 years. Aside from paying for prosecuting counsel in very serious crimes on a slightly more regular basis, and providing financial incentives via rewards to those who secured convictions (which also damaged the probity of the criminal justice system), government involvement in the prosecution process was little changed from 1500. Many other aspects of the system

---

4.   H. Fielding, *An Enquiry into the causes of the Late Increase of Robbers*, London, 1751, p.xiii.

were anachronistic. Arguably, in some ways, the American colonies had progressed faster and further than the mother country during the seventeenth century. Largely unencumbered by vested legal interests (before the late 1600s) and the 'dead hand' of tradition that was occasionally found in England, many early colonial procedural innovations were sensible reforms that anticipated future developments in the mother country, and were influenced by the contemporary debate in England. Thus, most American states effectively (if not always theoretically) abandoned benefit of clergy and attainder leading to forfeiture of property and corruption of the blood during the 1600s. The colonists, challenged by vast and thinly populated spaces, also frequently replaced the unwieldy English court structure with a slightly more coherent system.[5]

Nevertheless, a close study of the period also reveals that it is possible to exaggerate the 'irrationality' of the English criminal justice system of the era. It was not simply an interstitial period between medieval obscurantism and today's 'rationalism'; it is a mistake to see criminal justice history as purely being a story of steady progress towards a 'modern' system. Frequently, careful scrutiny reveals 'method in the madness'. It is wrong to assume that early modern Englishmen were necessarily unequipped to create appropriate institutions for their own, very different, society. Early modern criminal law enforcement was not

---

5.   B. Chapin, *Criminal Justice In Colonial America, 1606-1660*, Athens, The University of Georgia Press, 1983, pp.145-149.

solely an anachronistic survivor from an earlier, darker, age, but often had an underlying rationale, providing a relatively cost-effective means of fighting crime in an otherwise poor society. Inevitably, it used policing procedures, trial processes and punishments that were dictated by financial constraints and issues of public and private self-interest.[6] It is easy to sit in emotional judgment on the criminal justice system of the sixteenth and seventeenth centuries, to ignore its context and to retrospectively suggest alternatives. Indeed, it was not difficult at the time. Perhaps for this reason, Sir Thomas Smith was dismissive of works, such as More's *Utopia*, which devised plans for ideal commonwealths "such as never was nor never shall be, vaine imaginations, phantasies of Philosophers to occupie the time and to exercise their wittes". However, some of the law's apparent brutality reflected the realities of a society in which the margins of existence were small. Thus, its prescribed system of execution is horrific, until the brutal reality of many 'normal' deaths in this pre-anaesthetic era is considered.

Additionally, it is at least arguable that when radical change did come to the criminal justice system, in the latter part of the eighteenth century, it was not entirely beneficial. The early modern criminal justice system had some significant strengths (as well as numerous weaknesses), many of which are absent today. Its trials were informal,

---

6.   G. Fisher, "Making Sense of English Law Enforcement in the Eighteenth Century: A Response," *The University of Chicago Law School Roundtable*, 1995, p.510.

flexible and allowed for intimate participant involvement. They would be transformed, after 1750, gaining counsel but losing their inquisitorial elements, a process that would eventually result in the slowness, rigidity, partiality and technicality of the modern lawyer dominated adversarial system. Rather than setting off down this route, had eighteenth century Englishmen thought carefully about the type of tribunal that was best suited to their changed circumstances, they might have explored the inquisitorial procedure used in their own ancient coroners' courts, which were often surprisingly effective in investigating and determining the truth behind suspicious deaths, frequently with the most limited resources. Arguably, they provided an alternative, if flawed, model of ajudication, remaining premised on a neutral and independent search for the truth.

If the system was so inherently unsatisfactory, it must also be asked why most early modern Englishmen obeyed the law, for most of the time, even when the power to create and interpret it lay in the hands of relatively few individuals? One answer, as has been seen, lies in the high degree of 'legitimacy' ascribed to the era's criminal law and justice system by a majority of the country's inhabitants. Some have sought malign explanations for this apparently contradictory phenomenon. Thus, in *Property, Authority, and the Criminal Law*, Douglas Hay produced a straightforward analysis suggesting that, in the eighteenth century at least, the interests of a ruling class were advanced via a clever use of the country's criminal justice system. According to this analysis, the criminal courts intimidated the population by the frequent threat via, for example, the 'bloody code' and the progressive withdrawal of clergy, and much less frequent use, of the death penalty. The state allegedly bolstered such intimidation by employing dramatic 'spectacle' at executions to enhance the law's importance. However, it also issued pardons liberally to create an illusion of fairness and benevolent paternalism. This neutralized lower class dissent, allowing the upper class to rule in its own interests. Even some observers from a (broadly) similar political stance have suggested that such an analysis is slightly simplistic. Thus, in *Whigs and Hunters*, Professor E. P. Thompson argued that although the law was used to benefit the ruling class at the expense of the lower classes, it ultimately influenced (and arguably moderated) the behavior and ideology of the lawmakers themselves. Legal forms imposed inhibitions and limitations on the actions of England's rulers.[7]

The need for a less blatant, more subtle, paradigm is understandable. There are major problems in viewing early modern English criminal law as being simply a weapon of social oppression, representing the interests of the propertied classes and employed against those of the poor. Of course, law serves a vital function in defining social obligations, rights, and privileges. Competing social groups often hold differing views of such legal rights and duties, and some groups always have more of a vested interest in the existing order than others. Not surprisingly, those who

---

7.   See on this, M.C. Stein, "Law and Legitimacy in England, 1800-1832: Bringing Professors Hay and Thompson to the Bargaining Table," *Boston University Law Review*, 1988, vol. 68, pp.621-633.

could exercise power in early modern England often did so in their own interests and according to their own vision of society. Undoubtedly, the system had major imperfections and entrenched injustices. However, before the institutionalisation of law enforcement in the late eighteenth and nineteenth centuries, England's criminal justice system depended on the co-operation and participation of men from all social ranks apart from the very lowest. Over half of the adult male population were in some way involved, when churchwardens, constables and leet jurors are included, even more if members of the *ad hoc* hue and cry are added; this is far more than in the modern era. Relatively poor people were also fairly willing to use the criminal courts, at least if they were local to them. Without their input the system could not have operated at all. This placed major constraints on the ability of the political nation to enforce unpopular policies effectively. Where the law was seen as being devoid of legitimacy, as, for example, in the comparatively rare instances of socially sanctioned crime (such as poaching and smuggling), or where specific legislation was highly unpopular, such as Ship Money, criminal law enforcement was often largely ineffectual.

Such widespread participation probably reflected a popular realisation that the lives of very few would have been bettered by the replacement of existing arrangements with a situation of total lawlessness, one in which men lived "without a common power to keep them all in awe". This was the option usually offered by criminal action. Today, it is sometimes fashionable to mock the quest for 'order', and to suggest that it is a misanthropic attempt to impose regularity on essentially unpredictable human beings. However, such views are rarely ventured by those who have lived with acute disorder. It did not require a false consciousness for ordinary Englishmen to appreciate that an imperfect order was better than no order. As Thomas Hobbes observed an innate aspect of human nature is that people frequently seek to gain advantage where they might, and often the "way of one competitor to the attaining of his desire is to kill, subdue, supplant, or repel the other".[8] Most unsuccessful 'competitors' (or crime victims) were poor. Crime was not (and is not) usually a substitute for political action, nor was it politics pursued by other means. The well-protected ruling class of late medieval England had been able to dispense with effective criminal justice much more easily than had the poor in the turbulent fifteenth century. The same is probably true of their modern counterparts.

---

8.   T. Hobbes, *Leviathan*, 1651, p.48.

Bibliography

A Citizen in London. (1751) *The Vices of the cities of London and Westminster trac'd from their original; being an impartial detection of the true cause ... of the present growth of immorality.* Dublin: G. Faulkner.

Addison J. et al. (1711) "The Spectator, No. 232, Nov. 26, 1711" reproduced in *The Spectator*, London: Everyman edn., J.M. Dent, vol. 2 (1945).

Allen, Christopher. (1997) *The Law of Evidence in Victorian England.* Cambridge: Cambridge University Press.

Amussen, Susan Dwyer. (1994) "'Being Stirred to Much Unquiet-ness': Violence and Domestic Violence in Early Modern England" in *Journal of Womens History*, vol. 6, at pp.70-77.

Andrews, William. (1899) *Bygone Punishments.* London: W. Andrews & Company.

Anon (1552) *A Manifest detection of the moste vyle and detestable use of Diceplay.* London: Abraham Vele.

Anon (1573) *A briefe discourse of the late murther of Master George Saunders.* London: Henry Bynnemen.

Anon (1591) *The manner of the death and execution of Arnold Cosbie, for murdering the Lord Burke, who was executed at Wansworth town's end on the 27 of January 1591.* London: William Wright.

Anon (1600) *Kemps nine daies wonder. Performed in a daunce from London to Norwich. Containing the pleasure, paines and kinde entertainement of William Kemp betweene London and that Citty in his late Morrice.* London: printed by E.A. for Nicholas Ling.

Anon (1605) *The bloudy booke, or, The tragicall and desperate end of Sir John Fites (alias) Fitz.* London: printed for Francys Burton.

Anon (1606a) *A true Report of the horrible Murther, which was committed in the house of Sir Jerome Bowes, Knight, on the 29 day of February.* London: imprinted by H.L. for Mathew Lownes.

Anon (1606b) *The Horrible Murther of a young Boy of three yeres of age, whose sister had her tongue cut out.* London.

Anon (1607) *A true Report of the horrible Murther, which was committed in the house of Sir Jerome Bowes, Knight, on the 29 day of February, Anno Dom 1606.* London, H.L. for Mathew Lownes.

Anon (1608) *The Arraignement and burning of Margaret Ferne-Seede, for the murther of her late Husband.* London: Henry Gusson.

Anon (1609a) *A True Relation of the most inhumane and bloody murther of Master James Minister and Preacher of the word of God at Rockland in Norfolk.* London: printed for R. Bowan.

Anon (1609b) *Foure Statutes, Specially Selected and Commanded by his Maijestie to be carefully put in execution by all Justices and other Officers of the Peace throughout the Realme.* London: Robert Barker.

Anon (1618) *Newes from Perin in Cornwall.* London.

Anon (1621) *London's Looking-Glass: or The Copy of a Letter, written by an English Travayler, to the Apprentices of London.* Reproduced by Scholar Press, vol. 7, Oxford: Bodleian,

Anon (1623a) *The Life and Death of Griffin Flood, Informer.* London.

Anon (1623b) *Homily on Obedience of 1547, from certain sermons of homilies appointed to be read in churches, In the time of the late Queene Elizabeth.* London: John Bill.

Anon (1624) *The Crying Murther.* London.

Anon (1630) *A Proclamation for the better discovery and prevention of Burglaries, Robberies, and other Suppressing of felons and outlawes, their aiders and Abettors, by bringing them to bee answerable to the several lawes of the Several Realmes of England and Scotland.* London.

Anon (1631) *The Just Lawyer: His Conscionable Complaint against Auricular or Private Informing and Soliciting of Judges By their Menialls, Friends and Favorites.* London: George Purslowe.

Anon (1632) *The Laws Resolutions of Womens Rights: or, the Lawes Provision for Women.* London: John More.

Anon (1641a) *Murther, murther, Or, A bloody relation how Anne Hamton, dwelling in Westminster nigh London, by poyson murthered her deare husband.* London.

Anon (1641b) *Newes from the North: or a Relation of a Great Robberie.* London.

Anon (1641c) *The Apprentices Warning-Piece ...* London.

Anon (1641d) *The Spiritual Courts Epitomized, in a Dialogue betwixt two Proctors, Busie Body, and Scrape-all, and their discourse of the want of their former imployment.* London.

Anon (1643) *The humble Remonstrance and Complaint of Many thousands of poore distressed Prisoners in the prisones in and about the Citie of London.* London: printed for John Gibson.

Anon (1645) *Signes and Wonders from Heaven...And how 20 witches more were executed in Suffolk this last Assize.* London: I.H.

Anon (1647) *Bloody Newes from Dover, Being A True Relation of The great and bloody Murder, committed by Mary Champion (an Anabaptist) who cut off her child's head.* London.

Anon (1650) *The Order of Keeping A Court Leet and Court Baron.* London: printed for William Lee.

Anon (1652a) *A cry against a crying Sinne: or, a Just Complaint to the Magistrates, against them who have broken the statute Laws of God, by killing of men meerly for Theft.* London: Samuel Chidley.

Anon (1652b) *Notable and pleasant History of the Famous renowned Knights of the Blade, comonly called Hectors.* London: Richard Harper.

Anon (1655) *The Devil's Reign upon Earth Being a Relation of several Sad and bloudy Murthers committed, especially that of Sir George Sonds his Son, upon his own Brother.* London, printed for John Andrews.

Anon (1657a) *An Act for the Better Suppressing of Theft upon the Borders of England and Scotland, And for Discovery of High- Way Men and other Felons, At the Parliament begun at Warwick 17th Sept. 1656.* London: printed by H. Hills.

Anon (1657b) *A Full and the Truest Narrative of the most Horrid, Barbarous and Unparalled Murder, Committed on the Person of John Knight, Apprentice.* London, T. Mabb.

Anon (1659a) *The unhappy marksman. Or a perfect and impartial discovery of that late barbarous and unparalleled murther committed by Mr George Strangeways.* London: printed by T.N.

Anon (1659b) *The Caterpillars of this Nation Anatomised in a brief yet notable discovery of house-breakers, pickpockets, & c.* London.

Anon (1660) *A Perfect List of all Such Persons as by Commission under the Great Seal of England are now Confirmed to be Custos Rotulorum ...* London.

Anon (1662a) *Murther will Out: or, an Unrighteous Discharge, No Security to the Murtherer.* London.

Anon (1662b) *The Life and Death of Mrs Mary Frith, Commonly Called Mal Cutpurse.* London: printed for W.G. Ilberton.

Anon (1663a) *A True and Impartial Account of the Arraignment, Tryal, Examination, Confession and Condemnation of Col. James Turner.* London.

Anon (1663b) *A Cry Against Oppression and Cruelty.* London.

Anon (1663c) *The Speech and Deportment of Colonel James Turner at his execution in Leaden-Hall-Street, January 21, 1663.* London.

Anon (1663d) *Madam Mary Carleton, lately stiled The German Princess; Truely Stated: With an Historical Relation of her Birth, Education, and Fortunes.* London: Sam Speed at the Rainbow in Fleetstreet, and Hen Marsh at the Princes Arms.

Anon (1668) *The Tryals of such Persons (Peter Messenger, Richard Beasley ... as under the Notion of London-Apprentices were tumultuously assembled in Moore-Fields, and other places, on Easter Holidays last, under colour of pulling down [sic] Bawdy-houses. Taken at the Sessions in the Old-Bailey, on Saturday April 4, 1668.* London: Robert Pawlet.

Anon (1673) *The Bloody Lover: or, Barbarous News from Glocester.* London: P. Browesby.

Anon (1674a) *A True and Perfect Revelation of a Robbery & Murder Committed by five notorious Highwaymen, on Wednesday the 18th of this Instant March, near Colbrook, London.* London.

Anon (1674b) *The confession of the four highwaymen.* London.

Anon (1675a) *Murther will out, or, a true and faithful relation of an horrible murther commited thirty three years ago, by an unnatural mother, upon the body of her own child, about a year old, and was never discovered till this 24th Nov. 1675, by her own self.* London.

Anon (1675b) *The Bloody Innkeeper, or Sad and Barbarous News from Glocestershire.* London.

Anon (1676) *News from Sussex: Or, the Barbarous Robber.* London.

Anon (1677a) *A Caution to Married Couples: Being a true Relation How a Man in Nightingale lane Having beat and abused his Wife, Murthered a Tub-man that endeavoured to stop him from Killing her with a Half-pike.* London: printed for D.M.

Anon (1677b) *A true Relation of all the Bloody Murders that have been committed in and about the Citie and Suburbs of London, since the 4th of this instant June 1677.* London.

Anon (1677c) *Horrid News from St Martins, or unheard of murder and Poyson.* London.

Anon (1678a) *An exact account of the trials of the several persons arraigned at the sessions-house in the Old-Bailey for London and Middlesex. Beginning on Wednesday, December 11. 1678 and ending the 12th of the same Month.* London: printed by Gilham Hills.

Anon (1678b) *Strange and Lamentable News from Dullidge-Wells; or, The Cruel and Barbarous Father.* London: printed for D.M.

Anon (1679a) *The Narrative of the Confession and Execution of the three Prisoners at Tyburn.* London.

Anon (1679b) *Strange and wonderful News from Linconshire. Or a Dreadful account of a most inhumane and bloody murther, committed upon the body of one Mr. Carter, by the contrivance of his elder brother ... and how it was soon after found out, by the appearance of a most dreadful ... ghost, etc.* Lincoln.

Anon (1679c) *The Narrative of the Confession and Execution of the three Prisoners at Tyburn.* London.

Anon (1679d) *The Proceedings of the Sessions at the Old-Baily, August 27-28.* London.

Anon (1680) *The petition of Francis Gibson A poore prisoner in Derby Goale to the Right Worshipfull his Majesties Justices of the peace at the quarter sessions houlden at Derby the 5 of October 1680 humbly sheweth.* Derby.

Anon (1681) *The Tryal of Slingsby Bethel Esq.: upon an Indictment preferred by Robert Mason.* London: R. Harbottle.

Anon (1682a) *The Tryal and Condemnation of George Brosky alias ... Thynn.* London: printed for Thomas Basset.

Anon (1682b) *A True Relation of the Most Horrible Murther, Committed by Thomas White of Lane Green in the Parish of Auffley in the County of Salop, Gent', upon the Body of his Wife Mrs Dorothy White.* London.

Anon (1682c) *The Office of the Clerk of the Assize: Containing The Form and Method of the Proceedings at the Assizes, and general Gaol-delivery.* London: printed for Henry Twyford.

Anon (1684a) *Strange News from Piccadilly; of a most Horrible and Dreadful Robbery and Murder.* London: printed for Edward Mallet.

Anon (1684b) *Sad and dreadful news from Kings Street in Westminster, or a most lamentable relation of the untimely end of the Lady Phillips. Who was found strangled in her chamber, on the 12th of this instant November, giving an account of all the material circumstances, attending the murther of that unfortunate lady.* London: printed for L.C.

Anon (1684c) *The confession and execution of Letitia Wigington of Ratclif, who suffered at Tyburn, on Fryday the 9th of this instant September, 1681, written by her own hand in the Gaol of Newgate two days before her death, being Condemned for whiping her Apprentice Girl to Death.* London, printed for Langley Curtiss, On Ludgate -Hill.

Anon (1688) *A True Relation of a Horrid Murder Committed upon the Person of Thomas Kidderminster of Topley in the county of Hertford, Gent. At the Whitehorse-Inn in Chelmsford in the County of Essex, in the Month of April 1654.* London: H. Hills, Junior.

Anon (1690) *The distressed Mother: or Sorrowful Wife in Tears.* London.

Anon (1692a) *Fair warnings to murderers of infants being an account of the tryal, codemnation [sic] and execution of Mary Goodenough at the assizes held in Oxon in February, 1691/2.* London: printed for Jonathan Robinson.

Anon (1692b) *The Arraignment, Tryal, Conviction and Condemnation of Henry Harrison, Gent for the Barbarous Murther of Andrew Clenche.* London.

Anon (1693) *The Tryal of John Foster, for Stealing a Mag-Pye.* London.

Anon (1695) *The True Relation of the tryals at the Sessions of Oyer and Terminer, ... as particularly of E.Wigenton for whipping a girl to death at Ratcliffe. And J. Peetly, for shooting a gentleman in Queen-Street.* London.

Anon (1698) *An Account of the Proceedings against Capt Edward Rigby At the Sessions of Gaol Delivery held at Justice-Hall in the Old-Bailey, on Wednesday the Seventh Day of December, 1698 for intending to Commit the Abominable Crime of Sodomy on the Body of one William Minton Printed by Order of the Court.* London: F. Collins in the Old Bailey.

Anon (1699a) *The Tryal of Spencer Cowper, Esq., ... upon an Indictment for the Murther of Mrs Sarah Stout, a Quaker.* London.

Anon (1699b) *A dialogue between a Quaker and his neighbour in Hertford, about the murder of Mrs Sarah Stout.* Westminster.

Anon (1700) *The Compleat Constable,* Second Edition. London.

Anon (1701) *Hanging, not Punishment Enough, for Murtherers, High-way Men, and House-Breakers.* London: printed for A. Baldwin.

Anon (1705) *A Full and True Account of the Tryal, Examination, and Proceedings against Mr John Maugridge a Kettle-Drummer.* London.

Anon (1707) *Jack Hall Richard Low: A full and true account of the apprehending ... of Jack Hall ... and Richard Low, for shooting a constable near Grays-Inn-Lane ... together with one Stephen Bunch ... being three most notorious house-breakers ... With their examination ... and their commitment to Newgate ... November the 25th, 1707.* London.

Anon (1709) *The Secret History of Clubs.* London.

Anon (1711) *A true account of what past at the Old Bailey ... relating to the tryal of R. Thornhill Esq. Indicted for the murther of Sir Cholmley Deering.* Second Edition. London.

Anon (1715a) *The History of the Most Remarkable Tryals in Great Britain and Ireland in Capital Cases.* London: printed for A. Bell.

Anon (1727) *The Three and Thirtieth account of the progress made in the Cities of London and Westminster, And Places adjacent, By the Societies for Promoting a Reformation of Manners; By Furthering the Execution of the laws against Prophaneness and Immorality, and by other Christian Methods.* London.

Anon (1730) *The Proceedings at the Sessions of the Peace, and Oyer and Terminer, for the City of London, and County of Middlesex; on Friday the 28th, Saturday the 29th, and Monday the 31st of Angust, and Tuesday the 1st of September 1730 ...* London: T. Payne.

Anon (1722a) *An Account of the behaviour, Confession, and last Dying words of Arnold Coke Esq., and John Woodburne, Labourer.* London.

Anon (1722b) *The Whole Life History of Benjamin Child, Lately Executed for Robbing the Bristol Mail.* London.

Anon (1729) *Hell upon Earth: or the Town in an Uproar, occasion'd by The late horrible Scenes of Forgery, Perjury, Street-Robbery, Murder, Sodomy, and other shocking Impieties.* London: printed for J. Roberts in Warwick-Lane, and A. Dodd without Temple-Bar.

Anon (1731) *An Account & c. of a Murther committed in Criplegate Parish, Dec.16. 1695, related by Mr Smithies, Curate of that Parish; and attested by Dr Fowler, then Bishop of Gloucester.* London.

Anon (1734) *Select Trials, for Murders, Robberies, Rapes, Sodomy, Coining, Frauds, and other Offences*, vol. 1. London: printed for J. Wilford.

Anon (1742) *Select Trials at the Sessions-House in the Old Bailey, From the Year 1720, to this Time*, vol. 1. Dublin: printed by S. Powell, for G. Ewing and W. Smith in Dame-street.

Anon (1745) *The Proceedings on the King's Commissions of the Peace, Oyer and Terminer, and Gaol Delivery for the City of London; And also the Gaol Delivery for the County of Middlesex, held at Justice-Hall in the Old-Bailey, on Wednesday the 10th, and Thursday the 11th of July.* London: printed and sold by M. Cooper.

Anon (1764) *Select Trials for murder, robbery, burglary ... at the Sessions House in the Old-Bailey, from ... 1741 to the present year, etc.*, vols. 1-4. London

Anon (1776) *A Complete Collection of State -Trials, And Proceedings For High Treason, and other Crimes and Misdemeanours*, vols.1-4. London: T. Wright, Essex-Street, Strand.

Anon (1847) *A relation, or Rather A True Account of The Island of England ... About the Year 1500*, trans. Charlotte Sneyd. London: Camden Society.

Anon (1888) *Calendar of the Manuscripts of the Marquis of Salisbury at Hatfield House*, Part II. London: HMSO.

Anon (1914) *The Mary Carleton Narratives, 1663-1673. A missing chapter in the history of the English novel*. Cambridge [Mass.]: Harvard University Press.

Anon (1976) *The Boke of Justices of Peas* (first published c.1506). London: Facsimile Professional Books Ltd and New Jersey: Walter J. Johnson Inc.

Anon (1982) *Punishment and Crime in East Lothian 1600-1800*. Haddington: East Lothian District Library. Local History Publications.

Anon (1987) *Crime in the Vale of Evesham 1651-1670 WEA Evesham History Workshop*. Hereford: Hereford and Worcester County Libraries.

Aray, Martin (1599) *The Discoverie and Confutation of a Tragical Fiction, Devysed and Played by Edward Squyor, yeoman soldier, hanged at Tyburne the 23, November, 1598*. London.

Ashley, Sir Francis (1981) *The Casebook of Sir Francis Ashley JP, Recorder of Dorchester: 1614-1635*. Bettey, J.H. (Ed.). Dorset: Dorset Record Society.

Atkinson, B.A. (1726) *A sermon preach'd to the societies for the reformation of Manners at Salter's-Hall, On Monday, June 29, 1726*. London.

Aubrey, John (1982) *Brief Lives*. Baxter, R. (Ed.). Woodbridge: The Boydell Press.

B.L. (1559) *The Boke for a Justice of Peace*. London, Richard Tottil.

B.L. (1608) *The Lives, Apprehension, Arraignment & Execution, of Robert Throgmorton. William Porter. Iohn Bishop. Gentlemen. Who were all executed ... the 26. of Februarij, 1608 for certaine roberies, and a murther committed on Bagshot-Heath*. London: Edward Allde for Henry Gosson.

B.L. (1612) *The Arraignment of John Selman, who was executed neere Charing-Crosse the 7 of January, 1612, for a felony by him ...* London: printed by W.H. for T. Archer.

Babington, Anthony (1999) *A House in Bow Street*, 2nd edn. Chichester: Barry Rose.

Babington, Zachary (1677) *Advise to Grand Jurors in Cases of Blood*. London: Printed for John Amery.

Bacon, Sir Francis (1641) *Cases of Treason*. London: printed by the Assignes of John More.

Bacon, Sir Francis (1841) "The Use Of The Law," in Montagu, Basil (Ed.),*The Works of Francis Bacon*, vol. 3. Philadelphia: Carey and Hart, at pp. 247-253 (first published posthumously 1630 by the Assignes of John Moore; there is doubt as to the authenticity of its attribution).

Bacon, Sir Francis (1906) "On Judicature" in *The Essays*. London, Everyman edn., J.M. Dent.

Bacon, Sir Nathaniel (1915) *The official papers of Sir Nathaniel Bacon of Stiffkey, Norfolk as Justice of the Peace 1580-1620*. Saunders H.W. (Ed.), vol. 26, London: Royal History Society, Camden Third Series.

Baker, J.H. (1973) "Criminal Justice at Newgate 1616-1627: Some Manuscript Reports in the Harvard Law School" in *The Irish Jurist*, vol. 8 at p.316.

Baker, J.H. (1977) "Criminal Courts and Procedure at Common Law 1550-1800" in Cockburn, J.S. (Ed.), *Crime in England 1550-1800*. London: Methuen.

Baker, J.H. (1984) "Le brickbat que narrowly mist" in *Law Quarterly Review*, vol. 100, at pp.544-548.

Baker, J.H. (1990) "The English Law of Sanctuary" in *Ecclesiastical Law Journal*, vol. 2, at p.8

Baker, J.H. (1991) *The Inner Temple: A Brief Historical Description*. London: The Honourable Society of the Inner Temple.

Baker, J.H. (1998) "The Three Languages of the Common Law" in *McGill Law Journal*, vol. 43, at p.5.

Banner, Stuart (1998) "When Christianity Was Part of the Common Law" in *Law and History Review*, vol. 16, at p.27.

Barlow, Theodore (1745) *The Justice of Peace: A Treatise Containing the Power and Duty of That Magistrate*. London: Lintot.

Barnes, G. (1962) "Due Process and Slow Process in the Late Elizabethan-Early Stuart Star Chamber" in *The American Journal of Legal History*, vol. 6, at pp.221-315.

Barnes, Thomas (1955) "Examination Before A Justice in the Seventeenth Century" in *Notes and Queries for Somerset and Dorset*, vol. 27, at pp.39-42.

Barnes, Thomas (Ed.) (1959) *Somerset Assize Orders 1629-1640*. Frome: Somerset Record Society.

Barrett, Andrew and Harrison, Christopher (1999) *Crime and Punishment in England, a Sourcebook*. London: U.C.L. Press.

Barton, Dr (1700) *Dr Barton's Sermon Preached at St Mary-le-Bow, To the Societies For the Reformation of Manners, October 2nd, 1699*. London.

Beattie, J.M. (1986) *Crime and the Courts in England 1660-1800*. Oxford: Oxford University Press.

Beattie, J.M. (1991) "Scales of Justice: Defense Counsel and the English Criminal Trial in the Eighteenth and Nineteenth Centuries" in *Law and History Review*, vol. 9, no. 2, at pp.221-268

Beattie, J.M. (2001) *Policing and Punishment in London, 1660-1750*. Oxford: Oxford University Press.

Beccaria, Cesare (1767) *An Essay on Crimes and Punishments*. London: J. Almon.

Beckerman, John S. (1992) "Procedural Innovation and Institutional Change in Medieval English Manorial Courts" in *Law and History Review*, vol. 10, no. 2, at pp.197-252.

Beckerman, John S. (1995) "Toward a Theory of Medieval Manorial Adjudication: The Nature of communal Judgments in a System of Customary Law" in *Law and History Review*, vol. 13, at pp.1-23.

Beier, A.L. (1985) *Masterless Men: the vagrancy problem in England 1560-1640*. London: Methuen & Co.

Bellamy, J.G. (1973) *Crime and public order in England in the later middle ages*. London: Routledge.

Bellamy, J.G. (1998) *The Criminal Trial in Later Medieval England Felony Before the Courts From Edward I to the Sixteenth Century*. Toronto: University of Toronto Press.

Bentley, D.R. (Ed.) (1997) *Select cases from the twelve Judges' notebooks*. London: John Rees.

Berman, Harold J. (1996) "The transformation of English Legal Science: from Hale to Blackstone" in *Emory Law Journal*, vol. 45, at p.437.

Bernard, Nicholas, Dean of Ardagh (1710) *The Case of John Atherton, Bishop of Waterford in Ireland: fairly represented. Against a late partial edition of Dr. Barnard's relation, and sermon at his funeral ... With a brief account of a conspiracy against the life of Mr Robert Hawkins.* London: Luke Stokoe.

Betterton, Alec (1995) "The Guildhall, Lavenham (Suffolk, England)" in *History Today*, vol. 45, issue 1, at pp.22-26.

Bettey, J.H. (Ed.) (1981) *The Casebook of Sir Francis Ashley JP, Recorder of Dorchester: 1614-1635* Dorchester: Dorset Record Society.

Biddle, Esther (1662) *The Trumpet Of the Lord Sounded forth unto these Three Nations, by one who is a Sufferer for the Testimony of Jesus, in Newgate.* London.

Birkenhead, The Earl of (1926) *Famous Trials of History*, vol. 1. New York: Doubleday, Doran and Co.

Blackstone, William (1765-1769) *Commentaries on the Laws of England* (vols. 1-4). Oxford: Clarendon Press.

Blunden, E. (Ed.) (1953) *The Christ's Hospital Book.* London: Hamish Hamilton.

Boes, Maria R. (1999) "Jews in the Criminal-Justice System of Early Modern Germany" in *Journal of Interdisciplinary History*, vol. 30.3, at pp.407-435.

Bohun, Edmund (1693) *The Justice of Peace: His Calling and Qualifications.* London.

Brackett, John K. (1992) *Criminal Justice and Crime: In Late Renaissance Florence, 1537-1609.* Cambridge: Cambridge University Press.

Bridgeman, Sir Orlando (1969) "Newgate, 1663, A Letter of Sir Orlando Bridgeman, Chief Justice," in *American Journal of Legal History*, vol. 13, at pp. 384-389.

Brooks, C. (Ed.) (1997) *Communities and Courts in Britain 1150-1900.* London: Hambledon.

Brown, B.J. (1963) "The demise of Chance Medley and the recognition of provocation as a defence to murder in English Law" in *American Journal of Legal History*, vol. 7, at p. 314.

Brown, Keith M. (1990) "Gentlemen and Thugs in 17th Century Britain" in *History Today*, vol. 40, issue 10, at p.10.

Browner, Jessica A. (1994) "Wrong Side of the River: London's disreputable South Bank in the sixteenth and seventeenth century" in Essays in *History University of Virginia*, vol. 36, at pp.34-50.

Bulstrode, Whitlocke (1723) *The Third Charge of Whitlocke Bulstrode, Esq., To the Grand Jury, And other Juries of the County of Middlesex, at General Quarter-Sessions of the Peace held on the Fourth Day of October 1722, at Westminster-Hall*. London.

Bunyan, John (1765) *A Relation of the Imprisonment of Mr. John Bunyan, Minister of the Gospel at Bedford ... in November 1660*. London: James Buckland.

Burton, K.M. (Ed.) (1948) *A Dialogue between Reginal Pole and Thomas Lupset*. London: Chatto and Windus.

Butler, Samuel (1908) *Characters and Passages from Note-Books*. A.R. Waller (Ed.). Cambridge: Cambridge University Press.

Campbell, Ruth (1984) "Sentence of Death by Burning for Women" in *Journal of Legal History*, vol. 5, at pp.44-59.

Capp, Bernard (1996) "Serial killers in 17th-century England" in *History Today*, vol. 46, issue 3, at pp.21-31.

Carro, Jorge L. (1986) "Sanctuary: The resurgence of an age-old right or a dangerous misinterpretation of an abandoned ancient privilege?" in *University of Cincinnati Law Review*, vol. 54, at p. 747.

Cavendish, Richard (2001) "Execution of Captain Kidd" in *History Today*, vol. 51, issue 5, at p. 53.

Chadwick, Owen (1953) "The Case of Philip Nichols, 1731" in *Transactions of the Cambridge Bibliographical Society*, vol. 1, part 5, at pp.422-431.

Chapin, Bradley (1983) *Criminal Justice In Colonial America, 1606-1660*. Athens, (Ga): The University of Georgia Press.

Clavell, John (1628) *A Recantation of an Ill led Life. Or a discoverie of the High-way Law*. London.

Cobbett, William (1809-1826) *Cobbett's Complete Collection of State Trials and Proceedings for High Treason and other Crimes and Misdemeanors from the earliest period to the present time, vols.1-33*. London: R. Bagshaw and Longman & Co.

Cockburn, J.S. (1968) "The Northern Assize Circuit" in *Northern History*, vol. 3, at p.122.

Cockburn, J.S. (1969) "Seventeenth-Century Clerks of Assize - Some Anonymous Members of the Legal Profession" in *American Journal of Legal History*, vol. 13, at pp.315-327.

Cockburn, J.S. (1972) *A History of English Assizes, 1558-1714.* Cambridge: Cambridge University Press.

Cockburn, J.S. (1977a) "The Nature and Incidence of Crime in England 1559-1625: A Preliminary Survey" in *Crime in England 1550-1800.* Cockburn, J.S. (Ed.). London: Methuen, at pp.49-72.

Cockburn, J.S. (Ed.) (1977b) *Crime in England 1550-1800.* London: Methuen.

Cockburn, J.S. (1978) "Trial by the Book? Fact and Theory in the Criminal Process 1558-1625" in *Legal Records and the Historian.* Baker, J.H. (Ed.). London: Royal Historical Society at pp.60-79.

Cockburn, J.S. (1985) *Calendar of Assize Records, Home Circuit Indictments, Elizabeth and James 1: Introduction.* London, HMSO.

Cockburn, J.S. (1988) "Twelve Silly Men? The trial Jury at Assizes, 1560-1670" in *Twelve Good Men and True: The Criminal Trial Jury in England 1200-1800.* Cockburn J.S. and Green T.A. (Eds.). Princeton: Princeton University Press.

Cockburn, J.S. (1991) "Patterns of Violence in English Society: Homicide in Kent 1560-1985" in *Past and Present,* no. 130, at p.106.

Cockburn, J.S. (1994) "Punishment and Brutalization in the English Enlightenment" in *Law and History Review,* vol. 12, no. 1, at pp.155-179.

Coke, Sir Edward (1637) *A Little Treatise of Baile and Maineprize 2nd Edn.* London: printed for William Cooke.

Coke, Sir Edward (1642) *The Second Part of the Institutes of the Laws of England.* London, M. Fletcher.

Coke, Sir Edward (1644) *Institutes of the Lawes of England, Part Three, Concerning High Treason, and other Pleas of the Crown and Criminall causes.* London: W. Lee.

Coke, Sir Edward (1823) *The Fourth Part of the Institutes of the Laws of England.* New York, Gryphon.

Collym, Nicholas (1650) *A Briefe Summary of the Lawes and Statutes of England.* London.

Conley, Carolyn (1999) "The Agreeable Recreation of Fighting" in *Journal of Social History,* vol. 33, no. 1, at p.57.

Consett, Henry (1685) *The Practice of the Spiritual or Ecclesiastical Courts.* London.

Cooper, Thomas (1620) *The Cry and Revenge of Blood: Expressing the Nature and haynousnesse of wilfull Murther*. London: Nicholas Okes.

Cornett, Judy M. (1997) "Hoodwink'd by custom: The exclusion of women from juries in Eighteenth-Century English Law and Literature" in *William and Mary Journal of Women and the Law*, vol. 4, at p.1.

Coss, Graeme (1991) "God is a righteous judge, strong and patient: and God is provoked every day. A Brief History of the Doctrine of Provocation in England" in *Sydney Law Review*, vol. 13, at pp. 570-604.

Cressey, David (1996) "Gender Trouble and Cross-Dressing in Early Modern England" in *Journal of British Studies*, vol. 35, at p.463.

Cressey, David (2000) *Travesties and Transgressions in Tudor and Stuart England*. Oxford: Oxford University Press.

Croft, Edward (1677) *England's Great Happiness; or a Dialogue Between Content and Complaint*. London: Printing-Press in Cornhill.

Crompton, Richard (1594) *L'Authoritie et Jurisdiction Des Courts de la Maiestie de la Roygne: Nouelment collect & compose*. London.

Crompton, Richard (1606) *L'office et auctority de justices de Peace, in part collect per Sir Anthonie Fitzherbert Chivalier, un de les Justices del common Banke*. London: The Company of Stationers.

Curtis, T.C. and Hale, F.M. (1981) "English thinking about crime 1530-1620" in *Crime and Criminal Justice in Europe and Canada*, Knafla, Louis A. (Ed.), Canada: Wilfred Laurier University Press.

Curtis, T.C. and Sharpe, J.A. (1988) "Crime in Tudor & Stuart England" in *History Today*, vol. 38, issue 2, at pp.23-33.

D.M. (1677) *A true Relation of all the Bloody Murders that have been commited in and about the Citie and Suburbs of London, since the 4th of this instant June 1677*. London.

D'Ewes, Sir, Simmonds (MP) (1613) *A Compleat Journal of the Votes, Speeches and Debates, both of the House of Lords and House of Commons Throughout the whole Reign of Queen Elizabeth of Glorious Memory*. London.

Dalton, Michael (1655) *The Country Justice, Containing the practise of the Justices of the Peace out of their Sessions ... Now again Enlarged, with many Precedents and Resolutions of the Quares Contained in the former*

Impressions. London: Company of Stationers.

Dalton, Michael (1661) *The Country Justice, Containing the practise of the Justices of the Peace out of their Sessions ... Now again Enlarged, with many Precedents and Resolutions of the Quares Contained in the former Impressions.* London: Company of Stationers.

Davies, Owen (1999) "Witchcraft: The Spell that Didn't Break" in *History Today*, vol. 49, issue 8, at p.7.

Dean, M. (1996) *Law-Making and Society in Late Elizabethan England. The Parliament of England 1584-1601.* Cambridge: Cambridge University Press.

Defoe, Daniel (1704) *Giving Alms No Charity.* London.

Defoe, Daniel (1962) *A Tour Thro' the Whole Island of Great Britain.* London, Dent-Everyman.

Defoe, Daniel (1927) *The Poor Man's Plea in The Shortest Way with the Dissenters.* Oxford: Basil Blackwell.

De Veil, Sir Thomas (1747) *Observations on the Practice of a Justice of the Peace: Intended for Such Gentlemen as design to Act for Middlesex or Westminster.* London: printed for Edward Withers.

De Veil, Sir Thomas (1748) *Memoirs of the Life and Times, of Sir Thomas De Veil.* London.

Dougdale, Gilbert (1604) *A true discourse of the practices of Elizabeth Cauldwell.* London.

Dugdale, William (1666) *Origines Juridiales or Historical Memorials of The English Laws.* London: printed by F. and T. Warren.

Dvorak, James J. (1988) "Neonaticide: Less Than Murder?" in *The Northern Illinois University Law Review*, vol. 19, at p.173.

Edelstein, Laurie (1988) "An Accusation Easily to be Made? Rape and Malicious Prosecution in Eighteenth-Century England" in *The American Journal of Legal History* vol. XLII, no.4, at pp.351-390.

Edwards, George J. (1906) *The Grand Jury, An Essay.* Philadelphia: George T. Bisel Company.

Ekirch, A.R. (1991) "Bound for America: A Profile of British Convicts Transported to the Colonies, 1718-1775" in *Crime and Justice in American History, The Colonies and Early Republic.* E.H.Monkkonen (Ed.), Part 1, vol. 1, at pp.52-88. London: Meckler.

Elias, Norbert (1982a) *The Civilizing Process, vol. 1, The History of Manners.* Oxford: Blackwell's.

Elias, Norbert (1982b) *The Civilizing Process, vol. 2, State Formation and Civilisation.* Oxford: Blackwell's.

Ellis, Steven (1995) "Frontiers and power in the early Tudor state" in *History Today*, vol. 45, issue 4, at pp.35-42.

Elton, G.R. (1977) *Reform and Reformation: England 1509-1558.* London: Edward Arnold.

Elton, G.R. (1982) *The Tudor Constitution: Documents and Commentary*, 2nd edn. Cambridge: Cambridge University Press.

Elyot, Thomas (1962) *The Boke named The Governour.* London: Everyman edn., J. M. Dent & Co

Emsley, Clive (1999) "The origins of the Modern Police" in *History Today*, vol. 49, issue 4, at pp. 8-14.

Evans, Robin (1982) *The Fabrication of virtue: English prison architecture, 1750-1840.* Cambridge: Cambridge University Press.

Evelyn, John (1955) *The Diary of John Evelyn*, (vols. 1-6), E.S. De Beer (Ed.). Oxford: Clarendon Press.

Feeley, M. and Little, D.L. (1991) "The Vanishing Female: The Decline of Women in the Criminal Process, 1687-1912" in *Law and Society Review*, vol. 25, no. 4, at p.719.

Felson, Marcus (1994) *Crime and everday life. Insights and implications for society*, London: Pine Forge Press.

Fennor, William. (1930) "The Counter's Commonwealth" in *The Elizabethan Underworld*. Judges, A.V. (Ed.), London: Routledge.

Fielding, Henry (1751) *An inquiry into the causes of the Late Increase of Robbers.* London.

Fielding, Henry (1755) *Journal of a Voyage to Lisbon.* London: A.Millar

Finch, Heneage (1660) *An Exact and Impartial Accompt Of the Indictment, Arraignment, Tryal, and Judgment (according to Law) of Twenty Nine Regicides.* London: Andrew Crook & Edward Powel.

Fisher, George (1995a) "The Birth of the Prison Retold" in *Yale Law Journal*, vol. 104, at p.1235.

Fisher, George (1995b) "Making Sense of English Law Enforcement in the Eighteenth Century: A Response" in *The University of Chicago Law School Roundtable*, at p. 510.

Fisher, George (1997) "The Jury's Rise as Lie Detector" in *Yale Law Journal*, vol. 107, at p. 575.

Fitzgerald, P.J. (1963) "Crime, Sin and Negligence" in *Law Quarterly Review*, vol. 79, at pp.351-354.

Fleetwood, W. (1657) *The Office of a Justice of Peace, Together with Instructions, How and in What Manner Statutes shall be Expounded.* London: printed by Ralph Wood for W.Lee.

Fletcher, George (1976) "The Metamorphosis of Larceny" in *Harvard Law Review*, vol. 89, no. 3, at pp.469-530.

Fortescue, Sir John (1885) *The Governance of England: otherwise called the difference between the absolute and a limited monarchy.* Plummer, Charles (Ed.). Oxford: Clarendon Press.

Foucault, Michel (1979) *Discipline and Punish: The Birth of the Prison.* Harmondsworth: Penguin

Fox, George (1976) *George Fox - An Autobiography* (First Published 1694). Richmond (Indiana): Friends United Press.

Fox, George (1975) *The Journal of George Fox.* London: Religious Society of Friends.

Fraser, George MacDonald (1971) *The Steel Bonnets. The story of the Anglo-Scottish Border Reivers.* London: Barrie & Jenkins.

Fudge, Erica (2000) "Monstrous Acts. Bestiality in Early Modern England" in *History Today* vol. 50, issue 8, at p.20.

Fuller, William (1703) *Mr William Fuller's Trip to Bridewell: With A True Account of his Barbarous Usage in the Pillory.* London.

Gallanis, T.P. (1999) "The Rise of Modern Evidence Law" in *Iowa Law Review*, vol. 84, at p.499.

Gardner, Ralph (1655) *England's Grievance Discovered in Relation to the Coal-Trade.* London.

Gaskell, Philip (1952) "Henry Justice, a Cambridge Book Thief" in *Transactions of the Cambridge Bibliographical Society*, at pp.348-357.

Gaskill, M. (2000) *Crime and Mentalities in Early Modern England.* Cambridge: Cambridge University Press.

Gay, John (1721) *The Beggar's Opera.* London.

Gee, Henry and Hardy, William John (Eds.) (1896) "The Root and Branch Petition (1640)" in *Documents Illustrative of English Church History.* New York: Macmillan.

Geis, G. (1978) "Lord Hale, Witches and Rape" in *British Journal of Law and Society*, vol. 5, at pp.26-44.

Gent, Thomas (1832) *Thomas Gent's autobiography*, Hunter, Rev. Joseph (Ed.), London.

Gent, Thomas (1832) *The Life of Mr Thomas Gent, Printer of York*. London, Thomas Thorpe.

Gent, Frank J. (1982) *The Trial of the Bideford Witches*. Crediton: Privately Published.

Gladwin, Irene (1974) *The Sheriff: The Man and his Office*. London: Victor Gollancz.

Glazebrook, P.R. (1962) "The Merging of Misdemeanours" in *Law Quarterly Review*, vol. 78, at pp.560-569.

Goldie, Mark (1997) "The Hilton gang: terrorising dissent in 1680s London" in *History Today*, vol. 47, issue 10, at p.26.

Goodcole, Henry (1618) *A True Declaration of the happy Conversion, Contrition, and Christian preperation of F. Robinson*. London.

Goodcole, Henry (1635) *Heavens Speedie Hue and Cry sent after Lust and Murther*. London: N. and I. Okes.

Goodcole, Henry (1635) *The Adultresses Funerall Day*. London: N and I. Okes.

Gordon, Michael D. (1980) "The Invention of a Common Law Crime: Perjury and the Elizabethan Courts" in *American Journal of Legal History*, vol. 24, at p.145.

Gordon, Rev. (1745) *The Life and Circumstantial Account of the extraordinary and Surprising Exploits, Travils, robberies and Escapes of the Famous Jenny Diver*. London.

Gottfredson, M. and Hirschi, T. (1990) A *General Theory of Crime*. Stanford: Stanford University Press.

Gough Nichols, John (Ed.) (1852) *Chronicle of the Grey Friars of London*. London: Camden Society.

Gough, Richard (1981) *The History of Myddle*. Hey, David (Ed.) (originally written 1701). Harmondsworth: Penguin.

Gragg, Larry (1995) "A vagabond in paradise: Thomas Verney in Barbados" in *History Today*, vol. 45, issue 8, at pp. 40-47.

Greaves, Richard L. (1981) *Society and Religion in Elizabethan England*. Minneapolis: University of Minnesota Press.

Green, Anne (1650) *A Wonder of Wonders. Being a faithful narrative and true relation of one Anne Green ... who ... was condemned ... and hanged ... in Oxford ... and was afterwards beg'd for an anatomy ...* London.

Green, T.A. (1985) *Verdict According to Conscience: Perspectives on the English Criminal Trial Jury.* Chicago: University of Chicago Press.

Greenshields, Malcolm (1994) *An economy of Violence in Early Modern France: criminal Justice in the Haute Auvergne, 1597-1664.* University Park (Pa.): Pennsylvania State University Press.

Griffiths, Matthew (1980) "Kirtlington Manor Court, 1500-1650" in *Oxoniensia,* at pp.260-283.

Grigor, Francis (Ed.) (1917) *Sir John Fortescue's Commendation of the Laws of England: The Translation into English of De Laudibus Legum Angliae* (written c.1461-5, first published in Latin c.1537). London: Sweet and Maxwell.

Gwynfor Jones, John (1996) *Law, Order and Goverent in Caernarfonshire, 1558-1640.* Cardiff: University of Wales Press.

Hair, Paul (Ed.) (1972) *Before the Bawdy Court: Selections from Church Court and other records relating to the correction of moral offences in England, Scotland and New England, 1300-1800.* London: Elek Books Ltd.

Hale, G. (1614) *The Private Schoole of Defence. Or The Defects of Publique Teachers, exactly Discovered, by way of Objection and revolution. Together with the true practise of the Science, set downe in judicious Rules and Observations; in a Method never before expressed.* London: John Helme.

Hale, Sir Matthew (1683) *A Discourse touching Provision for the Poor.* London: printed for William Shrowsbery, at the Bible in Duke-Lane.

Hale, Sir Matthew (1713) *The History of the Common Law of England.* London: Published Posthumously by J.Walthoe, in the Savoy.

Hale, W. (Ed.) (1847) *A series of precedents and proceedings in criminal causes from 1475 to 1640; extracted from Act Books of Ecclesiastical Courts in the Diocese of London.* London: Francis and John Rivington.

Hall, Joseph (1608) *Characters of Vertues and Vices.* London: printed by Melch. Bradwood.

Hammer, C.I. (1978) "Patterns of Homicide in a Medieval University Town: Fourteenth-Century Oxford" in *Past and Present,* no.78, at p.11.

Hammond, J.L. and Hammond, Barbara (1920) *The Village Labourer 1760-1832: A Study in the Government of England before the Reform Bill.* London: Longmans.

Hanawalt, Barbara A. (1975) "Fur Collar Crime: the Pattern of Crime amongst the Fourteenth-Century English Nobles" in *Journal of Social History*, vol. 8, at pp.1-17.

Hanawalt, Barbara A. (1995) "Narratives of a Nurturing Culture: Parents and Neighbors in Medieval England" in *Essays in Medieval Studies*, vol. 12, at p.1.

Hardy, W. (1905) *Calendar to the Sessions Books and Sessions Minute Books, 1619 to 1657*, vol. 5. Hertford: Hertford County Records.

Harman, Thomas (1567) *A Caveat or Warning, for Common Cursitors vulgarly called Vagabones.* London: Wylliam Gryffith.

Harrison, Canon William (1577) *A Description of England in Raphael Holinshed's The First Volume of the Chronicles of England, Scotland and Ireland.* London: Imprinted for John Harrison.

Harrison, Canon William (1877) *A Description of England* (reproduction of 2nd book, 2nd edn., 1587). London: New Shakespeare Society.

Harrison, Canon William (1889) *Elizabethan England edited from the Description of England.* Rhys, Ernest (Ed.). London: Camelot Series.

Harrison, Christopher (1997) "Manor Courts and the Governance of Tudor England" in *Communities and Courts in Britain 1150-1900.* Brooks, C. (Ed.). London: Hambledon.

Havard, J.D. (1960) *The Detection of Secret Homicide.* London: MacMillan.

Hawles, Sir John (1680) *The English-mans right. A dialogue between a barrister at law and a jury-man.* London.

Hay, Douglas (1975) "Property, authority and the criminal law" in *Albions Fatal Tree: crime and society in 18th century England.* Hay, D. et al (Eds.). New York, Pantheon Books.

Hearnshaw, F.J.C. (Ed.) (1907) *Court Leet Records, vol. 1, Part III, 1603-1624.* Southampton: Southampton Record Society Publications.

Helmholz, R.H. (1987) *Canon Law and the Law of England.* London: The Hambledon Press.

Helmholz, R.H. (1990) "Origins of the privilege against self-incrimination: The role of the European Jus Commune" in *New York University Law Review*, vol. 65, at p. 962.

Hemphill, C. Dallett (2000) Review of "From Courtesy to Civility: Changing Codes of Conduct in Early Modern England" by Anna Bryson (New York: Oxford University Press) in *Journal of Social History*, vol. 33, issue 3, at p.747.

Hentzner, Paul (1889) *Travels in England during the reign of Queen Elizabeth.* London: Cassell & Co.

Herbert, George (1652) *A Priest to the Temple, or, The Countrey Parson his character, and Rule of Holy Life.* London: printed by T. Maxey for T. Garthwait.

Herrup, Cynthia B. (1985) "Law and Morality in Seventeenth- Century England" in *Past & Present*, no.105, at p.102.

Herrup, Cynthia B. (1987a) Review of "Crime Law and Society in Late Medieval and Tudor England" by Bellamy, J.G. (1984) in *American Journal of Legal History*, vol. 31, at p.164.

Herrup, Cynthia B. (1987b) *The Common Peace: Participation and the Common Law in Seventeenth Century England.* Cambridge: Cambridge University Press.

Herrup, Cynthia B. (1999a) "Finding the Bodies" in *GLQ: A Journal of Lesbian and Gay Studies*, vol. 5.3, at pp.255-265

Herrup, Cynthia B. (1999b) *A House in Gross Disorder: Sex, Law, and the Second Earl of Castlehaven.* New York: Oxford University Press.

Hext, Edward (1951) "Letter written by Edward Hext, a Somerset JP, to Lord Burghley on 25th September 1596" reproduced in *Tudor Economic Documents* (vol. 2). Tawney R.H. and Power E. (Eds.), London: Longmans.

Hill, L.M. (1966) "The Two-witness Rule in English Treason Trials: Some comments on the Emergence of Procedural Law" in *American Journal of Legal History*, vol. 12, at p.95.

Hitchcock, Robert (1580) "A Politic Plat for the honour of the Prince" in *Social England Illustrated: A Collection of XVIIth Century Tracts.* Arber, Edward (Ed.). Westminster: Archibald Constable, 1903.

Hobbes, Thomas (1651) *Leviathan.* London, Andrew Crooke.

Hobson, John (1988) "John Hobson's Diary", reproduced in *The Making of Barnsley Brian Elliot.* Barnsley, Wharncliffe Publishing Limited at pp.83-118.

Hoffer, Peter and Hull, N.E.H. (1981) *Murdering Mothers.* London: New York University Press.

Holcroft, William (1986) *William Holcroft His Booke' Local Office-holding in Late Stuart Essex.* Sharpe J.A. (Ed.). Chelmsford: Essex Record Office.

Howard, John (1929) (1st pub. 1777) *The State of the Prisons.* London: Everyman edn. J.M. Dent.

Howle, Henry (1990) "Henry Howle's Notebook" in *Kent Records, New Series.* Hull, Felix (Ed.), vol. 1, parts 1-3. Kent: Kent Archaeology Society.

Howson, G. (1970) *Thieftaker General: the rise and fall of Jonathan Wild.* London: Hutchinson.

Hudson, William (1792) *A Treatise on the Court of Star-Chamber.* London.

Hunnisett, R.F. (1998) *Sussex Coroners' Inquests 1603-1688.* London: Public Records Office.

Hurl-Eamon, J. (2001) "Domestic Violence Prosecuted: Women Binding Over Their Husbands for Assault at Westminster Quarter Sessions, 1685-1720" in *Journal of Family History,* vol. 26, no. 4, pp. 435-454.

Hurstfield, Joel (1973) *Freedom, Corruption and Government in Elizabethan England.* London: Jonathan Cape.

Hutton, Alfred (1892) *Old Sword-Play. The Systems of Fence in vogue during the XVIth XVIIth, and XVIIIth centuries with lessons arranged from the works of various ancient masters ... Containing fifty-seven plates, etc.* London: Grevel & Co.

Hutton, Sir Richard (1656) *The Reports of that Reverend and Learned Judge ...* London: printed by T. R. for H. Twyford and T. Dring.

Hutton, W. (1791) The History of Derby, London.

Ingram, M.J. (1984) "Ridings, Rough Music and the 'Reform of Popular Culture' in Early Modern England" in *Past and Present,* no.105, at pp.79-113.

Ingram, M.J. (1987) *Church Courts, Sex and Marriage in England 1570-1640.* Cambridge: Cambridge University Press.

Ingram, M.J. (1977) "Communities and Courts: Law and Disorder in early-Seventeenth-Century Wiltshire" in *Crime in England 1550-1800.* Cockburn, J.S. (Ed.). London: Methuen, at pp.110-134.

Ingram, M.J. (1996) "Reformation of Manners in Early Modern England" in *The Experience of Authority in Early Modern England.* Griffiths, P., Fox, A., Hindle, S. (Eds.). Basingstoke: Macmillan.

Ives, E.W. and Manchester, A.H. (Eds.) (1983) *Law, Litigants and the Legal Profession*. London: Royal History Society.

Jackson, Mark (1996) "Infanticide: historical perspectives" in *New Law Journal*, vol. 146, No 6736, at p.416.

Jacob, Giles (1709) *The Laws of Appeals and Murder*. London.

Jacob, Giles (1734) *The Compleat Parish Officer*, 7th edn. Republished by Wiltshire Family History Association, Salisbury (1996).

Jenkins, Philip (1986) "From Gallows to Prison? The Execution Rate in Early Modern England" in *Criminal Justice History*, vol. 7, at pp.51-71.

Johnson, Captain Charles (1734) *A General History of the Lives and Adventures of the Most Famous Highwaymen, Murderers, Street-Robbers*. London: J. Janeway.

Johnson, Samuel (1953) "Crime and Punishment" in *The Rambler*. London: Everyman edn. J.M. Dent.

Judges, A.V. (1930) *The Elizabethan Underworld*. London: Routledge.

Keeton, G.W. (1961) "Judge Jeffreys as Chief Justice of Chester 1680-1683" in *The Law Quarterly Review*, vol. 77, at pp. 36-68.

Kaye, J.M. (1967) "The Early History of Murder and Manslaughter, (part 2)", in *The Law Quarterly Review*, vol. 83, at pp.569-601.

Kelly, James (1998) "The pirate, the ambassador and the map-maker (Captain Bartholomew Sharpe)" in *History Today*, vol. 48, issue 7, pp. 49-55.

Kelyng, Sir John (1708) *A Report of Divers Cases in Pleas of the Crown, Adjudged and determined; in the Reign of the late King Charles II With Directions for Justices of the Peace and Others*. London: Isaac Cleave.

Kemp, William (1600) *Kemp's 9 daies vvonder. Performed in a daunce from London to Norwich*. London: E.A.

Kempt, Thomas (1909) *The Book of John Fisher, Town Clerk and Deputy Recorder of Warwick 1580-1581*. Warwick: Henry Cooke & Son.

Kent, Joan R. (1973) "Attitudes of Members of the House of Commons to the Regulation of 'Personal Conduct' in Late Elizabethan and Early Stuart England" in *British Institute of Historical Research*, vol. 46, at pp.41-71.

Kent, Joan R. (1981) "The English Village constable, 1580-1642: The nature and dilemmas of the Office" in *Journal of British Studies*, vol. 20 (2), at pp. 26-49.

Kent, Joan R. (1983) "'Folk Justice' and Royal Justice in Early Seventeenth-Century England: A 'Charivari' in the Midlands" in *Midland History*, vol. 8, at pp.70-85.

Kermode, J. and Walker, G. (Eds.) (1994) *Women, Crime and the Courts in Early Modern England*. London: UCL Press.

Kesselring, Krista (1999) "Abjuration and its Demise: the Changing Face of Royal Justice in the Tudor Period" in *Canadian Journal of History*, vol. 34, no.3, at p.345.

Kesselring, Krista (2001) "A Draft for the 1531 'Acte for Poysoning'" in *English Historical Review*, vol.116, at pp.894-899.

Ketch, John (1683) *The Apologie of John Ketch Esq.: The Executioner of London, in Vindication of himself as to the Execution of the Late Lord Russell, On July 21st 1683*. London: John Brown.

Kevorkian, Tanya (2000) "The Rise of the Poor, Weak, and Wicked: Poor Care, Punishment, Religion, and Patriarchy in Leipzig 1700-1730" in *Journal of Social History*, vol. 34, no.1, at p.163.

Kidderminster, Thomas (1688) *A true Relation of the horrid Murder committed upon the person of T. K. ... at ... Chelmsford, in ... April, 1654. Together with a true account of the ... discovery of the same nine years after; for which M. Drayne ... was executed in 1667*. London.

King, James VI and I (1597) *Daemonologie by King James VI of Scotland in the form of a dialogue, Book 3*. Edinburgh.

King, Peter (1992) "Legal Change, Customary Right, and Social Conflict in Late Eighteenth-Century England: The Origins of the Great Gleaning Case of 1788" in *Law and History Review*, vol. 10, no. 1.

Klerman, Daniel (2001) "Settlement and the Decline of Private Prosecution in Thirteenth-Century England" in *Law and History Review*, vol. 19, no.1, at pp.1-66.

Knafla, Louis A. (Ed.) (1981) *Crime and Criminal Justice in Europe and Canada*. Waterloo (Ontario): Wilfred Laurier University Press.

Knafla, Louis A. (1983) "'Sin of all Sorts Swarmeth': Criminal Litigation in an English County in the early Seventeenth Century" in *Law, Litigants and the Legal Profession*. Ives E.W. and Manchester A.H. London: Royal History Society, at pp.50-68.

Knafla, Louis A. (1994) *Kent at Law 1602. The County Jurisdiction: Assizes and Sessions of the Peace.* London: HMSO and PRO.

Kopel, David B. (1995) "It Isn't About Duck Hunting: The British Origins Of The Right To Arms" in *Michigan Law Review*, vol. 93, at pp.1333-1362.

Kyll, Thomas (1739) *The Trial of the notorious Highwayman Richard Turpin, at York Assizes on the 22nd day of March, 1739, before the Honourable Sir William Chapple, Kt. Judge of Assize.* York, 1739, at pp.1-3.

L.B. (1609) *Foure Statutes, Specially Selected and Commanded by his Maijestie to be carefully put in execution by all Justices and other Officers of the Peace throughout the Realme.* London: printed by Robert Barker.

L.L. (1617) *A True Relation of Most desperate Murder committed upon the Body of Sir John Tindall.* London: printed by Edw: All.de.

Lacour, Eva (2001) "Faces of violence revisited. A typology of violence in Early Modern rural Germany" in *Journal of Social History*, vol. 34, no. 3, at pp.649-668.

Langbein, John (1973) "The Origins of Public Prosecution at Common Law" in *The American Journal of Legal History*, vol. 17, at p.313.

Lambarde, William (1826) *A Perambulation of Kent, conteining the description, hystorie, and customes of that Shire* (first written 1570). London: Baldwin, Cradock, Joy & Co.

Lambarde, William (1583) *The Duties of Constables, Borsholders, Tithing men, and such other low Ministers of the Peace.* London.

Lambarde, William (1619) *Eirenarcha: Or of the Office of the Justices of Peace in Foure Books.* London: Company of Stationers.

Lambarde, William (1635) *Archeion, or, A Discourse on The High Courts of Justice in England.* London.

Lambarde, William (1962) *Ephemeris* in *William Lambarde and Local Government.* Read, Conyers (Ed.). New York: University Press Ithaca.

Landau, Norma (1984) *The Justice of the Peace 1679-1760.* Berkeley: University of California Press.

Landau, Norma (1999) "Indictment for Fun and Profit: A Prosecutor's Reward at Eighteenth-Century Quarter Sessions" in *Law and History Review*, vol. 17, at p.507.

Lander, J.R. (1989) *English Justices of the Peace 1461-1509.* London: Alan Sutton.

Landsman, Stephan (1990) "The rise of the contentious spirit: Adversary procedure in Eighteenth Century England" in *Cornell Law Review*, vol. 75, at p.497.

Landsman, Stephan (1998) "One Hundred Years of Rectitude: Medical Witnesses at the Old Bailey, 1717-1817" in *Law and History Review*, vol. 16, at p.445.

Lane, Roger (1998) Review of "The Civilization of Crime: Violence in Town and Country Since the Middle Ages" in *Journal of Social History*, vol. 31, no. 3, pp.750-753.

Langbein, John H. (1983) "Shaping the Eighteenth-Century Criminal Trial: A View from the Ryder Sources" in *University of Chicago Law Review*, vol. 50, at p.1.

Langbein, John H. (1994) "The historical origins of the privilege against self-incrimination at Common Law" in *Michigan Law Review*, vol. 92, at pp.1047-1085.

Langbein, John H. (1996) "Historical Foundations of the Law of Evidence: A View From the Ryder Sources" in *Columbia Law Review*, vol. 96 at pp.1168-1202.

Langeluddecke, H. (1997) "Law and order in seventeenth-century England: the organisation of local administration during the personal rule of Charles I" in *Law and History Review*, vol. 15, at pp. 49-76.

Langeluddecke, H. (1998) "'Patchy and Spasmodic'?: The Response of Justices of the Peace to Charles I's Book of Orders" in *English Historical Review*, vol. 113, no.454, at p.1231.

Laud, Archbishop William (1635) "Visitation Articles, 1635" in *Anglicanism*. More E. (Ed.). Harrisburg, PA: Morehouse Publishing at pp. 702-705.

Lawson, Peter C. (1986) "Property Crime and Hard Times in England, 1559-1624" in *Law and History Review*, vol. 4, at p.109.

Lawson, Peter C. (1988) "Lawless Juries? The Composition and Behaviour of Hertfordshire Juries, 1573-1624" in *Twelve Good Men and True: The Criminal Trial Jury in England 1200-1800*. Cockburn J.S. and Green T.A. (Eds.). Princeton: Princeton University Press.

Lawson, Peter C. (1998) "Patriarchy, Crime and the Courts: The criminality of Women in Late Tudor and Early Stuart England" in *Criminal Justice in the Old World and the New*. Smith, G.T. (Ed.). Toronto: Centre of Criminology, University of Toronto.

Leach, William (1652) *The Bribe-Takers of Jury-Men, Partiall, Dishonest, and Ignorant Discovered and Abolished*. London: printed by E.Cotes.

Le Blanc, Jean Bernard (1747) *Letters on the English and French Nations*, vol. 2. London: J. Brindley.

Lemmings, David (1988) "Blackstone and Law Reform by Education: Preparation for the Bar and Lawyerly Culture in Eighteenth-Century England" in *Law & History Revue*, vol. 16, p. 211.

Lenman, B. and Parker, G. (1980) "The State, the Community and the Criminal Law in Early Modern Europe" in *Crime & The Law: The Social History of Crime in Western Europe since 1500*. Gatrell, V.A.C. *et al* (Eds.). London: Europa.

Leyton, Elliott (1997) *Men of Blood: Murder in Modern England*. Harmondsworth: Penguin Books.

Lysons, Daniel and Lysons, Samuel (1806) *Magna Britannia; Being a concise topographical account of the several counties of Great Britain* (vols.1-6). London: T. Kadell and W. Davies.

MacFarlane, Alan (1970) *Witchcraft in Tudor and Stuart Essex*. London.

MacFarlane, Alan (1980) "Review Essay of 'Calendar of Assize Records Essex Indictments Elizabeth I'" in *American Journal of Legal History*, vol. 21, at pp.171-177.

MacFarlane, Alan and Harrison, Sarah (1981) *The justice and the mare's ale, law and disorder in seventeenth century England*. Oxford: Blackwell.

Mandeville, Bernard De (1725) *An Enquiry into the Causes of the Frequent Executions at Tyburn*. London.

Marcus, Richard L. (1984) "English Common Law: Studies in the sources: the Tudor treason trials: Some observations on the emergence of forensic themes" in *University of Illinois Law Review*, at p. 675.

Marriott, John (2000) "Sweep them off the streets (historical attitudes towards the poor in London, England)" in *History Today*, vol. 50, issue 8, pp. 26-28.

Mathews, Nancy L. (1984) *William Sheppard, Cromwell's Law Reformer*. Cambridge: Cambridge University Press.

McAuley, Finbarr and McCutcheon, J. Paul (2000) *Criminal Liability*. Dublin: Round Hall Ltd.

McCune, Pat (1991) "Justice, Mercy, and Late Medieval Governance" in *Michigan Law Review*, vol. 89, no.6, at pp.1661-1678.

McIntosh, Marjorie Keniston (1984) "Social Change and Tudor Manorial Leets" in *Law and Social Change in British History.* Guy, J.A. and Beale H.G. (Eds.). London: Royal Historical Society.

McIntosh, Marjorie Keniston (1991) *A community transformed: The manor and Liberty of Havering, 1500-1620.* Cambridge: Cambridge University Press.

McIntosh, Marjorie Keniston (1998) *Controlling Misbehaviour in England, 1370-1600.* Cambridge: Cambridge University Press.

MacKenzie, T.H. (1999) *Oakham Castle: A Guide and History.* Clough, Oakham: Rutland County Council.

Maynard, Sir John (1699) *The Case of a Murther in Hertfordshire. Found amongst the papers of that eminent lawyer, Sir John Maynard, etc.* London.

McMullan, John (1984) *The Canting Crew: London's Criminal Underworld 1550-1700.* New Brunswick (N.J.): Rutgers University Press.

McMullan, John (1987) "Crime, Law and Order in Early Modern England" in *British Journal of Criminology.* vol. 27, no.3, at pp. 252-274.

Melling, Elizabeth (Ed.) (1969) *Crime and Punishment, Kentish Sources* VI. Maidstone: Kent County Council.

Mercer, E.D. and Goodacre, K. (1965) *Guide to the Middlesex Sessions Records, 1549-1884.* London: GLRO.

Mercer, Sarah (1991) "Crime in Late-Seventeenth-Century Yorkshire: an Exception to a National Pattern?" in *Northern History*, vol. 27, at pp.106-119.

Metzmeier, Kurt X. (1996) "Preventive Detention: A Comparison of Bail refusal practices in the United States, England, Canada and other common law nations" in *Pace International Law Review*, vol. 8, at p.399.

Middleton, Wilhelm (1545) *The Boke For A Justyce of Peace, never so well and dylygently set forthe.* London.

Milward, John (1938) *The Diary of John Milward Esq., September 1666 to May 1668.* Robbins, Caroline (Ed.). Cambridge: Cambridge University Press.

Misson, M. (1719) *Memoirs and Observations in his Travels over England.* (J. Ozell, trans.). London.

More, Sir Thomas (1997) *Utopia* (Robinson, Ralph, Trans. 1st published 1516). Ware: Wordsworth Classics.

More, Sir Thomas (1557) *The History of King Richard the Third*. Richard Bear (Ed.) (1997). Oregon: University of Oregon.

More, Sir Thomas (1577) "The Deballaryon of Salem and Bizance 1533" from *The Works of Sir Thomas More*. London: reproduced by Scolar Press.

More, Sir Thomas (1931), "The History of King Richard the Thirde" (1st written c. 1513) in *The English Works of Sir Thomas More* (1st written c.1513) A.W. Reed *et al* (eds.) vol. 1. London: Eyre and Spottiswoode.

Moreton, Andrew (Daniel Defoe) (1725) *Every-Body's Business is No-Body's Business*. London.

Moreton, C. (1993) "Mid-Tudor trespass: a break in at Norwich 1549" in *English Historical Review*, vol. 107, at pp.387-398.

Morrill, J.C. (1976) *The Cheshire Grand Jury 1625-1659, A Social and Administrative Study*. Leicester: Leicester University Press.

Morris, N. and Rothman, D.J. (Eds.) (1995) *The Oxford History of the Prison*. Oxford: Oxford University Press.

Morris, T.A. (1999) *Tudor Government*. London: Routledge.

Mortimer, Levine (1963) "A More than Ordinary Case of 'Rape', 13 and 14 Elizabeth I" in *American Journal of Legal History*, vol. 7, p.159.

Naunton, Robert (1889) *Fragmenta Regalia*. London: Cassell & Co.

Nelson, Janet (2000) Review of "Providence in Early Modern England" by Alexandra Walsham in *History Today*, vol. 50, issue 5, at p.54

Nelson, William (1717) *The Law of Evidence*. London: R. Gosling.

Neville, C. J. (1994) "Keeping the peace on the northern marches in the later Middle Ages" in *English Historical Review*, vol. 109, at pp.1-25.

Oakley, A.F. (1971) "Sir John Reresby and the Moor - A 17th century Coroner's Inquest" in *History of Medicine*, vol. 3, at pp.27-31.

Ogle, Arthur (1949) *The Tragedy of the Lollard's Tower: The Case of Richard Hunne and its aftermath in the Reformation Parliament, 1529-1533*. Oxford: Pen-in-hand.

Oldham, James C. (1983) "The Origins of the Special Jury" in *University of Chicago Law Review*, vol. 50, at p.137.

Oldham, James (1994) "Truth-Telling in the Eighteenth-Century English Courtroom" in *Law and History Review*, vol. 12, no. 1, at pp. 95-122.

Osterberg, Eva (1996) "Criminality and the Early Modern State in Scandinavia" in *The Civilization of Crime: violence in town and country since the Middle Ages*. Johnson, J.A. and Monkkonen, E.H. (Eds.) Urbana: University of Illinois Press.

Overbury, Sir Thomas (1676) *A true and Perfect Account of the Examination, Confession, Tryal, Condemnation, and execution of Joan Perry, and her two sons, John and Richard Perry, For the Supposed Murder of William Harrison. Gent.* London: Rowland Reynolds.

Paton, Diana (2001) "Punishment, Crime, and the Bodies of Slaves in Eighteenth-Century Jamaica" in *Journal of Social History*, vol. 34, no. 4, pp.923-954.

Payling, S.J. (1998) "Murder, motive and punishment in fifteenth-century England: two gentry case-studies" in *English Historical Review*, vol. 113, no.450, at p.1.

Penn, W. and Mead, W. (1730) "The Trial of William Penn and William Mead, at The Old-Baily, For a Tumultous Assembly, the Ist, 3rd, 4th, and 5th of September, 1670" in *A Complete Collection of State-Trials, Proceedings upon High Treason and other Crimes and Misdemeanors, from the Reign of King Richard II to the End of the Reign of King George I*, vol. 2, 2nd edn. London, at p.606.

Pepys, Samuel (1971) *The Diary of Samuel Pepys*. Latham R. and Mathews W. (Eds.), vols. 1-11. London: Bell and Hyman.

Perry, Mary Elizabeth (1980) *Crime and Society in Early Modern Seville*. Hanover (N.H.): University of New England Press.

Petty, Sir William (1967) *The Petty Papers: Some Unpublished Writings of Sir William Petty* edited from the Bowood Papers by the Marquis of Lansdowne (vol. 1). New York: Augustus M. Kelley Publishers.

Phillimore, W.P.W. (Ed.) (1894) *Gloucestershire Notes and Queries*, vol. V, 1891-1893. London.

Platter, Thomas and Busino, Horatio (1995) *Journals of two travellers in Elizabethan and early Stuart England*. Razzell, Peter (Ed.). London: Caliban.

Plucknett T.F. and Barton J.C. (Eds.) (1974a) *1st Dialogue, 1523, St Germain's Doctor and Student*. London: Selden Society, London.

Plucknett T.F. and Barton J.C. (Eds.) (1974b) *2nd Dialogue, 1530, St.Germain's Doctor and Student*. London: Selden Society.

Porter, Roy (1997) "Bethlem/Bedlam: methods of madness?" in *History Today*, vol. 47, issue 10, at p.41.

Post, J.B. (1983) "Local Jurisdictions and Judgment of Death in Later Medieval England" in *Criminal Justice History*, vol. 4, at pp.1-21.

Potter, David (1997) "Rigueur de justice: Crime, Murder and the Law in Picardy, Fifteenth-Sixteenth Centuries" in *French History*, vol. 11, no. 3, at pp.265-309.

Pound, J.F. and Beier, A.L. (1976) "Debate, Vagrants and the Social Order in Elizabethan England" in *Past and Present*, no. 71, at pp.126-130.

Powell, Edward (1988) "Jury Trial at Gaol Delivery in the Late Middle Ages: The Midland Circuit, 1400-1429" in *Twelve Good Men and True: The Criminal Trial Jury in England 1200-1800*. Cockburn J.S. and Green T.A. (Eds.). Princeton: Princeton University Press.

Prest, Wilfrid (1967) "Legal Education of the Gentry at the Inns of Court, 1560-1640" in *Past and Present*, no. 38, at pp.20-39.

Prest, Wilfrid (1986) *The Rise of the Barrister: A Social History of the English Bar 1590-1640*. Oxford: Clarendon Press.

Pryme de la, Abraham (1870) *The Diary of Abraham de la Pryme*. Durham: Surtees Society.

Pulton, Ferdinando (1623) *De Pace Regis et Regni; Viz. A Treatise Declaring Which Be The Great And General Offences of the Realme*. London: Lincoln's Inn.

Pyson (1526) *Diversite de Courts et leur Jurisdictions*. London.

Quintrell B.W. (Ed.) (1981) *Lancashire JPs at the Sheriff's Table 1578-1694*. Lancaster: The Record Society of Lancashire and Cheshire.

Ramirez, Deborah A. (1994) "The Mixed Jury and the Ancient Custom of Trial by Jury De Medietate Linguae: A History and a Proposal for Change" in *Boston University Law Review*, vol. 74, at p.777.

Rawlings, Philip (1992) *Drunks, whores and idle apprentices: criminal biographies of the eighteenth century*. London: Routledge.

Rawlings, Philip (2001) *Policing: A Short History*. Cullompton: Willan Publishing.

Rayner, J.L. and Crook, G.T. (Eds.) (1926) *The Complete Newgate Calendar* (vols. 1-5). London: Privately printed for the Navarre Society.

Read, Conyers (Ed.) (1962) *William Lambarde and Local Government 1580-1588.* New York: Cornell University Press, Ithaca.

Redwood, B.C. (Ed.) (1954) *Quarter Sessions Order Book 1642-1649.* Lewes: Sussex Record Society, vol. 54.

Reresby, Sir John (1734) *The Memoirs of Sir John Reresby.* London.

Rice, James D. (1996) "The criminal trial Before and After the Lawyers: Authority, Law and Culture in Maryland Jury Trials, 1681-1837" in *American Journal Legal History*, vol. 40, at pp.455-475.

Rid, Samuel (1930) "Martin Markall, Beadle of Bridewell" in *The Elizabethan Underworld.* Judges A.V. (Ed.). London: Routledge.

Robbins, Caroline (Ed.) (1938) *The Diary of John Milward, Esq. September 1666-May 1668.* Cambridge: Cambridge University Press.

Roberts, Stephen (1982a) "Fornication and bastardy in Mid-Seventeenth Century Devon: how was the Act of 1650 enforced?" in *Outside the Law: Studies in Crime and Order 1650-1850.* Rule, J. (Ed.) at pp.1-14.

Roberts, Stephen (1982b) "Jury Vetting in the 17th Century" in *History Today*, vol. 33, issue 2, at pp. 25-29.

Robinson, Henry (1651) *Certain Consideration In Order to a more Speedy, Cheap, and Equall Distribution of Justice throughout the Nation.* London: Mathew Simmons.

Robinson, Henry (1653) *Certaine proposals in order to a new modelling of the lawes, and law-proceedings.* London: Mathew Simmons.

Robison, William B. (1988) "Murder at Crowhurst: A Case Study in Early Tudor Law Enforcement" in *Criminal Justice History*, vol. 9, at pp. 44-45.

Rogers, H.C.B. (1972) *Weapons of the British Soldier.* London: Sphere Books.

Rogers, Michael (1996) "Gerald Winstanley on Crime and Punishment" in *Sixteenth Century Journal*, vol. XXVII 3, at p.739.

Rokeby, Mr Justice (1887) *The Diary of Mr Justice Rokeby printed from a manuscript in the Possession of Sir Henry Peek, Bart.* London: Wyman & Sons.

Roper, William (1963) *The Life of Sir Thomas More, in Lives of Sir Thomas More.* E.G. Reynolds (Ed.). London: Everyman edn., J.M. Dent.

Rowse, A.L. (1961) *The England of Elizabeth - The Structure of Society.* London: Macmillan.

Rublack, Ulinka (1999) *The Crimes of Women in Early Modern Germany.* Oxford: Oxford University Press.

Ruff, Julius R. (2001) *Violence in Early Modern Europe 1500-1800.* Cambridge: Cambridge University Press.

Rule, John (Ed.) (1982) *Outside the Law: Studies in Crime and Order 1650-1850.* Exeter: Papers in Economic History, University of Exeter.

S.R. (1610) *Martin Mark-All, Beadle of Bridewell; His defence and Answere to the Belman of London.* London: John Budge.

Salmon, Thomas (1720) *Tryals for High-Treason, and other Crimes. With proceedings on bills of attainder, and impeachments. For three hundred years past,* vol. 4. London: D. Brown, etc.

Samaha, Joel (1975) "Gleanings from Local Criminal Court Records: sedition amongst the 'inarticulate' in Elizabethan England" in *Journal of Social History,* vol. 8, at p.62.

Samaha, Joel (1978) "Hanging for Felony: The Rule of Law in Elizabethan Colchester" in *Historical Journal,* vol. 21, at pp.763-782.

Samaha, Joel (1981) "The recognizance in Elizabethan Law Enforcement" in *American Journal of Legal History,* vol. 25, at pp. 189-204.

Savage, Thomas (1668) *Gods Justice against Murther, or the bloudy Apprentice executed. Being an exact ... relation of a bloudy murther committed by one T. Savage ... in Ratliffe upon the maid of the house his fellow servant, being deluded thereunto by the instigations of a whore.* London.

Saviolo, Vicentio (1595) *Vincentio Saviolo his Practise. In two Bookes. The first intreating of the use of the Rapier and Dagger. The second, of Honor and honorable Quarrels.* London: J Wolfe.

Sayles, G.O. (1959) *The Court of King's Bench in Law and History.* London: Selden Society.

Sayre, Francis Bowes (1928) "Criminal Attempts" in *Harvard Law Review,* vol. 41, at pp.821-859.

Schulte Herbruggen, H. (1983) "The Process against Sir Thomas More" in *Law Quarterly Review,* vol. 99, at pp.113-136.

Selden, John (1640) *A Briefe Discourse Concerning the Powers of the Peeres and Comons of Parliament, in point of Judicature.* London.

Shapiro, Barbara J. (1986) "To A Moral Certainty: Theories of Knowledge and Anglo-American Juries 1600-1850" in *Hastings Law Journal,* vol. 38, at p.153.

Sharpe, J.A. (1981) "Domestic Homicide in Early Modern England" in *Historical Journal*, vol. 24, at pp. 29-48.

Sharpe J.A. (1983) *Crime in Seventeenth Century England*. Cambridge: Cambridge University Press.

Sharpe, J.A. (1985) "Debate: The History of Violence in England. Some Observations" in *Past & Present*, no. 108, at p. 215.

Sharpe, J.A. (1993) "Lessons of History: Hard times revive law and order panic" in *The Independent* (London), April 12, 1993.

Sharpe, J.A. (1977) "Law-Enforcement in the Seventeenth-Century English Village" in *Crime and the Law*. Gatrell V.A.C. *et al* (Eds.). London: Europa.

Sharpe, J.A. (1999a) *Crime in Early Modern England 1550-1750*, 2nd edn. London: Longman.

Sharpe, J.A. (1999b) *The Bewitching of Anne Gunter: A Horrible and True story of football, witchcraft, murder and the King of England*. London: Profile Books.

Shaw, J. (1728) *The Practical Justice of Peace: or a Treatise shewing the power and authority of that office in all its branches, etc*. London, Thomas Ward.

Sheppard, William (1656) *The Whole Office of the County Justice of Peace*, 3rd Edition. London: W.Lee.

Shoemaker, R.B . (1991) *Prosecution and Punishment: Petty Crime and the Law in London and Rural Middlesex, c.1660-1725*. Cambridge: Cambridge University Press.

Silver, George (1599) *Paradoxes of Defence*. London: Edward Blount.

Sklansky, David A. (1999) "The Private Police" in *UCLA Law Review*, vol. 46, at p.1165.

Slobogin, Christopher (2000) "An end to Insanity: Recasting the role of mental disability in Criminal Cases" in *Virginia Law Review Association*, vol. 86, at p. 1199.

Smalbroke, Richard (1728) *Reformation necessary to prevent Our Ruine: A Sermon Preached to the Societies for Reformation of Manners, at St. Mary-le-Bow, on Wednesday, January 10th, 1727*. London: printed and sold by Joseph Downing.

Smith, Rev. M.G. (1982) "Pastoral Discipline and the Church Courts: the Hexham Court 1680-1730" in *Borthwick Papers*, no.62, York.

Smith, Richard (1695) *Mistaken Justice: or, Innocence condemn'd, in the person of Francis Newland, lately executed at Tyburn, for the ... murther of ... Francis Thomas. Being a true account of the evidence against him, etc.* London.

Smith, S.R. (1973) "The London Apprentices as Seventeenth- Century Adolescents" in *Past and Present*, vol. 61, at pp.149-161.

Smith, Simon (1996) "Piracy in early British America" in *History Today*, vol. 46, issue 5, at p.29.

Smith, Sir Thomas (1583) *De Republica Anglorum. The maner of Gouvernement or policie of the Realme of England* (written 1565). London: Henri Midleton for Gregorie Seton.

Smith, Captain Alexander (1719) *A Compleat history of the lives and robberies of the most notorious highwaymen ... for above an hundred years past*, vols. 1-3. London: Briscoe

Soman, Alfred (1980) "Deviance and Criminal Justice in Western Europe, 1300-1800: An Essay in Structure" in *Criminal Justice History*, vol. 1, at pp.3-28.

Somers, John Lord (1682) *The Security of English-Mens Lives, or the Trust, Power, and Duty of the Grand Jurys of England explained according to the fundamentals of the English government, etc.* London: printed for Benj. Alsop.

Spelman, Sir Henry (1626) *Archaeologus*, (vols. 1 and 2). London: Joannen Beale.

Spenser, Edmund (1884), "A Veue of the Present State of Ireland" (1st published 1596), in A.B. Grosart (ed.). *The Complete Works in Verse and Prose of Edmund Spenser*. London, privately published.

Spierenburg, Peter (1991) *The Prison Experience: Disciplinary Institutions and their Inmates in Early Modern Europe*. New Brunswick and London: Rutgers University Press.

Spraggs, Gillian (2001) *Outlaws and Highwaymen*. London: Pimlico.

Starkey, T. (1948) *A Dialogue between Reginal Pole and Thomas Lupset*, Burton, K.M. (Ed.). London: Chatto and Windus.

Staunford, Sir William (1557) *Les Plees Del Coron: divisee in plusiors titles & common lieux*. London

Staunford, Sir William (1607) *Les Plees Del Corone ...* London.

Steegman, Edward (1987) "Of History and Due Process" in *Indiana Law Journal*, Indiana, vol. 63, at pp.369-399.

Stein, Mitchell C. (1988) "Law and legitimacy in England, 1800-1832: Bringing Professors Hay and Thompson to the bargaining table" in *Boston University Law Review*, vol. 68, at p. 621.

Stephen, Sir James Fitzjames (1883) *A History of the Criminal Law of England*, 3 vols, London, Macmillan.

Stockdale, Eric (1977) *A Study of Bedford Prison*. Chichester: Philimore,

Stone, Lawrence (1967) *The Crisis of the Aristocracy 1558-1641*. Abridged Edition. Oxford: Oxford University Press.

Stone, Lawrence (1983) "Interpersonal Violence in English Society, 1300-1980" in *Past and Present*, no. 10, at p.22.

Stone, Lawrence (1985) "Debate: The History of Violence in England, A Rejoinder" in *Past & Present*, no.108, at p. 216.

Stow, John (1592) *The Annales of England, faithfully collected out of the most authenticall Authors, Records, and other Monuments of Antiquitie, from the first inhabitation untill this present yeere 1592*. London: imprinted by Ralfe Nebery.

Stow, John (1971) *A Survey of London. Reprinted from the text of 1603*, vol. 1. Introduced by Charles Lethbridge Kingsford. Oxford: Clarendon.

Strathern, Marilyn (1985) "Discovering 'Social Control'" in *Journal of Law and Society*, vol. 12, no. 2, at pp.111-134.

Styles, John (1988) "Crime in 18th Century England" in *History Today*, vol. 38, issue 3, at p.36.

Sym, John (1637) *Life's Preservative Against Self-Killing*. London.

T.C. (1618) *The Glory of England, or a True Description of many excellent prerogatives and remarkeable blessings, whereby she Triumpheth over all the Nations of the World*. London.

T.W. (1660) *The Clerk of Assize, Judges-Marshall, and Cryer: Being The True Manner and form of the proceedings at the Assizes and General Goale-Delivery, both in the Crown Courts, and Nisi Prius Court*. London: printed for Timothy Twyford.

Tawney, R.H. and Power, E. (Eds.) (1951) *Tudor Economic Documents*. London: Longmans.

Terill, Richard J. (1985) "William Lambarde: Elizabethan Humanist and Legal Historian" in *The Journal of Legal History*, vol. 6.2, at pp.157-178

Thomas, William (1657) *The Regulation of Law-Suits, Evidence, and Pleadings - An Assize-Sermon, By William Thomas, Preached at Caernarvon, 16th March 1657*. London.

Thornton, Tim (1995) "Cardinal Wolsey and the Abbot of Chester" in *History Today*, vol. 45, issue 8, at p.12.

Thurley, Simon (1998) "The lost Palace of Whitehall. (tercentenary reflections on the significance of the royal Palace)" in *History Today*, vol. 48, issue 1, at pp. 47-52.

Townshend, Henry (1967) *Notes of the Office of a Justice of Peace, 1661-3*. Hunt, R.D. (Ed.). Worcester: Worcestershire Historical Society.

Toynbee, Paget (Ed.) (1918-1925) *Supplement to the Letters of Horace Walpole*. Oxford: Clarendon Press, vol. III, at pp. 132-135.

Turnbull, Colin M. (1984) "The Individual, Community and Society: Rights and responsibilities from an anthropological Perspective" in *Washington and Lee Law Review*, vol. 41, at p. 77.

Twyford, H., Dring, T. and Place, F. (1660) *Justice Restored: Or a Guide For His Majestie's Justices of Peace*, 2nd edn. London: Th.Roycroft.

Twyford, Henry (1676) *The Office of the Clerk of Assize*. London.

Underdown, David (1985) *Revel, Riot & Rebellion, Popular Politics and Culture in England 1603-1660*. Oxford: Oxford University Press.

Van Caenegam, R.C. (1987) *Judges, Legislators & Professors: Chapters in European Legal History*. Cambridge: Cambridge University Press.

Van Dulmen, Richard. (E. Neu, Trans.) (1990) *Theatre of Horror: Crime and Punishment in Early Modern Germany*. Oxford: Polity Press.

Van der Heijden, Manon (2000) "Women as victims of sexual and domestic violence in 17th Century Holland: Criminal Cases of Rape, Incest and Maltreatment in Rotterdam and Delft" in *Journal of Social History*, vol. 33, no.33, at p.623.

Van Muyden, Madame (Trans. and Ed.) (1902) *A foreign View of England in the reigns of George I and George II; The letters of Monsieur Cesar de Saussure, to his Family*. London: John Murray.

Von Friedeburg, Robert (1990) "Reformation of Manners and the Social Composition of Offenders in an East Anglian Cloth Village: Earls Colne, Essex, 1531-1642" in *Journal of British Studies*, vol. 29, no. 4, at pp.358-9.

W.C. and Allde, F. (1624) *The crying Murther: Contayning the cruell ... Butcher[y] of Mr Trat. ... For this fact ... P. Smethwicke, A. Baker, C. Austen, and A. Walker, were executed.* London.

W.M. (Trans.) (1638) *The Sonne of the Rogue, or the Politicke Theefe. With the Antiquitie of Theeves.* London.

W.S. (1653) *Reports of that Learned and Judicious Clerk, J. Goldsborough Esq., Sometimes one of the Protonotaries of the Court of Common Pleas.* London.

Walter, John (1980) "Grain riots and popular attitudes to the law: Malden and the crisis of 1629" in *An ungovernable people: the English and their law in the 17th and 18th centuries.* Brewer, John and Styles, John. (Eds.). London: Hutchinson, at pp.47-84.

Walwin, William (1651) *Juries justified; or, A word of Correction to Mr Henry Robinson; For his seven Objections against the Trial of Causes by Juries of twelve men.* London: Robert Wood.

Ward, Edward (1709) *The Secret History of Clubs: particularly the Kit Cat, Beef-stake ... etc.* London.

Warner, Jessica (1999) "'Damn you, you informing bitch'. Vox populi and the unmaking of the Gin Act of 1736" in *Journal of Social History,* vol. 33, no.2, at p.299.

Warner, Jessica, Ivis, Frank and Demers, Andree (2000) "A Predatory Social Structure: Informers in Westminster, 1737-1741" in *Journal of Interdisciplinary History,* vol. 30.4, at pp. 617-634.

Warrington, J. (Ed.) (1956) *The Paston Letters* (vol. 1). London: Everyman Edition, J.M. Dent.

Watkin, Thomas Glyn (1984) "Hamlet and the Law of Homicide" in *The Law Quarterly Review,* vol. 100. at pp. 282-310.

Watson, Godfrey (1974) *The Border Reivers.* London: Robert Hale & Co.

Wesley Pue, W. (1983) "The Criminal Twilight Zone: Pre-Trial Procedures in the 1840s" in *Alberta Law Review,* vol. 21, at pp.335-364.

Wesley, Rev. John (1872) "Sermon 52 preached before the Society for Reformation of Manners On Sunday, January 30, 1763" in *The Works of the Rev. J. Wesley* (vols. 1-14). London: Wesleyan Conference Office.

Williams, C. (Ed.) (1967) *English Historical Documents 1485-1588,* vol. 5. London: Eyre and Spottiswoode.

Wilkinson, John (1618) *A Treatise Collected out of the Statutes of this Kingdom, and according to common experience of the lawes, concerning the Office and Authoritie of Coroners and Sherifes.* London.

Wilson, Ralph (1722) *A Full and Impartial Account of all the Robberies Committed by John Hawkins* ... 3rd edn. London: J.Peele.

Wormald, Jenny (1980) "Bloodfeud, Kindred and Government in Early Modern Scotland" in *Past and Present*, vol. 87, at pp. 54-97.

Wrightson, Keith and Walter, John (1976) "Dearth and the Social Order in Early Modern England" in *Past and Present*, no. 71, at pp.22-46.

Wrightson, Keith (1980) 'Two concepts of order: justices constables and jurymen in seventeenth century England" in *An ungovernable people: the English and their law in the 17th and 18th centuries'* Brewer, John and Styles, John (Eds.). London: Hutchinson.

Wrightson, Keith (1982) "Infanticide in English History" in *Criminal Justice History*, vol. 3, at p.1.

Wrightson, Keith (1996) "The Politics of the Parish in Early Modern England" in Griffiths T. P. *et al* (Eds.), The Experience of Authority in *Early Modern England*. Basingstoke: Macmillan.

Wrightson, Keith (1998) *English Society, 1580-1680*, Second Edition. London: Routledge.

Zaller, Robert (1987) "The Debate on Capital Punishment During the English Revolution" in *American Journal of Legal History*, vol. 31, at pp.126-144.

Zysberg, Andre (1980) "Galeres et galerians en France a la fin du xvii siecle: une image du pouvoir royal a l'age classique" in *Criminal Justice History*, vol. 1, at p.50.

Contemporary Journals and Newspapers Cited.

The Gentleman's Magazine

The London Gazette

Index